EDUCATION IN A COMPETITIVE AND GLOBALIZING WORLD

CONTINUING PROFESSIONAL DEVELOPMENT AND LIFELONG LEARNING

ISSUES, IMPACTS AND OUTCOMES

EDUCATION IN A COMPETITIVE AND GLOBALIZING WORLD

Additional books in this series can be found on Nova's website under the Series tab.

Additional e-books in this series can be found on Nova's website under the e-books tab.

PUBLIC HEALTH IN THE 21ST CENTURY

Additional books in this series can be found on Nova's website under the Series tab.

Additional e-books in this series can be found on Nova's website under the e-books tab.

EDUCATION IN A COMPETITIVE AND GLOBALIZING WORLD

CONTINUING PROFESSIONAL DEVELOPMENT AND LIFELONG LEARNING

ISSUES, IMPACTS AND OUTCOMES

GREG J. NEIMEYER
AND
JENNIFER M. TAYLOR
EDITORS

Nova Science Publishers, Inc.
New York

Copyright © 2012 by Nova Science Publishers, Inc.

All rights reserved. No part of this book may be reproduced, stored in a retrieval system or transmitted in any form or by any means: electronic, electrostatic, magnetic, tape, mechanical photocopying, recording or otherwise without the written permission of the Publisher.

For permission to use material from this book please contact us:
Telephone 631-231-7269; Fax 631-231-8175
Web Site: http://www.novapublishers.com

NOTICE TO THE READER

The Publisher has taken reasonable care in the preparation of this book, but makes no expressed or implied warranty of any kind and assumes no responsibility for any errors or omissions. No liability is assumed for incidental or consequential damages in connection with or arising out of information contained in this book. The Publisher shall not be liable for any special, consequential, or exemplary damages resulting, in whole or in part, from the readers' use of, or reliance upon, this material. Any parts of this book based on government reports are so indicated and copyright is claimed for those parts to the extent applicable to compilations of such works.

Independent verification should be sought for any data, advice or recommendations contained in this book. In addition, no responsibility is assumed by the publisher for any injury and/or damage to persons or property arising from any methods, products, instructions, ideas or otherwise contained in this publication.

This publication is designed to provide accurate and authoritative information with regard to the subject matter covered herein. It is sold with the clear understanding that the Publisher is not engaged in rendering legal or any other professional services. If legal or any other expert assistance is required, the services of a competent person should be sought. FROM A DECLARATION OF PARTICIPANTS JOINTLY ADOPTED BY A COMMITTEE OF THE AMERICAN BAR ASSOCIATION AND A COMMITTEE OF PUBLISHERS.

Additional color graphics may be available in the e-book version of this book.

Library of Congress Cataloging-in-Publication Data

Continuing professional development and lifelong learning : issues, impacts and outcomes / editors, Greg J. Neimeyer, Jennifer M. Taylor.
 p. cm.
 Includes index.
 ISBN 978-1-62100-767-8 (hardcover)
 1. Career development. I. Neimeyer, Greg J. II. Taylor, Jennifer M.
 HF5381.C68725 2011
 658.3'124--dc23
 2011038325

Published by Nova Science Publishers, Inc. † New York

Contents

Preface ix

Foreword xi

Section 1. Professional Development and Lifelong Learning 1

Chapter 1 Preparing Health Professional Students for Continuing Education and Continuing Professional Development 3
Kristin Kari Janke

Chapter 2 Continuing Nursing Education to Ensure a Competent Nursing Workforce 13
Kathy Chappell and Karen Drenkard

Chapter 3 Physician Lifelong Learning: Conceptualization, Measurement, and Correlates in Full-Time Clinicians, Academic Clinicians, and Medical Students 29
Mohammadreza Hojat, J. Jon Veloski and Joseph S. Gonnella

Chapter 4 Informal Learning, Incidental Learning, and Deliberate Continuing Education: Preparing Psychologists to Be Effective Lifelong Learners 71
James W. Lichtenberg and Rodney K. Goodyear

Chapter 5 Exploring the Relationship between Lifelong Learning, Continuing Education, and Professional Competencies 81
Jennifer M. Taylor, Greg J. Neimeyer, Mary Zemansky and Steven Rothke

Section 2. Regulatory Perspectives on Continuing Education and Professional Development 99

Chapter 6 Self-Assessment Guide and Professional Development Plan: Facilitating Individualized Continuing Professional Development 101
Rick Morris

Chapter 7	Continuing Professional Development: A Regulatory Perspective *Carol Webb and Jacqueline B. Horn*	135
Chapter 8	Disciplinary Actions by a State Board of Psychology: Do Gender and Association Membership Matter? An Update *Samuel Knapp and Leon VandeCreek*	155

Section 3. Continuing Education Mandates — 159

Chapter 9	Should Continuing Education Be Mandatory for Re-Licensure? Arguments for and against *Aimee Adams and Bruce S. Sharkin*	161
Chapter 10	A Review of Concerns in Regard to the Implementation of the CE Mandate in Illinois *Mary Zemansky*	183
Chapter 11	Do CE Mandates Matter? The Effects of CE Mandates on CE Participation *Greg J. Neimeyer, Jennifer M. Taylor, Mary Zemansky and Steven E. Rothke*	191

Section 4. Professional Development and Personal Well-Being — 201

Chapter 12	Continuing Education, Ethics and Self-Care: A Professional Life Span Perspective *Erica H. Wise and Clare M. Gibson*	203
Chapter 13	The Practitioner's Intense Search for Knowing in a Sea of Ambiguity: Answers from the Learning Triangle of Practice, Academic Research and Personal Life *Thomas M. Skovholt and Michael T. Starkey*	229
Chapter 14	Professional Competency and Personal Experience: An Exploratory Study *Jennifer M. Taylor, Greg J. Neimeyer and Douglas Wear*	249

Section 5. Societal Implications and Impacts — 263

Chapter 15	Lifespan Professional Development through Practice-Based Education: Implications for the Health Professions *Ronald M. Cervero*	265
Chapter 16	Competence, Education, Professional Development, Psychology, and Socio-Cybernetics *John Raven*	277

Chapter 17	Planning for Change in Psychology: Education, Outcomes, and Continuing Professional Development *Paul E. Mazmanian, Taylor E. Berens,* *Angela P. Wetzel, Moshe Feldman and Alan W. Dow*	**317**
Section 6. Future Directions		**343**
Chapter 18	Specialization and Life Long Learning *Ronald H. Rozensky and Nadine J. Kaslow*	**345**
Chapter 19	Reflection, Rethinking, and Looking Ahead *Jo Linder-Crow*	**359**
Chapter 20	Anticipating the Future of CE in Psychology: A Delphi Poll *Greg J. Neimeyer, Jennifer M. Taylor,* *Doug Wear and Jo Linder-Crow*	**377**
Index		**395**

PREFACE

What constitutes continuing professional development and what roles do these activities play in assuring professional competence and public protection? These questions are at the heart of "Continuing Professional Development and Lifelong Learning: Issues, Impacts and Outcomes" and are joined by a range of related questions that address current and best practices in professional development at individual, professional and societal levels. Through a variety of diverse perspectives, authors delve into critical issues related to lifelong learning and professional development and invite the reader to consider the roles and functions of continuing professional development, the problems and prospects associated with mandating it, and the continuing quest to translate effective learning into competent practice that is dedicated to the welfare of the consumer, on the one hand, and the generation of improved outcomes, at the other. Interested readers will range from current consumers to trenchant critics of the current health care system. Anyone interested in improving health care services and developing best practices, will find ample food for thought in the pages of "Continuing Professional Development and Lifelong Learning" that can be applied to better evaluating and facilitating ongoing professional competence and health care outcomes.

FOREWORD

The rapidly changing landscape of the health professions has carried with it significant implications for continuing professional education within these fields. These implications include a renewed commitment to lifelong professional learning, on the one hand, and a constructive critique of its central features, on the other. Both this commitment and this critique are the subject of this book. By highlighting the ongoing controversies and late-breaking developments within the field of contemporary continuing professional education, this book is designed to provide conceptual and empirical advances in a way that helps to support the field's principal objectives: the maintenance of professional competence and the protection of the public.

By looking at the field of continuing professional development through a set of six different lenses, we hope to be able to add clarity and detail to the contemporary concerns, considerations and controversies that animate the field's current conversations and will assuredly inform its rapidly developing future, as well. Each of these lenses is represented by a separate section of the volume, providing a window onto a distinctive feature or facet of the field.

The first section targets *Professional Development and Lifelong Learning* and explores the mechanisms and outcomes associated with inculcating the values of lifelong learning into a range of different professional training programs. Kristin Janke identifies a variety of useful methods and procedures for preparing students for lifelong professional learning within the context of pharmacy training. Her work highlights the critical role of an early introduction of lifelong learning values into our training programs, together with the skill sets that will help students maximize their learning across the course of their professional careers. Karen Drenkard and Kathy Chappell build on this account within the context of nursing, highlighting both the problems and prospects associated with instantiating lifelong learning values, attitudes and skills into professional training programs. Mohammadreza Hojat and his colleagues turn their attention towards physicians and detail the abundant benefits that follow from a strong commitment to lifelong learning. A remarkable range of professional accomplishments, achievements, and capacities are associated with high levels of lifelong learning, and Hojat et al.'s account combines conceptual clarity with empirical rigor in bringing these relationships into sharper focus. Next, James Lichtenberg and Rodney Goodyear discuss lifelong learning attitudes and competencies in graduate school and ways in which graduate schools can foster lifelong learning. Jennifer Taylor and her colleagues conclude this section with a consideration of the relationship between lifelong learning and aspects of professional competency. In an exploratory study of professional psychologists, they find links between levels of lifelong learning and professional self-efficacy and productivity.

Section two turns to look at *Regulatory Perspectives on Continuing Education and Professional Development*. Rick Morris outlines the innovative self-assessment system currently in place in Canada, articulating its conceptual underpinnings and detailing the processes and procedures that constitute it. Carol Webb and Jacqueline Horn provide an informed and informative overview of the emerging conceptualization of continuing professional education in psychology within the United States. This vision places a premium on the breadth of different educational sources and the capacity of professionals to adapt their education to their varying styles of learning. To conclude this section, Samuel Knapp and Leon VandeCreek provide a vivid snapshot of the potential value of professional affiliation and interaction in reducing professional liability and the disciplinary actions that occur as a result.

The longstanding controversies associated with *Continuing Education Mandates* are the target of the book's third section. Mandated continuing education is a common, though not universal, feature within the allied health professions, and this section turns to examine the implications and outcomes associated with these mandates. Aimee Adams and Bruce Sharkin review the full complement of arguments that figure prominently in the discussion of CE mandates, both in favor of, and opposed to, these mandates. Mary Zemansky builds on this work by providing what amounts to a case-based illustration of the reluctance and resistance associated with mandating CE. She outlines this opposition by drawing from her experience in the State of Illinois, the most recent state to enact a CE mandate for psychologists. Greg Neimeyer and his colleagues then ask the pointed question, "Do Mandates Matter?" and answer this question in relation to data concerning the impact of mandates on CE participation and perceptions.

The fourth section of the volume targets the relationship between *Professional Development and Personal Well-Being*. Erica Wise and Clare Gibson draw attention to the intimate relationship between personal adjustment and professional capacity. They provide a compelling account of the vital role of ongoing self-care in relation to ethical practice and professional competence. Thomas Skovholt and Michael Starkey further explore the interface between personal and professional domains, highlighting the endemic complexities and ambiguities that are part and parcel of professional practice and the existential realities that attend them. And finally, Jennifer Taylor and her colleagues cap off the fourth section of the volume by exploring the relationship between professional development, competencies and self-care. In their study of professional psychologists, their findings again underscore the critical role of personal adjustment and well-being in relation to a range of professional capacities and competencies.

The fifth section of the book widens the lens and brings broader *Societal Implications and Impacts* in to the field of vision. Ronald Cervero initiates this section by outlining a range of systemic and organizational features that are vital to the integrity of the field's still-developing mechanisms for providing professional development and ensuring professional competence. John Raven broadens this vision further still with his critical appraisal of contemporary practices and his astute analysis of the impediments that are endemic to current systems of continuing education and, indeed, educational systems themselves. Paul Mazmanian and his colleagues address the terms, outcomes and societal responsibilities implicit in the contract between ongoing professional development on the one hand, and the protection of the public through continuing professional competence, on the other. Each of the contributions in this fifth section of the book draws attention to the broader organizational, societal and cultural features that inform, and can impede, efforts to ensure ongoing professional development and the maintenance of competence.

The sixth and final section of the volume casts an eye towards the future. Ronald Rozensky and Nadine Kaslow identify the rapid advances in relation to specialization within the health professions broadly, and within psychology especially. Their incisive perspective brings clarity not only to the field's probable future but, importantly, also to the broader societal and professional forces and processes that will support and sustain those future developments. Jo Linder-Crow provides a set of thoughtful reflections on developments within continuing education across the health professions over time and looks to that history to inform a vision of the field's future, as well. Greg Neimeyer and his colleagues conclude the section and the volume with a Delphi Poll aimed at predicting the future of continuing education within psychology. The increasing specialization of the field, coupled with the decreasing half-life of professional knowledge loom large in their findings, throwing into high relief the significant cross-currents that are likely to buffet the field in the foreseeable future and place significant challenges on its mechanisms for continuing education and professional development.

Through the contributions of these scholars and practitioners we hope that this volume will sharpen the discussion regarding interdisciplinary trends and bring clarity to future developments within the field of ongoing professional development. Ultimately, the value of this volume may be best gauged by the questions is raises, rather than the answers that it provides. As George Kelly once remarked, "a pat answer is the enemy to a fresh question," and the primary purpose of this book is to generate a wide range of questions and concerns that may inform the discussions, deliberations and decisions that will that will shape the field's future in the very foreseeable future.

SECTION 1.

PROFESSIONAL DEVELOPMENT AND LIFELONG LEARNING

In: Continuing Professional Development ...
Editors: G. J. Neimeyer and J. M. Taylor

ISBN: 978-1-62100-767-8
© 2012 Nova Science Publishers, Inc.

Chapter 1

PREPARING HEALTH PROFESSIONAL STUDENTS FOR CONTINUING EDUCATION AND CONTINUING PROFESSIONAL DEVELOPMENT

Kristin Kari Janke[*]
University of Minnesota College of Pharmacy, US

ABSTRACT

Explicit development of self-directed and lifelong learning abilities is needed to create a foundation for success as practitioners. This chapter calls for faculty, continuing education (CE) professionals and clinicians supervising students to work together for focused attention on learning skill development in health professions curricula. In addition, the chapter poses questions related to enhancing CE preparation for consideration by faculty, clinical supervisors and CE professionals. Furthermore, it suggests continuing professional development (CPD) as a method to arm our students for success in responding to the daily demands for learning, as well as taking responsibility for their ongoing competency. The chapter concludes by discussing challenges to CPD and recommendations for implementing CPD with students.

Keywords: Continuing Education, Continuing Professional Development, Lifelong Learning

PREPARING STUDENTS FOR CONTINUING EDUCATION AND CONTINUING PROFESSIONAL DEVELOPMENT TRANSITION FROM STUDENT TO PRACTITIONER

In considering the career span of a health professional it is evident that a minority of the time is spent in formal, curriculum-based education and that the majority of time is spent learning on the job and through continuing education events and opportunities. Our students

---

[*] Correspondence regarding this paper may be directed to Kristin Kari Janke at janke006@umn.edu or University of Minnesota College of Pharmacy, 7-158 Weaver Densford Hall, 308 Harvard St. SE, Minneapolis, MN 55455.

spend 13 years in the K-12 system where, in large part, they are told what to study, how to study it and how they will be assessed. When they arrive at University, true, they make course selections. But within those courses they are again told what objectives to achieve, which resources to use and the standards and methods by which their learning will be judged. After 15 – 17 years of this process, they arrive in our health professions schools asking "where's the bar, and how high do I need to jump?". In other words, they are well accustomed to others telling them the requirements to succeed in learning. And they have become masters at meeting them.

Our students develop study skills. Every backpack is equipped with multiple colors of pens, highlighters and post- it notes. Laptops are ready, and a cry of panic goes out if the slide set is not available electronically. They know when they need to come to class and when they can review a recording (often at double speed). Students quickly discern which readings really need to be read and which can be skipped. They know the study environment that they need to be optimally efficient and successful (e.g., coffee shop or a quiet chair at home). They identify colleagues to study with. They even know how far in advance they need to start studying for a particular type of exam in a particular professor's course. In short, they learn to "drink from the fire hose" and manage the masses of information they are told to master. They are stressed, but they cope.

Then, everything changes. In most health professional curricula there is an identifiable point where learning changes. That point is associated with increased patient care responsibility. There's no stronger motivator than knowing that the care of a patient is in your hands. You better know what you're doing.

Initially, when faced with this transition, a student may think that their experiential learning will be preceptor-driven. The instructor will be replaced by a wise, practice-savvy practitioner. This person will *really* know what the student needs to master. They will be able to tell the student what they need to know or direct the student to it. They will be a great role model to shadow and mimic. They will be the safety net as the student steps forward to improve the patient's care. Indeed, preceptors do, to some extent, drive learning, replacing the instructor. They do move our students from nervous observer to competent practitioner.

But, let's look at this from the student's perspective. Talk to a student about to enter experiential training, and they will relay some interesting hopes. They may express a desire for their practice supervisor to assign them readings on new guidelines or clinical trials. They may look forward to being quizzed on procedures. They may envision themselves going home at night and revisiting their course notes, systematically reviewing each condition and therapeutic approach. In short, they may believe that they will study and learn in the usual ways, but it will all be more relevant and meaningful because it will be in practice.

Once they're a few weeks into this experiential work, however, our students quickly understand that the "syllabus" for experiential learning is subject to modification. Despite objectives for their time at the site, they find that their learning is powerfully driven by the patients they see. If a patient shows up with a rare condition, health professionals don't get to say "I didn't have a lecture on that". We need to respond. Our students also come to understand that their learning is influenced by their practice environment. New safety or performance standards can launch whole departments into continuous improvement processes, which inevitably, involve learning.

Somehow an individual student-practitioner's ongoing learning needs must be combined and integrated with the needs that arrive regularly because of particular patients and particular projects or initiatives at their practice. Somehow someone needs to ferret through all these needs and develop a reasonable approach for addressing them. But, there's no time. My patient needs my skills now and my boss needed my recommendations for this new therapeutic approach yesterday. This will be the struggle for the next forty years of their career.

Unfortunately, in many health professions curricula, little time is spent preparing students for the transition to more self-directed learning. The transition is often abrupt. Students go from being in the classroom one day to a work environment the next. Just as students are being asked to self assess, determine which resources will be most important to their ongoing learning and figure out how to manage their learning efforts learning is becoming more urgent with more consequences. In many respects it is "out of the frying pan and into the fire".

This paper calls for faculty and continuing education professionals to work together to create focused attention on learning skill development in health professions curricula. Explicit development of self directed and lifelong learning abilities is needed to create a foundation for success as practitioners. In addition, in order for students to appreciate the differences between didactic and experiential learning, increased coaching and learning support is required at the transition to practice. To that end, clinicians supervising students need to join the conversation.

PREPARATION FOR CE

In large part, our students are unprepared to maximize their involvement with continuing education (CE). The health professions would benefit from a creative dialogue on strategies for preparing our students to function well in the current CE system. Questions for faculty, clinical supervisors and CE professionals may help to jump start individual considerations and collective discussion.

Let's start with our faculty colleagues. How do health professional curricula prepare students to engage in CE? Explicit education is needed rather than assuming that effective strategies will be developed following immersion. Specifically, how can we better prepare students versed in self assessment? Self assessment is so important in identifying learning needs in preparation for program selection. Relatedly, how can we increase proficiency in the reflection and evaluative skills that aid new practitioners in assessing their practice and their patients' care? This analysis identifies areas for performance improvement that are often addressed via education. In preparation for the educational choices that will inevitably need to be made, how can we encourage the use of criteria for quality when evaluating available CE programs? Finally, how can we increase awareness of the strong factors that will be influencing their participation?

For instance, as CE professionals are acutely aware, barriers to participation in CE include time and accessibility (Marriott, 2007). Am I available that day/time? Can I get there (and park!) conveniently? Is it free (in some professions), covered by my employer or reasonably priced? Offering an alternative to live programming, Internet based programming addresses the need for convenience and cost-effectiveness. Not surprisingly, the majority of sites offer free programming and Internet based CE is projected to continue increasing (Harris, 2010).

While convenience and cost are important, they can become driving forces, rendering learning needs as secondary considerations. The fear is that practitioners will accumulate years of accessible, convenient, and well priced CE, which is not, in fact, directly matched to their learning needs. While these individuals may have met licensure requirements, their competency to practice may actually be declining. Knowing these possibilities provides additional fodder for discussion on how to best prepare students.

For clinical supervisors, a separate set of questions might be asked. For instance, how can we enhance our role-modeling of learning in practice? As an example, is there discussion with our students about the role of CE? When we participate in programs with our students, is there discussion of elements such as quality and bias? How would my students describe how I take my learning and apply it in practice? How I share it with others? How I build on what I've learned to better meet my patient's needs? While observation of practitioner learning is important, overt discussion of these topics can help assure that students understand what they're seeing. It also opens the door for questions on how selections are made, how learning is transferred to practice and how CE is supplemented with other forms of learning.

There are different opportunities for growth among the community of CE professionals. For instance, how have we connected with faculty and clinical supervisors to create conversation about preparing students? In addition, students often attend live CE programming. What tools or prompts are provided (e.g., self assessment checklists, learning planning documents) to help them make the most of their experience? Other opportunities for supporting students exist. How are they identified as students so that other participants can make an effort to welcome them and encourage them? Are there incentives for participation (beyond reduced fees), such as volunteer practitioner-mentors who will participate and discuss with them? Facilitating the transfer of learning is particularly important. To that end, what assistance is available to enhance students' ability to take their learning back to their patient care setting? These same tools would likely be meaningful and effective for practitioners as well.

PREPARATION FOR CPD

Currently, the preparation for optimizing CE participation is not sufficient. Students need experience thinking about their competency and designing plans to address their learning needs as they evolve over time. In addition, it must be recognized that CE only provides a fraction of a practitioner's learning (see Lichtenberg & Goodyear, 2012; Skovholt & Starkey, 2012). Questions from other health care providers, unique patient symptoms, and institution specific protocols all influence our need to learn, among many other factors. As we respond to these factors we're interpreting patient data and researching therapeutic approaches. We're consulting with colleagues, implementing new techniques and monitoring the effects of interventions. We're observing others as they provide care and "borrowing" the best of their approach. In short, practitioners are learning regularly as they care for patients and respond to their practice environment. We must arm our students to succeed in responding to the daily demands for learning, as well as taking responsibility for their ongoing competency.

One method for encouraging practitioner proactive engagement in learning is Continuing Professional Development (CPD). CPD has been defined as the responsibility for "systematic maintenance, development and broadening of knowledge, skills and attitudes, to ensure continuing competence as a professional, throughout their careers" (International Pharmaceutical Federation, p. 2). In addition to maintaining competency, goals of CPD include improving personal performance and enhancing career progression (Rouse, 2004a). CPD has been described as an ongoing, self-directed, structured, outcomes-focused cycle of learning and personal improvement (Dopp, 2010; Rouse, 2004b). Various groups in multiple professions have advocated for this concept, as well as organizations such as the Institute of Medicine (Institute of Medicine, 2010).

While engaging in CPD, health professionals must reflect on their practice and self-assess their performance and associated learning needs. This work is followed by planning of learning, acting on those plans, and eventually evaluating progress. Documentation of this process allows for peer review and support, along with regulatory or employer review, if applicable.

By educating students on CPD, we can annually transition large cohorts of CPD-ready new practitioners to practice. However, preparing CPD-ready new practitioners does not come without its challenges.

Connecting Seemingly Disparate Concepts: The health professions have long been recognized for their commitments to lifelong learning and self directed learning. In fact, as candidates are interviewed for entry into health professions schools they often comment on their attraction to the profession because they "love to learn". Candidates readily recognize that the curriculum will only be the beginning.

CPD, lifelong learning and self directed learning are not inconsistent. They fit well together. We need practitioners with a lifelong commitment to learning. We need them to be self-directed in their approach. CPD can bring these oft-discussed concepts to life by providing structure and process support. It is not uncommon for CPD programs to provide training, documentation tools and access to learning communities for ongoing support. In addition, CPD programs often encourage or provide review, whether that be by peers, employers or regulatory bodies. This review allows recognition of a practitioner's learning achievements. In essence, CPD can be viewed as a means to operationalize lifelong and self directed learning.

In addition, CPD is not at odds with CE. As practitioners assess their needs and develop learning plans, they will need continuing education to meet their learning goals. CE professionals also play a critical role in helping to develop CPD related tools, such as self assessments, documentation systems and review processes, as well as CPD training programs.

Successful implementation of CPD will require addressing the challenge of misconceptions and confusion around these seemingly disparate concepts. Continued communication about the interfaces between lifelong learning, self directed learning, continuing education and continuing professional development is needed. Faculty and clinical supervisors must be clear and articulate in conveying the relationships between these concepts to students, as well as their importance to optimal patient care.

Building Student Opportunities: Health professions curricula have historically provided some instruction related to some CPD-related skills, especially self assessment and reflection. However, these opportunities are often not taught consistently throughout the curriculum, reinforced through repeated practice or supported with quality feedback. In addition, CPD also requires skills in documentation and peer review. While curricula certainly address these topics, it's often not in relation to learning. Other CPD-related skills, such as learning planning and learning assessment, may have received limited instruction.

As a result, successful implementation of CPD with students will require a re-design of our curricular approaches to teaching learning related skills. Early exposure to these skills and exposure in both didactic and experiential settings is likely needed. In addition, students need opportunities to practice, receive feedback and practice again. Much like learning to write a SOAP note, student skills will develop over time.

Building Successful Practice-Based CPD Models. Students appreciate seeing examples of successful CPD implementation in practice environments. Even one local example of an employer using CPD as part of professional development or performance review can be incredibly powerful. Local models also provide a host of practitioners who can speak with students about the advantages of CPD, strategies for success and the impact it has on practice. Of course, models within each profession can also provide the quantitative and qualitative data necessary to encourage regulatory recognition of CPD.

Partnerships with Regulatory Boards. Ideally, new graduates would transition to CPD-friendly regulatory environments that are able to recognize learning documented by continuing education (CE) credits or quality CPD methods. The heart of a regulatory board's responsibility is continued competency. CPD can help to address the continued competency mandate (Konstantinides, 2010). Attention must be paid to troublesome, but not insurmountable issues, such as quality control, resources, auditing practices and review processes. Standards and guidelines for training, documentation, and credit determination will be needed.

Learn From and With Each Other. Simultaneously with advancing curricula, others are attempting to advance CPD in other environments. Coordination and cooperation is needed to avoid re-inventing the wheel. To be successful, task forces are helpful to support strategic planning, training, communication and evaluation around CPD initiatives. In addition, many organizations of health professionals have already examined CPD and developed policy statements in support. Students will want to know why CPD is important and who is supporting it. In addition, researchers have been called upon to help determine how to achieve the best learning outcomes when utilizing this process. Students will want to know the evidence supporting the development of these skills.

If we accept these challenges, the end result will be a cadre of CPD experienced new practitioners transitioning to a CPD-friendly regulatory environment. These new practitioners can then experience the professional rewards and satisfaction associated with CPD, as well as assist with the dissemination of this concept in practices.

CPD IN HEALTH PROFESSIONS CURRICULA

Each college or school will have a different response to the challenge of preparing students for continuing professional development. Following is one example and advice to other health professional educators based on that experience.

An Example: The CPD Portfolio. At the University of Minnesota College of Pharmacy, our CPD work occurs in the fourth (final) year, concurrent with our year long experiential education program. Every five weeks, student move to a new practice location and work with a new preceptor. It is an exciting year of exploration, seeing the diversity of pharmacy practice in community, ambulatory clinics, hospitals and many specialty areas such as managed care, care for the underserved and clinically focused specialty areas such as infectious disease or cardiology. However, students can become caught up and carried away in the experiences. They undoubtedly gain clinical skills, but they're moving very frequently from one preceptor to another. It often takes the preceptor time to understand their students' abilities, and then it's off to the next preceptor. In addition, a student's experience is strongly shaped by the particular patients at the site, at the moment. While reacting to the opportunities presented results in growth, regular conversations about learning objectives and proactive engagement in opportunities can improve the year long experience.

A CPD portfolio process was developed to help students tie together their eight, five week experiences. Students are required to submit a learning portfolio for evaluation quarterly. This includes one submission prior to beginning their experiential training and then three more submissions spaced through their final year (approximately 15 weeks apart). In addition, they share their learning portfolio with each new preceptor every five weeks as a means of introduction and to encourage conversations about learning needs and interests.

The portfolio consists of a Curriculum Vitae and Biosketch. These elements are critical in providing information on the student's background, experiences and interests. In addition, prior to rotations, students use StrengthsFinder 2.0 (Rath, 2007) and take the Clifton StrengthsFinder as a means to think about their professional development and various roles within the profession that may be a good fit. As a result, there are several assignments related to how the student might use and develop their strengths over the course of rotations.

At the beginning of the portfolio process, students are guided through a process of self assessment. This includes reviewing their performance in the curriculum, reviewing their performance on various recently completed curricular assessments, thinking about how they best learn and articulating their short and long term career goals. This document is the used to derive the objectives and learning plan for their first 15 weeks on rotation.

After their first 15 weeks, students submit a "status update" describing their progress in implementing their first learning plan and reflecting on their learning. This status update serves as the foundation for the learning plan for the next 15 weeks. Some unfinished objectives may be carried forward and new objectives may be added, along with ideas for learning activities and evaluation of their learning. This learning plan is then discussed with their preceptors as they enter each rotation.

Profile Personal Benefits: Students need to know how this process will benefit them. Comments from practitioners or students who have participated in CPD are helpful in setting the stage. These CPD-experienced individuals are able to address "Why?" and "To what benefit?". Ideally, the senior student/new graduate or practitioner will deliver the message themselves, but succinct quotations interspersed through slides and handouts can also be helpful. In addition, comments from those who have participated in CPD aid the students in seeing how this will benefit them beyond general satisfaction and confidence. Students can be walked through some exercises to help them articulate their career goals. And, their own goals can be used to illustrate how CPD can help them to develop the knowledge, skills and experiences to get there.

Emphasize Movement within the Profession: Explain the connection between curricular-based CPD initiatives and local initiatives and/or movements within the profession. In pharmacy, we're able to share several policy statements from national organizations supporting CPD, as well as findings from studies. Discuss how your faculty are watching trends within the profession and modifying the curriculum to be responsive. In our experience, following a face-to-face orientation with a few short editorials describing CPD needs and achievements within the profession has left students saying, "I thought CPD was a pretty good idea, but now I can really see why it is!". In other words, mentioning the CPD work within the profession once is helpful, but repeated revisiting and expansion on the profession's work is better.

Invest in Coaching and Support: Students will be working hard on their career goals, learning objectives and plans. Self assessments and reflections will not come easily for some. After their toils, students will want feedback. How did I do? Oftentimes, this is just the obstacle that causes faculty to resist CPD initiatives. Who will read and write comments? How will they find the time? If there are multiple people involved, how will we create consistency in grading? Creativity is often required at this juncture. In our case, rather than spread our 160 students per year across the faculty, or even a subset of the willing faculty, we decided to contract with four pharmacists to function as coaches and evaluators. In our model, each student is assigned to a pharmacist evaluator for the year. The same pharmacist sees all four submissions and can therefore see their progress. We hold quarterly meetings with the pharmacists to discuss student struggles, suggest ways to improve the process, norm on our grading practices and evolve how we're providing feedback. Each school will have unique circumstances to consider. However, investing in coaching and support is important.

Create a Dialogue about CPD Skills: Students will not be experts at this out of the gate. They need to understand that CPD involves a number of skills and, like all skill development, it takes time and repeated practice. It is also important to create a dialogue about their skill development. In our situation, students are in their final year and are spread around the state. Even a class session to discuss progress is impossible, as well as any one-on-one, face-to-face meetings. Creativity is required in developing an environment that supports conversation. One simple and successful strategy that we have used is to ask students where they would like feedback. Rather than us receiving their work and commenting on what we feel is important, the student makes a feedback request. They are asked to tell us what they would like feedback on, specifically, and why. This allows the student to say "I took your advice on objectives, and I think they're more measurable this time. But, can you confirm?" The feedback comments can then begin by addressing their request. Having repeated cycles of CPD submissions also helps in creating a dialogue. Again, with logistical, procedural and resource differences between health professions schools, one size will not fit all. However, consideration of how to create a dialogue with students about CPD skills is needed.

Recognize Excellence: Students love the thrill of achievement. Consider how you might recognize those with extraordinary work. It often makes intuitive sense to approach CPD with a pass/fail process. We need their work to meet a standard and for them to know if it does or doesn't. And it can be difficult to develop grading criteria or rubrics that will differentiate many levels of achievement. We may be inclined to "keep it simple". However, proficient/not proficient is often unsatisfying for our cohorts of high achieving students in the health professions. We have found that three levels of grading are helpful. We explain that we need their work to meet certain criteria (and provide documentation describing those criteria) and that passing will require that their work be satisfactory. However, in grading, we also have an "exceptional" rating (with defined criteria) to recognize those that are clearly working well above the standard. In addition, each year our evaluators recognize their top performing students with a simple email of congratulations. Students appreciate knowing where their work stood out. It provides them with confidence and motivation to continue. Although grading models will differ among various health professions curricula, methods for recognizing excellence should be a component of the evaluation process.

Conclusion

If we are to improve learning, the transition from student to practitioner requires more attention. Students need explicit support to help them navigate and engage optimally in the current CE system. In addition, they need practice in developing lifelong learning and self directed learning skills that can assist them in maintaining competency and responding to daily practice demands for learning.

Investing in CPD initiatives within health professions curricula, while challenging, can create large cohorts of CPD-ready practitioners graduating each year. These cohorts can then assist in disseminating CPD concepts in practice. To succeed, we must work together and focus our efforts on clarifying terminology and articulating the interfaces between seemingly disparate concepts in learning. In addition, we need to build opportunities for students to learn CPD skills, to build successful practice-based CPD models, to work with regulatory boards to seek recognition of CPD and to learn from one another as we tackle these challenges.

As we work with students in developing their CPD skills, we need to profile the personal benefits to them and emphasize how their CPD work in the curriculum connects with the CPD work happening within the health professions. We need to engage them in a dialogue about their CPD skill development and invest in coaching and supporting them. Finally, we need to recognize excellence so that students can gain confidence and maintain their motivation.

Preparing students for thirty or more years as a practitioner requires an intentional commitment to developing learning skills. To succeed, faculty, CE professionals and clinicians supervising students must challenge themselves to innovate within their areas of influence, implementing and refining strategies to assist students in their learning skills. We must also partner in developing curricular opportunities for students to optimize their engagement with continuing education and to gain significant experience to profit from their ongoing continuing professional development activities.

Biosketch

KRISTIN KARI JANKE'S work in continuing education began with her service as a Board Member on the Canadian Council for Continuing Education in Pharmacy in the mid-1990s. From 1998-2009, Dr. Janke was the Director of Continuing Education at the University of Minnesota College of Pharmacy. Dr. Janke currently serves on the Accreditation Council for Pharmacy Education (ACPE) Continuing Education (CE) Commission and was chair from 2007-2008.

Dr. Janke has teaching and scholarly interests in Continuing Professional Development (CPD). She teaches Minnesota's fourth year CPD Portfolio course, which is a required, year-long course that is completed concurrently with Advanced Pharmacy Practice Experiences (APPEs) and is designed to develop lifelong learning skills. She is a member of the ACPE Continuing Professional Development (CPD) Task Force, which has the goal of facilitating further profession-wide implementation and adoption of the CPD concept and approaches.

Dr. Janke served on the Editorial Board of the American Journal of Pharmaceutical Education, representing the Continuing Education Section of AACP, from 2000-2010. She has also served on the Pharmacy Education Panel for the Annals of Pharmacotherapy since 2003.

REFERENCES

Dopp, A.L., Moulton, M.R., Rouse M.J., & Trewet, C.B. (2010). A five-state continuing professional development pilot for practicing pharmacists. *American Journal of Pharmaceutical Education, 74*, 28.

Harris, J. M., Sklar, B. M., Amend, R. W. & Novalis-Marine, C. (2010). The growth, characteristics, and future of online CME. *Journal of Continuing Education in the Health Professions, 30*, 3–10.

International Pharmaceutical Federation. (2002). *FIP Statement of Professional Standards. Continuing Professional Development.* Retrieved from http://www.fip.org/www/uploads/database_file.php?id=221andtable_id=.

Institute of Medicine. (2010). *Redesigning continuing education in the health professions.* Washington, D.C.: The National Academies Press.

Konstantinides, G. (2010). Continuing professional development: The role of a regulatory board in promoting lifelong learning. *Innovations in Pharmacy, 1*, 14.

Lichtenberg, J.W., & Goodyear, R. K. (2011). Informal learning, incidental learning, and deliberate continuing education: Preparing psychologists to be effective lifelong learners. In G. J. Neimeyer, & J. M. Taylor (Eds.), *Continuing professional development and lifelong learning: Issues, impacts and outcomes* (pp. 73-81). Hauppauge, NY: Nova Science Publishers.

Marriott, J.L., Duncan, G.J., & McNamara, K.P. (2007). Barriers to pharmacist participation in continuing education in Australia. *Pharmacy Education, 7*, 11-17.

Rath, T. (2007). *StrengthsFinder* 2.0. New York, NY: Gallup Press.

Rouse, M.J. (2004a). Continuing professional development in pharmacy. *Journal of the American Pharmacists Association, 44*, 517-520.

Rouse, M.J. (2004b). Continuing professional development in pharmacy. *American Journal of Health System Pharmacy, 61*, 2069-2076.

Skovholt, T.M., & Starkey, M.T. (2011). The practitioner's intense search for knowing in a sea of ambiguity: Answers from the learning triangle of practice, academic research and personal life. In G. J. Neimeyer, & J. M. Taylor (Eds.), *Continuing professional development and lifelong learning: Issues, impacts and outcomes* (pp. 223-241). Hauppauge, NY: Nova Science Publishers.

In: Continuing Professional Development ...
Editors: G. J. Neimeyer and J. M. Taylor

ISBN: 978-1-62100-767-8
© 2012 Nova Science Publishers, Inc.

Chapter 2

CONTINUING NURSING EDUCATION TO ENSURE A COMPETENT NURSING WORKFORCE

Kathy Chappell and Karen Drenkard*
American Nurses Credentialing Center, US

ABSTRACT

This chapter reviews considerations and trends related to mandatory continuing nursing education to ensure a competent nursing workforce. This review includes a description of initial entry into the nursing profession, the history and current state of continuing education for all health professions, review of current literature, discussion of quantity versus quality of continuing education, economic implications of mandatory continuing education, and the link between competency and patient safety.

Keywords: Continuing Nursing Education, Competency, Mandatory Continuing, Education, Nursing Workforce

One critical element of a high-quality health care system is a competent nursing workforce. In an increasingly complex, technical and acute health care environment, it is essential that nurses are competent to perform their duties and must do so with little range for error. Competency is assessed at initial entry into the nursing profession but evaluating and ensuring competency over the life of a nurse is an increasingly difficult task. The knowledge and skills possessed upon initial entry must evolve radically over time due to fast-paced changes in the health care environment. In addition, nurses frequently move between different specialty areas, increase or decrease hours worked, or even leave the work force temporarily and return after a period of time. Maintaining competency can seem like an insurmountable task.

---

* Correspondence regarding this manuscript may be directed to: Kathy Chappell, 8515 Georgia Avenue, Silver Spring, MD 20910, Kathy.chappell@ana.org.

One strategy that many states have employed to ensure competency in the nursing work force as well as other health professions is mandatory continuing education. This chapter will review considerations and trends related to mandatory continuing nursing education to ensure competency. This review will include a description of initial entry into the nursing profession, the history and current state of continuing education for all health professions, review of current literature, discussion of quantity versus quality of continuing education, economic implications of mandatory continuing education, and the link between competency and patient safety.

NURSING LICENSURE AND ENTRY LEVEL COMPETENCY

Governance of health professionals is the responsibility of state governments as delegated by the federal government. States make decisions regarding licensure, scope of practice and discipline. Nurses are regulated by state boards of nursing. Laws and regulations governing the education and professional practice of nursing are enacted by a state board of nursing which is generally comprised of nursing professionals from across state regions as well as citizen members. Depending on state structure, the board of nursing may report to the state governor, another state official or to a state agency (National Council of State Boards of Nursing, 2010).

State boards of nursing are members of the National Council of State Boards of Nursing (NCSBN). The NCSBN works on behalf of the nursing profession and state boards to provide a forum for nursing leadership to advance the professional practice of nursing. One of the most important functions of the NCSBN is developing the entry level licensure exam for nursing, the National Council Licensure Examination or NCLEX. The NCLEX exam is recognized as the minimum competency for entry-level nursing in the United States. To be eligible for the NCLEX exam, an applicant must have graduated an approved professional nursing program or, if from a foreign country, pass an examination for graduates of foreign nursing schools. States may also grant reciprocity to nurses holding active licenses in other states (National Council of State Boards of Nursing, 2010).

While the NCLEX examination is recognized as the minimum competency standard for initial entry, there is no recognized standard to evaluate competency for practicing nurses. Many states have adopted mandatory continuing nursing education (CNE) requirements for re-licensure in an attempt to ensure competency however evidence supporting a direct relationship between CNE and competency is lacking. Some states require up to 15 hours of CNE annually or biannually while other states have no CNE requirement for re-licensure (Journal of Continuing Education Annual CE Survey, 2010). The National Council of State Boards of Nursing is evaluating the significant variability between states and the link between CNE and competency.

EVALUATING THE CURRENT STATE OF CONTINUING EDUCATION FOR ALL HEALTH CARE PROVIDERS

Continuing nursing education, as defined by the American Nurses Association (ANA) Scope and Standards of Professional Development 2000, is "systematic professional learning experiences designed to augment the knowledge, skills, and attitudes of nurses, and therefore enrich the nurses' contributions to quality health care and their pursuit of professional career goals" (American Nurses Assocation Scope and Standards, 2000). To qualify as CNE, knowledge gained from the educational activity must be generalizable regardless of employer of the nurse. In contrast, activities such as new employee orientation are not considered to fall under the category of continuing nursing education since the knowledge gained would not be considered generalizable outside of the organization.

Ensuring competency of the health care practitioner is not unique to nursing. The Accreditation Council for Continuing Medical Education (ACCME) and the Accreditation Council for Pharmacy Education (ACPE) are also grappling with evaluating, measuring and documenting the relationship between continuing education and competency for physicians and pharmacists. Within nursing, the American Nursing Credentialing Center (ANCC) works with continuing education providers to ensure the delivery of quality education while also evaluating outcomes of individual education activities and the value of CNE to nursing professional development.

In 1967, the President's Committee on Health Manpower issued a report addressing competency in the health care workforce. Four years later, New Mexico passed legislation mandating continuing education for physician re-licensure. By 1978, 20 more states issued similar legislation (O'Reilly, Tifft, & DeLena, 1982). There was debate among stakeholders regarding whether continuing education guaranteed competency, how many hours of education were required to maintain competency and how to best assess the learning needs of health care professionals. The fundamental questions raised more than 30 years ago have still not been answered.

Increasing focus on the competency of health care professionals has continued to evolve and was launched to the forefront of health care discussion when the Institute of Medicine of the National Academies (IOM) published its landmark report in 2000, "To Err Is Human: Building a Safer Health System." The report shocked the public, sparking anxiety and fear throughout the world when it described what those in the health care field knew intimately: it was and is dangerous to be a patient. The report did not, however, blame health care practitioners. Instead, the report focused on system issues that needed to be implemented, checks and balances, that would reduce the chance that an error could occur (Kohn, Corrigan & Donaldson, 2000). Strategies recommended by the IOM included the following:

- Establishing a national focus to create leadership, research, tools, and protocols to enhance the knowledge base about safety.
- Identifying and learning from errors by developing a nationwide public mandatory reporting system and by encouraging health care organizations and practitioners to develop and participate in voluntary reporting systems

- Raising performance standards and expectations for improvements in safety through the actions of oversight organizations, professional groups, and group purchasers of health care.
- Implementing safety systems in health care organizations to ensure safe practices at the delivery level.

While "To Err Is Human" focused primarily on the health care environment as opposed to the individual practitioner, the IOM followed with two publications in 2001 and 2003, "Crossing the Quality Chasm" and "Health Professions Education: A Bridge to Quality," that addressed the delivery of quality health care in relation to both appropriate and effective utilization of resources and reformation of health care education (Greiner & Knebel, 2003; IOM Report, 2000). These reports continue to be drivers for reforming the current health care system and have been widely cited by stakeholders including consumers, health care practitioners, health care organizations, regulation agencies, accrediting bodies, private foundations, educational institutions and governmental agencies.

In 2007, the Josiah Macy, Jr. Foundation, a privately endowed foundation whose mission is to improve the education of health professionals in the interest of the public, convened a conference on "Continuing Education in the Health Professions: Improving Healthcare Through Lifelong Learning" (Hager, Russell & Fletcher, 2008). The purpose of the conference was primarily to examine continuing education for medicine and nursing with a focus on how physicians and nurses "maintain and improve their knowledge and skills in order to provide safe, effective and high quality healthcare for their patients" (Hager, Russell & Fletcher, 2008). After evaluating the current system of continuing education, conference participants made the following observations:

- There is an overreliance on delivery of continuing education via lecture format.
- Continuing education is counted as a metric in hours as opposed to measuring change in knowledge, competence or performance.
- There is a lack of attention focused on clinicians evaluating and improving their own practice.
- There is a lack of emphasis on clinical questions arising from the delivery of patient care (learner-driven) as opposed to continuing education arising from needs determined by the provider (provider-driven).
- There is a lack of inter-professional collaboration in continuing education.
- There is a lack of focus on improving systems of care to improve the delivery of quality patient care.
- There is inadequate use of internet technology in the delivery of continuing education activities.
- There is a lack of rigor in the study of continuing education outcomes and/or effectiveness.

At the end of the conference, participants representing leadership in medicine, nursing and education established that the "quality of patient care is profoundly affected by the performance of health professionals." The purposes of continuing education, as outlined in the Macy report conclusions, include improving the quality of patient care by improving individual practitioner's knowledge, skills and attitudes; assuring continued competency of clinicians; assuring the delivery of safe and effective patient care; and providing accountability to the public (Hager, Russell & Fletcher, 2008).

Following the Macy conference on continuing education, stakeholders recommended establishing a national, inter-professional continuing education institution to advance the science of continuing education. The Macy Foundation formally requested that the Institute of Medicine (IOM) review the current state of continuing education and consider forming an institution. In response, the IOM formed the Committee on Planning a Continuing Health Care Professional Education Institute. The Committee's report, "Redesigning Continuing Education in the Health Professions" published by the IOM in 2010, examined the current system of continuing education for all health professionals, explored the creation of a national, inter-professional institution, and offered recommendations for how such an institute might operate.

The IOM 2010 report describes the current state of continuing education. According to the report, there are "major flaws in the way CE is conducted, financed, regulated, and evaluated. The science underpinning CE for health professionals is fragmented and underdeveloped" (IOM Report, 2010). After a comprehensive analysis of continuing education, the report details fundamental flaws in the current delivery of CE including participation in continuing education to meet regulatory or employer requirements as opposed to addressing an identified individual educational need; reliance on a didactic delivery method for content as opposed to an interactive or learner-driven method; provider as opposed to learner-driven content for continuing education activities; lack of inter-professional education opportunities or forums; inability to effectively evaluate achievement of educational objectives in an activity; influence of commercial interests on the content of educational activities; and significant variability in the regulation of continuing education (IOM Report, 2010).

Based on its previous reports in 2001 and 2003 and together with the findings of the Macy conference and its 2010 report on continuing education, the IOM recommends that a new system of continuing education be built upon a foundation of five core competencies including ability of the health care practitioner to provide patient-centered care, work collaboratively in inter-professional teams, utilize evidence-based practice, understand and apply quality improvement tactics and effectively utilize information technology (IOM Report, 2010).

CONTINUING EDUCATION FOR NURSES

While debate continues on how to reform the health care education system, nurses continue to seek quality continuing nursing education for both personal and professional needs. Many nurses pursue continuing education to fulfill personal learning goals or to achieve professional certification. In states with mandatory continuing education requirements for re-licensure, nurses are required to complete a specified number of continuing educa tion credit to be eligible for re-licensure. Considerable interest continues to be focused on the relationship between mandatory continuing education and nurse competency by nurses, boards of nursing and other organizations with vested interest.

Mandatory continuing education requires significant investment of human, financial and material resources but also ensures a revenue stream for the organizations that provide, administer and/or accredit continuing education programs.

Fundamentally, there is agreement that a high quality, technically competent workforce requires on-going continuing education after initial entry into the profession. Financial professionals, lawyers, engineers, teachers, and pilots all have mandatory continuing education requirements (IOM Report, 2010). In the nursing profession, no standardized mandatory continuing education requirement exists. States are able to independently decide whether to require continuing education for re-licensure and, if they choose to do so, decide how many hours are required for re-licensure. States make their decision lacking clear, definitive evidence that continuing nursing education positively impacts nurse competency. States, however, are under considerable pressure from consumers, regulatory agencies and health care organizations to ensure some measure of competency in the pool of licensed nursing professionals in their jurisdiction.

The National Council of State Boards of Nursing examined the relationship between continuing nursing education and nurse competency. In addition to developing and administering the NCLEX exam as evaluation of basic, entry-level competency, the NCSBN has developed guiding principles for the regulation of the professional practice of nursing that impact continuing nursing education including: protection of the health, safety and welfare of the public; due process rights for nurses; promotion of shared accountability for safe patient care; promotion of evidence-based standards of care; clarification of the scope and standards of practice; and standardization of regulation across all states (National Council of State Boards of Nursing, 2010).

The NCSBN conducts and funds research to advance the professional practice of nursing including studies to evaluate nurse competence. The 2010 NCSBN Research Agenda includes studies that support the following strategic objectives: patient safety, practice issues, nursing education, competence, discipline, data collection, evidence-based practice, quality and cost-effectiveness (National Council of State Boards of Nursing, 2010). One study, published in 2009, specifically addressed Post-Entry Competence of the practicing nurse. The study first examined descriptive characteristics of a cross-sectional group of nurses from entry level through practice at five years. The study then proceeded longitudinally by following entry level nurses with six to 18 months of experience over the next five years. The purpose of the study was to describe how nurse competency evolved over the time period, when significant change occurred and what competencies were required of nurses over the study period. Qualitative data was collected and analyzed resulting in a deeper understanding of the transition from education into practice as well as implications for both basic and continuing nursing education (National Council of State Boards of Nursing, 2010). The post-study final report recommended that continuing nursing education activities related to professional competence include: time management, delegation, collaborative practice, resource management, teamwork, in-depth pathophysiology and treatment in area of clinical practice, self-reflection, and role clarification (National Council of State Boards of Nursing, 2010).

REVIEW OF CURRENT LITERATURE

There is an abundance of literature about continuing nursing education, however studies evaluating the outcomes of continuing education (CE) in general have been poorly designed, utilized small sample sizes or lacked valid and reliable outcomes measures (IOM Report, 2010). Studies have not been replicable or generalizable. Outcome measures for individual activities have focused primarily on measures such as learner satisfaction with activity content or satisfaction with event location. Little emphasis has been placed on measuring "higher" level outcomes such as change in practice or effect on patient outcomes.

In "Redesigning Continuing Education in the Health Professions," the IOM's Committee on Planning a Continuing Health Care Professional Education Institute reviewed in excess of 18,000 articles on continuing education, knowledge acquisition, and inter-professional education. Review, analysis and comparison resulted in narrowing the final count of 62 studies and 20 systematic reviews and meta-analyses meeting inclusion criteria (IOM Report, 2010). The studies included learners from both medicine and nursing. Despite an overall weakness in study design limiting generalizable conclusions, there was some evidence that continuing education can positively and significantly impact patient outcomes by increasing or improving practitioner knowledge, skills, attitudes, or behaviors. Effective continuing education activities had some common elements. The educational design included a needs assessment and the activity content was specifically designed to address the identified gap. The educational activity employed an interactive learning style and used on-going learner feedback to increase learner engagement. The educational activity was provided in multi-modal format with time incorporated for learners to grasp content. If possible and appropriate, simulation was incorporated into the educational design. Moving forward, the IOM has recommended a research agenda that includes: identification of theoretical frameworks for educational design, determination of appropriate continuing education methodology for different learning situations, matching curriculum design to the appropriate outcome measure, and evaluation of the impact of different variables on learning (IOM Report, 2010).

Continuing education has been linked to improved employee satisfaction, higher employee retention rates, high employee self-esteem and promotion of an organizational culture of excellence (Levett-Jones, 2005). A relationship also exists between investment in continuing education opportunities for nurses and increased patient satisfaction, reduced length of stay, reduced incidence of complications, and reduction in patient mortality (Aiken, Smith & Lake, 1994; Levett-Jones, 2005). Although a relationship between continuing education and different variables exist, it is not evidence of causation. It may be that institutions that provide and promote continuing education for nurses have other characteristics that positively impact satisfaction, retention and outcomes.

An integrated literature review and meta-analysis published in the Journal of Advanced Nursing in 2006 by two Canadian nurse authors presented factors that facilitate or inhibit continuing nursing education and identification of methods to improve continuing education effectiveness. A total of 40 articles meeting inclusion criteria were reviewed. Factors that facilitated participation in continuing education included nurses' desire to improve professional knowledge, improve nursing skills, find personal satisfaction in the joy of learning, and increase self-assurance (Griscti & Jacano, 2006). Care must be taken in generalizing these findings to all nurses due to self-selection bias since only nurses who participated in continuing education were surveyed. There was no data from nurses who did not choose to participate in continuing education. Nurses were also more enthusiastic participants of continuing education when the content was presented in a participatory manner as opposed to didactic lecture format and when the content was primarily learner-driven (Griscti & Jacono, 2006).

In an article describing the evolution of accreditation in continuing nursing education, authors Dr. Whitehead and Dr. Lacey-Haun presented outcomes of a research study conducted by the National Council of State Boards of Nursing in 2002 to evaluate the link between continuing nursing education and development of professional competence. Surveys were sent to all licensed, active nurses in the United States and the response rate was 30%. Findings were analyzed by both nursing degree and state affiliation for licensure. Both registered and licensed vocational nurses collected more hours of continuing nursing education if they were licensed in a state with mandatory continuing education requirements, though the difference was not statistically significant when compared to nurses from states without mandatory requirements. Nurses in states with continuing education requirements collected significantly more hours of education unrelated to their current or future work (Whitehead & Lacey-Haun, 2008). This might be interpreted as nurses completing education requirements just to "check off the box" or, as the authors suggest, nurses working in states with mandated continuing education requirements may be more motivated to seek out educational events that award continuing education credit. Barriers to accessing continuing education cited most frequently included lack of time off work to attend continuing education activities and lack of reimbursement (Whitehead & Lacey-Haun, 2008).

QUALITY VS. QUANTITY - CONTINUING NURSING EDUCATION

State boards of nursing currently mandate the number of hours of continuing education that a nurse must accumulate for re-licensure. However, based on all available evidence, the number of total education hours is not a metric that results in clinical competency. In fact, there is essentially no mention of total hours in any discussion of reforming education for health care professionals. One significant challenge for the nursing profession is how to distinguish educational activities that result in improved or increased knowledge, attitudes, practices or behaviors and that positively impact the quality of health care for both patients and providers from those that do not.

The quality of an educational activity can be difficult to measure. Ideally, participation in any educational activity should result in a specific and measureable outcome for the learner. Many variables that affect the outcome of an educational activity can be controlled such as qualifications of the planners and presenters, the integrity of content, the teaching-learning strategies used, and whether the activity was designed to meet an identified learner need. Some variables that affect the outcome of the educational activity cannot be controlled however and the intended outcome may not be achieved for an individual learner. Uncontrollable variables may include lack of motivation by the learner, presentation style that is incongruent with a participant's learning style or environmental distractions during the educational activity (room/seats uncomfortable, etc.).

One strategy that can be used to distinguish high-quality educational activities is accreditation. Accrediting bodies review the capacity of an organization to provide quality continuing education including committed and accountable leaders; adequate human, financial and material resources; sound educational design processes; and on-going evaluation of outcomes. An accredited organization has voluntarily submitted to a rigorous external review and has demonstrated the ability to provide quality continuing education. The design of educational activities by accredited organizations must adhere to strict quality standards increasing the likelihood that identified outcomes will be achieved. States rarely distinguish quality of educational offerings for nurses by accreditation but rather require total number of hours regardless of quality. Advanced Practice nurses are required to complete significantly more hours of continuing education. Interestingly, nursing certification bodies do require that a percentage of hours submitted for re-certification are provided by accredited organizations (Journal of Continuing Nursing Education Annual CE Survey, 2010).

State-mandated continuing education for both physicians and pharmacists is similar to nursing. The Federation of State Medical Boards reports a range of zero to 50 hours annually for physician re-licensure (Federation of State Medical Boards, 2009). The Accreditation Council for Pharmacy Education reports approximately 15 hours annually for pharmacy re-licensure (D. Travlos, personal communication, March 31, 2010). State requirements for nursing range from zero hours to 15 hours per year for general nursing (Journal of Continuing Education Annual CE Survey). Advanced Practice nurse requirements range from zero hours to 50 hours per year (Journal of Continuing Education Annual CE Survey). Despite significant variability between states, there is no evidence that the quality of health care provided in states with mandatory continuing education requirements is different from states without mandatory requirements. There are too many variables that effect quality outcomes measures to be able to isolate the effects of continuing education on competency.

ECONOMIC IMPLICATIONS FOR MANDATORY CONTINUING NURSING EDUCATION

There are significant economic implications for state-mandated continuing nursing education requirements that affect individual nurses, nursing organizations, health care organizations, providers of continuing nursing education and state governments.

In states that require mandatory continuing nursing education for re-licensure, nurses must pay for courses or educational events that offer contact hours. Costs can range from several dollars per contact hour to $100 per contact hour or more. Nurses may not work and generate an income without a license therefore they are required to pay for and participate in continuing education activities. Nurses may also act as faculty or presenters for continuing education activities producing a revenue stream from teaching.

A variety of nursing organizations are impacted by mandatory continuing nursing education. State nursing associations may be providers of continuing education or approve others to provide continuing education, incurring both a cost for personnel required to administrate programs as well as a source of revenue from applicants. Accrediting bodies require an investment of resources to run programs as well as generate revenue from applicants. Academic institutions may provide continuing education as a source of revenue and costs may be minimal since faculty is already employed.

Health care organizations such as hospitals have a vested interest in ensuring nurses have access to continuing education in order to maintain an eligible workforce. Health care organizations may also provide continuing education to nurses as a public service. As Levett-Jones (2005) discussed in her article, health care organizations that provide continuing education for nurses may also be creating an environment that increases nursing satisfaction, increases patient satisfaction, increases nurse retention, and improves patient outcomes. State governments must devote human, financial and material resources to either administer or provide oversight for nursing continuing education. States that mandate continuing education must document and/or validate hours for individual nurses. According to the United States Department of Labor, Bureau of Labor Statistics Occupational Handbook 2010 - 2011, there are 2.6 million registered nurses in the United States (US Department of Labor, 2011). With 33 out of 57 states and U.S. territories requiring mandatory continuing education, over 1.5 million nurses are completing CE for re-licensure and state boards of nursing are tracking their requirements.

MANDATORY CONTINUING EDUCATION AND PATIENT SAFETY

One primary driver of mandated continuing education for health care professionals is patient safety. The delivery of high-quality, safe care is dependent on a competent workforce. As reported by the Institute of Medicine in "To Err is Human," thousands of patients die annually due to medical error. The total cost of medical errors in the United States including lost income, lost productivity, disability and health care costs amounts to millions of dollars annually (Kohn, Corrigan, & Donaldson, 2000).

Evaluating and ensuring competency for health care providers is a considerable challenge. Patients, health care providers, health care organizations, state governments and the federal government all have a vested interest in a competent professional health care provider however measuring and validating competency is difficult. Equally challenging is identifying the tactics that develop and maintain competency over time.

Many state boards of nursing have chosen or are considering mandated continuing nurse education to ensure competency. While some evidence exists to support continuing education as a strategy to maintain competency in the health care workforce, many could argue that the evidence is weak in both quality and results. Legally, should states mandate continuing education requirements for health care professionals in light of current evidence or should states focus resources on re-designing the current health care education system with the ultimate goal of creating a sound, evidence-based system that produces competent health care professionals?

LEGAL DEFINITION OF COMPETENCE – THE STANDARD OF CARE

Competence, related to the health care practitioner, is not a legal definition per se. Competence rather is determined in relation to a recognized standard of care. The standard of care may be determined by comparing the actions of one health care practitioner to a recognized peer or expert, the "reasonable standard of care." The comparison of actions may also be made to a recognized "national standard of care" (Furrow, Greaney, Johnson, Jost & Schwartz, 2008). In *Health Law: Cases, Materials and Problems, 6th Edition*, competency-based duty of care for physicians is defined as: "Each physician may with reason and fairness be expected to possess or have reasonable access to such medical knowledge as is commonly possessed or reasonably available to minimally competent physicians in the same specialty or general field of practice throughout the United States, to have a realistic understanding of the limitations on his or her knowledge or competence, and, in general, to exercise minimally adequate medical judgment" (Furrow et al., 2008). Similarly in nursing, the standard of care is considered to be "what a reasonably prudent nurse, under similar circumstances, would have done…a minimum standard of 'do no harm'" (Risk Management, ANA website, 2010).

The American Nurses Association published a position statement on Professional Role Competence in May 2008. Although not a legal document, ANA position statements do provide legislative bodies with guidance from the national nursing organization and can result in state-enacted legislation. The position statement for ANA Professional Role Competence states:

> The public has a right to expect registered nurses to demonstrate professional competence throughout their careers. ANA believes the registered nurse is individually responsible and accountable for maintaining professional competence. The ANA further believes that it is the nursing profession's responsibility to shape and guide any process for assuring nurse competence. Regulatory agencies define minimal standards for regulation of practice to protect the public. The employer is responsible and accountable to provide an environment conducive to competent practice. Assurance of competence is the shared responsibility of the profession, individual nurses, professional organizations, credentialing and certification entities, regulatory agencies, employers, and other key stakeholders. (ANA website, Risk Management, 2010)

The health care environment is increasingly acute and complex. Nurses' roles have expanded considerably in recent years and patients expect a high level of knowledge from nurses.

Competency of a nurse is evaluated when an adverse event occurs. Lack of competency, practicing outside a defined scope of practice, or practicing negligently can result in significant patient injury or loss of life. It can also result in judgments and significant monetary awards against health care providers, health care organizations and companies that insure both. State boards of nursing as well as other vested organizations want to ensure nurses practice competently to *prevent* an adverse event from occurring and therefore have implemented mandatory continuing education as one strategy to ensure competence.

RECOMMENDATIONS

Following the Institute of Medicine's report, "Redesigning Continuing Education in the Health Professions," state boards of nursing as well as other governmental and consumer groups have renewed interest in mandatory continuing education. A safe, high-quality health care system is only possible when health care providers practice competently. Exhaustive, expert evaluation of the current health care education system conducted by organizations such as the Josiah Macy, Jr. Foundation and the Institute of Medicine has revealed fundamental flaws and recommend a complete re-design of the system to ensure that participating in continuing education activities results in positive outcomes for patients, health care providers, and health care organizations.

In the absence of conclusive evidence that continuing education ensures competency, there is also a lack of evidence that continuing education harms patients, providers or organizations outside of a fiscal impact. Mandating participation in continuing education activities may force health care providers to engage in life-long learning when that they otherwise might not be motivated to do so. Nurses who regularly participate in continuing education, especially in states without mandated continuing education, are more likely to be those who are self-motivated, have good self-assessment skills and a desire for on-going professional development.

The mere act of attending a continuing education activity does not guarantee that learning will occur, however. As described in previous reports, the quality of the educational activity is one of the most significant factors of learner engagement, willingness to participate and satisfaction. Content provided that is not useful to the learner, is not presented in an interactive manner, and is not evaluated in terms of change in knowledge, attitudes, practices or behaviors can hardly be called continuing education. Instead, content as described might be more aptly referred to as "paying for a product" – hours of continuing education.

To create a competent nursing work force, certifying bodies could focus less on a metric of total hours of continuing education and devote resources to ensuring that nurses have easy access to high-quality, accredited continuing education. In addition, certifying bodies could require organizations that provide continuing education to identify measureable outcomes related to participation in CE activities. Finally, research could be conducted to evaluate if a relationship exists between continuing education and competency and, if so, identify variables that might impact the relationship.

Strategies to ensure access to high-quality, accredited continuing education for all nurses may require the investment of additional resources however the investment may also positively impact patient outcomes including reduced length of stay and reduced mortality; nursing outcomes such as improved satisfaction and improved retention; and organizational outcomes such as reduced employee turnover costs or adverse patient events. To ensure that all nurses are able to access CE, health care organizations may need to invest in additional information technology such as software or program updates, provide nurses with internet access or support nurses with time out of the clinical setting. Health care organizations may need to invest in the internal resources required to pursue accreditation by creating or expanding departments of education and teaching educators how to deliver content using best practices. Providers of continuing education may need to invest resources in delivering content in more interactive or web-based formats as opposed to traditional didactic lecture technique. Nurses may need to learn how to identify their own learning needs, evaluate their own level of competency and determine the best strategies to address their own performance gaps. Health care professionals of all disciplines will need to develop strategies to learn in multi-disciplinary settings, focusing on the strengths that each profession offers (see also Mazmanian, Berens, Wetzel, Feldman, & Dow, 2012).

Although the Institute of Medicine's Committee on Planning a Continuing Health Care Professional Education Institute has recommended a complete overhaul of the current health care education system, the strategies listed previously can be implemented now. State boards of nursing, nursing organizations, health care organizations, and providers of continuing education have an opportunity to work together creating an infrastructure that supports the delivery of quality continuing education and safe, high-quality patient care.

Under the proposed health care reform initiative, there may be opportunity to redesign the continuing education system for nurses and other health professionals quickly and comprehensively across all states. Attention is currently being focused on both access to health care services and the delivery of quality health care. In addition, there is considerable focus on evidence-based practice, standardization of practice, and comparative effectiveness research. Competency of the health care professional is one component of a quality health care system. To achieve safe, high-quality care, nurses and other care givers must be able to access, evaluate and utilize large amounts of health-related information. Nurses must be able to practice according to guidelines and standards. Nurses must be able to compare patient outcomes and identify opportunities for quality improvement or research to advance the scientific base for health care delivery. Nurses must be able to work collaboratively in teams with other health care providers. Continuing education has a role in achieving these goals.

Continuing education can provide nurses with skill sets required for them to perform competently. Participating in continuing education activities also has the potential to stimulate a desire for additional learning opportunities, increase professional satisfaction, improve patient outcomes, improve patient safety and improve nurse retention. To achieve these outcomes, however, continuing education activities need to be learner-driven, interactive, and easily accessible. Continuing education activities should be offered to inter-professional audiences and via multi-modal formats for different learning styles.

Should states mandate continuing education for nurses? The potential positive effects of participating in continuing education activities are compelling and the relative risk is small. Research may never be able to demonstrate a direct link between continuing education and competency for several reasons. There are multiple variables that can affect competency including but not limited to individual characteristics of the nurse, the quality of the health care environment, the influence of peers or mentors, quality of the nurse's academic preparation, and availability of educational offerings including non-continuing education activities such as in-service and work experience. Creating and maintaining a competent work force is such an essential component of a quality health care system, however, that mandatory continuing education should be supported, promoted and mandated for all nurses and other health care providers.

BIOSKETCHES

KATHY CHAPPELL, *MSN, RN* is currently the Director of the American Nurses Credentialing Center's Accreditation Program. A nurse for over 20 years, Kathy has a wide range of expertise including clinical practice as a direct care nurse in critical care and emergency nursing; hospital administration as an assistant head nurse and hospital supervisor; project management for programs such as the Magnet Recognition Program, NDNQI, quality improvement and shared governance; and hospital-system strategic planning for support of professional nursing practice including nursing clinical education, nursing student recruitment and research. As the Director of the Accreditation Program, Kathy is responsible for the accreditation of organizations as providers and approvers of continuing nursing education (Primary Accreditation), joint accreditation of organizations providing inter-professional continuing education (Joint Accreditation) and accreditation of courses validating nursing skills or skill sets (Nursing Skills Competency Program).

KAREN DRENKARD, *PhD, RN, NEA-BC, FAAN* is the Executive Director at the American Nurses Credentialing Center. She was appointed having served as the Sr. Director for Credentialing Operations and the Director of the Magnet Recognition Program® for the American Nurses Credentialing Center for three years. Drenkard comes to ANCC with nearly 10 years as the senior vice president of nursing/chief nurse executive of Inova Health System, a five hospital not for profit healthcare delivery system in northern Virginia. Drenkard was the principal investigator in HRSA funded research involving the implementation of a human caring model in acute care hospitals. She is currently an editorial advisor to *Journal of Nursing Administration* and *Nursing Administration Quarterly* (NAQ). She is on the Executive Committee of the National Advisory Council on Nursing Education and Practice (NAC-NEP), the Board of Visitors for the University of Pittsburgh School of Nursing and is a Board of Trustees member at Inova Loudoun Hospital. She is Fellow in the American Academy of Nursing. Drenkard received her doctorate (PhD) in nursing administration from George Mason University, is a 2003 Wharton Nurse Executive Fellow, and a Robert Wood Johnson Executive Nurse Fellow 2003-2006.

REFERENCES

Aiken, L.H., Smith, H.L, & Lake, E.T. (1994). Lower Medicare mortality among a set of hospitals known for good nursing care. *Medical Care, 32*, 771 - 785.

American Nurses Association. (2008). *Position statements: Professional role competence.* Retrieved from http://www.nursingworld.org/position/practice/role.aspx.

American Nurses Association. (n.d.). *Risk Management Series.* Retrieved from http://www.nursingworld.org/mods/archive/mod310/cerm102.htm.

American Nurses Association. (2000). *Scope and standards of professional development.* Washington DC: Author.

Douglas, J., Goodloe, L., & Pickral, J. (2010). Demonstrating competence for nurses in Virginia. *Virginia Nurses Today, 18*, 6.

Federation of State Medical Boards. (2009). Continuing medical education overview by states. Appendix.

Furrow, B.R., Greaney, T.L., Johnson, S.H., Jost, T.S., & Schwartz, R.L. (2008). *Health law: Cases, materials and problems* (6th ed.). St. Paul: Thompson-West.

Greiner, A.C., & Knebel, E. (Eds.). (2003). *Health professions education: A bridge to quality.* Washington, DC: The National Academies Press.

Griscti, O., & Jacono, J. (2006). Effectiveness of continuing education programmes in nursing: literature review. *Journal of Advanced Nursing, 55*, 449 – 456.

Hager, M., Russell, S., & Fletcher, S.W. (2008). *Continuing education in the health professions: Improving healthcare through lifelong learning,* The Josiah Macy, Jr. Foundation. Retrieved from: www.josiahmacyfoundation.org.

Institute of Medicine of the National Academies. (2001). *Crossing the quality chasm: A new health system for the 21st century.* Washington, DC: The National Academies Press.

Institute of Medicine of the National Academies. (2010). *Redesigning continuing education in the health professions.* Washington, DC: Committee on Planning a Continuing Health Care Professional Education Institute.

Journal of Continuing Nursing Education. (2010), Annual CE Survey. *Journal of Continuing Nursing Education, 41*, 4 – 11.

Kohn, L.T., Corrigan, J.M., & Donaldson, M.S. (Eds.). (2000). *To err is human: Building a safer health system.* Washington, DC: The National Academies Press.

Levett-Jones, T.L. (2005). Continuing education for nurses: A necessity or a nicety? *Continuing Education for Nurses, 36*, 230 – 233.

Mazmanian, P.E., Berens, T. E., Wetzel, A. P., Feldman, M., & Dow, A. W. (2012). Planning for change in psychology: Education, outcomes, and continuing professional development. In G. J. Neimeyer, & J. M. Taylor (Eds.), *Continuing professional development and lifelong learning: Issues, impacts and outcomes* (pp. 311-335). Hauppauge, NY: Nova Science Publishers.

National Council of State Boards of Nursing. *2010 Research agenda.* Retrieved https://www.ncsbn.org/1621.htm.

National Council of State Boards of Nursing. *Boards of nursing.* Retrieved from https://www.ncsbn.org/boards.htm.

National Council of State Boards of Nursing. *Guiding principles.* Retrieved from https://www.ncsbn.org/1325.htm.

National Council of State Boards of Nursing. *NCLEX examinations – Candidate information.* Retrieved from https://www.ncsbn.org/1213.htm.

National Council of State Boards of Nursing. *Post-entry competence study.* Retrieved from https://www.ncsbn.org/986.htm.

O'Reilly, P., Tifft, C.P., & DeLena, C. (1982). Continuing medical education: 1960s to the present. *Journal of Medical Education, 57*, 819 – 826.

United States Department of Labor, Bureau of Labor Statistics. *Occupational Outlook Handbook 2010 – 2011.* Retrieved from http://www.bls.gov/oco/ocos083.htm.

Whitehead, T.D., & Lacey-Haun, L. (2008). Evolution of accreditation in continuing education in America. *The Journal of Continuing Education in Nursing, 39*, 493 – 499.

Chapter 3

PHYSICIAN LIFELONG LEARNING: CONCEPTUALIZATION, MEASUREMENT, AND CORRELATES IN FULL-TIME CLINICIANS, ACADEMIC CLINICIANS, AND MEDICAL STUDENTS

Mohammadreza Hojat[*], J. Jon Veloski and Joseph S. Gonnella
Center for Research in Medical Education and Health Care,
Jefferson Medical College, Thomas Jefferson University, US

"If a medical degree is considered to be an indication of the completion of learning, it should be given at the time of a physician's retirement. Until then a physician is a student with a moral, ethical, and legal obligation to continue learning."

(Gonnella, Callahan, Louis, Hojat, & Erdmann, 2004, p.10).

ABSTRACT

Empirical research on lifelong learning in medicine has been scarce because of the ambiguity associated with its definition, as well as the lack of a psychometrically sound instrument to measure it. In this chapter, which is an expansion of our previous research, we present a definition of lifelong learning in medicine and report the psychometrics and correlates of an instrument (Jefferson Scale of Physician Lifelong Learning, JeffSPLL) that we began to develop in 2001 to specifically measure orientation toward lifelong learning among physicians and medical students. We collected survey data from 3,195 physicians who were classified into three groups: Full-time clinicians ($n=1,127$), academic clinicians ($n=1,612$), and others ($n=456$). The three underlying components of

---

[*] Correspondence regarding this manuscript may be direct to Dr. Hojat, Jefferson Medical College, 1025 Walnut Street, Suite 119, Philadelphia, PA 19107-5083, USA. E-mail: Mohammadreza.Hojat@Jefferson.edu.
This is an updated Chapter originally published in: Handbook of Lifelong Learning Developments, Editor: Margaret P. Caltone, pp. 37-78 (ISBN: 978-1-60876-177-7, © 2010 Nova Science Publishers, Inc.).

the JeffSPLL resulted from factor analysis including: "learning beliefs and motivation," "attention to learning opportunities," and "skills in seeking information." These factors correspond to the key features of lifelong learning often described in the literature, thus providing support for the construct validity of the JeffSPLL. Significant correlations between the JeffSPLL scores and the criterion measures of commitment to lifelong learning, learning motivation, information seeking skills, professional accomplishments, career satisfaction, and academic performance support the criterion-related validity of the JeffSPLL for both full-time clinicians and academic clinicians. The reliability coefficients (coefficient alpha and test-retest) of the JeffSPLL ranged from 0.72 to 0.86 in both groups of physicians. In another study, the JeffSPLL was adapted for administration to medical students with satisfactory psychometric support. Implications of the findings in monitoring the outcomes of medical educational programs, and investigating differences across academic medical centers and groups of medical students and physicians are discussed.

Keywords: Lifelong learning, physician, medical student, medical education, psychometrics, validity, reliability

INTRODUCTION

In the field of medicine, a commitment to rigorous learning throughout one's career has been described as an important element of professionalism (Arnold, 2002; Duff, 2002; Epstein & Hundert, 2002; Miflin, Campbell, & Price, 1999; Nelson, 1998; Nierman, 2002; Veloski & Hojat, 2006). Medical education is indeed a process of lifelong learning that begins in medical school, extends into graduate medical education, and continues throughout a physician's professional life (AAMC, 1999). Lifelong learning is vital for the provision of cutting edge, and safe medical care (Schrock & Cydulka, 2006) and for advances in medical research and biotechnological development. This is particularly crucial in the practice of medicine today due to the rapid expansion of medical information and technology.

Preparing medical students to become lifelong learners has received widespread attention by the professional organizations. For example, in the first of three reports of the Medical School Objectives Project (MSOP), prepared by the Association of American Medical Colleges (AAMC, 1999), it is recommended that medical students should develop skills and motivation "to engage in lifelong learning to stay abreast of relevant scientific advances." (available at: www.aamc.org/meded/msop/).

The Liaison Committee on Medical Education (LCME) recommended that medical school faculty "should foster in students the ability to learn through self-directed, independent study throughout their professional lives" (LCME, 2000). Principle 5 of the 9 Principles of Medical Ethics adopted by the American Medical Association's House of Delegates on June 17, 2001, specifies that "A physician shall continue to study, apply, and advance scientific knowledge...." (available at: http://ama-assn.org/ama/pub/category/2512.html). Teaching medical students to become lifelong learners has been the most consistent recommendation in virtually all proposals for the reform of medical education (Christakis, 1995). Lifelong learning was among five competencies considered to be extremely important by more than 75% of surveyed physicians (Finocchio, Bailiff, Grant, & O'Neil, 1995).

CONCEPTUALIZATION AND DEFINITION

Despite the emphasis placed on the importance of physicians' lifelong learning, no broadly accepted definition of the term has been proposed (O'Shea, 2003). Various terms have been used under the rubric of lifelong learning, including self-directed learning, self-educative approach, self-initiative learning, active learning, independent learning, contextual learning, continuing education, and distance learning. Although these terms may share some common elements, each has its own unique features.

Lifelong learning is a complex and multidimensional concept (McKenzie, 2001) that involves personal and motivational factors and learning skills as well as a value system, creativity, and empowerment (Longworth, 2001). This complexity is reflected in the following definition suggested by Longworth and Davies (1996) of the European Lifelong Learning Initiative: Lifelong learning is the development of human potential through a continuously supportive process which stimulates and empowers individuals to acquire all the knowledge, values, skills and understanding they will require throughout their lifetime and to apply them with confidence, creativity and enjoyment in all roles, circumstances and environments (cited in Longworth, 2001).

This broad definition encompasses complex notions, such as "human potential," "supportive process," "creativity," and "enjoyment," that are difficult to measure. For the practical purpose of developing an operational measure of physicians' lifelong learning, based on a review of relevant literature and panel discussions in a pilot study (Hojat et al., 2003), we define lifelong learning as follows:

> A concept that involves a set of *self-initiated activities* (behavioral aspect), and *information seeking skills* (capabilities) that are activated in individuals with *sustained motivation* (predisposition) to learn and the ability to *recognize their own learning needs* (cognitive aspect).

The four key concepts in this definition that are frequently described in the literature (Aspin, Chapman, Hatton, & Sawano, 2001; Bligh, 1993; Candy, 1991; Knowles, 1975) are in italics to underscore their importance. This conceptualization and definition of lifelong learning in medicine was supported in a recent doctoral dissertation study with medical students at Indiana University School of Medicine (Brahmi, 2007).

MEASUREMENT

Although a few research tools have been used to measure self-directed learning in the general adult population (Bligh, 1993; Guglielmino, 1977; Oddi, 1986), they are neither specific to physicians nor designed to address lifelong learning as conceptualized and defined above. For example, Guglielmino (1977) developed a Self-Directed Learning Readiness Scale (SDLRS) containing 58 Likert-type items (e.g., "I love to learn"). Bligh (1993) prepared a short version of the SDLRS that includes only 28 items. In a recent study with medical students, the construct validity of the SDLRS has been questioned (Hoban, Lawson, Mazmanian, Best, & Seibel, 2005).

Oddi (1986) developed another scale to identify personality characteristics of self-directed continuing learners, the Oddi Continuing Learning Inventory (OCLI), containing 24 items. Subsequent studies of the OCLI's validity were inconclusive (Oddi, Ellis, & Altman Robertson, 1990; Six, 1989).

The Jefferson Scale of Physician Lifelong Learning: There was a need in medical education research for a psychometrically sound instrument to measure physicians' orientation toward lifelong learning. In response to this need, in 2001 we began to develop the Jefferson Scale of Physician Lifelong Learning. Step-by-step procedures in the initial development of the Scale have been described in previous reports (Hojat, Gonnella, Nasca, & Veloski, 2004; Hojat, Veloski, Nasca, Erdmann, & Gonnella, 2006). To the best of our knowledge, this scale was the first and only instrument that could serve as an operational measure of physician lifelong learning. The first version of the Scale contained 19 items, each answered on a 4-point Likert-type scale (Strongly agree=4; Strongly disagree=1). The higher the score, the greater orientation toward lifelong learning.

Evidence in support of the psychometric properties of the Scale (construct validity, criterion-related validity, internal consistency reliability, and test retest reliability) was reported in two studies (Hojat et al., 2003; 2006). Further evidence in support of its psychometrics was reported in the second study, in which 444 physicians participated (Hojat et al., 2006). In the factor analysis of the 19 items of the Scale, four factors emerged: "professional learning beliefs and motivation," "scholarly activities," "attention to learning opportunities," and "technical skills in seeking information" (Hojat et al., 2006).

These four factors were similar to those found in our previous study involving 160 physicians (Hojat et al., 2003). For example, the "professional beliefs and motivation" factor in the second study corresponded to the two factors of "motivation" and "self-initiated learning" in the preliminary study. The "scholarly activities" factor in the second study corresponded with the "research endeavor" factor in the first study. The "attention to learning opportunities" factor that emerged in the second study corresponded to the "need recognition" factor in the first study. And finally, the "technical skills in information seeking" factor in the second study corresponded to the "technical skills" factor extracted in the first study. In addition, psychometric evidence supported its criterion-related validity, internal consistency reliability (coefficient alpha), and test- retest reliability (Hojat et al., 2003; 2006).

One of the limitations of the 19-item Scale was that some of its items (e.g., related to research activities) were not applicable to full-time clinicians who are not typically involved in formal research activities. It can also be presumed that lifelong learning priorities and activities of physicians who are involved exclusively in patient care (full- time clinicians) would be different from those who, in addition to patient care, are also involved in research and teaching (academic clinicians). Therefore, on the basis of the aforementioned presumption, it seemed beneficial to revise it so that it could be applicable to both groups of full-time clinicians and academic clinicians.

RESEARCH PURPOSES

We designed this study to revise the 19-item Scale so that it could be equally applicable to full-time clinicians as well as academic clinicians, and to study its validity and reliability after revision. In addition, we examined the correlations between scores of the revised Scale with criterion measures of research interest, learning motivation, information seeking skills, self-ratings of lifelong learning, the social desirability response style, career satisfaction, professional accomplishment, and indicators of academic performance before, during, and after medical school in the two groups of full-time clinicians and academic clinicians.

METHOD

Participants

The potential research participants included 5,553 living graduates of Jefferson Medical College between 1975 and 2000. Of this group 5,349 had deliverable mailing addresses. Research participants included 3,195 physicians of the aforementioned group who responded to a survey that was mailed in 2006. This represented 60% of those with deliverable mailing addresses and 58% of all living graduates in the selected time period. The respondents' ages (as of 2006) ranged from 29 to 66 years, with a mean and median of 46 and a standard deviation of 7.3. Women constituted 26% (n=826).

Research Instrument

A survey containing 42 items was mailed to the participants (Appendix A). Items 1, 2, and 3 addressed respondents' work status, work setting, and professional time per week devoted to various activities, respectively. Item 4 requested information about 11 professional accomplishments that presumably require continuous learning. Items 5 and 6 asked about respondents' satisfaction with their medical career and with their education at Jefferson, respectively, on a 10-point scale.

Items 7 to 25 of the survey included all 19 items of the Scale. (We describe the revisions in the Procedures section.) These items were answered on a 4-point Likert-type scale (1=Strongly Disagree, 4=Strongly Agree). For the purpose of studying the validity of the scale we included additional items in the survey. For example, 13 Likert-type questions about orientation toward lifelong learning and activities presumably associated with continuing medical education (26-27, 29-34, 36-38, 40-41 in Appendix A) were included. Also, three items (Items 28, 35, and 39) were adapted from the Zuckerman-Kuhlman Personality Questionnaire (ZKPQ) to detect the tendency to provide socially desirable responses (Zuckerman, Kuhlman, Joireman, Teta, & Kraft, 1993; Zuckerman, 2002). These three items were chosen from a 10-item "Infrequency" scale in the ZKPQ. The Infrequency scale was developed to detect intentionally false answers by identifying respondents who make responses that are unlikely to be true (Zuckerman, 2002). Finally, an item for measuring self-reported global ratings of lifelong learning was included in the survey (item 42, Appendix A) for the validity study.

Procedures

The Jefferson Scale of Physician Lifelong Learning (19-item) was refined based on the findings of two separate pilot studies to improve the clarity of the items, and to ensure that the items were relevant to the activities of physicians who were involved exclusively in patient care and others who, in addition to patient care, were also engaged in teaching and/or research. Participants in the first pilot study included 10 clinical faculty members at Jefferson Medical College who had been involved in medical education research. They were asked to review the wording of the 19 items to improve their clarity. All 10 faculty members responded, and the Scale was subsequently revised based on their feedback.

To incorporate feedback from practicing physicians, we undertook the second pilot study in which we asked 50 practicing physicians in the Jefferson Health System to further refine the contents and improve the clarity of the items of the Scale. A cover letter asked them to review the survey and make any suggestions to improve the clarity of the text in general. We also solicited the physicians' feedback on elements of the survey that addressed indicators of lifelong learning attitudes, orientation, and the activities of physicians involved in patient care and those who, in addition to patient care, were also involved in teaching, research, or in both. The survey was anonymous, and a copy of our previously published paper on physician lifelong learning (Hojat et al., 2003) was included to encourage cooperation.

Thirty physicians responded (60% response rate within four weeks) to the second pilot study. Based on their feedback, slight modifications were made to some items of the scale. For example, the item "I read professional journals every week" was slightly modified to "I read professional journals at least once a week." The modifications were significant only on the following item, which had read "I routinely attend grand rounds offered in my specialty regardless of whether a certificate of attendance is offered." It was changed to "I routinely attend continuing medical education programs to improve patient care."

Selection of Participants and Development of an Electronic Database: Identifying information (e.g., name, social security number, year of graduation, active or non-active status) for the potential participants was retrieved from the database of the Jefferson Longitudinal Study of Medical Education (Gonnella, Hojat, & Veloski, 2005; Hojat, Gonnella, Veloski, & Erdmann, 1996; information about the Jefferson Longitudinal Study of medical Education is also posted at: http://jdc.jefferson.edu/jlsme). Mailing addresses for these physicians were obtained from the Jefferson Alumni Office and were merged electronically with data from the Jefferson Longitudinal Study database. These data were maintained in a Microsoft Access database in which each graduate was assigned a confidential numerical code for the present study.

The purpose of these codes was to conceal respondents' identities and to maintain the confidentiality of individual information from the survey during data collection and data entry. These codes were also used as identifiers for merging data from the survey with those in the Jefferson Longitudinal Study of Medical Education. The codes also made it possible to follow-up on nonrespondents, correct addresses for those with address changes, and to identify those with invalid addresses. In addition, these codes allowed us to match respondents in the test-retest sample.

Mailing of the Surveys: Mailing labels were generated in the database for all physicians in the sample. A postcard was mailed to all potential research participants informing them about the study and that the survey would be mailed in two weeks. The purpose of a preliminary mailing of postcards was twofold. First, we wanted to identify any undeliverable addresses or changes of address. Second, we assumed that the postcard signed by two investigators (JSG and MH) could generate an expectancy among potential participants that could lead to a better response rate. Approximately two weeks after the postcards were mailed, 73 postcards were returned because of invalid addresses.

We sent the survey accompanied by a cover letter and an addressed postage-paid return envelope to the study sample with valid addresses. The full name of each physician, merged from the database, was printed on the cover letter which was signed by two investigators (JSG and MH). The confidential code was printed on the top right corner of the survey as well as on the cover letter and the mailing label to assure each coded survey was sent to the physician whose name was printed on the cover letter and the mailing address.

Approximately eight weeks after the initial mailing of the survey, the number of returned surveys declined to only a few per day. At this time, we sent the first reminder, which included a cover letter, a copy of the survey, and a return envelope to those who had not responded to the initial mailing. Approximately six weeks after the first reminders, the pace of returns had slowed to a few per week. We then mailed a second reminder, including a cover letter, the survey, and a return envelope, to the nonrespondents. A third reminder was mailed about eight weeks later. Information about the status of the survey, change of address, and invalid addresses for each individual participant was routinely updated in the Access database as we gradually received the surveys.

Retest Sample: To study the stability of responses, we mailed a second copy of the survey to a sample of 200 respondents to the first mailing with a brief cover letter. We received 132 completed surveys from the reliability study (66% response rate).

Merging Survey Data with Data from the Jefferson Longitudinal Study: Data from the returned surveys were entered into an electronic file and merged with data from the Jefferson Longitudinal Study of Medical Education (Gonnella, Hojat, & Veloski, 2005; Hojat, Gonnella, Veloski, & Erdmann, 1996; http://jdc.jefferson.edu/jlsme). Data included demographic information; performance measures before, during and after medical school; scores on medical licensing examinations (Parts 1, 2, and 3 of the NBME and Steps 1, 2, and 3 of the USMLE); and specialties.

PERFORMANCE VARIABLES

Relationships between scores of the Jefferson Scale of Physician Lifelong Learning and the following performance variables were examined in univariate and multivariate statistical models.

Measures of Performance Before Medical School: This set of measures included the following variables:

- scores on the Scholastic Aptitude Test (SAT) Verbal scales (taken in high school),
- scores on the SAT-Quantitative scale,
- scores on the Medical College Admission Test (MCAT),
- undergraduate grade point averages in science courses,
- undergraduate grade point averages in non-science courses, and

- interviewer ratings on the admission interview as an applicant to medical school.

The SAT scores obtained directly from the AAMC were self-reported and were available for 2,750 (86%) of the sample. The MCAT scores were available for almost all physicians in the sample. Subtests of the MCAT changed during the study period. For respondents who had graduated before 1982, we used the "Science" and "Verbal" subtests. For those who had graduated between 1982 and 1995, we used the "Science Problem Solving" and "Reading" subtests, and for those who graduated after 1995, we used the "Biological Sciences" and "Verbal Reasoning" subtests.

The respondents' admission interviews were rated on a 12-point scale, with a higher score indicating a more favorable rating. Demographic variables, such as gender and age at entrance to medical school, were also used in statistical analyses. The possible confounding effects of these demographic variables were controlled for in multiple regression analysis by examining the unique contribution of other variables in the model.

Measures of Performance during Medical School: In this set, we used the following variables:

- first-year grade point average (GPA) in medical school,
- second-year GPA in medical school,
- grades on objective examinations in six major clerkships in the third year of medical school (family medicine, medicine, obstetrics-gynecology, pediatrics, psychiatry, and surgery),
- average global ratings of clinical competence given to each of the six aforementioned third-year major clerkships,
- medical school class rank,
- scores on Part 1 of the licensing examinations of the National Board of Medical Examiners (NBME) or Step 1 of the United States Medical Licensing Examinations (USMLE), and
- scores on Part 2 of the NBME or on Step 2 of the USMLE.

The first- and second-year GPAs are based on objective examinations with reliability coefficients that are usually in the 0.70s or higher. Evidence in support of the short- and long-term predictive validity of these GPAs has been reported (Gonnella, Erdmann, & Hojat, 2004; Hojat, Gonnella, Erdmann & Veloski, 1997). Also, data supporting the predictive validity of global ratings of clinical competence in the six major clerkships are available for our graduates (Callahan et al., 2000).

Medical school class rank was calculated based on one-third weight given to performance measures in the basic sciences component of medical school education, and two-thirds to the clinical sciences component of medical school education. Evidence in support of the psychometrics and predictive validity of the medical school class rank has been reported (Blacklow, Goepp & Hojat, 1991; 1993). Students usually take Part 1 of the NBME or Step 1 of the USMLE at the end of the second year and Part 2 of the NBME or Step 2 of the USMLE in the fourth year of medical school.

Measures of Performance in First Year of Residency: The following set of variables was selected:

- average ratings in the postgraduate competence area of "knowledge and clinical capabilities,"
- average ratings in the postgraduate competence area of "professionalism,"
- scores on Part 3 of the NBME or Step 3 of the USMLE.

The physicians' postgraduate competence was rated on 24 items at the end of the first postgraduate year by either the residency program director or a faculty member most familiar with the residents' performance. The two components of postgraduate competence — "knowledge and clinical capabilities" (the science of medicine) and "professionalism" (the art of medicine) — emerged in a factor analytic study (Hojat et al., 2007). Data in support of the psychometric properties of these ratings have been reported for the original version of the rating form (Hojat, Veloski and Borenstein, 1986; Hojat, Borenstein and Veloski, 1988), as well as for the revised version (Hojat et al., 2007). Ratings of postgraduate clinical competence and scores on Step 3 of the USMLE (formerly Part 3 of the NBME) were available for about 75% of the study sample who had granted us permission for collecting such data.

This set of measures included the number of hours worked per week in "patient care," "administration," and "continuing medical education" (item 3, Appendix A).

Also, participation in any of the following 11 indicators of professional accomplishment (in the past five years) that presumably require continuous learning were used for the study of criterion-related validity of the lifelong learning scale (item 4 in Appendix A):

- publishing articles in peer-reviewed journals,
- presenting papers before a national professional group,
- conducting research,
- receiving a research or training grant,
- receiving a professional award or honor,
- holding an office in a national professional organization,
- serving on a professional committee (e.g., hospital, professional society),
- serving as an editor or editorial board member of a professional journal
- serving as a peer reviewer for a professional journal,
- sharing in the development of a new medical or surgical procedure, instrument, drug, or technique that was described in the literature, or
- presenting patient education or research findings on radio or television, in a newspaper, or before a community group.

STATISTICAL ANALYSIS

Data for the 19 items of the Jefferson Scale of Physician Lifelong Learning (7-25 in Appendix A) and the 16 items as the criterion measures for the validity study (26-41 in Appendix A) were separately subjected to principal component factor analysis (varimax rotation) to examine the underlying components of each set of items. Correlational methods (bivariate correlations, multiple regression) were used to examine the validity of the scale and to study the correlates of physician lifelong learning in the full-time clinicians and academic clinicians. Also, *t*-test and analysis of variance were used to detect group differences on the lifelong learning scores.

Measures of performance during medical school and on medical licensing examinations and ratings of clinical competence in residency training were linearly transformed to a standardized distribution with a mean of 100 and a standard deviation of 10 to allow the comparison of differences on a standard scale.

Statistical Versus Practical (Clinical) Significance: Because of the large sample size, small-group differences or negligible correlations could be statistically significant but practically (clinically) unimportant (Cohen, 1987; Hojat and Xu, 2004). Therefore, when appropriate, we examined the effect size estimates for statistically significant differences, correlations, or associations to assure that the statistically significant findings were practically (clinically) important as well.

For the purpose of determining the clinical significance of the findings, we used the operational definitions for the magnitude of effect size estimates suggested by Cohen (1987). For example, in comparisons of two means, we considered the magnitude of an effect size that was less than 0.25 to be clinically unimportant. Effect sizes less than 0.10 in chi-square analyses—as well as correlations with a magnitude of less than 0.10, or standardized regression coefficients less than 0.10—were also considered to be negligible, thus practically unimportant. The number of observations in different statistical analyses varies slightly as a result of missing data.

RESULTS

Comparison of Respondents and Nonrespondents

To examine the representativeness of respondents, we compared them with those who did not respond ($n=$ 2,262) on a number of variables. The respondents' mean age (as of 2006) was 46.8 years ($SD = 7.3$). The nonrespondents' mean age was 46.2 ($SD = 7.4$), and the effect size of the difference was only 0.06, which can be regarded as practically (clinically) unimportant. According to Cohen (1987), when comparing two means, effect sizes around 0.25 or less are considered small and clinically negligible, and those around 0.50 are moderate, while those around 0.75 and larger are clinically important (also see Hojat and Xu, 2004).

The respondents and nonrespondents were also compared by gender, ethnic group, and specialty. No significant gender difference was observed in response rates between men (58%) and women (60%) ($\chi2(1) = 2.23$, $p=0.14$). Among ethnic groups, African American physicians had the lowest response rate (39%), followed by Asians (50%), Hispanics (57%), and whites (60%). Although the association between ethnicity and response rate was statistically significant ($\chi2(4) =40.80$, $p<0.01$), the related effect size (0.07) was negligible. For chi-square tests, effect size estimates lower than 0.10 are negligible (Cohen, 1987). The response rate was highest among physicians in ophthalmology (65%) and lowest among those in hospital-based specialties (anesthesiology, pathology, radiology) (47%). The association was statistically significant, but practically unimportant ($\chi2(9) = 31.65$, $p<0.01$, effect size = 0.07).

Respondents and nonrespondents were also compared on measures of performance during medical school (GPAs in years 1 and 2, examination grades, and global ratings of clinical competence in year 3); ratings of global clinical competence in third year major clerkships; postgraduate competence ratings on "Knowledge and clinical capabilities" and "Professionalism"); and scores on medical licensing examinations (USMLE, Steps 1, 2, and 3 or, formerly, NBME, Parts 1, 2, and 3). The summary results are reported in Table 1.

As shown in the table, although all of the differences between the two groups of respondents and nonrespondents were statistically significant (using the *t*-test and Bonferroni correction), the effect sizes were all smaller than 0.25. While these findings generally suggest that nonrespondents were more likely than respondents to be African American, more likely to practice hospital-based specialties, and more likely to perform lower on selected measures of academic performance during and after medical school, none of the effect sizes of the differences reached the magnitude of clinical importance. These findings were consistent with those in another study in which it was found that research volunteers, compared to nonvolunteers, were more likely to be among high achievers in medical school (Callahan, Hojat & Gonnella, 2007).

Table 1. Effect Sizes of Differences between Respondents and Non-Respondents on Performance Measures (Entire Sample)

Performance Measures	Effect Size [1]
During Medical School	
GPAs in 1st and 2nd yr	0.08
Examination grades in 3rd yr	0.14
Global ratings of clinical competence (3rdyr)	0.19
1st Postgraduate Year-Ratings of Competence	
Knowledge and Clinical Capabilities	0.13
Professionalism	0.13
Licensing Examination	
USMLE Step 1/ NBME Part 1	0.05
USMLE Step 2 / NBME Part 2	0.13
USMLE Step 3 / NBME Part 3	0.11

[1] All differences were statistically significant (p<0.05) by t-test corrected for number of comparisons (Bonferroni's correction). However, all of the effect sizes were small in magnitude and considered negligible based on operational definition of effect size suggested by Cohen (1987). The effect size was calculated by the following formula: (mean for respondents minus mean for non-respondents)/pooled standard deviation.

Based on the aforementioned findings we concluded that the observed differences between respondents and nonrespondents on age, gender, ethnicity, specialty, measures of performance during and after medical school, and scores on medical licensing examinations were all negligible. Thus, we concluded that the respondents fairly represented the entire cohort of graduates of Jefferson Medical College during the study period with regard to the aforementioned variables.

CLASSIFICATION OF RESPONDENTS

We classified respondents into the following categories based on the number of hours per typical week they reported spending in patient care, teaching, research, and administration.

Full-Time Clinicians: Included 1,127 respondents (77% men) who reported spending more than 28 hours per week (FTE of 4 days) involved in patient care, *without* any involvement with teaching and research (0 hours/week in teaching and research).

Academic Clinicians: Included 1,612 respondents (75% men) who reported spending more than seven hours per week (FTE of one day) involved with patient care *and some* involvement with teaching or research (> 0 hours/week in teaching or research).

Other Physicians: The rest was a heterogeneous mix of physicians (*n*=456) involved mostly in administrative activities or research who were excluded from statistical analyses in which only full-time clinicians and academic clinicians were compared.

Factor Analysis of the Jefferson Scale of Physician Lifelong Learning

The underlying components of the 19 items of the Scale were examined for the entire sample by using principal components factor analysis followed by varimax rotation. Results are summarized in Table 2. As reported in the table, the four extracted factors with eigenvalues greater than 1 accounted for 60% of the total variance before rotation. Ten items had factor loadings greater than 0.35 on the first factor. This factor, which accounted for 33% of the variance, was considered to be a grand factor of the 19-item Scale involving "learning beliefs and motivation" (corresponding eigenvalue = 6.2). The following item had the largest factor loading on this factor: "Rapid changes in medical science require constant updating of knowledge and development of new professional skills."

Six items had factor loadings greater than 0.35 on the second factor, which accounted for 13% of the variance (eigenvalue = 2.3). Based on the content of the items with high factor loadings, this factor can be regarded as a construct involving "scholarly activities." The following item had the largest factor loading: "I publish articles in peer-review journals."

The third factor included three items with factor loadings greater than 0.35 and accounted for 8% of the variance (eigenvalue = 1.2). This factor was considered to be an underlying construct involving "attention to learning opportunities." The following item had the largest factor loading: "I routinely attend continuing medical education programs to improve patient care." *

Finally, only two items had factor loadings greater than 0.35 on the fourth factor, which accounted for 6% of the variance (eigenvalue=1.1). This factor was titled "Technical skills in information seeking." The following item had the largest factor loading: "I routinely search computer databases to find out about new developments in my specialty." All items were mono-factorial, with the exception of the following two items, which had loadings greater than 0.35 on two factors (bi-factorial items).

The first item was "I take every opportunity to gain new knowledge/skills that are important to my profession" (loading on factor 1 was 0.44 and 0.51 on factor 3). The other item was "I routinely attend annual meetings of professional medical organizations" (loading on factor 2 was 0.36 and on factor 3 was 0.47). Therefore, despite the changes in wording, the results of factor analyses confirmed the factor structure emerged in our previous studies (Hojat et al, 2003; 2006) with only minor changes in the magnitudes of factor coefficients.

Table 2. Summary Results of Factor Analysis of the 19-Item Jefferson Scale of Physician Lifelong Learning (Entire Sample)

Items[1]		Rotated Factor Coefficients			
		1	2	3	4
Factor 1: Learning Beliefs and Motivation					
1	Rapid changes in medical science require constant updating of knowledge and development of new professional skills.	**0.76**	0.08	0.07	0.05
2	I recognize my need to constantly acquire new professional knowledge.	**0.70**	0.1	0.23	0.09
3	I believe that I would fall behind if I stopped learning about new developments in my profession.	**0.61**	0.07	0.17	0.15
4	Life-long learning is a professional responsibility of all physicians.	**0.60**	0.01	0.15	0.05
5	One of the important goals of medical school is to develop students' life-long learning skills.	**0.57**	0.16	0.11	0.03
6	I enjoy reading articles in which issues of my professional interest are discussed.	**0.52**	0.05	0.23	0.14
7	I always make time for self-directed learning, even when I have a busy practice schedule and other professional and family obligations.	**0.48**	0.1	**0.35**	0.21
8	I read professional journals at least once every week.	**0.42**	0.1	0.33	0.24
9	Searching for the answer to a question is, in and by itself rewarding.	**0.39**	0.08	0.08	0.14
Factor 2: Scholarly Activities					
10	I publish articles in peer-reviewed journals.	0.07	**0.86**	0.05	0.14
11	I conduct research as a principal investigator or a co-investigator.	0.05	**0.80**	0.05	0.1
12	I give on average at least one presentation per year at a professional meeting.	0.09	**0.75**	0.13	0.16
13	I routinely exchange e-mail with colleagues.	0.13	**0.49**	0.2	**0.35**
14	I attend educational programs whether or not CME credit is offered.	0.26	**0.39**	0.33	0.09
Factor 3: Attention to Learning Opportunity					
15	I routinely attend continuing medical education programs to improve patient care.	0.32	0.07	**0.60**	0.03
16	I take every opportunity to gain new knowledge/skills that are important to my profession.	**0.44**	0.13	**0.51**	0.18
17	I routinely attend annual meetings of professional medical organizations.	0.16	**0.36**	**0.47**	0.1
Factor 4: Technical Skills in Information Seeking					
18	I routinely search computer databases to find out about new developments in my specialty.	0.22	0.23	0.19	**0.83**
19	My preferred approach in finding an answer to a question is to search the appropriate computer databases.	0.17	0.22	0.03	**0.58**
Eigenvalue	6.2	2.3	1.2	1.1	
% Variance	33	13	8	6	

[1] Items are listed by the order of the magnitude of the factor coefficient within each factor. Values greater than 0.35 are in bold. Items were answered on a 4-point Likert-type scale (1=strongly disagree, 4= strongly agree).

REVISING THE JEFFERSON SCALE OF PHYSICIAN LIFELONG LEARNING

The following steps were taken to revise the Jefferson Scale of Physician Lifelong Learning to make it applicable to both "full-time clinicians" and "academic clinicians." First, the content of the 19-item Scale was judged by participants of two pilot studies described earlier to determine the items' face validity for the two groups of full-time clinicians and academic clinicians. In these pilot studies the appropriateness of the items for measuring lifelong learning among full-time clinicians and academic clinicians was subjectively evaluated. Five items related to research and teaching activities were not considered by at least one-third of participants to be optimal indicators of lifelong learning for full-time clinicians who are not involved in research and teaching activities.

These five items happened to be those with high loadings on the second factor (scholarly activities) that emerged in factor analysis of the complete set of 19 items for the entire sample. We used the remaining 14 items with high loadings on the other three factors ("learning beliefs and motivation," "attention to learning opportunities," and "technical skills in information seeking") to create a shorter, revised version of the Jefferson Scale of Physician Empathy (acronym JeffSPLL, Appendix B). Thus, this 14-item revised version was considered to be appropriate for administration to both full-time clinicians as well as academic clinicians.

In another study, we examined the underlying factors of the 14-item JeffSPLL for full-time clinicians and academic clinicians (Hojat, Veloski & Gonnella, 2009). Three factors of "learning beliefs and motivation," "attention to learning opportunity," and "technical skills in seeking information" emerged from the 14-item JeffSPLL for both groups of physicians (Hojat et al., 2009). These findings suggest that the underlying construct of the JeffSPLL remained stable for different groups of physicians, and the construct of the JeffSPLL is consistent with the definition of the concept it purports to measure.

Furthermore, the fact that these mathematically derived factors are also conceptually relevant to the features of lifelong learning described by others (Bligh, 1993; Candy, 1991; Cole, 1998; Jennet & Swanson, 1994; Nelson, 1998; Schrock * Cydulka, 2006; Ward, Gruppen, & Regehr, 2002) provides support for the construct validity of the JeffSPLL.

Brahim (2007) asked students at Indiana University School of Medicine about their perceptions of features of lifelong learning in medicine. By content analysis of students' responses, Brahim concluded that the underlying construct of our scale reported in this and previous studies (Hojat et al., 2003, 2006, in press) was fully supported by her findings.

UNDERLYING CONSTRUCT OF THE CRITERION MEASURES

Responses to items 26 through 41 of the survey (Appendix A) for examining the criterion-related validity of the JeffSPLL and its factors were subjected to factor analysis (principal component factor extraction with varimax rotation). The results of the factor analysis are summarized in Table 3.

Table 3. Summary Results of Factor Analysis of the Criterion Measures (Entire Sample)

Criterion Measures		Rotated Factor Coefficients				
		1	2	3	4	5
Factor 1: Research Interest						
1	I consider myself a researcher as well as a clinician.	**0.86**	0.16	0.16	-0.05	0.06
2	I enjoy conducting research.	**0.81**	0.10	0.18	-0.06	0.08
3	Despite the demands on my time, I have found time to participate in clinical trials and other clinical investigations.	**0.79**	0.11	0.15	-0.01	0.03
4	In seeking answers to questions I routinely try to collect and analyze data.	**0.38**	**0.36**	0.16	-0.14	0.02
Factor 2: Intrinsic Motivation						
5	I can easily recognize what I need to learn with regard to the rapid advances in medicine	0.12	**0.59**	0.13	0.01	0.04
6	Regardless of my busy professional schedule, I always feel the motivation to learn about new advance in medicine.	0.15	**0.57**	0.10	-0.27	0.16
7	I frequently give up free time to keep up to date professionally.	0.21	**0.43**	0.07	-0.23	0.10
8	I can easily recognize my professional strengths and weaknesses.	0.01	**0.42**	0.06	0.00	0.03
Factor 3: Information Seeking Skills						
9	I can say that I am pretty competent in using a computer in database search, email, power point and word processing.	0.17	0.11	**0.84**	-0.02	0.00
10	I believe that every physician needs to be able to use the internet to keep up with new advances in medicine.	0.07	0.18	**0.52**	-0.07	0.01
11	I keep electronic health records of my patients	0.20	0.07	**0.36**	0.00	0.10
Factor 4: Extrinsic Motivation						
12	I am not interested in learning new things for the sake of learning, unless there is a practical need for it.	-0.08	-0.08	0.04	**0.62**	0.01
13	Learning cannot be initiated by itself. There should be an external factor to initiate it.	-0.01	-0.09	0.03	**0.55**	0.06
Factor 5: Social Desirability Response Style						
14	I never met a person that I did not like.	0.06	0.01	0.01	0.03	**0.77**
15	I have never been bored.	0.09	0.27	0.05	0.09	**0.31**
16	I never have any trouble understanding anything I read that first time I read it.	0.00	0.21	0.07	0.15	**0.28**
Eigenvalue		3.8	1.6	1.4	1.3	1.1
% Variance (before rotation)		24	10	9	8	7

Item are listed by the order of the magnitude of the factor coefficients within each factor. Values greater than 0.25 are in bold. Items were answered on 4-point Likert-type scale (1=strongly disagree, 4= strongly agree).

As shown in the table, five factors emerged, each with an eigenvalue greater than 1. These five factors accounted for 58 percent of the total variance, before rotation. Factor 1 can be regarded as a construct involving "research interest" (eigenvalue = 3.8, accounting for 24% of the variance). Four items had factor loadings greater than 0.35 on this factor. The following item had the largest factor loading (0.86): "I consider myself a researcher as well as a clinician." We expected that the scores of this factor would yield a larger validity coefficient with the total JeffSPLL for academic clinicians than for full-time clinicians due to the involvement of the former group in research activities.

Five items had factor loadings greater than 0.35 on the second factor (eigenvalue = 1.6, accounting for 10% of the variance). This factor, based on the content of the five items with high factor loadings, can be considered as a construct involving "intrinsic motivation." The following item had the largest factor loading (0.59): "I can easily recognize what I need to learn with regard to the rapid advances in medicine." We expected the scores for this factor to yield higher validity coefficients with scores of the "learning beliefs and motivation" and "attention to learning opportunities" factors of the JeffSPLL than with scores of the "technical skills in information seeking" factor for both groups of physicians.

Two items had factor loadings greater than 0.35 on factor 3, titled "computer skills" (corresponding eigenvalue = 1.4, accounting for 9% of the variance). The item with a higher factor loading (0.84) was "I can say that I am pretty competent in using a computer in database search, email, power point and word processing." We expected that scores of this factor would yield the highest validity coefficient with scores of the "technical skills in information seeking" factor of the JeffSPLL for both groups of physicians.

Two items had factor loadings greater than 0.35 on the fourth factor (eigenvalue = 1.3, accounting for 8% of the variance) (see Table 3). The content of these items indicated that this factor measures "extrinsic motivation" or learning motivated by external factors. The item with the higher factor loading (0.62) was "I am not interested in learning new things for the sake of learning, unless there is a practical need for it." We expected the scores for this factor to yield negligible or negative correlations with the total score and factor scores of the JeffSPLL, because of the assumption that lifelong learners are motivated by intrinsic forces primarily for the sake of learning not for obtaining certificates of attendance!

Finally, three items that were adapted from the ZKPQ to detect social desirability response style had the highest factor loading on the fifth factor, "social desirability response style." The item with the greatest loading (0.77) on this factor was "I never met a person that I did not like." Assuming that respondents completed the survey honestly, we expected no significant correlations between scores for this factor and the total or factor scores for the JeffSPLL. Otherwise, controlling for the effect of the social desirability style in all statistical analyses of the JeffSPLL would be necessary.

CRITERION-RELATED VALIDITY OF THE JEFFSPLL

We examined the criterion-related validity coefficients (Pearson product-moment correlations) between total scores of the JeffSPLL, and its factor scores (three factors), and the factor scores of the criterion measures (five factors) in both groups of full-time clinicians and academic clinicians separately. Weighted factor scores were used in these analyses. The summary results for the full-time clinicians and academic clinicians are reported in Table 4.

As predicted, high correlations among scores for the "intrinsic motivation" factor of the criterion measures and factor scores for "learning beliefs and motivation" ($r=0.41$ for full-time clinicians and $r=0.45$ for academic clinicians) and "attention to learning opportunities" ($r=0.41$ for full-time clinicians and $r=0.40$ for academic clinicians) were confirmed. Also, expectations of negligible or negative validity coefficients with scores of the "extrinsic motivation" factor of the criterion measure were supported. It is also interesting to note that as expected the correlations between "learning beliefs and motivation factor" of the JeffSPLL and scores on the "extrinsic motivation" of the criterion measure were significantly negative ($r=-0.35$) for both group of physicians. Similar results were obtained for the total scores of the JeffSPLL.

Table 4. Validity Coefficients Between Factor Scores and the Total Scores of the JeffSPLL and the Criterion Measure Factors for Full-Time Clinicians (FTC) and Academic Clinicians (ACAD)

Criterion Measure Factors	Factor Scores			
	Learning Beliefs and Motivation FTC (ACAD)	Attention to Learning Opportunities FTC (ACAD)	Technical Skills in Information Seeking FTC (ACAD)	JeffSPLL Total Scores FTC (ACAD)
Research Interest	-0.04 † (0.13)	0.04 † (0.07)	0.04† (0.11)	0.06 (0.34)
Intrinsic Motivation	0.41 (0.45)	0.41 (0.40)	0.16 (0.10)	0.50 (0.54)
Information Seeking Skills	0.07 (0.14)	0.06 (0.09)	0.47 (0.41)	0.33 (0.35)
Extrinsic Motivation	-0.35 (-0.35)	-0.16 (-0.21)	-0.06 (-0.02†)	-0.28 (-0.32)
Social Desirability Response style [1]	0.05† (0.03 †)	0.13 (0.06)	0.01† (0.01 †)	0.09 (0.05)
Global Rating of Lifelong Learning [2]	0.47 (0.49)	0.36 (0.36)	0.17 (0.13)	0.55 (0.58)

[1] Based on responses to a 3-item scale adapted from the Zuckerman-Kuhlman Personality Questionnaire (ZKPQ) used for detecting social desirability response bias.
[2] Based on response to a question asking physicians to rate themselves in lifelong on a 10-point scale.
† Non-significant ($p>0.05$), other correlations are statistically significant ($p<0.05$), however, correlations smaller than 0.10 in magnitude are considered negligible based on the operational definitions suggested by Cohen (1987).

As expected, no substantial correlation was found between scores on the three factors, and the total scores of the JeffSPLL and factor scores of the "social desirability response style," suggesting that the pattern of findings cannot be substantially distorted by the possibility of social desirability response bias. The total scores of the JeffSPLL were substantially correlated with the global ratings of lifelong learning (item 42, Appendix A) for full-time clinicians ($r=0.55$) and academic clinicians ($r=0.58$). These findings provide strong support for the criterion-related validity of the JeffSPLL for both groups of full-time clinicians as well as academic clinicians.

Descriptive Statistics and Reliability Coefficients for the JeffSPLL: Descriptive statistics of the JeffSPLL for the two groups of full-time clinicians and academic clinicians are reported in Table 5.

The mean score for full-time clinicians ($M=44.5$) was smaller than that for academic clinicians ($M=47.1$)($t(2752) =11.2$, $p<0.01$, effect size=0.37) indicating that academic clinicians expressed a stronger inclination toward lifelong learning than full-time clinicians. No significant difference was observed between the two groups on standard deviations of their corresponding scores.

Table 5. Descriptive Statistics and Reliability Coefficients for the JeffSPLL

	Groups	
	Full-Time Clinicians	Academic Clinicians
Means	44.5	47.1
Standard Deviation	5.5	5.3
25th percentile	41	43
50th percentile (median)	45	48
75th percentile	49	52
Actual range1	28-56	28-56
Coefficient alpha	0.85	0.86
Test-Retest2	0.72	0.77

[1] Possible range of scores: 14-56.
[2] Test-retest reliability was calculated for physicians who completed the survey for a second time within approximately four months between testing. The retest reliability sample size for full-time clinicians was 49, and for academic clinicians was 73.

Adapted from: Hojat, M., Veloski, J.J., and Gonnella, J.S. (2009). Measurement and correlates of physicians' lifelong learning. Academic Medicine. 84, 1066-1074, Copyright ©2009, Association of American Medical Colleges.

The Cronbach's coefficient alpha reliability was equally large for both groups (0.85, and 0.85, respectively), and test-retest reliability coefficients were at an acceptable range for psychological testing (0.72 and 0.77, respectively). Cronbach's coefficient alpha is an indicator of the internal consistency aspect of a test's reliability, and the test-retest reliability coefficient is an indicator of the test scores' stability over time. Test-retest reliability was calculated for the physicians who completed the survey twice approximately four months apart. The sample sizes for test-retest reliability were 49 (for full-time clinicians) and 73 (for academic clinicians).

The magnitude of the obtained reliability coefficients indicates that the scores of the JeffSPLL are not only internally consistent (coefficient alpha) but also are relatively stable over-time (test-retest reliability) for both groups of physicians. Score distributions for both groups are reported in Table 6.

CORRELATES OF THE JEFFSPLL SCORES

For each group of full-time clinicians and academic clinicians we examined the univariate and multivariate correlations between scores of the JeffSPLL and three sets of measures collected before, during, and after medical school.

Before Medical School: The following seven variables were included in the set of measures collected before medical school: Age at entrance to medical school (in years), gender (male=1, female=0); SAT (Verbal) and SAT (Quantitative) scores; undergraduate GPAs (in science courses); undergraduate GPAs (in nonscience courses); and ratings for medical school admission interview.

As we indicated earlier, because of the large sample size, correlations of negligible magnitude can be statistically significant but of no practical value. Using Cohen's suggested guidelines (1987) concerning the operational definition of effect size estimates in correlational analysis, we regarded any correlation coefficient less than 0.10 as an effect size that was practically (clinically) unimportant. We also used a similar cut-off point for the standardized beta coefficients in multiple regression analyses.

Table 6. Frequency Distributions and Cumulative Percentages of Scores of the JeffSPLL

	Groups			
	Full-Time Clinicians		Academic Clinicians	
Score	Frequency	Cumulative %	Frequency	Cumulative %
≤ 28	1	<1	1	<1
29-31	8	1	2	<1
32-34	33	4	7	1
35-37	61	9	42	3
38-40	153	23	148	12
41-43	215	42	238	27
44-46	226	62	250	43
47-49	178	78	310	62
50-52	144	90	317	82
53-55	93	99	244	97
56	14	100	51	100

The results of bivariate and multivariate correlations for the full-time clinicians and academic clinicians are reported in Table 7. As shown in the table, there was only one marginally significant inverse relationship between the JeffSPLL scores and undergraduate GPAs in nonscience courses for full-time clinicians (β=-0.10). All other relationships were negligible, suggesting that demographic variables and performance measures prior to medical school have no practical relevance to orientation toward lifelong learning in either group of physicians.

During Medical School: The following six variables were included among performance measures collected during medical school: First-year GPAs, second-year GPAs, third-year examination grades, third-year clinical competence ratings on six major clerkships, scores on Step 1 of the USMLE (formerly Part 1 of the NBME examinations), and scores on Step 2 of the USMLE (formerly Part 2 of the NBME examinations).

Bivariate and multivariate correlations and standardized regression coefficients for full-time clinicians and academic clinicians are reported in Table 8. As shown in the table, in the multivariate statistical models, the GPAs in the first year (negative correlation) and second years of medical school showed a statistically significant relationship with JeffSPLL scores in the full-time clinicians, but the magnitude of multivariate *R* was only 0.10 which is marginal according to our definition of clinical significance. The first-year GPAs' negative contribution to the model could have been an artifact of high correlations between the predictors. For academic clinicians, the only significant predictor of orientation toward lifelong learning was the competence ratings in the third-year core clerkships. Overall, we can conclude that performance measures during medical school do not yield a practically strong relationship with the JeffSPLL scores.

Table 7. Correlations between the JeffSPLL Scores, Demographics, and Performance Measures Before Medical School

	Groups			
	Full-Time Clinicians		Academic Clinicians	
	Bivariate	Beta	Bivariat	Beta
Performance Measures	R	Coefficient	r	Coefficient
Age at Entrance to Medical School	0.05†	-0.02†	0	-0.05†
Gender (Male=1, Female=2)	0.01†	0.02†	-0.01†	0.03†
SAT-Verbal	0.03†	0.03†	0.03†	0.09**
SAT-Quantitative	-0.07†	-0.08†	-0.03†	-0.09**
Undergraduate GPAs (Science Courses)	-0.07*	0.01†	-0.00†	-0.01†
Undergraduate GPAs (Non-Science	-0.09**	-0.10*	-0.02†	0.00†
Medical School Admission Interview Rating	0.02†	0.03†	0.00†	0.03†
Multiple R (Adjusted)		0.07†		0.07†

** $p<0.01$, * $p<0.05$, †p=Nonsignificant.

Table 8. Correlations between the JeffSPLL Scores and Performance Measures During Medical School

Groups				
	Full-Time Clinicians		Academic Clinicians	
	Bivariate	Beta	Bivariate	Beta
Performance Measures	R	Coefficient	r	Coefficien
1st Year GPAs	-0.02†	-0.14**	0.01†	-0.08*
2nd Year GPAs	0.04†	0.13*	0.04†	0
3rd Year Examinations	0.05†	0.01†	0.06*	0.01†
3rd Year Clerkships Competence	0.07*	0.05†	0.12**	0.11*
USLME-Step 1/NBME-Part1	0.03†	-0.03†	0.06*	0.08†
USLME-Step 2/NBME-Part2	0.06*	0.05†	0.07*	0.02†
Multiple R (Adjusted)		0.10*		0.12**

** $p<0.01$, * $p<0.05$, †p =Nonsignificant.

To examine the relationships between scores of the JeffSPLL and medical school class rank, we compared the JeffSPLL scores in three groups of physicians who were classified in the top 25%, middle 50%, and bottom 25% of medical school class rank. Summary statistical results are reported in Table 9.

Data reported in the table indicate that for both groups of full-time clinicians and academic clinicians, the JeffSPLL mean scores for the top 25% were higher than the bottom 25% in the class. The results of analysis of variance indicated that the differences were statistically significant, although the effect sizes were marginal (0.09, and 0.07 for full-time clinicians and academic clinicians, respectively). A positive correlation between self-directed learning scores and performance in medical school has been reported (Shokak, Shokar, Romeo & Bulik, 2002). However, our findings generally did not indicate a strong relationship between scores of the JeffSPLL and performance measures in medical school.

Table 9. Scores of the JeffSPLL by Top 25%, Middle 50%, and Bottom 25% of Medical School Rank

	Groups			
Medical School Rank	Full-Time Clinicians		Academic Clinicians	
	M	SD	M	SD
Top 25%	45.4	5.4	47.9	5.1
Middle 50%	44.7	5.5	47.1	5.3
Bottom 25%	44.2	5.6	46.5	5.3
F-ratio	3.18*		5.6**	

M=Mean, SD=Standard Deviation.
** $p<0.01$.
Adapted from: Hojat, M., Veloski, J.J., and Gonnella, J.S. (2009). Measurement and correlates of physicians' lifelong learning. *Academic Medicine. 84*, 1066-1074, Copyright ©2009, Association of American Medical Colleges.

First year of Residency Training: We examined the relationships between scores of the JeffSPLL and the following three measures of performance in residency: Average ratings on factors of "medical knowledge and clinical capability" and "professionalism" given by the directors of residency programs upon completion of the first year of residency, and scores in Step 3/Part 3 of the medical licensing examinations. Bivariate and multivariate correlations and standardized regression coefficients for three variables in the two groups of physicians are reported in Table 10. As the table illustrates, none of the three variables showed a practically significant relationship with scores of the JeffSPLL in full-time clinicians. However, for academic clinicians, performance of Part 3/Step 3 of medical licensing examinations could marginally predict the JeffSPLL scores ($R=0.12$, $p<0.01$).

PROFESSIONAL ACTIVITIES

We examined relationships between scores of the JeffSPLL and time devoted to the following professional activities: Patient care, administration, and continuing medical education (item 3, Appendix A).

Bivariate and multivariate correlations and standardized regression coefficients for the two groups of physicians are reported in Table 11.

As illustrated in the table, for both groups, the only practically significant correlation with the JeffSPLL was the time devoted to continuing medical education activities. However, this relationship was stronger for academic clinicians ($R=0.24$, $p<0.01$) than full-time clinicians ($R=0.15$, $p<.01$).

Professional Accomplishments: Results of correlational analyses of the JeffSPLL scores and 11 indicators of professional accomplishments (item 4, Appendix A) are reported in Table 12. The obtained bivariate correlations were practically significant for six indicators of professional accomplishments in full-time clinicians and for all accomplishment indicators in academic clinicians. For full-time clinicians, the largest correlation was found between scores of the JeffSPLL and physicians' presenting patient education or medical research findings in the public media ($r=0.23$). For academic clinicians, the largest correlation was obtained between scores of the JeffSPLL and physicians' serving as a reviewer for a professional journal ($r=0.28$) and also for physicians' publication and research activities ($r=0.27$).

Table 10. Correlations between the JeffSPLL Scores and Measures of Clinical Competence in Residency

	Groups			
	Full-time Clinicians		Academic Clinicians	
	Bivariate	Beta	Bivariate	Beta
Clinical Competence Measures	r	Coefficient	r	Coefficient
Medical knowledge and Clinical Capability[1]	0.05†	0.03†	0.06*	0.07†
Professionalism [1]	0.04†	0.01†	0.03†	-0.02†
Score on USMLE-Step3/NBME- Part 3	0.07*	0.05†	0.11**	0.10**
Multiple R (Adjusted)		0		0.12**

** $p<0.01$, * $p<0.05$, † p=Nonsignificant.
[1] Ratings given by the residency program directors on a 24-item rating form at the end of the first postgraduate year (Hojat et al., 2007).

Table 11. Correlations between Scores on the JeffSPLL and Time Per Week Devoted to Professional Activities

	Groups			
	Full-Time Clinicians		Academic Clinicians	
	Bivariate	Beta	Bivariate	Beta
Professional Activities	r	Coefficient	r	Coefficient
Patient Care	0.05†	0.06*	-0.07**	-0.04†
Administration	0.07*	0.07*	0.11**	0.07**
Continuing Medical Education	0.13**	0.12**	0.23**	0.22**
Adjusted R		0.15**		0.24**

** $p<0.01$; * $p<0.05$; † p=Nonsignificant.

In the multivariate statistical model, presentation of patient education and medical research findings had the largest unique contribution to the scores of the JeffSPLL in full-time clinicians ($\beta=0.18$). The largest standardized regression coefficients for academic clinicians were obtained for conducting research, receiving research or training grants, and serving as a reviewer for a professional journal ($\beta=0.09$). The adjusted multiple Rs were 0.26 and 0.36 for full-time clinicians and academic clinicians, respectively ($p<0.01$). These findings demonstrate that the unique contribution of the indicators of accomplishment were different in full-time clinicians and academic clinicians, which may reflect the learning priorities of the two groups.

Career Satisfaction: We examined the correlation between JeffSPLL scores and physician ratings of career satisfaction (item 5, Appendix A). Significant correlations were obtained between scores of the JeffSPLL and ratings of career satisfaction ($r=0.23$, $p<0.01$ in both groups). The significant link between JeffSPLL scores and measure of career satisfaction, as well as statistically and practically significant correlations with measures of professional accomplishments, provide additional support for the criterion-related validity of the JeffSPLL.

Table 12. Summary Results of Correlational Analyses of Scores on the JeffSPLL and Professional Accomplishments

Indicators of Professional Accomplishment[1]	Groups Full-Time Clinicians r[2]	β[3]	Academic Clinicians r[2]	β[3]
1. Published an article in a professional journal.	0.12**	0.04	0.25**	0.04
2. Presented a paper before a national professional group.	0.14**	0.06	0.27**	0.05
3. Conducted research, including clinical trials.	0.16**	0.09**	0.27**	0.09**
4. Received a grant for research or training.	0.05	0.03	0.27**	0.09**
5. Received a professional award or honor.	0.12**	0.03	0.17**	0.03
6. Held office in a national professional organization.	0.05	0.04	0.15**	0
7. Served on a professional committee (hospital, professional society).	0.12**	0.06*	0.17**	0.09**
8. Served as an editor, or on the editorial board of a professional journal.	0.02	0.02	0.17**	0
9. Served as a reviewer for a professional journal.	0.04	0	0.28**	0.09**
10. Shared in developing a new medical/surgical procedure, instrument, drug, or technique that was described in the literature.	0.07*	0	0.16**	0.02
11. Presented patient education/research findings on radio, on TV, in a news paper or before a community group.	0.23**	0.18**	0.19**	0.08**
Adjusted Multiple R	0.26**		0.36**	

** $p<0.01$, * $p<0.05$.
[1] A weight of 1 was assigned to those who had accomplished the indicated activity in the past five years, and a weight of 0 to those without such involvement.
[2] Bivariate correlations.
[3] Standardized regression coefficients.
Adapted from: Hojat, M., Veloski, J.J., and Gonnella, J.S. (2009). Measurement and correlates of physicians' lifelong learning. *Academic Medicine. 84*, 1066-1074, Copyright ©2009, Association of American Medical Colleges.

Satisfaction with Undergraduate Medical Education: Significant correlations were obtained between scores of the JeffSPLL and ratings of satisfaction with medical education at Jefferson. The magnitude of the obtained correlation reached the level of practical significance for the full-time clinicians ($r=0.20$, $p<0.01$), but was at the marginal level of practical significance in academic clinicians ($r=0.10$, $p<0.01$).

ADDITIONAL ANALYSES: GROUP COMPARISONS

We conducted additional analyses to compare the physicians' lifelong learning scores by gender and specialty in each group of full-time clinicians and academic clinicians. We also compared the physicians who participated in different educational programs in medical school with the other physicians in the sample.

SPECIALTY AND GENDER

We classified the respondents into ten categories according to their primary specialty, and examined the differences in the JeffSPLL scores among the male and female physicians in different specialties in full-time clinicians and academic clinicians (Table 13). Using two-way analysis of variance, followed by multiple-range post hoc mean comparison test (Duncan), we tested the main effects of specialty and gender and the interaction effects of specialty by gender in each group of full-time clinicians and academic clinicians. The two independent variables were medical specialty and gender, and the dependent variable was the JeffSPLL score. Data were analyzed separately for full-time clinicians and academic clinicians. The means and standard deviations of the JeffSPLL scores for men and women in different specialties and the summary results of the statistical analyses are reported in Table 13.

Specialty Differences: Among full-time clinicians, the highest mean scores of the JeffSPLL were obtained by those in internal medicine and hospital-based specialties (anesthesiology, pathology, radiology); and the lowest mean scores were obtained by those in emergency medicine, pediatrics, family medicine, and psychiatry. The Duncan post hoc mean comparison test showed that the mean scores of the physicians in internal medicine ($M=45.8$) and hospital-based specialties ($M=45.7$) were significantly higher than those in emergency medicine ($M=42.5$), pediatrics ($M=42.5$), family medicine ($M=43.6$), and psychiatry ($M=44.5$) ($p<0.01$). Physicians in emergency medicine and pediatrics scored significantly lower than those in obstetrics and gynecology ($M=45.2$), ophthalmology ($M=45.5$), and surgery ($M=44.6$).

Among academic clinicians, physicians in internal medicine scored significantly higher ($M=48.4$) than those in emergency medicine ($M=45.2$), family medicine ($M=46.2$), hospital-based specialties ($M=46.6$), and psychiatry ($M=46.7$). Also, those in emergency medicine scored significantly lower that physicians in obstetrics and gynecology ($M=47.5$), pediatrics ($M=47.1$), surgery ($M=47.1$), and ophthalmology ($M=46.9$).

Therefore, we can conclude that significant differences in orientation toward lifelong learning exist among physicians in various specialties, and that the pattern of differences varies for full-time clinicians and academic clinicians. However, there was one common finding in both groups showing that physicians in internal medicine obtained the highest scores while their counterparts in emergency medicine obtained the lowest scores on the JeffSPLL.

Gender Differences and Interaction Effect: As shown in Table 13, no significant difference was found between men and women who were full-time clinicians or academic clinicians. The findings that none of the gender by specialty interaction effects (for the full-time clinicians and academic clinicians) were statistically significant also indicate that the observed specialty differences on JeffSPLL scores were not confounded by gender effect.

SPECIAL PROGRAMS IN MEDICAL SCHOOL

We examined the JeffSPLL scores of full-time clinicians and academic clinicians who participated in the following four educational programs during medical school.

MD-PhD Degree Program: The study sample included 47 physicians (12 full-time clinicians which is approximately 1% of the group and 35 academic clinicians which is approximately 2% of the group). Eighteen of these physicians had participated in the combined MD-PhD program, and 29 had received their PhDs before entering the medical school. Those who earned both degrees were compared on the JeffSPLL scores with the rest with MD degrees in full-time clinician and academic clinician samples. Summary of statistical results are reported in Table 14.

As shown in the table, the mean JeffSPLL scores for physicians with MD and PhD degrees were higher than those with only an MD degree in both full-time clinicians and academic clinicians. However, the difference was statistically significant only in academic clinicians (effect size=0.39), not in full-time clinicians.

Combined BS-MD Program: The combined BS-MD program at Jefferson, which was initiated in 1964, enables participants to enter the program immediately after graduating from high school. Currently, it is a six-year program (it was a five-year program before 1984) whose participants earn their BS degree in an accelerated two-year program at Pennsylvania State University and earn their MD degree at Jefferson Medical College. Participants must be among the top 10 percent of graduates from their high school with high SAT scores. More detailed descriptions of the program have been published elsewhere (Arnold, Xu, Epstein, & Jones, 1996; Callahan, Veloski, Xu, Hojat, Zeleznik, & Gonnella, 1992; Jones, Arnold, Xu, & Epstein, 2000).

There were 296 physicians who graduated from this program (118 full-time clinicians, 178 academic clinicians). For a balanced comparison, we selected a group of 509 physicians (195 full-time clinicians, 314 academic clinicians) who could have been qualified for the program based on their high school achievement and SAT scores, but pursued the regular medical school curriculum (Table 14). We also selected another group of 418 physicians (178 full-time clinicians, 240 academic clinicians) who could not have been qualified for the program (based on their high school performance and SAT scores) as a third comparison group Finally, 1,505 physicians (629 full-time clinicians, 876 academic clinicians) with insufficient data to determine their eligibility for the program were included in a fourth comparison group.

The JeffSPLL scores of respondents who graduated from the combined BS-MD program were compared with the scores of the other three groups. The means, standard deviations and summary statistical results are reported in Table 14. Results of analysis of variance indicated no statistically significant differences among the four groups on the JeffSPLL scores in full-time clinicians and academic clinicians.

Physician Shortage Area Program: This program was initiated in 1975 to recruit medical students who intend to enter family medicine and practice in geographic areas experiencing a shortage of physicians. Studies of the program's graduates have confirmed its success in achieving its stated goals (Rabinowitz, 1983, 1988; Rabinowitz et al., 1999a, 1999b).

Table 13. Comparisons of Scores of the JeffSPLL by Specialty and Gender

Groups		Full-Time Clinicians			Academic Clinicians		
Specialties		Men	Women	Total	Men	Women	Total
		M (SD) {n}	M (SD) {n}	M (SD) {n}	M (SD) {n}	M (SD) {n}	M (SD) {n}
FM	Family Medicine	43.3 (4.8){170}	44.2 (5.3){67}	43.6 (4.9){237}	46.1 (5.1){141}	46.4 (5.0){72}	46.2 (5.1){213}
IM	Internal Medicine	45.9 (5.7){167}	45.1 (5.9){39}	45.8 (5.7){206}	48.4 (5.2){319}	48.5 (4.8){85}	48.4 (5.1){404}
PD	Pediatrics	42.3 (5.6){28}	43.5 (4.3){32}	42.9 (4.9){60}	47.2 (5.1){62}	47.1 (5.3){57}	47.1 (5.1){119}
SU	Surgery	45.6 (5.2){161}	44.6 (5.2){10}	45.5 (5.2){171}	47.1 (5.4){263}	46.0 (5.5){23}	47.1 (5.4){286}
EM	Emergency Medicine	42.5 (4.7){49}	42.5 (6.4){13}	42.5 (5.1){62}	45.3 (5.3){79}	44.9 (5.1){19}	45.2 (5.2){98}
OB	Ob/Gyn	44.3 (6.0){36}	46.2 (5.4){33}	45.2 (5.8){69}	47.6 (5.0){62}	47.3 (5.0){47}	47.5 (4.9){109}
APR	Anest/Path/Radio	45.6 (5.8){117}	45.6 (6.4){31}	45.7 (5.9){148}	46.2 (5.3){113}	47.4 (5.2){34}	46.6 (5.3){147}
OPH	Ophthalmology	45.5 (5.9){49}	45.6 (5.4){12}	45.5 (5.8){61}	46.9 (5.6){51}	47.1 (5.6){15}	46.9 (5.5){66}
PS	Psychiatry	44.5 (6.4){24}	44.7 (4.7){6}	44.5 (6.1){30}	46.8 (4.6){36}	46.4 (4.6){18}	46.7 (4.6){54}
O	Others	44.6 (5.4){60}	57.5 (4.4){14}	45.1 (5.4){74}	47.6 (5.7){83}	46.6 (6.1){28}	47.4 (5.8){111}
			Gender Differences				
Total Men		44.8 (5.5){861}			47.2 (5.3){1,209}		
Total Women		44.9 (5.5){257}			47.1 (5.2){398}		
		Specialty Differences					
Specialty		IM=APR>EM=FM=PD=P EM=PD<OB=OPH=SU=O			IM>APR=EM=FM=P EM<OB=OPH=PD=SU=O		
Gender		Men=Women			Men=Women		

For full-time clinicians: Specialty effect: $F_{(9, 1098)}=5.1$, $p<0.01$. Gender effect: $F_{(1, 1098)}=1.6$, $p=$Nonsignificant. Interaction effect: $F_{(9, 1098)}=0.72$, $p=$Nonsignificant.
For academic clinicians: Specialty effect: $F_{(9, 1587)}=3.71$, $p<0.01$. Gender effect: $F_{(1, 1587)}=0.32$, $p=$Nonsignificant. Interaction effect: $F_{(9, 1587)}=0.36$, $p=$Nonsignificant.

Table 14. Comparisons of Physician Who Graduated From Different Programs in Medical School on the JeffSPLL Scores

Groups	Full-Time Clinicians M (SD) {n}	Academic Clinicians M (SD) {n}
	MD-PhD Program [1]	
Participants	46.7 (7.3) {12}	49.0 (4.5) {35}
Others	44.7 (5.5) {1,108}	47.1 (5.3) {1,573}
	Combined BS-MD Degree Program [2]	
1. Participants	44.3 (5.4) {118}	47.4 (5.4) {178}
2. Qualified to participate	44.7 (5.7) {195}	47.6 (5.1) {314}
3. Not qualified to participate	44.8 (5.4) {178}	46.8 (5.4) {240}
4. Insufficient data	44.9 (5.5) {629}	47.1 (5.3) {876}
	Physician Shortage Area Program	
Participants	44.7 (5.3) {84}	46.7 (5.3) {75}
Others	44.8 (5.5) {1,036}	44.2 (5.3) {1,532}
	Delaware-Jefferson Program [4]	
Participants	42.6 (5.0) {79}	46.8 (5.2) {137}
Others	44.7 (5.5) {1,040}	47.2 (5.3) {1,469}

[1] For full-time clinicians, $t_{(1118)}=1.7$, $p=$ Nonsignificant; for academic clinicians, $t_{(1606)}=2.08$, $p<0.05$.
[2] For full-time clinicians, $F_{(3,1116)}=0.43$, p=Nonsignificant,; for academic clinicians, $F_{(3,1604)}=1.01$, p=Nonsignificant.
[3] For full-time clinicians, $t_{(1035)}=1.11$, p=Nonsignificant; for academic clinicians, $t_{(1605)}=0.78$, p=Nonsignificant.
[4] For full-time clinicians, $t_{(1117)}=2.28$, $p<0.05$; for academic clinicians, $t_{(1604)}=0.89$, p=Nonsignificant.

There were 159 physicians who participated in this program (84 full-time clinicians, 75 academic clinicians). These physicians were compared on their JeffSPLL scores to the non-participants. Statistical findings reported in Table 14 indicated no significant differences between program participants and non-participants.

The Delaware-Jefferson Program: The Delaware Institute for Medical Education and Research (DIMER) program is a joint medical education program involving the University of Delaware, the Medical Center of Delaware, and Jefferson Medical College. This program was initiated in 1970 for qualified residents of Delaware. Special consideration is given to students who elect to spend portions of their clinical clerkships at Delaware hospitals affiliated with the medical college. The ultimate goal of the program is to provide physicians who plan to care for the residents of Delaware.

There were 216 graduates of this program among respondents (79 full-time clinicians, 137 academic clinicians). They were compared on the JeffSPLL scores with the other physicians in each group of full-time clinicians and academic clinicians. Summary statistical results are reported in Table 14. As shown in the table, the mean JeffSPLL scores were lower for the participants of this program in both groups. The difference was statistically significant for full-time clinicians ($p<0.05$, effect size=0.38).

JeffSPLL Adapted for Administration to Medical Students

The JeffSPLL was originally developed for measuring orientation toward lifelong learning in physicians. In response to a need for a similar measure for administration to medical students, a group of medical education researchers at Virginia Commonwealth University Medical School in collaboration with us made some slight modifications in some of the items of the JeffSPLL to enhance their face validity for administration to medical students (Wetzel et al., 2010). The three-factor solution reported in the original scale was confirmed in the medical student version. The mean, standard deviation, Cronbach coefficient alpha, and test-retest reliability over two-month period were 43.52, 4.65, 0.77, and 0.65, respectively for 732 medical students (Wetzel et al., 2010). (See Appendix C for a copy of the adapted version for medical students.)

DISCUSSION AND CONCLUSION

During this era of exponential growth in medical knowledge and the rapid development of biomedical advances, it is important and timely to empirically study medical student and physician lifelong learning, its development, its predictors, and its outcomes. Based on our belief that a concept that is well-defined is a concept that is half measured, we discussed the conceptualization of lifelong learning, and presented a definition of the term. The elements described in our definition of physician lifelong learning mathematically emerged in our factor analytic study that confirmed the overlap between conceptualization and measurement of physician lifelong learning. In addition, our conceptualization of physician lifelong learning was supported in a doctoral dissertation research with medical students (Brahmi, 2007).

We believe that a concept begins to exist when it can be measured. Therefore, in addition to conceptualization, we refined the instrument for measuring orientation toward lifelong learning among full-time clinicians as well as academic clinicians and medical students. The procedures used in the development and refinement of the instrument and supporting psychometric evidence were consistent with the key standards for test development, test content, validity and reliability of educational and psychological testing outlined by professional organizations (AERA, APA, NCME, 1999). In addition to supportive conceptualization and psychometric evidence, the following features contribute to the strength of our findings.

Series of Interrelated Studies: This is our fourth in a series of interrelated studies on physician lifelong learning. The first was a study of 160 physicians in which step-by-step development of the first 19-item version of the Jefferson Scale of Physician Lifelong Learning was described (Hojat et al., 2003). The second study was conducted with 444 physicians to further examine the psychometrics of this Scale (Hojat et al., 2006). The third study used a national sample of 3,195 physicians to examine correlates of physician lifelong learning in both full-time clinicians and academic clinicians by using the 14-item JeffSPLL (Hojat et al., 2009). The study described here is an expansion of the last in the series. In addition to a nationwide sample, this study is unique in making a distinction between clinicians who are exclusively involved in patient care and those with additional involvement in research and teaching. The 14-item JeffSPLL used in this study is not only equally applicable to both groups of physicians, but the strong psychometric evidence supports its usefulness in either group. A recent study also provided psychometric support for the JeffSPLL in medical students (Wetzel et al., 2010).

Sample Representativeness: Although the fact that the sample of physicians graduated from one medical school may be a limitation of this study, other factors strengthen the results. For example, the participants had completed their residency training at 391 institutions throughout the United States and were practicing in 49 states in 2006. In addition, Jefferson Medical College, established in 1824, is similar to other large private medical schools in the country with regard to its four-year curriculum, composition of student body, attrition rate, and students' career choices. The gender composition of the study sample (26 % women) and specialty distribution (33% in primary care specialties of general internal medicine, family medicine, and general pediatrics, 5% obstetrics/gynecology, 4% each in anesthesiology, psychiatry, and general surgery, 2% pathology) were similar to national data for U.S. physicians (Smart, 2007). Also, the two types of career paths that were studied represent the majority of active physicians in this country. These factors strengthen the external validity (generalization) of the findings and mitigate the single institution limitation.

Social Desirability Response Bias: As with any self-report instrument, concern can be raised about the accuracy of responses and the effect of the "social desirability response bias" especially when the meaning of the questions is transparent. It is true that respondents to any self-report instrument can always place themselves in a socially desirable light by manipulating their responses and giving "positive" answers. The degree of social desirability response bias is a function of the test taker's belief in testing outcomes (Hojat, 2007). Obviously, when a test is used for selection or promotion, respondents may be more inclined to provide socially acceptable answers. However, the argument about the possible confounding effect of social desirability response bias in our findings can be refuted for the following reasons: First, our survey was administered in a "nonpenalizing" situation—respondents' identity was concealed and the confidentiality of their information was assured.

Second, the pattern of relationships in our criterion-validity study (e.g., obtaining higher correlations among conceptually relevant factor scores of the JeffSPLL and those of the criterion measures) indicates that social desirability response bias could not distort the expected internal relationships among variables.

Third, the negligible correlations we found between scores on the JeffSPLL and the measure of social desirability response bias suggest that social desirability did not substantially distort our research findings. Therefore, it was unnecessary to control for the effect of social desirability in our statistical analyses of the data.

Fourth, to examine the accuracy of responses, we compared physicians' self-reported publications with relevant information recorded in electronic databases for selected groups of 44 respondents who reported more than five publications in peer reviewed journals in the past five years. We also selected a sample of 42 physicians who reported no publications. We asked our medical-record librarian (blind to respondents' self-report information) to search relevant databases for information about the publications of the aforementioned physicians with and without publications.

A high concordance rate was observed between the respondents' own report of the number of publications and information extracted from electronic databases. The mean number of publications for those who published were 32 (self-report) and 30 (electronic database) which were not significantly different. We obtained a significant correlation of 0.85 ($p < 0.01$) between the self-report number of publications and publication record in electronic databases. Based on these findings, the argument that social desirability bias could have distorted the findings can be refuted.

Attitudes, Orientation, and Behavior: Another concern is that an individual's self- report of orientation toward lifelong learning may not necessarily reflect their actual lifelong learning behavior.

The link between attitude and behavior has been hotly debated among social and behavioral scientists (for a recent review, see Wallace, Paulson, Lord, & Bond, 2005). The belief is that when people form an attitude or orientation toward an issue, they are no longer neutral about that issue. Thus, they are likely to behave in a way that is consistent with their attitude about it (Sherif, Sherif, & Nebergall, 1965) to avoid unpleasant tension associated with "cognitive dissonance" (Festinger, 1964).

Attitudes often generate an affect, and a cognitive orientation that can lead to behavior. Because the measurement of actual behaviors requires a long period of observation to record a sufficient number of behavioral manifestations, social and behavioral scientists often use measures of attitudes as a proxy for the relevant behaviors. Despite this argument, satisfactory evidence would be necessary to support the validity and reliability of the measuring instrument. Such evidence in support of the validity and reliability of the JeffSPLL was provided in this study. In addition, the fact that we found significant correlations between scores on orientation toward lifelong learning and behavioral manifestations of lifelong learning (e.g., indicators of professional accomplishment) supports a strong link between orientation and its behavioral manifestation. It is important to note that measures of professional accomplishments are important behavioral manifestations of physicians' lifelong learning; however, the ultimate consequences of lifelong learning in medicine can be demonstrated by optimal patient care and positive clinical outcomes.

IMPLICATIONS FOR FUTURE RESEARCH

The JeffSPLL used in this study was specifically developed to measure orientation toward lifelong learning among full-time clinicians and academic clinicians. Further research however is needed to study the lifelong learning needs of the smaller number of physicians in career paths other than full-time clinicians and academic clinicians.

It is also desirable to conduct a predictive validity study to examine the relationships between the JeffSPLL scores and tangible clinical outcomes such as indicators of patient improvement, accuracy of diagnosis, patient compliance, patient satisfaction, etc. This will set an agenda for future research.

We must emphasize that despite the large sample sizes, the descriptive statistics reported in the present study can by no means serve as norms for comparative purposes. Therefore, it is desirable to develop tables of norms for the JeffSPLL from nationally representative samples of male and female physicians in different specialties, and for medical students. National norms could be used to evaluate an individual's score or to compare the mean scores of a particular group of physicians (e.g., female clinicians in pediatrics, or male academic clinicians in a medical school's internal medicine department) with a corresponding group of physicians at the national level. National norm tables can also be developed for medical students. This sets another agenda item for future research.

The availability of the JeffSPLL makes it possible to evaluate the educational outcomes of different programs in undergraduate and graduate medical education. For example, problem-based learning, evidence-based medicine, and the outcomes of continuing medical education programs designed to improve physician lifelong learning can be empirically assessed using the JeffSPLL. This suggests another line of future research.

Medical schools and residency programs have professional obligations to monitor the quality of their graduates using a variety of instruments in a longitudinal study design, including orientation toward lifelong learning to assure that their educational goals are being achieved and to provide feedback to their faculty and graduates. The instrument evaluated in this study has practical value to monitor educational programs in undergraduate and graduate medical education, and to empirically study the predictors and outcomes of physician lifelong learning. And that sets an additional agenda item for future research.

APPENDIX A. SURVEY OF PHYSICIAN LIFELONG LEARNING

Confidential

INSTRUCTIONS: Please answer all of the following questions that are applicable to you.

1. Your work status:
   a. Full-time (35 or more hours per week).
   b. Part-time (less than 35 hours per week).
   c. Not presently working (Skip to question 4).
2. Your primary work setting (select only one):
   a. Solo practice.
   b. Private practice with one or more physicians in the same specialty.
   c. Private practice in a multi-specialty group.
   d. Salaried medical school faculty.
   e. City, county, state, or federal government (including uniformed services).
   f. Other, please specify:
3. On average, how many hours per week do you typically devote to each of the following activities:
   a. Patient care (seeing patients and related activities) .   hours/week a1. Approximate number of patients per week:
   b. Teaching (medical students, residents)   hours/week
   c. Research   hours/week
   d. Administration (other than directly related to patient care).   hours/week
   e. Continuing medical education (e.g., reading, conferences, lectures)
   f. Other, please specify: hours/week

4. *INSTRUCTIONS:* Please circle the appropriate letter to indicate which of the following you have participated in or received recognition for during the past five years.

If yes, approximate number of times in past 5 years

a. Published an article in a professional journal   N   Y
b. Presented a paper before a national professional group N   Y
c. Conducted research, including clinical trials   N   Y
d. Received a grant for research or training   N   Y
e. Received a professional award or honor   N   Y
f. Held office in a national professional organization   N   Y

Instructions: Please indicate the extent of your agreement with each of the following statements by circling the appropriate number.

	Strongly Disagree	Disagree	Agree	Strongly Agree
13. I routinely search computer databases to find out about new developments in my specialty.	1	2	3	4
14. I believe that I would fall behind if I stopped learning about new developments in my profession.	1	2	3	4
15. I give on average at least one presentation per year at a professional meeting.	1	2	3	4
16. I conduct research as a principal investigator or a co-investigator	1	2	3	4
17. I attend educational programs whether or not CME credit is offered	1	2	3	4

Instructions: Please indicate the extent of your agreement with each of the following statements by circling the appropriate number.

	Strongly Disagree	Disagree	Agree	Strongly Agree
18. One of the important goals of medical school is to develop students' life-long learning skills	1	2	3	4
19. Rapid changes in medical science require constant updating of knowledge and development of new professional skills.	1	2	3	4
20. I always make time for self-directed learning, even when I have a busy practice schedule and other professional and family obligations.	1	2	3	4
21. I publish articles in peer-reviewed journals.	1	2	3	4
22. I recognize my need to constantly acquire new professional knowledge.	1	2	3	4
23. I routinely attend continuing medical education programs to improve patient care	1	2	3	4

	Strongly Disagree	Disagree	Agree	Strongly Agree
24. I take every opportunity to gain new knowledge/skills that are important to my profession.	1	2	3	4
25. My preferred approach in finding an answer to a question is to search the appropriate computer databases.	1	2	3	4
26. I can easily recognize what I need to learn with regard to the rapid advances in medicine.	1	2	3	4
27. I enjoy conducting research	1	2	3	4

Instructions: Please indicate the extent of your agreement with each of the following statements by circling the appropriate number.

	Strongly Disagree	Disagree	Agree	Strongly Agree
28. I have never been bored.	1	2	3	4
29. In seeking answers to questions I routinely try to collect and analyze data.	1	2	3	4
30. I consider myself a researcher as well as a clinician.	1	2	3	4
31. Despite the demands on my time, I have found time to participate in clinical trials and other clinical investigations.	1	2	3	4
32. I can easily recognize my professional strengths and weaknesses.	1	2	3	4
33. I can say that I am pretty competent in using a computer in database search, email, power point and word processing.	1	2	3	4
34. I keep electronic health records of my patients.	1	2	3	4
35. I never met a person that I did not like	1	2	3	4
36. Regardless of my busy professional schedule, I always feel the motivation to learn about new advances in medicine.	1	2	3	4

Instructions: Please indicate the extent of your agreement with each of the following statements by circling the appropriate number.

	Strongly Disagree	Disagree	Agree	Strongly Agree
37. I frequently give up free time to keep up to date professionally.	1	2	3	4
38. I believe that every physician needs to be able to use the internet to keep up with new advances in medicine	1	2	3	4

(Continued)

	Strongly Disagree	Disagree	Agree	Strongly Agree
39. I never have any trouble understanding anything I read the first time I read it.	1	2	3	4
40. I am not interested in learning new things for the sake of learning, unless there is a practical need for it.	1	2	3	4
41. Learning cannot be initiated by itself. There should be an external factor to initiate it	1	2	3	4
42. Please rate yourself in lifelong learning by checking a point on the following 10-point scale:	1	2	3	4

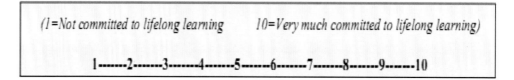

Any comments:

Thank you for your cooperation. Please return the completed questionnaire in the enclosed envelope to: Jefferson Medical College, Center for Research in Medical Education and Health Care, 1025 Walnut Street, Suite 119, Philadelphia, PA 19107.

Your completion and return of this survey is an indication of your agreement to voluntarily participate in this study, approved by the Thomas Jefferson University Institutional Review Board. ©Jefferson Medical College, 2006.

APPENDIX B. THE JEFFERSON SCALE OF PHYSICIAN LIFELONG LEARNING (JEFFSPLL)

Instructions: Please indicate the extent of your agreement with each of the following statements by circling the appropriate number

	Strongly Disagree	Disagree	Agree	Strongly Agree
1. Searching for the answer to a question is, in and by itself rewarding	1	2	3	4
2. Life-long learning is a professional responsibility of all physicians	1	2	3	4
3. I enjoy reading articles in which issues of my professional interest are discussed	1	2	3	4
4. I routinely attend annual meetings of professional medical organizations..	1	2	3	4

	Strongly Disagree	Disagree	Agree	Strongly Agree
5. I read professional journals at least once every week	1	2	3	4
6. I routinely search computer databases to find out about new developments in my specialty	1	2	3	4
7. I believe that I would fall behind if I stopped learning about new developments in my profession	1	2	3	4
8. One of the important goals of medical school is to develop students' life-long learning skills	1	2	3	4
9. Rapid changes in medical science require constant updating of knowledge and development of new professional skills	1	2	3	4
10. I always make time for self-directed learning, even when I have a busy practice schedule and other professional and family obligations	1	2	3	4

Instructions: Please indicate the extent of your agreement with each of the following statements by circling the appropriate number.

	Strongly Disagree	Disagree	Agree	Strongly Agree
11. I recognize my need to constantly acquire new professional knowledge	1	2	3	4
12. I routinely attend continuing medical education programs to improve patient care	1	2	3	4
13. I take every opportunity to gain new knowledge/skills that are important to my profession	1	2	3	4
14. My preferred approach in finding an answer to a question is to search the appropriate computer databases	1	2	3	4

APPENDIX C. JEFFERSON SCALE OF PHYSICIAN LIFELONG LEARNING (JEFFSPLL- MEDICAL STUDENT VERSION)

Instructions: Please indicate the extent of your agreement with each of the following statements by circling the appropriate number

	Strongly Disagree	Disagree	Agree	Strongly Agree
1. Searching for the answer to a question is, in and by itself rewarding	1	2	3	4

(Continued)

	Strongly Disagree	Disagree	Agree	Strongly Agree
2. Life-long learning is a professional responsibility of all physicians	1	2	3	4
3. I enjoy reading articles in which issues of medicine are discussed	1	2	3	4
4. I routinely attend meetings of student study groups	1	2	3	4
5. I read medical literature in journals, websites or textbooks at least once every week	1	2	3	4
6. I routinely search computer databases to find out about new developments in medicine	1	2	3	4
7. I believe that I would fall behind if I stopped learning about new developments in medicine	1	2	3	4
8. One of the important goals of medical school is to develop students' life-long learning skills	1	2	3	4
9. Rapid changes in medical science require constant updating of knowledge and development of new professional skills	1	2	3	4
10. I always make time for learning on my own, even when I have a busy class schedule and other obligations	1	2	3	4
11. I recognize my need to constantly acquire new professional knowledge	1	2	3	4
12. I routinely attend optional sessions, such as grand rounds, guest lectures, or clinics where I can volunteer to improve my knowledge and clinical skills	1	2	3	4
13. I take every opportunity to gain new knowledge/skills that are important to medicine	1	2	3	4
14. My preferred approach in finding an answer to a question is to consult a credible resource such as a text, computer database, or colleague				

© 2007 Jefferson Medical College. All rights reserved. Adapted for administration to medical students (Wetzel, Mazmanian, Hojat, et al. 2010).

Acknowledgments

This study was funded in part by an invitational grant from the National Board of Medical Examiners (NBME) Edward J. Stemmler, MD Medical Education Research Fund. The study, its findings, and interpretations of the outcomes do not necessarily reflect NBME policy, and NBME support provides no official endorsement. Thomas J. Nasca, MD played a significant role in the initial development of the Jefferson Scale of Physician Lifelong Learning when he was the Dean of Jefferson Medical College. He is now Chief Executive

Officer at the Accreditation Council for Graduate Medical Education. We would like to thank Dorissa Bolinski for her editorial assistance, and the Jefferson Alumni Office for providing us with the mailing addresses of study participants.

BIOSKETCHES

MOHAMMADREZA HOJAT, Ph.D. is Research Professor of Psychiatry and Human Behavior, and Director of the Jefferson Longitudinal Study of Medical Education at Jefferson Medical College of Thomas Jefferson University in Philadelphia, Pennsylvania. Dr. Hojat is a licensed psychologist in the Commonwealth of Pennsylvania, and has published more than 200 articles in peer-reviewed journals on educational, psychological, and social issues. Dr. Hojat has served as a coauthor of "Loneliness: Theory, Research, and Applications" (Sage Publications, 1987), and a coeditor of "Assessment Measures in Medical School, Residency, and Practice: The Connections" (Springer, 1993). His latest book "Empathy in Patient Care: Antecedents, Development, Measurement, and Consequences" was published by Springer in 2007.

JON VELOSKI, M.S. is Director of Medical Education Division, Center for Research in Medical Education and Health Care, Jefferson Medical College of Thomas Jefferson University. He is a coeditor of "Assessment Measures in Medical School, Residency, and Practice: The Connections" (Springer, 1993), and the author of many publications in medical education research.

JOSEPH S. GONNELLA, M.D. is Dean Emeritus, Distinguished Professor of Medicine, and Founder and Director of the Center for Research in medical Education and Health Care, Jefferson Medical College of Thomas Jefferson University. Dr. Gonnella is a recipient of many awards in medical education and health care research including the AAMC Abraham Flexner Award for Distinguished Service to Medical Education. He is the leading author of "Assessment Measures in Medical School, Residency, and Practice: The Connections" (Springer, 1993), and editor of "Clinical Criteria for Disease Staging" (The MEDSTAT Group, SysteMetrics Division, Ann Arbor, MI., 5th edition 2003).

REFERENCES

AAMC. (1999). Contemporary issues in medicine—Medical informatics and population health: Report II of the Medical School Objectives Project. *Academic Medicine, 74*, 130-141.

American Educational Research Association (AERA), American Psychological Association (APA), National Council on measurement in Education (NCME) (1999). *Standards for educational and psychological testing.* Washington, DC: AERA, APA, NCME.

Arnold, L. (2002). Assessing professional behavior: Yesterday, today, and tomorrow. *Academic Medicine, 77*, 28-37.

Arnold, L., Xu, G., Epstein, L. C., & Jones, B. (1996). Professional and personal characteristics of graduates as outcomes of differences between combined baccalaureate-MD degree programs. *Academic Medicine, 71*(Suppl.), S64-S66.

Aspin, D., Chapman, J., Hatton, M., & Sawano, Y. (2001). *International handbook of lifelong learning*. Dordecht, The Netherlands: Kluwer.

Blacklow, R. S., Goepp, C. E., & Hojat, M. (1991). Class ranking models for dean's letter of recommendation and their psychometric evaluation. *Academic Medicine, 66*, s10-s12.

Blacklow, R. S., Goepp, C. E., & Hojat, M. (1993). Further psychometric evaluation of a class ranking model as a predictor of graduates' clinical competence in the first year of residency. *Academic Medicine, 68*, 295-297.

Bligh, J. (1993). The S-SDLRS: A short questionnaire about self-directed learning. *Postgraduate Education for General Practice, 4*, 121-125.

Brahmi, F. A. (2007). Medical students' perception of lifelong learning at Indiana University School of Medicine. Doctoral Dissertation completed at the School of Library and Information Science, Indiana University.

Callahan, C. A., Hojat, M., & Gonnella, J. S. (2007). Volunteer bias in medical education research: An empirical study of over three decades of longitudinal data. *Medical Education, 41*, 746-753.

Callahan, C. A., Veloski, J. J., Xu, G., Hojat, M., Zeleznik, C.. & Gonnella, J. S. (1992). The Jefferson-Penn State B.S.-M.D. program: A 26- year experience. *Academic Medicine, 67*, 792-797.

Callahan, C., Erdmann, J. B., Hojat, M., Veloski, J. .J., Rattner, S., Nasca, T. J., & Gonnella, J. S. (2000). Validity of faculty ratings of students' clinical competence in core clerkships in relation to scores on licensing examinations and supervisors' ratings in residency. *Academic Medicine, 75*(Suppl.), S71-S73.

Candy, P. C. (1991). *Self-direction for life-long learning: A comprehensive guide to theory and practice*. San Francisco, CA: Jossey-Bass.

Christakis, N. A. (1995). The similarity and frequency of proposals to reform US medical education: Constant concerns. *Journal of the American Medical Association, 274*, 706-711.

Cohen, J. (1987). *Statistical power analysis for behavioral sciences*. Hillsdale, NJ: Lawrence Erlbaum.

Cole, T. B. (1998). Journal-based continuing medical education. *Journal of Medical Practice Management, 14*, 123-126.

Duff, P. (2002). Professionalism in medicine: An A-Z primer. *Obstetrics and Gynecology, 99*, 1127-1128.

Epstein, R. M., & Hundert, E. M. (2002). Defining and assessing professional competence. *Journal of the American Medical Association*, 287, 226-235.

Festinger, L. (1964). *Conflict, decision, and dissonance*. Stanford, CA: Stanford University Press.

Finocchio, L. J., Bailiff, P. J., Grant, R. W., & O'Neil, E. H. (1995). Professional competence in the changing health care system: Physicians' view on the importance and adequacy of formal training in medical education. *Academic Medicine, 70*, 1023-1028.

Gonnella, J. S., Callahan, E. J., Louis, D. Z., Hojat, M., & Erdmann, J. B. (2004). Medical education and health services research: The linkage. *Medical Teacher, 26*, 7-11.

Gonnella, J. S., Hojat, M., & Veloski, J. J. (2005). Abstracts: Jefferson Longitudinal Study of Medical Education. Philadelphia, PA: Jefferson Medical College. Access: http://jdc.jefferson.edu/jlsme.

Gonnella, J. S., Erdmann, J. B., & Hojat, M. (2004). An empirical study of predictive validity of number grades in medical school using three decades of longitudinal study: Implications for a grading system. *Medical Education, 38*, 425-434.

Guglielmino, L. M. (1977). *Development of the self-directed learning readiness scale* (Doctoral dissertation, University of Minnesota, 1977). *Dissertation Abstracts International, 38*, 6467A.

Hoban, J. D., Lawson, S. R. Mazmanian, P. E., Best, A. M., & Seibel, H.R. (2005). The self-Directed Learning Readiness Scale: A factor analysis study. *Medical Education, 39*, 370-379.

Hojat, M. (2007). *Empathy in patient care: Antecedents, development, measurement, and outcomes.* New York: Springer.

Hojat, M., Paskin, D. L., Callahan, C. A., Nasca, T. J., Louis, D. Z., Veloski, J. J., Erdman,…Gonnella, J. S. (2007). Components of postgraduate competence: Analysis of 30 years of longitudinal data. *Medical Education, 41*, 982-989.

Hojat, M., Veloski, J. .J. & Borenstein, B. D. (1986). Components of clinical competence ratings: An empirical approach. *Educational and Psychological Measurement, 46*, 761-769.

Hojat, M., & Xu, G. (2004). A visitor's guide to effect sizes: Statistical significance versus practical (clinical) importance of research findings. *Advances in Health Sciences Education, 9*, 241-249.

Hojat, M., Borenstein, B. D., & Veloski, J. .J. (1988). Cognitive and noncognitive factors in predicting the clinical performance of medical school graduates. *Journal of Medical Education, 63*, 323-325.

Hojat, M., Gonnella, J. S., Erdmann, J. B., & Veloski, J. J. (1997). The fate of medical students with different levels of knowledge: Are the basic medical sciences relevant to physician competence? *Advances in Health Sciences Education, 1*, 179-196.

Hojat, M., Gonnella, J. S., Nasca, T. J., & Veloski, J. *An operational tool for assessing physician lifelong learning.* (2004, May). Report submitted to the National Board of Medical Examiners. Edward J. Stemmler, MD, Medical Education Research Fund.

Hojat, M., Gonnella, J. S., Veloski, J. J., & Erdmann, J. B. (1996). Jefferson Medical College Longitudinal Study: A prototype for evaluation of changes. *Education for Health, 9*, 99-113.

Hojat, M., Nasca, T. J., Erdmann, J. B., Frisby, A. J., Veloski, J. J. & Gonnella, J. S. (2003). An operational measure of physician lifelong learning: Its development, components, and preliminary psychometric data. *Medical Teacher, 25*, 433-437.

Hojat, M., Veloski, J., Nasca, T. J., Erdmann, J. B., & Gonnella, J. S. (2006). Assessing physicians' orientation toward lifelong learning. *Journal of General Internal Medicine, 21*, 931-936.

Hojat, M., Veloski, J. J., & Borenstein, B. D. (1986). Components of clinical competence ratings: An empirical approach. *Educational and Psychological Measurement, 46*, 761-769.

Hojat, M., Veloski, J.J., & Gonnella, J. S. (2009). Measurement and correlates of physician lifelong learning. *Academic Medicine, 84*, 1066-1074.

Jennet, P. A. & Swanson, R. W. (1994). Lifelong, self-directed learning: Why physicians and educators should be interested. *Journal of Continuing Education for Health Professions, 14*, 69-74.

Jones, B. J., Arnold, L. Xu, G., & Epstein, L. C. (2000). Differences in the preparation and practice of male and female physicians from combined baccalaureate-MD degree program. *Journal of American Medical Women Association, 55,* 29-31.

Knowles, M. (1975). *Self-directed learning: A guide for learners and teachers.* New York: Association Press.

Liaison Committee on Medical Education (LCME). (2000). *Function and structure of a medical school.* Washington, DC: Author.

Longworth, N., & Davies, W. K. (1996). *Lifelong learning: New visions, new implications, new roles for the industry, government, education, and the community for the 21st century.* London: Kogan Page.

Longworth, N. (2001). Learning communities for a learning century. In D. Aspin, J. Chapman, M. Hatton, & Y. Sawano (Eds.), *International handbook of lifelong learning* (pp. 591-618). Dordecht, The Netherlands: Kluwer.

McKenzie, P. (2001). How to make lifelong learning a reality: Implications for the planning of educational provision in Austria. In D. Aspin, J. Chapman, M. Hatton, & Y. Sawano (Eds.), *International handbook of lifelong learning* (pp. 367-378). Dordecht, The Netherlands: Kluwer.

Miflin, B. M., Campbell, C. B., & Price, D. A. (1999). A lesson from the introduction of a problem-based, graduate entry course: The effects of different views of self-direction. *Medical Education, 33,* 801-807.

Nelson, A. R. (1998). Medicine: Business or professionalism, art or science? *American Journal of Obstetrics and Gynecology, 174,* 755-758.

Nierman, D. M. (2002). Professionalism and the teaching of clinical medicine: Perspectives of teachers and students. *Mt. Sinai Journal of Medicine, 69,* 410-411.

Oddi, L. F. (1986). Development and validation of an instrument to identify self-directed continuing learners. *Adult Education Quarterly, 36,* 97-107.

Oddi, L. F., Ellis, A. J., & Altman Robertson, J. E. (1990). Construct validity of the Oddi Continuing Learning Inventory. *Adult Education Quarterly, 43,* 62-70.

O'Shea, E. (2003). Self-directed learning in nurse education: A review of literature. *Journal of Advanced Nursing, 43,* 62-70.

Rabinowitz. H. K. (1983). A program to recruit and educate medical students to practice family medicine in the fourth year of medical school. *Journal of the American Medical Association, 249,* 1038-1041.

Rabinowitz, H. K. (1988). Evaluation of a selective medical school admissions policy to increase the number of family physicians in rural and underserved areas. *New England Journal of Medicine, 319,* 480-486.

Rabinowitz, H. K. Diamond, J. J., Hojat, M., & Hazelwood, C. E. (1999a). Demographic, educational, and economic factors related to recruitment and retention of physicians in rural Pennsylvania. *Journal of Rural Health, 15,* 216-218.

Rabinowitz, H. K., Diamond, J. J., Markham, F. W., & Hazelwood, C. E. (1999b). A program to increase the number of family physicians in rural and underserved areas: Impact after 22 years. *Journal of the American Medical Association, 281,* 255-260.

Schrock, J. W., & Cydulka, R. K. (2006). Lifelong learning. *Emergency Medicine Clinics of North America, 24,* 785-795.

Sherif, C. W., Sherif, M., & Nebergall, R. E. (1965). *Attitudes and attitude change: The social judgment-involvement approach.* Philadelphia, PA: W. B. Saunders.

Shokar, G. S., Shokar, N. K., Romeo, C. M., & Bulik, R.J. (2002). Self-directed learning: looking at outcomes with medical students. *Family Medicine, 34*, 197-200.

Six, L. E. (1989). The generality of the underlying dimensions of the Oddi Continuing Learning Inventory. *Adult Education Quarterly, 40*, 43-51.

Smart, D.R. (2006). *Physician characteristics and distribution in the U.S.* Chicago, IL: American medical Association.

Veloski, J. J., & Hojat, M. (2006). Measuring specific elements of professionalism: Empathy, teamwork, and lifelong learning. In D. T. Stern (Ed.), *Measuring medical professionalism* (pp. 117-145). Oxford, UK: Oxford University Press.

Wallace, D. S., Paulson, R. M., Lord, C. G., & Bond, C. F. (2005). Which behaviors do attitude predict? Meta-analyzing the effects of social pressure and perceived difficulty. *Review of General Psychology, 9*, 214-227.

Ward, M., Gruppen, L., & Regehr, G. (2002). Measuring self-assessment: Current state of the art. *Advances in Health Sciences Education, 7*, 63-80.

Wetzel, A.P., Mazmanian, P.E., Hojat, M., Kreutzer, K.O., Carrio, R.J., Carr, C.,… Rafiq, A. (2010). Measuring medical students' orientation toward lifelong learning: A psychometric evaluation. Academic Medicine (Supplement), 85, s41-s44.

Zuckerman, M., Kuhlman, D. M., Joireman, J., Teta, P., & Kraft, M. (1993). A comparison of three structure models for personality: The Big Three, the Big Five, and the Alternative Five. *Journal of Personality and Social Psychology, 65*, 757-768.

Zuckerman, M. (2002). Zuckerman-Kuhlman Personality Questionnaire (ZKPQ): An alternative five-factorial model *In* B. De Raal, & M. Perugini (Eds.), *Big five assessment* (pp.377-396). Seattle, WA: Hogrefe and Huber.

Chapter 4

INFORMAL LEARNING, INCIDENTAL LEARNING, AND DELIBERATE CONTINUING EDUCATION: PREPARING PSYCHOLOGISTS TO BE EFFECTIVE LIFELONG LEARNERS

James W. Lichtenberg[1,*] *and Rodney K. Goodyear*[2]
[1] University of Kansas, US
[2] University of Redlands, US

ABSTRACT

Psychology training programs bear some responsibility for preparing students to engage in lifelong professional learning, but the means of accomplishing this has received relatively little attention. In this commentary, we consider several lifelong learning attitudes graduate schools cultivate (curiosity, an interest in learning, and skepticism), we suggest lifelong learning competencies that graduate schools provide (information retrieval skills, critical reflection skills, objective self-awareness), and we discuss habits of lifelong learning that programs can encourage in their students (involvement in professional associations, seeking opportunities for new learning). Although many training programs already do much to prepare their graduates for lifelong learning and to enhance their readiness to learn from situations they had not anticipated, in many cases they do not engage students deliberately and planfully in preparation for lifelong learning.

Keywords: Life-long learning, life-long learners, graduate education, deliberate continuing education

---

[*] Correspondence regarding this manuscript may be directed to James W. Lichtenberg, University of Kansas, Dept. of Psychology and Research in Education, 1122 W. Campus-Road, J. R. Pearson Hall, Room 214, Lawrence, KS, 66045.

Author Note: An earlier version of the chapter was presented as part of the symposium, Examining the Mechanisms for Lifelong Learning in Professional Psychology (C. Belar, Chair), at the annual meeting of the American Psychological Association, Boston, August 15, 2008.

Educators, professional associations, accrediting bodies and organizations, licensing and certification boards, employers, third-party payers and the general public all have come to understand that professional training and education extends beyond simple *preparation for* one's professional career. It is an ongoing and integral part of the career itself. Professionals no longer can view the end of one's graduate training with relief from education (Collins, 2009).

This is as true of psychologists as for other professionals. Whereas doctoral programs provide students with threshold levels of competence for *entry-level practice,* alumni need then to be prepared to continue their professional development on their own initiative. For new graduates, some post-degree professional development will be in the service of continuing to develop expertise, which in any domain takes approximately 10 years (Ericsson, 1996). But in addition, the evolving nature of psychological science and practice knowledge requires that all psychologists continually incorporate new knowledge and skills into their work. We owe it to our clients and should regard lifelong learning as a professional imperative.

To be sure, a person will continually learn, regardless of his or her intent, for even the least involved or motivated person inevitably will have passive and other incidental learning experiences. Therefore, we should qualify the term *lifelong learning* at the outset. Despite the rhetoric, concern and emphasis placed on continuous professional development (CPD)—most especially within the medical profession, there is no generally-accepted definition of *lifelong learning*. However, paraphrasing the Commission for a Nation of Lifelong Learners' 1997 definition of *lifelong learning*, we offer the following:

> Lifelong learning is a continuously supportive process which stimulates and empowers individuals to acquire the knowledge, values, skills and understanding they require throughout their professional lifetimes and to apply them with confidence, creativity, and enjoyment in their various professional roles, circumstances, and environments.

This definition emphasizes lifelong learning as (a) continuous, (b) supportive, (c) stimulating and empowering, (d) incorporating knowledge, values, skills and understanding, (e) spanning one's professional career, (f) applied, (g) incorporating confidence, creativity and enjoyment, and (h) inclusive of the variety of professional roles, circumstances and environments the professional might encounter. Reflecting on these characteristics of lifelong learning, Collins (2009) commented that lifelong learning never stops, isn't done alone, is self-directed and active (rather than passive), involves more than simply what one knows, spans one's professional lifetime, is not just for knowledge sake, is positive and fulfilling, and covers the breadth of one's professional role and activities..

And although, as noted earlier, learning undoubtedly will occur even when unintended and even among the unmotivated, we wish to be clear that our concern is with is the psychologist who has:

> a lifelong commitment to learning, that is, someone whose top-level goals, the goals that govern major life plans, include learning goals. Thus, the lifelong learner appears to have more than a lively curiosity and a willingness to study, more even than a serious involvement in some subject matter. The lifelong learner treats learning itself as a valued

part of life and structures other activities in life so that they will serve learning. (Bereiter and Scardamalia, 1989, p. 361-362)

Figure 1 briefly summarizes several primary types of learning experiences we believe a psychologist is likely to have. The first of these, graduate training, employs a specific curriculum that guides students toward some level of common knowledge, using a sequence of experiences that should build on one another. But once students have graduated–and especially after attaining licensure–they have considerable latitude in what to learn and how. That learning is primarily "autodidactical" (Candy, 1991). Ziman (2003) asserted, for example, that "every scientist–indeed every professional scholar worthy of the name–has to be an autodidact" (p. 97)—to which we would add the practitioner, who must exercise self-direction in his or her continual professional development.

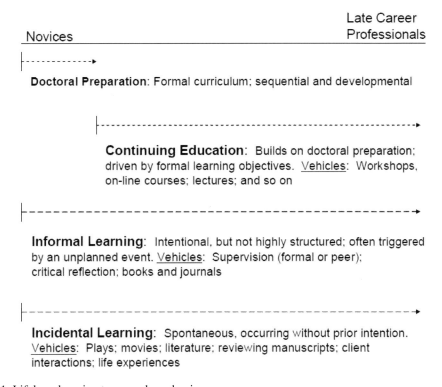

Figure 1. Lifelong learning types and mechanismz.

Of the several categories of learning that occur post-degree, self-direction is most evident with respect to informal learning and probably least so with incidental learning.

Hammond and Collins (1991) describe the process of *self-directed learning* as one in which:

> … learners take the initiative…for increasing self- and social awareness, critically analyzing and reflecting on their situations, diagnosing their learning needs with specific reference to competencies they have helped identity, formulating relevant learning goals, identifying resources for learning, choosing and implementing learning strategies, and reflecting on and evaluation their learning. (p. 13-14)

With *incidental learning*, the issue for the psychologist is being able to profit from unplanned events. Perhaps the notion of *planned happenstance* (e.g., Mitchell, Levin, & Krumboltz, 1999) is a useful one to entertain in this regard. It is a concept employed in career development, which in one sense is what lifelong learning is. Its premise is that the successful person will be able to capitalize on unanticipated situations.

Continuing education seems a sort of middle category between informal and incidental learning in regards to psychologists' degree of self-direction in learning: although CE programs have formal learning objectives and state and provincial psychology boards often will mandate specific amounts and types of continuing education, psychologists have considerable freedom in choosing which specific CE programs to take, from whom, and in what format. Therefore, psychologists have – and exercise – choices within these constraints.

Our particular concern in this chapter is with how training programs might prepare psychology students to engage effectively in lifelong learning; to maximize their effectiveness as autodidacts (with respect to informal learning and CE) and to optimize their ability to exercise "planned happenstance" (with respect to incidental learning). The American Psychological Association's (2002) *Guidelines and Principles for Accreditation of Programs in Professional Psychology* stipulate that a training program is to provide the means by which students can acquire "attitudes essential for life-long learning, scholarly inquiry, and professional problem-solving as psychologists in the context of an evolving body of scientific and professional knowledge" (p. 11). This speaks to the inculcation of the commitment to which Bereiter and Scardamalia (1989) spoke.

But this training guideline speaks only to attitudes and does not speak to competencies or practice. Moreover, even the attitudes are unspecified. In what follows, we will suggest some details that might be added to this barebones frame.

GRADUATE SCHOOL PREPARATION FOR LIFE-LONG LEARNING

Psychology training programs bear some responsibility for preparing students to engage in lifelong learning. But the means of accomplishing this has received relatively little attention and so in this section we outline what we consider to be three major components in graduate school preparation for lifelong learning. First, we consider several lifelong learning attitudes graduate school cultivate; second, we suggest lifelong learning competencies that graduate schools provide; and third, we discuss habits of lifelong learning, which programs encourage in their students.

Life-Long Learning Attitudes

Three lifelong learning attitudes seem especially important. These are curiosity, an interest in learning, and skepticism.

Curiosity: This is a key attribute to drive ongoing professional learning and has been addressed as such by educators at least as far back as Dewey (1938). Although often considered to be a trait-like quality in people, nevertheless, it is reasonable to believe that training must have some effect on curiosity, particularly through what faculty model in their own behavior. Moreover, graduate training can serve the critical function of shaping towards what that curiosity is directed: Curiosity is important, but insufficient, for unless it is channeled in particular ways, it may not produce relevant professional learning.

Interest in learning: Interest in learning shares some similarity with curiosity, but is sufficiently distinct to warrant specific attention. This interest is characterized by a willingness to make and learn from mistakes, while at the same time supported by confidence in one's ability to learn and openness to feedback (Collins, 2009). Interest in learning is also characterized by humility with respect what one knows and the recognition of the evolving nature of our field, the half-life of knowledge in our field (see Cronbach & Snow, 1977) and the need to upgrade and revise our knowledge base.

Skepticism: This is a key attitude for any scientist and one that all psychology students take away from their graduate programs, regardless of training model. Like curiosity, it is one of the attitudes Dewey (1938) advocated for practitioners. A psychologist's exercise of skepticism can take many forms. For example, it is not uncommon for a CE workshop presenter to be claiming extraordinary effectiveness for some treatment they or their associates have developed. A well trained psychologist should be asking for the evidence (and have the skills to evaluate the quality of that evidence).

Life-Long Learning Competencies

We have identified three competencies graduate programs instill to promote lifelong learning, though there certainly are others (e.g., see Collins, 2009). They range in their order of complexity.

Information retrieval skills: The most basic lifelong learning skills students will take from their academic training programs likely is that of finding information to answer professional questions that arise. The ability to find and use libraries is central and time honored. But psychologists also need to be able to find information in online databases, on the internet, and other places. As technologies continue to evolve, so too will the form these skills take. This also suggests that whereas programs provide essential information retrieval skills, it is a domain of skills that itself will require lifelong learning to enable the psychologist to keep abreast of developing technologies.

The ability to critically reflect on practice: Once psychologists have attained licensure in the U.S., they typically are not required to receive formal supervision. They need, therefore, to be able to self-supervise (cf., Dennin & Ellis, 2003) at this point. Goodyear (2006) proposed that this self-supervision–one form of lifelong learning--occurs primarily through critical self-reflection, which itself is a skill students learn through their participation in clinical supervision.

All supervisors are didactic to some extent, with those of some theoretical orientations (e.g., CBT) behaving more didactically than others. But much supervision is designed to help supervisees reach a deeper understanding of the situation and/or of alternative ways of thinking about it (e.g., "What do you suppose was going on to elicit that particular response to the client?" "What concerns do you have about employing that particular strategy with this client?" "What are you observing to conclude that this client is improving?"–and so on). In the process of doing this, the supervisee inevitably will internalize this stance and many of the particular ways of asking the questions. Put another way, the supervisor is modeling ways to think about the situation.

Objective self-awareness: Whether explicitly stated as such or not, objective self-awareness is a key goal in virtually all training programs. We list it here as a competence that can be taught—as one that will stand students in good stead as they begin practicing autonomously. It is a complementary–and perhaps prerequisite--skill to the self-supervision for which critical self-reflection is the vehicle. Students and professionals alike need to be able to determine what they need to learn and how to make and carry out a learning plan.

Habits of Professional Behavior

There is one other broad class of behavior that might best be labeled "habits of professional behavior." One concerns involvement in professional associations; the other concerns how and where one seeks new knowledge.

Involvement in professional associations: When APA's Commission on Accreditation reviews programs, it examines the extent to which graduates report being involved in professional associations as an indicator of the extent to which they are exhibiting attitudes toward lifelong learning.

Involvement in professional associations provides psychologists with formal and informal opportunities for learning. This includes research and professional presentations as well as CE workshops and the opportunity to stay abreast of the latest professional issues (healthcare policies, psychotherapy with women, GLBT, multicultural guidelines, custody evaluations, forensic practice, etc.) as well as matters of practice jurisprudence. It also affords opportunities to become involved in professional service that aids the profession while also enriching the individual psychologist through the perspectives it offers. In these and other activities, informal interactions with other psychologists help ensure current information about the field and a common way of thinking like a psychologist.

Seeking appropriate venues for new learning. Psychology faculty, especially those in scientist-practitioner programs, would like to believe that they develop in their students the habit of looking to professional journals for new and emerging knowledge. Unfortunately, the available data does not indicate that is the case (cf., Cohen, Sargent & Sechrest, 1986; Morrow-Bradley & Elliott, 1986). In fact, the work of highly experienced practitioners is more likely to be informed by literature, the cinema, and theater than by formal continuing education or self-study (Rønnestad & Skovholt, 2002).

But whether or not psychologists choose to read the scientific and professional literature, a good training program will have prepared them to seek objective information about their own work (e.g., by routinely using quantitative data to assessing their client progress) and how to evaluate it (e.g., see Clement, 1999).

CONCLUSION

APA's Board of Educational Affairs' competency task group focused on a "culture of competence" and the need for a seamless handing off of learning and assessment of competencies (see Kaslow et al., 2007; Leigh et al., 2007; Rubin et al., 2007). The thrust of the report was on the need to establish mechanisms to monitor continued competence as the person progressed from academic program, to internship, to postdoctoral fellowships, to licensing boards. The notion was that there need to be contingencies established and carried out to ensure the continued professional competence of practitioners. For example, analogous to making elderly drivers retake the performance portion of the driver's license exam to renew, psychologists might be made to retake the EPPP after so many years to assure that they have remained current in their knowledge and skills. (Within academic settings, the parallel is the notion of "post-tenure" review to evaluate and assure continued satisfactory performance in the areas of teaching and research, and within medical settings, physicians who practice internal medicine or one of the 19 subspecialities are required to take recertification exams from the American Board of Internal Medicine to ensure maintenance of competencies.) But even if those mechanisms were in place, it would not obviate the need for autodidactical and other life-long learning skills.

We believe training programs already are doing a great deal to prepare their graduates for important lifelong learning tasks and enhancing their readiness to learn from situations they had not anticipated. But we also believe that in many cases they are not thinking of these experiences as preparation for lifelong learning. We hope, through these comments, to help advance a discussion of how training programs might do a better and more deliberate job at this.

BIOSKETCHES

ROD GOODYEAR, Ph.D., received his doctorate from the University of Illinois, Champaign-Urbana. He is Emeritus Professor of Education (Counseling Psychology), University of Southern California where he directed the APA accredited counseling psychology program for 20 years and was serving as Associate Dean of Faculty when he left to join the University of Redlands faculty as Professor of Education. The primary focus of his scholarship has been on the training and supervision of psychologists. His book with Janine Bernard (*Fundamentals of Clinical Supervision*), in its fourth edition, is arguably the most used of its type in the world and has translations in Korean and Chinese. He has served on the American Psychological Association's Continuing Education Committee and on its Commission on Accreditation; has received the Council of Counseling Psychology Training Programs, Award for *Lifetime Contributions to Education and Training in Counseling Psychology* and has received the Fulbright-Yonsei Distinguished Lecturing Award in Korea. A Fellow of both the American Educational Research Association and the American Psychological Association, he has served as Editor of the *Journal of Counseling and Development* and currently serves on the editorial boards of several psychology journals.

JAMES LICHTENBERG, Ph.D., ABPP, received his doctorate from the University of Minnesota. He is Associate Dean for Graduate Programs and Research and Professor of Counseling Psychology at the University of Kansas where he has served as Director of Training for the doctoral program in counseling psychology for over 30 years—during which time has also served as Director of the University Counseling Center and as Chair of the Department of Counseling Psychology. He is a Fellow of the American Psychological

Association, the Association for Psychological Science, and the American Educational Research Association. He has served on and chaired the APA Commission on Accreditation and has chaired the Council of Counseling Psychology Training Programs. He has served as Chair of Education and Training Committee for the Society of Counseling Psychology and represented APA's Board of Scientific Affairs on the Association's Task Force on the Assessment of Competence in Professional Psychology. He is the recipient of the Council of Counseling Psychology Training Programs' *Award for Lifetime Contributions to Education and Training in Counseling Psychology.*

REFERENCES

American Psychological Association (2002). *Guidelines and principles for accreditation of programs in professional psychology.* Washington, DC: American Psychological Association.

Bereiter, C., & Scardamalia, M. (1989). Intentional learning as a goal of instruction. In L.B. Resnick (Ed.), *Knowing, learning and instruction: Essays in honor of Robert Glaser* (pp. 361-392). Hillsdale: Erlbaum.

Candy, P.C. (1991). *Self-direction for lifelong learning.* San Francisco: Jossey-Bass.

Clement, P.W. (1999). *Outcomes and incomes: How to evaluate, improve and market your psychotherapy practice by measuring outcome.* New York: Guilford.

Cohen, L. H., Sargent, M., & Sechrest, L. (1986). Use of psychotherapy research by professional psychologists. *American Psychologist, 41,* 198-206.

Collins, J. (2009). Education techniques for lifelong learning. *RadioGraphics, 29,* 613-622.

Commission for a Nation of Lifelong Learners (1997*). A nation learning: Vision for the 21st century.* Washington, DC: Commission for a Nation of Lifelong Learning.

Cronbach, L., & Snow, R. (1977). *Aptitudes and instructional methods: A handbook for research on interactions.* New York: Irvington.

Dennin, M. K., & Ellis, M. V. (2003) Effects of a method of self-supervision for counselor trainees. *Journal of Counseling Psychology, 50,* 69-83.

Dewey, J. (1938). *Experience and education.* New York: The Macmillan Company.

Ericsson, K. A. (1996). The acquisition to expert performance: An introduction to some of the issues. In K. A. Ericsson (Ed.), *The road to excellence: The acquisition of expert performance in the arts and sciences, sports and games* (pp. 1-50). Mahwah, NJ: Lawrence Erlbaum Associates.

Goodyear, R. K. (2006, June). *Supervision to foster reflective practice.* Presentation at the 2nd International Interdisciplinary Conference on Clinical Supervision, Buffalo, NY.

Hammond, M., & Collins, R. (1991). *Self-directed learning: Critical practice.* New York: Nichols.

Kaslow, N.J., Rubin, N.J., Bebeau, M.J., Leigh, I.W., Lichtenberg, J.W., Nelson, P.D., …Smith, I.L. (2007). Guiding principles and recommendations for the assessment of competence. *Professional Psychology: Research and Practice, 38,* 441-451.

Leigh, I.W., Smith, I.L., Bebeau, M.J., Lichtenberg, J.W., Nelson, P.D., Portnoy, S.M.,… Kaslow, N.J. (2007). Competency assessment models. *Professional Psychology: Research and Practice, 38,* 463-473.

Mitchell, K.A., Levin, A.S., & Krumboltz, J.D. (1999). Planned happenstance: Constructing unexpected career opportunities. *Journal of Counseling and Development, 77*, 115-124.

Morrow-Bradley, C., & Elliott, R. (1986). Utilization of psychotherapy research by practicing psychotherapists. *American Psychologist, 41*, 188–197.

Rønnestad, M. H. & Skovholt, T. M.(2002). Learning arenas of professional development: Retrospective accounts of senior psychotherapists. *Professional Psychology: Research and Practice, 32,* 181-187.

Rubin, N.J., Bebeau, M.J., Leigh, I.W., Lichtenberg, J.W., Nelson, P.D., Portnoy, S.M., …Kaslow, N.J. (2007). The competency movement within psychology: An historical perspective. *Professional Psychology: Research and Practice, 38,* 452-462.

Ziman, J. (2003). The scientist as autodidact. In J. Solomon, *Passion to learn: An inquiry into autodidacticism.* London: Routledge-Falmer.

Chapter 5

EXPLORING THE RELATIONSHIP BETWEEN LIFELONG LEARNING, CONTINUING EDUCATION, AND PROFESSIONAL COMPETENCIES

Jennifer M. Taylor[1,*], *Greg J. Neimeyer*[1], *Mary Zemansky*[2] *and Steven Rothke*[3]

[1] University of Florida, US
[2] Private Practice, Chesterton, Indiana, US
[3] Northwestern University, US

ABSTRACT

How do lifelong learning, continuing education, and professional competencies relate to each other? In a study of 413 Illinois psychologists, lifelong learning was found to be significantly related to all measured areas of professional competence, including greater involvement in professional and scholarly activities, higher levels of participation in continuing education, and stronger agreement with the need to evaluate learning and mandate continuing education. Findings are discussed in relation to the developing literatures on evidence-based continuing education and the lifelong commitment to the development and documentation of professional competencies.

Keywords: Continuing education, lifelong learning, professional development, competency

THE IMPORTANCE OF THE COMPETENT PSYCHOLOGIST

Over the last few decades interest in defining the competencies of a professional psychologist has increased. Competence has been defined in many ways. Borrowing from the medical profession, Epstein and Hundert (2002) define competence as "the habitual and

---

[*] Correspondence regarding this manuscript may be directed to Jennifer Taylor, Department of Psychology, University of Florida, P. O. Box 112250, Gainesville, FL 32611.

judicious use of communication, knowledge, technical skills, clinical reasoning, emotions, values, and reflection in daily practice for the benefit of the individual and community being served" (p.226). Competence builds upon foundational skills and knowledge in the profession and involves the ability to apply knowledge gained to clinical issues. Epstein and Hundert note that competence involves both a developmental component and a habit of the mind. Competence is developmental in the sense that it grows in complexity as one matures. In addition, competency involves certain important "habits of the mind," which include attentiveness, inquisitiveness, self-awareness, and openness to feedback, learning, and growth.

Within the field of psychology, the National Council of Schools and Programs of Professional Psychology (NCSPP) has identified core professional competencies for professional psychologists, such as research, evaluation, consultation and continued education (Peterson, Peterson, Abrams & Stricker, 1997). And, in 2002, foundational and functional competencies necessary for graduates of professional psychology programs were articulated at the Competencies Conference: Future Directions in Education and Credentialing (Kaslow, 2004). A "cube model" was created to highlight the interaction between foundational and functional competencies at each level of professional development (Rodolfa et al., 2005).

WHAT ARE COMPETENCIES IN PSYCHOLOGY?

Fouad et al. (2009) note that there is an important need for developing measurable, agreed-upon competencies in the field of psychology. They identified foundational and functional professional competencies and benchmarks across three professional development stages: preparedness for practicum, internship, and licensure. Within foundational competencies, these included competencies in the areas of professionalism, scientific knowledge and methods, ethical legal standards and policy, relationships, reflective practice, self-assessment, and self-care, among other areas. The first dimension, professionalism, includes professional values and ethics that encompass integrity, ethics in the field, and responsibility. This competency includes aspects of the professional identity, understanding who one is as a psychologist, knowledge about relevant issues in the field, and the ability to integrate both science and practice. The second dimension addresses competencies in scientific knowledge and methods. This includes the construct of scientific mindedness and an understanding of research and the application of research to practice. The third dimension, ethical legal standards and policy, includes competency in one's ethical conduct, knowledge of legal issues and the ability to apply and execute ethical decision making. The fourth dimension, relationships, includes competencies in affective skills and interpersonal relationships, and the ability to deal with difficult communication, integrate feedback from others, and relate with others. The fifth dimension, reflective practice, self-assessment, and self-care, includes competencies in understanding one's strengths and weaknesses and updating one's knowledge or skills, as necessary.

In recent years there has been a trend towards creating a "culture of competence" in the field of psychology (Roberts, Borden, Christiansen & Lopez, 2005; Belar, 2009), driven in part by the need for a more adequate, competency-grounded definition of preparedness for practice (Fouad et al., 2009). There are many challenges to assessing competencies, however.

Some of these relate to defining and developing appropriate measures to assess competencies, while others include convincing others that the comprehensive assessment of competencies is important (Lichtenberg et al., 2007; Neimeyer, Taylor & Wear, 2009).

FROM OTHER-ASSESSMENT TO SELF-ASSESSMENT: A DEVELOPMENTAL PERSPECTIVE ON EVALUATION OF COMPETENCIES

In the field's current state an intriguing shift occurs between the assessment of competencies in graduate school and the assessments of competencies post-licensure. In graduate school, students are evaluated on their effectiveness during practicum; during internship, students are evaluated on their clinical effectiveness at their internship site; and during the licensure phase, formal evaluations occur to assess one's understanding and effectiveness as a clinician. But what happens after a psychologist is licensed? Psychologists often shift from receiving evaluations on their competencies, as assessed by others, to the evaluation of their competencies as assessed by themselves. This shift from "other-" to "self-" assessment adds to the importance of engagement in learning throughout one's professional career. Because psychologists shift from being accountable to others to being accountable to themselves, it is imperative that they take the initiative to assess their strengths and weaknesses and to engage in continued learning to promote and enhance competent practice (see Linder-Crow, 2012).

LIFELONG LEARNING: A NECESSARY VEHICLE TO BUILDING AND MAINTAINING COMPETENCIES

While it is crucial that psychologists practice within their boundaries of competence, how can they be sure they are doing so? Lifelong learning is the key to building and maintaining competencies.

Lifelong learning has been defined in many ways, indicative of the complexity of the term. After a systematic review of the term, and a series of panel discussions, Hojat, Veloski, Nasca, Erdmann and Gonnella (2006) defined lifelong learning operationally, as "a concept that involves a set of self-initiated activities (behavioral aspect) and information seeking skills (capabilities) that are activated in individuals with a sustained motivation to learn and the ability to recognize their own learning needs (cognition)" (p. 931).

Lifelong learning, continuing education and professional development are necessary practices that begin in graduate school, continue through one's internship, and constantly develop and mature throughout one's professional life. In order to achieve and maintain competencies, lifelong learning and continuing education are necessary tools.

In fact, an essential reason why continuing education is mandated for many psychologists and others in health professions lies in the ethical importance of maintaining competencies (see APA, 2000). And one important way of maintaining competencies is, as the APA Ethical Principles of Psychologists and Code of Conduct (2010) Standard 2.01 states, to stay up-to-date in one's area of specialization, practicing only within one's bounds of competencies (see

Standard 2.01a, c). Psychologists are also reminded that in order to be competent, they must take action to remediate areas of weakness (see Standard 2.01b, d, e). Even more directly, Standard 2.03 states that, "Psychologists undertake ongoing efforts to develop and maintain their competence" (APA, 2010). It should be noted that the Ethical Standards are created by the American Psychological Association as enforceable rules for professional conduct, highlighting the imperative of taking steps to build and maintain competencies for ethical practice.

CONTINUING EDUCATION: THE LINK BETWEEN LIFELONG LEARNING AND PROFESSIONAL COMPETENCIES

To be an ethical psychologist is to be a competent psychologist and to be a competent psychologist is to be a lifelong learner. While lifelong learning is the vehicle for competencies, what is one vehicle for lifelong learning? One way to engage in lifelong learning is through continuing education (CE).

The emphasis on CE and lifelong learning has grown since the 1970s (Neimeyer & Taylor, 2010), with an increasing focus on the evaluation of CE effectiveness. In a nationwide study of 6,095 psychologists, most respondents reported high satisfaction with their CE experiences and the learning which occurred (Neimeyer, Taylor & Wear, 2009). Nearly 80% rated their past experiences with CE as good or excellent and approximately 65% reported learning a great deal or a moderate amount from their CE programs. Additionally, over 80% of the psychologists agreed or strongly agreed that they were more effective practitioners because of their CE experience, while 65% reported that what they learned from CE translated frequently or often to their clinical work. And while participants reported high satisfaction and the translation of the knowledge from their CE experiences, they also noted that CE helped them to become more ethical psychologists. Over 70% of psychologists strongly agreed or agreed that CE enabled them to become more knowledgeable about ethical issues, about 65% strongly agreed or agreed that CE helped them be more ethical in their clinical work, and about 60% felt that it reduced their professional exposure. Similar findings were also reported in another study by Neimeyer, Taylor and Philip (2010). Thus, studies suggest that continuing education can increase one's knowledge of the field and can promote more ethical behavior (see also Neimeyer, Taylor & Wear, 2011).

THE CURRENT STUDY

Given the importance of professional competencies and the reputed role of lifelong learning and continuing education in supporting their development, is it surprising that more work as not examined the relationship among these variables. Thus, the goal of this study was to examine these relationships in an effort to better understand the ways in which aspects of lifelong learning and continuing education may interact and support the ongoing development of professional competencies.

METHODS

Participants

In partnership with the Illinois Psychological Association (IPA), members of the IPA were invited to participate in an online survey regarding their attitudes and activities involving professional development and lifelong learning. Participants were provided with a survey link, which enabled them to anonymously complete the survey online. The survey was completed by 413 psychologists, which represented a response rate of about 67% of the total membership. The average age of the participants was 52 years old (SD = 11.9). The slight majority (61%) of respondents were female, while 39% were male, a distribution representative of IPA's total membership (60% female, 40% male). About 88% of the respondents were Caucasian, 4% were African American, 2% were American Indian or Alaskan, 1% was Asian, 1% was Hispanic or Latino, and 1% was multiracial. This distribution is consistent with the IPA's total membership of 94% Caucasian, 2% African American, 1% Asian, 1% Hispanic or Latino, 1% multiracial, and 2% Other.

Measures

Participants completed the survey online. The survey was part of a larger study on professional development and continuing education. For this study, three categories of variables were measure. They included lifelong learning, measures of professional competence and participation and perceptions of CE activities.

Each participant's orientation towards lifelong learning was measured through the Jefferson Scale of Physician Lifelong Learning (JSPLL; Hojat et al., 2003; Hojat et al., 2006). Because the scale was originally designed for physicians, the items were adapted for psychotherapists (see Appendix A), and renamed The Jefferson Scale of Psychotherapist Lifelong Learning (JSPLL), accordingly. The JSPLL consists of 19 items, each measured on a 4-point Likert scale. Lower scores represent lower orientations toward lifelong learning. The overall Cronbach's alpha for the modified JSPLL in this study was $r = .85$. The JSPLL consists of four subscales; the subscale for professional learning beliefs and motivation had a Cronbach's alpha of $r = .78$ (nine items), the subscale for scholarly activities had an $r = .80$ (four items), the subscale for attention to learning opportunities had an $r = .77$ (four items), and the subscale for technical skills in seeking information had an r = .62 (two items).

To measure competency, the Professional Competencies Scale was developed based on the conceptualization of Fouad et al. (2009), see Appendix B. The scale measured self-assessed competencies in six areas: professional identity (three items; Cronbach's alpha = .65), scientific mindedness (two items; Cronbach's alpha = .49), ethical conduct skills (three items; Cronbach's alpha = .76), affective skills (three items; Cronbach's alpha = .82), self-assessment skills (three items; Cronbach's alpha = .80), and interpersonal skills (two items; Cronbach's alpha = .68). The competency assessment consisted of 36 items and six subscales, measured on a 5-point Likert scale. Lower scores represented lower self-assessed competencies. The overall Cronbach's alpha for the complete competency assessment was .92.

Finally, a self-report assessment was used to assess participation in scholarly and professional activities, as well as participation and perceptions regarding CE activities. To measure involvement in scholarly and professional activities, a five item assessment was created that evaluated the extent to which individuals were involved in publishing papers, presenting papers, receiving professional awards and honors, serving on professional committees, and serving as reviewers for professional journals, on a 5-point Likert scale (1 = very infrequently; 5 = very frequently). Cronbach's alpha for this assessment was $r = .86$.

Participants were also to indicate the number of hours of formal and informal continuing education they had completed over the course of the previous year and to indicate their perceptions of their CE experiences along a range of dimensions.

Because the goal of the study was to explore the relationships between lifelong learning attitudes, competencies, and a number of professional variables, bivariate correlations were examined.

RESULTS

Levels of lifelong learning were found to be related to all measured dimensions of professional competence, involvement in scholarly and professional activities, agreement with the assessment of learning, and more positive perceptions of continuing education experiences and outcomes (see Table 1).

First, participants who reported higher degrees of lifelong learning also reported greater competencies in relation to their professional identity ($r = .63$), scientific mindedness ($r = .52$), ethical conduct skills ($r = .46$), affective skills ($r = .28$), self-assessment skills ($r = .24$), and interpersonal skills ($r = .20$), $p < .001$. Overall, lifelong learning was significantly related to perceived general competencies, $r = .54, p < .001$.

In addition, higher levels of lifelong learning were also related to more frequent publications in peer-reviewed journals ($r = .49$) and more frequent presentations at national conferences ($r = .52$), as well as the greater frequency of receiving professional awards or honors ($r = .37$), serving on professional committees ($r = .45$), and serving as a reviewer for a professional journal ($r = .46$).

Further, levels of lifelong learning were related to a greater investment in formal continuing education ($r = .25$) and informal continuing education ($r = .38$), $p < .001$, as well as stronger agreement with the idea that CE programs should include knowledge tests ($r = .16, p < .01$) and skills assessments over the material that they cover ($r = .26, p < .001$). Thus, those with the strongest commitments to lifelong learning tended to support more stringent evaluations of their learning.

In relation to the perceived outcomes of CE, lifelong learners reported greater agreement that CE contributed to their effectiveness in clinical practice ($r = .19, p < .001$) and enhanced their counselor self-efficacy ($r = .16, p < .01$), suggesting that those who have a higher commitment to lifelong learning also feel somewhat more confident in their clinical work.

Finally, in relation to CE mandates, those who reported higher levels of lifelong learning also reported stronger agreement that CE should be mandatory for license renewal ($r = .24, p < .001$). Lifelong learners additionally reported greater support for evidence-based continuing education in psychology ($r = .29, p < .001$).

Table 1. Correlation among Variables

	LLL	Competency	Pubs.	Present.	Awards	Committees	Reviewer	Formal CE	Informal CE	Knowledge tests	Skills tests	Effectiveness	Self-Efficacy	Mandated CE	EBCE
LLL	1	.54**	.49**	.52**	.37**	.45**	.46**	.25**	.38**	.16**	.26**	.19**	.16**	.24**	.29**
Competency		1	.13*	.13*	.18**	.22**	.13*	.15*	.30**	-.01	.10	.17**	.38**	.02	.10
Pubs.			1	.76**	.49**	.42**	.78**	-.09	-.26**	-.06	-.05	.10*	-.02	-.01	-.17**
Present.				1	.55**	.57**	.68**	-.12*	-.21**	-.13**	-.11**	.01	-.05	-.07	-.18**
Awards					1	.55**	.49**	-.17**	-.16**	-.14**	-.12*	-.06	-.06	-.07	-.22**
Committees						1	.45**	-.24**	-.22**	-.11	-.13*	-.07	-.13*	-.14**	-.16**
Reviewer							1	-.04	-.27**	-.08	-.06	.05	.05	-.05	-.15**
Formal CE								1	.15**	.05	.06	.19**	.11	.08	.08
Informal CE									1	-.04	-.01	.02	.07	.01	.05
Knowledge tests										1	.73**	.22**	-.04	.45**	.40**
Skills tests											1	.23**	.07	.43**	.43**
Effectiveness												1	.07	.38**	.18**
Self-Efficacy													1	-.02	.01
Mandated CE														1	.41**
EBCE															1

Note. Total N = 413. ** indicates significance at p < .01, * indicates significance at p < .05. LLL = Jefferson Scale of Psychotherapist Lifelong Learning; Pubs = publications written in peer-reviewed journals; Presentations = presentations given at national conferences; Awards = awards and honors received; Committees = service on professional committees; Reviewer = service as a reviewer for professional journals; Knowledge tests = CE should include knowledge tests; Skills = CE should include skills assessments; Effectiveness = CE has contributed to clinical effectiveness; Self-efficacy = counselor self-efficacy; mandated CE = agreement with mandated CE; EBCE = agreement with evidence-based continuing education in psychology.

DISCUSSION

An orientation towards lifelong learning was related to a number of variables: professional competencies, greater professional involvement, and greater confidence in one's clinical work. Within the competency domain, lifelong learning was related to competencies in one's professional identity, scientific mindedness, ethical conduct skills, affective skills, self-assessment skills and interpersonal skills. In line with the literature, Epstein and Hundert (2002) note that being a competent professional includes "habits of mind," a variable that comprises "observations of one's own thinking, emotions, and techniques, attentiveness, critical curiosity, recognition of and response to cognitive and emotional biases, [and] willingness to acknowledge and correct errors", a description that mirrors the definition of lifelong learning (p. 227). Thus, to be a competent psychologist *means* to be a lifelong learner. In a field that is marked by rapid advances on an ongoing basis, professional competence entails staying current, and staying current requires a commitment to ongoing learning.

Aside from its relationship with professional competencies, lifelong learning was also related to involvement in scholarly and professional activities, such as publishing and presenting professional papers, receiving more awards and honors, serving on more professional committees and serving more often as a journal reviewer. Lifelong learning was also related to higher levels of both formal and informal continuing education, a finding that suggests that lifelong learning is more than an attitude; it is an action. Lifelong learners also reported stronger agreement that CE has increased their clinical effectiveness, which may reflect their commitment to learning and to the translation of that learning in to practice.

Finally, lifelong learning was related to counselor self-efficacy. Psychologists who tend to be most confident with their clinical skills were also those who engaged in the highest levels of continued learning, highlighting the importance of keeping a curious, inquisitive mind (Epstein & Hundert, 2002). This finding suggests that an orientation towards lifelong learning might translate into more effective clinical practices and outcomes, as well, though it remains for future work to address these possibilities.

Limitations

The findings and implications from this study, however, should be interpreted in the context of the study's limitations, as well. Because self-report measures were used, demand characteristics and memory reconstruction, among other biases, may affect the interpretability of the findings. Furthermore, the present study used a competency instrument developed from recent conceptualizations regarding competencies in the field of psychology, but few measures of comprehensive competency in professional psychology exist. Several researchers have noted the need for accurate, full-range competency assessments (Belar, 2009; Epstein & Hundert, 2002; Kenkel, 2009; Lichtenberg et al., 2007;). Accurate assessments of competencies could lead to more effective research on ways to increase those competencies and could also directly lead to more effective clinical work.

Additionally, while relationships between competencies, lifelong learning and continuing education were examined, any causal relationships among these variables remain unclear. It is not clear, for example, whether greater involvement in lifelong learning creates more competent psychologists or if those who are more competent are simply more interested in engaging in continued learning. Alternatively, some third variable might account for the relationship between both of them, highlighting the need for future work to examine these relationships through models of mediation and moderation.

Finally, many of the correlations between variables were moderately strong, but a few correlations, though significant, were weak. Thus, although this study documents the relationship between aspects of lifelong learning, professional competence and continuing education, both the nature and the strength of those relationships require replication in future research prior to placing strong confidence in them on the basis of this exploratory study.

Implications and Conclusions

Nonetheless, findings from this study suggest that a passion for learning is related to many positive outcomes, including greater professional competency and openness to evaluation and growth. And if lifelong learning is related to so many important variables, how can the field of psychology foster lifelong learning for professionals? To create a culture of lifelong learning and competence, perhaps the first step starts with inculcating graduate students with the value of continual learning. Lifelong learning can be modeled by mentors through their ongoing curiosity and growth. Additionally, to create a culture of lifelong learning, the field of psychology needs more documented evidence of the benefits of lifelong learning. The availability of stronger evidence regarding the outcomes of higher levels of lifelong learning may generate greater acceptance of its value and efforts to support it. Lifelong learning, professional competencies and involvement in professional activities are important features in the field. As the field advances, these components will continue to be crucial to the identity and integrity of what it means to be a psychologist.

APPENDIX A

Jefferson Scale of Psychotherapist Lifelong Learning

1. Rapid changes in science require constant updating of knowledge and development of new professional skills.

    a. Strongly disagree
    b. Disagree
    c. Agree
    d. Strongly agree

2. I recognize my need to constantly acquire new professional knowledge.

    a. Strongly disagree
    b. Disagree

c. Agree
d. Strongly agree

3. Lifelong learning is a professional responsibility of all psychotherapists.

   a. Strongly disagree
   b. Disagree
   c. Agree
   d. Strongly agree

4. I believe that I would fall behind if I stopped learning about new developments in my profession.

   a. Strongly disagree
   b. Disagree
   c. Agree
   d. Strongly agree

5. One important mission of undergraduate education is to develop the habit of lifelong learning.

   a. Strongly disagree
   b. Disagree
   c. Agree
   d. Strongly agree

6. I enjoy reading articles in which issues of my professional interests are discussed.

   a. Strongly disagree
   b. Disagree
   c. Agree
   d. Strongly agree

7. I always make time for self-directed learning, even when I have a busy practice schedule and other professional and family obligations.

   a. Strongly disagree
   b. Disagree
   c. Agree
   d. Strongly agree

8. Searching for an answer to a question is, in and by itself, rewarding.

   a. Strongly disagree
   b. Disagree
   c. Agree
   d. Strongly agree

9. I review professional journals every week.

    a. Strongly disagree
    b. Disagree
    c. Agree
    d. Strongly agree

10. I actively conduct research as a principal Investigator or as a co-investigator.

    a. Strongly disagree
    b. Disagree
    c. Agree
    d. Strongly agree

11. I give on average at least one presentation at professional meetings in every given year.

    a. Strongly disagree
    b. Disagree
    c. Agree
    d. Strongly agree

12. I frequently publish articles in peer-reviewed journals.

    a. Strongly disagree
    b. Disagree
    c. Agree
    d. Strongly agree

13. I routinely exchange e-mail messages with my colleagues.

    a. Strongly disagree
    b. Disagree
    c. Agree
    d. Strongly agree]

14. I routinely attend presentations offered in my field regardless of whether a certificate for attendance is offered.

    a. Strongly disagree
    b. Disagree
    c. Agree
    d. Strongly agree

15. I routinely attend annual meetings of professional organizations.

    a. Strongly disagree
    b. Disagree
    c. Agree
    d. Strongly agree

16. I attend professional development programs regardless of whether CE credit is offered.

    a. Strongly disagree
    b. Disagree
    c. Agree
    d. Strongly agree

17. I take any opportunity to gain new knowledge/skills that are important to my profession.

    a. Strongly disagree
    b. Disagree
    c. Agree
    d. Strongly agree

18. My preferred approach in finding an answer to a question is to search the appropriate computer databases.

    a. Strongly disagree
    b. Disagree
    c. Agree
    d. Strongly agree

19. I search computer databases (e.g.. PSYCHLIT) to find out about new developments in my field.

    a. Strongly disagree
    b. Disagree
    c. Agree
    d. Strongly agree

APPENDIX B

Professional Competencies Scale

To what extent do you agree with each of the following in relation to your practice…

Professional Identity Scale

1. I keep up with advances in the profession.

   a. Strongly disagree
   b. Disagree
   c. Neither agree nor disagree
   d. Strongly agree

2. I contribute to the development and advancement of the profession and colleagues.

   a. Strongly disagree
   b. Disagree
   c. Neither agree nor disagree
   d. Strongly agree

3. I demonstrate integration of science in my professional practice.

   a. Strongly disagree
   b. Disagree
   c. Neither agree nor disagree
   d. Strongly agree

Scientific Mindedness Scale

1. I independently access and apply scientific knowledge and skills appropriately and habitually to the solution of problems.

   a. Strongly disagree
   b. Disagree
   c. Neither agree nor disagree
   d. Strongly agree

2. I readily present my own work for the scrutiny of others.

   a. Strongly disagree
   b. Disagree
   c. Neither agree nor disagree
   d. Strongly agree

Ethical Conduct Scale

1. I integrate an understanding of ethical-legal standards policy when performing all functional competencies.

   a. Strongly disagree
   b. Disagree
   c. Neither agree nor disagree
   d. Strongly agree

2. I demonstrate awareness that ethical-legal standards policy competence informs and is informed by all foundational competencies.

   a. Strongly disagree
   b. Disagree
   c. Neither agree nor disagree
   d. Strongly agree

3. I take responsibility for continuing professional development.

   a. Strongly disagree
   b. Disagree
   c. Neither agree nor disagree
   d. Strongly agree

Interpersonal Relationships Scale

1. I effectively negotiate conflictual, difficult and complex relationships including those with individuals and groups that differ significantly from myself.

   a. Strongly disagree
   b. Disagree
   c. Neither agree nor disagree
   d. Strongly agree

2. I maintain satisfactory interpersonal relationships with clients, peers, faculty, allied professionals, and the public.

   a. Strongly disagree
   b. Disagree
   c. Neither agree nor disagree
   d. Strongly agree

Affective Skills Scale

1. I seek clarification in challenging interpersonal communications.
   a. Strongly disagree
   b. Disagree
   c. Neither agree nor disagree
   d. Strongly agree

2. I demonstrate understanding of diverse viewpoints in challenging interactions.

   a. Strongly disagree
   b. Disagree
   c. Neither agree nor disagree
   d. Strongly agree

3. I accept, evaluate, and implement feedback from others.

   a. Strongly disagree
   b. Disagree
   c. Neither agree nor disagree
   d. Strongly agree

Self-Assessment Scale
1. I accurately identify my level of competence across all competency domains.

   a. Strongly disagree
   b. Disagree
   c. Neither agree nor disagree
   d. Strongly agree

2. I accurately access my own strengths and weaknesses and seek to prevent or ameliorate the impact on my professional functioning.

   a. Strongly disagree
   b. Disagree
   c. Neither agree nor disagree
   d. Strongly agree

3. I recognize when new or improved competencies are required for effective practice.

   a. Strongly disagree
   b. Disagree
   c. Neither agree nor disagree
   d. Strongly agree

BIOSKETCHES

JENNIFER M. TAYLOR received her M.S. in counseling psychology from the University of Florida. She is currently a Ph.D. candidate in the University of Florida counseling psychology program. Her research focuses on professional development and competencies, lifelong learning, continuing education, and mentoring.

GREG J. NEIMEYER received his Ph.D. in counseling psychology from the University of Notre Dame. He is professor of psychology in the Department of Psychology at the University of Florida and director of the Office of Continuing Education and Psychology at the APA. A fellow of the APA, he is also a member of the Department of Community Health and Family Medicine. His areas of research include professional development, epistemology and psychotherapy, and relationship development and disorder.

MARY ZEMANSKY obtained a Bachelor's degree in Psychology from UCLA in 1981 and received her Ph.D. in Clinical Psychology from California School of Professional

Psychology in 1985. She then completed a fellowship in geropsychology at Rancho Los Amigos Medical Center. She is a licensed clinical psychologist who has worked in hospital settings, academic institutions and most recently in private practice. Her areas of specialization include neuropsychology, aging, adolescent development, ethics and continuing education. She served for 15 years on the Illinois Psychological Association ethics committee and was chair for two terms. She is currently co-chair of the Continuing Education Task Force of the IPA. She does consultation work to a pediatric nursing home in Illinois.

STEVEN E. ROTHKE received his doctorate in Clinical Psychology from the University of Kentucky and is board certified in both Clinical Neuropsychology and Rehabilitation Psychology through the American Board of Professional Psychology. He has served as Director of the Neuropsychology Testing Laboratory and head of the Department of Psychology at the Rehabilitation Institute of Chicago. He is a Clinical Assistant Professor in the Departments of Psychiatry and Behavioral Sciences and Physical Medicine and Rehabilitation at Northwestern University Medical School. He is the Immediate Past-President of the Illinois Psychological Association where he served as President for 2007-2008 and 2009-2010 and co-chaired the task force to institute mandatory continuing education programming for psychologists in Illinois. Dr. Rothke evaluates and treats individuals with conditions such as brain injury, dementia, exposure to neurotoxins, post-traumatic stress disorder, and depression. He also consults to business and industry regarding fitness for duty, risk assessment, and need for job modifications to accommodate a mental or psychiatric disability.

REFERENCES

American Psychological Association. (2000). *Minutes of APA Council of Representatives*. Washington, DC: Author.

American Psychological Association. (2010). *Ethical principles of psychologists and code of conduct*. Retrieved from http://www.apa.org/ethics/code/index.aspx

Belar, C. D. (2009). Advancing the culture of competence. *Training and Education in Professional Psychology, 3*, S63-S65.

Epstein, R. M., & Hundert, E. M. (2002). Defining and assessing professional competence. *Journal of the American Medical Association, 287*, 226-235.

Fouad, N. A., Grus, C. L., Hatcher, R. L., Kaslow, N. J., Hutchings, P. S., Madson, M. B., Crossman, R. E. (2009). Competency benchmarks: A model for understanding and measuring competence in professional psychology across training levels. *Training and Education in Professional Psychology, 3*, S5-S26.

Hojat, M., Veloski, J., Nasca, T. J., Erdmann, J. B., & Gonnella, J. S. (2006). Assessing physicians' orientation toward lifelong learning. *General Internal Medicine, 21*, 931-936.

Hojat, M., Nasca, T. J., Erdmann, J. B., Frisby, A. J., Veloski, J. J., & Gonnella, J. S. (2003). An operational measure of physician lifelong learning: Its development, components and preliminary psychometric data. *Medical Teacher, 25*, 433-437.

Kaslow, N. J. (2004). Competencies in professional psychology. *American Psychologist, 59*, 774-781.

Kenkel, M. B. (2009). Adopting a competency model for professional psychology: Essential elements and resources. *Training and Education in Professional Psychology, 3*, S59-62.

Lichtenberg, J., Portnoy, S., Bebeau, M., Leigh, I. W., Nelson, P. D., Rubin, N. J...Kaslow, N.J. (2007). Challenges to the assessment of competence and competencies. *Professional Psychology: Research and Practice, 38*, 474-478.

Linder-Crow, J. (2011). Reflection, rethinking, and looking ahead. In G. J. Neimeyer, & J. M. Taylor (Eds.), *Continuing professional development and lifelong learning: Issues, impacts and outcomes* (pp. 353-370). Hauppauge, NY: Nova Science Publishers.

Neimeyer, G. J., & Taylor, J. M. (2010). Continuing education in psychology. In J. C. Norcross, G. R. VandenBos, & D. K. Freedheim (Eds.), *History of psychotherapy: Continuity and change* (pp. 663-671). Washington, DC: American Psychological Association.

Neimeyer, G. J., Taylor, J. M., & Philip, D. (2010). Continuing education in psychology: Patterns of participation and perceived outcomes among mandated and nonmandated psychologists. *Professional Psychology: Research and Practice, 41*, 435-441.

Neimeyer, G. J., Taylor, J. M., & Wear, D. M. (2009). Continuing education in psychology: Outcomes, evaluations, and mandates. *Professional Psychology: Research and Practice, 40*, 617-624.

Neimeyer, G. J., Taylor, J. M., & Wear, D. M. (2011). Continuing education in professional psychology: Do ethics mandates matter? *Ethics and Behavior, 21*, 165-172.

Peterson, R. L., Peterson, D. R., Abrams, J. C., & Stricker, G. (1997). The National Council of Schools and Programs of Professional Psychology education model. *Professional Psychology: Research and Practice, 28*, 373-386.

Roberts, M. C., Borden, K. A., Christiansen, M. D., & Lopez, S. J. (2005). Fostering a culture shift: Assessment of competence in the education and careers of professional psychologists. *Professional Psychology: Research and Practice, 36*, 355-361.

Rodolfa, E. R., Bent, R. J., Eisman, E., Nelson, P. d., Rehm, L., & Ritchie, P. (2005). A Cube model for competency development: Implications for psychology educators and regulators. *Professional Psychology: Research and Practice, 36*, 347-353.

Section 2.

Regulatory Perspectives on Continuing Education and Professional Development

In: Continuing Professional Development …
Editors: G. J. Neimeyer and J. M. Taylor

ISBN: 978-1-62100-767-8
© 2012 Nova Science Publishers, Inc.

Chapter 6

SELF-ASSESSMENT GUIDE AND PROFESSIONAL DEVELOPMENT PLAN: FACILITATING INDIVIDUALIZED CONTINUING PROFESSIONAL DEVELOPMENT

*Rick Morris**
College of Psychologists of Ontario, Canada

ABSTRACT

The *Self Assessment Guide and Professional Development Plan* is the cornerstone of the Quality Assurance Program of the College of Psychologists of Ontario. It is designed to assist members of the College to undertake an honest and personal assessment of their strengths, weakness or gaps in their current level of knowledge and skill. Through a series of questions and statements, the *Self Assessment Guide* encourages members to evaluate their knowledge and skill in their particular areas of practice and to assess their familiarity, understanding and adherence to a variety of statutes, professional standards and codes of ethics. Through the completion of the self review, members identify areas for professional enhancement to be achieved through an individualized educational plan reflective of their personal learning needs and style.

Keywords: Self assessment, professional development, individualized learning plan, self review

The College of Psychologists of Ontario is the governing body for psychological practitioners, *Psychologists and Psychological Associates,* in Ontario, Canada. Through the participation of the public and the profession, the College ensures the delivery of competent and ethical professional psychological services from qualified providers. In meeting its

---
* Correspondence regarding this manuscript may be directed to: Rick Morris, Ph.D., C.Psych., College of Psychologists of Ontario, 500-110 Eglinton Avenue West, Toronto, Ontario M4R 1A3, 416-961-8817, rmorris@cpo.on.ca.

legislated responsibilities, the College has developed and implemented a Quality Assurance Program, to "assure the quality of the practice of the profession and to promote continuing evaluation, competence and improvement among the members." [Health Professions Procedural Code, 1991, 1.(1)]. The Quality Assurance Program is a multifaceted approach including both self assessment and onsite peer review components. This chapter provides an overview of the Quality Assurance Program and details the self assessment component. Serving as a regulatory mechanism, the Quality Assurance Program targets the maintenance of professional competence and the protection of the pubic as its primary objectives.

PHILOSOPHY

In designing the Quality Assurance Program, of which the *Self Assessment Guide and Professional Development Plan* is a key component, a positive and enabling philosophy was incorporated. This philosophy can be summarized as:

- public protection through continuous improvement and lifelong learning; and,
- regulation through the positive advancement of the profession rather than through complaints and discipline processes.

The goal was to develop a Quality Assurance Program that was encouraging of self-improvement, continuous learning, and ongoing professional development. The program was built on the belief that conscientious practitioners regulate themselves in the provision of safe, effective and ethical services. In keeping with this philosophy, the Program was designed to reflect three basic assumptions about the members of the College. Psychologists and Psychological Associates:

- strive to act ethically and adhere to standards;
- are concerned about public protection and the welfare of their clients; and,
- are motivated not only to maintain the quality of service delivery but to strive for continuous improvement.

Self Assessment Guide and Professional Development Plan

The *Self Assessment Guide and Professional Development Plan* (see Appendix A) is the cornerstone of the Quality Assurance Program of the College of Psychologists of Ontario. First introduced in 1999, it is designed to assist members to undertake an honest and personal assessment of their strengths, weakness or gaps in their current level of knowledge and skill. Since its launch, there has been increasing interest by other psychology regulatory bodies in the College's approach to self-evaluation and professional development planning as an alternative to traditional programs based on counting continuous education hours.

Through a series of questions and statements, the *Self Assessment Guide* encourages members to evaluate their knowledge and skill in their particular areas of practice and to assess their familiarity, understanding and adherence to statutes and regulations, the

Standards of Professional Conduct (College of Psychologists of Ontario, 2005), the *Canadian Code of Ethics for Psychologists* (Canadian Psychological Association, 2000) and other guidelines that govern the profession. Through the completion of the self review, members identify areas for professional enhancement to be achieved through an educational plan reflective of their individual learning needs and style.

In most cases, individuals complete the self-evaluation privately. Some members however, choose to work with colleagues providing feedback to one another on the completeness of each others' self review and suggesting educational plans. When common areas for enhancement are noted, members may engage in joint learning activities to fulfill their *Professional Development Plans*.

THE PROCESS

Members are required to complete the *Self Assessment Guide and Professional Development Plan* every other year. Principle 1.4 of the *Standards of Professional Conduct* (College of Psychologists of Ontario, 2005), requires that "a member participate fully in all mandatory aspects of the College's quality assurance program."

The *Self Assessment Guide and Professional Development Plan* is a two-step process; a self review of a variety of aspects of one's practice conducted through the completion of the *Self Assessment Guide*; and, flowing from this, the design and implementation of an individualized *Professional Development Plan*.

In completing the *Self Assessment Guide*, members reflect upon identified differences between their current and desired levels of knowledge and skill, noting both areas of strength and weakness. As areas for enhancement are identified, these are recorded and become the basis for the *Professional Development Plan*. Following the completion of the self review, the *Professional Development Plan* is created based on the items identified. In creating the *Professional Development Plan*, members are encouraged not to focus solely on areas of deficiency, where the goal may be improvement or remediation. Members are also encouraged to consider areas of strength in their current knowledge and practice, where the professional development goal is to enhance already established skills.

The *Professional Development Plan* requires members to design their own continuing education program, both in content and methodology. The content of the program is dependent upon the member's self-identified educational objectives to be achieved in a manner designed to suit the member's individual needs and learning style. In addition to documenting plans related to current practice, that is, enhancing strengths or remediating deficiencies, the *Professional Development Plan* may also be used to document learning needs associated with areas of future practice a member may be considering.

NOTIFICATION

In the spring of each year the College notifies, by e-mail, those members who are required to complete the *Self Assessment Guide* and *Professional Development Plan* that year.

Members with odd registration numbers complete it in odd numbered years and even registration number members completing it in even years.

The *Self Assessment Guide* is available on the website of the College of Psychologists (www.cpo.on.ca), in MSWord and a writeable PDF format (http://www.cpo.on.ca/members-of-the-college/quality-assurance/index.aspx?id=124). It is available as a complete document, or each part may be accessed separately. Members may complete and save the form on their computers in whichever version they find most useful.

In addition to the blank forms, a sample, completed *Self Assessment Guide and Professional Development Plan* is included. This is provided as a guide to illustrate the way in which the process may be used for maximum benefit.

SUBMISSION TO THE COLLEGE NOT REQUIRED

The *Self Assessment Guide and Professional Development Plan* component of the Quality Assurance Program is founded upon principles of self-evaluation and continuous improvement. To encourage critical and honest self review, the *Self Assessment Guide and Professional Development Plan* is completed and retained by the member and normally is not submitted to the College. It was anticipated that if members were required to submit the completed *Self Assessment Guide* to the professional regulatory body this would inhibit honest and open self review and then detract from the value of the exercise.

While the completed *Self Assessment Guide and Professional Development Plan* normally is not submitted to the College, a member is required to make the most recent *Self Assessment Guide and Professional Development Plan* available to reviewers should the member be randomly selected to participate in the onsite *Peer Assisted Review* component of the Quality Assurance Program. As well, members who do not submit the required *Declaration of Completion* are required to forward their complete form to the College for review by the Quality Assurance Committee.

DECLARATION OF COMPLETION

Upon completing the Self Assessment Guide and Professional Development Plan, the member submits a *Declaration of Completion* to the College. In signing the Declaration, the member attests that: *I have reviewed my practice in psychology and documented this in the Self Assessment Guide. I have created a Professional Development Plan to address the continued professional developmental objectives I have identified. I understand that I must retain the completed Self Assessment Guide and Professional Development Plan in my files.*

The *Declaration of Completion* is the College's documentation that a member is participating in this mandatory component of the Quality Assurance Program. Only the Declaration must be submitted to the College, not the entire *Self Assessment Guide and Professional Development Plan*, provided that this is done in a timely fashion.

100% COMPLIANCE EXPECTED

The Quality Assurance Committee of the College of Psychologists monitors the completion of the *Self Assessment Guide and Professional Development Plan* and submission of the *Declarations of Completion*. The expected completion rate is 100%. Members are given three to four months notice in the year that they are required to complete the *Self Assessment Guide and Professional Development Plan*. This has proven to be adequate time to allow members to complete this requirement, permitting time for reflection and creativity, even among the busiest of members.

As the deadline approaches, an e-mail reminder is sent to those who have not yet submitted their *Declaration of Completion* encouraging them to do so by the deadline. Members who do not submit the *Declaration of Completion* are sent a formal letter from the Quality Assurance Committee reminding them of their obligation. This formal reminder provides a brief extension to the deadline. Members are informed that if the *Declaration of Completion* is not submitted by the new deadline, they will be required to submit the entire *Self Assessment Guide and Professional Development Plan* to the Quality Assurance Committee for review.

Those members who, regardless of the initial notification and reminders, are still remiss in submitting the *Declaration of Completion,* are sent a formal second reminder. This reminder notes that *Self Assessment Guide and Professional Development Plan* is past due and directs the member to submit the fully completed *Self Assessment Guide and Professional Development Plan* to the College for review. Submission of the *Declaration of Completion* alone is no longer sufficient.

REMINDERS SENT TO ENCOURAGE COMPLETION

By the initial deadline, approximately 65% of the members usually have submitted the *Declaration of Completion*. The first reminder letter is sent to the remainder. This reminder is successful in encouraging a response from the majority of those whose *Declaration of Completion* was outstanding. Of the total number of *Self Assessment Guide and Professional Development Plans* to be completed, less than one percent, equal to about 10 to 15 members, must be sent the second reminder.

While completion of the *Self Assessment Guide and Professional Development Plans* is required by the Standards of Professional Conduct (College of Psychologists of Ontario, 2005), the Quality Assurance Committee views its role as one of encouraging members to undertake this valuable self-evaluation with the resultant plan to address identified learning objectives. Therefore, providing a series of reminders is viewed as a necessary and important component of the process. The goal, in keeping with the philosophy underlying the Quality Assurance Program, is to encourage self review and ongoing continuing education, not to use the authority of the College to enforce compliance, unless absolutely necessary.

COMMITTEE REVIEW OF SELF ASSESSMENT GUIDE AND PROFESSIONAL DEVELOPMENT PLANS

Following the second reminder, the Quality Assurance Committee receives the completed *Self Assessment Guide and Professional Development Plans* for most of those outstanding. These often are accompanied by a letter of explanation regarding the lateness of the submission and an apology that reminders letters had to be sent. At a meeting of the Quality Assurance Committee, these are individually reviewed with consideration given to the quality of the self-evaluation and the educational plan created. Special note is taken of the connections and congruence between the areas of strength or weakness identified and the development plan proposed.

In most cases, the *Self Assessment Guide and Professional Development Plan* are completed comprehensively and demonstrate the considerable thought and attention paid to completing it. In such cases, the Quality Assurance Committee writes to the member indicating that the plan was reviewed and that the Committee had no comments regarding the *Self Assessment Guide and Professional Development Plan* itself. The Committee however, encourages the member to complete the required process and submit the *Declaration of Completion* in a more timely fashion in future.

On occasion, the review of *Self Assessment Guide and Professional Development Plan* finds sections that have been omitted, or more often, a learning plan that appears inconsistent with, or not directed toward addressing, the items identified as deficiencies or gaps in the self review. In such cases, the Quality Assurance Committee writes to the member noting these issues and asks for a response addressing specific questions or general comments regarding the concerns raised.

Each year, there are two or three members who, despite all the reminders, do not send in their *Declaration of Completion* or *Self Assessment Guide and Professional Development Plan*. Members who have not provided evidence of completion of the *Self Assessment Guide and Professional Development Plan* are referred to the Registrar of the College for further action as these members are not in compliance which their mandatory obligation to participate in the Quality Assurance Program.

EXTENUATING CIRCUMSTANCES

The initial notifications regarding the *Self Assessment Guide and Professional Development Plan* as well all reminders ask members to contact the College should there be extenuating circumstances which could interfere with their ability to complete the *Self Assessment Guide and Professional Development Plan* either by the deadline or at all. The College recognizes that challenging circumstances do arise for members who might otherwise readily comply with all College requirements. For example, members have encountered serious personal accidents or illness or serious problems concerning close family members which have made it necessary for them to suspend practice, putting their efforts into managing these personal circumstances. These situations are reviewed on a case by case basis and members may be granted a deadline extension, or depending on the circumstances, a deferral. In most cases, members are requesting an extension to the deadline and are diligent in complying within the extra time provided.

CONTENT

Self Assessment Guide

The *Self Assessment Guide and Professional Development Plan* is a self-evaluation tool designed to assist members to evaluate their current level of knowledge and skill. Items identified that require further review or some other action, are carried forward to the *Professional Development Plan*. The *Self Assessment Guide* is divided into sections prompting self review and subsequent *Professional Development Plan* creation in a variety of areas:

Part I	Legislation, Standards of Professional Conduct, Code of Ethics and Guidelines
Part II	Service to Clients
Part III	Teaching/Training and Research Activities
Part IV	Supervisory Activities
Part V	Current Areas of Practice and/or Services Provided
Part VI	Anticipated Areas of Future Practice
Part VII	Professional Development Plan
Part VIII	Reflection on Professional Development Plan

Part I. Legislation, Standards of Professional Conduct, Code of Ethics and Guidelines

Members are required to be familiar with, and adhere to, a variety of laws and codes related to professional practice. These include provincial and federal statutes and regulations, the *Standards of Professional Conduct* of the College of Psychologists, *2005* and the *Canadian Code of Ethics for Psychologists* (Canadian Psychological Association, 2000). Within these are a variety of requirements which apply to all members pertaining to topics such as confidentiality, consent to treatment and consent to access, disclosure or release of information, specific mandatory reporting obligations, and many others. These documents, considered to be relevant to all members regardless of area of practice or populations served, are listed in the first section of Part I of the *Self Assessment Guide*. In this section, members are asked to consider their familiarity with the content of the documents listed. It is not required that all of these materials be part of a member's professional library but it is important that they be sufficiently familiar with them and have ready access for reference, when needed. The section provides the member with a place to note both familiarity with the document and access to it.

Included in this section are the documents such as the:

- Psychology Act, 1991
- Professional Misconduct Regulation under the Psychology Act, 1991
- Standards of Professional Conduct, 2005

- Personal Health Information Protection Act, 2004
- Mandatory child abuse reporting obligations under the Child and Family Services Act, 1990

Depending upon the member's area of practice, practice setting, or population served, there are other pieces of legislation or standards that may impact on practice. In the second section of Part I, members are asked to consider additional documents for relevance to their practice and if relevant, indicate their level of familiarity and access. Additional space is provided to include other items which are not listed but the member believes to be important and relevant to their practice.

Examples of documents in this section include the:

- Children's Law Reform Act, 1990
- Education Act, 1990
- Mental Health Act, 1990
- Youth Criminal Justice Act, 2002

It is recognized that there are many statutes, standards or guidelines that may not apply to a particular member's practice. It is important however, that a member have sufficient familiarity with the documents listed to be able to discern whether or not closer attention need be paid to them.

Items that require further study or those to which the member currently does not have ready access are carried forward to the *Professional Development Plan* for action.

Most of the documents listed in the *Self Assessment Guide and Professional Development Plan* are readily available online from the websites of the College of Psychologists of Ontario, the Canadian Psychological Association or the provincial or federal governments. The *Self Assessment Guide* provides links to each document that is available online, and additional contact information for the document sources is provided, as well.

Each year, in preparing the next *Self Assessment Guide and Professional Development Plan*, the Quality Assurance Committee reviews and updates the list of documents, as necessary.

Part II. Service to Clients

This section of the *Self Assessment Guide* addresses practice issues related to a member's work with clients. It contains a variety of items drawn from the Standards of Professional Conduct (College of Psychologists of Ontario, 2005) and the Professional Misconduct Regulation (Ontario Regulation, 1993) under the Psychology Act, 1991. It is designed to assist members to review their practice against a list of important professional practice expectations. The importance of recordkeeping is highlighted in this section with an extensive series of questions related to this. The source for each item is provided to permit ready reference to the original document should the member wish to review a particular item.

Since the *Self Assessment Guide* only contains a subset of items from the Standards of Professional Conduct (College of Psychologists of Ontario, 2005) and the Professional Misconduct Regulation (Ontario Regulation, 1993), members are reminded of their responsibility to be familiar with the full documents. Due to the diversity of areas of psychological practice, not every item will necessarily apply to each member. Review of each item is necessary but having done so, members are permitted to indicate some are *Not Applicable* to their practice.

In completing this section, members indicate if they are compliant with the requirement listed or whether some action is required. Space is provided for the member to note when the required action was completed as a way tracking those which remain outstanding.

Examples of statements in this section include:

- My records contain the following information as per sections 9.2 and 9.3 of the revised Standards of Professional Conduct.

    - Identifying data (e.g., names, addresses, telephone numbers, dates of birth, sex, and referral source
    - Documentation of client consent regarding the collection, use and disclosure of personal health information
    - A copy of all reports received or sent by you on behalf of or for a patient/client
    - Assessment procedures used
    - Summary of findings

- I only provide services in my demonstrated areas of professional competence.
- I retain client files for a minimum of 10 years following the client's last contact or, in the case of clients under 18 years of age, for at least 10 years following the day they became or would have become 18.
- I have not entered into any arrangements such as a lease for use of premises or equipment; administrative services or the provision of supervision which provides for a fee or income splitting based on a percentage of fees invoiced or collected.
- I have made arrangements for safeguarding of patient/client records, in the event of my disability or death, and I have informed the College of these arrangements.
- I have made provisions for:

    - Storage of records in a secure place which guarantees privacy of access to the record.
    - Continuing patient/client care in the event of my disability or death.
    - Mandatory professional liability insurance.

Part III. Teaching/Training and Research Activities

Part III of the *Self Assessment Guide* relates to teaching/training and research activities in which many members of the College are involved. Some members carry out these activities in formal settings such as a university, college or funded research facility. It is recognized that in these settings, there are formal written policies with respect to ethics and conduct. Other members may engage in training or research activities within organizations that do not necessarily have formal written policies or codes. In either case, members are required to know the codes of ethics and policies related to these activities.

In contrast to the other parts of the *Self Assessment Guide* which contain detailed questions or statements for members to consider, Part III related to teaching/training or research activities is much briefer. In this section, members are simply asked to identify whether their work is conducted in a setting with formal codes or policies pertaining to teaching/training or research. In either case, one must indicate if there is action required with respect to ensuring familiarity with the appropriate ethical codes and policies regarding teaching/training or professional behavior with respect to conducting research.

Part IV. Supervisory Activities

Many members are involved in a range of supervisory activities in a variety of academic, institutional or private practice settings. These can include the supervision of members of the profession who are in the process of a qualifying for autonomous practice, supervision of students, or supervision of non-regulated providers such as psychometrists, therapists or counsellors. Part IV of the *Self Assessment Guide* asks members to consider whether the supervisory processes they have in place fulfill the requirements of the College. In addition, members are asked to consider their familiarity with two particular supervision documents, the *Supervision Resource Manual* (College of Psychologists, 2009) and Canadian Psychological Association's *Ethical Guidelines for Supervision in Psychology: Teaching, Research, Practice and Administration* (2009).

Examples of statements in Part IV include:

- I take full professional responsibility for all clients seen by my supervisee.
- I have adequate training, knowledge and skill to render competently all psychological services undertaken by my supervisee.
- Users of my supervisee's services are informed of his/her status and are given specific information as to his/her qualifications.
- In all fee-for-service arrangements, setting and receipt of fees remains my responsibility or that of the employing agency.

Part V. Current Areas of Practice and/or Services Provided

Part V of the *Self Assessment Guide* is less structured than the previous sections. In it, members list their current areas of practice, the services they provide and the populations served. A *Reference List: Areas of Practice and Services Provided* is presented at the end of the *Self Assessment Guide and Professional Development Plan*. This list, while comprehensive, is not considered to include all possible areas of practice or services offered, but is presented as a guide to assist members to consider the large variety of services they may offer.

Having completed a list of current areas of practice, members must identify any differences between their current and their desired levels of knowledge and skill. Given the open-ended nature of this section of the *Self Assessment Guide*, it is the most time consuming to complete as it requires consideration of the services provided and honest contemplation and evaluation of one's knowledge and skill. As differences between current and desired levels of knowledge and skill are identified, they are carried forward to the *Professional Development Plan* for consideration of steps to be taken to bridge any gaps.

Differences in current and desired levels of knowledge and skill need not only be areas of deficiency as members may evaluate their current level of knowledge and skill as quite satisfactory. As responsible professionals however, members are encouraged to undertake activities directed toward further enhancement through continued professional development.

Part VI. Anticipated Areas of Future Practice

Members of the College of Psychologists are required to practice only within their demonstrated areas of professional competence. As one's areas of interest develop or opportunities for professional growth arise, members often consider expanding or changing their authorized areas of practice. Part VI of the *Self Assessment Guide* encourages members to identify possible future areas of practice, when appropriate. Movement to expand into these areas of future practice need not be imminent, however members are encouraged to begin to think about possible changes allowing the necessary, often significant, lead time to set out and complete any required enhancement or retraining. The steps to be taken to fill any gaps between current and desired levels of the knowledge and skills may become part of the current *Professional Development Plan* or entries in this section may be noted solely for future consideration.

Part VII. Professional Development Plan

As each section of the *Self Assessment Guide* was completed, members have had the opportunity to note legislation or standards with which they are not as familiar as they would like. They have identified areas of the professional practice and client service in which they are may not be in compliance with or adequately meeting professional standards. Opportunities for further development or enhancement in teaching/training, research or supervisory activities have also been noted. In the final self review section of the *Self Assessment Guide* areas of practice in which there is a difference between current and desired levels of knowledge and skill have been identified. In addition, members have had the opportunity to consider areas of anticipated future practice and the knowledge and skill required to achieve the desired level of competence.

As these items are noted in completing the *Self Assessment Guide*, they are carried forward to Part VII, the *Professional Development Plan*, and an individualized learning plan is created. The *Professional Development Plan* permits the member to list the differences carried forward, identify the steps to be taken in addressing these differences and to specify the timeline during which the educational activity will be completed. Additional space is provided to record courses, workshops or other educational activities, noting the date and duration. The *Professional Development Plan* may address both areas of current practice where continued development of knowledge or skill is desired, and areas of future practice a member may be considering.

The *Professional Development Plan* is a tool that individual members use to plan, undertake and evaluate their personal continuing education program. The *Professional Development Plan* requires each member to design his or her own continuing education program, both in content and in methodology. The content of the program is dependent upon the member's self-identified developmental objectives, and each member designs the program to suit his or her individual needs and learning style.

Part VIII. Reflection on Professional Development Plan

During the two-year life cycle of the *Self Assessment Guide and Professional Development Plan* some items may become less relevant and some plans may change as one's career progresses. In maintaining the currency of the *Professional Development Plan* members are encouraged to note why a particular aspect included in the *Plan* may not have been carried out as anticipated when the *Plan* was originally developed. Reflecting upon the completion of the *Professional Development Plan* during its two-year cycle provides an ongoing record of the status of the member's professional development that can useful when next completing the *Self Assessment Guide* and developing an updated *Professional Development Plan*.

Next Steps

As the *Self Assessment Guide and Professional Development Plan* is completed every other year, there have now been six full completion cycles. Members whose *Self Assessment Guide and Professional Development Plan* are reviewed as part of the onsite *Peer Assisted Review* process provide positive anecdotal reports of the utility of the process, however this has not recently been evaluated more systematically. A survey evaluation of the usefulness of the process was conducted shortly after its introduction (College of Psychologist of Ontario, 2002). Through the use of a survey of 200 randomly selected members, information was obtained regarding the value of the process, the ease of completion and the overall acceptance of this approach by members. Plans are being made to conduct a survey review the *Self Assessment Guide and Professional Development Plan* with the participants once again; now that the profession has had ten years experience with it.

The previous results were very encouraging suggesting that members found the process of self-evaluation and professional education planning to be of value. In the earlier survey, respondents were asked to rate the effectiveness of the *Self Assessment Guide and Professional Development Plan* in helping them to: identify gaps between current and desired level of knowledge or skill; review relevant legislation and professional practice standards; understand their responsibilities when providing supervision; develop a plan to address their identified learning objectives; and, monitor their professional development activities. On each of these the response from the majority of members was very positively.

Members were given the opportunity to describe any changes to their professional practice which they could attribute to participation in the *Self Assessment Guide and Professional Development Plan* component of the Quality Assurance Program. Changes noted included increased awareness of specific areas of competence requiring improvement; closer attention to statutes and regulations and greater confidence in communicating these to clients; updating of consent to treatment and/or release of information processes and forms; and, a reminder to adequately discuss the limits of confidentiality with clients at the outset of service.

In considering the overall process, members commented that the *Self Assessment Guide and Professional Development Plan* was useful in affirming current positive practices. Others noted with appreciation, the flexibility to plan for one's own needs and the trust placed in members' integrity and willingness to self-monitor his/her professionalism and professional development. The *Self Assessment Guide and Professional Development Plan* was seen, by others, to encourage methodical self-scrutiny and a more systematic approach to professional development than might otherwise be achieved.

These earlier findings encouraged the College of Psychologists to develop and refine this self-evaluation and planning component of the Quality Assurance Program. Changes implemented based on additional member feedback will further enhance the *Self Assessment Guide and Professional Development Plan* process and the objective to promote the enhancement of professional competence through ongoing continuing education and development.

As a regulator, the College requires members to participate in ongoing continuing education and activities directed toward the maintenance of competence. In mandating this, the goal is to offer members a process that is flexible, constructive and encouraging of creativity, and one that permits the freedom to tailor their ongoing education to their individual learning styles, needs and opportunities.

APPENDIX A

THE COLLEGE OF PSYCHOLOGISTS OF ONTARIO

SELF ASSESSMENT GUIDE AND PROFESSIONAL DEVELOPMENT PLAN

Instructions and Forms Booklet

Quality Assurance Program

February/March 2012

Name: _____   Date Completed: _____

QUALITY ASSURANCE PROGRAM

SELF ASSESSMENT GUIDE AND PROFESSIONAL DEVELOPMENT PLAN

Introduction

All members holding Certificates of Registration as a Psychologist or Psychological Associate are required to complete the *Self Assessment Guide and Professional Development Plan*. This includes members whose registration status is *Regular, Inactive* or *Academic*. It is expected that all members will be engaged in continuous professional development directed toward maintaining and enhancing their level of knowledge, skill and experience in their area(s) of practice. Continuing professional development activities should be documented in the *Self Assessment Guide and Professional Development Plan*.

Through the use of the *Self Assessment Guide and Professional Development Plan*, members are required to undertake this self-review every second year. Members with odd numbered registration numbers complete the review in the odd numbered years and those with even registration numbers, in the even numbered years. Members with *Certificates Authorizing Supervised Practice* or *Certificates Authorizing Interim Autonomous Practice* must complete the *Self Assessment Guide and Professional Development Plan* every year.

In 2012, members with even registration numbers must complete the *Self Assessment Guide and Professional Development Plan* and submit the *Declaration of Completion*, attesting to this, to the College. The deadline for submission is Friday, June 29, 2012.

In completing this review, members may find that some sections are not applicable to their work. These sections may be noted as Not Applicable (N/A).

Note: A completed sample 2012 *Self Assessment Guide and Professional Development* form is available for reference on the College website.

Self Assessment Guide

The *Self Assessment Guide* is designed to assist members to evaluate their current level of knowledge, skill and experience and to identify areas in which they feel some further development or enhancement may be beneficial. The *Guide* is divided into the following sections:

- Legislation, Standards, Codes and Guidelines
- Service to Clients
- Teaching/Training and Research Activities
- Supervisory Activities
- Current Areas of Practice and/or Services Provided
- Anticipated Areas of Future Practice
- Professional Development Plan*
- Reflection on Previous Professional Development Plan
- Reference List of Areas of Practice and Services Provided

* Professional Development Plan

Following the completion of the self assessment, members are expected to create a *Professional Development Plan* to address items identified in the self-review. The plan may address both areas of current practice, where continued development of knowledge or skill is desired, as well as areas of future practice a member may be considering.

The *Professional Development Plan* is a tool that members may use to plan, track and evaluate their personal continuing education program. The *Professional Development Plan* permits each member to design his or her own continuing professional development program, both in content and in methodology. The content of the program is informed by the member's self-identified developmental objectives; designed to suit each member's individual needs and learning style.

Submission to College Not Required

The *Self Assessment Guide and Professional Development Plan* component of the Quality Assurance Program is founded upon principles of self-evaluation and continuous improvement. It is a tool to be completed and retained by each member and is not normally submitted, in full, to the College. Should a member be randomly selected to participate in the *Peer Assisted Review* component of the Quality Assurance Program however, the member will be required to have the most recent *Self Assessment Guide and Professional Development Plan* available.

Accompanying the *Self Assessment Guide and Professional Development Plan* is a *Declaration of Completion*. **This is to be signed and returned to the College by Friday, June 29th, 2012.** The *Declaration* asserts that: *I have reviewed my practice in psychology and documented this in the Self Assessment Guide. I have created a Professional Development Plan to address the continued professional developmental objectives I have identified. I understand that I must retain the completed Self Assessment Guide and Professional Development Plan in my files.*

The *Declaration of Completion* is the College's documentation that a member has participated in the Quality Assurance Program.

NOTE: Members, who do not submit the *Declaration of Completion* by the deadline, may be required to submit the full, completed *Self Assessment Guide and Professional Development Plan* for review by the Quality Assurance Committee of the College.

Confidentiality and Legislative Protection of Quality Assurance Material

The Regulated Health Professions Act (1994), the Personal Health Information Protection Act (2004) and the Quality of Care Information Protection Act (2004) provide for the protection of Quality Assurance information, held by a member, that was completed for the purpose of complying with the requirements of the College's Quality Assurance Program. A member's *Self Assessment Guide and Professional Development Plan* is not admissible in evidence in a civil proceeding. This information could be required by the College however, to the extent permitted by legislation.

PART I   LEGISLATION, STANDARDS OF PROFESSIONAL CONDUCT, CODE OF ETHICS AND GUIDELINES

Many statutes and regulations including the Standards of Professional Conduct, the Canadian Code of Ethics for Psychologists, as well as the child abuse reporting requirements under the Child and Family Services Act and the mandatory reporting obligations under the Regulated Health Professions Act, apply to all members. In the first section of Part I, please consider whether you are sufficiently familiar with the content of these documents. Members are not required to own these materials but it is important that members be familiar with, and have access to, them. Any needs identified with respect to these should be noted. Most of these documents are readily available online from the College, Canadian Psychological Association or the provincial and federal government websites. Links are provided for those documents available online, as well as a key to the contact information for the sources of the documents.

Depending upon your area(s) of practice and populations served, there are a number of other pieces of legislation or guidelines that may impact on your work. Review the items in the second section of Part I and, if they apply to your practice, indicate your level of familiarity and any other comments. In considering one's familiarity with this material, one should ensure that one knows enough about it to determine if it is relevant to one's practice. Please include on the 'Other' line, any items which are not indicated, but which you consider to be important to your practice. The College would appreciate being notified of significant omissions so these can be considered in future editions of the *Self Assessment Guide*.

If you identify a need for greater familiarity, the way in which this will be obtained should form part of your *Professional Development Plan*. Any needs you may have with respect to reviewing these materials or securing ready access to them should also form part of your *Professional Development Plan*.

Document and Source	Sufficiently Familiar Yes/No	Comments or Action to be Taken
Psychology Act, 1991 ①		
Regulations under the Psychology Act ① • Professional Misconduct • Registration • Quality Assurance and Advertising		
Regulated Health Professions Act and Health Professions Procedural Code, 1991 as amended ①		
Standards of Professional Conduct and Supplementary Notes, College of Psychologists of Ontario, September 2009 ②		
Canadian Code of Ethics for Psychologists, Third Edition, Canadian Psychological Association, Revised 2000 ①②		
Practice Guidelines for Providers of Psychological Services, Canadian Psychological Association, Updated 2001 ④		

Document and Source	Sufficiently Familiar Yes/No	Comments or Action to be Taken
Health Care Consent Act, 1996 as amended ①		
Personal Health Information Protection Act (PHIPA) (2004) ①		
Protection of Personal Information and Electronic Documents Act (PIPEDA) (2000) ⑤		
Mandatory obligation to report child abuse under the Child and Family Services Act, 1990 (s.72) as amended ①		
Mandatory obligation to report sexual abuse of a patient under the Health Professions Procedural Code of the Regulated Health Professions Act, 1991 (s.85) as amended ①		

The following documents **may not apply to all** providers of psychological services. Please complete the following chart for those which apply to your practice, marking the others as Not Applicable (N/A).

Document and Source	Sufficiently Familiar Yes/No	Comments or Action to be Taken
Accessibility for Ontarians with Disabilities Act, 2005 ①		
Automobile Insurance Rate Stability Act, 1996 & Statutory Accident Benefit Schedule, under the Insurance Act, 1996 as amended ①		
Child and Family Services Act, 1990 as amended ①		
Children's Law Reform Act, 1990 as amended ①		
Companion Manual to the Canadian Code of Ethics For Psychologists, Canadian Psychological Association, 2001 ④		
Corrections and Conditional Release Act (Canada) 1992 ⑤		
Ethical Guidelines for Psychological Practice Related to Child Custody and Access, Ontario Psychological Association, 1997 ③		
Guidelines for Child Custody Evaluation in Family Law Proceedings, American Psychological Association, 2010 ⑥		
Education Act, 1990 as amended ①		
Ethics in Research with Human Participants, American Psychological Association, 2000 ②		
Freedom of Information and Protection of Privacy Act, 1990 as amended ①		

Document and Source	Sufficiently Familiar Yes/No	Comments or Action to be Taken
Human Rights Code, 1990 as amended ①		
Mental Health Act, 1990 ①		
Municipal Freedom of Information and Protection of Privacy Act, 1990 as amended ①		
Public Hospitals Act, 1990 as amended ①		
Services and Supports to Promote the Social Inclusion of Persons with Developmental Disabilities Act, 2008 ①		
Standards for Education and Psychological Testing, American Psychological Association, 1999 ②		
Substitute Decisions Act, 1992 ①		
Workplace Safety and Insurance Act, 1997 as amended ①		
Youth Criminal Justice Act, 2002 as amended ⑤		
Other: _____		

RESOURCES

① Publications Ontario, http://www.e-laws.gov.on.ca/navigation?file=home&lang=en (English) or http://www.e-laws.gov.on.ca/navigation?file=home&lang=fr (French)
50 Grosvenor St. Toronto, Ontario M7A 1N8.
(416) 326-5300, Toll Free (800) 668-9938

② College of Psychologists of Ontario, www.cpo.on.ca
110 Eglinton Avenue West, Suite 500, Toronto, Ontario, M4R 1A3.
(416) 961-8817, Toll Free (800) 489-8388

③ Ontario Psychological Association, www.psych.on.ca
21 St. Clair Avenue East, Suite 403, Toronto, Ontario M4T 1L8. (416) 961-5552

④ Canadian Psychological Association, www.cpa.ca
151 Laurier Avenue West, Suite 702, Ottawa, Ontario, K1P 5J3. (613) 237-2144

⑤ Federal Publications, http://laws.justice.gc.ca/en/index.html (English) or
http://laws.justice.gc.ca/fr/index.html (French)
425 University Avenue, Suite 401, Toronto, Ontario M5G 1T6. (416) 860-1611

⑥ *American Psychologist*, 1994, 49(7) 677-680. American Psychological Association, www.apa.org
(800) 374-2721

PART II SERVICE TO CLIENTS

This section is applicable to practitioners in their work with clients. It contains a variety of items drawn from the Standards of Professional Conduct and the Professional Misconduct Regulation. Completion of this part will assist you in thinking about your work relative to these very important areas of professional practice. You may find that some items do not apply to your practice and these can be marked as Not Applicable (N/A). Items that require further review or some action should be noted and carried forward to your *Professional Development Plan*. Please note that this section does not list every Standard or every item included in the Professional Misconduct Regulation to which members are responsible to adhere.

The Standards of Professional Conduct and Professional Misconduct Regulation
Note: Numbers at the end of the following statements refer to an applicable Standard of Professional Conduct) (SPC) or Professional Misconduct Regulation (PM)

Item	Yes/No	Action Required (Yes/No) Comments
I only provide services in my demonstrated areas of professional competence. [SPC 5.1]		
I engage in activities to remain current to the scientific and professional developments in areas directly related to the services that I provide.		
I retain client files for a minimum of 10 years following the client's last contact or, in the case of clients under 18 years of age, for at least 10 years following the day they became or would have become 18. [SPC 9.4]		
Upon the request of my client or their legal representative, I provide another member of the College with original or raw results or data.[SPC14]		
I do not accept gifts of more than token value from my clients. [SPC 12.6]		
I participate fully in all mandatory aspects of the Quality Assurance Program. [SPC 1.4]		
I am aware of the harassment provisions of Principle 13 of the Standards. [SPC 13]		
I inform my client of the limits of confidentiality before or at the commencement of my involvement with them. [PM 11]		
I inform my client of the charges to be levied for my services before or at the commencement of a service. [PM 22] and work out the method of setting fees and other charges with my clients at the earliest possible opportunity.[SPC 10.1]		
I do not accept prepayment for services but, with my client's agreement, I may accept a retainer to be held in trust and applied against services rendered. [SPC 10.4]		
I do not offer a reduction in fee for prompt payment. [PM 28]		

Item	Action Required (Yes/No) Comments
I obtain informed consent with respect to the delivery of all psychological services unless otherwise permitted or required by law. [SPC 7.2]	
I obtain informed consent with respect to the collection, use and disclosure of personal information and personal health information unless otherwise permitted or required by law. [SPC 8.1]	
I have not entered into any arrangements such as a lease for use of premises or equipment; administrative services or the provision of supervision which provides for a fee or income splitting based on a percentage of fees invoiced or collected. [SPC 10.5]	
I make reasonable efforts to ensure that all transmissions of information, either in hard copy or electronically, protects the privacy of the client record. [SPC 9.6.2]	
I ensure that any record, certificate, report or other document is not false, misleading or otherwise improper. [PM 20]	
I have notified the College of any offenses of which I have been found guilty as per the RHPA.	
I have made provisions for: - Storage of client records to ensure they are safe and protected from loss, tampering or unauthorized use or access; - Maintenance of psychological tests and supplies in a secure place; - Maintenance of records of all bills presented to patients/ clients and payments received; - Continuing patient/client care in the event of my disability or death; - Mandatory professional liability insurance; - Office and personal injury liability, as appropriate.	

Record Keeping
My records contain the following information as per sections 9.2 and 9.3 of the revised Standards of Professional Conduct. (Dependent upon whether a member's practice is with individuals or corporations, not all of these may apply)

Item	Yes/No	Action Required (Yes/No) Comments
Identifying data (e.g., names, addresses, telephone numbers, dates of birth, sex, and referral source)		
Documentation of client consent regarding the collection, use and disclosure of personal health information		

Item	Yes/No	Action Required (Yes/No) Comments
Documentation of client consent to treatment in the record, as needed		
Description of services provided and the date of every relevant and material contact with the client or consultation about the client		
Documentation, in the record, that the limits of confidentiality have been discussed		
Relevant information about every material service activity related to the client including:		
Assessment procedures used		
Summary of findings		
Periodic description of client progress		
Documentation that fees have been discussed		
A copy of any service contract between you and the patient/client		
A copy of all reports received or sent by you on behalf of, or for, a patient/client		
The name, address and telephone number of the organization, firm, corporation, or community, and the name and position of the primary contact person		
The name(s), and title(s) of the person(s) who can release confidential information about the organization, firm, corporation, entity, or community		

PART III TEACHING/TRAINING AND RESEARCH ACTIVITIES

Many members are involved in teaching or training activities and/or research. For some members, these activities are carried out in formal settings such as universities or funded research facilities that have formal written policies with respect to ethics and conduct in teaching/training and/or research. Other members conduct these activities in their work settings within organizations that do not necessarily have formal written policies or codes of ethics and conduct. If you are involved in teaching or training and/or research activities, please complete these parts. Should you assess that further review or action is required, this should be carried forward to your *Professional Development Plan*.

TEACHING/TRAINING ACTIVITIES

Item	Yes/No	Action Required (Yes/No) Comments
I teach or train in a setting which has formal written codes of ethics and policies regarding professional behaviour to which I must adhere and I am familiar with these.		

OR

I teach or train in a setting that does not have formal written codes of ethics and policies but I am familiar with codes of ethics and policies regarding professional behaviour with respect to teaching and training.		

RESEARCH ACTIVITIES

Item	Yes/No	Action Required (Yes/No) Comments
I conduct research under the auspices of a fund granting body or research facility that has formal written codes of ethics and policies regarding professional behaviour to which I must adhere and I am familiar with these.		

OR

I conduct research at a setting which is not under the auspices of a fund granting body or research facility but I am familiar with codes of ethics and policies regarding professional behaviour with respect to conducting research.		

PART IV   SUPERVISORY ACTIVITY

Members are involved in numerous supervisory activities in a variety of academic, institutional or private practice settings. If you are engaged in supervisory activities, please complete Part IV and carry forward any items that require further review or action to your *Professional Development Plan*.

Item	Yes/No	Action Required (Yes/No) Comments
I am familiar with the Supervision Resource Manual, 2nd Edition, March 2009 published by the College.		
I am familiar with the Ethical Guidelines for Supervision in Psychology: Teaching, Research, Practice, and Administration, Canadian Psychological Association, 2009		
I assume full professional responsibility for all clients seen by my supervisee.		
I have adequate training, knowledge and skill to render competently all psychological services undertaken by the supervisee.		
I provide supervision appropriate to the knowledge, skills and competence of the supervisee.		
I ensure clients are informed: a) of the professional status and qualifications and that all services are reviewed with and conducted under my supervision; b) of my identity and how they can contact me; c) that a meeting can be arranged at their request or the request of the supervisee d) that I will have access to all relevant, confidential information about the client required for me to provide adequate supervision.		
All billing and payments for services are in my name.		
Public announcements of service are offered only by me or in my name.		
In all fee-for-service arrangements, setting and receipt of fees remains my responsibility or that of the employing agency.		
My name, clearly identifying me as the supervisor and my contact information is clearly identified on all reports and formal correspondence.		
I countersign all written reports and formal correspondence prepared by *non-regulated providers*, under my supervision.		
I encourage my supervisee to engage in ongoing professional development.		

PART V   EVALUATION OF CURRENT AREAS OF PRACTICE AND/OR SERVICES PROVIDED

List your current areas of practice or the services you provide. At the back of this booklet is a *Reference List: Areas of Practice and Services Provided* that might be helpful in fully describing your services and activities. This list is provided as a guide and is not intended to be all-inclusive.

Identify any differences between your current and desired levels of knowledge or skill. Please consider both areas requiring improvement and areas where enhancement is desired. Having identified these differences, you should begin to think about how these might be addressed through continuing professional development. Please describe these differences and carry them forward to be addressed in your *Professional Development Plan*.

Areas of Practice/Services Provided	Differences Between Current and Desired Levels of Knowledge and Skill

PART VI   ANTICIPATED AREAS OF FUTURE PRACTICE

Members often consider expanding or changing areas of practice. This section entitled *Anticipated Areas of Future Practice* will allow you to identify future areas of practice you may be considering and to evaluate your current status with respect to the knowledge, skill and experience necessary to practice in this new or expanded area. Identify any differences between your current and desired levels of knowledge, skill and experience, and begin to develop your *Professional Development Plan*.

NOTE: Changing Areas of Practice - Retraining Plans

According to the Registration Regulation (Ontario Regulation 533/98) members of the College, "shall practise the profession only within those areas of the member's competency that are authorized by the College or under the supervision of a member who has competency in those areas." [10(2)1] If you are considering a change in your practice that could include either a change in area of practice, in activity and/or in clients served, a retraining plan, approved by the Registration Committee of the College, may be required. If you are unsure if the changes you are contemplating constitute a change in your area of practice, you are encouraged to contact the Registration Committee. Please refer to the Guidelines For Change of Area of Competence for Autonomous Practice Members.

Areas of Future Practice or Services to be Provided	Differences Between Current and Desired Levels of Knowledge and Experience

PART VII PROFESSIONAL DEVELOPMENT PLAN

A *Professional Development Plan* is created by each member to address any differences between the current and desired levels of knowledge, skill or experience identified through the self assessment.

Differences Identified Through Self Assessment	Developmental Plan to Address Differences	Time Line	Course, Workshop, Activity

Other Continuing Professional Development

In addition to addressing self-identified differences between one's current and desired level of knowledge, skill and experience members should also list any other continuing professional development activities undertaken to enhance practice and professional development.

Course, Workshop, Activity	Date	Hours

PART VIII   REFLECTIONS ON PREVIOUS PROFESSIONAL DEVELOPMENT PLAN

During the two year life of the *Self Assessment Guide and Professional Development Plan* some items may become less relevant and some of your plans may change. It is helpful to note, as a reminder to yourself, why a particular aspect of your *Professional Development Plan* may not have been carried out at all or in the manner expected. As well, you may wish to make other comments about the completion and effectiveness of the *Professional Development Plan*. This is information can provide an ongoing record of the status of your professional development and may be very useful in two year's time when completing your next *Self Assessment Guide and Professional Development Plan*.

<u>Comments on Professional Developmental Plan</u>

Reference List: Areas of Practice and Services Provided

Populations

Infants	Seniors
Children	Couples
Adolescents	Families
Adults	Organizations

Conditions Assessed and/or Treated - Types of Difficulties or Issues

Abuse; sexual, physical, emotional	Chronic Pain	Medical; e.g., cancer, stroke
Addiction; e.g., alcohol, gambling, drugs, etc.	Cognitive issues; giftedness, delays, limitations	Palliative care
		Physical disabilities
AIDS and HIV	Death and dying	Psychiatric disorders
Anxiety	Depression	Separation, Divorce
Attention deficit disorder	Eating disorders	Sexuality
Autism	Brain injury	Sexual dysfunction
Behaviour problems	Learning disabilities/problems	Sports and Performance
Capacity to make decisions	Lifestyle issues	Other

Services Provided

Assessment
Addiction
Adoption
Child Custody/Welfare
Corrections/Forensic
Designated Capacity Assessor (SDA)
Disability
Industrial/Organizational
Neuropsychology
Mental Health and Well Being
Parenting Capacity
Educational/Learning
Vocational/Career
Rehabilitation/Insurance

Diagnosis
Behavioural Disorders
Developmental Disabilities
Mental Health/Psychiatric Disorders
Personality Disorders

Other
Research
Supervision
Teaching/Training

Treatment
Biofeedback
Cognitive Behavioural Therapy
Counselling
Crisis Intervention
Desensitization Training
Group Therapy
Hypnotherapy
Individual Therapy
Psychotherapy

NOTES

NOTES

The College of Psychologists of Ontario
110 Eglinton Ave W, Suite 500
Toronto, Ontario M4R 1A3

Tel: (416) 961-8817/(800) 489-8388   Fax: (416) 961-2635
e-mail: cpo@cpo.on.ca   website: www.cpo.on.ca

BIOSKETCH

RICK MORRIS is the Deputy Registrar/Director, Professional Affairs for College of Psychologists of Ontario. He has a Ph.D. in psychology from the University of Toronto and worked principally in children's mental health before joining the staff of the College in 1996. He is well known among members of the College, psychologists and psychological associates, for his work as practice advisor to both members and the public who have ethical dilemmas and practice or legislative queries. Dr. Morris makes numerous presentations to both members and other groups throughout Ontario on a variety of professional practice topics and has been invited to speak on many occasions, at psychology conferences in both Canada and the United States. He is the Chair of the Association of Canadian Psychology Regulatory Organizations, the national association of regulators of psychology in Canada. Dr. Morris is a fellow of the Association of State and Provincial Psychology Boards and is a recipient of the Barbara Wand Award for excellence in the areas of ethics and standards from the Ontario Psychological Association.

REFERENCES

Canadian Psychological Association. (2000). *Canadian code of ethics for psychologists* (3rd ed.). Ottawa: Author.

Canadian Psychological Association. (2009). *Ethical guidelines for supervision in psychology: teaching, research, practice and administration.* Ottawa: Author.

College of Psychologists of Ontario. (2002). The quality assurance program, status update: Part 1. *The Bulletin, 19,* 6-9.

College of Psychologists of Ontario. (2005). *Standards of professional conduct.* Toronto: Author.

College of Psychologists of Ontario. (2009). *Supervision Resource Manual.* Toronto: Author.

Health Professions Procedural Code. (1991). Schedule to the Regulated Health Professions Act, 1991, SO 1991, c. 18, as amended.

Ontario Regulation. (1993). Professional misconduct. O. reg. 801/93 *Psychology Act*, 1991. SO 1991, c. 38, as amended/.

Chapter 7

CONTINUING PROFESSIONAL DEVELOPMENT: A REGULATORY PERSPECTIVE

Carol Webb[1,*] and Jacqueline B. Horn[2]
[1] Emory University, US
[2] University of California, Davis, US

ABSTRACT

The issue of how psychologists maintain and enhance their competence is a significant issue for professional psychology and for licensing boards in their obligation to protect the public. It is the responsibility of health care regulatory agencies to ensure that their licensees/registrants are competent to practice when they first become licensed; but in recent years licensing boards have paid more attention to ensuring that their licensees/registrants maintain competency to practice throughout their careers. This chapter identifies and discusses the issues relevant to maintenance of competence that relate to regulation, and includes a discussion of some of the ethical issues involved in the provision of continuing education. A preliminary model that replaces the current reliance on continuing education workshops as the primary means of ensuring maintenance of competence is presented. Finally, recommendations specific to ensuring competence are addressed.

Keywords: Continuing education, continuing competence, psychology regulation, psychology licensing

The issues of lifelong learning, continuing education, and continuing professional competence have received significant attention in the psychological literature in the past few decades (e.g., VandeCreek, Knapp, & Brace, 1990; Wise et al., 2010). The awareness that learning does not end when one's formal education is complete, and that professionals should continue to update their skills, enhance their existing knowledge, and reexamine their

---
[*] Correspondence regarding this manuscript may be directed to Carol Webb, Ph.D., at cwebb@emory.edu.

professional attitudes throughout their careers, is central to this focus, both for professional psychology and for licensing boards in their obligation to protect the public.

The continuing professional development of its members is one feature that defines a profession. Historically, the way psychologists have achieved and ensured this ongoing professional development has been by participation in Continuing Education (CE), which often has meant formal learning activities conducted in classroom or workshop settings. Continuing Professional Development (CPD), however, is a broader concept, referring to the continuing development of the multi-faceted *competencies* needed for quality professional performance in one's area of practice. Whereas CE activities should help to update and refine knowledge, CPD activities should help to update and refine competencies.

CPD activities have as their foundation a continuing learning process, starting after completion of graduate school and continuing as long as the psychologist is engaged in professional activities. CPD, therefore, stands as a professional obligation of every psychologist, and at the same time, is also a prerequisite for enhancing the quality of professional psychology, for helping to ensure the ongoing competence of psychologists, and ultimately to provide the best psychological services to the public.

It is the ethical obligation of psychologists to practice competently (APA, 2002; CPA, 2000), and governments in the United States (U.S.) and Canada have established boards in each of the states and provinces to regulate the profession of psychology and to protect the public from the incompetent or unethical practice of psychology licensees. The shaping, reshaping and development of a psychologist involves responding to changing societal and individual needs in the context of evolving science and professional activities (WFME, 2003). CPD is essential to maintaining professional competencies, to remedy and/or update gaps in knowledge and skills, to review professional attitudes, and to enable professionals to respond to the challenges of rapidly growing knowledge and technology, as well as changing practice requirements and structures in which that practice occurs.

In the following pages we will examine the issues relevant to the maintenance of competence that relate to the regulation of psychology. We will propose that a broader understanding of lifelong learning, continuing education, and continuing professional development is necessary to follow the mandate under which psychology's licensing boards operate, that of consumer protection. We will discuss a model for CPD that serves as a first step toward providing the range and kinds of activities that could be used to help ensure this continuing professional development and one that offers a methodology for ensuring the continuing psychological competence important for the profession and critical for the public. Additionally, we will look to the future of psychology regulation and describe what we think ultimately will be necessary for the profession and for professional regulation, whose obligation it is to ensure that psychologists continue to remain competent practitioners in order to protect the public.

History of Continuing Educaton and Psychology Licensure

In 1945, Connecticut became the first state to have an independent licensing act for psychology, and by the late 1970's, all 50 states had psychology licensing acts. With the creation of the Psychologists Registration Act in 1960, Ontario was the first Canadian province to establish a licensing act for psychologists; now, licensing laws have been established in all 10 provinces. The purpose of all licensure laws was, and is, to protect the public from incompetent or unethical professional practice (DeMers & Schaffer, 2011).

Psychology licensing boards, therefore, are charged with regulating the profession of psychology in order to ensure that the public who utilizes those services is both protected from incompetent or unethical practice and enjoys the benefits of psychological services as practiced by competent psychologists. In carrying out their mandates, psychology licensing boards determine the types of education and training needed in order for individuals to become licensed, describe the kinds and amount of supervised professional experience needed prior to those individuals becoming licensed, and develop and administer examinations that assess both knowledge of psychology and of the laws and regulations that govern the profession of psychology in their jurisdictions. Regulatory boards, through legislative mandate, also determine what is required for psychologists to be able to maintain and renew their licenses, always with an eye toward consumer protection.

In 1957, Maryland became the first state to legislate mandatory CE for psychologists as a way to try to ensure the ongoing professional competence of its licensees. Since that time, legislation has emerged requiring some form of mandatory CE in 46 of the 54 U.S. states and territories and in 6 of the 10 Canadian provinces that make up the membership of the Association of State and Provincial Psychology Boards (ASPPB), the association comprised of all the regulatory agencies in the U.S. and Canada.

In 1998, the *ASPPB Model Act for Licensure of Psychologists* included for the first time a provision for *mandatory* CE, representing a distinct shift in perspective from previous iterations of their model act that had not addressed the necessity of mandatory CE. Mandatory CE was seen as one way to ensure the ongoing competence of licensed psychologists. In 1999, ASPPB established its first CE Task Force, and by 2001, ASPPB had published its *Guidelines for Continuing Education*, with recommendations for licensing boards to *require* CE of its licensees, noting at the time that several states and provinces, while not currently mandating CE, had legislation in place that would allow this (ASPPB, 2001). At the time of this writing, 52 of the 64 jurisdictions that regulate psychology in the U.S. and Canada mandate CE for their licensees, with several other jurisdictions in the process of making CE a requirement. As with other requirements established by licensing boards, CE requirements are quite varied, depending on jurisdiction (Daniels & Walter, 2002; see also Adams & Sharkin, 2012).

The public may assume that professional regulatory boards are ensuring that their licensees maintain competence to practice. A recent survey (AARP, 2007) indicated that the public overwhelmingly thinks that health care professionals *should* be required to demonstrate their competence periodically; and the majority of those same individuals support states establishing guidelines for evaluating that competence.

The psychology licensing boards in the U.S. and Canada that mandate CE for their licensees do so at a rate comparable to other health and mental health regulatory agencies. Medicine requires mandatory CE in 87% of its U.S. jurisdictions and in 60% of its Canadian jurisdictions; pharmacy's CE requirements are mandatory in all of its jurisdictions, both in the U.S. and Canada; and dentistry has mandatory CE required in 94% of its jurisdictions in the U.S. and 80% of its Canadian jurisdictions (Webb, Horn, Boll, Brown & Yarrow, 2010). Of the 63 U.S. and Canadian jurisdictions that are members of the American Social Work Board, the social work equivalent of ASPPB, 60 mandate CE and/or proof of continuing competency at license renewal, as demonstrated by attendance at continuing education workshops or in continuing education classes (51/53 U.S. states and territories and 9/10 Canadian provinces) (ASWB, 2009).

REVIEW OF CONTINUING COMPETENCY AND REGULATION

The need for health care professionals to maintain their competence and stay abreast of new developments in their discipline seems obvious, both to the public and to professional groups. Consumer advocacy, research and public policy groups such as the Citizens Advocacy Center, the Cochrane Collaboration and the Pew Commissions have addressed this need for many years now. Additionally the field of medicine has taken the lead in the U.S. in addressing issues pertaining to the maintenance of competence through their specialty certification boards and the Institute of Medicine (IOM).

The Pew Health Professions Commission issued four landmark reports between 1989-1999 addressing the need for health care reform in the delivery of health care services, in the education and training of health care professionals and in the regulation of the health care workforce. The Pew Commission Task Force on Health Care Workforce Regulation (Finocchio et al., 1998) recommended the following changes (among others) in order to more effectively protect the public and ensure the ongoing competence of health care professionals:

1. National standards for scope of practice and continuing competency requirements
2. More consumer representation on regulatory boards and oversight agencies
3. Legislation to assist with professional mobility and practice across state boundaries

With regard to the issue of the need for regulatory boards to require the demonstration of continued competence, this report acknowledged that CE workshops are insufficient to ensure continuing competency, and that most licensing boards do not require their licensees to demonstrate their continuing competence. They discussed the advantages of state licensing boards pairing with private credentialing and certification groups (in psychology, one example would be the American Board of Professional Psychology (ABPP)) to assist with the demonstration of continuing competence and contrasted health care efforts with efforts from other professions. For example, they report that pilots are mandated by the Federal Aviation Administration to be recertified at regular intervals on both medical and professional competency measures.

The Pew Commission recommended a review of continuing competence for the health care professions no less than every seven years, with more frequent reviews for those who are older or who have demonstrated need for remediation. They add that these reviews should include reexaminations, specialty certification, peer reviews, self-assessment, mandatory CE for license renewal, mandatory disclosure of malpractice or other disciplinary actions, and mandatory reporting of any criminal actions. This report, however, did not address the specifics of how to measure continuing competence; rather, it advised that this should be left to the professional groups.

The Citizens Advocacy Center (CAC) (Swankin, LeBuhn & Morrison, 2006), in a report commissioned by the Association of Retired Persons (AARP), addressed the need for continuing competence among health care professionals from a consumer perspective. They reported that with the increasing complexity and innovations in knowledge and technologies, the need for maintaining and enhancing competence is more essential than ever. They also asserted that regulators are *not* currently ensuring that licensees in the health care workforce are maintaining their competence, but that it *should* be the place of licensing boards to do so. They proposed a regulatory model that "includes periodic *assessment* of knowledge, skills, and clinical performance; development, execution, and documentation of an *improvement plan* based on the assessment; and periodic *demonstration* of current competence" (p. iii original emphases). The assessment and documentation of knowledge and skills can utilize a variety of methods including:

> written or oral examinations, peer review, consumer satisfaction surveys, records review, self-reflection leading to self-directed learning program portfolios, evaluation by standardized patients, on-site practice review, performance evaluations, and continuing education based on needs assessment and followed by a test or other verification that the course material has been absorbed. (Swankin, LeBuhn & Morrison, 2006, p. iv)

These methods of assessment are highly relevant to evaluating the effectiveness of CPD activities in psychology.

The CAC made a number of recommendations focused on reforming the way in which continuing competence is assessed. Included in these recommendations were proposals to replace CE requirements for re-licensure with mandated CPD requirements that "must include (a) assessment; (b) development, execution, and documentation of a learning plan based on the assessment; and (c) periodic demonstrations of continuing competence…through a variety of legally defensible, psychometrically sound, evidence-based methods" (p. 38). Additionally they recommended that licensing boards should themselves evaluate which methods of CPD are effective to maintain competency in the "knowledge, skills, attitudes, judgment, abilities, experience, and ethics necessary for safe and competent practice in the setting and role of an individual's practice at the time of re-licensure" (p. 38). They also asserted that licensing boards should partner with credentialing and specialty boards to assist in the demonstration of continuing competency.

If health care professions could abide by these recommendations, it seems that the goal and duty of licensing boards to ensure continuing competence would be fulfilled. In psychology, however, as well as most of the other health care disciplines, there remain many obstacles. The first of the CAC recommendations, for instance, requires mandated CPD activities at each licensure renewal period and also requires documentation through "legally defensible, psychometrically sound, evidence-based methods" (p. 38). Currently, the state of psychology research in methods of delivering or assessing effectiveness in CPD activities has not evolved to the point where that recommendation can be met (Neimeyer, Taylor, & Wear, 2009). Another recommendation is that state regulatory agencies should conduct pilot projects to assess and measure methods to evaluate the efficacy of various methods of CPD. While a noteworthy idea, state and provincial licensing boards for psychologists do not have the financial or staffing resources, or the scientific expertise, to conduct such projects. For a variety of reasons it is highly impractical to think that licensing boards will be able to manage projects like these for some time to come.

A third recommendation refers to the idea that licensing boards should outsource the assessment and documentation of continuing competency to other professional groups. In fact, medicine has embraced that concept, and physicians who are Board Certified through the American Board of Medical Specialties (ABMS) are now required to undergo periodic reevaluations of their competency in order to maintain their board certification (ABMS, 2011). Physicians are required to complete a four-step process that includes licensure, lifelong learning and self-assessment, demonstration of specialty-specific updated skills and knowledge, and involvement in practice audits and assessments; that is, demonstrating that they are effectively utilizing evidence-based practices in their work with patients. In psychiatry for example, board certified psychiatrists are required to present evidence of maintenance of competence every 10 years, and this evidence must include a self-assessment of what new information is needed to maintain competence, at least 30 CE credits each year, chart reviews, peer-assisted performance reviews, patient feedback, and an evaluation of whether improvements in practice performance have actually occurred. And finally, each board certified psychiatrist must pass a multiple-choice examination on current research and clinical updates in his or her specialty (American Board of Psychiatry and Neurology, 2009).

These requirements place the field of medicine far ahead of psychology in being able to demonstrate continuing competence for its licensees. Medicine has a long history as an organized profession as well as hundreds of thousands of members. More than 80% of physicians are board certified (ABMS, 2011(b)), as compared to less than 5% of psychologists, making ABMS requirements for the maintenance of competence serve as protections for the public by actually enhancing the medical care that is offered to consumers. The Federation of State Medical Boards (FSMB), the physician equivalent of ASPPB, has endorsed CPD requirements for maintaining a medical license to include the self-assessment, assessment of knowledge and skills, and performance in practice components identified above (FSMB, 2008, 2010).

More recently, the IOM (2010) released a report reviewing the field of CE and offered 10 recommendations, including the establishment of a public-private institute solely devoted to CPD. This institute would collaborate with all of the health care professions to determine the content and evidence base for CPD. Additionally, the IOM proposed that this institute would address issues of regulation and financing of CPD. Two of the recommendations, quoted below, specifically address the need for more understanding through research regarding the maintenance of competence:

"Recommendation 2: To achieve the new vision of a continuing professional development system, the planning committee should design an institute that:

(a) Creates a new scientific foundation for CPD to enhance health professionals' ability to provide better care;
(b) Develops, collects, analyzes, and disseminates metrics, including process and outcome measures unique to CPD;
(c) Encourages development and use of health information technology and emerging electronic health databases as a means to provide feedback on professionals' and health system performance;

(d) Encourages development and sharing of improvement tools (e.g., learning portfolios and assessment resources) and theories of knowledge and practice (e.g., peer review systems for live documentation, such as wikis) across professions;
(e) Fosters interprofessional collaboration to create and evaluate CPD programs and processes; and
(f) Improves the value and cost-effectiveness of CPD delivery and considers ways to relate the outputs of CPD to the quality and safety of the health care system." (p. 8).

"Recommendation 4: The Continuing Professional Development Institute should lead efforts to improve the underlying scientific foundation of CPD to enhance the knowledge and performance of health professionals and patient outcomes by:

(a) Integrating appropriate methods and findings from existing research in a variety of disciplines and professions,
(b) Generating research directions that advance understanding and application of new CPD solutions to problems associated with patient and population health status,
(c) Transforming new knowledge pertinent to CPD into tools and methods for increasing the success of efforts to improve patient health, and
(d) Promoting the development of an inventory of measurement instruments that can be used to evaluate the effectiveness and efficiency of CPD." (p. 9).

The idea of a public-private inter-professional institute devoted to the continuing professional development not only of health care professionals, but of all professionals engaged in applied work, is an intriguing one, and one that potentially could result in both enhanced professional competence and improved patient/client outcomes. National standards for continuing competence for psychologists, and effective means to deliver programs and assess outcomes, could be incorporated by state licensing boards as requirements for licensure renewal. Psychologists offer a unique resource to the development and implementation of such an institute, with education and training in research methodology and application of evidence-based principles. It will be imperative that psychologists are actively involved in this institute.

ASPPB Task Force and Model for CPD

In 2009, in light of the competency movement and other recent developments in the field of psychology (Kaslow et al., 2004; Rodolfa et al., 2005), the ASPPB Board of Directors decided to update its *Guidelines for Continuing Education* and appointed a Task Force to (1) revise and update the current *Guidelines* (2) study the role that regulatory bodies can have in assuring that licensed psychologists maintain their competence and (3) make recommendations to regulatory bodies on how to implement maintenance of competence. The Task Force reviewed research on CE in psychology and CE in general, approaches to maintaining and enhancing competence taken by other professions, the role and effectiveness of self-assessment, and several other areas of research from a regulatory perspective. Upon completion of these reviews, the ASPPB six-person Task Force determined that a broader construct than that associated with traditional CE was needed in order to provide licensing boards with the best model for assessing and determining competence. The Task Force decided that the new guidelines would encompass this broader perspective, but also decided that updated guidelines should only be the beginning of work toward this broader perspective. Ultimately this group became known as the Maintenance of Competency and Licensure Task Force (MOCAL), indicating a long-term view that would begin with the *ASPPB Guidelines for Continuing Professional Development* and end with specific suggestions and solutions for ways to attain and measure the ongoing competence of psychology licensees.

As indicated previously, we believe that current CE activities update and increase the knowledge necessary to practice competently, but that CPD activities must update and increase both the knowledge *and* the other components of competence (e.g., skills and attitudes) necessary for effective practice. More importantly, psychology's regulatory boards must be able to demonstrate that they are taking steps to ensure that their licensees maintain competence to practice throughout their careers, something already assumed by the public (e.g., Finlayson & Dewar, 2001; Neuberger, 2000; Swankin et al., 2006). To that end, the Task Force proposed a new model for CPD.

The MOCAL model for CPD uses the competencies identified by a national sample of psychologists through the most recent practice analysis for the Examination for Professional Practice of Psychology (EPPP) (ASPPB, 2010). Additionally, the Task Force understands and agrees with the APA definition of CE that states:

> Continuing education (CE) in psychology is an ongoing process consisting of formal learning activities that (1) are relevant to psychological practice, education, and science; (2) enable psychologists to keep pace with emerging issues and technologies; and (3) allow psychologists to maintain, develop, and increase competencies in order to improve services to the public. (APA, 2009, p. 2.)

The MOCAL model for CPD builds upon a completed doctoral program in psychology so it is not a substitute for the basic academic education and training needed for entry to the field of psychology. Instead, it provides psychology's regulatory agencies with specific recommendations they can use to help ensure that their licensees have continued to refine and update their skills and knowledge, and ultimately, will provide a way to help ensure that consumers of psychological services are both protected from incompetent or unethical practice and are able to utilize the services of competent psychologists.

As indicated previously, this model takes into account what the research literature tells us about what does and what does not work in CE as it is currently offered, and what other professions have done to ensure the continuing competent practice of their licensees (ASPPB, 2010; IOM, 2010). The conclusions that can be drawn from this research are:

1. CPD is necessary and expected. Current models of CE cannot be demonstrated to be sufficiently effective in producing outcomes necessary for the maintenance of competence, so models that allow for a variety of CPD activities that psychologists can adapt and focus on their areas of greatest needs could be useful.
2. Further delineation of treatment guidelines is critical for the field to provide more specificity as to what psychologists need to know and the procedures they should use to promote improved client or patient outcomes.

3. Careful monitoring of CPD activities is important to assure consumers, professionals and the public alike, that the activities are faithful to principles of evidence based-practice. CPD providers should be obligated to specify the foundations on which their offerings are based, that is, identifying the sources of the material they present distinguishing between empirical research, applied experience, and/or theoretical concepts. Each of these areas has an important contribution to maintaining competence, and preferably CPD activities would integrate research, applied experience, and theoretical concepts with elements of patient/client characteristics in each of the activities.
4. Current methods of assessing CPD outcomes are inadequate. Most focus on affective reactions to the activity (which we now recognize may not be related to later professional behavior) and on self-report regarding the extent and value of knowledge acquired. As yet, it is not possible to fully assure ourselves that many CPD activities directly enhance declarative or procedural knowledge, transfer from the CPD activity into the workplace, address the variety of competencies identified as important for practice, or enhance practice outcomes.
5. Research suggests a variety of ways that psychology can strengthen the relationship between CPD and educational/client/practice outcomes that should be incorporated into any model. CPD is most effective for ensuring professional competence when individuals are involved in a variety of activities that occur over time, that include formal follow-up, and that reduce professional isolation (ASPPB, 2010, p. 15-16).

Table 1.

CPD Activity	Value of Credits by Activity
Professional	
1. Peer Consultation (case consultation groups, peer supervision, journal clubs, regional research groups; mentoring; recipient of consultation receives credit unless learning is reciprocal)	1 hour = 1 credit
2. Practice Outcome Monitoring (assessing patient/client outcomes via questionnaire)	1 patient/client = 1 credit
3. Professional Activities (serving on psychological association boards or committees, scientific grant review teams, or board member of regulatory body)	1 year = 10 credits
4. Conferences/Conventions (attendance time as distinguished from CE credits)	1 conference day = 1 credit
Academic	
5. Academic Courses (Taking a graduate-level course from a regionally accredited institution related to psychologist's area of practice)	1 semester long course = 20 credits
6. Instruction (teaching a course in a regionally accredited institution; full day workshop presentation; only counts first time teaching or presenting)	1 course/1 full day workshop = 20 credits
7. Publications (writing for peer-reviewed publications, book chapter, or editor or coeditor of publication)	1 publication = 10 credits
Continuing Education	
8. Approved Sponsored CE (workshops; must be from a recognized approved sponsor as defined below)	1 hour = 1 credit

CPD Activity	Value of Credits by Activity
9. Self-directed learning (reading, videos, unsponsored activities)	1 hour = 1 credit
Board Certification	
10. Board Certification (can count for 100% of required CPD in the year that certification is awarded)	Certification awarded = 40 credits

Table 1 presents the ASPPB model for CPD that takes into consideration what has been learned from reviewing CPD and CE literature and includes a credit system versus the system of hours now in place in most jurisdictions, and uses for this example 40 required credits per licensure renewal time frame.

It is anticipated that psychologists will participate in a variety of CPD activities to fulfill requirements for licensure renewal in this model. If the CPD activity requires sponsorship, an approved sponsor must provide it. Qualifying programs include those offered by the American Psychological Association or any of its sponsors approved through the American Psychological Association CE Sponsor Approval System (CE-SAS), the Canadian Psychological Association Continuing Education Sponsor Review Program, the Academies of the Specialty Boards of ABPP, regionally accredited colleges and universities, Category I Continuing Medical Education (CME) of the American Medical Association and the Canadian Medical Association, and Continuing Legal Education through the American and Canadian Bar Associations, if relevant to the practice of psychology.

It could well be that most psychologists already engage in a number of these activities and maintain their competence routinely. There is no known data that elucidates the frequency or severity of "psychological errors" committed by less than competent practitioners, nor is there research that demonstrates that clients are receiving less than optimal services from practitioners. It is possible that this model will allow psychologists to "count" more of what they are already doing as evidence of continued competence rather than require more CPD activities from them for licensure renewal. The model provides more flexibility for licensees and broadens the range of acceptable activities for regulatory bodies.

ETHCIAL AND CONFLICT OF INTEREST ISSUES

The ethical and conflict of interest issues pertinent to the regulation of maintenance of competence are related to two broad spheres - money and influence. Continuing education for psychologists, physicians, pharmacists, and professionals in other disciplines offers the opportunity for businesses to make large profits, as well as to influence those professionals who attend their programs to utilize particular intervention and assessment methods and materials, pharmaceuticals, and/or equipment. Many for-profit companies offering CE for psychologists can easily be found on the internet and through bulk advertising that comes in the mail to most licensed psychologists. CE for psychologists is also provided by non-profit organizations including APA, educational and training institutions, state psychological associations, and other professional groups. The opportunity for conflict of interest difficulties is boundless for all of these organizations. Indeed, conflict of interest issues within Continuing Medical Education (CME) for both physicians and pharmacists has reached historic proportions as commercial industries (including the pharmaceutical industry) provided over $1.5 billion of support for CME in 2008 alone (IOM, 2010). As a result, the accreditation council for CME, their sponsor approval agency, has had to develop rigorous and detailed regulations concerning the disclosure of conflicts of interest before and during CME sessions. Additionally, universities and medical schools also require faculty to disclose conflict of interest issues annually in relationship to the research and intervention grants they receive in order to avoid ethical challenges to the outcomes of their scientific endeavors. Recently, universities and medical schools have sanctioned faculty members who violate those required disclosures.

To date, psychology fortunately has avoided many, but not all, of these conflicts. However, as more jurisdictions allow psychologists prescriptive authority, there will need to be more attention paid to the regulation of CE and CPD by sponsor approving agencies so that the possible influence of commercial industry is managed appropriately and openly disclosed. Psychologists who market equipment or psychological tools and techniques for personal or professional profit should also be required to disclose their affiliations with the commercial companies prior to their CE presentations being accepted or presented.

Most jurisdictions that require CE as a condition for licensure renewal allow for CE to be acquired through a variety of sponsors, and almost all allow for APA- approved programs. The CE-SAS is part of the APA Continuing Education Committee (CEC) and has as its mission to develop and manage the mechanisms and methods by which CE programs are evaluated for quality assurance purposes (APA, 2009). The resulting list of standards and criteria serve as a guide for groups seeking APA approval and are reasonably rigorous. It is interesting to consider though, that the organization approving sponsors for CE programs (APA) also has one of the largest offerings of approved CE programs. While we are confident that there are firewalls in place between the CE-SAS and APA's Office of Continuing Education, the perception of the potential for conflict of interest still exists. Further, it is unclear how effectively the CE-SAS monitors approved sponsors for compliance to their standards, and although there are sanctions in place if those standards are violated (see http://www.apa.org/ed/sponsor/about policies/policy-manual.pdf), these may not be widely known or understood.

It may be useful for APA to consider a sponsor approval program that functions as an independent, non-profit agency totally outside of the larger APA, directed by members of a number of professional organizations (e.g. APA, ASPPB, ABPP, CCTC, APPIC) and by representatives of the public. Such a sponsor approval system could eliminate the possible perception of conflict of interest.

A GLIMPSE TO THE FUTURE

As psychology matures as a discipline, a number of advances in CPD will need to occur. In order to accomplish the regulatory goal of ensuring the continuing competence of psychologists, these advances must include development and adherence to national standards of education and training for entry-level professionals, development of accepted competencies for practice, development and assessment of specialty standards of training and practice, and a commitment to not only lifelong learning, but to the assessment and demonstration of lifelong learning.

NATIONAL STANDARDS

Much more attention has been paid to the *development* of competent entry-level psychologists than has been paid to how practitioners *maintain* competency throughout their careers. Even so, there are great variations among training programs and training models so that there exists a deepening divide in our discipline between the "scientists" and the "practitioners." Further, there are many different applied fields within psychology, including non-health care related ones. Until recently, the APA has only accredited training programs in clinical, counseling, school or combined psychology. Currently there is an option for other applied fields to become accredited, although to date, none have done so. APA-accredited training programs self-identify as scientist-practitioner, clinical-scientist, practitioner-scholar and a myriad of other labels to distinguish themselves from each other in their emphasis and focus on either science or practice. We even have different degrees (Ph.D., Psy.D.) to further distinguish our training models. APA has accredited programs from all of these models, adhering to the "thousand blooming flowers" notion of quality (Benjamin, 2001).

The APA Commission on Accreditation's acceptance and endorsement of the idea that adherence to the expressed model of training is what is evaluated and valued, rather than the ability of training programs to demonstrate that students acquire accepted competencies, has made the job of regulation of practice much more difficult. Recently, however, it seems there has been a shift toward the development, and hopefully adherence to, more unified standards of training. It is essential that all trainees who intend to become licensed to deliver health care services graduate from their training programs with a similar set of skills, knowledge, professional values, reasoning abilities and performance for psychology to continue to grow as a respected and substantial member of the health care professions. Likewise, it is incumbent on the regulatory community to develop and adhere to national standards for education, supervised experience, and examination performance so that licensing boards require the same entry-level qualifications for all psychologists. Additionally it is important that psychology regulatory bodies also agree on and enforce similar, if not uniform, requirements for CPD at licensure renewal. When psychology can agree and implement national standards for licensure at the entry level, ensuring the maintenance of competency becomes more feasible, consumers will be better protected.

Recommendation

APA, APPIC, ASPPB, ABPP and other stakeholders should agree on and implement national standards for education, accreditation, supervised professional experience, licensure, and re-licensure.

COMPETENCE

There have been many advances in our field over the last 10 years in the area of identifying and defining the competencies needed to practice (Kaslow, 2004; Kaslow et al., 2004; Rodolfa et al., 2005). The 2002 APPIC sponsored Competencies Conference established parameters for competencies necessary for psychological practice, and the extremely valuable and important follow-up workgroups developed benchmarks for those competencies (Fouad et al., 2009) and offered a means to assess those competencies (Kaslow et al., 2009). However, while the benchmarks document identified the functional and foundational competencies necessary for the first three levels of professional development - readiness for practicum, readiness for internship, and readiness for entry to practice - the workgroup did not address the next level of professional development, maintenance of competence over time.

ASPPB (2010), through its most recent practice analysis, identified six core competencies for the professional practice and regulation of psychology. They are Scientific Knowledge; Evidence-Based Decision Making/ Critical Reasoning; Interpersonal and Multicultural Competence; Professionalism/ Ethics, Assessment; and Intervention/ Supervision/ Consultation. These competencies are utilized in the development of questions for the national licensing exam for psychology, the EPPP, which is the only national measure of readiness to practice that exists at this time. The six competencies identified by the practice analysis are similar to the primary competencies identified by the 2002 Competency Conference, but based more exclusively on the applied practice of psychology rather than also including teaching and training realms. ASPPB has also begun investigating how alternative methods of assessing competence could be used to evaluate entry-level qualifications of applicants for licensure through the initiation of its Task Force on Competency Assessment.

Recommendations

APA should continue the excellent work of the Benchmarks and Assessment workgroups and expand the focus to include identifying, defining, and outlining methods of assessment for ongoing competence. A natural starting point for the more detailed definitions and behavioral anchors needed for the next level of professional development, ongoing professional competence, would be to utilize the core competencies already identified by both APA and ASPPB.

ASPPB should continue to maintain and refine the EPPP, as a test of the scientific, ethical and applied knowledge necessary for entry-level practice. The timing of taking the EPPP should be reexamined, and ASPPB and the training community should consider having students take it at the end of their graduate education. Research suggests that the closer to the end of their graduate training individuals take the EPPP, the more likely they are to pass (Shaffer, Lipkins, Rodolfa, Webb & Horn, in press). ASPPB and other stakeholders should continue to address alternative methods of assessing competence beyond scientific knowledge and either enhance the EPPP to include these measures or develop an additional examination to directly assess competence. Once entry-level competency-based examinations are developed and utilized, developing competency-based examinations to assess ongoing competence will be more practical.

SPECIALIZATION

If it is true in psychology as it is in medicine, that over time practitioners develop areas of specialty and their practice narrows, then the issue of the assessment of maintenance of competence necessarily must address issues of specialization. While at entry-level, both training and assessment of knowledge and competence tend to be broadly focused, ongoing training and assessment may need to be tailored to reflect what psychologists are actually doing in their day-to-day practices. In medicine, this is accomplished through medical specialty boards. In psychology, while there are specialty certification boards, most notably ABPP, relatively few psychologists become board certified. It will be an impossible task for licensing boards to be able to develop examinations or other assessment procedures for all of the specialties in psychology. Therefore, it seems that psychology will need to evolve further in the realm of specialty board certification in order for any meaningful reevaluation for continuing competency to occur.

There are some organizations within psychology that have been working on defining and developing criteria for the recognition of specialties (e.g., Council of Specialties (CoS), Commission for the Recognition of Specialties and Proficiencies in Professional Psychology (CRSPPP)), and their work needs to continue and grow so that there is universal recognition and acceptance of what a specialty is and the method by which one becomes a specialist. Further, it seems that there are a number of board certification groups that exist in psychology, with various levels of credibility. From a regulatory perspective, licensing boards will be much more amenable to accepting assurances of maintenance of competence from one recognized board certification body that has as its members all of the recognized specialties. Currently, it seems that ABPP is the organization that most closely meets that requirement. Fortunately ABPP recognizes specialties in both health care and other applied areas. One of psychology's strengths is the breadth of the discipline. There are many settings within health care as well as outside of health care that utilize psychological principles and services, and regulation of maintenance of competence issues are relevant to all of these applied areas.

Recommendations

APA, our training institutions, and other professional groups should encourage their members to become board certified in whatever specialty that is appropriate for them, and board certification should become a requirement for those applied psychologists who work at hospitals, community mental health centers, academic institutions or in private practice settings where third party payers are billed.

ABPP and other credible and legitimate board certifying groups should join together and cooperate to develop one universally recognized board certification body, and develop requirements for ongoing maintenance of certification for each specialty.

LIFELONG LEARNING

The commitment to lifelong learning is one that our profession has valued for a long time. Indeed, it is believed that most psychologists not only value lifelong learning, but engage in it on a regular and as needed basis. However, psychology and many other disciplines lag in the assessment and demonstration of lifelong learning. The IOM (2010) recommendation for a private-public institute devoted to the development of valid and reliable methods of learning that address the acquisition of knowledge, the application of that knowledge to practice, and the assessment of whether changes in practice are reflected in improved outcomes, may be the critical variable needed in order to significantly advance this field. However, at this point, with economic and other challenges facing our nation, it does not seem reasonable to wait for that kind of institute to be created.

APA is in the process of developing treatment guidelines, having already developed a number of practice guidelines. These guidelines, which utilize evidence-based principles of effective interventions, relationship stances, common factors, etc., are essential to be able to assess areas where one may need more time and effort to maintain or enhance competence. The APA CE Sponsor Approval System (APA, 2009) requires that CE programs adhere to a set of criteria that includes theoretical, scientific and/or practice bases of credibility. Recently APA's CE Sponsor Approval System added requirements that CE programs be supported by scientific findings. These standards and criteria are rigorous if applied uniformly to not only APA CE, but to all of its subsidiaries as well. Most states have a number of APA-approved CE sponsors that develop and offer CE.

ASPPB is in the process of developing updated CPD guidelines for state licensing boards to use at licensure renewal. These guidelines, discussed above, include more options to maintain and enhance competency than are currently offered by traditional CE workshops. We see these guidelines as a step toward a more comprehensive system for achieving CPD. More research about the efficacy of different training delivery methods is needed to help guide licensing boards and ASPPB in knowing what kinds of activities are most likely to lead to maintaining competence. Further, research that determines which type of learning activity is associated with improved outcomes would also be extremely useful, although for psychology, this is probably a very difficult task. New and creative assessment methodologies may need to be developed in order to accomplish this task.

Recommendations

Psychology should be included in the development and implementation of a private-public institute devoted to maintenance of competence for all health care professionals.

APA, ABPP, ASPPB and other professional groups should develop assessment strategies to link CPD activities to improved client outcomes.

APA and other groups should develop innovative CPD activities, perhaps using the tremendous technological advances we have seen in recent years as aids. For example, it now may be possible to offer virtual peer consultation groups, or cyber-based supervision using recognized problem- or disorder- specific experts as part of APA's CE offerings, or to develop databases of appropriate and valid patient or client outcomes by treatment method and type of problem(s) or disorder(s).

APA should investigate developing an independent sponsor approval agency comprised of members of a variety of professional organizations.

APA should devise a way to make aspects of sponsor applications public so that people who sign up to take CE from these sponsors can have a way to ensure that sponsors are adhering to what they said they would do. This could allow for multiple quality assurance checks, not only from APA but from consumers who take CE courses from APA-approved sponsors. APA should also consider requiring objective measures of learning at the conclusion of programs, not only for online CE programs, but also for those that are attended in person; and should consider adding follow-up measures of what was learned and how that learning may have (or have not) been transferred into practice. While these objective measures of learning may not reflect a parallel improved outcome in an applied setting, they could represent a step towards a change in how psychologists view their responsibilities for the maintenance of competence.

ASPPB should continue to review and revise CPD guidelines and encourage jurisdictions to adopt uniform standards for CPD.

2025

From a regulatory perspective, it is anticipated that in the next 10-15 years there will be a valid, reliable and universal system in place for the demonstration and assessment of continuing competence for psychologists. Many more psychologists will be board certified in a number of cohesive and well-defined specialties, in both health care and other applied areas. The idea of reassessment of competence will be included in teaching of professional values as part of professional training programs and psychologists will expect that there will be periodic evaluations for the length of their professional careers.

The continuing competency system will probably include a periodic review of all licensed psychologists' competence as demonstrated through CPD activities, self- and peer-assisted assessments of need and documentation of methods to meet those needs through practice audits and patient or client feedback, and a reexamination of knowledge, skills, and attitudes. While the idea of reexaminations may seem an anathema to many, it is not an unreasonable expectation. Consumers of psychological services have a right to expect that their providers will remain competent, and will be able to demonstrate their competence through valid methods of assessment. Licensing boards have an obligation to ensure that their licensees are competent, both when initially licensed and throughout their professional careers. ASPPB, as the foremost authority in the regulation and credentialing of psychologists, is working on the development of these possibilities through the creation and support of the MOCAL and Competency Assessment Task Forces. With the collaboration of professional organizations in psychology (e.g., ASPPB, ABPP, APA) and in other disciplines (e.g., Medicine, Social Work), it is anticipated that these goals can be achieved.

BIOSKETCHES

DR. CAROL WEBB is a member of the Board of Directors of the Association of State and Provincial Psychology Boards (ASPPB) and currently is serving as President-Elect of the association. As a member of the ASPPB Board of Directors, Dr. Webb chairs the Mobility Committee and also chairs the ASPPB Task Force for the Maintenance of Competence and Licensure (MOCAL). She is on the Georgia State Board of Examiners of Psychologists, having been appointed initially in 2002 and reappointed in 2008, and she served as its President for three years. Dr. Webb the Director of Internship Training at Emory University School of Medicine/Grady Health Systems and has a private practice with Peachtree Psychological Associates in Atlanta, GA. She supervises predoctoral interns, postdoctoral fellows, psychology practicum students, and psychiatry residents at Emory/Grady in adult and child psychotherapy and in the Psychiatric Emergency Service.

DR. JACQUELINE HORN is a member of the Board of Directors of the Association of State and Provincial Psychology Boards (ASPPB) and currently serves in the third year Member-at-Large position. As a member of the ASPPB Board of Directors, Dr. Horn chairs the Item Development Committee for the Examination for Professional Practice in Psychology (EPPP) and is a member of the ASPPB Task Force for the Maintenance of Competence and Licensure (MOCAL). She was a member of the California Board of Psychology from 2002-2009, and served at its President for three years. She was a member of the Ethics Committee of the California Psychological Association from 1993-2002. For the past 30 years, Dr. Horn has been a Lecturer in Psychology at the University of California, Davis, and she maintains a private practice as well.

REFERENCES

AARP. (2007). *2007 Virginia member survey: Health care quality*. Retrieved from http://www.aarp.org/research.

Adams, A., & Sharkin, B. S. (2011). Should continuing education be mandatory for re-licensure? Arguments for and against. In G. J. Neimeyer, & J. M. Taylor (Eds.), *Continuing professional development and lifelong learning: Issues, impacts and outcomes* (pp. 157-178). Hauppauge, NY: Nova Science Publishers.

American Board of Medical Specialties. (ABMS) (2011). *Maintenance of certification*. Retrieved from http://www.abms.org/Maintenance_of_Certification/ABMS_MOC.aspx.

American Board of Medical Specialties. (ABMS) (2011 b). *Board certification editorial background*. Retrieved from http://www.abms.org/news_and_events/media_newsroom/pdf/abms_editorialbackground.pdf.

American Board of Psychiatry and Neurology. (2009) *Maintenance of certification for psychiatry*. Retrieved from http://www.abpn.com/moc_psychiatry.htm.

American Psychological Association. (2002). Ethical principles of psychologists and code of conduct. *American Psychologist, 57,* 1060-1073.

American Psychological Association. (2009) *Standards and criteria for approval of sponsors of continuing education for psychologists*. Retrieved from http://www.apa.org/ed/sponsor/about/standards/manual.pdf.

American Social Work Board. (2009). *Social work regulatory board CE policies*. Retrieved from http://www.aswb.org/SWL/conteducation.asp.

ASPPB *Study of the practice of licensed psychologists in the United States and Canada*. (2010). Retrieved from http://www.asppb.net/files/PA_Executive_Summary_2010.pdf.

Association of State and Provincial Psychology Boards. (2001). *ASPPB guidelines for continuing education.* Retrieved from http://www.asppb.net/i4a/pages/index.cfm?pageid=33.

Association of State and Provincial Psychology Boards. (2010). Draft *proposal: Continuing professional development guidelines.* Retrieved from http://www.asppb.net/files/Final_draft_CPD_report[1].pdf.

Benjamin, L.T. Jr. (2001). American psychology's struggles with it's curriculum. *American Psychologist, 56*, 715-747.

Canadian Psychological Association. (2000). *Canadian code of ethics for psychologists* (3rd edition). CPA: Ottawa, ON.

Daniels, A.S., & Walter, D. (2002). Current issues in continuing education for contemporary behavioral health practice. *Administration and Policy in Mental Health, 29*, 359-376.

DeMers, S.T., & Schaffer, J.B. (2011). The regulation of professional psychology. In Knapp, S., Gottlieb, M, Handelsman, M. & VandeCreek, L. (Eds). *Handbook of Ethics,* Washington, D.C.: American Psychological Association.

Federation of State Medical Boards. (2008). *Special Committee on Maintenance of Licensure*. Retrieved from http://www.fsmb.org/pdf/Special_Committee_MOL_Draft_Report_February2008.pdf.

Federation of State Medical Boards. (2010). *Maintenance of Licensure Policy*. Retrieved from http://www.fsmb.org/pdf/mol-board-report-1003.pdf.

Finlayson, B., and Dewar, S. (2001). Reforming complaint systems: UK and New Zealand. *The Lancet, 358*, 1290.

Finocchio, L.J., Dower, C.M., Blick, N.T., Gragnola, C.M., & the Taskforce on Health Care Workforce Regulation. (1998). *Strengthening Consumer Protection: Priorities for Health Care Workforce Regulation*. San Francisco, CA: Pew Health Professions Commission.

Fouad, N.A., Grus, C.L., Hatcher, R.L., Kaslow, N.J., Hutchings, P.S., Madson, M.B.,...Crossman, R.E. (2009). Competency benchmarks: A model for understanding and measuring competence in professional psychology across training levels. *Training and Education in Professional Psychology, 3*, S5-S26.

Institute of Medicine. (2010). *Redesigning Continuing Education in the Health Professions*. Washington, DC: The National Academies Press.

Kaslow, N. J. (2004). Competencies in professional psychology. *American Psychologist,59*, 774-781.

Kaslow, N. J., Borden, K. A., Collins, F. L., Forrest, L., Illfelder-Kaye, J., Nelson, P. D., Willmuth, M. E. (2004). Competencies Conference: Future directions in education and credentialing in professional psychology. *Journal of Clinical Psychology, 80*, 699-712.

Kaslow, N.J., Grus, C.L., Campbell, L.F., Fouad, N.A., Hatcher, R.L., & Rodolfa, E.R. (2009). Competency assessment toolkit for professional psychology. *Training and Education in Professional Psychology, 3*, S27-S45.

Neimeyer, G.J., Taylor, J.M., & Wear, D.M. (2009). Continuing education in psychology: Outcomes, evaluations and mandates. *Professional Psychology: Research and Practice, 40,* 617-624.

Neuberger, J. (2000). The educated patient: New challenges for the medical profession. *Journal of Internal Medicine, 247,* 6-10.

Rodolfa, E. R., Bent, R. J., Eisman, E., Nelson, P. D., Rehm, L., & Ritchie, P. (2005). A cube model for competency development: Implications for psychology educators and regulators. *Professional Psychology: Research and Practice, 36*, 347-354.

Schaffer, J.B., Lipkins, R., Rodolfa, E., Webb, C., & Horn, J.B. (in press). The examination for professional practice in psychology: New data – practical implications. *Training and Education in Professional Psychology.*

Swankin, D., LeBuhn, R.A., & Morrison, R. (2006). *Implementing continuing competency requirements for healthcare practitioners.* AARP: Washington.

VandeCreek, L., Knapp, S., & Brace, K. (1990). Mandatory continuing education for licensed psychologists: Its rationale and current implementation. *Professional Psychology: Research and Practice, 21,* 135-140.

Webb, C., Horn, J.B., Boll, T., Brown, R., & Yarrow, C. (2010, October). *Continuing professional development: Looking to the future.* Paper presented at the annual meeting of the Association of State and Provincial Psychology Boards, Savannah, GA.

Wise, E., Sturm, C.A., Nutt, R.L., Rodolfa, E., Schaffer, J.B., & Webb, C. (2010). Life-long learning for psychologists: Current status and a vision for the future. *Professional Psychology: Research and Practice, 41,* 288-297.

World Federation for Medical Education. (2003). *Continuing professional development (CPD) of medical doctors: WFME global standards for quality improvement.* WFME Office: University of Copenhagen, Denmark.

In: Continuing Professional Development …
Editors: G. J. Neimeyer and J. M. Taylor

ISBN: 978-1-62100-767-8
© 2012 Nova Science Publishers, Inc.

Chapter 8

DISCIPLINARY ACTIONS BY A STATE BOARD OF PSYCHOLOGY: DO GENDER AND ASSOCIATION MEMBERSHIP MATTER? AN UPDATE[1]

Samuel Knapp[1],* and Leon VandeCreek[2]
[1] Pennsylvania Psychological Association, Harrisburg, PA, US
[2] Wright State University, US

ABSTRACT

Using archival data consisting of licensing board adjudications and membership lists of the Pennsylvania Psychological Association over a 14-year period (1997-2010), the authors found that the likelihood of being disciplined by the Pennsylvania State Board of Psychology was higher for men and for psychologists who did not belong to their state psychological association. However, gender and association membership interacted (nonmember male psychologists had the highest risk of committing ethical infractions and even nonmember female psychologists had disciplinary rates higher than female members), suggesting that only certain males are at the highest risk for an infraction. The data suggest the importance of professional connectedness in reducing risks of being disciplined.

Keywords: Ethics, Disciplinary Action, Gender, State Psychological Association Membership

---

[1] This chapter updates an article that appeared in Volume 41, Fall, 2009 edition of Focus on 31, the newsletter of Division 31, State, Provincial, Territorial Psychological Association Affairs. We thank Division 31 For giving us permission to reprint portions of that article.

* Dr. Knapp is employed by PPA and is partially responsible, among other responsibilities, for ethics education for the state association. Dr. VandeCreek is a past-President of PPA.
Correspondence regarding this manuscript may be directed to Samuel Knapp, 76 Country Lane, Landisville, PA, 17538.

A salient goal of all professionals is to work at a high level of skill throughout their careers. Attaining such a goal requires continued dedication and a willingness to engage in life-long learning (Wise, 2010). Certainly, it is worthwhile to learn as much as possible about the personalities, training experiences, and practice patterns of those who excel in their profession. Conversely, it is worthwhile to learn as much as possible about those who fail to excel.

This study looks at psychologists who fell short of their career goals on at least one measure, being disciplined by their state board of psychology. This study measured the relationship between gender, state association membership, and the likelihood of being disciplined by the State Board of Psychology. We used archival data consisting of descriptions of licensing board adjudications found in the newsletters of the Pennsylvania State Board of Psychology newsletters and the membership lists of the Pennsylvania Psychological Association (PPA) over a 14-year period (1997-2010). During this time period, the State Board of Psychology published notices of 193 adjudications against psychologists (an additional 11 adjudications were made against non-psychologists for practicing psychology without a license).

Continuing education violations accounted for 41% of all adjudications, followed by sexual contact with patients (10%) and non-sexual boundary violations (10%). Among all infractions, male psychologists were involved in 123 and female psychologists in 66 (in 4 cases the gender of the individual could not be determined). This difference was significant $\chi 2$ (1, 188) =24.6. $p < .0001$. Of the 38 disciplinary actions involving boundary violations, 31 were against male psychologists.

Determining the gender distribution was not straightforward. The gender analyses assumed that the number of females slightly exceeded the number of male psychologists during this time period. Although the State Board of Psychology keeps no data on the gender of licensees, assumptions were made concerning the gender distribution of psychologists in Pennsylvania from the annual member surveys of the Pennsylvania Psychological Association which found that 47% of state association members were female in 1998 (Knapp & Keller, 1998), and 55% were female by 2009 (Knapp & Keller, 2009). Using these data to generate an estimate, a decision was made to consider the population of psychologists to be 53% female over the period covered by this study. We believe that this generalized to the entire population of all licensed psychologists, because the trend for the increased number of women psychologists is consistent with nation-wide trends in psychology (Cynkar, 2007).

Nonmembers of PPA were involved in 143 infractions and members in 50. Based on our estimate of 40% association membership, this difference was significant $\chi 2$ (1, 192) = 16.9, $p < .0001$. Of the 38 disciplinary actions involving boundary violations, 31 were against nonmembers.

Determining the percentage of psychologists who belong to the state association was not straightforward. The number of licensed psychologists varies over the course of the two-year license renewal period and is highest before licenses expire on November 30 of odd years, and lowest at the beginning of each renewal period on December 1 of odd years. The number of licensed psychologists who belong to the state association is highest at the end of the calendar year, and lowest at the beginning of the calendar year when the number of members dropped for non-payment of dues is highest. Consequently, the percentage of licensed psychologists who belong to the state association varies between 40% and 50%, depending on which figures are used. For purposes of this study, we estimated the percentage of licensed psychologists who belonged to the state association by using the number of licensed association members in January 2009 just after a number of members were dropped for non-payment of dues. Thus, in this study, we assumed that PPA members constituted 40% of the population of licensed psychologists, although the estimate might be low.

Membership interacted with gender. Of the 189 violations in which the gender of the psychologists could be verified, 92 were committed by non-member males, 47 by non-member females, 31 by member males, and 19 by member females. Of the 38 disciplinary actions involving boundary violations, 25 were committed by non-member males, six by non-member females, six by member males, and one by a member female.

In conclusion, nonmembers had higher disciplinary rates than members do. The only other study we know of that looks at the same issue found that orthopedic surgeons who belonged to their professional association had a lower frequency of malpractice complaints than non-members (Kilmo, Daum, Brinker, McGruire, & Elliot, 2000). The reasons for the correlation between association membership and disciplinary actions are unclear. Perhaps the consultation and education that PPA provides to its members helps them to reduce risks of being disciplined. Or perhaps psychologists who are more conscientious, more interested in connecting with other psychologists, or more committed to honest self-assessments (Wise, 2010) self-select themselves into professional associations. Perhaps both factors are present.

Gender was also related to the risk of a disciplinary action, especially for boundary violations. The reasons for this relationship are unclear. Perhaps the gender effect occurs because male psychologists, as a group, tend to be older and have had more years of practice in which a licensing board complaint could be filed. Perhaps male psychologists do not have the same level of social skills as female psychologists and are less able to develop and maintain productive relationships with patients, or keep appropriate boundaries.

Nonetheless, the data do not suggest an inherent or across the board risk of ethical misconduct by male psychologist. Gender and association membership interact (non-member male psychologists have the highest risk of committing ethical infractions and even nonmember female psychologists had disciplinary rates higher than female members) suggesting that only certain males are at the highest risk for an infraction. Cullari (2009) found that the average male psychologist in Pennsylvania who was disciplined was 55 years old with 23 years of experience. Data from this study and that of Cullari suggest that older and socially isolated males are at the highest risk of being disciplined by a licensing board. The data suggests that disciplinary rates might be decreased by encouraging psychologists to become more socially connected with their peers.

BIOSKETCHES

SAMUEL KNAPP, Ed.D., ABPP, has been the Director of Professional Affairs for the Pennsylvania Psychological Association since 1987. His primary area of interest is in professional ethics. Dr. Knapp is co-author of *Practical ethics for psychologists: A positive approach* and Editor-in-Chief of *Handbook on Ethics* to be published by the American Psychological Association.

LEON VANDECREEK, Ph.D., ABPP, is Professor of Psychology at the School of Professional Psychology at Wright State University in Dayton, Ohio. His primary area of interest is in professional ethics. Dr. VandeCreek is co-author of *Practical ethics for psychologists: A positive approach* and an Associate Editor of *Handbook on Ethics*.

REFERENCES

Cynkar, A. (2007 June). The changing gender composition of psychology. *Monitor on Psychology, 38*, 46-47.

Cullari, S. (2009 June). Analysis of Board of Psychology Disciplinary Actions: 1990-1997. *Pennsylvania State Board of Psychology newsletter.* Retrieved from http://www.dos.state.pa.us/portal/server.pt/community/newsletters/19087.

Kilmo, G., Daum, W., Brinker, M., McGruire, E., & Elliott, M. (2000). Orthopaedic medical malpractice: An attorney's perspective. *American Journal of Orthopaedics, 29*, 93-97.

Knapp, S., & Keller, P. (1998). *Annual Survey of PPA members.* Unpublished data.

Knapp, S., & Keller, P. (2009). *Annual Survey of PPA members.* Unpublished data.

Wise, E. (2010). Maintaining and enhancing competence in professional psychology: Obsolesence, life-long learning, and continuing education. *Professional Psychology: Research and Practice, 41,* 288-292.

Section 3.

Continuing Education Mandates

Chapter 9

SHOULD CONTINUING EDUCATION BE MANDATORY FOR RE-LICENSURE? ARGUMENTS FOR AND AGAINST

Aimee Adams* and Bruce S. Sharkin
Kutztown University, US

ABSTRACT

Should continuing education (CE) be mandatory for psychologists? This question has been debated for many years and continues to elicit intense scrutiny. In this chapter, a brief overview of the history and current status of mandatory continuing education (MCE) in the United States is provided, followed by arguments for and against MCE. Relevant literature to support each argument is cited. In particular, the issue of whether MCE ensures competent professional practice is critically examined. The chapter concludes with suggestions for modifying the current system of MCE in order to be more uniform across states and more relevant to the professional practice of psychology.

Keywords: Mandatory continuing education, continuing education, professional competence, professional psychology, pros and cons

The issue of whether continuing education should be mandatory for psychologists has been debated and contested for many years (e.g., Hellkamp, Imm, & Moll, 1989; Sharkin & Plageman, 2003; VandeCreek & Brace, 1991) and continues to be scrutinized (e.g., Neimeyer, Taylor, & Wear, 2009). Although continuing education is sometimes referred to as continuing professional education and continuing professional development, for consistency this chapter will refer to it as continuing education (CE) and mandatory continuing education (MCE). Following a brief overview of the history and current status of MCE, this chapter will

---

* Correspondence regarding this manuscript may be directed to Aimee Adams, Dept. of Counseling and Psychological Services, Kutztown University, 127 Beck Hall, P.O. Box 730, Kutztown, PA, 19530. (610) 683-4072.

examine arguments for and against making CE mandatory, citing relevant literature to support each argument. In addition to existing research, we will cite anecdotal evidence such as observations of the first author in her role as CE program coordinator for a regional psychological association approved as a CE sponsor by the American Psychological Association (APA). We have two goals for this chapter: (1) to critically examine the question of whether CE needs to be mandatory to ensure competent professional practice and (2) to stimulate continuing debate on this issue. The chapter will conclude with suggestions for modifying the current system of MCE and implications for future research.

HISTORY AND CURRENT STATUS OF MCE

According to the APA Council of Representatives, CE is an "ongoing process consisting of formal learning activities" (APA, 2000). The Association of State and Provincial Psychology Boards (ASPPB, 2010) defines CE as "an ongoing process to maintain and enhance professional competence in the psychologist's area of practice or specialty." In contrast to graduate training (which focuses on development of new skills), CE is aimed at refining existing skills and learning new ones, as well as maintaining awareness of changes in knowledge and clinical interventions (Daniels & Walter, 2002). MCE for re-licensure consists of requiring psychologists to undertake a variety of learning experiences in order to enhance the services they provide and ensure their competency (Melnyk et al., 2001).

There is a long-standing tradition within the field of psychology that education beyond graduate studies and licensure is necessary to maintain competence. Maryland was the first state to mandate CE for psychologists in 1957 (Melnyk et al., 2001). Throughout the 1960s and 1970s, more states followed suit. Jones (1975) noted that although the need for CE had been recognized for years, external pressures made the issue more immediate. For example, the movement to mandate CE for psychologists was influenced by legislation requiring doctors of medicine and other healthcare professionals to prove their participation in CE for license renewal. Consumers, and state and national governments, all exerted pressure on psychology and other health care professions to adopt MCE requirements (Hellkamp et al., 1989). During the 1960s and 1970s, there was a decrease in consumer trust in medical professionals as well as growing demands for accountability and proof of competency in the wake of increasing numbers of malpractice suits. This paved the way for MCE to become an important way for professions to reassure consumers that practitioners were competent.

The American Association of State Psychology Boards (a precursor to the ASPPB) encouraged member boards to mandate CE for licensure renewal; by 1975, three states had already done so and eight others were considering similar legislation (Jones, 1975). There was also a movement within the profession to encourage CE, an attitude that was reflected in the Vail Conference recommendation that CE should be a part of professional training. In addition, managed care organizations influenced behavioral health providers to undergo additional training beyond the graduate level (Hoge, 2002).

By 1989, 20 states and Puerto Rico had some form of MCE (Hellkamp et al., 1989). This reflected a 122% increase from nine states prior to the 1980s. In 1992, the ASPPB included MCE in their Model Act for Licensure of Psychologists, which served as a guide for states in developing their licensure requirements (ASPPB, 1992). In 2001, the ASPPB Committee on

Education and Training issued guidelines for CE that could be adopted by state and provincial boards (Melnyk et al., 2001). The guidelines recommended that every licensed psychologist should complete at least 20 hours per year of CE meeting criteria adopted by the board, with at least a portion of the 20 hours in each renewal period consisting of training in ethics and legal issues. The guidelines also provided recommendations for program formats and types, program content, instructor qualifications, record keeping, and exemptions.

By 2002, 40 jurisdictions mandated that CE be required as a part of re-licensure (Daniels & Walter, 2002), and by 2006 that number grew to 43 states plus the District of Columbia (APA, 2006a). With the recent passing of MCE legislation in Illinois, the current figure is 44 states, plus the District of Columbia. Interestingly, CE requirements were legally challenged in 1942, but have not been overturned in courts since that time (Melnyk et al., 2001).

Despite the ASPPB's recommendation of 20 hours per year (Melnyk et al., 2001), a certain portion of which should be devoted to ethical and legal issues, the actual requirements for MCE vary widely by state. It is important to note that these requirements can change due to changes in state legislation. Variations occur in whether CE is mandatory, the number of hours required, and the period of licensure renewal. There is also variability in whether certain topics are required to be covered and, if so, how many hours must be devoted to them (see Table 1). For example, while Alaska, Arkansas, and Idaho all require 20 hours of CE annually, they vary in terms of whether they require courses in ethics and, if so, how many. The number of hours required per year also varies widely (e.g., 9 in North Carolina; 10 in Kentucky, Massachusetts, and West Virginia; 12 in Nebraska and South Carolina; 15 in Nevada, Pennsylvania, and Wyoming; 25 in Kansas and Oregon; and 30 in Arizona and Vermont). The renewal period during which CE must be completed ranges from annually (e.g., Alaska) to every three years (e.g., New Mexico), with the majority of states requiring that hours be completed biannually. Psychology is not the only mental health discipline that is plagued by inconsistencies in continuing education requirements. Social work, psychiatry, counseling, and marriage and family therapy, all have CE requirements that vary by state in terms of whether it is mandated and, if so, how many hours must be completed (Daniels & Walter, 2002).

All states that mandate CE recognize the APA and its approved sponsors as an acceptable form of CE and most accept graduate courses from approved institutions. The types of other activities that are acceptable and how many hours can be devoted to them vary from state to state (see Table 2). Activities that are approved by certain states include, teaching a course, presenting or publishing research, serving as a journal editor, attending psychological association meetings, and providing or receiving clinical supervision. Most states restrict the number of hours that can be obtained from non-APA-approved programs as well as the number that can be achieved through home study or other non-interactive learning activities. There are also some states that require a certain amount of hours from each of several categories. For example, Tennessee requires that the 40 hours of CE completed biannually be dispersed among three types: Type I is CE offered by APA-approved education providers, Type II is CE that is primarily psychological in nature or relevant to the science and practice of psychology (e.g., regional or state psychological association offerings, graduate courses in an APA-approved graduate psychology program), and Type III includes less structured learning experiences such as clinical peer consultation groups, teaching and presentations, and publications.

Table 1. Continuing Education Requirements by State

State	CE Mandated?	Hours/ Years	Ethics Hours/ Years	Other Hours
Alabama	Yes	20/1	N/A	
Alaska	Yes	40/2	3/2	
Arizona	Yes	60/2	4/2	4 in domestic violence/2
Arkansas	Yes	20/1	N/A	
California	Yes	36/2	Required, hours not specified	1 course domestic violence 1 course in aging (1 time requirements)
Colorado	No	N/A	N/A	
Connecticut	No	N/A	N/A	
Delaware	Yes	40/2	N/A	
District of Columbia	Yes	30/2	3/2	3 in cultural competence/2
Florida	Yes	40/2	3/2	2 in domestic violence/6 2 in medical malpractice /2
Georgia	Yes	40/2	3/2	3 cultural diversity in 1st renewal period (if not taken pre-licensure)
Hawaii	No	N/A	N/A	
Idaho	Yes	20/1	4/3	
Illinois	Yes*			
Indiana	Yes**	40/2	6/2	
Iowa	Yes	40/2	6/2	6 in state law/risk management for 2nd renewal
Kansas	Yes	50/2	3/2	6 in diagnosis and treatment of mental disorders/2
Kentucky	Yes	30/3	3/3	
Louisiana	Yes	30/2	2/2	2 forensics hours can be substituted for ethics hours
Maine	Yes	40/2	3/2	3 in supervision/2*** 20 in current/future practice area
Maryland	Yes	40/2	3/2	3 in cultural competence/2
Massachusetts	Yes	20/2	N/A	
Michigan	No	N/A	N/A	N/A
Minnesota	Yes	40/2	N/A	
Mississippi	Yes	20/2	2/2	

State	CE Mandated?	Hours/Years	Ethics Hours/Years	Other Hours
Missouri	Yes	40/2	N/A	
Montana	Yes	40/2	N/A	
Nebraska	Yes	24/2	N/A	
Nevada	Yes	30/2	6/2	
New Hampshire	Yes	40/2	6/2	
New Jersey	No			
New Mexico	Yes	40/2	5/2	4 in cultural diversity/2
New York	No			
North Carolina	Yes	18/2	3/2	
North Dakota	Yes	40/2	3/2	
Ohio	Yes	23/2	3/2	
Oklahoma	Yes	20/1	3/1	
Oregon	Yes	50/2	4/2	
Pennsylvania	Yes	30/2	3/2	
Puerto Rico	Yes	45/3	N/A	
Rhode Island	Yes	24/2	N/A	
South Carolina	Yes	24/2	N/A	
South Dakota	Yes	"some" (not specified)	N/A	
Tennessee	Yes	40/2	3/2	
Texas	Yes	12/1	3/1	
Utah	Yes	48/2	6/2	
Vermont	Yes	60/2	6/2	
Virginia	Yes	14/1	1.5/1	
Washington	Yes	60/3	4/3	
West Virginia	Yes	20/2	3/2	
Wisconsin	Yes	40/2	6/2	
Wyoming	Yes	30/2	N/A	

Note. * Legislation mandating CE has been passed, but hours requirements are still under consideration.

** Only psychologists who are endorsed as "health services providers in psychology" are mandated to complete CE.

*** For psychologists providing supervision.

Table 2. Examples of Activities Qualifying for MCE Credit by Selected States (Number of Hours Permitted, if Applicable)

State (Total CE Hours Required)	Graduate Course	Professional/ Board Meeting	Article/ Chapter Authorship	Book Authorship	Teaching Course	Teaching Seminar/ Workshop	Home Study	Conference Presentation
Alaska (40)	X		X (20)	X (20)	X (≤ 13)	X (≤ 13)	X (≤ 20)	X (20)
Arizona (60)	X (≤ 20)	X (≤ 10)	X (≤ 20)	Yes (≤ 20)			NS	X (≤ 20)
Arkansas (20)	X (≤ 20/course)	X (≤ 4)	X (1st time)	X (1st time)	X (1st time)	X (1st time)	X (≤ 19)	X (1st time)
Delaware (40)	X	No	X (≤ 15)	X (≤ 40)	X (1st time)	X (one time)	NS	X (≤ 8 per presentation)
District of Columbia (30)	X		X (≤ 15)	X (≤ 15)		X (≤ 15) includes prep time	NS	X (≤ 15)
Idaho (20)	X	X (≤ 6)	X	X	X course preparation (≤ 6)		6 individual, 10 online	X (≤ 6 per presentation)
Indiana (40)	X	X (journal club)			X (prep time only)	X (prep time only)	X (≤ 10)	
Louisiana (30)	X	X (≤ 12)			X (15 hours/ credit hour, includes prep time	X (if approved CE program)		
Maine (40)	X		X (for literature review)	X (for literature review)	X (≤ 10, prep time only)	X (≤ 10, prep time only)	X	
Minnesota (40)	X		X (≤ 20)	X (≤ 40)	X (1st time)		X	
Nebraska (24)	X (1st time)		X (1st author; 8 hours)	X (1st author; 16 hours)	X (1st time; 15 hours)	X (if approved CE program)	X	
Nevada (30)	X						X (≤ 15)	
New Hampshire (40)	X		X (≤ 5)	X (≤ 10)	X (10 for new course, 5 for thorough update)	X (≤ 10, prep time only)	X (≤ 20)	
New Mexico (40)	X		X (2-8 depending on authorship)	X (≤ 15)		X (≤ 8)	X (≤ 25)	X (≤ 4) except poster
North Carolina (18)		X	Only prep as self-study (≤ 9)	Only prep as self-study (≤ 9)	Only prep as self-study (≤ 9)	Only prep as self-study (≤ 9)	NS	Only prep as self-study (≤ 9)

State (Total CE Hours Required)	Graduate Course	Professional/ Board Meeting	Article/ Chapter Authorship	Book Authorship	Teaching Course	Teaching Seminar/ Workshop	Home Study	Conference Presentation
North Dakota (40)	X		X 5 per article, 15 per chapter	X (20 per book)			X (≤ 20)	X (5 per presentation)
Oklahoma (20)	X		X (10 each)	X (10 each		X (if not employed as a teacher)	NS	
Pennsylvania (30)	X		X (≤ 10)	X (≤ 10)	X (≤ 15) (once every 4 years)	X (≤ 15) (for approved sponsor) once every 4 years	X (≤ 15)	
South Carolina (24)	X	X (≤ 12)	X	X	X (1st time)		NS	
Tennessee (40)	X		X (22)	X (22)	X (≤ 22)	X (≤ 22)	X	X (≤ 22)
Utah (48)	X (no limit)				X (≤ 10)		X (≤ 18) internet or distance	
Vermont (60)	X	X (≤ 30)	X (≤ 30) writing time	X (≤ 30) writing time	X (≤ 30) prep time	X (≤ 30)	X (≤ 30)	X (≤ 30) prep time
Virginia (14)			X (≤ 4) one time	X (≤ 4) one time	X (≤ 4) one time, prep included	X (≤ 4) one time, prep included	NS	
West Virginia (20)	X (no limit)		X (≤ 6)	X (≤ 6)	No	X (≤ 10) (presentation time only)	NS	
Wisconsin (40)	X (≤ 20)		X (≤ 20)	X (≤ 20)	X (≤ 20) 1st time	X 1st time	NS	X 1st time
Wyoming (30)	Activities not specified	10 hrs must be APA or NASP, 20 hrs can be WPA or WSPA					NS	

Note. NS = Not specified. States were randomly selected for inclusion in this table.

The ASPPB (Melnyk et al., 2001) recommended that compliance with MCE requirements be monitored through random audits of 10% of all license renewal applications, as well as audits of all individuals whose licenses were subject to board action. In addition, they recommended that each license-renewal applicant sign a document attesting to the completion of the MCE requirements. They also suggested that psychologists should retain proof of attendance for at least two licensing cycles. As with the other aspects of MCE, the actual policies on compliance enforcement and record keeping vary widely by state. For example, psychologists licensed in Idaho must retain records for five years and are subject to random audits, while psychologists in California must submit records of attendance for all MCE programs, except when they are automatically reported by the organization offering the program. Overall, it is clear that there are variations in virtually all aspects of MCE, from whether it exists to how it is implemented. It is possible that this variability is due in part to the lack of consensus within the profession about whether CE should be mandated and, if so, under what conditions. The arguments offered for and against MCE are numerous and can provide some insight into the reasons for the lack of consistency in MCE in psychology.

Arguments for MCE

Perhaps the most often cited argument for mandating CE for psychologist re-licensure is that it ensures that practitioners stay current on newly emerging research and best practices in psychology. Although empirical data supporting the argument that CE leads to greater competence has been lacking for many years, this argument has face validity and CE is assumed to improve psychologists' competence and practice.

Many years ago, Dubin (1972) lamented the "minimal interest" that psychologists showed in CE. He argued that a doctorate in psychology has a half-life of 10-12 years, suggesting that much of the information obtained during graduate study is outdated after this period of time. VandeCreek, Knapp, and Brace (1990) proposed that, due to the increase in the rate of expansion of knowledge, that half-life is growing increasingly shorter. Currently, assessment of competence occurs primarily when psychologists are initially licensed and are required to take the Examination for Professional Practice of Psychology (EPPP), which covers a range of topics in psychology. Many states also require that new licensure applicants take a state exam, which ranges from a written exam on state statutes to an oral case presentation. Competence is also assessed at this stage via proof of completion of minimum education and supervision requirements, as well as supervisor evaluations of the applicant. All of these requirements are meant to ensure that psychologists possess the minimal competence necessary to provide services to the public (Rubin et al., 2007). With the exception of proof of compliance with CE mandates, there is no formal assessment of competence beyond the initial licensure. Rubin et al. note that in states without mandates, the only indicators of competence are psychologists' self-evaluation, public complaints to licensure boards, and the personal motivation of psychologists to engage in lifelong learning. Proponents of MCE argue that psychologists must participate in CE in order to be knowledgeable about changes in our understanding of psychological theories and interventions, and that mandates ensure they will do so.

Several researchers have explored whether MCE leads to greater competence. Sharkin and Plageman (2003) found that 45% of participants in their study reported that CE participation often made them more effective clinicians (41% reported this sometimes occurs, 11% reported rarely feeling more effective as a result of CE). More recently, Neimeyer et al. (2009) surveyed a national sample of psychologists on their experiences with CE. They found that the majority of participants (79%) reported feeling satisfied with their CE experiences. The majority of participants also reported moderate to high levels of learning (64%) and frequently translating their learning into their professional practice (64%) as a result of participation in the programs. Respondents also reported that participating in CE made them more effective psychologists, reduced their professional liability, and made them more aware of ethical issues. Although this data is limited to self-report, it suggests that psychologists perceive CE to be useful in making them more competent professionals. Clearly, more research is needed in this area to further support these findings.

The issue of whether MCE improves competence among professionals has been examined more extensively in fields other than psychology. Studies have shown that within physical health professions, CE enhances practitioner knowledge, skills, and attitudes (e.g., Young & Willie, 1984), and improves practitioner competence and patient outcomes (e.g., Davis et al., 1999). For example, Davis et al. (1999) reviewed 14 studies on CE programs in medicine that were published between 1993 and 1999. They concluded that CE interventions have an effect on physician performance and patient outcomes, but only when the programs are interactive (versus didactic). Clearly, there is a need for research on the various outcomes of MCE in psychology, but it is possible that the positive outcomes achieved in physical health professions also occur for psychologists. According to VandeCreek et al. (1990), factors that contribute to successful CE programs for psychologists include having a clearly identified target audience, participants who are motivated to learn, participants who are aware of gaps in their knowledge and skills, clear learning objectives, active participation of participants in the program, and supervised application opportunities after the program.

Even in the absence of empirical evidence establishing that CE improves competence and is necessary to avoid obsolescence, many would agree that a goal of lifelong learning is something all professionals should work to achieve. Wise (2010) went so far to state that "…it would be untenable to presume that foundational academic training, in and of itself, provides sufficient preparation for a full career of competent professional practice" (p. 289). One could argue that these are arguments for striving for lifelong learning rather than for MCE. Perhaps we can trust psychologists to be intrinsically motivated to engage in CE and there is not a need to force them to do so by making their re-licensure contingent upon completing CE hours. To really address the issue of whether mandates are necessary, we must explore whether they have an impact on practitioners' willingness to participate in CE and their actual CE behavior.

Research shows that there is variability among psychologists' self-reports in terms of whether they would continue to attend CE programs if they were not mandated to do so. For example, VandeCreek et al. (1990) found that 25-30% of practitioners might not participate in CE if they were not mandated to do so. Sharkin and Plageman (2003) found that 38% of Pennsylvania psychologists reported they would not continue to take the required number of CE hours if they were not mandated by the state to do so. Perhaps, then, mandates serve to encourage those individuals who are not intrinsically motivated to engage in formal CE. It is important to note that these studies assessed willingness to engage in *formal* CE; it is possible that those psychologists who would not participate in formal programs might engage in other forms of learning, such as reading journals and case consultations. However, as noted by Neimeyer et al. (2009), more research is needed to determine whether this is the case.

In terms of actual CE behavior, Phillips (1987) estimated that between 25% and 30% of practitioners would not engage in CE unless mandated to do so. There is empirical support for the argument that mandating CE ensures that more psychologists participate in formal CE activities. Some have expressed concern that increased participation in CE may be inaccurately attributed to mandates. Brown, Leichtman, Blass, and Fleisher (1982) surveyed Maryland psychologists before and after the state mandated CE. They concluded that it was the increased *availability* of CE programs following the mandate, as opposed to the mandate itself, which led to higher attendance at formal preregistered CE programs and workshops. In contrast, Hellkamp et al. (1989) noted that when Ohio had a voluntary CE system, only 25% of members of the state psychological association joined the CE system, and even fewer members maintained up-to-date records of their learning activities.

There is more recent evidence that psychologists in states that mandate CE participate in significantly more CE activities than those practicing in non-mandating states (Neimeyer, Taylor, & Philip, 2010a; Neimeyer et al., 2009). For example, Neimeyer et al. (2010a) found that Phillips' (1987) estimate held true in their national sample, reporting that 25% of the licensed psychologists they surveyed who practiced in states without mandates completed less than five CE hours per year (only 1.4% of psychologists in mandated states completed less than 5 hours). They also found that psychologists in non-mandating states reported participating in an average of one-third fewer CE programs as compared to psychologists in mandated states. Therefore, although many psychologists are self-motivated to engage in lifelong learning and actually exceed the number of hours required for re-licensure (Fagan, Ax, Liss, Resnick, & Moody, 2007; Neimeyer et al., 2009), mandates may serve to motivate those individuals who might otherwise neglect their professional development. Even for those who are self-motivated to learn, setting aside time to engage in CE can be quite challenging and mandates can serve as an incentive to prioritize lifelong learning that might otherwise fall by the wayside.

One concern about MCE, which will be explored further in the next section of this chapter, is that it may inadvertently pressure psychologists to select programs primarily to meet mandate requirements rather than to improve their professional competency. However, there is some evidence that psychologists choose CE programs primarily on the basis of the program topic (Sharkin & Plageman, 2003; Neimeyer, Taylor, & Wear, 2010b), with factors such as cost, convenience, and location being important but not primary considerations. There is also evidence that psychologists select topics based not just on interest but on perceived need for more education in that area (Fowler & Harrison, 2001). Neimeyer et al. (2010b) also suggested that their finding that psychologists in different work settings (e.g., medical setting, private practice, etc.) exhibited differences in the types of CE programs they selected refutes the notion that MCE leads psychologists to focus more on practical concerns than on improving their professional competency when choosing programs. However, it is notable that 93% of participants in their study cited convenience as an important consideration and 85.4% reported that cost was a critical factor.

Another argument for MCE is that it helps to define the profession and ensure consumer confidence. There is evidence that the public expects that licensed professionals will remain current and competent in their areas of practice and that they will undergo regular assessment of their professional skills (e.g., AARP, 2007). Consumer advocacy groups have campaigned for mandatory continuing professional development for healthcare professionals and regular assessment of competence (e.g., Swankin, LeBuhn, and Morrison, 2006). As noted, other fields such as medicine and its specialties also mandate CE. MCE may provide the field with credibility and increase consumer confidence. As with the argument of increased competence, there are no existing data to support this claim, but it does have face validity. Furthermore, the *Ethical Principles of Psychologists and Code of Conduct* (APA, 2010) highlights the need for psychologists to obtain training to ensure they are competent. The Code states that, "Psychologists provide services, teach, and conduct research with populations and in areas only within the boundaries of their competence, based on their education, training, supervised experience, consultation, study, or professional experience" (Principle 2.01(a)). Furthermore, Principle 2.03 (Maintaining Competence) states that "Psychologists undertake ongoing efforts to develop and maintain their competence." Thus, it seems that psychologists have an ethical imperative to engage in lifelong learning, both in order to meet the standards of the profession and to reassure consumers of their competence.

Favorable attitudes towards MCE among many psychologists have been reported as another argument in support of mandates. A 1989 survey of executive officers of state and provincial psychology boards indicated that the states without MCE would personally favor an MCE requirement in their state and that those states with MCE favored the requirement. Research also shows that the majority (75%) of psychologists surveyed in Pennsylvania (a state with MCE) are in favor of MCE (Sharkin & Plageman, 2003). Recently, Neimeyer et al. (2009) documented that psychologists in states with MCE have more favorable attitudes toward CE mandates than do psychologists in states without mandates (84.3% versus 55.3%). Overall, however, 77.6% of their respondents (across mandated and non-mandated states) reported they agreed or strongly agreed with CE mandates. Although it seems that there is strong support for MCE among many psychologists, a number of arguments against mandates have also been raised. Reasons for opposition to MCE will be explored in the following section.

ARGUMENTS AGAINST MCE

Although increased competence is one of the most frequently cited arguments for MCE, opponents counter that there is a lack of substantial empirical evidence to support this claim. There is no guarantee that attending a CE program will lead to learning or increased competence, or that participants will apply the knowledge they acquire to their practice. Outcome data is typically limited to proof of attendance, which usually involves completion of a self-report evaluation of the program (including learning outcomes) by participants. The APA Sponsor Approval System offers templates for evaluation forms, but their content and structure are determined by the individual or organization offering the program. Thus, the majority of data available on the outcomes of MCE are based on un-validated, self-report evaluation forms completed at the end of programs or self-report research surveys; therefore, there are no objective data indicating that MCE leads to greater professional competence for psychologists.

In addition, CE participants may not be invested in providing accurate data on the evaluation forms. In her time as CE coordinator for a local psychological association, the first author often observed participants hurriedly completing their evaluation forms with seemingly little attention to the individual items. Factors such as prior education and motivation also influence competency and are not assessed by evaluation forms. Further, evaluation forms only measure learning outcomes for the specific topic covered in the program being evaluated. When compared to a comprehensive competency measure such as the EPPP, such measures seem to be inadequate representations of professional competency. The outcome measures also fail to assess learning outcomes such as the application of new skills and knowledge to clinical practice. Data on the learning outcomes of other qualifying CE activities (i.e., informal activities such as case consultation and supervision) are even more limited and it is difficult to draw general conclusions about their effectiveness due to the lack of uniformity of required proof of completion by state.

Another limitation of available outcome data (based on large scale surveys and individual program evaluations) is that they may be influenced by social desirability. Given that measures of social desirability were not included in the surveys previously cited, it is impossible to determine this empirically. However, it is possible that survey respondents are influenced by social desirability when responding to questions such as those about their reasons for selecting programs, their willingness to attend programs regardless of mandates, and whether or not they complete other work during the program. Likewise, psychologists completing self-evaluations at the end of programs may rate their knowledge and skill acquisition as higher than it actually is due to a wish to appear competent. Taken together, these assessment issues significantly limit the profession's ability to determine whether CE mandates lead to increased professional competence. This also prevents the field from using such data to modify existing practices in an effort to improve the CE system.

Kaplan (1974) long ago noted that mandating CE is appropriate for a field such as medicine due to the rate of new discoveries and the related need for practitioners to maintain updated knowledge. However, he argued that the same is not true of psychology, stating "There is no scientific proof that new methods of treating emotional distress are superior to older methods" (p. 114). Although one can argue that new discoveries and treatment approaches are continually emerging within the field of psychology (especially now as compared to when Kaplan made his argument nearly 40 years ago), it is still debatable whether psychologists who employ existing methods need to learn new approaches in order to practice competently. Although this is certainly an argument that warrants significant scrutiny, it is nonetheless a consideration in the argument against mandating CE.

A practical drawback to MCE is the financial burden it places on psychologists. This may be an unfair burden on practitioners, particularly those employed in private practice or other settings where CE programs are not offered or paid for as a benefit of employment. The 1994 APA Study on Mandated Continuing Education (Phillips, 1994) found that 29.3% of psychologists in states without MCE spent less than $500 on CE per license renewal period, while only 19.9% of psychologists in states with mandates spent less than $500. Notably, 81% of psychologists in all states reported spending less than $2,000 per renewal period. Unless they work in a setting that provides access to free CE or subsidizes CE attendance, many psychologists must personally bear the financial responsibility of meeting CE requirements (Fagan et al., 2007). Practitioners may also face the issue of cancelling clients in order to attend programs, thereby leading them to experience the "double jeopardy" of forfeiting billable hours while spending money on CE programs. Sharkin and Plageman (2003) found that while the majority (78%) of participants in Pennsylvania indicated they can obtain the 30 required hours biannually without difficulty, a small minority (6%) indicated they can rarely or never do so. For those individuals with particular challenges such as income, accessibility, etc., the mandates may constitute an undue burden. A similar argument is that mandating all professionals to engage in CE is unfair; that is, practitioners should not have government or professional restrictions placed upon them unless they demonstrate inferior performance (Hellkamp et al., 1989).

In addition to the responsibility placed on psychologists, MCE also places a financial burden on state licensing boards to properly monitor compliance. For example, the state of California must pay to monitor compliance based on online submission of proof of attendance by psychologists. This burden on state licensing boards has led some professions to question mandates in the past. In 1981, for instance, the National Association of Social Workers dropped their MCE requirements due to the cost of ensuring compliance (Hellkamp et al., 1989). Although the NASW eventually reinstated their MCE requirements (48 hours every two years), it is clear that there were concerns about the costs associated with MCE. An early survey of state and provincial psychology board executive officers found that several non-mandating states cited the burden on the board as one barrier (Hellkamp et al., 1989). For example, at that time Mississippi indicated that inadequate finances would prevent them from implementing MCE. Perhaps improvements in technology and more cost-efficient methods to monitor compliance have contributed to an increase in the number of boards willing to take on the responsibilities associated with MCE, but the financial burden remains a concern for opponents of mandates. Often, that burden gets passed on to psychologists in the form of licensure renewal fees.

Another concern about MCE is that even those practitioners in mandating states largely self-select the programs they will take to meet requirements. Although 32 states currently mandate completion of a single ethics program for licensure renewal, the selection of which courses to take is left to the discretion of the individual. On the one hand, this process allows practitioners to select those programs that are most relevant to their workplace, the population they treat, and the roles they perform as a psychologist (e.g., evaluator, therapist, etc.). Indeed, Neimeyer et al. (2010b) found significant differences in topic selection among psychologists as a function of their work settings. On the other hand, Daniels and Walter (2002) expressed concern that this allows practitioners to select programs that do not lead to the "diversity or depth of knowledge" needed to practice remain abreast of changes in evidence-based practice.

Stated another way, there is concern that mandates may motivate clinicians to complete CE only to achieve re-licensure. They could focus more on the number of hours offered and the convenience of completing the hours (in terms of time, cost, and location) versus the quality and relevance of the training. As a CE coordinator, the first author has noted that many psychologists made a habit of attending most, if not all, of the CE trainings offered by the organization (a local psychological association). Informal polling of these psychologists revealed that they often took the trainings because of the convenient location, the discount offered to association members, and the opportunity for networking with colleagues. Given the wide range of topics covered in the trainings, it was possible that these psychologists were at times attending trainings that were not directly related to their practice but were compelled to attend because of these other factors. As noted previously, researchers have found that psychologists do cite cost and convenience as important factors in their selection of CE activities, but they cite program topic as the most important factor (Sharkin & Plageman, 2003; Neimeyer et al., 2010b). Perceived need for more education in a particular area is also an important selection factor (Fowler & Harrison, 2001). MCE may also encourage a focus on completing hours versus other factors, as psychologists may see a need to simply obtain the needed number of hours in order to maintain licensure. Research does bear out these concerns to some extent. Sharkin and Plageman (2003) found that, while the majority (65%) of their sample reported they rarely or never attend CE programs just for the hours, a third of the sample admitted that they sometimes or often do so. Certainly, more empirical research is needed on how factors other than increasing competence in areas relevant to their areas of practice influence psychologists' choice of CE programming, as well as whether mandating CE contributes to this type of selection process.

A similar concern is that psychologists may be discouraged from seeking out opportunities for learning that would benefit their practice but which do not satisfy mandate requirements. For example, some states either do not allow supervision or consultation to qualify for MCE or limit the number of hours that can be obtained through these activities. Early studies of psychologists' CE activities suggested that they engaged in a variety of activities but that they preferred personal contacts with other professionals (Allen, Nelson, & Scheckley, 1987) and reading books (Allen et al., 1987; Brown et al., 1982) over formal workshops. Although many states do allow psychologists to submit activities for Board approval, this process is time-consuming and approval is not guaranteed. Given limited time to devote to CE, psychologists may avoid valuable sources of learning in favor of formal, structured programs that automatically meet MCE requirements. In some cases, these programs may meet criteria for APA sponsorship but provide little in the way of increased knowledge and competence. Thus, practitioners may forfeit valuable experiences that could lead to greater competence and service provision in order to satisfy mandates.

MCE can also shift the focus for some psychologists from lifelong learning to simply meeting requirements. In the first author's experience, there were a number of situations in which practitioners requested credit in spite of not meeting the requirements. For example, even when practitioners missed a large portion of the program because of arriving late or leaving early, they still insisted on receiving all of the CE credits. If the emphasis is primarily on completing credits, practitioners may select programs they are not interested in and utilize the training time to complete other work. Sharkin and Plageman (2003) found that most respondents denied doing so, but again this is self-report data that could be influenced by social desirability. Both of the current authors have noticed this occurring at a wide range of programs. As long as they complete an evaluation form participants still receive credit for attendance, but they may have learned very little as a result of focusing on other work or otherwise not engaging in the material. This is similar to the argument in education against "teaching to the test" as it shifts the focus from learning and increasing competence to learning the narrow set of skills for which they will be tested. In the case of CE, that gets narrowed down to one factor: being able to prove one attended a sufficient number of CE hours. Perhaps if it was not mandated, practitioners could choose those programs that they are most interested in and would therefore (theoretically) learn something more relevant to their practice.

Whereas some states require that a certain number of hours be completed in ethics or other special content areas such as domestic violence, this is not the case in other states.

Likewise, most states do not require hours in the practitioner's specialty, if applicable. One exception is Maine, which requires that 20 of the required 40 hours biannually be completed in the psychologist's current or future area of practice. There is also no formal process for helping practitioners determine their personal areas of growth and learning needs. In the absence of such processes, practitioners are left to self-select their CE activities. Ideally, they will undergo a personal process of determine knowledge deficiencies, and selecting and engaging in those activities that will help them fill those gaps. However, research has shown that self-assessment of knowledge gaps is usually poor without training (e.g., Dunning, Heath, & Suls, 2004), suggesting that many practitioners may be inadequately prepared to effectively self-assess their own learning needs.

In addition to the concerns about the focus on receiving credits, opponents of MCE argue that, with MCE, individuals and organizations offering CE may focus more on meeting sponsorship criteria than on providing quality programming. CE training has indeed become a profitable industry. The process of obtaining APA sponsorship approval is a time consuming and expensive process that may be unrealistic for some program providers to pursue. If they cannot obtain co-sponsorship from an approved organization, psychologists in mandating states may be less likely to attend these trainings because they will not receive the necessary credit for attendance. They may divert their limited time and funds to approved programs, even if they are less relevant to their practice than the non-approved programs. This could lead (and may already have led) to programming of poorer quality that still meets criteria and to limited competition in the market.

There are also philosophical arguments against MCE. In the late 1990s and early 2000s, psychologists successfully petitioned to prevent the Michigan Psychological Association and the Michigan state licensing board from adopting MCE requirements. Petitioners cited their belief that MCE infringes on psychologists' autonomy and professional judgment in selecting CE activities. In addition, they claimed that MCE allows "bureaucratic entities" rather than the individual practitioner to decide what type and amount of information should be learned (Kavanaugh, 2002). Opponents of MCE in Michigan cautioned that shifting to a mandatory system would prevent practitioners from having the freedom to select a diversity of programs that would allow them to practice as they see fit. Some opponents (e.g., McLoughlin, 2000) have suggested that state organizations may support mandates because they stand to benefit financially from them by offering programs that meet MCE requirements.

TO MANDATE OR NOT TO MANDATE: SHOULD THAT BE THE QUESTION?

Perhaps the question should not be merely whether or not to mandate CE for re-licensure, but how to structure and enforce mandates. Existing mandates focus on the number of hours completed and may require that certain content areas be covered. However, there are no standardized assessments of learning needs and, with the exception of un-validated, self-report evaluation forms, there is no evidence of learning outcomes based on CE. Although a full discussion of the issues with evaluation is outside of the scope of this chapter, it is important to note that the evaluation forms are retained by the sponsoring organization in order to meet the documentation requirements for the sponsors approved by APA. Proof of "competency" of psychologists is limited to certificates of attendance for formal programs or documentation of engaging in other approved activities. Perhaps a more valid approach to mandating and documenting CE would be to alter the evaluation system.

VandeCreek et al. (1990) highlighted the need for psychology to follow the example set by other fields by demonstrating a connection between their participation in CE and their actual practice. They suggested pre- and post-tests, taped demonstrations of skills learned during the program, and submission of proof of competence (e.g., scored test protocols, client records altered to maintain confidentiality, etc.) as potential means for assessing whether skills were acquired during the training. Advances in technology, such as on-line communication, could make these strategies more feasible for today's practitioner. Interestingly, in their national survey of psychologists, Neimeyer et al. (2009) found that most psychologists prefer the use of participant satisfaction ratings over knowledge or skills assessments in evaluating what they learn at CE programs. Only 44.4% of their participants agreed that objective knowledge tests to gauge learning should be a part of CE evaluation and even fewer (29%) agreed with skills assessments to determine whether they are able to apply the knowledge gained during programs. Given the reluctance among the majority of practitioners to make changes to the current evaluation system, a shift towards these models is likely to fuel as much debate as has the issue of whether or not CE should be mandated. However, without a shift to more evidenced-based outcome evaluations, the field of psychology will continue to be unable to answer one of the most critical questions in the debate over MCE: Does CE participation lead to greater competency?

A report by the APA Task Force on the Assessment of Competence in Professional Psychology (APA, 2006b) outlined several recommendations for competency evaluation. It included the recommendation that graduate training programs teach self-assessment skills and that CE programs include self-assessment. The current MCE system in most states does not provide sufficient guidance to psychologists in assessing their learning needs and choosing appropriate programs, and such training would help to address this issue. In addition, attention to multi-method, multi-informant evaluation, as well as sensitivity to individual and cultural diversity during the assessment process, were highlighted in the report. The report also suggested that psychometrically valid competency assessment tools should be developed and that structured post-licensure assessment of competence be considered. Finally, the report recommended that the profession of psychology come to a consensus on core competencies (both general and specific) and that criteria needed to be considered "expert" in these competencies be made public. As a result of this recommendation, an Assessment of Competency Benchmarks Work Group (ACBWG) (2007) was formed and proposed 12 core competencies, identified indicators of levels of competency, and identified appropriate assessment measures for them. Ideally, future mandates would incorporate this more structured approach to assessing CE learning outcomes, not only to document professional competency, but also to empirically inform changes to MCE. Research is also needed on the utility of the recommendations of the ACBWG and on the psychometric properties of competence assessments.

Another consideration for modifying mandates is that perhaps psychologists with a specialty should take a certain number of CE credits within that specialty in order to maintain their status as a specialist. One of the initial goals of mandating CE was to ensure the public was being protected from incompetent practitioners. However, if we continue with the current system of simply making sure psychologists accrue a certain number of hours with no accountability, that goal may never be achieved. Even for those without a specialty, there may be a benefit to the field identifying critical competencies as advocated by the ACBWG and ensuring that some hours be devoted to them.

Leigh et al. (2007) argued that psychology lags behind other health care professions in that it does not require formal post-licensure assessment in addition to CE. Hellkamp et al. (1989) noted that professional competency can be demonstrated through the CE model or through the examination/peer review model. Historically, psychologists favor MCE over examination requirements for re-licensure (e.g., Vitulano & Copeland, 1980). Perhaps another solution to modifying the existing CE structure is to require psychologists to re-take the licensure exam or to borrow from other fields that use performance-based assessments throughout practitioners' careers (Leigh et al., 2007). Moving toward an examination model would bring its own set of issues but could be a more stringent way of assessing competence than the current system. Alternatively, the peer review model consists of colleagues judging the quality of work a professional has performed (Stricker & Cohen, 1984). Certainly, these approaches could be combined with MCE and research could help to determine whether there is a relationship between CE participation and learning outcomes as assessed via peer review or examination.

One clear issue with the current MCE system is the lack of uniformity among states in terms of factors such as the number of CE hours mandated, the types of content required, the types of activities that are approved, and the procedures for monitoring compliance. One challenge this may present for practitioners is that portability of their license from state to state may be limited. For those practitioners who are licensed in more than one state, they must maintain awareness of multiple requirements and any changes that arise. Likewise, practitioners who move to another state must learn the requirements for each new state in which they practice. Practitioners in states with mandates and those who are mandated to complete more hours could rightly argue that they have a burden unequal to that of their peers in other states. In addition, consumers in states without mandates have a right to demand that practitioners in their state meet the same requirements of those in other states. It seems then, that greater consistency is needed in the occurrence and implementation of mandates.

The ASPPB (Melnyk et al., 2001) has previously issued guidelines for MCE and it appears that many states have adopted at least a portion of them. In 2010, the ASPPB Task Force on Maintenance of Competence and Licensure (MOCAL) issued a *Draft Proposal of Guidelines for Continuing Professional Development* (CPD) (Webb et al., 2010), and at the time of this publication, feedback was being solicited on the document. This draft changes the language from CE to Continuing Professional Development and changes "hours" to "credits" to reflect the fact that some activities cannot easily be counted as hours. Similar to the 2001 guidelines, it is recommended in the current draft that psychologists be mandated to complete 40 credits biannually or 20 credits per year if the renewal period is not two years. The draft also specifies which types of activities should be allowed and encourages practitioners to select from a range of activities (i.e., peer consultation, practice outcome monitoring, instruction, and approved sponsored CE) by making most of them worth only a percentage of the total required credits. This draft document helps to address one of the arguments against MCE: that mandates encourage psychologists to focus on formal programs that meet the criteria for mandates. By encouraging practitioners to utilize a range of activities to accrue the required number of hours, the current recommendations may increase the likelihood that CE participation will actually lead to increased competence. Finally, the guidelines provide specific recommendations for the verification of each type of activity (i.e., a verification form with number of hours with a patient and de-identified patient questionnaire to prove participation in assessing practice outcomes). In addition to the feedback being solicited, the ASPPB's International Congress on Licensure, Certification, and Credentialing in Professional Psychology would be another excellent forum to address these issues.

For their part, states should consider adopting more uniform guidelines to ensure that consumers in all states can seek care from qualified clinicians. Research shows that many psychologists favor a single, national CE requirement (Fagan et al., 2007) similar to that instituted for nationally certified school psychologists (NASP, 1989). The diversity of interests, learning styles, and learning needs among psychologists necessitates some individual control over the selection of topics and activities. However, greater uniformity is needed in terms of the number of hours required, the topics that must be covered, and the types and number of approved activities. Perhaps even the reporting procedures could benefit from being more standardized, although this is one area of MCE that states may prefer to retain control over given that they will need to provide the resources to enforce reporting procedures.

Finally, although there is quality control of MCE programs, whether it is based on APA approval or other criteria, it is possible for a program to meet these criteria without being of high quality or leading to increased competence among participants (i.e., because of their prior level of training, level of engagement in the program, etc.). There may be a need to change the format of programs based on evidence from other fields that some types of training (e.g, interactive techniques) are more effective than others (e.g., didactic, non-interactive programs) (Davis et al., 1999). Changes to MCE requirements should take research on learning outcomes into account and more research should be done within psychology to determine the most effective types of learning activities.

Conclusion

Clearly, there are many arguments for and against MCE. Proponents believe that CE leads to greater professional competence and service delivery and that without mandates psychologists will not engage in lifelong learning at sufficient levels or at all. Further, they cite the favorable attitudes towards mandates among practitioners and the ethical principles of our profession that require ongoing efforts to maintain competence for ethical practice as arguments for MCE. Available empirical data is limited, but overall indicates that many psychologists are in favor of mandates, are satisfied with their CE experiences, and feel that CE participation leads to increased competence. Opponents argue that there is little empirical evidence for the effectiveness of CE in psychology, MCE places an undue financial burden on practitioners and states, and mandates shift the motivation for practitioners from lifelong learning to meeting re-licensure requirements. It seems that a number of the arguments against MCE, including the lack of evidence of its effectiveness and the lack of uniformity among states' requirements, reflect a need for more research on CE and a movement towards greater uniformity in requirements. Rather than being arguments against mandates, they seem to serve as arguments for reform of MCE. The issue of whether CE should be mandatory and how it should be implemented has been debated for years and will likely continue to be debated for years to come. Psychology needs to prioritize our understanding of the best ways to facilitate lifelong learning in order to improve service delivery. With their skills in research, education, and assessment, psychologists have much to contribute to the understanding of the topic of CE.

BIOSKETCHES

AIMEE C. ADAMS, received her PhD in counseling psychology from Lehigh University. She is an assistant professor and faculty counselor at Counseling and Psychological Services at Kutztown University. In addition, she is an adjunct faculty member at Lehigh University in the Counseling Psychology Department and College of Education.

Dr. Adams' research interests include professional practice issues, legal/ethical and policy issues, counselor multicultural competence, and college counseling issues. She has presented at numerous regional, state, and national conferences on topics including policies on mandated assessment in college counseling, ethical issues in college counseling, and college students' expectations for counselor multicultural competence. She has published articles and a book chapter on topics including racial identity, off-campus counseling referrals for university students, and sexual violence education policy.

Dr. Adams served as the Continuing Education chair of a regional psychological association for two years and continues to consult with the person in this role. She currently serves as president-elect for a regional psychological association and as and treasurer for a state psychological association. She has served as a conference proposal reviewer for the American Counseling Association and is a member of the American Counseling Association and American Psychological Association.

BRUCE S. SHARKIN received his Ph.D. in counseling psychology from the University of Maryland in 1989. Dr. Sharkin is an associate professor and Administrative Director of the Department of Counseling and Psychological Services at Kutztown University in Kutztown, Pennsylvania. Dr. Sharkin is the author of *College students in distress: A resource guide for faculty, staff, and campus community* (2006) and a forthcoming book, *Being a college counselor on today's campus: Roles, contributions, and special challenges,* to be published in November of 2011. Dr. Sharkin has served as an editorial reviewer for the *Journal of College Counseling, Journal of Counseling Psychology,* and *Journal of Counseling and Development.* Dr. Sharkin is currently an editorial advisory board member for the American Counseling Association Publications office.

REFERENCES

AARP. (2007). *Strategies to improve health care quality in Virginia: Survey of residents age 50+*. Washington, DC: AARP.

Allen, G. J., Nelson, W. J., & Sheckley, B. G. (1987). Continuing education activities of Connecticut psychologists. *Professional Psychology: Research and Practice*, 18, 78-80.

APA (American Psychological Association). (2000). *Minutes of APA Council of Representatives*. Washington, DC: APA.

APA (American Psychological Association). (2006a). *State provincial mandatory continuing education in psychology (MCEP) requirements: 2006 survey results.* Retrieved from https:www.apa.net.

APA (American Psychological Association). (2006b). *Report of the APA task force on the assessment of competence in professional psychology.* Washington, DC: APA.

APA (American Psychological Association). (2007). *Assessment of competency benchmarks work group: A developmental model for the defining and measuring competence in professional psychology.* Washington, DC: APA.

APA (American Psychological Association). (2010). *American Psychological Association ethical principles of psychologists and code of conduct: 2010 Amendments.* Retrieved from http://www.apa.org/ethics/code/index.aspx.

ASPPB (Association of State and Provincial Psychology Boards) (1992). *ASPPB model act for licensure and registration of psychologists.* Retrieved from https://www.asppb.net/.

ASPPB (Association of State and Provincial Psychology Boards). (2010). *ASPPB model act for licensure and registration of psychologists.* Retrieved from https://www.asppb.net.

Brown, R. A., Leichtman, S. R., Blass, T., & Fleisher, E. (1982). Mandated continuing education: Impact on Maryland psychologists. *Professional Psychology, 13,* 404-411.

Daniels, A. S., & Walter, D. A. (2002). Current issues in continuing education for contemporary behavioral health practice. *Administration and Policy in Mental Health, 29,* 359-376.

Davis, D, Thomson, M., Oxman, A., & Haynes, R. (1995). Changing physician performance: A systematic review of the effect of continuing medical education strategies. *JAMA: Journal of the American Medical Association, 274,* 700-705.

Davis, D., Thomson O'Brien, M. A., Freemantle, N., Wolf, F. M., Mazmanian, P., & Taylor-Vaisey, A. (1999). Impact of formal continuing medical education: Do conferences, workshops, rounds, and other traditional continuing education activities change physician behavior or health care outcomes? *JAMA: Journal of the American Medical Association, 282,* 867-874.

Dubin, S. S. (1972). Obsolescence or lifelong education: A choice for the professional. *American Psychologist, 27,* 486-498.

Dunning, D., Heath, C., & Suls, J.M. (2004). Flawed self-assessment: Implications for health, education, and the workplace. *Psychological Science in the Public Interest, 5,* 69-106.

Fagan, T. J., Ax, R. K., Liss, M., Resnick, R. J., & Moody, S. (2007). Professional education and training: How satisfied are we? an exploratory study. *Training and Education in Professional Psychology, 1,* 13-25.

Fowler, E., & Harrison, P. L. (2001). Continuing professional development needs and activities of school psychologists. *Psychology in the Schools, 38,* 75-88.

Hellkamp, D., Imm, P., & Moll, D. (1989). Mandatory continuing education (MCE): Desirable or undesirable? A survey of executive officers of state psychological associations. *The Journal of Training and Practice in Professional Psychology, 3,* 33-46.

Hoge, M. (2002). The training gap: An acute crisis in behavioral health education. *Administration and Policy in Mental Health, 29,* 305-317.

Jones, N. F. (1975). Continuing education: A new challenge for psychology. *American Psychologist, 30,* 842-847.

Kaplan, R. (1974). Continuing education and licensure. *Professional Psychology, 5,* 114.

Kavanaugh, P. (2002). Mandatory continuing education (MCE) – industrializing and deprofessionalizing psychology. *MSPP News.* Retrieved from http://www.academyanalyticarts.org/kava15.htm.

Leigh, I. W., Smith, I. L., Bebeau, M. J., Lichtenberg, J. W., Nelson, P. D., Portnoy, S.,…Kaslow, N. J. (2007). Competency assessment models. *Professional Psychology: Research and Practice, 38,* 463-473.

McLoughlin, C. (2000). On mandatory continuing education. *MSPP News.* Retrieved from http://www.academyprojects.org/lemclo2.htm.

Melnyk, W., Allen, M., Nutt, R., O'Connor, T., Robiner, B., Linder-Crow, J., & Pacht, A. R. (2001). *ASPPB guidelines for continuing professional education.* Retrieved from http://www.asppb.net/files/public/Publication_Test.htm.

NASP (National Association of School Psychologists). (1989). *Continuing professional development program.* Washington, DC: NASP.

Neimeyer, G. J., Taylor, J. M., & Philip, D. (2010a). Continuing education in psychology: Patterns of participation and perceived outcomes among mandated and nonmandated psychologists. *Professional Psychology: Research and Practice, 41,* 435-441.

Neimeyer, G. J., Taylor, J. M., & Wear, D. M. (2009). Continuing education in psychology: Outcomes, evaluations, and mandates. *Professional Psychology: Research and Practice, 40,* 617-624.

Neimeyer, G. J., Taylor, J. M., & Wear, D. (2010b). Continuing education in psychology: Patterns of participation and aspects of selection. *Professional Psychology: Research and Practice, 41,* 281-287.

Phillips, L. E. (1987). Is mandatory continuing education working? *Journal of Continuing Education in the Health Professions, 7,* 57-64.

Phillips, L. E. (1994). *A study of mandatory continuing education.* Washington DC: APA.

Rubin, N. J., Bebeau, M., Leigh, I. W., Lichtenberg, J. W., Nelson, P. D., Portnoy, S…Kaslow, N. J. (2007). The competency movement within psychology: An historical perspective. *Professional Psychology: Research and Practice, 38,* 452-462.

Sharkin, B. S., & Plageman, P. (2003). What do psychologists think about mandatory continuing education? A survey of Pennsylvania practitioners. *Professional Psychology: Research and Practice, 34,* 318-323.

Stricker, G. & Cohen, L. (1984). APA/CHAMPUS peer review project: Implications for research and practice. *Professional Psychology: Research and Practice, 15,* 96-108.

Swankin, D., LeBuhn, R., & Morrison, R. (2006). Implementing continuing competency requirements for health care practitioners. *American Association of Retired Persons, Washington, D.C.* Retrieved from http://aarp.org/ppi.

Webb, C., Boll, T., Brown, R., Horn, J., Yarrow, C., & Pippin, C. (2010). *Report of ASPPB Task Force on Maintenance of Competence and Licensure (MOCAL).* Retrieved from https://www.asppb.net/.

Wise, E. (2010). Maintaining and enhancing competency in professionally psychology: Obsolescence, life-long learning, and continuing education. *Professional Psychology: Research and Practice, 41,* 289-292.

VandeCreek, L., & Brace, K. (1991). Mandatory continuing education in the health professions. *Journal of Training and Practice in Professional Psychology, 5,* 23-36.

VandeCreek, L., Knapp, S., & Brace, K. (1990). Mandatory continuing education for licensed psychologists: Its rationale and current implementation. *Professional Psychology: Research and Practice, 21,* 135-140.

Vitulano, L. A., & Copeland, B. A. (1980). Trends in continuing education and competency demonstrations. *Professional Psychology, 11,* 891-897.

Young, L., & Willie, R. (1984). Effectiveness of Continuing Education for Health Professionals: A Literature Review. *Journal of Allied Health 13,* 112-123.

Chapter 10

A REVIEW OF CONCERNS IN REGARD TO THE IMPLEMENTATION OF THE CE MANDATE IN ILLINOIS

*Mary Zemansky**
Private Practice, Chesterton, Indiana, US

ABSTRACT

Despite psychologists' general acceptance that Continuing Education can benefit their professional development, they also harbor ongoing concerns as to the efficacy of the processes involved in attaining it. This paper examines commentary from list serve members in regard to a CE mandate which becomes effective for Illinois psychologists in 2012. Areas of concern that were identified included: the type of CE content that would be permitted to satisfy the requirement, financial costs associated with compliance, adequacy of training offered, and hesitancy over the regulations surrounding compliance. A number of these issues have previously been successfully addressed by other states, which forms a basis of existing knowledge from which solutions can be devised. Such information can be disseminated via timely and relevant presentations to psychologists seeking to meet the CE requirements.

Keywords: Mandates, continuing education, lifelong learning, professional development

The history of mandated Continuing Education (CE) in psychology dates back over 50 years, and has been marked by varied opinions as to the efficacy of its intention to achieve ongoing professional development. The State of Illinois recently approved legislation that mandates CE for psychologists, allowing an opportunity to revisit points of contention surrounding such mandates (see Adams & Sharkin, 2012) within the context of professional psychology in general and healthcare more broadly. This chapter provides an overview of the

---

* Correspondence regarding this manuscript may be directed to Mary Zemanksy, 206 S. Calumet Road Suite E, Chesterton, IN, 46304.

more significant issues and controversies which were identified during the development of the Illinois legislation and that may possibly inform the implementation of the mandates as they are introduced at the time of the 2012 licensing cycle.

BACKGROUND

In July of 2010 lawmakers in Illinois approved legislation that provides a mandate for continuing education for psychologists, making Illinois the 44th jurisdiction (43 states and the District of Columbia) to require CE for the maintenance of a license in clinical psychology. This accomplishment was achieved over the course of many years by a number of individuals within the Illinois Psychological Association (IPA) working diligently to advance a proposal to enact such a requirement to ensure that psychologists within the state were meeting standards that were similar to their peers for licensing. The need for continuing education was identified as part of the strategic plan for the IPA Council in 2005-2006. An array of task force members subsequently reviewed literature within the health care field and collected information on the implementation of CE in other states. Both academic psychologists as well as clinicians provided input on the proposal; comments were solicited online from Illinois Psychological Association listserv members to address concerns over the amount, type and guidelines for CE requirements. A unique opportunity was thereby provided to raise and debate concerns about mandatory CE prior to its implementation.

This situation led to some interesting revelations regarding the concerns of psychologists about the proposal. When invited to offer feedback, members of IPA identified a number of issues that caused them reservations about the CE process. Many of these comments were integrated into the final recommendation offered to the Department of Financial and Professional Regulation (IDFPR), which is currently in the process of establishing written rules to manage the CE requirement. The description that follows is a sampling of opinions, and is not intended to represent the views of all psychologists who hold an Illinois license.

FEEDBACK ON AREAS OF CONCERN

While the majority of psychologists felt strongly about mandating CE, there were varied opinions as to how the legislation should compare with other mandates already in place in other licensing jurisdictions throughout the nation, which vary widely (Daniels & Walter, 2002). There was considerable sentiment that mandating only Category I units would discredit efforts of the membership to engage in the more informal types of CE recognized in many states as Category II. The intent of the proposal, however, was to allow psychologists more freedom and flexibility in the acquisition of Category II CE by purposefully not specifying types and amounts of this kind of learning that needed to be tracked. It was also strongly felt that the requirement (in the IPA proposal) of 23 units per licensing cycle was "too much"; one intrepid individual suggested that the two-year time frame to meet requirements might not allow the opportunity to participate in "worthwhile" programs which would enhance his skills in a given area, causing him to resort to taking courses that were irrelevant to his needs in order to comply with the regulations. Still others termed the hour requirement a potential "hassle and an expense without much benefit", implying that numbers of hours do not translate into beneficial learning experiences. There was also a comment that there should not be a requirement in ethics and risk management because the content is "too repetitive" and does not bring that much to the development of the practitioner. The proposal regarding a CE mandate was carefully developed to address such issues; the number of mandatory Category I units, for example, was based upon examining the requirements of other states to ensure that the hours required was comparable to other states. As for the inclusion of ethics training, this is believed to lead to improved quality of services and the reduction of costly mistakes that can easily be prevented, based on feedback from the APA insurance Trust as well as the Illinois State Board of Psychology (see Knapp & Vandecreek, 2012). Additionally, other states include mandatory CE in this area, with the intention of maintaining and developing competency within the field (American Psychological Association, 2000); in fact, the topic of ethics is the single most frequently required content area mandated by state boards in psychology (Neimeyer, Taylor & Wear, 2011; Wise et al., 2010).

Several individuals cited concern regarding the absence of evidence that CE makes an impact on the practice of psychology. Commentators cited studies that have shown that CE has a negligible effect on clinical performance and that there is no empirical basis indicating that CE improves quality of care. However, findings from multiple surveys indicate that most psychologists utilize CE to keep abreast of professional developments and advance their clinical knowledge, and a vast majority of those practitioners found their CE experiences has practical utility for their work with patients and makes them more effective as clinicians (Neimeyer, Taylor & Wear, 2009; Sharkin & Plageman, 2003). This stance also minimizes the findings from continuing education studies in other professions as being irrelevant to the profession of psychology, including Continuing Medical Education (CME) research which indicates that such training is effective in producing enhanced clinical skills. The evidence-based care approach intends to identify specific applied skills that enhance clinical practice and elevate the standard of care, and is likely to advance the utility of CE in furthering professional growth.

Certainly there is a lack of consensus among psychologists as to what constitutes effective CE. Many respondents felt that offerings thus far have been unimpressive in their content, presenters and cost; one individual cited "big companies with schlocky presentations" as a major detriment to his interest in attaining CE. While a means of systematically rating the quality of CE programs is lacking, the APA as well as state associations have developed standards for CE approval that address quality issues at a basic level. The fact that many professions have adopted CE as a means of keeping its members up-to-date on new developments in the field legitimizes its use to some extent. Lacking a viable alternative to educate professionals on practice trends, assist them in actively acquiring new skills or achieving the level of expertise expected by a public seeking professional services leaves CE as the best means to accomplish such goals.

Other respondents were quite insistent upon including weekend courses and/or post-graduate trainings as the means to achieve their CE units, advocating for "one-stop shopping" to dispense with the requirement in a relatively efficient manner. States have allowed such workshops to count as Category I but have set a limit on the number of units that can be obtained in this manner, usually 50% of the total accumulated over a renewal period. This was done to ensure that a breadth of issues could be covered within the CE requirements, since some individuals might choose to accumulate all their units within a weekend course rather than view CE as a process of ongoing learning which covers a broad base of knowledge. There are a number of states that mandate specific coursework be completed either each cycle or at least one cycle post-licensure, but allow professionals to choose areas of their own interest to fulfill the remainder of the requirement (see Adams & Sharkin, 2012, for examples).

The availability of home study or distance learning programs was also raised, with some psychologists finding this option a positive addition to the CE offerings but many others questioning its efficacy. CE research in other fields shows that isolated learning experiences do not provide much in the way of measurable increases in the knowledge base of its participants, arguing against the solo practitioner taking a course in isolation on his or her home computer. The CME literature has concluded that the most effective physician performance and clinical outcome improvements occur after programs emphasizing interactive sessions (problem-based learning) over didactic training (Davis et al., 1999; McGuickin & Burke, 2002), and this could serve as a model for psychology to follow. The need for peer feedback appears to be essential in impacting one's professional perspective and preventing lapses in judgment that might lead to potential problems (Linder-Crow, personal communication). Since methods of knowledge acquisition are rapidly changing in the technological world, more opportunities are being offered with sophisticated programs which permit live interaction with other professionals and thereby allow questions and insights to be shared, such as Webinars (Daniels & Walter, 2002). Distance learning, organized and directed learning experiences that occur when the instructor and student are not in direct visual or auditory contact, is also undergoing refinement through programs available on the internet. The administration of home study CE through organizations such as the American Psychological Association has helped to legitimize this process and provided a breadth of topics for training.

Quite a few psychologists mentioned the financial costs of CE, citing it as a "hardship" due to ever-shrinking insurance reimbursements and ever-mounting costs for malpractice insurance and other practice maintenance. These individuals were concerned that traveling to and participating in CE coursework was not only an expense, but took away valuable time from their practices and therefore their income stream. While this issue is a sensitive one, the IPA proposal suggested that costs (financial as well as time) are minimal when weighed against the benefits to the profession of psychology. The 1994 APA Study on Mandated Continuing Education (Phillips, 1994), for example, found that 81% of psychologists across the country spent less than $2000 per year on their continuing education, with substantial percentages spending less than $500. This appears to be a reasonable price to pay in order to bring psychologists into conformity with other licensed mental health professionals in Illinois, all of whom mandate CE. Psychologists' participation in CE makes a statement to the public that our profession is compliant with the generally accepted need to keep clinical skills updated through ongoing learning within the field. When psychology is willing to be accountable, it can convey the intent to oversee how care is dispensed to those served by the profession.

A few psychologists believed that Illinois has managed quite well thus far to produce quality services without having to join other states in mandating CE requirements. The true nature of this is unknown; one means to assess this is to determine the number of complaints about competency that the licensing Board receives each year (but such information is not made available). While it is known that basic skills are acquired during graduate school and internship, it is unclear how to integrate evolving knowledge within the field once a license has been granted. Daniels and Walter (2002) state that following the attainment of the license to practice psychology, CE is geared toward refining of existing clinical skills, mastery of changes in the knowledge base and clinical techniques, and development of new skills. Still other psychologists within the state still contended that self-monitoring is sufficient for CE accumulation, and thus a mandate was not necessary. These individuals noted that many psychologists already attend CE of their free will and are updating their knowledge and skills on a regular basis. They added that having requirements established by the state would take away their "autonomy" to make decisions as to which types and topics of continuing education are most relevant for them, and advocated for Illinois to remain distinct in allowing its psychologists to determine their own standards of care. While the ability to objectively identify and resolve shortcomings in training may apply to some individuals in the field, this view ignores the research that clearly shows there are a percentage of "CE laggards" (Phillips, 1991) who will fail to update their skills unless required to accomplish this (Neimeyer et al., 2009; Neimeyer, Taylor & Philip, 2010).

A couple of people commented on the need for "grandfathering" for those psychologists in practice over 20 years. In essence, they did not find it fair that a person who has practiced for a given time should have to comply with obtaining as many units as new practitioners, since many of their cohorts are in the process of scaling down their practices to a part-time status. The argument against this view has been made by other jurisdictions, and raises the concern that individuals who have been out of their academic training for the longest time probably stand the most to gain from updating their skill levels. While no provision was made based on seniority, the proposal suggested to offer postponement or waiver of the requirements to individuals with prolonged illness or disability, or those who are active duty military personnel. It should be noted that such individual perspectives do not represent general trends; the number of years that psychologists have spent in practice, for example, has not generally been linked to their overall support (or lack thereof) of CE mandates (Neimeyer et al., 2009).

Finally, the mistrust of regulatory agencies was cited as posing potential problems regarding implementation and flexibility of the rules that will ultimately be made concerning the CE mandate. Individuals questioned the ability of the Illinois Department of Financial and Professional Regulation to adequately define the most appropriate needs of psychologists, citing the rules as being "potentially adversarial" in scope. Individuals also raised concerns that the implementation of consequences for failing to meet those requirements might be too "harsh", and questioned how the procedure to monitor the achievement of these standards would be "fair and reasonable". One psychologist rightly noted that once the rules were written, any changes would require additional legislation to amend it. The IPA has addressed such concerns by offering their proposal to IDFPR for their consideration in drafting the implementation rules. The proposal details are only recommendations and may or may not be accepted by IDFPR as the final rules by which CE mandates will be defined. The details of the mandate (e.g., number and types of hours required) are administrative rules of the IDFPR and not written in the Licensing law (which only states that the department can set a mandate); this makes it much easier to make changes in the future (i.e., new law is not needed) if experience proves the initial rules ineffective or if the empirical research in the field indicates the need for different rules.

Conclusion

Overall, while many of the concerns that were raised by practicing psychologists in relation to mandated CE in the State of Illinois have validity, most of the issues can be addressed by proper interpretation and implementation of the requirements once these have been defined by the state. This legislation provides the field with a wealth of opportunities to refine CE programs to psychologists, including topics relevant to new graduates whose interests may be profoundly different from those seasoned veterans in the field. It seems likely that the number of CE offerings in Illinois, from a variety of sources, will increase as a function of the new mandates (Brown et al., 1982). The state psychological association has indicated its intention to provide more accessible CE in terms of availability (geography and frequency) and cost, and plans are being developed to present information to the IPA membership to raise awareness of the mandate. Feedback from psychologists will continue to be sought as CE offerings are being developed and promoted to ensure that the content is meeting the clinical needs of a wide array of practitioners in a timely and thoughtful manner. Ultimately, the goal is to encourage best practices in relation to the development and maintenance of professional competencies, and to support mechanisms that provide documentation to this effect in the increasingly evidence-based world of professional practice.

Acknowledgments

The author would like to express her appreciation to Illinois Psychological Association list serve members for their timely input on the CE mandate, along with the many individuals who have served on the IPA CE Task Force throughout the years. She would especially like to thank her co-chair of the IPA CE Task Force, Steven Rothke, Ph.D., for his invaluable comments on the draft of this chapter.

Biosketch

MARY ZEMANSKY obtained a Bachelor's degree in Psychology from UCLA in 1981 and received her Ph.D. in Clinical Psychology from California School of Professional Psychology in 1985. She then completed a fellowship in geropsychology at Rancho Los Amigos Medical Center. She is a licensed clinical psychologist who has worked in hospital settings, academic institutions and most recently in private practice. Her areas of specialization include neuropsychology, aging, adolescent development, ethics and continuing education. She served for 15 years on the Illinois Psychological Association ethics committee and was chair for two terms. She is currently co-chair of the Continuing Education Task Force of the IPA. She does consultation work to a pediatric nursing home in Illinois.

REFERENCES

Adams, A., & Sharkin, B.S. (2012). Should continuing education be mandatory for re-licensure? Arguments for and against. In G. J. Neimeyer, & J. M. Taylor (Eds.), *Continuing professional development and lifelong learning: Issues, impacts and outcomes* (pp. 157-178). Hauppauge, NY: Nova Science Publishers.

American Psychological Association. (2000). *Minutes of the APA Council of Representatives.* Washington, D.C.: Author.

Brown, R.A., Leichtman, S.R., Blass, T., & Fleisher, E. (1982). Mandated continuing education: Impact on Maryland Psychologist. *Professional Psychology, 13,* 404-411.

Daniels, A., & Walter, D. (2002). Current issues in continuing education for contemporary behavioral health programs. *Administration and Policy in Mental Health, 29,* 359-376.

Davis, D., O'Brien, M.T., Freemantle, N., Wolf, F.M., Mazmanian, P., & Taylor-Vaisey, A. (1999). Impact of formal continuing medical education: Do conferences, workshops, rounds, and other traditional continuing education activities change physician behavior or health care outcomes? *Journal of the American Medical Association, 282,* 867-874.

Knapp, S., & Vandecreek, L. (2012). Disciplinary actions by a state board of psychology: Do gender and association membership matter? An update. In G. J. Neimeyer, & J. M. Taylor (Eds.), *Continuing professional development and lifelong learning: Issues, impacts and outcomes* (pp. 151-154). Hauppauge, NY: Nova Science Publishers.

Linder-Crow, J. (2008). Personal communication with the first author.

McGuckin, C., & Burke, D. (2002). Best evidence medical education in psychiatric training. *Australasian Psychiatry, 10,* 348-352.

Neimeyer, G.J., Taylor, J.M., & Philip, D. (2010). Continuing education in psychology: Patterns of participation and perceived outcomes among mandated and nonmandated psychologists. *Professional Psychology: Research and Practice, 41,* 435-441.

Neimeyer, G.J., Taylor, J.M., & Wear, D.M. (2009). Continuing education in psychology: Outcomes, evaluations, and mandates. *Professional Psychology: Research and Practice, 40,* 617-624.

Neimeyer, G.J., Taylor, J.M., & Wear, D.M. (2011). Continuing education in professional psychology: Do ethics mandates matter? *Ethics and Behavior, 2,* 165-172.

Phillips, L.E. (1987). Is mandatory continuing education working? *Mobius, 7,* 57-64.

Phillips, L.E. (1994). *A study of mandatory continuing education.* Washington, D.C.: American Psychological Association.

Sharkin, B.S., & Plageman, P. M. (2003). What do psychologists think about mandatory continuing education? A survey of Pennsylvania practitioners. *Professional Psychology: Research and Practice, 34,* 318-323.

Wise, E.H., Sturm, C.A., Nutt, R.L., Rodolfa, E., Schaffer, J.B., & Webb, C. (2010). Lifelong learning for psychologists: Current status and a vision for the future. *Professional Psychology: Research and Practice, 41,* 288-297.

Chapter 11

DO CE MANDATES MATTER? THE EFFECTS OF CE MANDATES ON CE PARTICIPATION

Greg J. Neimeyer[1,*]*, Jennifer M. Taylor*[1]*,*
Mary Zemansky[2] *and Steven E. Rothke*[3]

[1] University of Florida, US
[2] Private Practice, Chesterton, Indiana, US
[3] Northwestern University, US

ABSTRACT

Previous research has noted higher levels of CE participation in states with CE mandates then without them. The current study explored the impact of CE mandates in the State of Illinois, which recently (2011) enacted, but had not yet implemented, a CE mandate for license renewal. A survey of psychologists in the state compared those who were aware of the mandate with those who were not yet aware of it terms of their levels of participation in formal and informal CE. Results indicated that an awareness of the mandates was associated with higher levels of formal CE, but not informal forms of professional development. Findings are discussed in relation to the literature on mandated CE and its role in ensuring professional competencies and public confidence.

Keywords: CE Mandates, Professional Development, Continuing Education, Professional Competencies

Formal continuing education (CE) in psychology is the spawn of the 1960's, born of an age of social activism and the public demand for greater professional accountability (Ross, 1974). The arrival of *mandatory* CE followed soon thereafter (Neimeyer & Taylor, 2010), delivering to the field of professional psychology an offspring that would suffer well-documented developmental challenges in the years ahead. As late as 1975 only three states

---

[*] Correspondence regarding this chapter may be directed to Greg J. Neimeyer, Department of Psychology, University of Florida, P. O. Box 112250, Gainesville, FL 32611.

had adopted mandatory CE in psychology (Jones, 1975), and even 15 years later only 19 states had enacted legislated CE mandates. The developmental delay associated with mandatory CE was not fully redressed until the 1990s when the rate of new CE mandates nearly doubled, leaving the field with 41 mandating jurisdictions by the year 2003. Today, 44 jurisdictions (43 states and the District of Columbia) have CE mandates for psychology while others continue to consider quality assurance mechanisms to fulfill the functions that CE is designed to accomplish.

In this chapter we explore the impact of CE mandates on participation in CE activities. The central orienting question is whether CE mandates matter or whether, as VandeCreek, Knapp, and Brace (1990) have wondered, the profession can "count on the integrity of individual practitioners to maintain competence" (p. 136) in the absence of a legal mandate to support what is already an ethical imperative (see Wise & Gibson, 2012).

CONCERNS AND COMPLEXITIES

The evidence, it turns out, is mixed. On the one hand, psychologists commonly report that they would participate in CE even in the absence of any mandate to do so (VandeCreek et al., 1990), and they cite a variety of factors that drive their participation, such as intrinsic interest in the topics, the need to remain current in the field, and the importance of redressing areas of perceived weakness (Neimeyer et al., 2010b). And whether they are from mandating or non-mandating states, psychologists generally report high (and comparable) levels of overall satisfaction with their CE experiences, with 70-80% indicating that they are satisfied or very satisfied with their professional development activities (Fagan, Ax, Liss, Resnick & Moody, 2007; Neimeyer, Taylor & Wear, 2009; Sharkin & Plageman, 2003).

Notwithstanding this generally favorable image, however, there has been longstanding concern that it may not accurately reflect some sizeable minority of practitioners who, in the absence of a legal mandate to do so, might not maintain a commitment to continuing education. Phillips (1987) estimated this group to be about 25-30% of licensed psychologists who, in the absence of a legislated mandate, would likely become what he termed, "CE laggards," participating only minimally, if at all, in ongoing efforts to maintain the currency of their professional knowledge and enhance their professional competencies.

In the absence of clear data to support these projections, however, many professionals influenced licensing jurisdictions and, understandably, resisted enacting CE mandates (see Zemansky, 2012) on the simple premise that a legal mandate of this sort had insufficient warrant. Relatedly, part of the discussion focused on the "costs and benefits" of mandated CE, with detractors arguing, for example, that mandating CE traded the known disadvantages associated with these mandates (principally cost and inconvenience) against its unknown advantages, given that the field has yet to produce compelling evidence that CE actually accomplishes its stipulated objectives in relation to the maintenance of competence and the protection of the public (see Neimeyer et al., 2009; Wise et al., 2011). Moreover, continuing concern also focused on whether the increases in the completion of formal CE that might accompany CE mandates might come at the expense of a range of informal CE, such as reading books and journals, attending conferences, or consulting colleagues. In short, one of the "hidden costs" of mandating formal CE might be to reduce the flexibility associated with pursuing a range informal forms of professional development and in this way compromise the fundamental premise of self-governed or "autodidactic" (Candy, 1991) learning that governs the CE process.

WEIGHING THE EVIDENCE

Evidence bearing on these issues comes from two primary types of studies; one "between-subjects" and one "within-subjects." The between-subjects studies consist largely of surveys that compare the rates of CE participation in CE-mandating and non-mandating states. The within-subjects studies examine the nature of CE participation within a state prior to, and following, its enactment of CE mandates.

"Between-Subjects" Research: Regarding the first approach, perhaps the strongest evidence bearing on these issues comes from the recent work of Neimeyer et al. (2009), which surveyed over 6,000 licensed psychologists across the country in relation to their CE participation in the previous year. By comparing the levels of CE participation among psychologists within mandated and non-mandated jurisdictions, Neimeyer et al. noted some striking differences. Results indicated that nearly 20% of those who operated without CE mandates completed fewer than 5 hours of CE per year (in contrast with fewer than 6% of those from mandating states), and nearly half of them completed fewer than 10 hours of CE. Subsequent work replicated these findings within an independent sample of more than 1,100 licensed psychologists (Neimeyer et al., 2010a), noting that 25% of the psychologists from non-mandating states completed fewer than five CE credits per year (compared with fewer than 9% of those from CE mandating states). These figures correspond closely to the earlier estimates regarding the probable percentage of "CE laggards" noted by Phillips (1987), lending credence to those projections.

In a further piece of research along these same lines, Neimeyer, Taylor and Wear (2011) examined differences in the participation rates of psychologists in CE programs dedicated to the topic of ethics. Within the United States, 18 states currently mandate the completion of an ethics program as a precondition to license renewal, whereas the others do not. The researchers argued that differential participation in ethics programs would represent an especially stringent test of the impact of CE mandates because ethics is widely regarded as the most important topic for CE (Wise et al., 2011) and is the single most commonly completed CE program across the board (Neimeyer et al., 2010b). If ever there was an instance in which CE mandates may not matter, the authors argued, it may well be in the area of ethics where "enlightened self-interest" alone may drive high rates of participation and obviate the need for any legal mandates.

What Neimeyer et al. (2011) found, however, was that ethics mandates did indeed matter; in the absence of a mandate only about 40% of the more than 5,000 psychologists they surveyed had completed an ethics program in the preceding year, compared to nearly two-thirds of those from within ethics-mandating states. So even in relation to CE programs that generate the highest levels of interest and participation (Neimeyer et al., 2010b; Wise et al., 2010), it appears that CE mandates enhance participation.

Given that CE mandates seem to matter, Neimeyer et al. (2011) turned towards a related question, seeking to identify whether the opposition to these mandates was located predominantly among those "CE minimalists" who, in the absence of a mandate, participate in little or no CE activity. To explore this possibility, the researchers examined the 1,083 psychologists in their non-mandated sample to determine whether those with the lowest levels of participation also had the highest levels of opposition to CE mandates. They operationally defined "CE minimalists" as those psychologists who had completed five or fewer CE credits in the previous 12 months, which would place them into the bottom 20% of their peers (Neimeyer et al., 2009). They then compared this group to the remainder of the sample of non-mandated psychologists (i.e., those who had completed more than five CE credits) in relation to their levels of agreement regarding mandating CE. Results revealed significant differences in the predicted direction. The "CE minimalists" were also the ones who expressed the greatest reservations about mandating CE, lending support to the earlier speculation that the opposition to CE mandates may be led precisely by those who may participate in it least (Neimeyer et al., 2009).

"Within-Subjects" Research: In addition to these "between subjects" studies, a second approach to identifying the impact of CE mandates on the completion of CE is a "within subjects" approach. Unfortunately, there is only one published study of this type in the current literature in professional psychology (Brown, Leichtman, Blass & Fleisher, 1982). In this study, Brown and his colleagues (1982) studied levels of participation in formal and informal CE prior to, and following, the enactment of CE mandates in the State of Maryland. By surveying psychologists within that state regarding a wide range of their professional development experiences, Brown et al. were able to determine that the CE mandates were related to significant increases in the completion of formal CE courses without, importantly, reducing levels of participation in informal forms of learning and professional development. Brown et al. found that the increased participation in formal CE occurred, in part, as a result of the increase in the number of CE programs that were offered as a result of the mandate. Interestingly, however, the increased availability and participation in formal CE did not detract from the continuing participation in informal forms of professional development, which remained consistent. This later finding ran counter to concerns expressed earlier in the literature that informal CE might fall prey to formal CE if the latter were mandated, on the assumption that the two forms of professional development might work in a hydraulic fashion with the increase in one coming at the expense of the other.

Consistent with the findings of Brown et al. (1982), recent work has repeatedly found that the correlation between levels of formal and informal CE is a *positive*, not a negative, one (Taylor, Neimeyer & Wear, 2012), a finding which has been reported in the medical literatures, as well (see Hojat, Veloski & Gonnella, 2012). This, in turn, has prompted researchers to speculate that formal CE mandates may actually contribute to a "culture of competence" that enhances, rather than detracts, from other forms and sources of learning. Further work is needed, however, to determine the exact nature of the relationship between participation in formal and informal forms of professional development. It remains unclear, for example, whether there is any sort of causal relationship between the two forms of learning or whether they are both responsive to some third, causal factor. It is clear, for instance, that as a commitment to lifelong learning increases, so too, do the levels of participation in both formal and informal forms of professional development (see Hojat et al., 2012). This, in turn, may underscore the importance of instilling lifelong learning attitudes early in the course of professional training to sustain a subsequent commitment to ongoing professional development.

THE CURRENT STUDY

In addition to the "between subjects" and "within subjects" approaches to identifying the impact of mandated CE on CE participation, the current study represents a third approach to the issue. This study essentially assesses the "prospective impact" of a CE mandate by examining the relationship between CE participation and the awareness of an impending CE mandate following its legislated enactment, but prior to its actual implementation. Specifically, the State of Illinois passed a piece of legislation in July of 2010 that mandates CE for license renewal beginning with the 2012 renewal cycle. Shortly after the passing of the legislation, but prior to its actual implementation, we conducted a survey of psychologists in the state. Because the legislation had just been enacted, but the mandates were not yet implemented, some psychologists were aware of the impending mandates and others were not. The central question we addressed was whether or not an awareness of the impending mandate was associated with higher levels of CE participation in anticipation of its actual implementation.

In collaboration with the Illinois Psychological Association, a survey was distributed to their membership through the membership listserv. Members were asked to participate by providing their perceptions regarding continuing professional development and were provided a link to an online survey that they could complete interactively and submit anonymously.

In all, 413 psychologists completed the survey, for a response rate of approximately 67% of the total membership who are licensed clinical psychologists. The mean age of the respondents was 52 years of age (SD=11.9). Sixty-one percent of the respondents were female and 39% were male, a distribution that is consistent with the larger membership of the Association (60% female; 40% male). Overall, approximately 4% of the respondents were African American, 2% were American Indian or Alaskan, 1% was Asian, 1% was Hispanic or Latino, and 1% was multi-racial, while 88% were Caucasian. These percentages are generally consistent with the distribution of ethnicity across the entire membership, which is as follows: 2% African-American, 1% Asian, 1% Hispanic or Latino, and 1% multi-racial, with 94% Caucasian and 2% other.

Respondents accessed and completed the survey online as part of a larger study continuing education and professional development. The survey included questions regarding whether they were aware of the new CE mandates ("Are you aware of the pending new requirements for CE in Illinois?", Yes or No), and items concerning the number of hours they spent in the previous year completing formal and informal continuing education and professional development activities. They also indicated their overall level of support for mandated CE by indicating the extent to which they agreed with the statement that, "continuing education should be mandated for license renewal", using a five-point rating scale that ranged from "strongly agree" (5) to "strongly disagree" (1).

In all, 222 respondents indicated that they were aware of the new CE mandates and 188 of them indicated that they were not aware of the new mandates. To examine the potential impact of the CE mandates on CE-related behavior, we compared the two groups in relation to the number of hours of formal and informal professional development that they reported having completed in the previous year.

RESULTS AND DISCUSSION

To explore the relationship between an awareness of the new CE mandates and professional development behavior, we first conducted a multivariate analysis of variance (MANOVA) using Awareness (Aware, Not Aware) as the independent variable and the number of reported hours of formal and informal CE as the dependent variables. A MANOVA was used to protect against the stepwise accumulation of Type-1 error that results from the use of serial univariate analyses (ANOVAs) and to control for the expected dependencies between the dependent variables (i.e. formal and informal CE).

The results of the MANOVA were significant, $F(2,338) = 6.11$, $p=.002$, demonstrating the overall differences between the two groups along both variables analyzed collectively. We then conducted two ANOVAs as follow-ups in order to determine the relationship between awareness of the mandates and the levels of participation in the two different forms of professional development (formal and informal CE).

Results along the measure of formal CE were significant, $F(1,339) = 12.11$, $p=.001$. As predicted, psychologists who were aware of the new CE mandates completed significantly higher levels of formal CE ($M = 18.26$; $SD = 15.30$) than did those who were unaware of the new mandate ($M= 13.05$; $SD = 11.18$). This difference is consistent with the findings of previous research comparing levels of CE completion among psychologists in CE-mandating and non-mandating jurisdictions, where the latter consistently report completing approximately one-third fewer CE credits than the former (Neimeyer et al., 2009).

Although this finding is consistent with the notion that an awareness of the new CE mandate resulted in increased CE participation, no causal relationship can be inferred from these results. It could just as well be the case that psychologists who are more active participants in formal CE were more aware of the impending mandates, with the participation increasing their awareness rather than the awareness increasing their participation. Furthermore, it is possible that there is no causal relationship between the awareness of the mandates and greater participation in CE in either direction. Instead, the relationship might be accounted for by a third variable that is causally related to the increase in both of these variables. One candidate in this regard would be the overall commitment to lifelong learning (see Hojat et al., 2012). Higher levels of lifelong learning attitudes, for example, might contribute both to higher levels of participation in CE and to a heightened awareness of regulations pertaining to professional development.

Support for this latter possibility might be found in a comparison of the levels of *informal* CE completed by respondents who were, and were not, aware of the new formal CE mandates. If levels of *informal* CE also increased in relation to an awareness of the formal CE mandates, this might argue in favor of a third factor, such as overall commitment to lifelong learning, as the potential causal agent. But if informal levels of CE did *not* increase with awareness, while levels of formal CE did, this finding might be more consistent with the potentially causal role of awareness in increasing the completion of formal CE, without affecting the levels of informal CE which lie outside the jurisdiction of the mandate.

Results of the comparison supported this latter conclusion; levels of informal CE were unrelated to the awareness of the CE mandate, $F(1,339) =.02$, $p=.89$. Levels of informal continuing education were comparable for those psychologists who were aware ($M = 147.97$;

$SD = 136.15$) and were not aware ($M = 144.83$; $SD = 152.32$) of the new mandates regarding formal CE.

Without clear evidence regarding the outcomes associated with formal CE, however, it remains to be seen whether there are demonstrated differences that are related to different levels of CE participation (Wise et al., 2010). For now what seems to be emerging most visibly is that CE mandates clearly matter, if only in relation to the levels of participation in CE. In the absence of CE mandates psychologists complete fewer formal CE activities. Whether these differences in CE participation translate into differential outcomes, such as improved practices, enhanced services, or better patient care, remains to be seen and is likely to be a central focus of the field's ongoing development as a profession that is committed to best practices in an increasingly evidence-based health care world.

BIOSKETCHES

GREG J. NEIMEYER received his Ph.D. in counseling psychology from the University of Notre Dame. He is professor of psychology in the Department of Psychology at the University of Florida and director of the Office of Continuing Education and Psychology at the APA. A fellow of the APA, he is also a member of the Department of Community Health and Family Medicine. His areas of research include professional development, epistemology and psychotherapy, and relationship development and disorder.

JENNIFER M. TAYLOR received her M.S. in counseling psychology from the University of Florida. She is currently a Ph.D. candidate in the University of Florida counseling psychology program. Her research focuses on professional development and competencies, lifelong learning, continuing education, and mentoring.

MARY ZEMANSKY obtained a Bachelor's degree in Psychology from UCLA in 1981 and received her Ph.D. in Clinical Psychology from California School of Professional Psychology in 1985. She then completed a fellowship in geropsychology at Rancho Los Amigos Medical Center. She is a licensed clinical psychologist who has worked in hospital settings, academic institutions and most recently in private practice. Her areas of specialization include neuropsychology, aging, adolescent development, ethics and continuing education. She served for 15 years on the Illinois Psychological Association ethics committee and was chair for two terms. She is currently co-chair of the Continuing Education Task Force of the IPA. She does consultation work to a pediatric nursing home in Illinois.

STEVEN E. ROTHKE received his doctorate in Clinical Psychology from the University of Kentucky and is board certified in both Clinical Neuropsychology and Rehabilitation Psychology through the American Board of Professional Psychology. He has served as Director of the Neuropsychology Testing Laboratory and head of the Department of Psychology at the Rehabilitation Institute of Chicago. He is a Clinical Assistant Professor in the Departments of Psychiatry and Behavioral Sciences and Physical Medicine and Rehabilitation at Northwestern University Medical School. He is the Immediate Past-President of the Illinois Psychological Association where he served as President for 2007-2008 and 2009-2010 and co-chaired the task force to institute mandatory continuing education programming for psychologists in Illinois. Dr. Rothke evaluates and treats individuals with conditions such as brain injury, dementia, exposure to neurotoxins, post-traumatic stress disorder, and depression. He also consults to business and industry regarding fitness for duty, risk assessment, and need for job modifications to accommodate a mental or psychiatric disability.

REFERENCES

Brown, R. A., Leichtman, S. R., Blass, T., & Fleisher, E. (1982). Mandated continuing education: Impact on Maryland Psychologist. *Professional Psychology, 13*, 404-411.

Candy, P. C. (1991). *Self-direction for life-long learning: A comprehensive guide to theory and practice.* San Fransisco: Jossey-Bass.

Fagan, T. J., Ax, R. K., Liss, M., Resnick, R. J., & Moody, S. (2007). Professional education and training: How satisfied are we? An exploratory study. *Training and Education in Professional Psychology, 1*, 13-25.

Hojat, M., Veloski, J. J., & Gonnella, J. S. (2012). Physician lifelong learning: Conceptualization, measurement, and correlations in full-time clinicians and academic clinicians. In G. J. Neimeyer, and J. M. Taylor (Eds.), *Continuing professional development and lifelong learning: Issues, impacts and outcomes* (pp. 33-72). Hauppauge, NY: Nova Science Publishers.

Jones, N. F. (1975). CE: A new challenge for psychology. *American Psychologist*, 842-847.

Neimeyer, G. J., & Taylor, J. M. (2010). *Continuing education in psychology*. In J. C. Norcross, G. R. VandenBos, D. K., and Freedheim (Eds.), History of Psychotherapy: Continuity and Change (pp. 663-671). Washington, DC: American Psychological Association.

Neimeyer, G. J., Taylor, J. M., & Philip, D. (2010a). Continuing education in psychology: Patterns of participation and perceived outcomes among mandated and nonmandated psychologists. *Professional Psychology: Research and Practice, 41*, 435-441.

Neimeyer, G. J., Taylor, J. M., & Wear, D. W. (2009). Continuing education in psychology: Outcomes, evaluations and mandates. *Professional Psychology: Research and Practice, 40*, 617-624.

Neimeyer, G. J., Taylor, J. M., & Wear, D. (2010b). Continuing education in psychology: Patterns of participation and aspects of selection. *Professional Psychology: Research and Practice, 41*, 281-287.

Neimeyer, G. J., Taylor, J. M., & Wear, D. (2011). Continuing education in professional psychology: Do ethics mandates matter? Ethics mandates matter? *Ethics and Behavior, 21*, 165-172.

Phillips, L. E. (1987). Is mandatory continuing education working? *Mobius, 7*, 57-64.

Ross, A. O. (1974). Continuing professional development in psychology. *Professional Psychology*, 122-128.

Sharkin, B. S., & Plageman, P. M. (2003). What do psychologists think about mandatory continuing education? A survey of Pennsylvania psychologists. *Professional Psychology: Research and Practice, 34*, 318-323.

Taylor, J. M., Neimeyer, G. J., & Wear, D. (2012). Professional competency and personal experience: An exploratory study. In G. J. Neimeyer, and J. M. Taylor (Eds.), *Continuing professional development and lifelong learning: Issues, impacts and outcomes* (pp. 243-255). Hauppauge, NY: Nova Science Publishers.

VandeCreek, L., Knapp, S., & Brace, K. (1990). Mandatory continuing education for licensed psychologists: Its rationale and current implementation. *Professional Psychology: Research and Practice, 21*, 135-140.

Wise, E. H., Sturm, C. A., Nutt, R. L., Rodolfa, E., Schaffer, J. B., & Webb, C. (2010). Lifelong learning for psychologists: Current status and a vision for the future. *Professional Psychology: Research and Practice, 41*, 288-297.

Wise, E. H., & Gibson, C. M. (2012). Continuing education, ethics and self-care: A professional life span perspective. In G. J. Neimeyer, and J. M. Taylor (Eds.), *Continuing professional development and lifelong learning: Issues, impacts and outcomes* (pp. 199-222). Hauppauge, NY: Nova Science Publishers.

Zemansky, M. (2012). Reviewing objections to the implementation of CE. In G. J. Neimeyer, and J. M. Taylor (Eds.), *Continuing professional development and lifelong learning: Issues, impacts and outcomes* (pp. 179-185). Hauppauge, NY: Nova Science Publishers.

Section 4.

Professional Development and Personal Well-Being

Chapter 12

CONTINUING EDUCATION, ETHICS AND SELF-CARE: A PROFESSIONAL LIFE SPAN PERSPECTIVE

Erica H. Wise and *Clare M. Gibson*
Department of Psychology
University of North Carolina at Chapel Hill, US

ABSTRACT

For professional psychologists there is a strong link between self-care and competence. Principle A of the 2002 APA Ethics Code reminds us that "Psychologists strive to be aware of the possible effect of their own physical and mental health on their ability to help those with whom they work". This chapter provides a broad overview of our ethical responsibilities and a framework for effective decision making in the areas of self-care and competence. Using the perspective of professional development, policies and research related to self-care and competence in graduate training and professional practice are reviewed and discussed. In addition, the implications of several lines of relevant research will be considered including challenges to engaging in effective self-assessment and self-care and the positive impact on therapist well-being and client outcomes of mindfulness training. Professional vignettes and recommendations for best practices in professional practice and graduate training are described.

Keywords: Continuing education, self-care, ethics, competence

In this chapter we will present a broad framework for integrating principles of effective self-care into continuing education workshops, graduate training and professional practice. The primary author (EHW) is a Clinical Professor, directs the training clinic, supervises and teaches graduate level courses in the clinical Ph.D. program at UNC Chapel Hill. She has

---

[*] Contact information: Department of Psychology, CB #3270, University of North Carolina at Chapel Hill, Chapel Hill, NC 27599-3270. Email: ewise@email.unc.edu. Phone: 919-962-5034.

extensive experience as an ethics educator and consultant on ethical and legal issues in the practice of psychology. She is past chair of the APA Ethics Committee and the North Carolina Psychology Board; she currently co-chairs the North Carolina Psychological Association (NCPA) Professional Affairs and Ethics Committee and serves as a frequent ethical and legal consultant to psychologists and attorneys in North Carolina. She has more recently become interested in professional competencies and in integrating self-care into graduate teaching, supervision, continuing education (CE) workshops and scholarly writing. The co-author (CMG) is an advanced graduate student at UNC Chapel Hill who will be completing an internship at the Veterans Affairs Maryland Health Care System-University of Maryland Baltimore Consortium. Her clinical and research interest is in psychotherapy for severe mental illness. She served as a graduate member of the NCPA's Colleague Assistance Committee (CAC) for two years. As a member of the CAC she was active in developing continuing education workshops on self-care and contributed to the NCPA's newsletter with an article about self-care in graduate students.

In a departure from traditional academic writing style, the authors incorporate a first person account of the personal and professional journeys that lead to their involvement in self-care with the hope that we will inspire others to integrate self-care into their professional endeavors. Following the narratives we will propose an integrated vision for the field.

A PERSONAL AND PROFESSIONAL JOURNEY (ERICA'S STORY)

I have always been drawn to the adage "You teach best what you most need to learn" (attributed to the author Richard Bach). This saying seems to capture something that is deeply meaningful to me; possibly it is the notion that even the most intellectual of our pursuits can be subtly influenced by aspects of ourselves that are outside of our conscious awareness. Or maybe it is the inherent truth that is embedded in the apparent paradox. In any case, this saying is particularly applicable to me when I turn to a consideration of my involvement in the teaching and practice of self-care. As a frequent workshop presenter on ethical and legal issues in professional psychology and as a faculty educator and supervisor in a doctoral clinical psychology program, I frequently address considerations (albeit indirectly) of self-care with my professional colleagues and graduate students. While it is not clear that self-care is what I *teach best* (per the quote above), it is almost certainly what I most need to learn. Early in the process of gathering resources in my preparation for writing this chapter I realized that I would not be writing a detached academic treatise on continuing education and self-care for psychologists. In fact, this is a topic that I am simply not able to keep meaningfully separate from my personal/private self. I would even argue that there is an intrinsic parallel between this topic and my experience in writing this chapter in that effective self-care is firmly rooted in the fundamental notion that many of the distinctions that we draw between our personal/private and professional selves are illusory (Mahoney, 1991).

THE PERSONAL-PROFESSIONAL DIMENSION IN PSYCHOLOGY

Contradictory messages about the distinctions that can be drawn between the personal/private and professional lives of professional psychologists can be readily discerned in our professional belief system and in our key published documents. For example, in its Introduction and Applicability section, the APA Ethics Code (2002) informs us that the professional activities (broadly defined) to which the code applies "…shall be distinguished from the *purely private conduct* of psychologists, which is not within the purview of the Ethics Code." (p.1061, italics added). So, what is "purely private conduct"? Presumably, anything that occurs when we are not at work. This is a totally clear decision rule…right? But let's explore further. Consider that in making the argument that self-care is an ethical imperative, it is common practice to quote Principal A of the 2002 APA Ethics Code which states that "Psychologists strive to be aware of the possible effect of their own physical and mental health on their ability to help those with whom they work". (p. 1062). Suddenly the distinction between the purely private/personal and the professional is no longer a bright line. This is the sort of ethical nuance that fascinates those of us who tend to reflect on such issues.

How is this discrepancy relevant to my story? As a self-professed academic "ethics nerd," I was not particularly interested in self-care and didn't actually see its relevance to my own academic scholarship, teaching, supervision or clinical practice. I will describe below the events that have shaped my interest in this area and have encouraged me to better appreciate the complex interface between ethical practice as a psychologist, professional competence, effective self care and the essential role that continuing education can play in linking these areas. In fact, the very process of writing this chapter is another step in a professional and personal journey that has increasingly allowed me to integrate these issues in my work and life.

HOW TO INCORPORATE SELF-CARE INTO AN ETHICS CE WORKSHOP?

I have been active in the North Carolina Psychological Association (NCPA) since early in my career. Just over five years ago, at a time when I had recently completed several terms as a member and chair of the North Carolina Psychology Board and was serving as co-chair of the NCPA Professional Affairs and Ethics Committee, I was contacted by my colleague (Steve Mullinix) who was then chair of the NCPA Colleague Assistance Committee (CAC), to discuss a program development request that had come from the NCPA Program Committee. The request was an intriguing one: to develop a formal Category A continuing education workshop for psychologists in North Carolina that would integrate self-care and ethics. As I initially considered this request I was completely stumped.

For many years I had presented traditional ethics and legal issues workshops and taught a graduate seminar that focused on complex ethical dilemmas in various areas of psychological practice, teaching and research. I just did not see how these areas could be coherently integrated into a workshop. Nor, was I particularly interested in self-care, which at the time seemed to be a rather fuzzy concept to me; something that fit best in a self-help book or discussed in a 12-step meeting. However, I was also intrigued with exploring the notion of reducing the risk of ethical problems through a consideration of positive psychology and stress management. Initially we struggled to develop the theme and focus for this workshop to which we had already committed ourselves (in retrospect this may not have been the most prudent course of action). As I and many others have frequently noted, albeit anecdotally, psychologists who are isolated, highly distressed or overwhelmed seem to be more likely to engage in unprofessional conduct. Conversely, it is commonly understood that ethical or legal complaints are universally a source of tremendous stress for psychologists. These initial realizations began to give us a sense of direction for the project and became our first conceptual toe hold in considering the interface between ethics and self-care.

As we reviewed the literature, we were impressed by the formulation of the *stress-distress-impairment-improper behavior continuum for psychologists* as identified by the APA Advisory Committee on Colleague Assistance (ACCA, n.d.) and realized that this construct could serve as an organizing principal for our workshop. As defined by ACCA, *stress* refers to how our bodies react to external or internal demands, *distress* to the subjective state of experiencing anxiety, pain or suffering, *impairment* to resultant compromised professional functioning and *improper behavior* to the resultant unethical or incompetent practice. With these ideas in mind I carefully re-read the APA Ethics Code and it became clear, somewhat belatedly in the workshop preparation process, that the standards on competence were directly related to self-care. In fact, as I worked to develop the didactic ethics content, I was struck by how easily the concepts (once identified) flowed. Since that time I have gradually become more familiar with the burgeoning literature on self-care for professionals in general and for psychologists in particular (this topic will be considered in more detail later in the chapter).

THE FIRST ETHICS AND SELF-CARE WORKSHOP

With some trepidation on my part we arrived to present our first integrated ethics and self-care workshop at a professional development conference in early 2005. Its title was rather convoluted: "Avoiding ethical and legal complaints: Self-Care and lessons learned..." Despite its somewhat daunting title, the workshop was well attended. In fact, the initial cap on enrollment was expanded several times to include additional participants. It was a large group and it was helpful that there were many friends and colleagues in attendance. Because the workshop was designed with the intention of meeting the North Carolina Psychology Board mandated three hours of CE in ethical and legal issues, we were careful to include substantial ethics content.

The basic elements of this initial workshop included:

1. Ethical underpinnings and concepts
2. A self-assessment exercise
3. The analysis of self-care vignettes
4. Strategies for self-care

It is interesting to note that this basic structure has been, for the most part, retained over time. The ethics content is described in detail in the next section of this chapter. The self-assessment exercise was adapted from the work of Ellen Baker (2002). In its current version, the 11 items on the self-assessment questionnaire are:

1. Briefly describe what makes a "good day" for you at work. In contrast, what makes a "bad day"?
2. Briefly, what personal attributes or life history experiences do you think led you to the field of psychology?
3. Is your work as a psychologist different from what you anticipated? If so, how?
4. What have been the significant periods / challenges during your career related to professional or personal stresses? What did you do to cope during those times?
5. What would you say are your current professional concerns / stressors?
6. Have you ever considered leaving the field? If so, why?
7. How do you know when you're under stress?
8. How might your stress affect those around you?
9. What has been most helpful for you regarding taking care of yourself and maintaining resiliency in your professional and personal life?
10. What do you consider your greatest challenge regarding self-care?
11. Given what you know now about yourself and the field of psychology, would you choose the same profession over again? Why?

In terms of structure, participants were asked to complete the questionnaire on their own and then to discuss their written responses with a partner. We were amazed to note in the initial workshop that it was difficult to get the attention of the audience back to us once they began sharing responses with each other; they did not want to stop talking. In this initial workshop the self-assessment activity was highly ranked and participants clearly stated in their post-workshop feedback that they had wanted to devote more time to it. In response we have added additional time for this exercise in subsequent workshops. Their response was in stark contrast to our concern that it might not generate much interest or engagement. Clearly, this activity tapped a deep chord in participants, many of whom initially acknowledged that they had signed up for the workshop primarily to receive mandatory ethics CE credits. Later it occurred to us that these questions are remarkably similar to those that are commonly asked during the initial session of couples therapy; in essence, we are taking a history of the participants' relationship with psychology. Intense emotions were generated in the process of remembering and discussing one's initial attraction to the field and areas of current stress, disappointment or disillusionment. Similarly, reconnecting to what is positive seemed to generate appreciation and gratitude. Participants were strikingly open in their willingness to share reactions and concerns in dyads and with the larger group. It was likely important that we explicitly encouraged participants to be mindful of their own boundaries and to only share what they wished and what felt comfortable to them.

Following the self-assessment exercise we presented and discussed a range of challenging ethical vignettes that related to the management of personal and collegial stress, expanding practice areas (out of choice or necessity) and other related topics. The vignettes were processed in small groups using an ethical decision making model and the analyses were shared with the full group. The vignettes generated animated discussion and were frequently identified as a highly valued aspect of the workshop. Finally, in this initial workshop, we presented and discussed basic principles of self-care, ethical risk management strategies and tips for how to respond in the event of an ethics complaint. As has become common practice in this workshop model, this initial workshop ended with a request for each participant to commit to several specific self-care strategies.

In later iterations of this workshop, we have explicitly introduced elements of positive psychology and Dialectical Behavior Therapy; in particular emotion regulation, mindfulness and interpersonal effectiveness (Linehan, 1993) and multicultural diversity. Later in the chapter I will make some practical suggestions for how this basic workshop template can be adapted for specific professional groups. It has become increasingly clear that this interactive workshop incorporated key components of successful continuing education in that participants were intellectually and emotionally engaged. In addition, through the discussion of vignettes we incorporated elements that represented practice situations common to participants' work setting. For a detailed discussion of criteria to consider in developing effective continuing education programs for psychologists, see Knapp and Sturm (2002) and Sturm (2010).

ETHICS, COMPETENCE AND SELF-CARE

Why is it useful to embed self-care in the context of ethics and competence? Perhaps most importantly, as is suggested in this chapter, these concepts are naturally interrelated. It is also a well-documented finding that the inclusion of ethics content tends to make workshops more appealing to potential participants. In a recent survey of over 6,000 psychologists concerning their participation in continuing education, ethics was the most frequently selected topic (Neimeyer, Taylor & Wear, 2010). Of course, the fact that 29 (57%) of the states that mandate continuing education have specific requirements for ethics content (Wise, 2010) may account for some of the popularity of this topic. While the frequency of its selection may very well be influenced by regulatory mandates, there does seem to be a genuine interest in ethics among psychologists, given that it is the most frequently attended CE course even within non-mandating jurisdictions (Neimeyer et al., 2010).

In this section I will provide an overview of ethical principles and content related to the interface between ethics, self-care and competence. In addition to establishing a theoretical foundation for the interrelatedness of these topics, this section is also intended to provide a starting point for the development of workshops in this area. Strategies to increase interest and impact are strongly recommended. Examples of vignettes are included throughout this section in order to illustrate the underlying principles. As mentioned above, the basic approach taken in this chapter can be integrated into a CE workshop on this topic and adapted for specific participant groups.

As a starting point for this discussion of ethics related to competence and self-care, let's consider the root meaning of the term competence and the implications of a more active and dynamic conceptualization of the term:

> The etymology of the term is germane. Competent is the present participle of the term "compete." In Latin, "competere," or to strive together, is derived from com = with and petere = to seek or to strive (American Heritage Dictionary, 1970, p. 271). This suggests that the early meaning of the term had active roots related to being qualified to compete; with special applicability to physical competition and sport. This more active

connotation is consistent with current thinking about competence as a dynamic set of skills and attributes that are context specific and evolve throughout one's professional life. (p. 627, Wise, 2008).

Competence is a cornerstone of the Ethics Principles of Psychologists and Code of Conduct (APA, 2002). In the aspirational portion of the code, the last sentence of Principle A: Beneficience and Nonmaleficence states that: "Psychologists strive to be aware of the possible effect of their own physical and mental health on their ability to help those with whom they work" (APA, 2002, p. 1063). As discussed earlier, this general principal draws our attention to the impact of our health (broadly defined) on our professional competence. The enforceable standards related to competence are contained in Standard 2. Several of the standards that are most relevant to self-care will be reviewed with relevant vignettes (adapted from Wise, 2008 and prior workshops) that are designed to elicit discussion of the underlying ethical issues, dilemmas and applications to professional functioning and practice.

ETHICAL STANDARDS RELATED TO COMPETENCE AND PERSONAL PROBLEMS

In any discussion of continuing education and self-care it is important to be mindful of the potential for impairment and improper behavior (to borrow terminology from the APA ACCA). The enforceable standards that are directly related to the distressed end of the self-care continuum are located within Standard 2 *Competence*. Because of its particular relevance, I will quote Standard 2.06 *Personal Problems and Conflicts* in its entirety:

(a) Psychologists refrain from initiating an activity when they know or should know that there is a substantial likelihood that their personal problems will prevent them from performing their work-related activities in a competent manner.
(b) When psychologists become aware of personal problems that may interfere with their performing work-related duties adequately, they take appropriate measures, such as obtaining professional consultation or assistance, and determine whether they should limit, suspend, or terminate their work-related duties (p. 1065).

As you read the following vignette (adapted from Wise, 2008), consider what it might be like to find yourself in this situation:

> You have noticed that you have begun to lose interest in your clinical practice. The problems that your clients tell you are beginning to sound alike, and you find it hard to stay awake in sessions. Several clients have asked you if you are feeling OK, and recently several have gotten hurt or angry when you have briefly nodded off during sessions. It has become increasingly difficult to return phone calls to clients and to other professionals. You have noticed that you are not sleeping well at night, your energy is low and you feel listless. You have been feeling increasingly overwhelmed by your administrative workload, and you have several custody reports that are weeks overdue. Your family and friends have mentioned that you seem tired and distracted. You have

also noticed that you are relying on alcohol to unwind in the evenings since you are unable to relax even though you are exhausted.

The concerns embedded in this vignette range from those that may be transient (e.g., having a stressful day or too little sleep on a short-term basis) to highly concerning "red flag" indicators of significant professional dysfunction (e.g., increased alcohol consumption, generalized burn out and avoidance of professional duties). In particular, the failure to attend to clearly identifiable professional responsibilities that impact the lives of others (such as late custody reports) significantly increases the likelihood of direct negative impact of our problems on the lives of our clients (improper behavior) and the risk of a formal complaint. Anecdotally, when adapted versions of this vignette have been presented to particular groups of psychologists, it is not uncommon for participants to state with a wry sense of humor that I have "seen into their lives" or have "read their minds." There is a profound poignancy in explicitly capturing in a targeted vignette the stressors that apply to different professional settings or levels of professional development. A consideration of this vignette tends to foster discussion of when to become concerned about one's functioning and potential barriers to seeking the support of friends or professional assistance even when we are truly in need. These discussions can tap into the typically unexpressed belief systems of psychologists. In addition to experiencing a general reluctance to recognize when personal distress has moved beyond the transient and manageable, a factor that frequently emerges in discussion of impairment vignettes is that it may in fact *not* be economically feasible for many psychologists to substantially limit or suspend their practice during transient periods of stress. For psychologists in private practice settings, there may be significant disincentives to "limit, suspend or terminate" work-related duties. Overhead continues and we tend to feel responsible for our clients. Similarly, colleagues in academic or agency settings experience different but powerful disincentives for taking time away from professional responsibilities for purely personal reasons. Some participants have discussed the importance of arranging work and personal obligations so that there can be some flexibility in the event of particularly stressful times. In her section, Clare will discuss the disincentives that are experienced in graduate training.

In general, sound self-care practices and effective early warning systems are much preferred and more likely to be implemented by psychologists. However, if there is substantial distress and a high likelihood of professional misconduct, it is most definitely preferable to limit or suspend practice rather than to potentially cause harm to a client or become subject to disciplinary proceedings. In reality, most situations fall along a continuum of severity. If psychologists practice affirmative self-care and remain alert to early signs of distress, they can decrease the likelihood of becoming significantly impaired and thereby needing to limit or suspend practice. Of course, there are also situations in which illness, trauma or major loss necessitates such measures no matter how careful the psychologist has been to engage in positive self-care. The discussion of these vignettes in small groups followed by full group discussion most often leads to the recognition of the central considerations outlined in this section in a way that tends to naturally emerge from the discussion. It is to be hoped that these discussions will have a positive impact on psychologists' future decision making in both the good times and the not so good.

Standard 1.04 of the APA Ethics Code, Informal Resolution of Ethical Violations, states that psychologists attempt to resolve ethical concerns by bringing them to the attention of the individual "if an informal resolution appears appropriate." The appropriateness of informal resolution is based on a consideration of whether substantial harm has already occurred or is likely to occur. If this risk is high, formal reporting under Standard 1.05 is probably indicated. In fact, we generally have broad discretion to address concerns with colleagues, although this is an area of considerable discomfort and professional debate. Based on my three terms as a member of the North Carolina Psychology Board, I am convinced that there are many situations in which concerned and caring colleagues might have effectively intervened before a disciplinary matter came to the attention of the regulatory board. As you read the following vignette (adapted from Wise, 2008), imagine yourself in the situation described, note the emotional reactions that might be triggered and consider how you might respond.

> You work in a large group private practice. During a coffee break in your office, a colleague tells you that he has continued to be emotionally devastated by the recent break-up of his 20+ year marriage. He tells you that he is considering meeting socially outside of sessions with a female client who is also dealing with the end of a long-term relationship. He tells you that he has mentioned his situation to her during several therapy sessions in order to let her know that he understands her pain. He tells you that the client was very empathic and that he thinks they could both use some additional emotional support. He emphasizes that they would just have coffee and talk after work. He wants your consultation regarding the ethical propriety of his engaging in this proposed behavior.

Most of us would readily recognize that this psychologist has already stepped onto a slippery slope and is poised to slide towards professional misconduct. At the point described in the vignette, high potential exists for harm to his client and his professional career. Less clear is how we might effectively intervene as a colleague. Few of us are prepared to have such difficult conversations with colleagues, although doing so might be one of the more important helping acts that we can undertake. In an ethics workshop we might encourage discussion of how we would respond, what would make this difficult for us and so forth. I explicitly tell participants that my hope is that having discussed the vignette in our workshop will result in a greater likelihood of addressing this issue with a colleague if ever confronted with this situation.

Psychologists must also consider approaching a colleague who has *not* explicitly requested assistance. In the following vignette (adapted from Wise, 2008), concern is raised by the receptionist in your practice who requests anonymity. While I would encourage you to take seriously the receptionist's concern about letting Dr. J know that she has expressed concern, her wishes must be weighed against the importance of approaching your colleague. It may not be possible to open a discussion with Dr. J without stating the cause for your concern. In addition to a consideration of the interpersonal and power dynamics inherent in this situation, the analysis of this vignette can also provide a useful and intellectually stimulating discussion of confidentiality in various clinical and non-clinical relationships.

> You work in a large group private practice. You come in to work 30 minutes before your first appointment to catch up on paperwork and the receptionist asks to talk privately with her. You step into the small kitchen and the receptionist tells you that she has become increasingly concerned about Dr. J, your colleague and practice partner. The

receptionist has noticed that Dr. J has been late for appointments and that several of his clients have called to cancel return appointments. In addition, she tells you that she has noticed that his breath smells of alcohol when he returns from lunch. She thinks that someone should know about this, but she doesn't want to "get into trouble" with Dr. J.

As in the previous vignette, being confronted with potentially impaired or improper behavior by a colleague is a stressful situation. In this second vignette, there are many elements of ambiguity; we do not know for certain the extent (if any) of Dr. Jones's impairment or its potential impact on clients. Clients cancel appointments for many different reasons and the receptionist may be mistaken about the smell of alcohol. It is even possible that the receptionist is angry at Dr. J about an unrelated issue. Of course, a common thread in such situations is the manner in which our personal health and functioning *can* directly impair our clinical competence. In the vignette it is not clear exactly what the administrative structure is of the practice or whether you yourself might be held accountable in some way for Dr. J's misconduct (if such is occurring). Does Dr. J need substance abuse treatment or is this all a misunderstanding? If the only source of concern is the receptionist's communication to you, how would you proceed if you decided to discuss the issue with Dr. J. How would you raise your concerns? In discussing potential responses, suggested strategies tend to vary widely, with some participants advocating for the gathering of more information. This might lead to a discussion of what role is appropriate for us with a colleague; should we attempt to quietly investigate? Some advocate for intervening forcibly whereas others state emphatically that they would most likely "do nothing." The variability in reactions to the vignette and to suggested potential steps that one might take is in itself useful to note. Overall, the point can be made that as a profession, we frequently fail to effectively intervene with ourselves or with our colleagues prior to the point at which distress or impairment leads to improper behavior.

ETHICAL STANDARDS RELATED TO COMPETENCE AND PROFESSIONAL PRACTICE

Standard 2.01(c) *Boundaries of Competence* states that "Psychologists planning to provide services, teach or conduct research involving populations, areas, techniques, or technologies new to them undertake relevant education, training, supervised experience, consultation, or study" (p. 1065). This standard is relevant to self-care in that it is common to recommend diversification of practice in order to stay current with trends in the field and as a strategy for maintaining energy and commitment. This standard sets forth the clear expectation that psychologists use defensible professional judgment and a cogent self-assessment process when they choose to expand their scope of practice. Although our ethics code recognizes a range of strategies, including more informal self-directed methods for expanding practice, regulatory boards are more likely to set objective, explicit requirements for seeking to move into new areas of practice. More generally, an inherent ethical tension exists between the conservative goal of practicing within the bounds of one's current competence and the desire to expand practice, provide services in emergent situations or where there is limited access to competent practitioners. Along with 2.01(d) which addresses situations in which a fully trained psychologist is not available, these two standards are carefully crafted to provide a judgment rule; they are not intended to provide a carte blanche for incompetent practice. The following vignette (adapted from Wise, 2008) is an example of how this ethical dilemma might be incorporated into a vignette for discussion in a CE workshop:

> Dr. A lives in a rural community and is one of two psychologists within a 100-mile radius. She has begun to receive more referrals of adolescent females who engage in self-harming behaviors, such as intentional cutting and burning. In practice for over 20 years, Dr. A is aware that her early psychodynamic training may not be the most effective treatment for achieving behavioral, emotional and cognitive change in such individuals, although she believes that the psychodynamic orientation offers a useful underpinning for case formulation. Dr. A attends an intensive week-long continuing education workshop that focuses on Dialectical Behavior Therapy and subsequently develops an email and telephone consultation relationship with the instructor. This relationship includes payment for ongoing case consultation as well as suggestions for additional study. Dr. A continues to read widely in this area including basic texts and outcome research. She is also aware of the personal stress related to work with this population and makes it a particular point to balance her case load and to actively engage in self-care behaviors that provide an effective counterpoint to her emotionally demanding psychotherapy practice. She is a member of her state association and has organized a state-wide consultation group for psychologists who are working with high risk and self-harming clients.

Let's consider whether Dr. A is approaching this issue in an appropriate and defensible manner: She is aware that her foundational academic training and supervised experience does not fully prepare her to work with this population in a manner that integrated current best practices, although her psychodynamic case formulation skills and her general expertise are certainly relevant. She undertakes formal continuing education, engages in ongoing self-study and seeks regular consultation with an expert and with colleagues who are engaged in similar work. Although this area of practice is arguably high stress, she finds it to be satisfying and it provides her with a sense of making a meaningful contribution. Overall, in this vignette, Dr. A does seem to be approaching her expanded practice in a thoughtful manner that indicates appropriate care for her clients and herself.

In contrast, let's consider the situation of a psychologist who is tempted to step beyond current training in a manner that has some likelihood of creating professional risk for the psychologist substandard care for the family. Standard 2.01(f) addresses the need for additional training for psychologists who wish to function in forensic roles or settings: "(f) When assuming forensic roles, psychologists are or become reasonably familiar with the judicial or administrative rules governing their roles" (p. 1065). In particular, forensic practice is an area in which even highly competent psychologists may not always know what they don't know. This vignette (adapted from Wise, 2008) can be used to explore the positive wish to expand into new areas of practice and the risks that can ensue:

> Dr. B has always been intrigued by legal matters and had actually considered going to law school before she decided to train to be a psychologist. She enjoys watching courtroom dramas and wonders how she would hold up if she were interrogated on the stand as an expert witness. She receives a call from an attorney friend who is looking for a local mental health professional to evaluate his client who is a mother involved in a

highly conflicted divorce. He asks if Dr. B would be willing meet with his client and then to informally render her opinion on whether or not his client is the better parent in a letter to the judge. The attorney states that he would not need a "formal evaluation", but just needs a "letter to the court". He further tells her that the father has been abusive and that he wants to make sure that the children are safe. The attorney also tells her that the father is very demeaning about the mental health profession and would most definitely not agree to participate in an evaluation. Dr. B is initially tempted to agree to take on this intriguing and lucrative referral, but requests time to consider the offer. She consults with several knowledgeable colleagues and reads the relevant chapter in a book on professional ethics and risk management. Dr. B concludes that she does not have adequate training to perform this evaluation and that her role as described by the attorney would be neither appropriate nor in the best interest of this family. With some regret, she declines the referral.

In discussing this vignette we might consider the *pulls* that Dr. B. is experiencing to step beyond her competence without adequate training and preparation. The use of a vignette can assist participants in more fully exploring the internal (emotional and intellectual) and external (informational) resources that may be needed for effective decision-making. In our foundational training, Domain B (e) in the Guidelines and Principles for the accreditation of programs in professional psychology requires programs to inculcate "Attitudes essential for life-long learning, scholarly inquiry, and professional problem solving as psychologists in the context of an evolving body of scientific and professional knowledge." (2008, p. 12). It is clear that psychologists will need this "attitude" in order to become effective life-long learners, so that they will be able to most effectively adapt to the rapid changes in the field and in our culture.

SELF-CARE CONTENT FOR WORKSHOPS

In recent years there has been a proliferation of self-care articles and books for psychologists; authors agree that it is essential for psychologists to proactively implement effective self-care strategies (e.g., Barnett, Baker, Elman & Schoener, 2007; Brucato & Neimeyer, 2009; Pope & Vasquez, 2005; Norcross & Barnett, n.d.; Norcross & Guy, 2007). In one survey of psychologists (Mahoney, 1997), respondents reported a relatively high rate of psychological distress with one third of respondents reporting anxiety or depression during the previous year. More than 40% of those surveyed reported episodes of emotional exhaustion during the previous year. Clearly (and not surprisingly) psychologists are not immune from personal problems. There has been increasing interest in our profession in examining the complex relationship between impairment and competence to practice (e.g., Mahoney, 1997; Baker, 2002; Webb, 2006). In her section, Clare will provide a more detailed overview of this literature as it relates to graduate students in professional psychology.

TAKING A BROAD AND FLEXIBLE APPROACH TO SELF-CARE

Traditionally, colleague assistance programs have focused on professionals abusing substances. While this is a critical area of attention, evidence suggests a broader range of personal concerns impact competence, and thus need to be addressed individually and collectively. Specific self-care content can be drawn from many sources. In particular, Norcross and Barnett (n.d.) provide an excellent framework for incorporating self-care into a continuing education workshop. They recommend the flexible incorporation of 12 basic principles (excerpted below):

1. Valuing the Person of the Psychotherapist
2. Refocusing on the Rewards
3. Recognizing the Hazards
4. Minding the Body
5. Nurturing Relationships
6. Setting Boundaries
7. Restructuring Cognitions.
8. Sustaining Healthy Escapes
9. Creating a Flourishing Environment
10. Undergoing Personal Therapy
11. Cultivating Spirituality and Mission
12. Fostering Creativity and Growth

Workshops can incorporate a discussion of these basic principles with a consideration of broad and general strategies that tend to be more effective than specific techniques.

POSITIVE PSYCHOLOGY

The incorporation of elements of positive psychology is very effective in self-care workshops, especially since many participants may not be familiar with basic findings in the field. There are many approaches to elaborating on specific self-care content. For example, participants might be reminded that there is research to support the notion that wealth is only weakly related to happiness both within and across nations, particularly when income is above the poverty level (Diener & Diener, 1996), or that activities that make people happy in small doses (such as shopping, good food and making money) do not lead to fulfillment in the long term, indicating that they tend to have quickly diminishing returns (Myers, 2000; Ryan & Deci, 2000). Similarly, there is research to suggest that people who express gratitude on a regular basis have better physical health, optimism, progress toward goals, well-being, and help others more (Emmons & Crumpler, 2000) and that trying to maximize happiness can lead to unhappiness (Schwartz, Ward, Monterosso, Lyubomirsky, White & Lehman, 2002). In particular, many of these findings have clear connections to items 11 and 12 on the Norcross and Barnett list above.

STRATEGIES FOR ADAPTING WORKSHOPS

How can self-care workshops be effectively adapted for specific participants? My primary suggestion is so simple that we sometimes neglect to consider and implement it: just ask! When I am invited to present to a group whose area of practice is not very familiar to me, I discuss in depth with my contact person the general concerns and stressors that the psychologists are likely to be experiencing. I then ask that a question be posted on the group's listserv regarding self-care or ethical dilemmas and concerns. I request that the responses be sent directly to me. I almost always receive a few and sometimes many. In either case, these responses provide critical insight into the issues being faced. With careful attention to de-identification, I incorporate these concerns into didactic material and vignettes. I have presented workshops for internship training directors, counseling center training directors and for psychologists in rehabilitation settings, large research-oriented medical centers and state hospitals, to name just a few.

INNOVATIVE PROGRAMS IN THE STATE PROVINCIAL AND TERRITORIAL PSYCHOLOGICAL ASSOCIATIONS

Although there are many examples of innovative self-care programming across the United States, I am going to focus on North Carolina and Pennsylvania as two states that have been particularly effective in engaging psychologists in a meaningful consideration of self-care.

North Carolina Psychological Association

The NCPA Colleague Assistance Committee has been very active in developing self-care workshops for psychologists in our state. In addition to partnering in the development of the initial self-care workshop in 2005, they have provided workshops on topics such as resiliency over the life span in which psychologists discussed stressors and coping strategies in groups based on years in practice, resiliency in tough economic times which focused on strategies for coping with the current recession and perceiving and responding to overt and subtle threats at work. These workshops have maintained a positive focus and have provided an excellent forum for the discussion of critical issues that impact self-care and competence.

Pennsylvania Psychological Association

Sam Knapp has long been a leader in this area. While a full consideration of his work is outside of the scope of this chapter, he graciously shared a few general principles for inclusion (personal communication). In particular, he suggests framing self-care workshops in a positive context. The Colleague Assistance Committee of the PPA emphasizes positive psychology, the importance of community, mindfulness and a sense of greater meaning. They embed self-care content in a non-threatening and non-guilt-inducing context. They make ample use of the association newsletter and have recently started an ethics blog. I would encourage anyone interested in developing this approach for their state psychological association to review Sam Knapp's body of work on behalf of psychologists in Pennsylvania.

Of course, the consideration of self-care issues should not emerge only during the years of professional practice, long after first encountering whatever stressors it may present. Instead, it is important to take a proactive position that explores self-care issues from the earliest periods of professional training. Understanding the impact of early training in terms of the beliefs and behaviors of graduate students and faculty role models provides a sobering, yet hopeful perspective. In addition, an examination of the current accreditation standards that shape our foundational academic training in professional psychology provides insight into why self-care remains more likely to be what we say than what we do.

PERSONAL JOURNEY TO SELF-CARE: PERSONAL-PROFESSIONAL DIMENSION (CLARE'S STORY)

The topic of self-care has been integral to my graduate school experience. Early in training I learned in a particularly painful and profoundly personal way the importance of attending to my well-being and preventing distress from affecting my clinical and academic work when my mother unexpectedly passed away in the spring of my second year of graduate school. In our program we begin clinical work in our second year, so I was still very new to clinical work at that point. After taking time off to attend the funeral services and be around family, I realized that I was simply not prepared to come back to my caseload of five clients. Furthermore, in one of those not uncommon twists of fate, one of my clients had similarly just experienced the death of a family member. My initial expectation was that I ought to come back to school, reschedule my clients for return appointments as soon as possible, and fully jump back into my coursework and research responsibilities. This seemed like the appropriate course of action. The lesson learned over many years as a diligent student was that the demands of academic training take precedence over all else.

After my return to Chapel Hill, I quickly realized that this plan was not going to work for me. I felt overwhelmed and could not imagine sitting with a client through an emotionally intense session or dispassionately discussing loss with the client who had recently lost a family member. After consultation with supervisors and advanced graduate students, I decided that it would be best to take some more time off from my clinical duties and to refer out my client who also had a death in the family (I worked with my supervisor to manage this process in a clinically and ethically appropriate manner). The faculty was very supportive and allowed me flexibility in completing assignments. However, practicing this self-care was not without its costs. There were both external and internal stressors. It was not an easy decision to attend to my self-care because like many graduate students I had developed a strong and previously unquestioned conviction that I needed to work through personal struggles no matter what. Despite the support and my decision to give myself some time, I still felt the pressure of clients waiting to be seen and getting the work submitted that was piling up as I grieved the loss of my mother.

When I returned to my clinical and academic duties it was business as usual. The world had kept going and I had to catch up. I felt somewhat rested from my break, albeit overwhelmed by my workload. Importantly, the decision to reenter my work required self-assessment. The importance of self-assessment in such situations is touched upon in Ethical Standard 2.06. While jumping back into one's work can be seen as comforting and a needed distraction, it may also prevent complete recovery from stressful life events. Careful self-reflection and consultation is needed to decide when it is best to go back to work and when it is prudent to take additional time for ones' self.

I learned early in my career that psychologists' personal lives intersect with their professional lives (see Mahoney, 1991). The point of this intersection is not always clear, though. I came to appreciate the difficulty of identifying how life stress negatively impacts one's professional life. The process can be very subtle. Students can quickly move down a path of distress, impairment and burnout if they are not aware of how their personal lives affect their professional duties. I was grateful to be surrounded by supervisors who helped guide me through the process so that I was not faced with the further stress of an immediate return to clinical work or from having my academics suffer.

When the NCPA's Colleague Assistance Committee (CAC) sent an email looking for a graduate student member of their committee during the beginning of my fourth year of graduate school, I was immediately drawn to the idea, having already experienced a very personal appreciation for psychologist self-care. I had developed a commitment to self-care as a result of my personal experience, as well as observing my fellow graduate student peers. I had noticed that many of my peers in graduate school struggled with self-care and that the failure to adequately attend to it took a toll on their clinical and academic work. I hoped that I could become an advocate for graduate student self-care through my involvement in the CAC.

My participation with the CAC has had benefits for me and for the committee. I have become more aware of my self-care. I have also learned early in my professional life about the obstacles that practicing psychologists face in maintaining their self-care and issues that I had yet to consider as a graduate student. For example, I assisted in creating and collecting data for two surveys that were subsequently used to inform two NCPA workshops, namely the impact of the economy on psychologists and another on workplace safety. I compiled both specific and open-ended responses to questions about "pearls of wisdom" and things learned by psychologists in each of the surveys. This cultivated an appreciation for the emotional distress that psychologist face, as well as their resiliency. Importantly, my CAC participation has reminded the practicing psychologists on the committee about the stressors faced by graduate students and the need to attend to implementing self-care at the graduate level of training. The NCPA CAC has now conducted self-care workshops at graduate programs throughout North Carolina. It is clear from the graduate students' responses at these workshops that they are experiencing distress and that they are in need of learning the importance and practice of self-care. The stress and distress endorsed, as well as the desire for learning more about self-care applied to all students regardless of whether they were on a clinical or research career trajectory. In addition to my membership as a graduate student, the NCPA CAC also has an intern and early psychologist on the committee. In this way, the CAC can address the unique challenges that are associated with the various stages of professional development. The work that is being done by the NCPA CAC is informed by a relatively small body of research on graduate student stress and self-care that is summarized below.

DATA ON STRESS AND SELF-CARE IN PSYCHOLOGY GRADUATE STUDENTS

I am not unlike other graduate students in professional psychology programs. Graduate students face a great deal of stress. Many students are juggling numerous duties and responsibilities. Since I am a graduate student and have been well trained to use research to bolster my points, I will provide some data on stress and self-care in psychology graduate students. Cushway (1992) found that 59 percent of clinical psychology graduates students identified as being in distress while in graduate school. In one study, the primary stressors for psychology graduate students were time constraints, difficulty working with faculty and limited financial resources (Cahir & Morris, 1991). Interestingly clinical psychology graduate students more specifically report stress around not attending to their self-care (Dorff, 1998). If unattended to, students are at risk of entering into a vicious cycle where the demands of graduate school initiate stress and their stress is exacerbated by not having the skills to reduce the effect of stress on their work.

Along with coursework, program requirements and teaching comes the new role of being a therapist. Indeed, students report that this contributes to their stress in graduate school (Rodolfa, Kraft & Reilley, 1988). Some reasons for this stress is that less experienced psychologists tend to feel compelled to "fix" their clients, more responsible for client's well-being and are more likely to feel incompetent if their interventions are not effective (Rodolfa et al., 1988). I have certainly found this to be the case in my experience. It has been hard to set boundaries with clients as I wanted to be available to them at the expense of my needs. It was also a slow realization that there were many parts of my clients' lives that were not in my control. If they lost a job, got a separation, or relapsed, I initially felt the burden of these setbacks. Thoughts such as, "If only I had used this intervention they may have not gone back to alcohol," or "If we had focused more on her relationship, this divorce would not have happened…" This has also been a particular issue for me since I specialize in the treatment of the severely mentally ill. My work with this population has been challenging as I am forced to recognize my limitations as a therapist. Aside from feeling powerless over symptoms, many people with severe mental illness struggle with other stressors such as lack of social support and financial resources. It has been emotionally difficult to recognize that I am unable to "cure" all areas of their life. The therapist role is a unique struggle that graduate students in professional psychology confront. We are often not fully equipped to emotionally process this new responsibility.

The good news is that some research shows that clinical psychology graduate students tend to have personality and psychological traits that may help them cope with stress (e.g., extraverted, outgoing, agreeable; Brooks, Holttum, & Lavendar, 2002). Another protective factor is that graduate students tend to be deeply committed to their chosen field of psychology. This commitment to psychology may be an explanation for low levels of professional burnout in clinical psychology graduate students (e.g., Clark, Murdock & Koetting, 2009). Although graduate students may have baseline trainee characteristics that help them cope with stress in graduate school, these need to be reinforced and promoted by programs, and faculty.

COMPETENCE IN TRAINEES AND ETHICAL STANDARDS

It is critical for programs to incorporate self-care in their training. The most compelling reason for this is that life stress can seriously harm students' clinical and academic work. Unlike graduate students in other academic departments, graduate students in professional psychology degree programs are directly providing services to members of the public. As was noted earlier, Principle A of the 2002 APA Ethics Code reminds us that we must be aware of the effects that personal life can have on clinical responsibilities. Similarly, in the enforceable Standards 2.06 (a) and (b), it is further documented that psychologists must refrain from starting an activity where their problems will impair competence. In the event that problems are present, the psychologist must take some type of action to determine whether they should limit work duties. In my case, I sought consultation from my clinical supervisor and an advanced graduate student. Based on the feedback, I temporarily scaled back on my clinical duties.

The issue of competence frequently arises for graduate students. We are evaluated throughout graduate school by clinical and academic supervisors. These evaluations are created by programs and are influenced by APA competence standards. Interestingly, self-care is not currently explicitly included as a core competence in the Commission on Accreditation (CoA) accreditation standards; the APA accreditation Domain B standards of life-long learning converge on this issue of self-care, but do not explicitly address it.

Although self-care is not currently identified as a core competency by CoA, its significance for trainees has been reflected in the competency literature. The Assessment of Competency Benchmarks Work Group was commissioned in 2005 to reevaluate the core competencies for training programs. The Benchmarks Work Group outlined 15 core competencies at three levels of training in the Benchmarks Work Group document, with self-care being identified as a core competency (Fouad et al., 2009). The Benchmarks document is informative but not enforceable. Without the CoA mandating self-care within professional psychology accreditation standards, graduate programs are not currently obligated to ensure that students are learning and integrating self-care issues into their professional lives. Specifically, the Benchmarks Workgroup defines the self-care competence as "attention to personal health and well-being to assure effective professional functioning." For trainees preparing for practica, the essential component for self-care is "understanding of the importance of self-care in effective practice; knowledge of self-care methods; attention to self-care." And, for students preparing for internship, the essential component is defined as "monitoring of issues related to self-care with supervisor; understanding of the central role of self-care to effective practice" (Fouad et al., 2009, p. S11). Another recent influential article on competency similarly endorses self-care as a core competency in trainees. Kamen, Veilleux, Bangen, VanderVeen and Klonoff (2010) administered a competency questionnaire to 641 graduate students in clinical psychology doctoral programs. "Trainee characteristics" was identified as a core competency. The identified characteristics included aspects converging on self-care such as seeking support from friends, balancing work and fun, and tolerating emotion. These aforementioned competency initiatives clearly highlight self-care as a core competency component. Hopefully, this research can be applied and integrated into training programs' curricula.

Training programs are preparing graduate students for a lifetime in clinical work, research and teaching. As part of those programs, it is necessary to start integrating the topic of self-care as has been done with multicultural competence since the mid 1990's. Students report actually not knowing where to start with self-care and how to integrate it into their professional life. One study found that 82% of clinical psychology graduate students would like more attention paid to self-care in their training programs (Montgomery, 2009). This must occur at both the individual and national level.

HOW TO INTEGRATE SELF-CARE INTO GRADUATE PROGRAMS: MACRO- AND MICRO-LEVEL CONSIDERATIONS

In this section I will synthesize my personal and professional experience and make recommendations about what students and programs can do to promote learning of self-care. What follows is an expansion on an article written for the NCPA newsletter in my role as the graduate student member of the CAC (Gibson, 2011).

Clearly, self-care is critical to graduate student functioning. Currently there are no mandated standards in this area. Given the Benchmarks Workgroup's recommendations, it seems possible that self-care will eventually be integrated into the standards for accrediting programs. Until then, the question remains, what can programs and students do now to help promote self-care?

The first suggestion is to openly promote psychotherapy. In some professional psychology training programs, psychotherapy is highly recommended or even required (e.g., psychodynamically oriented programs; McWilliams, 2004); however, many programs do not mandate or specifically encourage psychotherapy. This may unintentionally maintain the stigma attached to psychotherapy and reduce the likelihood of graduate students seeking their own therapy. Indeed, students are less likely to seek out their own therapy if they believe the faculty does not value psychotherapy (Dearing, Maddux & Tangney, 2005). Of course stigma and faculty are not the only barriers to psychotherapy. Dearing et al. (2005) found that other barriers to seeking psychotherapy are cost, time, and confidentiality. Money is a stressor for students and the cost of psychotherapy can be prohibitive for students. Campus counseling centers would be a reasonable alternative for students, but these are sometimes practicum sites. Students may be apprehensive about training in a center where they received mental health services. Psychology graduate students are pressed for time and another meeting in the day may actually be more stressful than helpful.

Given some of the complications around receiving therapy, programs may want to consider making cost-effective therapy readily available to students. One example of this comes from our clinical program at UNC-Chapel Hill. In the past, students in the program were told that the program administrative assistant had a list of local therapists who had agreed to work on a pro-bono basis. There were some problems with this process, though. For one, there was no consideration for confidentiality. Students would have to ask for the "list." Second, this list had not been updated in years. Some of the therapists were no longer in practice or had moved. Third, not many students knew this list was available. It was not advertised anywhere; students had to ask around, thereby compromising both anonymity and confidentiality.

A UNC graduate student colleague realized that this process of getting the "list" was arduous and not responsive to students who might be in need of psychotherapy. She took the initiate to streamline this process for students so that confidentiality was respected. First, she called the therapists on the list to find out who was still in practice and willing to work on a sliding scale for graduate students. She sent out an email to therapists in the area inquiring who would be willing to be added to this list. An updated list of local therapists was created and included in the clinical handbook. Clinical students could then easily access psychotherapy options. Importantly, the accessibility of this resource demonstrates that the UNC clinical program is open to students seeking therapy. This is a simple and effective tool that programs could adapt.

Graduate faculty and clinical supervisors serve as professional models. This professional modeling includes self-care. But, as Erica pointed out earlier, psychologists struggle with effectively attending to their own self-care. Thus, it is critical for them to first attend to their stress management and to model this for their students. Unsurprisingly, there are reports that graduate students do not have adequate role models for self-care (DeAngelis, 2002). Faculty and supervisors are strongly encouraged to consider their influence on students. When they practice their own self-care they can communicate this to trainees. In my own experience, I have been influenced by my supervisors' advice about taking care of myself and observing their methods of integrating self-care into their lives.

The social support literature repeatedly documents the protective elements of relationships (Taylor et al., 2000). Within the graduate student and stress literature, sense of community (SOC) has shown to be an important variable. SOC is defined as a sense of belonging to a community, working towards a common goal, and a belief that the community will meet one's needs (Chavis & Newbrough, 1986). SOC is more comprehensive and inclusive than social support. It provides a sense of meaning and commitment. Clark et al. (2009) found that SOC predicted burnout and career satisfaction in counseling psychology graduate students. This finding speaks to the importance of fostering a SOC in graduate programs. Programs should not overlook the importance of socials and events that bring students together. It also highlights the academic and emotional benefits of student and faculty collaboration.

In the same study that explored SOC, Clark et al. (2009) analyzed specific social relationships, such as peers, family and mentors. The authors found that the advisor relationship was strongly related to stress in doctoral students. Interestingly, the advisor relationship was the only relationship predictive of burnout. That is, as compared to friends and family, it was the advisor-student relationship that was most strongly predictive of burnout. This certainly underscores the importance of the advisor relationship in graduate programs. Advisors should be mindful of their role in students' well-being and ensure they attend to the relationship. One way that this relationship can be fostered is through regularly scheduled individual meetings.

The beneficial effects of participation in a community extend beyond graduate school, of course, and into professional practice. Knapp and VandeCreek (2012) have noted the relationship between membership in a state psychological association and a reduction in the number of actions brought against psychologists' licenses for ethical misconduct. The intentional development of a sense of community (SOC) can serve as an important factor that supports the well-being of the therapist and his or her capacity to practice effectively and ethically.

Most importantly, issues of self-care need to be integrated into professional training at the earliest opportunity, as part of their graduate training programs. Students have shown that they are unsure how to attend to their well-being. Thus, programs can start to integrate self-care into courses and within in-house workshops. Rather than seeing self-care as a discrete topic to be taught in a class, it can very easily be interwoven within the curriculum. Appropriate classes for this topic are in clinical didactics, psychotherapy classes or ethics courses. In addition, issues related to graduate student self-care can be the focus of workshops or seminars throughout year. The NCPA Colleagues Assistance Committee (CAC), for example, has held workshops at a variety of graduate programs including UNC-Chapel Hill. These workshops put self-care on students' radar, provide them a space to discuss their struggles, and normalize the stressors of graduate school.

SELF-CARE AT THE STUDENT LEVEL

While programs and the APA can work to promote self-care, students can take initiative to start attending to their well-being early in their professional lives. The most effective way to attend to self-care is to monitor stress and coping. Some forms of psychotherapy that emphasize an attunement to the therapists own feelings have been found to be positively related to levels of self-care (Brucato & Neimeyer, 2009). Students can start to become mindful of the stress-distress continuum and monitor their own stress levels (see Epstein, Seigel & Silberman, 2008). It is easy to get carried away with the stress of graduate school and overlook its impact on clinical and academic work. Students should remember that early intervention can help prevent impairment and burnout.

In the event that students are experiencing stress, they may consider utilizing their social support system. Increased social support has been cited as an effective coping strategy in reducing graduate student stress (Montgomery, 2009). Students may also find it helpful to normalize their distress by talking to other graduate students. Many internships offer support groups for interns to process the stress around clinical work. Perhaps graduate programs can similarly implement voluntary process groups. In fact, this is a time when it may be most needed since graduate students are new to their provider role.

Students should also consider seeking out counseling to cope with stress. Regardless of whether students are more research oriented, graduate school is a stressful period and all students can benefit from psychotherapy. One specific intervention that has been found to be efficacious for graduate students is mindfulness training. Shapiro, Brown and Biegel (2000) found that mindfulness training prevented psychological stress, decreased negative affect and rumination, and increased positive affect in trainees. Another study found that mindfulness training in trainees was even related to better outcome in their clients (Grepmair et al., 2007).

CONCLUSION

It is critical for graduate students to start to identify when their level of stress is impacting their work and life. Attending to stress early on in training can set the stage for healthy professional habits. Self-care is a valuable area to focus on as it has a significant impact on personal and professional satisfaction. Moreover, self-care directly minimizes the risk of ethical problems arising from impairment and results in good clinical practice. It is therefore imperative for the APA and CoA to strongly encourage or even mandate that programs integrate the learning of self-care into foundational doctoral training. An important reality to consider, though, is that it can be arduous and painstaking for programs to alter their already packed curriculum. However, if the learning of self-care principles and strategies can be interwoven into the already existing curriculum (e.g., a self-care module could be included in a psychotherapy or ethics course), it would likely ease the transition into program requirements. We may not be too far off from such a curriculum adjustment given the Benchmarks Workgroup recent competency recommendations. In the end, though, programs, students, and the clients they treat may all become beneficiaries of the increased attention to issues of self-care.

BIOSKETCHES

ERICA H. WISE is Clinical Professor and Director of the Psychology Training Clinic for the Department of Psychology at UNC-Chapel Hill. She teaches doctoral level courses that focus on clinical theory and practice, ethics and diversity. She is a former chair of the APA Ethics Committee and the North Carolina Psychology Board. She is a frequent presenter and consultant on ethical issues in clinical psychology. Her professional interests include education and training, psychotherapy outcome research and applications of ethics and self-care in academic and professional practice settings. She strives to incorporate high standards of professional practice and self-care into all of her endeavors.

CLARE M. GIBSON is an advanced clinical psychology doctoral student at UNC-Chapel Hill. She completed her bachelor's degree at Binghamton University with highest honors. Clare's clinical and research interests are in psychotherapy for severe mental illness and treatment in the early course of psychosis. Her dissertation is evaluating the impact of intranasal oxytocin on social cognition and social functioning in schizophrenia. Clare's involvement in professional psychology has included two years as a graduate student member of NCPA's Colleague Assistance Committee (CAC). Clare will be completing her internship at the Veterans Affairs Maryland Health Care System-University of Maryland Baltimore Consortium.

REFERENCES

Advisory Committee on Colleague Assistance (n.d.). *The stress-distress-impairment continuum for psychologists*. Retrieved April 30, 2011 from the American Psychological Association, Practice Organization Web site: http://www.apapracticecentral.org/ce/self-care/colleague-assist.aspx

American Heritage Dictionary of the English language. (1970). New York: American Heritage.

American Psychological Association (2002). Ethical principles of psychologists and code of conduct. *American Psychologist*, 57, 1060-1073.

Baker, E. (2002). Caring for ourselves as psychologists. *Register Report*, 2-7.

Barnett, J.E. Baker, E.K., Elman, N.S. & Schoener, G.R. (2007). In pursuit of wellness: The self-care imperative, *Professional Psychology: Research and practice, 38,* 603-612.

Brooks, J., Holttumm, S., & Lavender, A. (2002). Personality style, psychological adaptation, and expectations of trainee clinical psychologists. *Clinical Psychology and Psychotherapy, 9,* 253-270.

Brucato, B., & Neimeyer, G.J. (2009). Epistemology as a predictor of therapists' self-care and coping. *Journal of Constructivist Psychology, 22,* 269-282.

Cahir, N. & Morris, R.D. (1991). The psychology stress questionnaire. *Journal of Clinical Psychology, 47,* 414-417.

Chavis, D. M., & Newbrough, J. (1986). The meaning of "community" in community psychology. *Journal of Community Psychology, 14,* 335-340.

Clark, H.K, Murdock, N.L., & Koetting, K. (2009). Predicting burnout and career choice satisfaction in counseling psychology graduate students. *The Counseling Psychologist, 37,* 580-606.

Cushway, D. (1992). Stress in clinical psychology trainees. *British Journal of Clinical Psychology, 31,* 169-179.

Diener, E. & Diener, C. (1996). Most people are happy. *Psychological Science, 3,* 181-185.

DeAngelis, T. (2002). Normalizing practitioners' stress. *Monitor on Psychology, 33,* 62–64.

Dearing, R.L., Maddux, J.E., & Tangney, J.P. (2005). Predictors of psychological help seeking in clinical and counseling psychology graduate students. *Professional Psychology: Research and Practice, 36,* 323-329.

Dorff, T. (1998). A needs assessment of the stressors and coping resources of graduate students in clinical psychology. (Doctoral dissertation). Retrieved from EBSCOhost. (Accession number 1998-95010-122).

Emmons, R. A. & Crumpler, C.A. (2000). Gratitude as a human strength: Appraising the evidence. *Journal of Social and Clinical Psychology, 19,* 56-69.

Epstein, R.M., Seigel, D.J., & Silberman, J. (2008) Self-monitoring in clinical practice: A challenge for medical educators. *Journal of Continuing Education in the Health Professions, 28,* 5-13.

Fouad, N. A., Grus, C. L., Hatcher, R. L., Kaslow, N. J., Hutchings, P., Madson, M. B., ... Crossman, R. E. (2009). Competency benchmarks: A model for understanding and measuring competence in professional psychology across training levels. *Training and Education in Professional Psychology, 3,* S5-S26.

Gibson, C.M. (2011, March/April). Self-care for graduate students: Tips for programs *and* students. *North Carolina Psychological Association Newsletter, 63,* 4.

Grepmair, L, Mitterlehner, F., Loew, T., Bachler, E., Rother, W., & Nickel, M. (2007). Promoting mindfulness in psychotherapists in training influences the treatment results in their patients: A randomized, double-blind, controlled study. *Psychotherapy and Psychosomatics, 76,* 332-338.

Kamen, C., Veilleux, J. C., Bangen, K. J., VanderVeen, J. W., & Klonoff, E. A. (2010). Climbing the stairway to competency: Trainee perspectives on competency development. *Training and Education in Professional Psychology, 4,* 227-234.

Knapp, S., & Sturm, C. (2002). Ethics education after licensing: Ideas for increasing diversity in content and process. *Ethics and Behavior, 12,* 157-166.

Knapp, S., & VandeCreek, L. (2012). Disciplinary actions by a state board of psychology: Do gender and association membership matter? An update. In G. J. Neimeyer, and J. M. Taylor (Eds.), *Continuing professional development and lifelong learning: Issues, impacts and outcomes* (pp.151-154). Hauppauge, NY: Nova Science Publishers.

Linehan, M.M. (1993). *Skills training manual for treating borderline personality disorder.* New York, NY: The Guilford Press.

Mahoney, M.J. (1991) *Human Change Processes: The Scientific Foundations of Psychotherapy.* New York: Basic Books.

Mahoney, M. (1997). Psychotherapists' personal problems and self-care patterns. *Professional Psychology: Research and Practice, 28*, 14-16.

McWilliams, N. (2004). *Psychoanalytic Psychotherapy: A Practitioner's Guide.* New York, NY: The Guilford Press.

Montgomery, C. (2009). *Professional psychology training programs: Program interventions and prediction of doctoral student stress and life satisfaction.* (Doctoral dissertation). Retrieved from PsycINFO. (Accession number 2010-99160-403).

Myers, D.G. (2000). The funds, friends, and faith of happy people, *American Psychologist, 55*, 56-67.

Neimeyer, G.J., Taylor, J.M., & Wear, D. (2010). Continuing education in psychology: Patterns of participation and aspects of selection. *Professional Psychology: Research and Practice, 41*, 281-287.

Norcross, J.C., & Guy, J.D. (2007) *Leaving it at the office: A guide to psychotherapist self-care.* New York: Guilford.

Norcross, J.C. & Barnett, J.E. (n.d.). *Self-Care as Ethical Imperative.* Retrieved April 30, 2011 from the National Register web site: http://www.e-psychologist.org/index.iml?mdl=exam/show_article.mdlandMaterial_ID=80.

Pope, K. S., & Vasquez, M.J.T. (2005) *How to survive and thrive as a therapist: Information, ideas, and resources for psychologists in practice.* Washington, DC: American Psychological Association.

Rodolfa, E. R., Kraft, W. A., & Reilley, R. R. (1988). Stressors of professionals and rainees at APA-approved counseling and VA medical center internship sites. *Professional Psychology: Research and Practice, 19*, 43-49.

Ryan, R. M., & Deci, E.L. (2000). Self-determination theory and the facilitation of intrinsic motivation, social development, and well-being. *American Psychologist, 55*, 68-78.

Schwartz, B., Ward, A., Monterosso, J., Lyubomirsky, S., White, K., & Lehman, D.R. (2002). Maximizing versus satisfying: Happiness is a matter of choice. *Journal of Personality and Social Psychology, 83*, 1178-1197.

Shapiro, S.L., Brown, K.W., & Biegel, G.M. (2000). Teaching self-care to caregivers: Effects of mindfulness-based stress reduction on the mental health of therapists in training. *Training and Education in Professional Psychology, 1*, 105-115.

Sturm, C. A. (2010). Challenges in implementing continuing professional education. *Professional Psychology: Research and Practice, 41*, 292-294.

Taylor, S. E., Klein, L. C., Lewis, B. P., Gruenewald, T. L., Gurung, R. A, & Updegraff, J. A. (2000). Biobehavioral responses to stress in females: Tend-and befriend, not fight-or-flight. *Psychological Review, 107*, 411-429.

Webb, K. (2006). Self-evaluation: How am I doing in my practice? *The North Carolina Psychologist, 58*, 1 and 16.

Wise, E.H. (2008). Competence and scope of practice: Ethics and professional development. *Journal of Clinical Psychology: In Session, 65,* 626-637.

Wise, E.H. (2010) Maintaining competence in professional psychology: Obsolescence, life-long learning and continuing education. *Professional Psychology: Research and Practice, 41,* 288-292.

In: Continuing Professional Development ...
Editors: G. J. Neimeyer and J. M. Taylor

ISBN: 978-1-62100-767-8
© 2012 Nova Science Publishers, Inc.

Chapter 13

THE PRACTITIONER'S INTENSE SEARCH FOR KNOWING IN A SEA OF AMBIGUITY: ANSWERS FROM THE LEARNING TRIANGLE OF PRACTICE, ACADEMIC RESEARCH AND PERSONAL LIFE

Thomas M. Skovholt[1],* and Michael T. Starkey[2]
[1] University of Minnesota, US
[2] University of Rhode Island, US

> No one who, like me, conjures up the most evil of those half-tamed demons that inhabit the human breast, and seeks to wrestle with them, can expect to come through the struggle unscathed.
>
> (Freud, cited in Schneider and May, 1995, p. 19)

ABSTRACT

In this chapter, we introduce several guides that serve as our knowledge base in the helping professions, while paying close attention to managing ambiguity and developing wisdom. Practitioners are often exposed to profound and complex human problems, and these existential tensions can remind practitioners of their own state of being. This can make the work confusing. In searching for answers practitioners become aware that there are no steadfast, ready-made solutions to ease client pain. In a field filled with so much uncertainty, professional education across the lifespan becomes vital. But where should practitioners turn for their education? We propose that practitioner expertise is like a learning triangle, with lessons from practice, research and theory, and the practitioner's personal life. All three sides are vital for optimal practitioner functioning.

Keywords: Uncertainty, Wisdom, Practice, Research, Personal Life, Learning Triangle

---

[*] Correspondence regarding this manuscript may be directed to Thomas M. Skovholt, Ph.D., 160 EdSciB, 56 East River Rd., Minneapolis, MN 55455.

Counselors and psychotherapists have a unique vantage point, one that is rivaled by few professions. The opportunity to help people navigate their lives—to sit with others while they create meaning and gain insight, to be trusted with unadulterated vulnerability—is an unmatched privilege. The material clients present is complex, mysterious, and sometimes distressing, a world full of wonderment, awe, pain, and despair. The view of that world, therefore, can be inspiring and frightening, and the profession is chosen by those who are willing to constantly enter this ambiguous arena.

Part of a "guild of healers" (Yalom, 2002, p. 259), counselors and psychotherapists are regarded with both great respect and quiet suspicion (Guy, 1987). Most individuals seek treatment to ease psychic pain, and practitioners are thought to play a large part in relieving that pain (Beutler et al., 2005). Day in and day out, practitioners—for hours on end—enter the client's personal world. These exchanges are often wrought with themes of loss, betrayal, isolation, and trauma. From those therapist-client exchanges emerge an unpredictable constellation of emotions: sadness, anger, terror, anxiety, shame, joy, and wonderment. This encounter is vitally important for the client and also significant for the counselor or psychotherapist. Therapist self-care and resilience is of central importance in this equation (Skovholt & Trotter-Mathison, 2011).

Not many professions offer the opportunity to view the human condition in the way that the counseling and therapy professions offer. Client stories of pain and struggle are not only a part of the work, they are also necessary. Working with clients to disinfect those wounded parts seems to be richly rewarding for practitioners (Starkey, 2010). This reward has a shadow, however. Counselors and psychotherapists, in order to help clients move through pain, bear witness to some of the most horrific acts of humanity, alongside some of the most prosocial, altruistic acts. Working so closely with the human condition can create feelings of powerlessness, anger, sadness, frustration, along with joy and excitement. This is the affective territory, one that counselors and psychotherapists cannot avoid. The effect of listening to and being immersed in existential pain is not an emotionally uninvolved job; it appears that it is nearly impossible for practitioners to not be affected personally by the practice of psychotherapy (Skovholt & Trotter-Mathisen, 2011; Starkey, 2010).

Being a counselor or psychotherapist influences all aspects of a person's being. In a study of how the work affects the practitioner, a consistent finding emerged: the work affects all aspects of the practitioner's life (Starkey, 2010). Participants of the study spoke at length about how being a counselor or psychotherapist influences, on a deep level, their everyday existence and serves as a fulfillment of the practitioner's identity. According to the participants, counselors and therapists are as vulnerable as clients, and experience the joy of being alive, as well as life's ever present shadow: meaninglessness, sickness, being alone, and the march towards death (Yalom, 2002). The work of therapy seems to help the practitioner approach and engage all these aspects of living—the inspiring as well as the frightening.

As a result of practice, counselors and psychotherapists develop a broad lens into the workings of human life (Starkey, 2010). This lens seems to allow a view of the human condition that few see. Because of this, practitioners are exposed to a wide range of human thought, emotion, and experience, which, in turn can open them to experiences within themselves that may have otherwise been left dormant. Now, this can be both burden and opportunity. Indeed, Yalom (2002) echoes this when he stated that the profession requires:

arduous, never-ending self-scrutiny and inner work...But that very requirement is more privilege than burden because it is an inbuilt strategy against stagnation. The active therapist is always evolving, continuously growing in self-knowledge and awareness. How can one possibly guide others in an examination of the deep structures of mind and existence without simultaneously examining oneself? (p. 256)

Perhaps one of the greatest benefits practitioners encounter at work is learning from and being helped by clients (Starkey, 2010; Kottler, 2003; Ronnestad & Skovholt, 2003; Yalom, 2002). Not many professions primarily focus on the challenges, lessons, and hopes of life, and how to engage them more fully. Clients may come to therapy with a desire to piece together a broken, sometimes shattered, life. Not only are we privy to the client's pain, we are also witness to the client's courage and resiliency while confronting that pain. (Skovholt et al., 2004; Starkey, 2010). In fact, Carl Jung "claimed that therapy work[s] best when the patient [brings] the perfect salve for the therapist's wound and that if the therapist doesn't change, then the patient doesn't either" (Yalom, 2002, p. 107).

Many times clients come to the space of the therapeutic hour with expectations—both overt and covert—that their problems will be solved, that they will receive an answer to a fundamental question about human existence. Such questions include: How shall I live? What meaning does my life have? How can I move on from an incredible loss? Questions like these ensue day after day, and at the heart of these questions lies a yearning to live more fully, more freely, and more authentically. Either unconsciously or consciously, clients believe that the counselor or psychotherapist has the answer, that the practitioner can quell the circling storm.

THE PRACTITIONER'S INTENSE SEARCH FOR ANSWERS IN ORDER TO EASE CLIENT PAIN

Counselors and psychotherapists, then, are driven by an intense search for answers to ease client pain (Skovholt & Starkey, 2010). The goal is to find definitive answers for the client, like the proverbial hot knife cutting through butter. A client has a problem to solve; the practitioner seeks an answer to give. Oftentimes, though, there are no concrete, steadfast answers. Indeed, some would argue (e.g., Yalom, 2002) that it is not the counselor or psychotherapist's job to teach the client how to love, how to recover from a profound loss, or how to nurture one's self. Instead, it is the practitioner's job to help the client identify and remove obstacles that are precluding optimal growth. But, just as there are as many questions as clients, there are just as many obstacles—if not more. So, where does the beneficent practitioner turn for answers? And, perhaps more importantly, how can the practitioner tolerate the ambiguity that is so inherent to the counseling and psychotherapy professions?

In counseling and psychotherapy's not so distant past, a push towards empirically supported treatments came to the forefront (e.g., Chambless & Hollon, 1998; Kendall, 1998). One of the well-intentioned ideas behind this movement was to manualize therapy: to assess a distressed person, place a diagnostic label on him or her, and then follow a manual to guide treatment decisions. It could be argued that the goal was to make clinicians masters of technique, to find problems and use a specific solution. This is very much the medical model: diagnose, treat, repeat. However, any practitioner who has practiced for a period of time recognizes that working with clients is not this simple. Practitioners deal with a very murky reality, one that often changes within the course of clinical treatment (Yalom, 2002). As more clinical material emerges, clients become more complex. Shouldn't treatment follow suit? Unfortunately—or perhaps fortunately—the practitioner's office becomes an environment of increasing complexity and uncertainty.

It is the job of the practitioner, then, to accept uncertainty while striving for certainty (Skovholt & Starkey, 2010). Counselors and psychotherapists begin to realize that the circle of not knowing grows as quickly as the circle of knowing and that ambiguity is an intimate part of the counseling and therapy professions. True knowing is a desert mirage: just as a person approaches, the mirage moves away; the longed-for nourishment is out of reach again and never grasped—a frustrating realization for the advancing graduate student and young professional (Skovholt & Starkey, 2010). In any given therapeutic hour, there is so much material: what is said and not said, what is nonverbally communicated. In this way, counselors and psychotherapists have a uniquely difficult job. The task of taking in ambiguous information, of making sense out of it, of helping a client work through difficult material can be intimidating. Indeed, Reed (2006) discusses 33 variables that are interacting in any given counseling or psychotherapy session. If there are 33 variables interacting in any given session, this leaves 1,089 different possibilities of exploration in any given hour. It is easy to see that the sheer ambiguity of the work can confuse, baffle, and even frighten.

This paradoxical quest—the intense search for answers while accepting the swampy reality of human complexity—is a life-long journey, and one not confined only to clients or the practitioner's office. Practitioners are also human confronting the same existential realities as their clients (Starkey, 2010; Yalom, 1989). The idea that counseling and therapy might be a paint by numbers application is enticing. All the practitioner would have to do is learn a method, a technique, an empirically supported treatment, or a manualized approach, and apply it. Unfortunately, the client is not a canvas to paint, but rather a living, thinking human being with difficult problems. Because counselors and psychotherapists share similar existential tension, the problems encountered by clients are often our own. What makes this more difficult is that answers to life's big questions (e.g., what is the meaning of my life? or How shall I live in the face of death?) are so convoluted and multifaceted, that an answer for one person will be completely different for another.

Uncertainty has been a thorn in the side of human kind for millennia: "The unexplained—especially the fearful unexplained—can not be tolerated for long…Giving a name to chaotic, unruly forces provides us with a sense of mastery or control" (Yalom, 1995, p. 84). However, there is an excitement that can come with the unknown. Consider, for example, a new path discovered or even the entrance into parenthood. With each of these there is likely to be a mixture of excitement and trepidation. The practitioner who can learn to accept ambiguity and work with it may expect a renewed sense of vitality in the work, for with ambiguity comes a sense of newness, of something to be discovered.

The hallmark feature of counseling and psychotherapy is ambiguity. This profession lacks a research-sought precision, which is craved by practitioners. When discussing the topic, Yalom (1989) states:

> Indeed, the capacity to tolerate uncertainty is prerequisite for the profession. Though the public may believe that therapists guide patients systematically and sure-handedly

through predictable stages of therapy to a foreknown goal, such is rarely the case: instead…therapists frequently wobble, improvise, and grope for direction. (p. 13)

So, one question beckons: how do practitioners manage the ambiguity, the uncertainty, and negotiate the convoluted material? The first task is the career-long process of reluctantly accepting the world of uncertainty. There is a second task, a more formidable one, indeed: the acquisition of personal wisdom (Skovholt & Starkey, 2010).

THE DEVELOPMENT OF PERSONAL WISDOM

Some discussion about applying a treatment to a particular problem or client has already been put forth. In an editorial by Garry Cooper (2011), he describes a similar move towards providing psychology graduate students with a curriculum of strict science and empirically supported treatments, espoused by Timothy Baker, Richard McFall, and Varda Shoham, which Cooper referred to as "the Baker report" (Cooper, p. 11). There have been criticisms of the Baker report, which include an argument that the Baker report advocates a too narrow and rigid view of counseling and psychotherapy. The critics contend that this report ignored relational factors that have consistently been related to positive outcome.

Cooper (2011) goes on to argue that "rather than moving in the direction of quantitative science, some believe that today's therapists should look for greater understanding of their fundamental task to the age-old concept of wisdom" (p. 11). He cites Heidi Levitt—a researcher at the University of Massachusetts, Boston—who is adamant that the acquisition of therapeutic wisdom lies well outside of providing manualized treatments and knowing the clinical research. Indeed, she and a colleague (Elizabeth Piazza-Bonin) studied a group of therapists who had been identified by their peers as exemplifying wisdom in psychotherapy. They wanted to discover what these therapists thought the task of therapy to be and characteristics these wise therapists had in common. They found that this group of therapists did not consider themselves problem solvers or technical robots; rather, these therapists emphasized empathetic listening and recognizing the importance of drawing on their own life experiences to properly attune to their clients' experiences. Cooper goes on to report, "rather than moving quickly to resolve their clients' doubts, questions, and confusion, they were at home with tolerating and exploring life's messy ambiguities" (p. 12). And, according to Cooper, Levitt argues this:

> Rather than reward students who come up with answers, we should teach students to spend more time on learning to develop questions…Maybe we should admit students by looking at their interpersonal skills, their capacity for empathy, and their ability to tolerate ambiguity. (p. 12)

In a related vein, a study of Master Therapists (Jennings & Skovholt, 1999; Skovholt, Jennings, & Mullenbach, 2004) showed the therapist's personal qualities make therapeutic differences. Their personal qualities were not one-dimensional, though. These elite therapists were highly developed on several different domains. They embodied different cognitive characteristics (e.g., a voracious appetite for learning), relational characteristics (e.g., an uncanny ability to engage clients deeply), and emotional characteristics (e.g., a refined sense of self-awareness), and the fusion of these domains helped them proceed in times of great uncertainty. The master therapists in these studies taught that therapeutic mastery involved developing, on many different (and deep) levels, as a person. Indeed, Wampold (2007) reported: "there is increasing evidence that it is the therapist and not the treatment per se that is responsible for therapeutic change" (p. 868).

Learning a technique takes a few hours: anyone can learn the basics of diaphragmatic breathing to help someone decrease anxiety in a matter of minutes. Do these techniques work? Of course they do. The argument here, though, is that the practice of counseling and psychotherapy is much more complex than applying a set of techniques to a person. To really sit with someone as he or she moves through pain and out to the other side of life meaning, enrichment, and purposeful living takes more than technical expertise. It takes wisdom as a human being, a task that takes years to master. Bales and Staudinger (2000) say this about the topic: "wisdom [is] an expertise in the conduct and meaning of life... knowledge and judgment about the essence of the human condition and the ways and means of planning, managing, and understanding a good life" (p. 124). Becoming a wiser and more mature human being is an elusive, slippery, and difficult road to traverse; indeed, it is a life long journey (Skovholt & Starkey, 2010).

These two tasks—striving towards personal maturity and wisdom, and searching for certainty while accepting uncertainty—are by no means reserved for the classroom. Being a counselor or psychotherapist has far-reaching effects on the practitioner (Starkey, 2010). Thus, to become a good clinician, the practitioner's person—his or her sense of self—has to be affected. Many of the participants in the Starkey study talked about the sacredness of the profession and how being a practitioner provides a sense of personal meaning. One said this:

> I like to think [practicing psychotherapy] has deepened me...I think the experience of being with people as they are moving in their life in ways that are increasingly gratifying to them is pretty damn rewarding, and moving with people through a lot of pain and out through the other side is also...I think there is a sacredness about what we do that's very apparent to me... (p. 53)

Another participant in Starkey's (2010) study talked about the profession in this way: "I'm very proud of it; I think it's a noble profession...It stimulates me to continue to study the field because I feel it's a sacred obligation to do the job properly" (p. 53). The sacredness that comes with practice is felt on a very deep, personal level. Therefore, practice and practitioner are not easily separated, which makes it vitally important for the practitioner to learn not only about technique, not only about interpersonal styles, not only about the mind's defensive structures, but also to learn deeply about oneself, how one contributes to the process, and, indeed, how to live the best possible life.

Two premises at the core of counseling and psychotherapy are these: this field is uncertain and greater personal wisdom helps the mature therapist to not only understand uncertainty, but to embrace it as well (Skovholt & Starkey, 2010; Duncan, 2010). This is the foundation of good work—the development of expertise and the drive towards mastery starts here. One question ensues, though: how does the maturing counselor or therapist begin to accept uncertainty and develop personal wisdom? We suggest that three guides exist to help the practitioner navigate the search for therapeutic wisdom, traverse the therapeutic terrain, and begin the path towards therapeutic excellence.

THE PRACTITIONER'S LEARNING TRIANGLE

There is no passivity in wisdom. The path towards therapeutic mastery is not one-dimensional, and it is a very active process. Graduate schools in counseling and psychotherapy are concerned with the following questions: What sources of knowledge are acceptable for practitioner development? Where do practitioners get their best ideas for the highly complex and difficult counseling and therapy enterprise? What epistemology—practitioner experience, personal life, or academic research—can we use? And, finally, and perhaps most importantly: which are acceptable?

The data for practice comes from an integration of larger guiding principles of theory and research, the rich experience database of practice, and lessons from the personal life of practitioners (Skovholt & Starkey, 2010). This is a learning triangle. One side contains the enormous knowledge base that comes from insights gained from reflective practice. A second is made of the useful theory and research applied to helping clients live richer, more meaningful lives. The third side of the triangle is comprised of the practitioner's life which offers wisdom about the human story. There exists a great tension in the profession about the use of these three knowledge bases. Each on its own provides us with rich data, but each, when used exclusively, is not necessarily sufficient to understand the complex nature of a client's life. All three sides are necessary to form the epistemological triangle of knowledge for the practitioner.

Wampold (2007) says that counselors and psychotherapists walk a tightrope between the accepted world of science and medicine and the less accepted world of the religious, spiritual and cultural. What is proposed here is a balance of knowledge among all aspects of practice, a model that legitimizes all three sides of the triangle.

Being a counselor or psychotherapist is a job that affects the practitioner on many profound levels (Starkey, 2010). The identity of the therapist is so important to therapeutic outcome (Norcross & Guy, 2007), that it cannot be just a job; practice becomes a way of life. Many of the participants in Starkey's study discussed how the difference between personal and professional life is an arbitrary distinction. Others discussed recognizing the desire to be helpers from a very young age. In this way, being a psychotherapist is a manifestation of the self, which can be an insurmountable privilege: "One of our preeminent satisfactions is the ability to integrate vocation with our identity…what we do with who we are" (Norcross & Guy, 2007, p. 186).

To have a vocation that allows for fulfillment of the self is a great opportunity. It appears as if, day in and day out, counselors and psychotherapists are given the opportunity to manifest very intimate, very deep parts of themselves. Some counselors and psychotherapists speak of how they were made to practice counseling and psychotherapy, of how being a counselor or psychotherapist is such a huge part of their identity. One person in Starkey's (2010) study thinks being a counselor or psychotherapist is a calling or a mission as if something deep within will not rest until she has found what she was looking for (see also Norcross & Guy, 2007). Counselors and psychotherapists seem to be drawn to this work because of an innate drive to understand other people, to help them through pain, to be with them as they come out the other side of despair (Kottler, 2003). If we look at it from these perspectives, counseling and psychotherapy cannot just be learned in a classroom, the learning has to be multifaceted. This is where the three sides of the triangle are so useful.

PRACTICE AS A SIDE OF THE TRIANGLE

> My patients have been—here, as always—my richest source of learning, and I am indebted to them.
>
> (May, 1972, p. 15)

A wide scale, international study of counselors and psychotherapists found that interaction with clients was the number one source of learning and professional development (Orlinsky & Ronnestad, 2005). These practitioners reported that their own hundreds and hundreds of hours of practice were the foundation of how they learned how to be an effective practitioner. It is nearly impossible to sit with clients who try to give meaning to their innermost experiences and not be affected by this interaction. Attempting to put a number on how many utterances of a particular word or how many nonverbal expressions were made during a therapeutic interaction is a daunting task and likely an impossible one, so it makes sense that experienced therapists rate their clients as their number one source of knowledge (Ronnestad & Skovholt, 2003). As practitioners sit with clients to help them move through pain, there is an intimate view into how client problems develop (Skovholt & Starkey, 2010). Research tries to capture commonalities among the multifaceted ways existence pain develops. However, as practitioners work with clients, we are exposed to the astounding variability of human life. Arguably, research attempts to control ambiguous phenomena, but as practitioners continue to be exposed to many different clients, there comes a realization that much of what a human being endures cannot be quantified. This is why learning from practice is so vital for developing expertise (Chi et al., 1988; Stahl et al., 2009).

The seat of the counselor and psychotherapist is a privileged one (Starkey, 2010). Counselors and psychotherapists witness, on a daily basis, the unfolding of a human life. Working with clients as they move through incredible pain can be awe-inspiring and a fertile ground for learning. The participants in Starkey's study reported that being a counselor or psychotherapist offers a very honored seat where client acts of resilience, courage, and growth are witnessed.

So far, the discussion has been about how counselors and psychotherapists learn about practice from their clients. Another type of learning occurs as a result of practice: lessons in the process of being alive and of moving through pain (Starkey, 2010). Generally, clients seek counseling and psychotherapy because they are in some sort of distress. It is easy to believe that exposure to so much pain and suffering on a daily basis may be burdensome to a practitioner. Interestingly, however, the opposite seems to be true. The respondents of Starkey's study stated that they were largely fortified by being exposed to so much human suffering. To be with clients who are in pain actually gave them tools to deal with their own wounds and their own suffering. So, not only are counselors and psychotherapists learning how to help other clients from practice but they are also learning how to help themselves during times of distress.

A close reading of many books written by prominent counselors and psychotherapists reveals that they dedicate their work to their clients. One reason for this is that most of their learning has come from clients with whom they have worked so intimately. Similarly, most psychology professors forego the use of literature and scholarship on teaching and use their own teaching and experiences in the classroom to guide their own teaching style and method.

(Thomas Brothen, teaching award winner in psychology, personal communication, September 3, 2007). Other examples, such as judging client readiness or the timing of interventions, come from many, many hours of interacting with clients.

As part of their graduate training, beginning counselors and psychotherapists are so often exposed to the "right way" of working with clients. Examples have been given above about empirically supported treatments and manualized interventions. These movements tell us that practice should be guided by research— positive and well-intentioned ideas. However, as counselors and therapists become more and more exposed to client problems, they learn about the limitations of the scientific method. The work is dominated by single case studies, not large numbers of people who were chosen by strict inclusion criteria. The tales that clients tell are wrought with so many different emotions and so many different variables that quantification of this material is to simplify human experience. The research method is handy here, but not completely useful. Yet, to use reflection on practice as a sole contributor to one's knowledge about practice is also problematic. This is why the use of the other two sides of the triangle becomes so important.

Counselors and psychotherapists who are both a part of the practice and research cultures (e.g., a professor who has a private practice) reported that they seldom used research findings in their practice (Lebow, 2006). Of course, this does not mean that research should be abandoned and practitioners should have free range to do as they please. There are two potential interpretations of this finding. First interpretation: practitioners should use research more in their work; the second: researchers need to start researching ideas that are more relevant to the practicing counselor or psychotherapist. Perhaps it should be both.

Many clinicians entered the helping professions in order to help other people, to be involved in the process of client growth and satisfaction. As a consequence of this pursuit, counselors and psychotherapists incur indelible benefits to their personhood (Starkey, 2010). The work allows practitioners to fulfill deep personality yearnings and allows a manifestation of those yearnings in everyday contact with clients. Watching clients change and grow gives practitioners the vicarious benefit of the challenge to be constantly growing and learning. It is important for practitioners to recognize and accept that they will be helped by their clients, for they are the greatest source of learning.

Clients can also help put the clinician's own problems in perspective: they offer a unique view of the human condition, which can provide a sense of universality—that humans are not alone in their suffering, that the deepest cravings of human life are all a part of what it means to be human. Even a person's darkest impulses are a part of what it means to be alive. It can be beneficial to help clients embrace their shadow, help them gain some compassion for that shadowed nature, and in so doing, helps practitioners come to terms with their own shadow, with those parts of themselves they find repulsive, shameful, or even wonderful.

Practitioners help people immerse themselves in the deepest questions of existence: why do we live, how do we live fully in the face of death, how do we take responsibility for creating our own path, and how do we create meaning in a world full of uncertainty? In helping clients answer these questions, practitioners *must* examine those questions for themselves. This allows for a richer and more meaningful existence.

ACADEMIC RESEARCH AS A SIDE OF THE TRIANGLE

It is the synergy of "ideas-plus-relationship" that creates real therapeutic power.

(Yalom, 2008, p. 204)

Above, we discussed the power of learning from clients, which occurs within the context of the therapeutic relationship. It cannot be stressed enough that the therapeutic relationship holds the real healing power of any course of counseling or psychotherapy (Yalom, 2008; Yalom, 1980). Yet, the ideas that have been put forth in our field have tremendous power as well. Yalom (2002) makes this point:

> Last it has always struck me as an extraordinary privilege to belong to the venerable and honorable guild of healers. We therapists are part of a tradition reaching back not only to our immediate psychotherapy ancestors, beginning with Freud and Jung and all their ancestors—Nietzsche, Schopenhauer, Kierkegaard—but also to Jesus, the Buddha, Plato, Socrates, Galen, Hippocrates, and all the other great religious leaders, philosophers, and physicians who have, since the beginning of time, ministered to human despair. (p. 258-259)

Our field is founded on great thinkers and great ideas. Indeed, the research method helps practitioners navigate the ambiguous therapeutic interaction. Research has brought forth very important psychological ideas has helped answer some very difficult questions posed by prominent psychologists. For example, Hans Eysenck (1952, cited in Clarkin & Levy, 2005) declared that psychotherapy was as beneficial as receiving no treatment at all. He cited research he had done, which found that people engaged in psychoanalysis actually had worse cure rates than people not treated. This spawned an army of studies hoping to demonstrate the positive efficacy of counseling and psychotherapy. Clarkin and Levy report this about the outcome of these studies: "Thanks in large part to researchers' responses to Eysenck's charge, we now know, generally speaking, that psychotherapy does indeed help people" (p. 194). A comprehensive summary of the mountain of research completed on counseling and psychotherapy can be found in *Bergin and Garfield's Handbook of Psychotherapy and Behavior Change* (Lambert, 2005). What one concludes after reading this volume is that counseling and psychotherapy work, and these approaches work quite well. This is the empirical research world that dominates university life. Professors are expected to not only teach but to also conduct research and publish in well-regarded peer-reviewed journals. Academic psychology professors and researchers are early pioneers who carved out the roads practitioners travel so effortlessly. They are invaluable ancestors. Studies completed by researchers who have somehow found a way to operationalize very complex psychological phenomena have stood the test of time. These studies have helped both researchers and practitioners work more effectively and have furthered the field in ways that are difficult to articulate.

Many students begin their academic careers in what Ronnestad and Skovholt (2003) call the "lay-helper" phase, where these students are drawn to the world of counseling and psychotherapy because they have had success in helping family members, friends, and strangers through difficulties in life. Without any training, graduate students in this phase of development rely on intuition and their own experiences to help people through problems. Inexperienced graduate students at this stage are asked by their programs to think about the human condition through the eyes of those who have gone before them. In a way, these students are asked to abandon earlier ways of helping and asked to adopt a more objective, research-supported way of working with clients (Ronnestad & Skovholt, 2003).

This is the traditional scientist-practitioner model. Programs that espouse this model teach their students to be research aficionados—to learn what works with clients and why. Students are urged to approach research findings with skepticism so that, when the time comes to do their own research, they can find more effective ways of working with people. As discussed above, some programs have adopted manualized treatment approaches (Chambless & Hollon, 1998; Karekla, Lundgren & Forsyth, 2004). These guides can help practitioners navigate the ambiguity of the consultation room. Learning a method like this is a valuable way to learn something: a practitioner (trained to be a skilled diagnostician) chooses a treatment based on the diagnosis. The therapy then follows a prescribed set of interventions shown in the research lab to be effective in helping someone with that particular problem. This is the paint by numbers approach.

As more research is completed, however, a more complex picture is painted and more controversy over what is effective is encountered. Some of this research has found that there are factors common to all treatment approaches (e.g., client and therapist characteristics) that predict the best client outcome (Wampold, 2001; Luborsky et al., 2002). Wampold's (2001) research has shown that there is not one intervention that outshines another to provide the most meaningful change.

Research gives practitioners a rough map of how to work with clients. Human beings share many similarities. So, one intervention that works with one person will likely translate into working with another person. However, clients live primarily in a subjective world. Because of this, generalizing treatments will be ambitious at best (Skovholt & Starkey, 2010).

The participants of Starkey's (2010) study spoke not only of their intense desire to keep learning but they also spoke to the obligation for further inquiry. The counselor and psychotherapist's job is like detective work: "In a unique way, the work of the psychotherapist is not unlike that of Sherlock Holmes" (Norcross & Guy, 2007, p. 24). There is a constant search, under the surface, for why client problems developed, how they can best be treated, and a continuous monitoring of how well the treatment is working (Norcross & Guy, 2007). This is the research method.

How much more complex can this pursuit be? Counselors and psychotherapists work intimately to try and understand the human mind, which can be, aside from understanding the intricate workings of the universe, one of the most challenging tasks one can undertake. And this is a powerful source of professional satisfaction (Starkey, 2010). Counselors and psychotherapists learn about the human condition, how it is assembled, and benefit greatly from this continuous learning. Even the most senior practitioners in Starkey's study talked about how they continue to learn. One participant talked about how he is grateful to those psychologists who have gone before him. He reported that because of them, he continues to learn and discover so much about the human condition.

As with the limitations of learning only from practice, there are several limitations of learning only from the research. Alan Kazdin (2004) makes this point about the science/practice rift: "The limitations of contemporary research related to how therapy is studied greatly restrict the extent to which the results from therapy research are likely to be generalizable to clinical practice" (p. 560).

Research has given practitioners an immense database of psychological content. We know now, more than ever, what puts together the human mind, what tears it down, and how to repair it. But, as Yalom (2008) aptly points out: "The effective therapist should never try to force some area of content: therapy should not be theory-driven but relationship-driven" (p. 204). To rely exclusively on this side of the triangle poses some danger of not really being "with" a client and can perhaps force the agenda of the counselor or psychotherapist rather than the client. When this happens, the treatment becomes more about the clinician and not as much about the client.

The importance of this side of the triangle cannot be overlooked, and theory and research need to be an intimate part of any practitioner's toolbox. Wise explorers make sure they have maps with them before they leave for an expedition. The same is true for the wise practitioner: the research method provides a map for the landscape of the human life. Growing counselors and psychotherapists attend several years of graduate school, spend hundreds of hours in supervision during practicum and internship, and have to take a licensing exam before being allowed to practice independently. There is tremendous opportunity for learning about the nature of existence this way. Indeed, master therapists have been found to have a voracious appetite for learning (Jennings & Skovholt, 1999), so embracing this side of the triangle is essential for continued development.

PERSONAL LIFE AS A SIDE OF THE TRIANGLE

> Question: What is the therapist's most valuable instrument? Answer (and no one misses this one): the therapist's own self.
>
> (Yalom, 2002, p. 40)

There is an incredible richness to our own lives. As we navigate our lives, we experience a world full of wonder, pain, loss, awe, and a host of other emotions that give meaning to what it is to be human. As practitioners, we learn from our own lives that we are not immune to the demands of existence. We live our lives alongside our clients. To pretend that their pain is not our pain is a disservice not only to our clients but to ourselves. Yalom (1989) captures this nicely when he writes:

> Though…psychotherapy abound[s] with the words patient and therapist, do not be misled by such terms: these are everyman, everywoman stories. Patienthood is ubiquitous; the assumption of the label is largely arbitrary and often dependent more on cultural, educational and economic factors than on the severity of pathology. Since therapists, no less than patients, must confront these givens of existence, the professional posture of disinterested objectivity, so necessary to scientific method, is inappropriate. We psychotherapists simply cannot cluck with sympathy and exhort patients to struggle resolutely with their problems. We cannot say to them you and your problems. Instead, we must speak of us and our problems, because our life, our existence, will always be

riveted to death, love to loss, freedom to fear, and growth to separation. We are, all of us, in this together. (p. 14, italics his)

Wise counselors and psychotherapists keep their existential struggles at the forefront of experience. When practitioners are able to recognize that they are just as vulnerable to the problems of life, the therapeutic relationship changes (Yalom, 2008). There are no more barriers to authentic relating—no masks worn, no pretending that the clinician is immune to existence pain—and this will often foster a more genuine therapeutic relationship, the fundamental healing force of any course of counseling or psychotherapy (Yalom, 2008; 1980).

As we discover more about ourselves through personal reflection and openness to experiencing life, client problems can be understood on a completely different level. As practitioners go through life, we, just as much as our clients, form attachments to people. Practitioners can be guaranteed that we will, at some point, lose important people in our lives. This personal world of loss contains tremendous value for practitioners: clients need them to be experts in this area because a large percentage of clients make the journey to the practitioner's office because of loss. There are many theories of how to help someone through a loss, many research studies completed on the grieving process, which can be very helpful to the practitioner. However, if counselors or psychotherapists are to really understand, we must come to understand loss and suffering on a personal, emotional level. Not only do practitioners need to understand grief and mourning, it is important for us to develop an awareness of all human thought, emotion, and experience.

Oftentimes, counselors and psychotherapists got into the field for very personal reasons. A recent book published—*Voices from the Field: Defining Moments in Counselor and Therapist Development* (Trotter-Mathison, Koch, Sanger, & Skovholt, 2010)—highlights how important personal lifeThe authors of this edited volume solicited essays from practitioners about critical incidents in their lives—personal or professional—that had significant influences on both themselves and their practice. The stories contain personal anecdotes of cancer, suicide, confrontation with death, birth, cultural experiences, and a myriad of other human stories that, on a very profound level, influenced the practitioner and his or her professional life.

Some very prominent practitioners in this field speak to the incredible lessons we can learn from personal life. Derald Wing Sue (2005), for example, said this: "I will never forget that incident [of racial harassment as a child]. It taught me several important lessons in life that have remained with me to this day and form the basis of my professional work" (p. 75). He goes on to say this: "Strive to integrate both your professional and personal journeys. If you are able to do that, the dichotomous distinction we often make between work and personal life becomes less an either/or choice and more a manifestation of your total being" (p. 82).

Counseling and psychotherapy can be consumed with darkness, pain, longing, death, and the confrontation with evil. Some of this serves to insulate and fortify the practitioner (Starkey, 2010; Yalom, 1980), but one cannot battle the forces of darkness all day long and expect to come through the battle untouched. In what other profession is it commonplace to go straight into the storm? It is difficult to imagine that a sailor would steer his or her vessel right into the heart of a storm, or a pilot, seeing a thunderstorm to the west, would turn the plane towards the flashes of light and rumbling clouds. But that is exactly what makes counseling and psychotherapy effective, and counselors and psychotherapists have to be willing to steer the vessel towards the darkest part of the storm. In order to best do this with people, counselors and therapists undergo years of training so that they know the general landscape of human problems. As practitioners develop and sit with more clients, wisdom can emerge from helping so many people. But, those experiences are not enough. To be most effective, practitioners need to immerse themselves in their own lives and learn a great deal from living as a human being. We as counselors and psychotherapists are also intimately involved in existence. We are not immune to life's harsh realities. If we are to be most effective with clients, we must realize and accept that we are human. This not only helps us connect with clients, this can also provide clients with a sense of universality where they begin to understand that we—their counselor or psychotherapist—are also affected by life. This deepens the therapeutic relationship (Yalom, 2008).

Similarly, if one is to take pause and reflect on the nature of existence, it is difficult to not be overtaken by a sense of awe and wonderment. The very fact that humans breathe, walk, communicate, and are able to reflect on the human condition seems absurd. The human life is immensely amazing, and counselors and psychotherapists should cherish the opportunity to immerse themselves in delving deeply into the human condition. Part of the awesomeness of life is the human being's capacity to suffer. Viktor Frankl (2006) showed that there is the opportunity for meaning in suffering by finding and creating his own meaning while a prisoner in a concentration camp. If practitioners confront their suffering and pain and move with it and through it, they recognize their own resilience, their own courage, and they are made stronger by this journey. Clients and their suffering can remind the practitioner of their own, which is a perfect opportunity to reflect on it and seek to work through it.

There is no such thing as therapeutic detachment, of removing the counselor or therapist from the encounter (Bugental, 1990; Ganzer, 2007; Lum, 2002). Practitioners are always intimately involved in the process, and, in order to be truly effective, counselors and psychotherapists must bring the fullness of themselves to the encounter. In order to do this, it is so important for counselors or therapists to reflect on and bring forth the fullness of their person. Indeed, Norcross and Guy (2007) state this about counselors and therapists: "The evidence tells us that successful psychotherapy is a product of many components, all of which revolve around, and depend upon, the individual psychotherapist" (p. 5).

As people accumulate experiences over the lifespan, great lessons can occur from living. This is an important and powerful knowledge source and a vital side to the practitioner's learning triangle. However, the influence of the practitioner's own emotional life can both distort and illuminate (Skovholt & Starkey, 2010). Therefore, the research and practice sides of the triangle help to offset the subtle distortions that may bubble up from this epistemological pool. There are several good ways to cultivate learning from this side of the triangle. One way to do this is to engage in personal counseling or psychotherapy. This is a wonderful way to learn about what it means to be alive and what it means to be a client. In fact, one of the most important learning experiences for advanced counselors and psychotherapists is engagement in their own therapy (Ronnestad & Skovholt, 2003; Daw & Joseph, 2007). Another way to foster this side of the triangle is for the practitioner to be in constant reflection of the self. As an understanding of the self deepens, this opens up avenues for more accurate empathy, for really joining a client in the depths of being, and for making the therapeutic relationship more authentic and genuine.

THE TRIANGLE AS A WHOLE

I am human, and nothing human is alien to me.

(Terence, cited in Yalom, 2008, p. 199)

At the core of a good course of counseling and psychotherapy is a deep, profound meeting of two people. Counselors and psychotherapists have a difficult task while engaging another person's life: to be both a participant in that person's experience and to be detached enough to maintain an observer role that is so necessary to effective work (Yalom, 1989). In this sense, practitioners must engage clients on several different levels. To retain objectivity and remain at an optimal distance from client problems, it is important for counselors and psychotherapists to know the broad map (the research method) of how human problems develop. A reflection on practice is also key to success here: the learning that occurs from working with so many people is so vital to professional development that it cannot be ignored or even given reduced credence. Practitioners must remember, too, that we are involved in existence, that we were thrown into this world without a map and expected to live with purpose, vitality, and in harmony with others (Bugental, 1965). This can be a very difficult thing to do, not only for clients but also for us. So, disinterested passivity and complete objectivity are impossible in this work. Counselors and psychotherapists are involved, on a very intimate level, with the material clients present. Indeed, Carl Jung (1989) once wrote, "The doctor cannot be effective unless he himself has been affected" (p. 134). Herein lies the importance of the third side of the triangle—the personal.

Learning is a constant companion to the counselor and psychotherapist. Optimal functioning as a practitioner involves an openness to learning (Ronnestad & Skovholt, 2003), and professional stagnation can occur if counselors and psychotherapists close themselves off to learning experiences. As practitioners develop—from the first practicum to the final client—there is much exposure to variability, the unknown, and the ambiguous. To work with this territory on a daily basis can be both frightening and awe-inspiring. Anxiety often diminishes as the practitioner matures and gains more experience (Ronnestad & Skovholt, 2003). However, this does not mean that ambiguity disappears with experience. In fact, reliance on technique and the "correct" way to perform therapy is often characteristic of beginning counselors and psychotherapists. This can be seen as a way of controlling the uncertain. As practitioners mature and gain more experience, there is less reliance on technique and more utilization of the self, which makes practice more ambiguous, shifting from external expertise to internal expertise (Ronnestad & Skovholt, 2003). Thus, the learning triangle can be an effective guide to optimal learning across the professional lifespan.

However, an optimal balance of all three sides of the triangle is key. Isosceles, scalene, or obtuse triangles do not benefit the counselor or psychotherapist very much. What we propose is an equilateral triangle, one with equal sides and angles. Each side of the triangle can offer valuable learning and insights to counselors and psychotherapists at all stages of the novice/seasoned professional continuum.

Remember, too, that the counselor and psychotherapist's identity is often wedded to his or her professional role (Starkey, 2010). To restrict learning in any way can be seen as a restriction of being. Practicing counseling and psychotherapy has a deep, salutary influence on the being of the counselor and psychotherapist. As a result of working so closely with the immense variability of the human situation, practitioners are changed by the work—we enjoy many personal benefits from helping others through pain, and we derive personal life meaning from this work (Starkey, 2010). There are hazards, of course, as with any other meaningful activity, but the benefits seem to outweigh the hazards. Indeed, Starkey's (2010) study showed that confrontation with despair on a daily basis actually serves to fortify rather than torment.

We know that most aspects of the counselor and psychotherapist's life seem to be changed by practice:

> I am not the same person who began to practice counseling and psychotherapy more than 30 years ago in an army hospital. And the changes in me are not solely those worked by time, education, and the life circumstances shared by most of my generation. A powerful force affecting me has been my participation in so many lives. A psychotherapist had best recognize that the profession will continually press on her or him to change and evolve...This work is exciting, constantly changing, demanding, exhausting, frightening, stimulating, dangerous, socially borderline, culturally essential, and much else—but the one thing it is not is boring!...Finally, and in some ways most importantly, being a psychotherapist has meant having a window on the human soul. Such a hard thing to try to say what that means. For me it has been acutely, poignantly important. It has given me what I think I always lacked before: a ground on which to stand in being alive, a foundation upon which to build an outlook for my own life and on life and death as our common heritage and fate. I believe in my deepest heart that I have realized more of my possibilities through this life than I could have in any other way. And I am grateful. (Bugental, 1978, p. 149-150)

One salient phrase from this quote is that the counseling and psychotherapy professions constantly place a pressure on practitioners to change and to grow. We cannot remain stagnant; the work is simply too demanding and too complex to think that we know everything about human existence. We must continue to uncover layers of experience previously unknown, to seek out the uncertain and embrace it, to love and live the questions that are not yet answered. We must continue to engage existence in ways that are increasingly vital for us. We must not tell ourselves that existential problems are reserved for the afflicted, the weak, or the poor in spirit. We must tell ourselves that we share the same fate our clients do. Indeed, we must seek to live the lives we want our clients to live and help them do the same.

BIOSKETCHES

TOM SKOVHOLT has lived a bi-cultural (university and practice) professional life for more than three decades. Living in both of these cultures as a teacher and researcher in one, and practitioner in the other for many, many years has had a major impact on his views of epistemology and related topics. Credentials include LP, ABPP and Fellow of APA. His teaching, writing and consulting is about practice in the caring professions such as counseling, therapy, teaching and health care. Books include *The Resilient Practitioner (2nd Edition 2011), Master Therapists, Voices from the Field: Defining Moments in Counselor and*

Therapist Development, The Evolving Professional Self and *Skills and Strategies for the Helping Professions.* He is a professor of counseling psychology at the University of Minnesota and has taught in Turkey and Singapore. Awards include University of Minnesota Morse Teaching Award and in 2010, the Lifetime Contributions to Education and Training by the Council of Counseling Psychology Training Programs and in 2011 and the Susan T. Rydell Outstanding Contributions to Psychology Award by the Minnesota Psychological Association.

MICHAEL STARKEY recently earned his Ph.D. from the University of Minnesota and is currently completing his post-doctoral hours at the University of Rhode Island Counseling Center. His clinical, writing, and research interests include practitioner development and existential issues in psychotherapy.

REFERENCES

Bales, P. B. & Staudinger, U. M. (2000). Wisdom: A metaheuristic (pragmatic) to orchestrate mind and virtue toward excellence. *American Psychologist, 55,* 122- 136.

Beutler, L. E., Malik, M., Alimohamed, S., Harwood, T. M., Talebi, H., Noble, S., & Wong, E. (2005). Therapist variables. In M. J. Lambert (Ed.), *Bergin and Garfield's handbook of psychotherapy and behavior change* (5th ed.) (pp. 227-306). New York: Wiley.

Bugental, J. F. T. (1990). *Intimate journeys: Stories from life-changing therapy.* San Francisco: Jossey-Bass.

Bugental, J. F. T. (1978). *Psychotherapy and process: The fundamentals of an existential-humanistic approach.* Reading, MA: Addison-Wesley.

Bugental, J. F. T. (1965). *The search for authenticity: An existential-analytic approach to psychotherapy.* New York: Holt, Reinhart, and Winston.

Chambless, D. L., & Hollon, S.D. (1998). Defining empirically supported therapies. *Journal of Consulting and Clinical Psychology, 66,* 7-18.

Chi, M.T.H., Glass, R. & Farr, M.J. (Eds.). (1988). *The nature of expertise.* Hillsdale, NJ: Lawrence Erlbaum Associates.

Clarkin, J.F., & Levy, K.N. (2005). The influence of client variables on psychotherapy. In M. J. Lambert (Ed.), *Bergin and Garfield's handbook of psychotherapy and behavior change* (5th ed.) (pp. 194-226). New York: Wiley.

Cooper, G. (2011). Clinician's digest: Wise therapists or technicians? *Psychotherapy Networker, 35,* 11-12.

Daw, B., & Joseph, S. (2007). Qualified therapists' experience of personal therapy. *Counselling and Psychotherapy Research, 7,* 227-232.

Duncan, B. L. (2010). Wizards, humbugs, or witches: Identity, uncertainty, and discovery. In B. L. Duncan (Ed.), *On becoming a better therapist* (pp. 145-162). Washington, DC: American Psychological Association.

Frankl, V.E. (2006). *Man's search for meaning.* Boston: Beacon.

Ganzer, C. (2007). The use of self from a relational perspective. *Clinical Social Work Journal, 35,* 117-123.

Guy, J. D. (1987). *The personal life of the psychotherapist.* New York: John Wiley and Sons.

Jennings, L., & Skovholt, T.M. (1999). The cognitive, emotional, and relational characteristics of master therapists. *Journal of Counseling Psychology, 46,* 3-11.

Jung, C.G. (1989). *Memories, dreams, and reflections.* New York: Vintage.

Karekla, M., Lundgren, J. D., & Forsyth, J. P. (2004). A survey of graduate training in empirically supported and manualized treatments: A preliminary report. *Cognitive and Behavioral Practice, 11,* 230-242.

Kazdin, A.E. (2004). Psychotherapy for children and adolescents. In M.J. Lambert (Ed.), *Bergin and Garfield's handbook of psychotherapy and behavior change* (5th ed.) (pp. 543-589). New York: Wiley.

Kendall, P.C. (1998). Empirically supported psychological therapies. *Journal of Consulting and Clinical Psychology, 66,* 3-6.

Kottler, J.A. (2003). *On being a therapist (3rd ed.).* San Francisco: Jossey-Bass.

Lambert, M.J. (Ed.). (2004). *Bergin and Garfield's handbook of psychotherapy and behavior change* (5th ed.). New York: Wiley.

Lebow, J. (2006). *Research for the psychotherapist: From science to practice.* New York: Routledge.

Luborsky, L., Rosenthal, R., Diguer, L., Andrusyna, T. P., Berman, J. S., Levitt, J. T., …Krause, E. D. (2002). The dodo bird verdict is alive and well-mostly. *Clinical Psychology, 9,* 2-12.

Lum, W. (2002). The use of self of the therapist. *Contemporary Family Therapy, 24,* 181-197.

May, R. (1972). *Power and innocence.* New York: Delta.

Norcross, J.C., & Guy, J.D. (2007). *Leaving it at the office: A guide to psychotherapist self-care.* New York: The Guilford Press.

Orlinsky, D. E., & Ronnestad, M.H. (2005). *How psychotherapists develop: A study of therapeutic work and professional growth.* Washington, D.C.: American Psychological Association.

Reed, G.M. (2006). What qualifies as evidence of effective practice? In J.C. Norcross, L.E. Beutler, & R.F. Levant (Eds.) *Evidence-based mental health* (pp. 13-23). Washington, DC: American Psychological Association.

Ronnestad, M.H., & Skovholt, T.M. (2003). The journey of the counselor and therapist: Research findings and perspectives on development. *Journal of Career Development, 30,* 5-44.

Schneider, K. J., & May, R. (1995). *The psychology of existence: An integrative, clinical perspective.* New York: McGraw-Hill.

Skovholt, T.M., Goh, M., Upidi, S., & Grier, T. (2004). The resilient multicultural practitioner. *The California Psychologist, 37,* 18-19.

Skovholt, T.M., Jennings, L., & Mullenbach, M. (2004). Portrait of the master therapist: The highly-functioning self. In T.M. Skovholt, & L. Jennings (Eds.), *Master Therapists: Exploring expertise in therapy and counseling* (pp. 125-146). Boston, MA: Allyn and Bacon.

Skovholt, T.M., & Starkey, M.T. (2010). The three legs of the practitioner's learning stool: Practice, research/theory, and personal life. *Journal of Contemporary Psychotherapy, 40,* 125-130.

Skovholt, T.M., & Trotter-Mathison, M. (2011). *The resilient practitioner: Burnout prevention and self-care strategies for therapists, counselors, teachers, and health professionals.* Second Edition. New York: Routledge.

Stahl, J. V., Hill, C. E., Jacobs, T., Kleinman, S., Isenberg, D., & Stern, A. (2009). When the shoe is on the other foot: A qualitative study of intern-level trainees' perceived learning from clients. *Psychotherapy: Theory, Research, Practice, Training, 46,* 376-389.

Starkey, M.T. (2010). *The psychological influence of therapists' professional lives: The effects of exploring the deep.* Unpublished doctoral dissertation. University of Minnesota.

Sue, D.W. (2005). The continuing journey to multicultural competence. In R.K. Coyle, & Bemak (Eds.), *Journeys to professional excellence: Lessons from leading counselor educators and practitioners* (pp. 73-84). Alexandria, VA: American Counseling Association.

Trotter-Mathison, M., Koch, J.M., Sanger, S., & Skovholt, T.M. (2010). *Voices from the field: Defining moments in counselor and therapist development.* New York: Routledge.

Wampold, B. (2007). Psychotherapy: The humanistic (and effective) treatment. *American Psychologist, 62,* 857-873.

Wampold, B. (2001). *The great psychotherapy debate.* Mahwah, NJ: Lawrence Erlbaum Associates, Inc.

Yalom, I.D. (2008). *Staring at the sun: Overcoming the terror of death.* San Francisco: Jossey-Bass.

Yalom, I.D. (2002). *The gift of therapy.* New York: Harper Collins.

Yalom, I. D. (1995). *The theory and practice of group psychotherapy* (4th ed.) New York: Basic Books.

Yalom, I.D. (1989). *Love's executioner.* New York: Basic Books.

Yalom, I.D. (1980).*Existential psychotherapy.* New York: Basic Books.

In: Continuing Professional Development …
Editors: G. J. Neimeyer and J. M. Taylor
ISBN: 978-1-62100-767-8
© 2012 Nova Science Publishers, Inc.

Chapter 14

PROFESSIONAL COMPETENCY AND PERSONAL EXPERIENCE: AN EXPLORATORY STUDY

Jennifer M. Taylor[1,*], *Greg J. Neimeyer*[1] *and Douglas Wear*[2]
[1] University of Florida, US
[2] Antioch University-Seattle, US

ABSTRACT

This study examines the relationship between aspects of psychologists' personal life (e.g., stress levels, self-care, life satisfaction and life adjustment) and their professional experience (e.g., professional self-efficacy, perceived competency and participation in informal and formal CE). In a study of 71 practicing psychologists, results revealed a range of significant relationships between personal and professional domains. Levels of stress, for example, were strongly and inversely related to levels of professional self-care, life satisfaction, life adjustment, and perceived competence, while professional development activities were related to higher levels of professional self-efficacy and perceived competence. Findings are discussed in relation to empirical studies in the field of CE and professional competencies, and the need to continue to explore the boundaries between personal experience and professional development and competence.

Keywords: Continuing education, competency, self-care, personal experience

Continuing education can be defined as "an ongoing process consisting of formal learning activities that (1) are relevant to psychological practice, education, and science, (2) enable psychologists to keep pace with emerging issues and technologies, and (3) allow psychologists to maintain, develop, and increase competencies in order to improve services to the public and enhance contributions to the profession" (APA, 2000). Continuing education is designed to promote and extend professional competencies. Professional competencies have been described in many ways but some of their most common components include critical

---

[*] Correspondence regarding this manuscript may be directed to Jennifer Taylor, Department of Psychology, University of Florida, P. O. Box 112250, Gainesville, FL 32611.

thinking skills, interpersonal relationship skills, knowledge of self, field-based knowledge and skill development, and certain personality traits and attitudes (Elman, Illfelder-Kaye & Robiner, 2005; Hatcher & Lassiter, 2007; Wise, 2008). Although continuing education is designed to promote ongoing professional development, the actual relationships between continuing education, professional competencies and personal well-being remain largely unknown. The primary purpose of this chapter is to explore these relationships in greater detail.

PERSONAL ADJUSTMENT AND PROFESSIONAL COMPETENCIES

The relationship between aspects of personal well-being and professional functioning has been the subject of considerable attention. At the extreme, personal impairment has been linked to professional dysfunction (Guy, Poelstra & Stark, 1989) which, in turn, has given rise to the increased need to attend to aspects of professionals' self-care (see Wise & Gibson, 2012). Beyond the realm of impairment itself, aspects of personal maturation and adjustment have figured prominently in the conceptualization of professional development. Skovholt and Starkey (2010), for example, have drawn attention to what they call the "three legs of the practitioner's learning stool," noting that personal maturation, scholarly development and ongoing clinical experience all play important roles in developing professional competence (p.125). They note the significant role that personal experiences, such as loss, grief and recovery, can carry for instance, in relation to our ability to empathize with suffering. As Skovholt and Starkey state, "In order to be most effective with clients, therapists need to realize and accept their own humanness" (p.129). Thus, drawing a distinction between personal experiences and professional capabilities may be illusory given the interdependence between the two. This is consistent with the "common factors" research that suggests that treatment outcomes are more reliant on the personal traits and characteristics of the therapist than on the particular theoretical orientation or interventions that are employed (Wampold, 2007).

In short, research from a variety of perspectives indicates that one's personal life can influence one's professional competencies, and vice versa. Some typical aspects of a psychotherapist's personal life that may affect, or be affected by, a psychotherapist's professional life include one's stress level, self-care, life satisfaction and perceived life adjustment, all of which will be explored in greater detail.

Preliminary research has already indicated that stress can impact levels of professional functioning, and psychotherapists may be particularly vulnerable in this regard. In fact, in a study of members of the Minnesota Psychological Association, many psychologists reported serious mental health problems and stressors and even more reported observing these features in their colleagues (Brodie & Robinson, 1991). For example, 47% of psychologists reported experiencing depression, while 84% reported observing it in their colleagues; 60% reported feeling burnt out or overworked, while 81% reported observing it in their colleagues; 49% reported experiencing relationship problems, while 78% observed this in their colleagues; 10% reported suicidal attempts or ideation, while 29% observed this in colleagues; and 7% acknowledged substance abuse as a problem, while 52% observed this problem in their colleagues. Furthermore, in an Iowa survey of psychotherapists, more than half of the participants reported depression and relationship problems (Deutsch, 1985), while other studies have reported that substance abuse, feelings of isolation, emotional exhaustion, anxiety, depression, and relationship issues are also relatively common experiences among psychotherapists (Elliott & Guy, 1993; Mahoney, 1997; Rupert, Stevanovic & Hunley, 2009). Moreover, psychologists are not immune to the impact of early traumatic experiences either, and research has indicated that many psychologists have endured abuse or other forms of early childhood trauma (Elliott & Guy, 1993; Radeke & Mahoney, 2000; Pope & Feldman-Summers, 1992; Pope & Tabachnick, 1994).

Of course, the practice of psychotherapy itself can be stressful, too, and it is not uncommon for psychologists to experience what many researchers term "compassion fatigue" (Figley, 1995; Showalter, 2010; Sprang, 2010). Compassion fatigue is the consequence of the "caring cycle," which is characterized by a cycle of empathy, involvement and attachment with clients, followed by termination of the therapeutic relationship (Skovholt, Grier & Hanson, 2001). Burnout and stress can result from the therapist's repeated experience of the caring cycle. This process can lead therapists to feel emotionally exhausted, which may then have a negative effect on their professional functioning.

Related work has noted the impact of stressful personal, as well as professional, relationships on professional functioning. In a recent study of 497 psychologists, greater conflict between work and family, for example, was significantly related to greater emotional exhaustion, negative, pessimistic attitudes toward clients and lower feelings of accomplishment (Rupert et al., 2009). For this reason, self-care is an essential element of professional renewal and has been cited as a key ingredient in preventing burnout (see Brucato & Neimeyer, 2009) on the one hand, and maximizing professional competencies on the other (see Wise & Gibson, 2012).

Self-care is comprised of activities that enable an individual to maintain physical and emotional well-being. Self-care behaviors can include a wide range of activities such as exercise, a healthy diet and personal hygiene, as well as activities associated with personal renewal, relaxation and recovery. Participating in hobbies, reading, personal therapy and vacations are all examples of diverse self-care behaviors that may reduce levels of stress and contribute to emotional well-being (Mahoney, 1997).

Past studies suggest that self-care is related to a range of positive outcomes, such as psychological adjustment (preventing burnout and aiding in personal growth and wellbeing) and ethical outcomes (reducing the risk of ethical violations) (Porter, 1995; Brucato & Neimeyer, 2009). As Barnett (2007) has noted, the primary objective is not to eliminate stress but to cope with it adaptively, rather than maladaptively. Maladaptive coping (e.g., through drugs or alcohol) can contribute to ineffective, or even harmful, practice (Barnett, 2007). To be an ethical and competent psychologist means to be a psychologist who practices effective self-care (see Wise & Gibson, 2012). Brucato and Neimeyer (2009) note that self-care can help to prevent the negative effects of stress, which can then translate into more effective therapy.

And finally, in relation to life satisfaction, although psychotherapists generally report high levels of life satisfaction, they also report experiencing significant stressors and negative life experiences. Research suggests that 80% of psychotherapists report feeling emotionally depleted from their work, 24% report financial security problems, 17% report relationship problems, 19% report sleep problems and low self-confidence, 24% report anxiety problems, 20% report being overweight, 19% report depression, and 19% report childhood abuse

(Radeke & Mahoney, 2000). These stressors can negatively impact one's life satisfaction. In fact, Stevanovic and Rupert (2009) call attention to the term "work-family spillover," noting that family conflict, lack of work-family balance and spillover can have a negative effect on one's personal and professional lives. In their work, family stressors significantly mediated the relationship between overall life satisfaction and emotional exhaustion from work and significantly mediated the relationship between family support and emotional exhaustion. Thus, overall levels of stress and personal adjustment can be important predictors of professional functioning.

THE ROLE OF CONTINUING EDUCATION

The relationship between continuing education and professional competencies has been a conceptually clear, but empirically elusive, one (Neimeyer, Taylor and Wear, 2009; Wise, 2010). Conceptually, continuing education is, by definition, specifically designed to contribute to the ongoing maintenance and development of professional competencies (e.g., APA, 2000). The American Psychological Association's definition of CE, for example, specifically identifies it with activities that "allow psychologists to maintain, develop, and increase competencies in order to improve services to the public and enhance contributions to the profession". From a conceptual standpoint, therefore, CE is expected to play a key role in the ongoing development and maintenance of professional competencies.

But, as Wise (2010) and others have noted, despite promising indications in this regard, it is not clear that CE has fully satisfied these expectations regarding its critical role in promoting professional competencies. On the positive side, research has consistently demonstrated practitioners' perceptions regarding the positive impact of CE on their professional practice (Sharkin & Plageman, 2003; Neimeyer et al., 2009; Neimeyer, Taylor & Philip, 2010a; Neimeyer, Taylor & Wear, 2011). Sharkin and Plageman (2003) reported that 45% of the participants in their study felt as though their CE participation made them more effective clinicians. Likewise, Neimeyer et al. (2009) found that the majority of the participants in their nationwide survey of psychologists (64%) reported moderate to high levels of learning from their CE experiences, with much of this learning translating into their practices. In summarizing their research, Neimeyer et al. (2009) note that the overall pattern of their findings "reflect an image of CE as a robustly favorable experience for psychologists who, at least from their own perspectives, learn substantial amounts and translate this learning into more informed, effective, and ethical professional practice" (p. 620).

Notwithstanding these positive appraisals, independent evidence of the effectiveness of CE is harder to come by (see Adams & Sharkin, 2012; Wise & Gibson, 2012). In part this is because, outside the area of medicine, there are no controlled studies of the effects of CE (Daniels & Walter, 2002). Extrapolations from research within medicine are instructive for this reason and these provide a mixture of evidence in this regard. Some studies have shown that continuing medical education (CME) enhances levels of knowledge and skills, as well as selected patient outcomes (Davis et al., 1995). While didactic programs consistently register no demonstrable impact on physician behavior or healthcare outcomes (Bloom, 1995), more interactive CME programs that include skill rehearsal and feedback do seem to translate both into behavioral changes and health-related outcomes (Davis et al., 1999). The bottom line seems to be consistent with VandeCreek and Brace's (1991) earlier observation that CE *can* be effective, but that the attention to best practices may be essential to that effectiveness. And, unfortunately, it appears as though the most commonly utilized methods of CE instruction (i.e. didactic presentations) are also the least effective methods (Bloom, 1995; Institute of Medicine, 2010; Neimeyer et al., 2009; Wise & Gibson, 2012).

While the link between CE and professional functioning has been the subject of considerable attention, less attention has been devoted to the link between CE and personal adjustment and functioning. On the face of it, this seems reasonable, at least insofar as CE is directed primarily at enhancing clinical skills and updating professional knowledge. On the other hand, there is reason to believe that enhanced levels of competence might be related to lower levels of stress and higher levels of personal well-being. And, as CE programs turn to address issues of personal, as well as professional, interest, like reducing professional liability or enhancing self-care, this training might be expected to become associated with reduced stress and enhanced personal adjustment and well-being, as well.

Consistent with this idea, one study discovered that CME was inversely related to levels of stress, burnout, and job dissatisfaction (Kushnir, Cohen & Kitai, 2000). The correlations, although modest ($r = -.18$ to $-.27$), provide one source of support for the likelihood that professional activities (such as CE) can have an effect on one's personal life and vice versa. A range of conceptual models, however, would support this probable link, too, by emphasizing the critical role of continuing education in affecting the attunement and well-being of therapists, and their ability to assess and monitor their professional abilities and capacities across different contexts and time (Lichtenberg & Goodyear, 2012).

The present study explores the relationship between personal and professional domains and examines the potential roles of formal and informal CE in supporting positive factors within each of these domains. In this study we investigated the relationship among two sets of variables. The first consisted of a range of and personal characteristics (i.e., current stress levels, self-care, life satisfaction and life adjustment) and the second concerned aspects of their professional functioning (i.e., professional self-efficacy, perceived competency and participation in both formal and informal continuing education), all of which were expected to be related to aspects of professional competencies.

METHODS

Seventy-one practicing psychotherapists from the APA Practice Organization participated in the present study examining the interaction between personal characteristics and professional attitudes and activities. Participants ranged in age from 31 years old to 79 years old ($M_{age} = 54.7$, $SD = 10.0$), with, on average, 23.5 years in practice ($SD = 11.6$). The slight majority of the participants were female (52.1%), and 97.2% were White/European American, 1.4% African American/Black, and 1.4% Other. These percentages approximate the American Psychological Association's broader membership which includes 1.8% African American, 2.2% Hispanic, 2% Asian,.4% multiracial, and 24.6% not specified (Center for Psychology Workforce Analysis and Research, 2007).

Participants were given several assessments designed to measure the relationship between personal and professional variables. Personal variables were assessed using measures of perceived stress, self-care, life satisfaction, and life adjustment. The Perceived Stress Scale was used to measure levels of personal stress (Cohen, Kamarck & Merlmestein, 1983). The Perceived Stress Scale is a widely used, 14-item assessment designed to measure the amount of stress an individual is currently experiencing. A self-report measure of self-care was also used; participants were asked, "How would you evaluate your overall level of self-care as a therapist?" (0 = pretty low/negligent, 40 = pretty high/vigilant). The Satisfaction with Life Scale (Diener, Emmons, Larsen & Griffin, 1985) was also used and is a five-item survey designed to measure life satisfaction and one component of subjective well-being. In addition, we used a self-report measure of overall life adjustment, consisting of a five-point rating scale (1 = very poorly adjusted, 5 = very well adjusted), to examine one's perceived adjustment to life.

Professional variables were assessed using measures of therapist self-efficacy, a self-report measure of perceived competency, and self-report measures of involvement in formal and informal CE. The Counselor Self-Efficacy Scale (Melchert, Hays, Wiljanen & Kolocek, 1996) was used as a measure of therapist self-efficacy. It consists of a 20-item survey designed to measure therapeutic knowledge and skill competencies. In addition, a self-report measure of professional competency was used, asking participants to indicate how competent they viewed themselves as being in relation to their professional practice, on a scale of 1 (marginally competent) to 5 (exceptionally competent). Further questions asked participants to indicate the number of hours they had spent in formal and informal continuing education during the previous year. Bivariate correlations were used to examine the relationship between variables.

RESULTS AND DISCUSSION

Results supported the relationship between aspects of the therapists' personal lives and a range of professional characteristics and activities. For example, greater perceived professional competence was significantly related to lower levels of stress ($r = -.52$), but higher levels of self-care ($r = .29$), counselor self-efficacy, ($r = .51$), life satisfaction ($r = .43$), and life adjustment ($r = .41$), $p < .05$, see Table 1. These findings highlight the potential interrelationship between aspects of professional and personal functioning in a way that supports previous work in this area (Mahoney, 1997; Brucato & Neimeyer, 2009; see also Wise & Gibson, 2012).

Relatedly, as Table 1 depicts, levels of reported stress were consistently related to lower levels of personal and professional functioning, while levels of self-care were positively related to this same range of variables. These patterns of findings again highlight the relationship between personal adjustment and professional functioning, underscoring the potentially critical role of responsible self-care in support of maximizing professional effectiveness (see Wise & Gibson, 2012).

Regarding the role of continuing education, it is noteworthy that higher levels of participation in formal CE activities were related both to higher levels of self-care ($r = .29$), on the one hand, and to perceived professional competence ($r = .24$), on the other, $p < .05$. The completion of informal CE was also related to perceived professional competence ($r = .27$), $p < .05$. The nature of these findings support the potential value of continuing education in relation to one of its primary purposes: to support professional development and the maintenance of professional competencies.

Table 1. Correlation Among Variables

	Stress	Life Satisfaction	Life Adjustment	Self-care	Self-efficacy	Competence	Formal CE/year	Informal CE
Stress	1	-.70*	-.65*	-.49*	-.41*	-.52*	.00	-.03
Life Satisfaction		1	.60*	.49*	.26	.43*	.09	.03
Life Adjustment			1	.46*	.43	.41*	.12	-.08
Self-care				1	.28*	.29*	.09	-.07
Self-efficacy					1	.51*	.07	.24
Competence						1	.24*	.27*
Formal CE/year							1	.32*
Informal CE/year								1

Note. Total N = 71. * indicates significance at $p < .05$.

Relatedly, it is worth noting that a positive relationship was found between the amount of formal and informal continuing education that was completed ($r = .32$, $p < .05$). This finding supports other findings (e.g., Taylor, Neimeyer, Zemansky & Rothke, 2012) and suggests that the two forms of professional development may not work in opposition to one another. Instead, formal CE may contribute to a "culture of competence" that supports the participation in a broader range of professional development activities that extend, as well, to informal educational activities, such as reading journals or books, attending conferences or consulting with colleagues.

IMPLICATIONS AND CONCLUSION

The results of this study carry implications for better understanding the relationship between aspects of personal adjustment and professional functioning, on the one hand, and the relationship between each of these and aspects of continuing education, on the other. Levels of perceived stress, life satisfaction and adjustment were examined in relationship to aspects of personal self-care, professional self-efficacy and perceived competence, as well as levels of participation in formal and informal CE activities.

Personal Adjustment and Professional Competencies

In the personal domain, lower levels of stress and higher levels of self-care, life satisfaction and life adjustment were related to higher levels of perceived professional competencies and therapist self-efficacy. This finding is consistent with related work that suggests the favorable effect of self-care and personal well-being on professional functioning. While causal inferences cannot be made, it seems likely that there is a reciprocal effect at work in which better adjustment contributes to more effective professional functioning and vice versa, though the precise nature of this relationship deserves further study.

The Role of Continuing Education

In addition, formal and informal continuing education were both significantly related to perceived professional competency. This finding is consistent with the notion that continuing education may have beneficial effects on one's proficiency as a clinician, though again, the causal nature of this relationship has yet to be determined.

Further, while a number of studies on CE and CME have related continuing education to professional variables, such as participant satisfaction (see Sharkin & Plageman, 2003; Fagan, Ax, Liss, Resnick & Moody, 2007; Neimeyer et al., 2009, 2010a) and clinical outcomes (see Rubel, Sobell & Miller, 2000), little research has examined the potential relationship between CE and aspects of personal well-being. Overall, participation in professional development activities in this study was not strongly related to levels of personal well-being, as measured by levels of perceived stress, life satisfaction or adjustment.

The precise reasons for the lack of relationships in this regard remain unknown, but they may stand testament to the premium professional development activities place on the acquisition of new knowledge and technical skills rather than personal awareness, balance or adjustment. Given the recurring relationships that have been noted between aspects of personal and professional functioning, however, perhaps continuing education activities should dedicate greater attention to the development of personal qualities that are presumed to contribute substantially to professional competencies. As explicit targets of formal and informal CE, for example, perhaps greater self-awareness, mindfulness, emotional attunement and self-care, for example, represent the personal and interpersonal skills sets that would enhance the relationship between CE and personal well-being and adjustment (see Skovholt et al., 2001; Wise & Gibson, 2012).

Alternatively, it may be that the relationship between CE and personal factors is present, but only in defined contexts. Some research suggests, for example, that workplace settings that offer many opportunities for updating professional development aid in lower stress and greater work satisfaction for their employees (Kushnir et al., 2000). It remains for future studies, however, to explore in greater detail the potential impact of CE participation on aspects of personal adjustment and well-being.

CONCLUSION

Results from this study provide a glimpse into the relationship between CE and the ongoing development of professional competencies. Findings suggest that personal experience, as well as express professional development, contribute to perceived professional competence.

The present study suggests that there is a connection between the CE and professional competencies, but the nature and strength of this connection remain unclear. While professional competency was significantly correlated with levels of formal and informal CE participation, the nature of this relationship requires further attention. It is not clear, for example, whether there is any causal relationship between these variables. It is tempting to attribute higher levels of perceived competency to the completion of more formal and informal CE activities, but the correlational nature of these findings do not permit any causal interpretations. It may be that higher CE participation contributes to greater competencies or that higher perceived competence translates into greater CE participation. Alternatively, it may be that there is no causal connection between these two sets of factors, but that a third variable operates to increase both of them. As an example, a greater commitment to lifelong learning may act to increase both the participation in CE activities and the development of greater professional competencies, and tentative work would suggest the likelihood of such an effect (see Hojat, Veloski & Gonnella, 2012). Future work should direct more systematic attention to the relationship between professional competence and participation in CE activities in order to clarify the role that CE may play in maintaining or enhancing effective clinical practice. Nonetheless, findings from this study suggest that there is an important relationship between one's personal well-being and professional functioning, one's perceived competency and professional self-efficacy. This suggests the potential value of CE programs that attend to aspects of personal well-being as a prospective mechanism for enhancing professional functioning and competence. Explicit attention to issues of increased self-care and reduced stress, for example, could translate into measurable differences in clinical efficacy and outcomes.

Future work might benefit from continuing efforts to examine the relationship between aspects of personal adjustment and professional functioning. It is especially noteworthy in this regard that current conceptualizations of professional competency place a premium on a variety of personal qualities (interpersonal relationships, self-awareness, tolerance for ambiguity, emotional awareness) that are uncommon targets of continuing education programs, per se. By contrast, most CE programs tend to emphasize assessment and intervention in relation a variety of disorders (Neimeyer, Taylor & Wear, 2010b), where the emphasis is placed on conceptual and technical skills pertaining to those disorders rather than the personal awareness or capacities of the therapist. Future work might productively examine the impact of both formal and informal CE that expressly targets the adjustment, growth and development of the therapist's personal qualities as a mechanism for enhancing their professional capacities. Work such as this might, in turn, provide empirical support for current conceptual notions regarding competence, and in this way, help align that work with the increasingly evidence-based world of professional development and continuing education.

BIOSKETCHES

JENNIFER M. TAYLOR received her M.S. in counseling psychology from the University of Florida. She is currently a Ph.D. candidate in the University of Florida counseling psychology program. Her research focuses on professional development and competencies, lifelong learning, continuing education, and mentoring.

GREG J. NEIMEYER received his Ph.D. in counseling psychology from the University of Notre Dame. He is professor of psychology in the Department of Psychology at the University of Florida and director of the Office of Continuing Education and Psychology at the APA. A fellow of the APA, he is also a member of the Department of Community Health and Family Medicine. His areas of research include professional development, epistemology and psychotherapy, and relationship development and disorder.

DOUGLAS M. WEAR received his Ph.D. in clinical psychology from the University of Wyoming. He is the president of Wear and Associates, Inc., executive director of the Washington State Psychological Association, director of Antioch University Seattle Psychology and Community Counseling Clinic, chair of the APA Continuing Education Committee, and past chair of APA Council of Executive Director of State and Provincial Psychological Associations. His research and professional interests include professional development, supervision, management, consulting, and coaching.

REFERENCES

Adams, A., & Sharkin, B. S. (2012). Should continuing education be mandatory for re-licensure? Arguments for and against. In G. J. Neimeyer, & J. M. Taylor (Eds.), *Continuing professional development and lifelong learning: Issues, impacts and outcomes* (pp. 157-178). Hauppauge, NY: Nova Science Publishers.

American Psychological Association. (2000). *Minutes of APA Council of Representatives.* Washington, DC: Author.

Barnett, J. E. (2007). Who needs self-care anyway? *Professional Psychology: Research and Practice, 38*, 603-612.

Bloom, B. S. (2005). Effects of continuing medical education on improving physician clinical care and patient health. *International Journal of Technology Assessment in Health Care, 21*, 380-385.

Brodie, J., & Robinson, B. (1991). MPA distress/impaired psychologists survey: Overview and results. *Minnesota Psychologist, 27*, 627-686.

Brucato, B., & Neimeyer, G. (2009). Epistemology as a predictor of psychotherapists' self-care and coping. *Journal of Constructivist Psychology, 22*, 269-282.

Center for Psychology Workforce Analysis and Research. (2007). *Demographic characteristics of APA members by membership status.* Retrieved from http://www.apa.org/workforce/publications/06-member/table-1.pdf.

Cohen, S., Kamarck, T., & Merlmestein, R. (1983). A global measure of perceived stress. *Journal of Health and Social Behavior, 24*, 385-396.

Daniels, A. S., & Walter, D. A. (2002). Current issues in continuing education for contemporary behavioral health practice. *Administration and Policy in Mental Health, 29*, 359-376.

Davis, D., Thomson, M., Oxman, A., & Haynes, R. (1995). Changing physician performance: A systematic review of the effect of continuing medical education strategies. *Journal of the American Medical Association, 274*, 700-705.

Davis, D., Thomson O'Brien, M. A., Freemantle, N., Wolf, F. M., Mazmanian, P., & Taylor-Vaisey, A. (1999). Impact of formal continuing medical education: Do conferences, workshops, rounds, and other traditional continuing education activities change physician behavior or health care outcomes? *Journal of the American Medical Association, 282*, 867-874.

Deutsch, C. J. (1985). A survey of therapists' personal problems and treatment. *Professional Psychology: Research and Practice, 16*, 305-315.

Diener, E., Emmons, R. A., Larsen, R. J., & Griffin, S. (1985). The satisfaction with life scale. *Journal of Personality Assessment, 49*, 71-75.

Elliott, D. M., & Guy, J. D. (1993). Mental health professionals versus non-mental-health professionals: Childhood trauma and adult functioning. *Professional Psychology: Research and Practice, 24*, 83-90.

Elman, N. S., Illfelder-Kaye, J., & Robiner, W. N. (2005). Professional development: Training of professionalism as a foundation for competent practice in psychology. *Professional Psychology: Research and Practice, 36*, 367-375.

Fagan, T. J., Ax, R. K., Liss, M., Resnick, R. J., & Moody, S. (2007). Professional education and training: How satisfied are we? An exploratory study. *Training and Education in Professional Psychology, 1*, 13-25.

Figley, C. R. (1995). *Compassion fatigue as secondary traumatic stress disorder: An overview*. In C. R. Figley (Ed.), Compassion fatigue: Coping with secondary traumatic stress disorder in those who treat the traumatized. New York: Brunner/Mazel.

Guy, J. D., Poelstra, P. L., & Stark, M. J. (1989). Professional distress and therapeutic effectiveness: National survey of psychologists practicing psychotherapy. *Professional Psychology: Research and Practice, 20*, 48-50.

Hatcher, R. L., & Lassiter, K. D. (2007). Initial training in professional psychology: The practicum competencies outline. *Training in Professional Psychology, 1*, 49-63.

Hojat, M., Veloski, J. J., & Gonnella, J. S. (2012). Physician lifelong learning: Conceptualization, measurement, and correlations in full-time clinicians and academic clinicians. In G. J. Neimeyer, & J. M. Taylor (Eds.), *Continuing professional development and lifelong learning: Issues, impacts and outcomes* (pp. 33-72). Hauppauge, NY: Nova Science Publishers.

Institute of Medicine. (2010). *Redesigning continuing education in the health professions*. Washington, DC: The National Academies Press.

Kushnir, T., Cohen, A. H., & Kitai, E. (2000). Continuing medical education and primary physicians' job stress, burnout and dissatisfaction. *Medical Education, 34*, 430-436.

Lichtenberg, J. W., & Goodyear, R. K. (2008, August). Preparing psychologists for lifelong learning. In C. D. Belar (Chair), *Examining the Mechanism for Lifelong Learning in Professional Psychology*. Symposium conducted at the meeting of the 2008 American Psychological Association Conference, Boston, MA.

Mahoney, M. J. (1997). Psychotherapists' personal problems and self-care patterns. *Professional Psychology: Research and Practice, 28*, 14-16.

Melchert, T. T., Hays, V. L., Wiljanen, L. M., & Kolocek, A. K. (1996). Testing models of counselor development with a measure of counseling self-efficacy. *Journal of Counseling and Development, 74*, 640-644.

Neimeyer, G. J., Taylor, J. M., & Philip, D. (2010a). Continuing education in psychology: Patterns of participation and perceived outcomes among mandated and nonmandated psychologists. *Professional Psychology: Research and Practice, 41*, 435-441.

Neimeyer, G. J., Taylor, J. M., & Wear, D. (2009). Continuing education in psychology: Outcomes, evaluations and mandates. *Professional Psychology: Research and Practice, 40*, 617-624.

Neimeyer, G. J., Taylor, J. M., & Wear, D. (2010b). Continuing education in psychology: Patterns of participation and aspects of selection. *Professional Psychology: Research and Practice, 41*, 281-287.

Neimeyer, G. J., Taylor, J. M., & Wear, D. (2011). *What does it mean to be a competent psychologist?* Unpublished manuscript.

Pope, K. S., & Feldman-Summers, S. (1992). National survey of psychologists' sexual and physical abuse history and their evaluation of training and competence in these areas. *Professional Psychology: Research and Practice, 23*, 353-361.

Pope, K. S., & Tabachnick, B. G. (1994). Therapists as patients: A national survey of psychologists' experiences, problems, and beliefs. *Professional Psychology: Research and Practice, 25*, 247-258.

Porter, N. (1995). Therapist self-care: A proactive ethical approach. In E. J. Rave, and C. C. Larsen, *Ethical decision making in therapy: Feminist perspectives* (pp. 247-266). New York, NY: Guilford Press.

Radeke, J. T., & Mahoney, M. J. (2000). Comparing the personal lives of psychotherapists and research psychologists. *Professional Psychology: Research and Practice, 31*, 82-84.

Rubel, E. C., Sobell, L. C., & Miller, W. R. (2000). Do continuing education workshops improve participants' skills? Effects of a motivational interviewing workshop on substance-abuse counselors' skills and knowledge. *The Behavior Therapist, 23*, 73-77, 90.

Rupert, P. A., Stevanovic, P., & Hunley, H. A. (2009). Work-family conflict and burnout among practicing psychologists. *Professional Psychology: Research and Practice, 40*, 54-61.

Schoener, G. R. (2007). Do as I say, not as I do. *Professional Psychology: Research and Practice, 38*, p. 610-612.

Sharkin, B. S., & Plageman, P. M. (2003). What do psychologists think about mandatory continuing education? A survey of Pennsylvania psychologists. *Professional Psychology: Research and Practice, 34*, 318-323.

Showalter, S. E. (2010). Compassion fatigue: What is it? Why does it matter? Recognizing the symptoms, acknowledging the impact, developing the tools to prevent compassion fatigue, and strengthen the professional already suffering from the effects. *American Journal of Hospice and Palliative Medicine, 27*, 239-242.

Skovholt, T. M., Grier, T. L., & Hanson, M. R. (2001). Career counseling for longevity: Self-care and burnout prevention strategies for counselor resilience. *Journal of Career Development, 27*, 167-176.

Skovholt, T. M., & Starkey, M. T. (2010). The three legs of the practitioner's learning stool: Practice, research/theory, and personal life. *Journal of Contemporary Psychotherapy, 40*, 125-130.

Sprang, G. (2010). Compassion satisfaction, compassion fatigue, and burnout in a national sample of trauma treatment therapists. *Anxiety, Stress and Coping: An International Journal, 23*, 319-339.

Stevanovic, P., & Rupert, P. A. (2009). Work-family spillover and life satisfaction among professional psychologists. *Professional Psychology: Research and Practice, 40*, 62-68.

Taylor, J. M., Neimeyer, G. J., Zemansky, M., & Rothke, S. E. (2012). Exploring the relationship between lifelong learning, continuing education, and professional competencies. In G. J. Neimeyer, & J. M. Taylor (Eds.), *Continuing professional development and lifelong learning: Issues, impacts and outcomes* (pp. 83-99). Hauppauge, NY: Nova Science Publishers.

VandeCreek, L., & Brace, K. Mandatory continuing education in the health professions. *Journal of Training and Practice in Professional Psychology, 5*, 23-36.

Wampold, B. (2007). Psychotherapy: The humanistic (and effective) treatment. *American Psychologist, 62*, 857-873.

Wise, E. H. (2008). Competence and scope of practice: Ethics and professional development. *Journal of Clinical Psychology: In Session, 64*, 626-637.

Wise, E. H. (2010). Maintaining competence in professional psychology: Obsolescence, lifelong learning and continuing education. *Professional Psychology: Research and Practice, 41*, 288-292.

Wise, E. H., & Gibson, C. M. (2012). Continuing education, ethics and self-care: A professional life span perspective. In G. J. Neimeyer, & J. M. Taylor (Eds.), *Continuing professional development and lifelong learning: Issues, impacts and outcomes* (pp. 199-222). Hauppauge, NY: Nova Science Publishers.

SECTION 5.

SOCIETAL IMPLICATIONS AND IMPACTS

In: Continuing Professional Development ...
Editors: G. J. Neimeyer and J. M. Taylor

ISBN: 978-1-62100-767-8
© 2012 Nova Science Publishers, Inc.

Chapter 15

LIFESPAN PROFESSIONAL DEVELOPMENT THROUGH PRACTICE-BASED EDUCATION: IMPLICATIONS FOR THE HEALTH PROFESSIONS

Ronald M. Cervero[*]

College of Education
Institute for Evidence-Based Health Professions Education
The University of Georgia, Athens, Georgia, US

ABSTRACT

There has been much recent discussion by leaders and scholars in the health professions about redesigning systems of lifespan professional development, highlighted by the Institute of Medicine's report, *Redesigning Continuing Education in the Health Professions* (2010). In this context, the chapter characterizes the current system of continuing professional development, summarizes the evidence base for dimensions of the proposed system, and identifies four key characteristics of the proposed system. In the current system, continuing professional development is: 1) Devoted mainly to updating practitioners about the newest developments, 2) Transmitted in a didactic fashion, 3) Offered by a pluralistic group of providers that do not coordinate their work together, 4) Using "seat time" to re-credential practitioners, and 5) Often paid for by vendors who stand to benefit from the learning. The redesigned system will involve four fundamental changes, including moving: 1) from a pre-service to a lifespan focus, 2) from content updates to practice-based learning, 3) from un-coordinated events to a curriculum, and 4) from re-credentialing based on participation to re-credentialing based on learning and practice.

Keywords: Continuing professional development, lifelong learning, practice-based education, evidence-based continuing education

---

[*] Correspondence regarding this manuscript may be directed to Ronald M. Cervero, Professor and Associate Dean. College of Education, University of Georgia, Aderhold Hall G-10Y, 110 Carlton St., Athens, GA 30602. (706) 542-2221 (office); (706) 542-0360 (fax).

BACKGROUND AND PUPROSE

The fundamental purpose of continuing professional development is to "facilitate the successful performance of practitioners in the diverse practice characteristic of professional work" (Houle, 1980, p. 12). This purpose stands in dramatic contrast to the most frequently encountered form of continuing professional development:

> It is dominated by the informational update. In what is typically an intensive two or three-day short course, a single instructor lectures and lectures and lectures fairly large groups of business and professional people, who sit for long hours in an audiovisual twilight, making never-to-be-read notes at rows of narrow tables covered with green baize and appointed with fat binders and sweating pitchers of ice water. (Nowlen, 1988, p. 23)

This picture is as universally recognizable to people in any profession as it is criticized for being largely ineffective in improving professional practice. Indeed, the familiarity of this picture would be funny if the importance of continuing professional development were not so great. The most fundamental issue that must be continually addressed is: "What is the problem for which continuing professional development is the answer?" It is clear that the problem has been conceived as "keeping practitioners up-to-date on the profession's knowledge base." In fact, keeping professionals up-to-date is as close to a unifying aim as continuing professional development has.

This lack of connection between the goals and the methods of continuing professional development has been noted by many scholars and leaders across the professions for several decades (Cervero, 1988; Cervero & Daley, 2010; Dryer, 1962; Houle, 1980; Miller, 1967). In the past five years, however, leaders in the health professions have stated that the negative consequences of this disconnect are no longer acceptable and have begun to seek governmental and profession-wide policy solutions. Of all of these approaches to the problem, the most visible has been the publication of the Institute of Medicine's (IOM) report, *Redesigning Continuing Education in the Health Professions* (2010). The report opens with the problem stated in its most stark terms:

> Continuing education (CE) is the process by which health professionals keep up to date with the latest knowledge and advances in health care. However, the CE "system," as it is structured today, is so deeply flawed that it cannot properly support the development of health professionals. CE has become structured around health professional participation instead of performance improvement. This has left health professionals unprepared to perform at the highest levels consistently, putting into question whether the public is receiving care of the highest possible quality and safety. (Institute of Medicine, 2010, p. ix)

The importance of these policy proposals for redesigning the system of continuing professional development cannot be overstated. We have known for decades how to design continuing professional development so that it achieves the outcomes of improved professional practice and patient care. There have been numerous reports of practical approaches and a significant scientific evidence base about successful approaches to continuing professional development. Thus, changing the system is more of a political problem than a knowledge problem. In this light, the purposes of this chapter are to: 1) Characterize the current and proposed system of continuing professional development, 2) Summarize the evidence base for dimensions of the proposed system, and 3) Identify four key characteristics of the proposed system.

THE CURRENT SYSTEM OF LIFESPAN PROFESSIONAL DEVELOPMENT

At the current time, the picture of "a single instructor lecturing and lecturing large groups of professionals" is still easily recognizable as the predominant form of continuing professional development. We do not yet have a similarly recognizable picture of a system of continuing professional development towards which we can move. The major reason for this lack of a unifying picture is that the professions are in a transitional stage, experimenting with many different purposes, forms, and institutional locations for the delivery of continuing professional development. These systems, such as they are, are incredibly primitive. I would characterize them as:

A. Devoted mainly to updating practitioners about the newest developments,
B. Transmitted in a didactic fashion,
C. Offered by a pluralistic group of providers (workplaces, for-profits,
D. associations, and universities) that do not coordinate their work together,
E. Using "seat time" to re-credential practitioners, and
F. Often paid for by vendors who stand to benefit from the learning.

Relatively speaking, these systems of continuing professional development are in their infancy. By way of analogy, the field is in the same state of development as pre-service education was 100 years ago. Medical education serves a useful point of comparison. In his 1910 report on medical schools in Canada and the United States, Flexner (1910) found that only 16 of 155 schools expected that their incoming students would have **any** previous college education and he recommended closing the ones that did not. It is unlikely that anyone in 1910 would have predicted the structure of medical education today. Likewise, systems of continuing education are likely to grow through this transitional period to achieve an equivalent coherence, size, and stature as the pre-service stage of professional education.

Proposals to construct a "lifelong" system of professional development are not new. The first such system was proposed 50 years ago for physicians in the Dryer Report, "Lifetime Learning for Physicians" (1962). Dryer's Joint Study Committee, which was sponsored by all the medical establishment's major governing bodies, proposed a system to be constructed across the three phases of the professional development: pre-service education, induction/residency, and continuing education. Significantly, the report recommended a focus on improving practitioner's clinical judgment as opposed to updating them on the newest developments:

Education for medicine must move from objectives placing such great emphasis upon the acquisition of information toward objectives more effectively promoting the ability to select, organize, and evaluate information in a way that will stimulate curiosity and foster the kind of critical perception which the judgments of a learned profession will increasingly require. (Dryer, 1962, p. xiv)

In a similar vein, the field of psychology has recently also proposed a system for using lifelong learning to maintain practitioners' continuing competence in the article titled, "Lifelong Learning for Psychologists: Current Status and a Vision for the Future" (Wise et al., 2010).

At the present time, then, there is widespread consensus that change is needed and is likely to be driven by external forces. The recent report of the Association of American Medical Colleges and the American Association of Colleges of Nursing offers a vision for this new system:

We envision a continuum of health professional education from admission into a health professional program to retirement that values, exemplifies, and assesses lifelong learning skills; emphasizes inter-professional and team-based education and practice; employs tested, outcomes-based continuing education methods; and links health professional education and delivery of care within the workplace. (AAMC and AACN, 2010, p. 3)

Drawing upon its previous reports for reshaping the health care system, and especially the health professions systems in its *Health Professions Education: A Bridge to Quality* (Greiner & Knebel, 2003), the IOM (2010) lays out a similar vision for a system of continuing professional development that ensures health professionals can: 1) Provide patient-centered care, 2) Work in interprofessional teams, 3) Employ evidence-based practice, 4) Apply quality improvement, and 5) Use health informatics. Each of these proposals for a system of lifespan professional development diverges sharply from the systems that are in place now for each profession.

CAN CONTINUING PROFESSIONAL DEVELOPMENT IMPROVE PRACTICE AND PATIENT HEALTH OUTCOMES?

The health professions have experimented with a practice-based model of continuing professional development since the 1960s. This model that focuses on health professionals' practice, not the newest research findings, was signaled by the question in the title of the article, *Continuing Education for What?* (Miller, 1967). With this article and many practical experiments in practice-based learning, Miller and others ushered in a new era of continuing professional development (Manning, 2003). For example, Storey reported on a project where physicians recorded the clinical problems they faced over a two-day period as a basis for understanding their educational needs (Storey, 1966). The succeeding decades have seen an incredible elaboration and extension of this educational model (Davis & Fox, 1994; Fox, Mazmanian, & Putnam, 1989). This emphasis on health professionals' practice has led to hundreds of research studies that sought to understand the link between continuing professional development and practice and patient health outcomes. These studies, many of which were randomized clinical trials (e.g., Tu & Davis, 2002), have shown that educational interventions under the right conditions can make a difference in health professionals' practice and patient health outcomes. Over the past 15 years, there have been several significant meta-analyses of these individual research studies (e.g., Bloom, 2005; Davis, Thomson, Oxman, & Haynes, 1992, 1995; Forsetlund et.al., 2009; Mansouri & Lockyear, 2007; Mazmanian & Davis, 2002; Robertson, Umble, & Cervero, 2003; Umble & Cervero, 1996) that can inform the redesign of systems of continuing professional development. These meta-analyses have asked two fundamental questions: 1) Can CPD improve practice and patient health outcomes?, and 2) What are the mechanisms of action that lead to positive changes in these outcomes?

I briefly summarize four of the meta-analyses by way of showing the consensus of evidence in response to these two questions. Umble and Cervero (1996) summarized 16 meta-analyses of continuing education for health professionals that were published between 1977 and 1993. They identified two waves of meta-analyses that asked whether CE can have an impact on practice and patient care. The first wave of eight publications asking the question, "Does CE have an impact?" found that CE can more easily change professionals' knowledge and competence than their practice and patient care. The second wave of eight publications (4 of which were statistical meta-analyses) found the primary influences on change were: Having conducted a needs-assessment for practice change, program intensity, learners from same practice setting, and administrative support and policy incentives for practice changes. They recommended that new research should focus on the question of why, not if, CE has an impact on practice change and patient care. Robertson et al. (2003) published an update seven years later of 15 new impact syntheses that had been published between 1994 through 2002. This article reinforced the central conclusions of the 1996 synthesis, showing that CE can have an impact, with knowledge and competence easier to change than practice and patient care. The primary influencers of improved outcomes were that CE a) is based on practice-based needs-assessment, b) is ongoing, c) uses interactive learning methods, and d) is contextually relevant.

The most rigorous meta-analysis was completed by the Agency for Health Research and Quality (Marinopoulos et. al., 2007). This report used 136 individual articles and nine systematic reviews to determine the "Effectiveness of Continuing Medical Education." The report used a broad definition of CME that included delivery formats as diverse as lectures, problem-based learning, and point of care learning. As with the two previous meta-analyses, CME was shown to be effective. However, its impact was less consistent as outcomes moved from knowledge to patient care: Knowledge (22 of 28, 79% of studies), attitudes (22 of 26, 85%), skills (12 of 15, 80%), practice behavior (61 of 105, 58%), clinical practice outcomes (14 of 33, 42%). The report concluded that there was not sufficient evidence to determine the impact of contextual factors, but did find that: a) live media is more effective than print, b) multimedia is more effective than single media interventions, c) multiple exposures are more effective than a single exposure, and d) simulation methods are effective for improving psychomotor and procedural skills.

Reinforcing many of the conclusions of the previous studies, the IOM report's chapter on "Scientific Foundations of Continuing Education" (2010) concluded from the evidence that effective CE: a) incorporates needs assessments, b) is interactive, c) employs ongoing feedback to learners, d) uses multiple methods of learning, and e) simulates the clinical setting. In summary, the overall conclusions from the evidence are that: 1) Continuing professional development *can improve* health professionals' practice and patient health outcomes, and 2) There is an *emerging consensus* about practice-based education's mechanisms of action that are likely to improve practice and patient health outcomes.

WHAT IS THE FUTURE OF LIFESPAN PROFESSIONAL DEVELOPMENT?

We are now entering a transformational era of constructing systems of continuing professional development. Although these systems have many dimensions, I focus on four that are likely to represent fundamental changes, including moving: 1) from a pre-service to a lifespan focus, 2) from content updates to practice-based learning, 3) from un-coordinated events to a curriculum, and 4) from re-credentialing based on participation to re-credentialing based on learning and practice.

From Pre-Service Focus to Lifespan System

The IOM Report correctly points out that there is a "lack of a coordinated vision" for continuing professional development across the health professions. This critique and the call for a "system" resonate with previous analyses of the problem and its consequences. An incredible amount of resources, financial and human, are used to support three to six years of professionals' pre-service education. Until recently, however, little systematic thought was given to what happens during the following 40 years of professional practice. Many leaders in the professions believed that the years of pre-service professional education, along with some refreshers, were sufficient for a lifetime of work. However, with the rapid social changes, the explosion of research-based knowledge, and spiraling technological innovations, many of these leaders, as exemplified in the Report, now understand the need to continually prepare people for 40 years of professional practice through continuing education.

Beginning in the 1960s, we began to see embryonic evidence for systems of continuing education. The 1970s saw the beginning of what is now a widespread use of continuing education as a basis for re-licensure and re-certification. By the 1980s organized and comprehensive programs of continuing education were developed in engineering, accounting, law, medicine, psychology, pharmacy, veterinary medicine, social work, librarianship, architecture, nursing home administration, nursing, management, public school education, and many other professions. During that decade, many professions also developed their systems of accreditation for providers of continuing education. In building these systems of continuing professional development, we can expect to see clearer connections to the entire continuum of professional development, including the phase of pre-service education and as well as the critical induction/residency phase. These connections are likely to include an alignment of curricula across the lifespan, a better coordination of providers for all three phases, and a more seamless credentialing system across the lifespan.

From Content Updates to Practice-Based Learning

Education and learning in the third stage of the continuum of professional education have a great advantage over the other two stages in promoting effective practice. They occur in a place and time when professionals are most likely to have a need for better ways to think about what they do. But to exploit this natural advantage, we need to find ways to better integrate continuing professional development, both in its content and educational design, into professionals' ongoing individual and collective practice. Practice-based education across the continuum of professionals' education offers a strategy that will define the systems of continuing professional development (Hager, Russell, & Fletcher, 2008). For example, practice-based learning models are also now at the center of reform proposals in the first two stages in the continuum of medical education (Association of American Medical Colleges [AAMC], 2004; Accreditation Council for Graduate Medical Education, 2007). The past 40 years has seen an incredible elaboration and extension of this practice-based educational model (Cervero, 1988; Daley, 2000; Eraut, 1994; Eraut, 2001; Houle, 1980; Nowlen, 1988). This movement to practice-based learning is now at the forefront of educational agendas throughout the professions (Cervero, 2001; Moore & Pennington, 2003; Thorpe, Woodall, Sadler-Smith, & Gold, 2004). The IOM Report supports this move with the recommendation to integrate continuing professional development into the quality improvement processes in healthcare.

From Uncoordinated Events to an Organized Curriculum

In the health professions' pre-service and induction/residency programs, there are fixed curricula, courses, and timeframes. These educational programs are highly regulated by accrediting bodies in order to assure competence upon entry to practice. This is true universally for both the classroom and clinical portions of these two first two stages of professional education. Once professionals enter into practice, however, the locus of responsibility for the curriculum of professional development shifts almost entirely to the individual. There are a small number of organizations that require participation in a formal course that covers a specific topic as part of the requirements for re-credentialing, usually related to the ethics of professional practice. However, in medicine there is a movement towards using general competencies that would structure the re-credentialing of medical specialties in the United States (Spivey, 2005). The six general competencies, which have been accepted by all the major stakeholder groups across the continuum in medical education, are focused on developing knowledge and skills related to patient care, medical knowledge, practice-based learning and improvement, interpersonal communication skills, professionalism, and systems based-practice (Miller, 2005). These competencies, however, do not constitute a comprehensive curriculum because no course content is prescribed. Rather, the processes of "self-directed learning" and "directed self-learning" are used to determine the curriculum. In the self-directed learning process, the American Board of Medical Specialties states that "physicians should evaluate their practice and their need to learn and define and receive help in defining areas of learning need as well as methods and resources to assure satisfaction of those needs in the process of improvement" (Miller, 2005, p. 154). What is new, however, comes from the process of "directed self-learning" that requires the specialty boards to help physicians "in identifying those areas of need and also to direct learners toward improvement mechanisms, taking care to make sure there is a balance established between self-directed learning and learning that is other directed. Both must be addressed" (Miller, 2005, p. 154).

From Re-Credentialing Based on Participation to Learning and Practice

Policymakers responsible for licensing, certification and accreditation will develop systems that move from accumulating credits based on participation in continuing professional development to rewarding effective individual and system learning (Davis & Willis, 2004; Regnier, Kopelow, Lane, & Alden, 2005). Looking across the professions globally, it is clear that all existing re-credentialing programs are based on the central premise articulated by Houle (1980) over 25 years ago: "To achieve its greatest potential, continuing education must fulfill the promise of its name and be truly continuing—not casual, sporadic, or opportunistic...This fact means essentially that it must be self-directed" (p. 12). Houle, however, recognizes that "reliance cannot be solely based on self-direction" (p. 12) because adult learners are not always in the best position to know what they do not know in terms of maintaining competency. The emerging recertification scheme that calls for the active involvement of medical specialty boards is the first example in which other stakeholders help practitioners construct their own professional development curriculum. There are many substantive reasons for not prescribing a standard curriculum for professional development across the lifespan. Thus, the involvement of professional bodies and employing organizations in partnering with individual practitioners to develop those curricula for re-credentialing may become the model across the professions over the next 20 years.

TRANSFORMING SYSTEMS OF CONTINUING PROFESSIONAL DEVELOPMENT

Are we truly at a transformational time for redesigning systems of continuing professional development? The IOM Report noted that the time is now, perhaps hoping it could serve as the Flexner Report for continuing professional development:

> Significant change in health professions education is not unprecedented. Specific to medicine, the ...Flexner report was published in 1910. The report dramatically changed the culture and landscape of undergraduate medical education in the United States. At the time of the Flexner Report, many observers...had concerns about the perceived lack of standardized prerequisites and curriculums across medical schools; the reliance on education through lectures and memorization, not at a patient's bedside; and the proprietary nature of medical education. These concerns...mirror today's concerns about continuing education of all health professionals. (IOM, 2010, p. 21)

Houle's (1980) commentary suggests that this transformation, while seemingly a distant hope, is more likely when seen in a grand historical context:

Learning must occur throughout the lifespan and must assume new and more complex forms. The plans to establish basic educational programs for those entering the professions were thought in the first quarter of [the 20th] century to be visionary, but they have been realized at levels far beyond those of the original dreams. Continuing education will follow the same pattern of growth; what we hardly dare prophesy today will be seen by later generations as efforts to achieve a manifest necessity. (Houle, 1980, p. 302)

The leaders of workplaces, professional associations, universities, and governments have both a tremendous opportunity and a clear responsibility to further develop the systems of continuing professional development for the health professions. As with any humanly-constructed system, the building of a coordinated system for any profession, much less across the health professions, is a political process. This process will be marked by fundamental struggles over the educational agenda and the competing interests of the educational agenda and the political-economic agendas of the multiple stakeholders for continuing professional development. As a political process, then, it is crucial that all of the stakeholders participate in a substantive way in negotiating these agendas for continuing professional development. For the immediate and long-term negotiation of these struggles will define whether continuing professional development can make a demonstrable impact on the quality and safety of health care in the United States.

BIOSKETCH

RONALD M. CERVERO is Associate Dean for Outreach and Engagement in the College of Education and Co-director of the Institute for Evidence-Based Health Professions Education at the University of Georgia. He is also a Professor in the Department of Lifelong Education, Administration, and Policy. He earned his M.A. in the social sciences and his Ph.D. in adult education at The University of Chicago. Professor Cervero has published extensively, with particular emphasis in the areas of continuing education for the professions and the politics of adult education. Two of his books have received the Cyril O. Houle World Award for Literature in Adult Education: *Effective Continuing Education for Professionals* in 1989 and *Working the Planning Table: Negotiating Democratically for Adult, Continuing, and Workplace Education* in 2006.

REFERENCES

Accreditation Council for Graduate Medical Education. (2007). *Common program requirements: General competencies.* Retrieved September 18, 2008, from http://www.acgme.org/outcome/comp/compFull.asp.

Association of American Medical Colleges (2004). *Educating doctors to provide high quality medical care: A vision for medical education in the United States.* Washington, DC: Author.

Association of American Medical Colleges and the American Association of Colleges of Nursing. (2010). *Lifelong learning in medicine and nursing: Final conference report*. Washington, DC: Author.

Bloom, B. S. (2005). Effects of continuing medical education on improving physician clinical care and patient health. *International Journal of Technology Assessment in Health Care, 21*, 380-385.

Cervero, R. M. (1988). *Effective continuing education for professionals*. San Francisco: Jossey-Bass.

Cervero, R. M. (2001). Continuing professional education in transition, 1981-2000. *International Journal of Lifelong Education, 20*, 16-30.

Cervero, R. M., & Daley, B. J. (2010). Continuing professional education: Multiple stakeholders and agendas. In P. Peterson, E. Baker, & B. McGaw (Eds.), *International encyclopedia of education (3rd ed.), Vol. 1* (pp. 127-132). Oxford: Elsevier.

Daley, B. (2000). Learning in professional practice. In V. Mott, & B. Daley (Eds.), *Charting a course for continuing professional education: Reframing professional practice* (pp. 33-42). New Directions in Adult and Continuing Education, 86. San Francisco: Jossey Bass.

Davis, D., & Fox, R. (1994). From Banff to Beaver Creek: Consensus building in CME. In D. Davis, & R. Fox (Eds.), *The physician as learner: Linking research to practice* (pp. x-xvii). Chicago: American Medical Association.

Davis, D. A., Thomson, M. A., Oxman, A. D., & Haynes, R. B. (1992). Evidence for the effectiveness of CME: A review of 50 randomized controlled trials. *Journal of the American Medical Association, 268*, 1111-1117.

Davis, D. A., Thomson, M. A., Oxman, A. D., & Haynes, R. B. (1995). Changing physician performance: A systematic review of the effect of continuing medical education strategies. *Journal of the American Medical Association, 274*, 700-705.

Davis, N. L., & Willis, C. E. (2004). A new metric for continuing medical education credit. *The Journal of Continuing Education in the Health Professions, 24*, 139-144.

Dryer, B. V. (1962). Lifetime learning for physicians: Principles, practices, and Proposals [Entire issue]. *Journal of Medical Education, 37*.

Eraut, M. (1994). *Developing professional knowledge and competence*. London: Falmer.

Eraut, M. (2001). Do continuing professional development models promote one-dimensional learning? *Medical Education, 35*, 8-11.

Flexner, A. (1910). *Medical education in the United States and Canada*. New York: Carnegie Foundation for the Advancement of Teaching.

Forsetlund, L., Bjorndal, A., Rashidian, A., Jamtvedt, G., Obrien, M.A., Wolf, F.,…Oxman, A.D. (2009). Continuing education meetings and workshops: Effects on professional practice and health care outcomes. *Cochrane Database of Systematic Reviews* (2): CD003030.

Fox, R. D., Mazmanian, P. E., & Putnam, R. W. (Eds.). (1989). *Changing and learning in the lives of physicians*. New York: Praeger.

Greiner, A.C., & Knebel, E. (Eds.). (2003). *Health professions education: A bridge to quality*. Washington, DC: The National Academies Press.

Hager, M., Russell, S., & Fletcher, S. W. (2008). *Continuing education in the health professions: Improving healthcare through lifelong learning*. New York: Josiah Macy, Jr. Foundation.

Houle, C. O. (1980). *Continuing learning in the professions*. San Francisco: Jossey-Bass.

Institute of Medicine. (2010) *Redesigning continuing education in the health professions.* Washington, DC: The National Academies Press.

Manning, P. R. (2003). Practice-based learning and improvement: A dream that can become a reality. *The Journal of Continuing Education in the Health Professions, 26,* S6-S9.

Mansouri, M., & Lockyear, J. (2007). A meta-analysis of continuing medical education effectiveness. *Journal of Continuing Education in the Health Professions, 27,* 6- 15.

Marinopoulos, S. S., Dorman, R., N., Wilson, L.M., Ashar, B.H., Magaziner, J.L., Miller, R.G.,…Bass, E.B. (2007). *Effectiveness of continuing medical education.* Evidence report/technology assessment no. 149. Rockville, MD: Agency for Healthcare Research and Quality.

Mazmanian, P. E., & Davis, D. A. (2002). Continuing medical education and the physician as a learner. *Journal of the American Medical Association, 288,* 1057-1060.

Miller, G. E. (1967). Continuing education for what? *Journal of Medical Education, 42,* 320-326.

Miller, S. H. (2005). American Board of Medical Specialties and repositioning for excellence in lifelong learning: Maintenance of certification. *The Journal of Continuing Education in the Health Professions, 25,* 151-156.

Moore, D. E., & Pennington, F. C. (2003). Practice-based learning and improvement. *Journal of Continuing Education in the Health Professions, 23,* S73-S80.

Nowlen, P. M. (1988). *A new approach to continuing education for business and the professions: The performance model.* New York: Macmillan.

Regnier, K., Kopelow, M., Lane, D., & Alden, E. (2005). Accreditation for learning and change. *The Journal of Continuing Education in the Health Professions, 25,* 174-182.

Robertson, M. K., Umble, K. E., & Cervero, R. M. (2003). Impact studies in continuing education for the professions: Update. *The Journal of Continuing Education in the Health Professions, 23,* 146-156.

Spivey, B. E. (2005). Continuing medical education in the United States: Why it needs reform and how we propose to accomplish it. *The Journal of Continuing Education in the Health Professions, 25,* 134-143.

Storey, P. B. (1966). National plan of the American Medical Association. *American Journal of Cardiology, 17,* 893-898.

Thorpe, R., Woodall. J., Sadler-Smith. E., & Gold, J. (2004). Studying CPD in professional life. *British Journal of Occupational Learning, 2,* 3-20.

Tu, K., & Davis, D. (2002). Can we alter physician behavior by educational methods? Lessons learned from studies of the management and follow-up of hypertension. *Journal of Continuing Education in the Health Professions, 22,* 11-22.

Umble, K. E., & Cervero, R. M. (1996). Impact studies in continuing education for health professionals: A critique of the research syntheses. *Evaluation in the Health Professions, 19,* 148-174.

Wise, E.H., Sturm, C.A., Nutt, R. L., Rodolfa, E., Schaffer, J.B., & Webb, C. (2010). Lifelong learning for psychologists: Current status and a vision for the future. *Professional Psychology: Research and Practice, 41,* 288-297.

In: Continuing Professional Development …
Editors: G. J. Neimeyer and J. M. Taylor
ISBN: 978-1-62100-767-8
© 2012 Nova Science Publishers, Inc.

Chapter 16

COMPETENCE, EDUCATION, PROFESSIONAL DEVELOPMENT, PSYCHOLOGY, AND SOCIO-CYBERNETICS

John Raven[*]
University of Edinburgh, Edinburgh, Scotland

ABSTRACT

What is the source of the widespread feeling that many professionals have not behaved professionally? Not usually a deficit in techno-rational knowledge (although such presumed deficits are precisely what is targeted in most attempts to fix the problem). More often the problem has been failure to build up a personal store of relevant up-to-date specialist knowledge. Still more often it stems from deficits in *tacit* knowledge … (unverbalised) knowledge of ways of *doing* things. But most often it stems from a failure to consider the wider needs of clients and a disregard of the consequences of rule-bound actions grounded solely in disciplinary knowledge. In other words, by failure to engage with issues which lie *outside* the individual's domain of specialist knowledge. In such a context, the concept of certifiable professional competence becomes an oxymoron.

The problem in psychology is exacerbated by the fact that many widely accepted thoughtways and procedures have serious shortcomings. As a result, many actions based upon them have undesirable consequences for individuals, institutions, and society. They must therefore be considered unethical.

For these reasons, seeking to restrict the actions of professionals to those which fall within a domain of certifiable techno-rational competence, and requiring them to regularly update that knowledge, is dangerous. More helpful might be a requirement to demonstrate that one has, in one way or another, contributed to the development of the profession.

Keywords: Competency, professional development, socio-cybernetics, lifelong learning

---

[*] Correspondence regarding this manuscript may be directed to John Raven, 30 Great King Street, Edinburgh EH3 6QH, Scotland or jraven@ednet.co.uk.

This chapter addresses issues having to do with the competence and professional development of people working with human resources in such areas as education and organisational and public management.

It is based on research that my colleagues and I have conducted in homes, schools, workplaces, and public management over the past half century.

My basic theme is that our technico-rational knowledge of such things as human development, the nature of competence, assessment, and management is so thin and so heavily based on such inadequate and misleading – indeed damaging – models and procedures, that it would be a mistake to require people working in these areas to engage in professional development activities conceived of as doing such things as taking further courses. My own position is that, if it is felt that continuing professional development does need to be authenticated, what would be needed would be evidence of it having *contributed to the development of the profession*. This would mean demonstrating that one had been doing such things as trying to influence the constraints that limit the effectiveness of psychologists, striving to develop new theoretical frameworks to handle previously neglected problems, and finding new ways of doing things. Doing any of these things would involve an ethical commitment to going well beyond the customary call of duty; doing things one does *not* know how to do. What would be required would be *professional* competence going well beyond what is currently considered to be one's area of certified technical competence.

An example may help to clarify the point. The word "education" comes from the Latin root "educere", which means "to draw out." This implies, and most teachers, pupils, parents, and educational philosophers agree, that the primary task of an educator is to draw out the diverse talents of children, pupils, students, subordinates, other course participants, or apprentices. Yet most teachers don't do this, pointing to many constraints that prevent them from doing so. The conclusion is stark: They cannot be considered to be competent teachers unless they set about, personally and through their professional associations, seeking to influence those constraints. Yet most teachers will claim, first, that it not within their remit to seek to influence such constraints, second that they are not *able* ... that is, they lack the competencies that are required ...to do so, and, third, that such activity is actually proscribed by professional/legal regulations to the effect that they work *only* within their domain of certified specialist competence.

More pointedly, so far as this chapter is concerned, the deficits in teachers' understandings of human competence (including professional competence), its development and assessment, and the determination of behaviour more generally are, in large part, due to oversights *on the part of psychologists.* We have failed to provide teachers with appropriate concepts and tools in these areas. Setting out to develop these understandings and tools – and understand why we have not, in the past, done more to develop them (and doing something about those constraints) – would require *psychologists* to engage in activities going well beyond what is currently regarded as their domain of professional competence. Thus, paradoxically, psychologists cannot be considered to be professionals *unless* they do these things. This turns out to be a rather general problem. Its resolution hinges not merely on developing an understanding of the nature, development, assessment, and deployment of generic, high-level, transferable competencies but also those required (i.e., the societal understandings required) to assert *professional* competence.

To re-state and re-phrase this: *Competence as a psychologist depends, among other things, on setting out to understand and influence the wider social forces that have deflected research psychologists from some of the most important topics they should have been investigating. This involves working outside their domain of certified technico-rational competence. More basically still, understanding the social forces that primarily control human behaviour must lie at the heart of any science which claims to be devoted to understanding and predicting human behaviour. Yet understanding these social forces has not, in the past, been seen as central to the mission of psychology.*

STUDIES DESIGNED TO CLARIFY EDUCATIONAL OBJECTIVES

I begin by very briefly summarising – and thus necessarily over-stating – some results from a number of opinion surveys carried out among parents, pupils, teachers, 20-to-30 year-old year old ex-pupils, and employers in many countries.

The overwhelming majority of those who were interviewed[1] thought the main goals of education include developing such qualities as the confidence and initiative required to introduce change (actually, it was the most widely endorsed goal among our adolescent pupils), problem-solving ability, the ability to work with others, the ability to make one's own observations, and the ability to understand how organisations and society work and play an active part in them. More generally, they include helping people to develop and get recognition for, the diverse, often idiosyncratic, talents they possess. The objectives said to be most important do include helping people to acquire the credentials that appear to control entry to jobs, but the impact of this is tempered by widespread recognition that the formal knowledge on which such certificates are based is in reality *un*important[2].

Few schools do much work in these areas[3]. Goodlad (1983) made the point forcefully by saying that, in general, the activities in which most pupils are engaged for most of the time in most schools do not merit description as academic or intellectual. They fail to nurture such qualities as judgment, analytic ability, the ability to interpret, the ability to communicate, the ability to reconcile different points of view, or critical thinking.

The quest to understand the reasons why schools generally neglect their main goals and what needs to be done to generate more appropriate arrangements forms the basis for much that will be said in this chapter.

---

[1] Morton-Williams et al., 1968; Goodlad, 1983; Johnston & Bachman, 1976; Flanagan & Russ-Eft, 1975; Flanagan, 1978; De Landsheere, 1977; Bill et al., 1974; MacBeath et al., 1981; Raven, 1977: Raven et al., 1975a, b; Andersson, 2001b.

[2] 73% of our adolescent pupils said that it was very important for schools to help them to do as well as possible in external examinations, but only 27% that it was important to learn about aspects of subjects not required for examination purposes. These figures compare with 83% who said it was very important for schools to help them "Develop the confidence and initiative required to introduce change". Their answers to other questions confirm that they correctly recognise that mastering the content they spend so much time studying and on which they are tested is largely a waste of time. I say "correctly" because the fact is that such knowledge has a half-life of a year. People forget 50% in one year, 75% in two years, 87.5% in three years and so on. It is also out of date when it is taught and fails to relate to the problems with which pupils will have to engage later in life.

[3] Goodlad, 1983; HMI, 1990; Galton et al.,1980, ORACLE; Raven et al., 1985; Johnston, 1973; Johnston and Bachman, 1976; Fraley, 1981.

STUDIES OF COMPETENCE IN WORKPLACES AND SOCIETY

There are many reasons why it is important to ask whether the opinions summarised above are founded in reality. One is that it may well be argued that our competence as psychologists depends mainly on high-level competencies like those enumerated by parents, teachers, and students and that the focus in any professional development activities should therefore be on nurturing such competencies. Another is that the answer one gets to the question depends on the methodology employed in research seeking an answer ... and this is often deficient for reasons which call into question many widely accepted practices.

In the course of hundreds of studies[4] conducted using fine-grained methodology – and especially *Behavioural Event Interviewing* (a variant of Flanagan's *Critical Incident Technique*) – it has been shown that effective organisations call on even their "low-level" employees (lavatory attendants, machine operatives, bus drivers, sales people, etc.) to utilise high-level competencies. For example, a compilation of "effective" behaviours observed among machine operatives (Flanagan & Burns, 1955) included examples of them studying the way the organisation in which they worked functioned and working out for themselves what they should be doing and then doing it without having to be given instructions. However, as researchers like Kanter (1985), Schön (1983), and Cunningham (2001) have shown, even observations at this level fail to do justice to the diverse subtle contributions that people in effective organisations make to the emergent properties of problem-identification-and-solving networks[5] which are rarely discussed. These diverse contributions include not only intervening in the internal structure of the organisation (by, for example, getting together with colleagues to influence those above one) but also seeking to understand and influence external constraints and opportunities ... such as those offered by the market or arising from the operation of politico-bureaucratic systems. We will return to this later because it has assumed increasing importance as our work has progressed.

The issue of diversity is important. Researchers have shown that there are many different *types* of effective physicians and scientists ... and none of them are predicted by college grades (Price et al., 1971; Taylor & Barron, 1963). Occupational categories are particularly unhelpful. Psychologists, for example, do all sorts of different things (ranging from running countries and organisations through helping distressed individuals to designing educational programmes, editing journals, and thinking through serious conceptual issues). Such heterogeneous professional groupings are therefore perhaps best understood as sociological groupings which operate mainly to protect their members by erecting barriers to entry. And indeed, as Steiner (1999) has shown, these entry requirements have been raised consistently –

---

[4] Many of the earlier studies are summarised in Raven (1984, 1997), and Spencer and Spencer (1993).

[5] In 1985, Kanter, very usefully, introduced the term "parallel organisation activity" to describe these activities. The term is important because it draws attention to the fact that that this non-hierarchical work does not replace the normal day to day hierarchical and defined-task-oriented activities of the organisation. Rather, they go on alongside – in parallel with – them. However time and resources are specifically set aside for them and all members of the organisation are involved. During this time, fluid, non-hierarchical, groupings form around emergent and previously half-noticed "problems". The members of these groups contribute in many different ways and a deliberate effort is made to recognise these diverse contributions. And staff are encouraged to work with other people engaging with similar problems both within the organisation and outside. Such collaboration generates new ideas and establishes and maintains a network of contacts to provide help and support when difficulties arise.

thus reinforcing the notion that additional "training" is required – without there being any significant change in the nature of the activities actually carried out by those who gain entry.

A couple of studies are of particular relevance here because they deal with *professional* competence.

One is Schön's (1983, 2001) study of how professionals think in action. He argues that the claim of *most* of those who describe themselves as professionals is without foundation. They do not live up to the norms and values they or their professional organisations espouse. He cites lawyers who have no real interest in justice or compassion, physicians who have little interest in the equitable distribution of quality health care, and scientists and engineers who care little about the beneficence and safety of their technologies.

He then goes on to examine the behaviour of some architects, designers, engineers, psychotherapists, and town planners whom he *would* be prepared to describe as professionals. They engage in activities going well beyond the boundaries of their job descriptions and engage with many issues which others would be inclined to overlook. To find ways forward, they engage in "experimental conversations with the problem" often re-defining it and extending its boundaries. The "real problems" lie *outside* the areas of technical competence that their training equipped them to handle; yet they are crucial to their competence, and especially their claim to be professionals. Hence the importance of Schön's (1983, 2001) claim that what is needed is not technico-rational competence but "the abilities required to deal with the swamp" (i.e., the competencies required to deal with situations in which the problems are unclear, messy, confused, and incapable of technical solution). Perhaps of particular interest here is these professionals' engagement with *systems* processes. Whereas many of those working with societal problems (such as malnutrition) propose discipline-based solutions drawing on the technical knowledge of their own particular discipline, the need is for systems-oriented understanding and intervention, which is to be sharply distinguished from "multi-disciplinary" intervention based on independent inputs suggested by a variety of "disciplines".

Also of interest here is Hattie's (2009) meta-analysis of more than 800 meta-analyses of the contribution to pupil "achievement" (traditionally measured) of 138 variables widely considered important to determine school success. Despite the gross limitations of the input and outcome measures, Hattie's conclusion is that effective teachers are extraordinary people characterised by high levels of dedication and personal competence. One of the most important things they do is to continuously seek feedback from their pupils and use it to reconsider their goals and reflect on, and improve, the quality of their teaching. They study the barriers the pupils have encountered and, when they find that their own activities have not had the desired effect, restructure what they are doing so as to achieve their objectives. This stands in stark contrast to the more common interpretation of "feedback" – which tends to be viewed as feedback *to pupils* of some kind of mark or score unaccompanied by any attempt to understand and remedy the problems which have prevented the pupils "doing better" (i.e., arriving at "The Correct Answer").

At the heart of this shift in understanding of the educational process lies a move from thinking of the task of "teaching" as involving "telling" to thinking of it as "managing development".

Another study that is of interest here is Adams and Burgess's (1989) study of teacher competence. Through an extended action-research process, they discovered that different teachers felt that they contributed in very different ways the process of schooling and education *conceived of as a whole*. Thus some teachers felt they had made a particular contribution to developing effective relationships with parents, others to getting the building improved, others to helping pupils with social difficulties, and so on. The *varieties* of teacher competence, physician competence, salesman competence, scientist competence, managerial competence and so on is something with which we, as psychologists, need to come to terms.

The studies mentioned above forcefully raise questions about the *criteria* to be applied when considering or assessing occupational and professional competence. One thing we have seen is that multiple and barely discussed contributions are required to create climates or cultures of enterprise or intelligence. Different people contribute in different ways, and the talents required to make these contributions in an important sense do not exist except in a context of complementary, if not congenial, contributions made by others.

*In*competence

What are the implications of these findings for the professional competence of teachers and psychologists? It can hardly be considered *ethical* to keep so many for so long in such environments. It is therefore an *ethical* requirement – a *professional* requirement – for psychologists and teachers to try to do something about it[6]. What competencies do they need to do *that*? And how can we prepare students to be competent thinkers throughout their lives? We will return to these questions.

Here we should note something else ... something to do with *incompetence* and the demand for certificates supposedly testifying to professional competence.

Surveys reported by Schön (1983, 2001) and Ilott (2001) show that vast numbers of people either have direct experience of, or are acutely aware of, instances of professional incompetence among doctors, lawyers, nurses, social workers and others. This experience includes the widespread observation that many "professionals" find ways of meeting "targets" (including taking content-based courses purporting to contribute to professional development) that have been laid down for them or creating the impression of following mandatory procedures *without* delivering the benefits they are expected to deliver to clients (Seddon, 2008).

And here is the catch. The response of politicians and most professional organisations to such observations on the part of the public has been to introduce "quality control" procedures *based on assessments of technico-rational knowledge*. Hence the proliferation of demands for certificates of "competence" to carry out the most menial tasks and the proscription of actions which go beyond what these areas. Hence the endless regulations about of which Schön's professionals complained so loudly.

Yet, as the work of Schön (1983, 2001), Hogan (1990), Becher (2001), Ilott (2001), and others has shown, incompetence is not the obverse of competence. The main sources of

---

[6] It will, of course, be objected that things have changed since these data were collected. But Andersson's (2001a,b) data hardly support it. In broad terms, one-third liked school, one-third just about tolerated it, and one-third found it a thoroughly destructive experience. Throughout my career as a researcher I have heard statements to the effect that "Yes, it used to be like that, but, in the last couple of years, things have changed". Whenever these beliefs have been checked they have turned out to lack foundation. Perhaps more convincing is the fact that, time after time, as the truth has dawned, one tranch of trumpeted reforms has been replaced by another equally lacking in an understanding of the kinds of problems discussed in this chapter - and thus unlikely to be successful.

*in*competence do not arise from deficits in the technico-rational knowledge. Nor do they even arise mainly from deficits in the kinds of competencies highlighted above. Rather, they arise from failure to *exercise* those competencies. They stem from a lack of *professionalism.*

Our incompetence *as psychologists* stems mainly from failure to do the things we should be doing to contribute to collective activity, and, in particular, from our failure to influence the social and political climate and structures which mainly determine what we do and the research which gets carried out.

The Importance of Beliefs about Society

Before leaving the question of competence and incompetence, and especially professional competence, it is important to return to another quality which pupils, teachers, parents, and employers said it was very important for pupils to develop, namely the ability to build up one's own understanding of how society works and, especially, the ability to intervene to improve its operation.

With a view to checking the validity of such claims, I interviewed a cross section of workers, ranging from street sweepers and blacksmiths to the chief executives of transnational corporations (Raven & Dolphin, 1978). I opened the interviews by asking my informants to tell me something about their jobs and their lives. Before long, they would be sitting on the edge of their chairs telling me about some problem they had. I would then ask "What could you do about that?" One after another they said "There's nothing I could do about it; the government should do it – but it's not my job to influence the government". Somewhat taken aback, I proceeded to arrange for our participation in a couple of national surveys around the topic (Raven & Litton, 1982; Raven & Whelan, 1976). These confirmed my initial observations: By and large people felt that only the government should tackle their problems. I was shocked. But then an interesting thing happened. An economist colleague pointed out that, in all countries of the EU, some 45% of GNP is spent directly by their central governments. But this is not the end of the story; the figure does not include expenditures by local governments or the nationalised or quasi-nationalised industries. When these are added in, the total comes to some 65%. And even this is not all. By requiring people to insure their cars, their health, meet endless regulations regarding health and safety and so on, governments "control" much more of total expenditure. We calculated 75%. Wow. The people were right (again!). So the importance of being able to build up one's own understanding of how society works, which involves much more than understanding the formal political system, turns out to be even more important than most people think. Indeed, it turns out that people's beliefs about society, how it works, and their place in it are, despite their neglect by psychologists, some of the most important determinants of behaviour. But there are good reasons why teachers and psychologists shy away from the area. Encouraging people to analyse and think about these processes and develop the strategies required to intervene in them is, as Harold Rugg (Robinson, 1983; Rugg, 1926) and others (e.g., those running the UK Schools Council Humanities and Integrated Science Projects) discovered to their cost, not only controversial but dangerous. Yet it cannot be too strongly emphasised that the ability to understand and influence social forces and invent ways of handling the value conflicts involved is a crucial competence to be possessed by – one would like to say "all", but that is not the case – citizens – especially those responsible for education and for bringing innovative programmes of psychological research and new forms of public management into being.

The Contrary View

Most psychologists would take issue with much of what I have said about the importance of high-level generic competencies in the workplace, citing numerous impressive studies which appear to show exactly the opposite. These include those brought together by such authors as Gottfredson (1997), Schmidt and Hunter (1998), Jensen (1998), and Ree, Earles, and Teachout (1994). Such studies seem to point unarguably to the conclusion that, as Ree et al. put it, *"g and not much else"* is important.

The discrepancy between the conclusions emanating from these two streams of research stems from what seems, on the surface, to be a difference in methodology. However, it, in reality, reflects a basic difference in the thoughtways (paradigms) on which the studies are built. Although this was highlighted by none other than the father of *g,* Charles Spearman, almost a century ago, the accepted criteria for high quality measurement taught in most advanced courses, and demanded by most journal editors, almost preclude the development of a more appropriate paradigm.

Spearman wrote:

Every normal man, woman, and child is ... a genius at something ... It remains to discover at what ... This must be a most difficult matter, owing to the very fact that it occurs in only a minute proportion of all possible abilities. It certainly cannot be detected by any of the testing procedures at present in current usage.

What he means to say, although he didn't fully realise it, is that it requires the development and adoption of an alternative way of thinking about and "assessing" individual differences. Or, more bluntly, that the current paradigm renders most people's most important talents invisible. It therefore deprives them of opportunities to get recognition for and utilise them. In reality, a more extreme statement turns out to be justified: it denigrates them.

The implications of these observations (and this will become a recurring theme of this chapter) are twofold. On the one hand, they urge us to resist offering, or participating in, "professional development" activities which will lead to further embedment of inappropriate thoughtways and procedures. On the other hand, they underscore the notion that we have a professional responsibility to contribute to the development of a more appropriate framework. It is to the development of the understandings and competencies required to do this that activities concerned with the professional development of psychologists need most importantly to be directed.

But hand in hand with the task of developing a more appropriate psychometric paradigm comes the task of clarifying the *nature* of these competencies; developing better ways of thinking about them.

Building on the work of McClelland et al. (1958), I have argued (Raven, 1984, 1997, 2001a, b) that a two *stage* or two *component* framework is required to think about and assess competence. First, we need to find out what it is that the person concerned is strongly motivated to do. And then, *and only then,* we need to establish which of a series of cumulative and substitutable components of competence, such as thinking about the nature of the task being undertaken, bringing to bear relevant habits and information, monitoring the effectiveness of thought and action, creativity, and persuading other people to help, the individual being assessed brings to bear in his or her efforts to undertake the activity.

It does not make sense to seek, as most psychometricians seek to do, to try to assess "initiative", "creativity", or even "the ability to think" (problem identification and solving ability; meaning-making ability) generically – independently of the activity being undertaken. These are all complex, difficult, and demanding activities that no one will undertake unless they are strongly and intrinsically motivated to carry out the activity.

So the whole development and assessment process looks very different from that most commonly envisaged when people speak about such things as the promotion of self-assessment through professional development activities. The shifts are from teaching as telling to teaching as nurturing growth, from a focus on *content* (to be mastered) to nurturing *competence,* from "ability" to "abilit*ies*", from assessment as scores on measures generated to meet the requirements of classical test theory and which presuppose that the ability can be "measured" out of context, to finding ways of detecting (making descriptive statements about) the components of competence brought to bear in the course of undertaking specific, personally valued activities.

These observations imply a two-*stage* (*not* a two-factor) assessment procedure. It is necessary to first find out what the person being assessed is strongly and intrinsically motivated to do, and then, and only then, which of these components of competence he or she tends to bring to bear to carry out the task (he or she will not display these components of competence unless engaged in a task they care about). In other words, what this means is that we need a *descriptive* model analogous to those used in chemistry and biology to think about competence and its assessment. This may be contrasted with the *variable*-based models so common in physics.

The difficulty posed by the studies of workplace competence reviewed by myself (Raven, 1984, 1997) and Spencer and Spencer (1993) as well as those being developed by psychologists involved in the "strengths" based movement (e.g., Buckingham & Clifton, 2005) is that their authors adopt idiosyncratic frameworks to describe the competencies needed in the occupational group or organisation studied. If we are to move forward it will be necessary to develop a common, agreed, set of descriptors – as in chemistry and biology.

I developed a preliminary version of what may be a more appropriate framework in my 1984 book *Competence in Modern Society*. Two key (if preliminary) observations were that the kinds of things people might be strongly motivated to do (i.e., activities they could be said to value) seemed to be endless, while the components of competence that might be brought to bear to carry out those activities seemed more limited in number.

In concluding this section I would like to reiterate the basic points being made here. On the one hand, attempts to introduce such things as licensing arrangements requiring people to demonstrate familiarity with traditional procedures is to be resisted. On the other hand, any claim to professionalism by those working in the area needs to be supported by evidence of a commitment to advance the development of psychological theory and practice in the area.

Nurturing Competence: The Importance of Developmental Environments

Over the past half century we have studied the development of competence in homes, schools, and workplaces. I will summarise some of the results in a moment. But, although it may at first appear to be of tangential relevance, I should first comment on the way in which psychologists have generally sought to investigate the effects of the environment on human characteristics.

Quite apart from the widespread gross misuse of multiple regression techniques in research studies (APA, 1999), most of those working in the area have sought to determine the relative importance of a variety of environmental variables by running correlations between scores on ability "variables" and environmental "variables". But ask yourself where biologists or chemists would have got to if they had tried to classify all animals or substances in terms of one, two, five, or 16 variables (analogous to g, "fluid" and "crystallised" "intelligence", "Big Five", or 16 "personality" factors) and then tried to establish the part played by different aspects of the environment in generating this variance by calculating the correlations with 10 variables purporting to measure the environment.

The outcome doesn't bear thinking about! But it is worth noting that, had they proceeded in this way, they would have been entirely unable to account for some of the simplest things, such as the transformations that occur in, for example, chemistry (e.g., as one pours sulphuric acid onto copper) or the development of complex ecological niches as in symbiosis. While reflecting on the implications of this, note that the properties of copper sulphate cannot be predicted by combining the individual properties of copper, sulphur, and oxygen in any kind of linear way, and those three substances are not recognisably "the same" when studied in combination and when considered individually. Psychologists who have sought monotonic relationships (in which a change in one variable is expected to produce some incremental change in another) between individual and environmental "variables" are unable to account for (or, indeed, even recognise) such things as the transformations that occur in homes, schools, and workplaces as mentors' values engage with those of tutees and, through the release and modelling of components of competence, produce dramatic changes (Jackson, 1986; Winter, McClelland, & Stewart, 1981).

Now to draw out the implications for the way in which we think of professional competence. What we have here is the promulgation of a way of thought that *cannot* meaningfully engage with the nature of human competence and its development. It is unethical (diversionary) to promote it. On the other hand, the field cries out for the *development* of psychological theory and practice. Thus there is no shortage of opportunities for psychologists to contribute to these developments. However, as we will see later, there are endless constraints on their doing so ... so it becomes even more important for psychologists, if they are to claim to be professionals, to seek to advance understanding of, and influence, those constraints.

Developing Competence in Schools

As has been mentioned, extensive studies have shown that few of the activities that characterise most schools are likely to lead to the development of high-level competencies.

However, there are exceptions. In the course of our own research we observed that, as described below, when teachers set out to nurture high-level competencies through inter-disciplinary, enquiry-oriented, group-based, project work largely conducted in the environment around the school, huge numbers of talents, at best only marginally related to *g*, come to light.

This is hugely important for at least two reasons. First, these talents are invisible, unrecognised, neglected, and, indeed, stifled, if one accepts the framework for thinking about individual differences adopted by most psychologists – including those providing courses purporting to enhance professional competence in the area. Second, the work illustrates one way in which these diverse talents can be nurtured, released, and harnessed to create climates or cultures of enterprise or intelligence. From this follows a dramatic reorganisation of most peoples' thoughtways. "Intelligence" is to be understood as an *emergent property of a group* rather than an individual characteristic. Furthermore, this intelligence depends on releasing and harnessing a huge variety of individual talents that are scarcely related to intelligence as conventionally understood. Thus, conventional ways of thinking are unethical – destructive of both individuals and society.

When we first visited the school we found the pupils engaged, more or less full-time, in a project designed to get something done about the pollution in the local river (see Raven, Johnstone, & Varley, 1985).

Some pupils decided that the first thing to do was to measure the pollution in the river. Some of them then set about collecting samples of the river water and trying to analyse it. This took them to the not-so-local university where they worked with lecturers trying to engage with this (apparently difficult) problem. Note that these pupils were developing the *competencies* of the scientist: the ability to identify problems, the ability to invent ways of investigating them, the ability to obtain help, the ability to familiarise themselves with a new field, and the ability to find ways of summarising information. Other pupils decided that more progress was to be made by studying the dead fish and plants along the river bank. Still others argued that all this was beside the point; the river was clearly polluted, and the problem was to get something done about it. Some then set about drawing pictures of dead fish and plants from the river bank with a view to releasing community action. The objective was not to depict what was seen *accurately,* but to represent it in such a way as to evoke emotions that would lead to action. While the "scientists" mentioned above sought to report the results of their work in what might be termed a classic academic format, other pupils again argued that that was irrelevant and set about generating slogans, prose, and poetry that would evoke emotions that would lead to outrage and action. Thus the *criteria* for what constituted effective reading and writing differed markedly from those which dominate most classrooms, and they varied from pupil to pupil. Still other pupils argued that, if anything was to be done about the river, it was necessary to get the environmental standards officer to do his job. (It turned out that he knew all about the pollution but had done nothing about it.) This led some pupils to set up domino-like chains to influence politicians and public servants. This in turn led the factory that was causing the problem to get at the pupils' parents saying that, unless this teacher and her class was stopped, they would all lose their jobs. Unabashed, some pupils set about examining the economic basis for the factory's claims.

Note that this teacher was not so much concerned with enhancing pupils' specialist *knowledge* in each of these areas[7] as to nurture a wide range of *different* **competencies** in her pupils. These competencies were not limited to substantive areas of investigation but also included the ability to contribute to group processes, including such things as the ability to put people at ease, the ability to defuse the intolerance which develops between people who contribute in very different ways to a group process (e.g., the intolerance of "artists" for "scientists"), the ability to publicise the observations of the quiet "ideas person", and the ability to "sell" the benefits of the unusual educational process to parents. The teacher in fact devoted considerable attention to highlighting the different types of contribution which different children were making to the group process. As a result, they stopped thinking of each other in terms of "smart vs. dumb" and instead noted what each was good at.

It is important to repeat that what was happening here required those concerned to make *descriptive statements* about each individual pupil's talents and areas of knowledge and expertise. Despite the assumptions which many of those who have grown up in the current climate of assessment bring with them, this could not be achieved by trying to arrange them on scales "measuring" these different abilities because a *different set of scales* would be required to record the talents of each child.

Note, also, that the class's ability to achieve its objective was dependent on *an emergent culture of intelligence or enterprise* which involved harnessing the *diverse* contributions of the pupils and *not* on individual champions or "high ability" pupils. More than that, many of the competencies individual pupils could develop and display were entirely dependent on other pupils creating an appropriate "environment" made up of "supporting" activities. Such competencies could only be said to *exist* in such a context.

In short, what we have here is a demonstration of not merely the feasibility but actual importance of moving from thinking in terms of "ability" to abilit*ies*, of moving from viewing education as primarily concerned with conveying *content* to seeing it as being mainly concerned with nurturing *competence*, and from thinking of "intelligence" as a relatively unalterable, individual quality to something which is a distinctly alterable characteristic of a group. It also requires us to think of the processes involved in a way analogous to those that would be required to think about the development of different species within an ecological niche and the characterisation of the niche as a whole.

Although implied by what has been said, it is useful to underline that the teachers' and pupils' notion of *what was to be learnt* was different. Pupils were to learn to lead, to invent, to put people at ease, to find ways of doing the impossible, to create political turbulence, etc. The objective was not that they should "learn" in the sense of acquiring stocks of standard, formal, low-level, verbalised *knowledge*. The ability to build up idiosyncratic combinations of up-to-date specialist knowledge, and tacit knowledge, yes – but that was different.

---

[7] It is important to note that, even if the teacher's objective had been to enhance the pupils' knowledge, documenting that knowledge would have posed insuperable problems for evaluators steeped in classical measurement theory. This stems from the fact that the knowledge would, on the one hand, have consisted of unique combinations of up-to-date specialist knowledge (i.e., it would have largely been idiosyncratic) and, on the other hand, would have been comprised of unverbalised, and often unconscious, knowledge of *ways of doing things* (i.e., it would mainly have consisted of *tacit* knowledge).

It cannot be too strongly emphasised that the hijacking of the term "learning" to mean learning *content* has to be strenuously resisted. One has *always* to ask learning *(to do)* **what?**

A similar ploy can be used to challenge widely accepted thoughtways about abilities. There is a tendency to seek to, for example, arrange people in a hierarchy according to their "creativity". But it is clear that one of the pupils mentioned above displayed a great deal of creativity in the course of orchestrating classroom (and political) disruption, another while putting others at ease, and another while finding ways to undertake a scientific study. One has always to ask: "Creativity (etc.) *in relation to carrying out which kinds of activity*?"

Developing Competence in Homes

Parents play an important role in nurturing the competencies of their children[8]. I will use the term *developmental environment* to refer to a kind of environment more likely to be created by parents who try to identify the particular interests and talents of each of their children and then create situations in which their children can undertake activities they care about – and, in the process, practice and develop high level competencies like the ability to problematise, find information, persuade other people to help, monitor the effectiveness of their behaviour, and so on.

Having set up a situation in which children can practice observing, inventing, adventuring, communicating, experimenting, and thinking whilst undertaking activities they care about, these parents intervene only occasionally. They do this sensitively when they sense an opportunity to assist their children through what Vygotsky (1978, 1981) might have termed a zone of proximal development. They help their children to conceptualise, to notice and resolve discrepancies between the expected results of their actions and the actual results, and to think about things which are not immediately present. They encourage them to think about the future and the long-term personal and social consequences of their actions and to act on those insights. They share their values and their view of the world with their children. They let them know that they think it is *important* to think, invent, adventure, and be in charge of one's destiny. They lead their children to become sensitive to cues which tell them that things are not working out as they had hoped, or even that they are getting out of control and that they should therefore either stop or get help. In this way their children learn to adventure into the unknown, secure in the knowledge that they can detect when things are going wrong and that they will be able to re-gain control.

We will later return to the vitally important question of why more teachers – and especially university lecturers – do so little to facilitate the development of such competencies in their students.

School vs. Home "Education" (or "Professionals" vs. "Amateurs"?)

One of my aims in this chapter is to call into question most conventional notions of what is meant by professionalism and professional development and, in particular, to underline the

---

[8] In addition to our own work reference may be made to the work of Kohn (1969, 1977); Sigel (1985, 1986); Sigel & McGillicuddly (1984); McGillicuddy-DeLisi (1982).

need to define professionalism as involving contributions *outside* one's domain of specialist technico-rational knowledge and, especially, contributing to the development of professional understanding.

Thus far, I have reviewed material which suggests: (a) that education involves a great deal more than schooling; (b) that parents are their children's most important educators, not in the sense that they do the things that schools do, but in the sense that they deploy sensitive strategies to facilitate the development of a wide range of important motivational dispositions and components of competence (including the ability to perceive, think, read, and communicate); and (c) that parents promote school success and cognitive development *indirectly*, by fostering such qualities as the ability to think for oneself, understand how systems work, and confidence in dealing with adults.

When one turns to an area of competence development in which teachers often claim particular professional competence, namely nurturing the ability to read, it again emerges (Tizard et al., 1982) that many parents (i.e., amateurs) are more effective than most teachers (i.e., professionals). One reason is that, as Francis (1982) found, parents tend to embed reading with their children in a meaningful, ongoing, joint activity. They provide different kinds of assistance depending on the child's previous experience with particular words. They vary what they do with the child's expectation of the text and with the child's (and their own) beliefs about the purpose of the reading session. When they help children to clarify meanings, they take account of the particular context in which the word is used and its function in the sentence. They relate the material they read to the child's interests. They spend a lot of time thinking about children's specific difficulties and trying to invent ways of helping them to overcome them.

When it comes to writing, one again finds that, whereas teachers tend to focus on low-level components of the task (such as on the *form* of letters and the format of sentences) parents tend to encourage their children to write about things they care about, and, in so doing, lead their children discover the deeper structure of language. They also develop idiosyncratic ways of communicating effectively by using such devices as allusion and innuendo. Many parents encourage their children to write messages with a view to influencing other people. Their success (or otherwise) in this endeavour provides the children with feedback about the effectiveness of their strategies.

It is often claimed that the main reason most teachers don't do these things has to do with class sizes. But this is actually not among the main causes of the discrepancy. Dewey had one adult to every four pupils in his school, but still only about 5% did what he enjoined them to do (Fraley, 1981). In an Educational Home Visiting project we evaluated (Raven, 1980), there was one teacher to every child and their task was to model mothering behaviour! *Still* most of them did not do the things many mothers do "instinctively". Part of the problem was that they felt obliged to conform to their image of what a *teacher* does. But other reasons included the fact that they did not know what the children's interests were and felt that they did not have the time to sit around and wait for this to emerge. After all, they were paid to be there to make something happen. Because they did not know what the children's motives were, they had little opportunity to harness them to create opportunities to feed the growth of important components of competence like seeking out and acting on self-generated feedback in order to undertake an activity more effectively. They had few opportunities to engage the child in activities that were important to them (the teachers) and then both model competent behaviour for the child and engage the child in thinking about constraints and inventing ways forward. Besides, their priorities in child development often conflicted with those of the mother. The mother might not want the child to ask questions or even to find written material which would enable them to pursue their own interests "Goodness knows what he might find poking about in books".

One of the things we have here is evidence of psychologists' general neglect of external determinants of behaviour. If we are to claim competence *as psychologists* we have to pay much more attention to these. If we are to claim to be *professional* psychologists, we have to join together with others to get something done about the pervasive neglect of such factors in the conceptual and research base which guides our profession.

But what would be a *professional* response to the material summarised above. One conclusion might be that we need to do much more to clarify the nature of developmental environments and the barriers which prevent most teachers and many parents creating them. Drawing such a conclusion would open up endless opportunities for psychologists to contribute to the development of their profession.

As far as professional development is concerned, it is clear that one thing we do *not* need is a requirement that teachers and psychologists demonstrate that they have undertaken activities (such as reading or taking courses) to bring them up to date with "developments" within the dominant paradigm of schooling and education. Equally, it is clear that one of the things we do need is opportunities for teachers and psychologists to contribute to the development of new ways of thinking, new tools, and new social arrangements. Backing up one step, what this would seem to mean is that it is necessary, if teachers and psychologists wish to claim to be professionals, for them to be involved in *promoting* such developments.

Developing Competence in Higher and Further Education

There can be little doubt that Higher and Further education *should* be primarily concerned with the development of generic, transferable, high-level competencies. Indeed, unless it does so, it is difficult to justify current arrangements because only a minority of students pursue careers related to their discipline of study. For example, in 1990, over 40% of graduates in history from British universities and nearly 40% of graduates in physics went into marketing, management services, or financial work. Graduates from physics, the biological sciences, and foreign languages enter almost as wide a range of jobs as do graduates from English, history, and the social sciences (Association of Graduate Careers Advisory Services, 1992). The vast majority claim that they have ceased to use any of the specialist knowledge they so painfully acquired at college after two years at work.

Once again it emerges that most higher education fails to nurture important high-level competencies [see Jacob (1956) and studies conducted by McClelland and his colleagues (e.g. Winter et al., 1981)]; although, as usual, the vast majority of studies in the area, such as those brought together by Pascarella and Terenzini (1991), fail to examine such issues.

However, when an appropriate methodology is adopted, it becomes clear that there are exceptions (see Winter et al., 1981; Mentkowski, 2000). Paradoxically, one the major groups of institutions that actually do nurture them consists of colleges that are widely accused of "elitism": namely "Ivy League" colleges in the US and their equivalents in Britain[9]. The other main group consists of colleges with a special mission, such as Bennington and Alverno.

As in schools, it emerges that certain forms of joint project-based education are particularly important. Also – and, for the sake of brevity, I did not dwell on it in connection with school education – exposure to mentors who share the students' concerns and provide role models especially of the normally private components of competence which make for effective behaviour. By engaging students in their own research, mentors, for example, not only portrayed high-level competencies in such a way that the students could "catch" them but involved the students, as apprentices, in those very activities. Thus students became involved in puzzling over half-identified and barely verbalised problems and undertaking "experimental interactions with the environment" to clarify both the nature of the problem and the effectiveness of strategies being employed. For example, a tutor might say (but not in so many words) "We seem to have a problem here. I'm not sure what it is. But if we do *this*...Whoops, NO!; that was a mistake. But what that means is…". And so on. In such ways students came to develop the confidence and competence needed to adventure into the unknown. More than that, they came to think it was *important* to do so. Also important were demanding, Socratic-like, interactions which challenged the way students thought and led them to change those thoughtways and assumptions, to engage in critical thinking, and enhanced their ability to muster arguments and persuade.

Once again, as in the contrast between parenting and schooling, it is clear that these are personal interactions which cannot easily be incorporated into large-scale programmes. Despite this, one institution, the School of Independent Studies at what was then the North East London Polytechnic (NELP) (see Stephenson, 2001), did at least illustrate how this could be done.

The concept of capability, which underlay the programme, had its origins in a *Capability Manifesto* drawn up by the Royal Society for Arts in 1980. This viewed capability as an all-round quality, observable in what Weaver (1994) described as the ability to engage appropriately and sensitively in "purposive and sensible" action, not just in familiar and highly focused specialist contexts but also in response to new and changing circumstances. This was seen to involve ethics, judgements, the self-confidence to take risks, and a commitment to learn from the experience. A capable person has culture, in the sense of being able to "decide between goodness and wickedness or between beauty and ugliness" (Weaver, 1994).

The programme began with an *Exploration Stage*, lasting 10 to 12 weeks, in which students were encouraged to review their values, priorities, strengths, and developmental needs and helped to plan, and negotiate approval for, their individualised developmental programme; continued with a *Progress Review Stage* running through the main study phase, in which students were helped to monitor and review their progress; and ended with a *Demonstration Stage*, in which students set out to show what they had learnt to do by applying it to real situations relevant to their intended career. Such a framework could well be adopted by others seeking to nurture the diverse competencies of professionals, including psychologists.

---

[9] It is of interest that the main beneficiaries of these programmes are people who have not, in any sense, been directly involved – i.e., members of the community as a whole – and not the participating individuals themselves. Note the importance of this finding from the point of view of underlining the importance of *comprehensive* evaluations.

Once things got to the stage of evaluating both the overall programme and individual students' development, the problem, with which we are now all too familiar, namely that all the students developed in different directions (see Stephenson, 2001), reared its ugly head. However, an ingenious solution was found. Instead of seeking to assess outcomes directly, the process of validation moved to validating the individual *programmes of study* and then testifying to the fact that the students had followed those programmes (Adams, Robbins, & Stephenson, 1981). It was argued that, if students had engaged an appropriate *process,* the outcomes, especially the idiosyncratic *knowledge* outcomes, which Lester (2001) has shown (contrary to all conventional wisdom) it is logically *impossible* to assess, would have been achieved.

It may be mentioned in passing that we have shown that similar arrangements can be made in schools. If it can be shown that a teacher has created a "developmental environment" in his or her classroom, the competencies pupils have developed become *visible*. These build on the invisible idiosyncratic, expert, formal and tacit, knowledge base the student has built up. This process could well find wider application in the evaluation of group-based personal development programmes among adults.

Something else of considerable importance may be noted in passing. A similar shift toward understanding process and *inferring* outcomes underlies a move from trying to apply positivistic, reductionist models in evaluation toward "illuminative" evaluation based on a study of the *processes* involved. *Most* important outcomes cannot be "measured" in the conventional sense.

As might be anticipated, it was not too many years before the progamme was, to all intents and purposes, closed down, in part because the external quality control agency (HMI) was uncomfortable with this shift from positivistic to illuminative evaluation methods.

But there was another interesting twist of direct relevance to the theme of this chapter. As might be anticipated on the basis of what was said earlier, those discipline-based NELP lecturers who *did* set about nurturing high-level competencies were accused of unprofessional conduct because they had strayed outside what was taken to be their domain of specialist knowledge (O'Reilly, 2001).

Unfortunately, there are yet other barriers to generalising educational activities of the kind encountered in institutions like Oxbridge, Alverno, and NELP.

One group of these relates to values conflicts. This will assume increasing importance as this chapter progresses. Indeed, at one level, it can be said that the most important problem in education is to come to terms with the diversity of values; a statement that is underlined in the subtitle of one of my most important books (Raven, 1994).

Other barriers to wider dissemination of competence-based education into universities are revealed in Schön's (1987) book *Educating the Reflective Practitioner.* He and Argyris spent over a decade trying to introduce activities designed to promote the development of the kinds of competence that he had, in *The Reflective Practitioner,* shown to be so important into MIT. They failed miserably. One reason was that the lecturers were not much interested in enhancing the competence of their students. They were locked into a framework in which the publication of bulletproof studies within their disciplines was the primary requirement. The peer review process ensured that publications putting forward insights which went *beyond* the data but were not tested *within* them would be rejected. More specifically, this prohibition extended to most research adventuring outside what were currently conceived to be the boundaries of the "discipline". Clearly such lecturers provided no role model for ethically-guided adventurous research and action involving comprehensive inputs and evaluation.

Less expected was the reaction of the students. Basically, they said "No one can tell if I am a competent manager or not. So what I will have to do is focus on getting myself promoted. That means parading the latest 'in' terms and phrases in front of my boss. That is exactly what the entire 'educational' system has encouraged me to do and advanced me for doing. No problem".

So here we have further insights into why the educational system as a whole does not do the things which most people, in a sense, want it to do (i.e., the things which are, in fact, the most important from the point of view of nurturing occupational and societal competence). Handling them requires systems thinking: How does the system work? What is driving it? How can I deal with some of the constraints which prevent me doing what should be done? These themes will become a major concern as this chapter progresses.

Developing Competence in Workplaces

The way in which managers nurture the talents of subordinates emerges incidentally, but in a most interesting and revealing way, in a study conducted using Behavioural Event Interviewing by Klemp, Munger and Spencer in 1977. But to understand the significance of what these managers (actually Naval Officers) were doing in the staff development area, attention must first be drawn to some of the other things they did that differentiated them from other officers. Even though they were working in what might be taken to be an archetypical command-and-control organisation (the US Navy), one of the most striking things they did was initiate new developments themselves; they did not wait to be given instructions. Like Hattie's teachers, they publicly set goals, encouraged feedback from their subordinates to help them monitor how well things were going, *and changed the goals if it emerged that a goal was inappropriate or that problem was not what it had been taken to be.* Likewise, they did not sit around complaining about the orders that came from higher up in the hierarchy, they got together with other officers at their own level to influence those above them. They themselves did not issue orders but set about mustering arguments and persuading people to do the things that they felt needed to be done. And they did not offer punitive feedback but rather encouraged people to monitor the effectiveness of their own behaviour and change the goals and the strategies where necessary.

So here indeed were some distinctive role models from whom subordinates could learn how to behave competently. But then these officers engaged in some distinctly unusual activities to facilitate the development of subordinates. On the one hand, they encouraged their subordinates to join them in doing *their* job. (Many managers fear that, if they were to do such a thing, the subordinates would oust them from their position.) When they were working with subordinates in this way they were able to lead those subordinates not only to observe, but actually *to share in* many of the normally private components of effective behaviour. They were able to share the opening *feelings* that suggested that they had an encountered some kind of problem, their struggles as they tried to "think" about it in various ways and rejected most of their initial "thoughts" because they did not square with all the facts (in other words, as they conducted mental "experimental interactions with the problem"). Then, still unclear about what the problem was, they might initiate some kind of overt action, quickly discover that it did not produce the desired result, and use this feedback to clarify the nature of the problem and the effectiveness of their strategy.

Furthermore, once they realised that the overlap between their motivational predispositions and those of a particular subordinate was insufficient to permit effective role modelling to occur, some of them sought out other managers who did share their subordinate's motives and placed those subordinates with him or her with a view to developing the components of competence in the context of undertaking those activities. Some of the teachers and parents whose work we described earlier did similar things.

ASSESSMENT

One of my objectives in this chapter has been to alert readers to some of the dangers inherent in thoughtways and procedures commonly advocated in universities and liable to be taught in continuing professional development courses in the education/human resources area and to suggest ways in which psychologists could, instead of taking courses, contribute to the continuing development of their profession.

So the logical next step is to turn to the assessment of competence.

But, before doing that, it is useful to highlight some fundamental problems associated with the concept of evidence based practice, and especially the notion of payment by demonstrated results; in education, personal development, and psychotherapy.

Most of the researchers working in the area have more or less proceeded on the assumption that "nothing could be simpler" than demonstrating change (or the lack of it). Simply administer some test before and after an intervention and subtract the initial from the subsequent scores.

Nothing could be more misleading! In the first place, as we have seen, there are not, and, if one works within the traditional measurement paradigm, cannot be, "measures" of the most important outcomes (or, to tell the truth, measures of the inputs or processes involved). The effective study of processes calls for the adoption of an ecological-type model with many and recursive feedback loops.

But, even if one ignores these problems, it emerges that most of the studies are extremely misleading and damaging. Yet they have had dramatic effects on practices and procedures which influence millions, if not billions, of people worldwide.

In actuality, we are here talking about what might be taken to be a number of different things: 1) the assessment of (relative) change in groups over time or in response to different treatments, including such things as administrative arrangements (that was what Hattie's meta-meta-analysis of 800 *meta*-analyses of tens of thousands of studies was all about), 2) the demonstration of *individual* change so as to be able to do such things as compare the relative effects of different treatments (e.g., drugs) on the same individual, and 3) the calculation of individual responsiveness *scores*, as in the calculation of personal "learning potential" scores by subtracting the pre- from post-intervention test scores (these difference scores then being correlated with other variables in an effort to do such things as clarify who responds).

One basic problem, although it is not the most fundamental, is that, incredible as it may seem, tests developed according to Classical Test Theory are unfit for (this) purpose.

The basic problem is that such tests do not yield equal-interval scales. Thus a score difference of, say, five points at one point in the scale is not the same thing as a score difference of five points at another point in the scale.

One implication of this is that the conclusions drawn from, for example, the thousands of studies purporting to compare the relative gains made by "more" and "less" able students in response to alternative educational and administrative practices are open to serious question. In fact it turns out that the findings can be easily reversed by even such a simple change as employing a test of the same "ability" but having a different level of difficulty.

Likewise, since a "learning potential" (gain) score of five means very different things at different points in the scale, any attempt to relate such scores (without reference to the point in the scale from which they are drawn) to other things, such as "environmental" (e.g., socio-economic) variables are likely to be seriously misleading.

In technical terms, the truth is that such change scores are heavily dependent on: 1) the absolute difficulty of the test, 2) the shape of the Test Characteristic Curve, and 3) the sector of the curve on which the change is measured (see Prieler and Raven, 2008 for details). To solve the problem it is necessary either to generate tests having linear Test Characteristic Curves or to make complex calculations using speciality computer programs.

The second basic problem arises from the tendency of most evaluators to focus on single outcomes in a manner not merely encouraged by, but often demanded by, reductionist science. Yet any educational or developmental process has a range of outcomes, some of them desired and desirable, some undesired and undesirable, some short and some long term, some on individuals, some on society (what is good for the individual may be bad for society), and varying from individual to individual.

The problem may be captured by saying that most evaluations purporting to support "evidence based practice" are insufficiently *comprehensive*.

In fact, as Prieler and Raven (2008) show, two important transformations in conventional thinking emerge if one pursues this issue. One is that the quality of an evaluation is to be judged more in terms of its *comprehensiveness* (its ability to get a rough fix on all important outcomes for different sorts of people, for individuals and the society in which they live, and in the short and the long term) than by the accuracy of its measures of particular outcomes or the "sophistication" of its analytic techniques.

Unfortunately, even this statement is not strong enough. Many effective educational/developmental processes are *transformational.* They do not result in people becoming "better" or "worse" along some predetermined "dimension". Instead they do such things as release previously existing components of competence into some activity the potentiality of which was not previously even suspected (see, for example, Jackson, 1968 for schoolchildren, Stephenson, 2001 and Winter et. al., 1977 for University students, and Hughes, 1998 for adults.)

Kazdin (2006) has underlined similar points in relation to psychotherapy. It *cannot* be meaningfully evaluated using a few pre-determined tests.

But worse is to come. These competencies are not merely released or triggered by some chance encounter with another person or problem. Their very existence depends on there being a supportive, if not necessarily congenial, context. And the effects of these collective interactions emerge not merely at the individual level (as in, for example, the strength of a single plant) but, more importantly, in a form that is analogous to an index of the viability of an ecological niche in a particular context. Suffice it to say that, in a single field, there are many hundreds of types of grass, no one type being the "fittest" in any general sense, and that the proportions of different strains varies with the balance of other plants, animals, and nutrients within a huge variety of niches.

These observations point to some of the most basic problems with research in the area. To move forward it will be necessary to move away from the kinds of procedures embraced by reductionist science to those hinted at in our earlier references to "illuminative" research and what might be described as an "ecological" image, not merely of the educational process, but of science itself.

Once again, the dangers are clear in relation to requiring psychologists to enroll in "professional development" courses built around the received wisdom. More than that, in this case, it is apparent that there is a need for professional commitment to work *outside* the profession to undo the damage that has been caused by basing policy on studies that have, in the past, adopted inappropriate methods and procedures.

THE ASSESSMENT OF COMPETENCE

So far I have summarised some of our work on the nature, development, and assessment of competence that highlights an apparently incomprehensible lacuna in the research psychologists have carried out in the past; a lacuna which has had serious negative consequences for individuals, organisations, and society. As a result, failure to undertake the necessary research must therefore be considered both unethical and unprofessional. Yet the design and conduct of the research that is needed would challenge the paradigms which currently dominate our field and, indeed, call into question many basic assumptions of reductionist, positivistic science itself. To get it done it would be necessary to intervene in poorly understood social and political processes currently considered to be outside the domain of psychology. This would invite a challenge to our professionalism which only a reconsideration, along the lines Schon has indicated, of what it *means* to claim to be a professional could resolve.

As has been shown, most mainstream psychometric frameworks fail to recognise most of the talents most people possess. They make it impossible to mount meaningful evaluations of educational, personal development, and clinical (e.g., psychotherapeutic) programmes and policies. Worse, as Spearman noted, their use within schools drives education out of these institutions because they focus teachers', pupils', parents', employers', administrators' and politicians' attention on the goals that are assessed and thus deflect attention from the most important qualities pupils possess and which society urgently needs to set about nurturing and utilising. What could be more unethical?

And the previous paragraph understates the problem, because most of the tests used in schools lack both construct and predictive validity. Concerning predictive validity, it is now well known from Schmidt and Hunter's (1998) meta-analyses that scores on educational tests correlate hardly at all with performance outside the school system.

As to construct validity, I have already laboured the point that they cannot legitimately be viewed as ways of assessing peoples' knowledge because their most important knowledge is both idiosyncratic and tacit.

But all these observations are really secondary to the primary point. And that is that psychologists have failed to provide parents, teachers, university lecturers, managers or any of those involved in personnel development, assessment, and selection with appropriate ways of thinking about and identifying the diversity of talents that are available. As a result, neither educational nor psychological researchers are able to mount meaningful evaluations of individuals or educational programs or policies.

A vague awareness of these things, combined with much more articulate unease about the uses to which test scores are put, has led to widespread criticism of testing.

The response of bodies like the International Test Commission has been interesting, if predictable. It has been to retreat into specification of technico-rational requirements for tests and testers. These rely heavily on widely endorsed, but poorly understood, concepts like "validity". Yet, as Messick (1995) and I have shown, one cannot validate tests using the procedures widely advocated in text books. So, once again, "professional development" courses set up to disseminate the standards set by such bodies and certifying such things as competence in testing, courses which inculcate the received wisdom on psychometrics and test construction, are liable to prove *dysfunctional.* One *cannot* assess things like "creativity" or even "the ability to think" in prescribed manner.

Laudable though the objective of, like the Joint Committee, setting standards prescribing that "only reliable and valid tests may be used in the evaluation of people and programs", their *effect* is to render many important personal qualities and the effects of policies and educational and social activities invisible. Since there are no good measures of the main objectives and outcomes of the kind of interdisciplinary, competency-oriented, enquiry-based, education discussed earlier, the requirement that only reliable and valid tests be used in their evaluation induces researchers to use only *irrelevant* tests unrelated to many of the objectives and possible unintended and undesirable consequences of both the programmes being evaluated and any programmes with which they are compared. As Kazdin (2006) has put it, such standards lead evaluators to employ what amount to arbitrary selections of measures unrelated to either the objectives of the programme or any analysis of its probable effects. This not only renders the positive outcomes of these activities invisible, it also ensures that many negative effects, especially of conventional educational activities and health care programmes, go undetected and undiscussed; indeed, they become almost undiscussable.

BARRIERS TO THE DEVELOPMENT OF AN EFFECTIVE EDUCATION SYSTEM AND A PRELIMINARY DISCUSSION OF THE MANAGEMENT AND ORGANISATIONAL ISSUES INVOLVED

There are many reasons why schools tend to neglect their main goals. These include the absence of a shared, formal understanding of how to nurture the desired qualities and how to find out whether one has done so, and, especially, how to nurture and recognise the huge variety of talents which are to be found in any classroom. They include an inability to handle the value conflicts that surface as soon as one tries to introduce educational programmes that actually set out to nurture high-level competencies or promote diversity. They include an inability to initiate a network of experiments aimed at different aspects of "the problem" and make appropriate arrangements to learn from those experiments.

So far as I can see, if society is to handle the values conflicts involved it would be necessary to create a variety of distinctively different educational programmes which actually do nurture different talents, to document the differential consequences of each of these in a comprehensive way, and to feed that information to the public so that pupils and parents can make informed choices between them. This stands in stark contrast to the notion that (very limited) information deemed relevant to such decisions should be fed upward in a bureaucratic system to politicians who take decisions binding on all. In short, it involves the evolution of new concepts of bureaucracy and democracy (see Raven, 1995, 2000, 2010a).

So, whose job is it to carry out the activities mentioned in the last paragraph? As far as I can see, it has to be the job of public servants. It becomes their job is to create a variety of options in every community, to ensure that they are comprehensively evaluated, and to feed this information to the public. More fundamentally, their task becomes that of promoting a ferment of innovation and learning. This means encouraging everyone in the system to experiment in their own areas and to support those trying to do so in related areas. It means facilitating the evolution of comprehensive evaluations. It means facilitating a move away from methodologies grounded in positivistic thinking and promoting an understanding of the kinds of "illuminative" methodology mentioned earlier and, in particular, examining the results of the experiments that have been initiated to draw out their implications for understanding the currently invisible *systems* processes that are deflecting the activities from their goals. Creating a ferment of innovation also means acting on the information which becomes available in an innovative way (i.e., as part of a recursive cycle of experimentation, learning and adjustment) in the long-term public interest.

If they are to do these things, there will need to be a sea-change in beliefs about the role of public servants. It will be necessary to generate new job descriptions for them, and it will be necessary to evolve new staff and organisational appraisal systems to find out how well they are doing.

How to get them to pay attention to such evaluations of their work? The answer was, in some sense, provided by John Stuart Mill in 1859. One way to make it more likely that people will act in the long term public interest instead of their own personal interests is to expose their behaviour to the public gaze. Or, as Mill put it, making "visible to everyone who did everything and by whose default anything was left undone". So what is required is a network of overlapping monitoring/supervisory groups as distinct from a form of accountability supposedly feeding information through extended bureaucratic chains to distant multi-purpose assemblies composed of what Adam Smith (1776) and John Stuart Mill described as committees of ignoramuses. Would the public participate in such arrangements? Make no mistake about it, when people can have an *influence,* as is very rarely the case in the context of what currently passes for democracy, they participate.

In reality, despite the negative comments I have made about the market process, it is important to understand the problem it was meant to solve and how it was meant to work. Adam Smith (1776) and Fred Hayek (1948) advocated it as an answer to a very basic question which is still with us; namely, how to create a society which will innovate and learn without central direction; one which will harness the expert information which is widely dispersed in the hearts, heads, hands, and tools of billions of people. The proposal was for an *organic* system with multiple feedback loops which did not depend on decisions by committees of wise men. Indeed, it was argued that the very concept of a wise man was an oxymoron. The reason was that, if someone initiates some activity at one location and someone else another activity at another location, no one can tell in advance what will happen when the two things come together. To pick up Ridley's (2010) memorable image, the problem is to facilitate the process whereby ideas evolving in different ecological niches have sex with each other and produce unpredictable, previously unimaginable, outcomes! It follows that, as Smith asserted, key information required to take wise decisions not only is not, but *cannot,* be available. On the other hand, through the market process, individuals could use their pennies to influence on the direction of development. They could "vote" separately on thousands of issues. They could invest in enterprises they liked the sound of and choose between a myriad of goods and services. They did not have to vote for politicians (whom they did not trust) offering only alternative *packages* of policies and largely unresponsive to feedback. They could change their decisions over time as they saw how things worked out.

For a variety of reasons it is up to psychologists to come up with a better answer to Smith and Hayek's question based on our understandings of organisational arrangements, the sources of (and deterrents to) managerial and professional competence, staff guidance, placement, and development systems, and staff and organisational appraisal systems. And we need to do so pretty quick since the two main models competing for public attention at the present time (current forms of "the market" and current forms of politico-democratic management via bureaucracy) are widely discredited, thereby producing alienation and apathy.

A Re-Formulation of the Problem

To re-state the problem in other terms: The need is for a better design for a socio-cybernetic system for the management of society.

To clarify, cybernetics is concerned with the study of guidance and control systems in animals and machines. One has to say animals, otherwise people think only of manmade systems, like missiles. But as soon as one says animals it is clear that one is concerned with understanding and mapping guidance systems which depend on multiple feedback loops many of which do not pass through any central nervous system. So socio-cybernetics is concerned both with understanding the social forces that control the behaviour of people in society (and regularly undermine well-intentioned social action) and designing better socio-cybernetic guidance systems for society.

Since psychology is centrally concerned with understanding the causes of human behaviour, it is clear that psychologists should be playing a major role in helping to develop an understanding of these processes and designing a better management system for society.

Let's turn now to the last issue mentioned when summarising the problems that need attention if we are to create an effective educational system; namely, the need to create a ferment of innovation, experimentation, and learning. There are so many things to be done that they could not possibly be centrally decreed. No blueprint is possible. The question then is to how to create a *learning society,* a society which will innovate and learn *without* central direction[10]. On the face of it, it would seem that organisational psychologists should be able to make some important contributions to the design of such a system.

But the *most* important lesson we learned at this point in our work was that the contributors to the abject failure of the so-called educational system do not operate independently but form a network, or system (using the word in another sense), of recursive and mutually supportive feedback loops. This network seems to have the capacity to perpetuate, even extend and elaborate, itself. It becomes virtually impossible to change any one part without changing others; otherwise the changes one has made are either negated by the reactions of the rest of the system or produce unanticipated, and often unwanted, changes elsewhere.

This network of feedback loops is sketched in Figure 1.

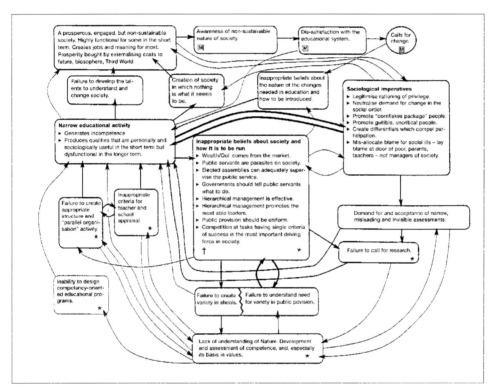

*Intervention in these cells would help change the nature of the qualities nurtured and rewarded in the system. Motives which could be harnessed to do this are marked Ⓜ.

†These need to be replaced by acceptance of the need to make managed economies work – to find way of giving effect to information concerning the public long term interest, the need to explicitly create variety and information on the personal and social consequences of the options, and to find ways of holding public servants accountable for, and getting them to sit in, the long-term public interest. This means systematic, broadly based, evaluation and participative democracy.

Figure 1. Feedback loops driving down quality in education.

Among other things, the Figure shows:

1. That the dominance of the activities with which schools are preoccupied arises from:

---

[10] Those who are ready to take the plunge may care to note that something still deeper is implied by the term "Learning Society". It is what the system, qua system, learns to do or stop doing that it is most important to influence – not the learning of the individuals within it.

a. A series of sociological imperatives (e.g., that schools assist in legitimising a hierarchical society and deciding who will be promoted into the higher ranks). (It follows from this, and this has important implications for the way we tend to think about solutions to the problems reviewed earlier, that what happens in schools is not mainly determined by the wishes of parents, teachers, pupils, employers, ministers of education or anyone else but, at least to a significant extent, by what is assessed in the sociological process of allocating position and status.);
b. Inappropriate beliefs about the nature of the changes that are needed in education itself, the management of the educational system, and the management of society;
c. Society's failure to initiate research which would yield useful insights into such things as the nature of competence and how it is to be fostered and assessed;
d. The absence of (a) systematically generated variety in, and choice between, educational programmes which have demonstrably different consequences and (b) information on the consequences of each of these alternatives;
e. Failure to create climates of innovation within schools[11] and
f. Inadequate dissemination of the results of research into the nature, development, and assessment of generic high-level competencies, and, especially, the implications of the values basis of competence.

2. That this narrow educational process has a series of knock-on effects which finally contribute to its own perpetuation. The competencies and beliefs that are nurtured and inculcated in schools reinforce a social order which offers major benefits to "able" people who do what is required of them without questioning that order. That society creates endless work which gives meaning to people's lives (but does little to enhance the general quality of life) and creates wealth at the expense of the biosphere, future generations, and the Third World. The formal and informal "educational" system helps to teach a host of incorrect beliefs which collectively result in nothing being what it is popularly or authoritatively said to be. This double-talk makes it extremely difficult to conduct any rational discussion of the changes needed in society. The sociological imperative that schools help to legitimise the rationing of privilege contributes to the demand for, and encourages acceptance of, narrow, invisible, and mislabelled assessments. Those predisposed to acquire these "qualifications" are not inclined to see the need for, or to commission, genuine enquiry-oriented research or notice other talents in their fellows. Teachers who become aware of the hidden competencies of their "less able" students experience acute distress. The lack of understanding of the nature of competence leads to a failure to underline the need for a variety of value-based educational programmes and thus to the perpetuation of narrow educational activity.

---

[11] The requisite developments are fully discussed in Chapter 8 of Managing Education for Effective Schooling (Raven, 1994) but especial reference may again be made to Kanter's (1985) notion of "parallel organisation activity".

3. That the main motives for change are widespread awareness that there is something seriously wrong with the educational system, and, more specifically, that it fails miserably in its manifest task of identifying, nurturing, recognising, and utilising most people's motives and talents. The most commonly proposed solutions to this problem, based as they are on other misunderstandings, are, however, inappropriate. However, another motive for change stems from increasing recognition that we have created a non-sustainable society and that basic change in the way society is run is essential.
4. That there are a number of points at which it should be possible to intervene in this network of feedback loops to create an upward spiral. These might involve:
    a. Changing the way we run society, introducing more, and more appropriate, social research and evaluation activity, and finding ways of holding public servants and politicians accountable for seeking out and acting on information in an innovative way in the long-term public interest;
    b. Introducing the "parallel organisation" activities[12] that are required to promote innovation within schools;
    c. Establishing a greater variety of distinctively different, value-based, educational programmes and providing information on the short and long-term, personal and social, consequences of each;
    d. Creating public debate about the forms of supervision (the nature of the democracy) needed to ensure that public servants seek out and act on information in an innovative way in the public interest; and
    e. Disseminating what is already known about the nature, development, and assessment of competence and its implications.

Standing further back from the figure what we see is that:

(1) It is impossible to achieve significant benefits by changing any one part of the system, such as curriculum or examinations or professional training on its own, without simultaneously making other changes; otherwise the effects of the change will either be negated by the reactions of the rest of the system or produce counterintuitive, and usually counterproductive, changes elsewhere. On the other hand, it is equally clear that command-and-control-based system-wide change based on uninformed opinion will achieve little.
(2) Pervasive, *systems-oriented,* changes are required to move forward. But these changes, although collectively system-wide, cannot be centrally mandated because there are too many new things to be done.
(3) Since what happens is not determined by the wishes of any particular group of people but *by the operation of the system itself* the widespread tendency to single out and *blame* parents, pupils, teachers, psychologists, public servants, or politicians is entirely inappropriate. *Their* behaviour is mainly determined by the system. One needs to take these systemic forces seriously and ask how they can be harnessed in

---

[12] See footnote 5.

an analogous way to that in which marine engineers harness the potentially destructive forces of the wind: They will not go away!

(4) It is vital to generalise the observation made in (3): We need to fundamentally reframe the way we think about the causation of behaviour in a way which parallels one of the transformations Newton introduced into physics. Before Newton, if objects moved or changed direction, it was because of their *internal* properties: they were *animated.* After Newton it was mainly because they were acted upon by a network of invisible *external* forces which could nevertheless be mapped, measured and harnessed. Observation (3) implies that we need a similar transformation in the way we think about the causes of human behaviour.

(5) The network of forces depicted (a) has the effect of driving attempts to deal with the problems based on single-variable common-sense interventions ever more narrowly, and ineffectively, around the triangle in the top left hand corner of the Figure, and (b) diverts attention from the developments, indicated in the bottom part of the Figure, that are so essential to move forward.

(6) The *causes* of the symptoms (and thus the appropriate place to start reform) are far removed from those symptoms.

(7) The system does not merely reproduce itself; it leads to the production of ever more elaborate versions of itself; it is self-elaborating; autopoietic[13].

In the foregoing, we have repeatedly used the word "force". We must now take up the question of the nature, or status, of these "forces". Viewed in one way, Figure 1 is analogous to a map of the interacting gravitational forces controlling the movements of the planets. But, if so, the nature of the *social* forces involved has yet to be elucidated. What is clear is that the links in the figure are not flows of e.g., resources as in the models developed by Forrester in 1961 and disseminated by Meadows, Meadows, and Behrens (1972). Nor are they flows of "information" as in networks of e-mails. Nor are they flows of, for instance, people from one section of the "educational system" to another. The contents of the boxes are not people or stocks of food or components. Only if the feedback loops really do represent *forces* of some kind does it make sense to ask how they can be harnessed (as in the forces acting on a sailing boat) or amplified or damped down (as in electrical energy flowing through a radio).

Put like that, it suggests that the need is to find ways of mapping, measuring, and harnessing social forces in a manner analogous to those adopted by physicists and engineers. And I have spent many years trying to do this [see e.g. Raven & Navrotsky (2001) and Raven (2010b)]. However, as was stressed earlier, the field of cybernetics encompasses the study of such things as the multiple, non-hierarchical, guidance and control systems that operate within organisms or within ecological niches. Unfortunately, in trying to do these things, biologists and ecologists encounter much the same problems as we do here.

Just to spell out the implications of these observations: on the one hand, it is clear that common-sense based "solutions" to the problems of the educational system are not going to work, so there is no point in enjoining administrators, teachers, or psychologists to attend

---

[13] i.e., in some sense self-organising, self-reproducing, and self-extending. The problem with the word "self-organising" on its own is that it is frequently taken to absolve the user from the need to explain how the process works. What we have seen here is that the "self-organising" processes of the educational system involve a whole series of mutually reinforcing and recursive feedback loops both within the educational system and in relation to the wider society.

courses devoted to their promotion. On the other hand, there is endless scope for adventurous research to advance understanding in the area. Thus while, yes, there is need, through professional development activities, to release, nurture, and create conditions for harnessing all of the competencies that are so crucial to the creation of cultures of innovation and intelligence, the chief focus of professional development activities has to be on finding ways of enabling and encouraging all members of the profession to contribute to the development of the profession. Paradoxically, doing *that* will mean working *outside* our areas of certified professional competence.

But to return to the point, our problem here is to find ways of understanding, mapping, and harnessing these social forces: the forces that primarily determine the behaviour of organisations and people.

In my efforts to do this I was introduced to what at first seemed a very promising lead, which does indeed illustrate the feasibility of trying to make progress along these lines. However, it incidentally yielded some dramatic illustrations of the counterintuitive, and usually counterproductive, effects of common-sense based interventions into poorly understood systems that are well worth examining.

The work deals with the complex and recursive feedback loops among the hundreds of variables that contribute to such things as quality of life, economic well-being, mortality, population, pollution, agricultural production and the consumption of resources.

The basic model showing these interactions was developed by Forrester in 1961 (see Forrester, 1971), formed the basis of the famous "Club of Rome" report *Limits to Growth* in 1972 (Meadows et al., 1972).

One of the things Forrester (1971) shows is that, if things are left pretty much as they are, industrialization will eventually be suppressed by falling natural resources.

But if science and technology find a way of avoiding resource depletion, which is an "obvious" "solution" to the problem, the outcome is even less desirable. Population and capital investment are then able to rise until a pollution crisis is created. Pollution then acts directly to reduce birth rate, increase death rate, and depress food production. In this case, population, which peaks in 2030, declines by 83% within 20 years. Forrester (1971) notes that this would be disaster of unprecedented proportions.

It would be interesting to review further findings from the work. But, as mentioned earlier, this lead did not live up to its initial promise. This was precisely because Forrester (1971) did *not* find ways of including the kinds of *social* forces shown in Figure 1 in their model. As a result, the implementation (or otherwise) of their recommendations becomes dependent on social and economic forces which lie outside it. One can no more identify the relative importance of a variety of possible interventions into the social guidance and control system in this area than one could in relation to the educational system.

To say a little more about this, consider Figure 1, which was based on the systems diagrams, now termed systemograms, published by Morgan (1986). Useful though they are, there is a fundamental problem. It is not possible to assess and weight the relative importance of the feedback loops that are depicted in such a way to be able to assess the likely effect of any proposed intervention. This remains a central problem to be addressed if we are to move forward.

Nevertheless, several things are already clear. One is that, if one is to intervene effectively in socio-cybernetic systems, we need some basic understanding of the system we are dealing with. And then we need to make numerous, *systems-oriented*, interventions.

Ironically, generating an understanding of a system depends on diffuse experimentation coupled with comprehensive evaluation and a deliberate effort to elucidate the implications of the effects of the action, both intended and unintended, for our understandings the system itself. It is quite possible that a diffuse network of such experiments might lead to some kind of assessment of the relative weights to be attached to each of the feedback loops.

THE WAY FORWARD

In developing our map of some of the systems processes that control the operation of the so-called "educational" system, we have attempted to follow the injunctions of House (1991), Parlett (1972, 1976), and Hamilton, Jenkins, King, MacDonald, and Parlett (1977) to use psychological data to illuminate a hidden network of social forces which overwhelmingly determines our behaviour and our theories. Many will claim that, as psychologists, we should not have done this or that we have "gone way beyond our data" in doing it. Yet, if we, as psychologists, wish to claim either to be serious students of the determinants of behaviour or that we aspire to apply science to benefit society, there is no doubt that we need to take the study of such forces seriously.

But clearly we will not engage with this task if we continue to work within the images and definitions of our role that we have accepted in the past. We need to actively articulate and promote a new image of ourselves and the role we can play in society. To put this another way, if we are to ferment the paradigm shifts that are required, or if we are to contribute as we would like to society, it is crucial for psychologists, *as part of our professional responsibilities,* to seek to understand, and find ways of intervening in, the omnipresent social forces which we have now seen control so much of our behaviour. Yet few of those who have noted the need for a sea change in thinking about the nature, development and assessment of competence believe it is part of their job to try to bring it about, still less to intervene in the network of social forces we have described.

How then to design a better guidance and control system for the management of the educational system and society more generally? There are many examples of more effective organisational arrangements to be found in research into individual organisations. Examples include those contributed by Schon (1971), Kanter (1985) Deming (1980), Johnson and Broms (2000), Kohn (1969), Semler (2001) and Erdal (2008).

Bookchin (2005) has underlined that what is common to these developments is that they involve moves toward "organic" structures.

In saying this he seeks to make a connection with the fact that the functioning of organisms is dependent on multiple, mostly non-hierarchical, feedback processes. Most functions, such as the maintenance of body temperature, are dependent on multiple feedback processes the majority of which do not pass through the central nervous system.

Bookchin (2005) then notes that it is so with many preliterate societies. Many have no chief, no hierarchy, no formalised religion, no written language, and no formal government structure. And the activities undertaken by individuals within them change depending on the needs of the whole.

One way of summarising what emerges from many of the studies of modern organisations alluded to earlier is that organisations benefit greatly if they can move toward organic structures.

Unfortunately, as Bookchin (2005) shows, the trend, seemingly since time immemorial, has been inexorably toward centralised command-and-control structures. This despite the repeated demonstration, not only that these run into enormous problems and generally fail to deliver high quality of life for most of those who participate in them, but also of the viability and success of alternatives.

The question is, then, why this trend has continued so inexorably and eliminated most of the successful alternatives.

This becomes a crucial question which organisational and other psychologists must answer if they wish to advance more successful management arrangements in connection with private or public institutions.

There is a strong tendency to attribute it to the doings of evil capitalists. Yet our work on the educational system shows that the process has too many components to support the view that it has been designed by an elite. What is most striking is that the system has evolved further and further along its current trajectory despite the repeated demonstration that the vast majority of pupils, parents, teachers, ex-pupils, and employers want it to move in exactly the opposite direction and despite the existence of a number of alternatives.

Bookchin (2005) attributes the overall trend in society to a "self-organising" process in which the central theme is the perpetuation and legitimisation of hierarchy.

It is this sociological need for hierarchy which drives the creation of huge amounts of essentially senseless work which constitutes the 'economic' system but, as Lane (1991) and Marks et al. (2006) show, does little to enhance quality of life. Unfortunately, a serious by-product of this senseless work (often focussed on materialistic goods) is the destruction of our habitat and thus, in due course, the elimination of our species.

There is not space to elaborate this thesis here (but see Raven, 2009). Suffice it to say that it is urgent for psychologists and others to study the socio-cybernetic processes that are contributing to this evolutionary trend and find ways of intervening in it.

AN INCIDENTAL, BUT PERHAPS REVOLUTIONARY, OBSERVATION

At this point we may draw out to a, somewhat paradoxical, but strikingly revolutionary, thought that seems to have emerged in our discussion. This is that what we have said essentially involves turning psychology inside out. It means de-animating human behaviour in the way Newton de-animated the behaviour of moving objects. It means attributing much of what we and others do to the invisible social forces that act upon us rather than to individual motives or values. Of course this is an over-statement because we have seen that these forces select and promote certain sorts of people who seem more adapt at promoting the "functions" of the system. Nevertheless there is something of an irony in suggesting that the way forward involves promoting the use of psychology to de-psychologise human behaviour.

And so to recap: early in this chapter it became clear that we need a new framework, or paradigm, to guide our thinking about competence and its development and assessment. But study of why the educational system has not in the past operated in a more professional way highlighted a more fundamental problem. This is that the behaviour of both our institutions as wholes and individuals within them is primarily determined by networks of mutually supportive and recursive *external* forces. This observation in turn affects our understanding of competence because it thus emerges that our competence is centrally dependent on understanding and harnessing these forces. More than that, it means that, if we are to claim special expertise in the area of understanding and predicting human behaviour we have to de-animate psychology: to turn it inside out. This is not to say that we should neglect individual psychology any more than the discovery of Newton's laws of motion mean that we should ignore the differences between different species of bird. But what it does mean is that, as professionals, it is incumbent on us to press for study of these forces. If we are to do these things we will need to press, not only for the development of new technico-rational knowledge but, more basically, for a move away from our current enthrallment with positivistic, reductionist, science. If we are to do any of these things we will need to reconsider what it means to be a professional; what professional competence involves.

CONCLUSION

In this chapter we have seen that:

1. Much received wisdom relating to the nature, development, and assessment of competence is inadequate. Worse, that much of its application has undesirable, indeed unethical, consequences for individuals and society. It follows that it would be unprofessional, indeed unethical, to require participation in "continuing professional development" activities conceived of as requiring enrollment in such things as courses to update participants' technico-rational knowledge.
2. There are endless opportunities to contribute to the evolution of better ways of thinking about, nurturing, and assessing competence. Unfortunately, dealing with the social forces which have, in the past, prevented psychologists doing these things calls for involvement in activities which are currently viewed as outside of psychology, and which many would therefore regard as going beyond their understanding of what it takes to be regarded as a professional psychologist. Nothing could be further from the truth; indeed, recognition of the importance of seeking to understand and find ways of intervening in these networks of forces has major implications for the way psychologists think about the determinants of behaviour and our understanding of competence in particular.
3. Our own research, including our work on the barriers to effective work in the area, suggests many leads which might be followed up in attempts to move forward.
4. While it *would* be possible to offer off-the-job programmes to nurture the competence of psychologists, those who set out to provide them would face serious challenges overcoming which would call for exceptional levels of competence and commitment going well beyond what most would regard as the legitimate calls of duty.

5. A more fruitful basis on which to move forward might be to require organisations to set aside time for what Kanter (1985) has usefully designated "parallel organisation activity" and to require psychologists to produce evidence that they have contributed to such activities.

6. What happens in the educational system, and society more generally, is not determined by the values or priorities of parents, pupils, teachers, employers, ministers of education or anyone else but by a network of recursive autopoietic social forces which few have sought to map or understand. Common-sense based interventions in these networks are either negated by the operation of the rest of the system or have counterintuitive, and usually counterproductive, effects.

7. The two key developments are required if we are move forward (i.e., to find ways of tackling the social and "environmental" problems which confront us) are (a) to develop better ways of thinking about, mapping, measuring and harnessing the social forces mentioned above, and (b) to design a new, organic, socio-cybernetic system for the management of society. In this connection, it was suggested that one way of looking at the task would be to see it as pointing the need to devise a new answer to Adam Smith's attempt to formulate arrangements that would lead to a society which would innovate and learn without central direction.

8. For the domain of psychology in general, we need a number of paradigm shifts as basic as those Newton introduced into physics. We need to "de-animate" our explanations of behaviour and see it as being primarily controlled by networks of invisible forces which can nevertheless be mapped, measured, and harnessed as effectively as Newton's observations made it possible to map, measure, and harness invisible physical forces; although a more appropriate image of the developments that are needed might be provided by attempts to map the interactions occurring in ecological niches.

9. Even more basically, if such developments are to occur, it will be necessary, though our professional development activities, to promote a movement away from a reductionist to what might be called a more ecological image of the scientific process itself.

BIOSKETCH

JOHN RAVEN. Perhaps the most important strand in John Raven's life work has been that which began with studies of what parents, pupils, teachers and employers wanted from the educational system. The barriers to delivering these outcomes included deficiencies in understanding of the requisite developmental (curriculum) processes and ways of testifying to the diverse outcomes. But more important was failure to come to terms with the sociological functions of the system and inappropriate (command-and-control-oriented) images of the way institutions, and especially public provision, should be managed. Yet, over time, something still more important came to the fore. What happened seemed to be controlled, not by people's priorities, but by a network of recursive and mutually reinforcing socio-cybernetic feedback loops. This prompted the realisation that we are all daily driven to do many things we are not personally predisposed to do. These insights led, first, to further work on public management, and especially the developments needed to create a sustainable society, and, second, to the notion that, just as it was necessary to de-animate explanations of the behaviour of moving objects in physics, so it will be necessary to de-animate our explanations of human behaviour and come to see it as being mainly determined by networks of invisible external forces rather than individual predispositions.

REFERENCES

Adams, E. A., Robbins, D., & Stephenson, J. (1981). *Validity and validation in higher education. Research papers 1-4 and summary report.* London: North East London Polytechnic, School of Independent Studies.

Adams, E., & Burgess, T. (1989). *Teachers' own records.* Windsor, England: NFER-Nelson.

Andersson, B-E. (2001a). *Blow up the school!* Paper presented at the NFPF conference in Stockholm, 15-17 March.

Andersson, B-E. (2001b). *School is good for many, but bad for too many. Voices from Students about their school situation.* Mimeographed paper. Stockholm: Institute of Education, Department of Child and Youth Studies.

Andersson, B-E., & Strander, K. (1999). *Perceptions of school and future adjustment to life. A longitudinal study between the ages of 18 and 25.* Stockholm, Sweden: Stockholm Institute of Education, Box 47 308, S-100 74.

APA Task force on Statistical Inference. (1999). See: L. Wilkinson and Task Force on Statistical Inference. (1999). Statistical methods in psychology journals: Guidelines and explanations. *American Psychologist, 54,* 594-604.

Association of Graduate Careers Advisory Services. (1992). *What do graduates do?* Cambridge: Hobson's Publishing.

Bachman, J. G., O'Malley, P. M., & Johnston, J. (1978). *Adolescence to adulthood: Change and stability in the lives of young men.* Ann Arbor, MI: Institute for Social Research.

Becher, T. (2001). The incapable professional. In J. Raven and J. Stephenson (Eds.), *Competence in the learning society.* New York: Peter Lang.

Bill, J. M., Trew, C. J., & Wilson, J. A. (1974). *Early leaving in Northern Ireland.* Belfast: Northern Ireland Council for Educational Research.

Bookchin, M. (2005). *The ecology of freedom: The emergence and dissolution of hierarchy.* Oakland, CA: AK Press.

Buckingham, M., & Clifton, D. O. (2005). *Now, discover your strengths: How to develop your talents and those of the people you manage.* Winchester, UK: Pocket Books.

Csikszentmihalyi, M., & LeFevre, J. (1989). Optimal experience in work and leisure. *Journal of Personal Social Psychology, 56,* 815-822.

De Landsheere, V. (1977). *On defining educational objectives.* Oxford: Pergamon Press.

Deming, W. E. (1980). Improvement of quality and productivity through action by management. *National Productivity Review, 1,* Winter, 12-22.

Department of Education and Science (1989). *National curriculum: From policy to practice.* London: HMSO.

Erdal, D. (2008). *Local heroes - How Loch Fyne Oysters embraced employee ownership and business success.* London: Viking

Flanagan, J. C. (1978). *Perspectives on improving education from a study of 10,000 30-year-olds*. New York: Praeger Publishers.

Flanagan, J. C., & Burns, R. K. (1955). The employee performance record. *Harvard Business Review, 33*, 95-102.

Flanagan, J. C., & Russ-Eft, D. (1975). *An empirical study to aid in formulating educational goals*. Palo Alto, CA: American Institutes for Research.

Flynn, J. R. (2000). *How to defend humane ideals*. Nebraska: University of Nebraska Press.

Forrester, J. W. (1971). *World dynamics*. Waltham MA: Pegasus Communications. (2nd ed., 1973, has an added chapter on physical vs. social limits.)

Forrester, J. W. (1971/1995). *Counterintuitive behavior of social systems.* Original text appeared in the January, 1971, issue of the *Technology Review* published by the Alumni Association of the Massachusetts Institute of Technology. All figures are taken from *World Dynamics* by Jay W. Forrester, Pegasus Communications, Waltham MA. http://sysdyn.clexchange.org/sdep/Roadmaps/RM1/D-4468-2.pdf.

Fraley, A. (1981). *Schooling and innovation: The rhetoric and the reality*. New York: Tyler Gibson.

Francis, H. (1982). Language teaching research and its effect on teachers in early education. In A. Davies (Ed.), *Language and learning in home and school*. London: SCRC/Heinemann.

Galton, M., & Simon, B. (1980). *Progress and performance in the primary classroom*. London: Routledge and Kegan Paul.

Galton, M., Simon, B., & Croll, P. (1980). *Inside the primary classroom*. London: Routledge and Kegan Paul.

Goodlad, J. (1983). *A place called school*. New York: McGraw Hill.

Gottfredson, L. S. (Ed.) (1997). Intelligence and social policy. *Intelligence, Whole Special Issue, 24*, 1-320.

Gow, L., & McPherson, A. (Eds.). (1980). *Tell them from me: Scottish school leavers write about school and life afterwards*. Aberdeen: University Press.

Hamilton, D., Jenkins, D., King, C., MacDonald, B., & Parlett, M. (Eds.). (1977). *Beyond the numbers game*. London: MacMillan Education.

Hattie, J. A. C. (2009). *Visible learning: A synthesis of over 800 meta-analyses relating to achievement*. London, England: Routledge; Taylor and Francis.

Hayek, F. A. (1948). *Individualism and economic order*. Chicago: University of Chicago Press.

Hewison, J., & Tizard, J. (1980). Parental involvement and reading attainment. *British Journal of Educational Psychology, 50*, 209-215.

Heynes, R.W., Veroff, J., & Atkinson, J. W. (1958). A scoring manual for the affiliation motive. In J. W. Atkinson (Ed.), *Motives in fantasy, action and society*. New York: Van Nostrand.

HMI (Scotland). (1980). *Learning and teaching in primary 4 and primary 7*. Edinburgh: HMSO.

HMI. (1978). *Primary education in England: A survey by H.M. inspectors of schools*. London: Department of Education and Science, HMSO.

Hogan, R. (1990). Unmasking incompetent managers. *Insight, May 21*, 42-44.

House, E. R. (1991). Realism in research. *Educational Researcher, 20*, 2-9.

Hughes, S. J. (1998). *Developmental effects of participation in a large group awareness training.* (Doctoral dissertation, University of Minnesota, 1998).

Ilott, I. (2001). Incompetence: An unspoken consensus. In J. Raven, & J. Stephenson (Eds.), *Competence in the Learning Society.* New York: Peter Lang.

Ilott, I., and Murphy, R. (1999). *Success and failure in professional education: Assessing the evidence.* London: Whurr Publishers.

Jackson, P. W. (1968). *Life in classrooms.* New York: Holt Rhinehart and Winston.

Jackson, P. W. (1986). *The practice of teaching.* New York: Teachers College Press.

Jacob, P. E. (1956). *Changing values in college.* New York: Harper Bros.

Jensen, A. R. (1998). *The g factor: The science of mental ability.* Westport, CN: Praeger.

Johnson, H. T., & Broms, A. (2000). *Profit beyond measure.* New York, NY. Free Press.

Johnston, L. D., & Bachman, J. G. (1976). Educational institutions. In J. F. Adams (Ed.), *Understanding adolescence* (3rd Ed.) (pp. 290-315). Boston: Allyn and Bacon.

Kanter, R. M. (1985). *The change masters: Corporate entrepreneurs at work.* Hemel Hempstead: Unwin Paperbacks.

Kazdin, A. E. (2006). Arbitrary metrics: Implications for identifying evidence-based treatments. *American Psychologist, 61,* 42-49.

Klemp, G. O., Munger, M. T., & Spencer, L. M. (1977). *An analysis of leadership and management competencies of commissioned and non-commissioned Naval Officers in the Pacific and Atlantic Fleets.* Boston: McBer.

Kohn, M. L. (1969/77). *Class and conformity: A study in values* (2nd Ed.). Chicago IL: Chicago University Press. (1st Ed.: Dorsey Press.)

Kohn, M. L., & Schooler, C. (1982). Job conditions and personality: A longitudinal assessment of their reciprocal effects. *American Journal of Sociology, 87,* 1257-86.

Kohn, M. L., Slomczynski, K. M., & Schoenbach, C. (1986). Social stratification and the transmission of values in the family: A cross-national assessment. *Sociological Forum, 1.*

Lane, R. E. (1991). *The market experience.* New York: Cambridge University Press.

Lester, S. (2001). Assessing the self-managing learner: A contradiction in terms. In J. Raven, & J. Stephenson (Eds.), *Competence in the learning society.* New York: Peter Lang.

MacBeath, J., Mearns, D., Thomson, B., & How, S. (1981). *Social education: The Scottish approach.* Glasgow: Jordanhill College of Education.

McClelland, D. C., Atkinson, J. W., Clark, R. A., & Lowell, E. L. (1958). A scoring manual for the achievement motive. In J. W. Atkinson (Ed.), *Motives in fantasy, action and society.* New York: Van Nostrand.

McGillicuddy-DeLisi, A. V. (1982). The relationship between parents' beliefs about development and family constellation, socio-economic status and parents' teaching strategies. In L. M. Laosa, & I. E. Sigel (Eds.), *Families as learning environments for children* (pp. 261-299). New York: Plenum.

Marks, N., Simms, A., Thompson, S., & Abdallah, S. (2006). *The (un)happy planet index: An index of human well-being and environmental impact.* London: New Economics Foundation.

Meadows, D. H., Meadows, D. L., & Behrens, W. W. (1972). *The limits to growth: A report for the Club of Rome's Project on the predicament of mankind.* London: Macmillan.

Mentkowski, M., & Associates (2000). *Learning that lasts. Integrating learning, development, and performance in college and beyond.* San Francisco: Jossey-Bass.

Messick, S. (1989). Meaning and values in test validation: The science and ethics of assessment. *Educational Researcher, 18(2)*, 5-11.

Messick, S. (1995). Validity of psychological assessment. *American Psychologist, 50*, 741-749.

Mill, J. S. (1859/1962). *Representative government*. London: Dent.

Morgan, G. (1986). *Images of organization*. Beverly Hills, CA: Sage.

Morgan, G. (Ed.). (1983). *Beyond method*. London: Sage.

Morton-Williams, R., Finch, S., Poll, C., Raven, J., Ritchie, J., & Hobbs, E. (1968). *Schools council enquiry one: Young school leavers*. London: HMSO.

O'Reilly, D. (2001). Competence and incompetence in an institutional context. In J. Raven and J. Stephenson (Eds.), *Competence in the learning society*. New York: Peter Lang.

Parlett, M. (1972). Evaluating innovations in teaching. In H. J. Butcher and E. Rudd (Eds.), *Contemporary problems in research in higher education*. New York: McGraw Hill.

Parlett, M. (1976). Assessment in its context. *Bulletin of Educational Research: Evaluation and Assessment, 11*, Summer.

Pascarella, E. T., & Terenzini, P. T. (1991). *How college affects students*. San Francisco, CA: Jossey-Bass.

Price, P. B., Taylor, C. W., Nelson, D. E., et al. (1971). *Measurement and Predictors of Physician Performance: Two Decades of Intermittently Sustained Research*. Salt Lake City: University of Utah, Department of Psychology.

Prieler, J., & Raven, J. (2008). Problems in the measurement of change (with particular reference to individual change [gain] scores) and their potential solution using IRT. In J. Raven and J. Raven (Eds.) *Uses and abuses of intelligence: Studies advancing Spearman and Raven's quest for non-arbitrary metrics* (pp. 173-210). Unionville, New York: Royal Fireworks Press; Edinburgh, Scotland: Competency Motivation Project; Budapest, Hungary: EDGE 2000; Cluj Napoca, Romania: Romanian Psychological Testing Services SRL.

Raven, J. (1977). *Education, values and society: The objectives of education and the nature and development of competence*. London, U.K.: H.K. Lewis, New York: The Psychological Corporation.

Raven, J. (1980). *Parents, teachers and children: An evaluation of an educational home visiting programme*. Edinburgh: Scottish Council for Research in Education.

Raven, J. (1984). Some limitations of the standards. *Evaluation and Program Planning, 7*, 363-370.

Raven, J. (1984/1997). *Competence in modern society: Its identification, development and release*. Unionville, New York: Royal Fireworks Press. www.rfwp.com (First published in 1984 in London, England, by H. K. Lewis.)

Raven, J. (1994). *Managing education for effective schooling: The most important problem is to come to terms with values*. Unionville, New York: Trillium Press; Edinburgh, Scotland: Competency Motivation Project.

Raven, J. (1995). *The new wealth of nations: A new enquiry into the nature and origins of the wealth of nations and the societal learning arrangements needed for a sustainable society*. Unionville, New York: Royal Fireworks Press; Sudbury, Suffolk: Bloomfield Books.

Raven, J. (2000). Rethinking democracy. *The Good Society 9*, 31-37.

Raven, J. (2001a). The assessment of competence. In J. Raven and J. Stephenson (Eds.), *Competence in the learning society*. New York: Peter Lang.

Raven, J. (2001b). The conceptualisation of competence. In J. Raven and J. Stephenson (Eds.), *Competence in the learning society*. New York: Peter Lang.

Raven, J. (2009). The emergence of hierarchy, domination and centralisation: Reflections on the work of Murray Bookchin. *Journal for Perspectives of Economic, Political, and Social Integration, 14,* 11-75.

Raven, J. (2010a). Advancing and defeating the PEGS agenda: Socio-cybernetics and Murray Bookchin. *The Good Society, 19,* 79-88.

Raven, J. (2010b). *Conceptualising, mapping, and measuring social forces.* Retrieved from http://eyeonsociety.co.uk/resources/scio.pdf

Raven, J., & Dolphin, T. (1978). *The consequences of behaving: The ability of Irish organisations to tap know-how, initiative, leadership and goodwill.* Edinburgh: Competency Motivation Project.

Raven, J., Johnstone, J., & Varley, T. (1985*). Opening the primary classroom*. Edinburgh: Scottish Council for Research in Education.

Raven, J., & Litton, F. (1982). Aspects of civics education in Ireland. *Collected Original Resources in Education, 6,* F4E7.

Raven, J., & Navrotsky, V. (2001). The development and use of maps of socio-cybernetic systems to improve educational and social policy. *Journal of Mental Changes, 7,* 19-60.

Raven, J., & Whelan, C. T. (1976). Irish adults' perceptions of their civic institutions. In J. Raven, C. T. Whelan, P. A. Pfretzschner, & D. M. Borock, *Political Culture in Ireland*. Dublin: Institute of Public Administration.

Ree, M. J., Earles, J. A., & Teachout, M. S. (1994). Predicting job performance: Not much more than *g*. *Journal of Applied Psychology, 79,* 518-524.

Ridley, M. (2010). *The rational optimist: How prosperity evolves.* London: Fourth Estate.

Robinson, D. W. (1983). *Patriotism and economic control: The censure of Harold Rugg.* (Doctoral dissertation, Rutgers University, 1983).

Schmidt, F. L., & Hunter, J. E. (1998). The validity and utility of selection methods in personnel psychology: Practical and theoretical implications of 85 years of research findings. *Psychological Bulletin, 124,* 262-274.

Schneider, C., Klemp, G. O., & Kastendiek, S. (1981). *The balancing act: Competencies of effective teachers and mentors in degree programs for adults.* Boston: McBer and Co.

Schön, D. (1971/73). *Beyond the stable state.* London: Penguin.

Schön, D. (1983). *The reflective practitioner.* New York: Basic Books.

Schön, D. (1987). *Educating the reflective practitioner.* San Francisco, CA: Jossey-Bass.

Schön, D. (2001). The crisis of professional knowledge and the pursuit of an epistemology of practice. In J. Raven, & J. Stephenson (Eds.), *Competence in the learning society.* New York: Peter Lang.

Seddon, J. (2008). *Systems thinking in the public sector: The failure of the reform regime ... and a manifesto for a better way.* Axminster, UK: Triarchy Press.

Semler, R. (2001). *Maverick!: The success story behind the world's most unusual workplace.* London: Random House.

Shiva, V. (1998). *Biopiracy: The plunder of nature and knowledge.* London: Green Books.

Sigel, I. E. (1986). Early social experience and the development of representational competence. In W. Fowler (Ed.), *Early experience and the development of competence*. San Francisco, CA: Jossey-Bass.

Sigel, I. E. (1986). Reflections on the belief-behavior connection: Lessons learned from a research program on parental belief systems and teaching strategies. In R. D. Ashmore, & D. M. Brodzinsky (Eds.), *Thinking about the family: Views of parents and children*. Hillsdale, NJ: Erlbaum.

Sigel, I. E. (Ed.). (1985). *Parent belief systems: The psychological consequences for children*. Hillside, NJ: Erlbaum.

Sigel, I. E., & McGillicuddy-DeLisi, A. V. (1984). Parents as teachers of their children: A distancing behavior model. In A. D. Pellegrini, & T. D. Yawkey (Eds.), *The development of oral and written language in social contexts*. Norwood, NJ: Ablex.

Smith, A. (1776/1981). *The wealth of nations*. Penguin Books: Harmondsworth, Mddx.

Spearman, C. (1926). *Some issues in the theory of g (including the Law of Diminishing Returns)*. Address to the British Association Section J – Psychology, Southampton, England, 1925. London: Psychological Laboratory, University College: Collected Papers.

Spencer, L. M., & Spencer, S. M. (1993). *Competence at work*. New York: Wiley.

Steiner, D. (1999). Searching for educational coherence in a democratic state. In S. L. Elkin, & K. E. Soltan (Eds.), *Citizen competence and democratic institutions*. University Park, PA: Pennsylvania State University Press.

Stephenson, J. (2001). Inputs and outcomes: The experience of independent study at NELP In J. Raven and J. Stephenson (Eds.), *Competence in the learning society*. New York: Peter Lang.

Taylor, C. W., & Barron, F. (Eds.). (1963). *Scientific creativity: Its recognition and development*. New York: Wiley.

Tizard, B., & Hughes, M. (1984). *Young children learning: Talking and thinking at home and school*. London: Fontana.

Tizard, J., Schofield, W. N., & Hewison, J. (1982). Collaboration between teachers and parents in assisting children's reading. *British Journal of Educational Research, 52*, 1-11.

Veroff, J. (1958). A scoring manual for the power motive. In J. W. Atkinson (Ed.), *Motives in fantasy, action and society*. New York: Van Nostrand.

Vygotsky, L. S. (1978). Mind in society: The development of higher psychological processes. In M. Cole, V. John-Steiner, S. Scribner, & E. Souberman (Eds.), ... Cambridge, MA: Harvard University Press.

Vygotsky, L. S. (1981). The genesis of higher mental function. In J. V. Wertsch (Ed.), *The concept of activity in society psychology*. Annank, NH: Sharpe.

Weaver, T. (1994). Knowledge alone gets you nowhere. *Capability, 1*, 1–6.

Winter, D. G., McClelland, D. C., & Stewart, A. J. (1981). *A new case for the liberal arts*. San Francisco: Josey-Bass.

Chapter 17

PLANNING FOR CHANGE IN PSYCHOLOGY: EDUCATION, OUTCOMES, AND CONTINUING PROFESSIONAL DEVELOPMENT

Paul E. Mazmanian[1],*, Taylor E. Berens[2], Angela P. Wetzel[3], Moshe Feldman[1] and Alan W. Dow[4]

[1] Office of Assessment and Evaluation Studies,
Virginia Commonwealth University, School of Medicine, US
[2] HABITS Lab, Department of Psychology,
University of Maryland Baltimore County, US
[3] Virginia Commonwealth University, School of Education, US
[4] Chair, Medication Safety Committee, Virginia
Commonwealth University, School of Medicine, US

The lives of some men and women are structurally shaped by the fact that they are deeply versed in advanced and subtle bodies of knowledge, which they apply with dedication in solving complex practical problems. They learn by study, apprenticeship, and experience, both by expanding their comprehension of formal disciplines and by finding new ways to use them to achieve specific ends, constantly moving forward and backward from theory to practice so that each enriches the other. Such people protect one another and are sometimes extended special protection by society far beyond that granted to other citizens. The price of protection is vigilance against poor performance and unethical behavior, and that vigilance is exercised by the privileged person, by others of similar specialization, and by society. These people are called professionals.

- Cyril O. Houle (1980)

---

* Correspondence regarding this manuscript may be directed to Paul E. Mazmanian, Associate Dean, Office of Assessment and Evaluation Studies, Virginia Commonwealth University, School of Medicine, Box 980466, Richmond, VA 23298.

Abstract

Lifelong learning is linked to psychologists' ethical commitment to develop and maintain their competence, and in turn, their competence is associated with improved outcomes for patients. No single theory of lifelong learning appears to predominate in psychology education; there is no universally recognized curriculum and no commonly accepted set of tools to guide psychologists through what is arguably the longest and most complex phase of their career learning. The science to explain outcomes and to inform models of continuing education planning is reviewed and found incomplete. Resources to support continuing education and advocacy for the profession are discussed. Leaders in psychology are asked to consider support for a public-private institute for continuing professional development in the health professions.

Keywords: Education, continuing, development, professions, institute, outcomes

In this chapter, the development of psychology as a profession is described, including the education, training, and qualifications of the psychology workforce in the United States of America. An interpretive review and appraisal of educational interventions is presented, with a model for measuring outcomes in continuing education. The interrelated roles of finance, science, and advocacy for education and psychology are summarized. Finally, the profession of psychology is asked whether a public-private institute for continuing health professional development might provide a valuable resource to practitioners, educators, scientists, and policy makers interested in the delivery of psychology services.

Defining the Profession

There may be no universally held answer to the question of what constitutes a profession, but there are three schools of thought to help understand the development of psychology as a profession. Each offers an alternative perspective for interpreting the work of those who provide psychological services to individuals or groups.

The *static approach,* pioneered by Abraham Flexner (1915), asserted "there are certain objective standards that can be formulated" to distinguish professions from other occupations. He identified six characteristics as essential for an occupation to claim professional status. Professions must: 1) involve intellectual operations, 2) derive their material from science, 3) involve definite and practical ends, 4) possess an educationally communicable technique, 5) tend to self-organization, and 6) be altruistic. This is called the static approach because objective criteria firmly discriminate between those occupations that are inherently professions and those that are not. Once this distinction is made, it is unlikely that those occupations not considered professional could develop into professions; yet, many occupations striving for higher status apply these criteria to decide whether their occupation is a profession (Cervero, 1988).

Compared to the static approach, the *process approach* offers gradation. The question of whether an occupation absolutely is or is not a profession gives way to several questions, each relating to a valued characteristic of the occupation. Conceptually, two fundamental questions are applied: To what extent does the occupation possess this valued characteristic? How is the occupation working toward its further refinement? When asked of psychology, the questions might be: To what degree do providers of psychological services demonstrate discrete mastery of their practice, and what are they doing to increase that control?

The process approach differs from the "yes or no" determination required with the static approach, because all occupations are viewed as existing on a continuum of professionalization. The highest values of the occupations are championed, and the overriding question becomes: How professionalized is the occupation? Within the process approach, there are no clear-cut boundaries separating professions from other occupations. Developed professions may, in fact, deprofessionalize within the process approach (Cervero, 1988).

The *socioeconomic approach* contrasts with both static and process approaches. It assumes there is no such thing as an ideal profession and no criteria necessarily associated with it. An occupation is commonly regarded by the general public as a profession or it is not. The title "profession" is ascribed in honor. It is a collective symbol, suggesting its members are highly valued by a society. Having achieved status and privileges, the recognition of an occupation as a profession is both socially constructed and socially granted. In the broadest sense, it is simply opposite of the word amateur: the professional baseball player, dancer, and cook earn a livelihood devoted to an activity, as opposed to being only transiently or professionally engaged (Flexner, 1915).

The privilege of the professional results not from a random process but from a political struggle, with varyingly high degrees of social and economic rewards accorded the winners; the price of protecting privilege is vigilance against poor performance and unethical behavior (Houle, 1980; Ameringer, 1999; Sullivan, 2005). That vigilance is to be exercised by the privileged person, by others of similar specialization, and by society (Ameringer, 2008; Houle, 1980; Wise, 2010).

THE PSYCHOLOGY WORKFORCE OF THE UNITED STATES

While there are several ways to define the profession, there are numerous activities, work environments, specialties, and education al opportunities for those comprising the profession. The US Bureau of Labor Statistics describes psychologists as studying mental processes and human behavior by observing, interpreting, and recording how people and other animals relate to one another and the environment. Psychologists look for patterns that will help them understand and predict behavior using scientific methods, principles, or procedures to test their ideas. Like other social scientists, psychologists formulate theories, or hypotheses, which are possible explanations for what they observe. But unlike other social science disciplines, psychologists often concentrate on individual behavior and, specifically, on the beliefs and feelings that influence a person's actions. Through such research, psychologists learn much that can help increase understanding between individuals, groups, organizations, institutions, and cultures (USBLS, 2010).

The American Psychological Association (APA), a scientific and professional organization representing psychologists in the United States, upholds a set of ethical principles and a code of conduct subject to continuous review and revision and intended to guide psychologists toward the highest ideals of the profession (APA, 2010). Standards are maintained for psychologists' work-related conduct, including a personal commitment and lifelong effort to act ethically; to encourage ethical behavior by students, supervisees, employees, and colleagues; and to consult with others concerning ethical problems.

In 2008, 170, 200 psychologists were estimated to be working in the US. The Bureau of Labor Statistics (USBLS, 2010) counts psychologists in three major categories: 1) clinical, counseling, and school psychologists, approximating 152,000, 2) industrial-organizational psychologists, numbering 2,300, and 3) all other psychologists, estimated at 15,900. Between 2008 and 2018, the largest growth in employment among these three groups is projected at 26%, for industrial-organizational psychology; followed by 14%, for all other psychologists; and 12% in clinical, counseling, and school psychology. About 34% of psychologists are self-employed, mainly as private practitioners and independent consultants (USBLS, 2010). Overall, USBLS predicts job opportunities will be best for those with a doctoral degree in a subfield, such as clinical health, and for those with a master's degree in industrial-organizational psychology. Prospects will be limited for those with a bachelor's degree (USBLS, 2010).

Education, Training, and Qualifications

The APA accredits doctoral training programs and select institutions that provide internships for doctoral students in clinical, counseling, and school psychology. Although a master's or doctoral degree, and a license, are required for most psychologists, a doctoral degree usually is required for independent practice. Psychologists with a Ph.D. or Doctor of Psychology (Psy.D.) qualify for a wide range of teaching, research, clinical, and counseling positions in universities, health care services, elementary and secondary schools, private industry, and government. A doctoral degree generally requires about five years of full time graduate study, culminating in a dissertation based on original research. A specialist degree or its equivalent is required in most states for an individual to work as a school psychologist, although some states credential school psychologists with master's degrees. A specialist (Ed.S.) degree in school psychology requires a minimum of two years of full time graduate study (at least 60 graduate semester hours) and a one year full time internship during the third year. People with a master's degree in psychology may work as industrial-organizational psychologists. They also may work as psychological assistants, conducting research under the direct research of doctoral-level psychologists. A master's degree in psychology requires at least two years of full time graduate study. A bachelor's degree in psychology qualifies a person to assist psychologists and other professionals in community mental health centers, vocational rehabilitation offices, and correctional programs. (See Figure 1.)

Psychologists in a solo or group practice or those who offer any type of patient care – including clinical, counseling, and school psychologists – must meet certification or licensing requirements in all states and the District of Columbia. Licensing laws vary by state and by type of position and require licensed or certified psychologists to limit their practice to areas in which they have developed professional competence through training and expertise. All states require that applicants pass an examination. Most state licensing boards administer a standardized test and many supplement the test with additional oral or essay questions. Most states require continuing education for renewal of the license. Clinical and counseling psychologists usually need a doctorate in psychology, an approved internship, and one to two years of professional experience.

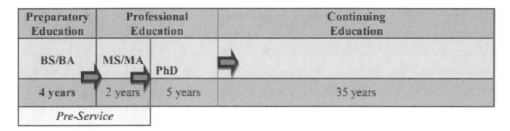

Figure 1. Preparatory, professional, and continuing education in psychology.

The American Board of Professional Psychology (ABPP) recognizes professional achievement by awarding specialty certification in thirteen different areas, such as psychoanalysis, rehabilitation, forensic, group, school, clinical health, and couple and family. To obtain board certification in a specialty, candidates must meet general criteria which consist of having a doctorate in psychology, as well as state licensure. Each candidate must then meet additional criteria of the specialty field, which is usually a combination of post-doctoral training in their specialty, several years of experience, and professional endorsements, as determined by the ABPP. Applicants are required subsequently to pass the specialty board examination.

Lifelong Learning and Continuing Education in Psychology

As with other professions, the need to keep up to date with new developments is considered a lifelong necessity by members of the profession of psychology and by society, although decisions regarding what to learn are made chiefly by individual practitioners. Lifelong learning presents as a value in psychology. The APA Code of Ethics requires that psychologists undertake ongoing efforts to develop and maintain their competence (APA, Section 2.03). The guidelines for the accreditation of doctoral programs in psychology require that the value of lifelong learning be taught as part of foundational academic training (Commission on Accreditation, APA, 2009) but there is no single theory of lifelong learning that predominates in psychology education, no universally recognized curriculum, and no commonly accepted set of tools unique to the exploration of learning across the stages of a professional psychologist's career. If lifelong learning for the professional occurs, it continues systematically or sporadically until retirement, disability, or death.

The APA regards continuing education as an ongoing process consisting of formal learning activities that 1) are relevant to psychological practice, education, and science, 2) enable psychologists to keep pace with emerging issues and technologies, and 3) allow psychologists to maintain, develop, and increase competencies in order to improve services to the public and enhance contributions to the profession (APA, 2000). The APA offers a system of sponsor approval and credit for continuing education. Approved sponsors include APA divisions, state and regional psychological associations, departments of psychology or other divisions within universities or colleges, professional schools of psychology, private organizations, professional societies and associations, hospitals, medical schools, mental health centers, government agencies, and individuals (APA, 2006). Any organization seeking recognition as a sponsor of continuing education must submit an application to APA's Continuing Education Committee, a group composed of members, appointed by APA's Board of Educational Affairs, who have expertise in continuing education (CE) program planning, administration, and evaluation, and who broadly represent the major fields of psychology. The Committee reviews applications from organizations and provides approval if the organization meets the guidelines provided in APA's "Standards and Criteria for Approval of Sponsors of Continuing Education for Psychologists." The standards include: 1) A statement of goals that reflect the notion that CE builds upon doctoral study in psychology, 2) Effective program management, 3) Satisfactory educational planning strategies and instructional methods, 4) Curriculum content that is related to well-established psychological principles or to ethical, legal, statutory or regulatory issues, or that is based on content that extends current theory, methods, or practice, 5) Program evaluation that may improve future programs, 6) Learning activities that meet the standards of APA's Standards document, and 7) Accurate and complete promotional and advertisement (APA, 2009). Once an organization receives approval as a sponsor, they may offer CE programs and courses for psychologists with the understanding that all CE activities will be conducted in compliance with the Standards and Criteria. The sponsor must complete an Activity Summary Form yearly, which lists all activities offered and includes promotional documents. The number of CE credits associated with a particular course or activity corresponds to the number of hours required to participate (APA, 2006). Objective measures of learning or higher level outcomes are uncommon features of continuing education in psychology (Neimeyer, Taylor, & Wear, 2009).

OUTCOMES AND BACKWARD PLANNING TO ASSESS THE EFFECTIVENESS OF CONTINUING EDUCATION

The prevalence of CE activities is a function of the demand for professional growth opportunities and the supply of available CE options. In turn, demand is driven by internal and external forces. Psychologists may be motivated internally as professionals by an orientation toward lifelong learning and a commitment to uphold professional standards that benefit their ongoing professional development. Alternatively, external motivating factors may include regulatory bodies that monitor to determine whether professional standards are being met, sometimes through methods of assessment for achievement of minimum levels of knowledge or competence, but more often through required numbers of CE credits that are audited occasionally for compliance. Multiple instructional strategies are available for CE planners and psychology professionals choosing how and when to engage in their continuing professional education. Table 1 presents a conceptual framework for planning and assessing the continuing education of psychologists. The model is revised from Moore, Green, and Gallis (2009). Variables align to guide practice and to suggest a research agenda for the continuing education of psychologists. The framework includes attendance as a method or data source for measuring *participation* at level 1. At level 2, participants' *satisfaction* with the setting and delivery of the continuing education activity is measured. Questionnaires completed by attendees is the method typically used to collect such data. Participant satisfaction ratings represent the most common form of assessment of CE in psychology (Neimeyer et al., 2009). *Declarative knowledge* (level 3A) is the degree to which participants state what the CME activity intended them to know. The data can be collected through pre- and post-tests of knowledge or through self-report of knowledge gain. *Procedural knowledge* (level 3B) is the degree to which participants state how to do what the CE activity intended them to know how to do, with pre- and post-tests of knowledge and subjective self-reports of knowledge gain forming the major sources of data. Attitudes, defined as a favorable or unfavorable evaluation toward a referent concept (Ajzen & Fishbein, 1980), serve as a potentially important outcome for CE in psychology. For example, the growing use of evidence-based practices (EBP) in mental health services has been identified as an important goal, and attitudes toward incorporating EBP into practice can serve as an indicator of progress toward this goal (Aarons et al., 2010).

Table 1. Outcomes Framework for Planning and Assessing the Continuing Education of Psychologists

Outcomes Framework	Description	Sources of Data
Participation LEVEL 1	Number of psychologists who participate in the educational activity	Attendance records
Satisfaction LEVEL 2	Degree to which expectations of participating psychologists were met regarding the setting and delivery of the educational activity	Questionnaires/surveys completed by attendees after an educational activity, focus groups
Learning: Declarative Knowledge LEVEL 3A	The degree to which participating psychologists state *what* the educational activity intended them to know	Objective: Pre- and post-tests of knowledge Subjective: Self-report of knowledge gain
Learning: Procedural Knowledge LEVEL 3B	The degree to which participating psychologists state *how* to do what the educational activity intended them to know how to do	Objective: Pre- and post-tests of knowledge Subjective: Self-reported gain in knowledge (e.g. reflective journal)
Competence LEVEL 4	The degree to which participating psychologists *show* in an educational setting *how* to do what the educational activity intended them to be able to do	Objective: Observation in educational setting (e.g. peer assessment and chart stimulated recall.) Subjective: Self-report of competence
Performance LEVEL 5	The degree to which participating psychologists *do* what the educational activity intended them to be able to do in their practices	Objective: Observed performance in clinical setting; client charts; administrative databases Subjective: Self-report of performance
Client health LEVEL 6	The degree to which the functional outcome of clients improves due to changes in the practice behavior of participating psychologists	Objective: Health status measures recorded in client charts or administrative databases Subjective: Client self-report of health status
Community health LEVEL 7	The degree to which the health status of a community improves due to changes in the practice behavior of participating psychologists	Objective: Epidemiological data and reports Subjective: Community self-report

It is reasonable to teach attitudes as content at levels 3a and 3b, with use of valid and reliable measures for assessment at levels 2, 3a, or 3b, but conceptual clarification is required to guide design decisions taken on a project-by-project basis. All such measures should closely target the intended objectives of CE in psychology, but objective measures of learning are not common elements in the current CE research in psychology (Neimeyer, Taylor, & Phillip, 2010a). At level 4, *competence* is the outcome measured, defined as the degree to which participants show, in an educational setting, how to do what the CE activity intended them to do. Observation of behavior in controlled conditions and self-report of competence are central sources of data for measuring competence. At level 5, participants demonstrate *performance,* the degree to which they do what the CE activity intended them to do in their practices. Observation of performance in the setting of care, client charts, and administrative databases, as well as self-reports of performance, are major sources of data for measuring performance, yet the direct demonstration of new skills and their translation into practice are absent currently from the CE literature in psychology (Neimeyer et al., 2010a). *Client health* is the degree to which the health status of those treated improves due to changes in the practice behavior of participants: this is level 6. Functional status measures recorded in client charts, administrative databases, as well as client self-report of health status form the major sources of data at level 6. At level 7, *community health* is the degree to which the health status of a community changes due to adjustments in the practice behavior of CE participants. Prevalence and incidence of diseases or disorders are central sources in a compendium of epidemiological data available to assess changes in community health.

The outcomes framework may be used to plan and assess the effectiveness of continuing education for psychologists. In developing continuing education for psychologists, leaders may choose to implement a backward planning model (Wiggins, 1998). Starting with the end in mind at level 7, and working backward through levels 6, 5, 4, 3B, 3A, 2, and 1, the planner continuously analyzes gaps between current performance and desired performance at each level, until no gap is detected at level 7. CE interventions can be designed accordingly to target specific gaps using education and instructional design theory and evidence based best practices. For example, using the World Health Organization Composite International Diagnostic Interview (WMH-CIDI) for diagnostic assessment and the World Health Organization Psychiatric Disability Assessment Schedule (WHO-DAS) to assess role impairment, Alegria and colleagues (2008) found racial and ethnic minority populations in the US receive less access and reduced quality care for depression, as contrasted to non-Latino whites. Starting at the end of the outcomes framework, level 7 (community health), recent studies (e.g., Alegria, 2008; Yeung, 2007) show a continuingly high prevalence of depression in the United States, with increased evidence of gaps in mental health care and outcomes for racial and ethnic minorities. Thus, at level 7, the gap between the current health status of racial and ethnic minorities and the desired health status may suggest a need for continuing education designed to reduce or eliminate the disparity.

The next step for the CE planner is to determine whether there is a gap at level 6 (client health) between the current health status of clients with depression and what national and local guidelines suggest it should be. This might be determined by reviewing the client charts of a psychologist or group of psychologists to learn whether improvements are found over time on the WHO-DAS for a select cohort of patients, including racial and ethnic minority populations and non-Latino whites. Quality of treatment for depression, for example, may be defined as: a) four or more specialty or general health provider visits in the past year, plus antidepressant use for 30 days or more; or b) eight or more specialty mental health provider visits of at least 30 minutes in length, with no antidepressant use (Wang, 2000).

If a gap exists in practices at level 6, the next step for a CE planner is to determine whether a gap exists between what the psychologists in these practices currently do and what they should do at level 5 (performance), to promote the best mental health for racial and ethnic minorities and non-Latino whites with depression. Sources include a review of charts for compliance and completed WMH-CIDI interviews with a sample of clients.

If a gap was detected in the performance of certain psychologists, the next step would be to determine whether there is a gap at level 4, psychologist competence, to show what the psychologist could do and what knowledge, attitudes, or skills he or she actually demonstrates in a controlled educational environment.

Finally, if a gap were detected in the competence of certain psychologists, the next step would be to determine if there is a gap at level 3B, procedural knowledge, between the knowledge a psychologist should describe and what he or she actually did describe. Similarly, a gap detected in the attitudes of select psychologists would show how a psychologist feels toward behaving in a proposed way and how he or she actually behaves.

It is generally understood that once presented with the information, most psychologists would be able to pass a test on how to increase access and improve the quality of care provided to racial and ethnic minority clients; there would be very limited opportunity to detect a gap at level 3B. As a result, it makes sense to plan most learning activities for psychologists focused at level 4, competence, while selectively assessing procedural knowledge that provides a foundation for behavior.

To succeed in reducing the gap in access and care for depression in ethnic and racial minorities, it is unlikely that a single psychologist or a group of psychologists could achieve the desired outcome without integrating the responsibility for access to and quality of care across other health professions. Simply relying on present education and health care systems without considering the unique barriers to quality care is unlikely to affect the pattern of disparities observed: populations reluctant to come to the clinic for depression care may have correctly anticipated the limited quality or access available to them (Alegria, 2008). Multidisciplinary action is required; yet, the formal continuing education of psychologists infrequently engages other health professionals.

Reliability and Validity Evidence

Like much of the testing in other professions, assessment along the continuum of psychology education suffers from a dearth of studies reporting use of reliable instruments. But to ensure that accurate interpretations inform ongoing education, measures for assessment and evaluation must be considered carefully, and selected based upon the best available evidence. Clear reporting of instrument development, including evidence for reliability and validity, is a responsibility of the instrument developer; critical evaluation of such evidence is an essential obligation of the instrument consumer. The good faith efforts of both parties are required for effective instrument development and application (DeVellis, 2003; Streiner & Norman, 2008).

The *Standards for Educational and Psychological Testing* (1999) provide preeminent guidance on best practices for developing an argument for construct validity of an instrument through accumulated reliability and validity evidence from five key sources – test content, response process, internal structure, relationships with other variables, and consequences of testing. Factor analysis is one technique useful for establishing validity evidence based on internal structure in instrument development. Reviews of factor analysis for instrument development in psychology, medical education, and education more generally indicate common errors in selecting factor analysis methods and inadequate reporting of methods and results; this limits the potential for replication and verification by other researchers and the evaluation by potential educators who may seek to apply the instrument in their practice (Fabrigar, Wegener, MacCallum, & Strahan, 1999; Henson, Capraro, & Capraro, 2004; Henson & Roberts, 2006; Norris & Lecavalier, 2010; Park, Dailey, & Lemus, 2002; Pohlmann, 2004; Wetzel, 2011; Worthington & Whittaker, 2006). Focused more broadly on multiple sources of reliability and validity evidence, reviews in subsets of medical education, such as measures of professionalism (Jha, Bekker, Duffy, & Roberts, 2007) and measures for evaluating clinical teaching (Hutchinson, Aitken, & Hayes, 2002), suggest insufficient reporting, limiting the ability of the consumer to effectively evaluate the instrument (Beckman Ghosh, Cook, Erwin & Mandrekar, 2004; Hutchinson et al., 2002; Jha et al., 2007; Lubarsky, Charlin, Cook, Chalk, & van der Vleuten, 2011; Ratanawongsa et al., 2008; Shaneyfelt et al., 2006; Tian, Atkinson, Portnoy & Gold, 2007; Veloski, Fields, Boex & Blanks, 2005). Evidence from a comprehensive review of medical education literature, specifically framed using the *Standards for Educational and Psychological* Testing (1999), indicates a large pool of instruments including measures at levels 2, 3A (declarative knowledge and attitudes), and 4, with only limited reliability and validity evidence based on a few narrow sources, specifically test content and internal structure (Wetzel, 2011). What appears lacking is further evidence to indicate how scores on the instrument relate to other theoretically related or unrelated variables, how scores on the instrument may predict important expected outcomes, or whether scores on the instrument remain stable or change over time, as anticipated by the theoretical understanding of the construct (Wetzel, 2011). Investigation of these sources of evidence requires time and more detailed research designs, including longitudinal studies. The report from the American Psychological Association Task Force on the Assessment of Competence in Professional Psychology (2006) called for the definition of competencies for professional psychology and for psychometrically sound assessment methods ranging up to level 4, competence. Subsequent reports elaborate competencies, their benchmarks, and toolkits for assessment (Fouad et al., 2009; Kaslow et al., 2009). From these instruments with limited supporting evidence, researchers and educators derive important implications about learners and curricular programs. At this writing, no review similar to those in medical education was apparent for reliability and validity evidence in psychology education.

Rater Training to Enhance Reliability and Validity

Observing and rating behavioral performance in controlled settings and on the job is resource-intensive and challenging, but important for understanding the effectiveness of CE interventions on demonstrated skills at levels 4 and 5 of the outcomes framework. Self-report methods are often biased (Davis et al., 2005) and using audit of patient charts or administrative reports mostly focus on outcomes rather than capturing specific behaviors targeted by the CE intervention. Rater training techniques can be used to increase the reliability and validity of observational performance ratings (Evans et al., 2009; Woehr & Huffcutt, 1994). Rater training includes 4 main components: 1) orientation to the purpose of the ratings and rating tool, 2) rater error training, 3) performance dimension training, and 4) frame of reference training. Orientation to the purpose and rating tool helps raters understand the context and consequence of the ratings they will be making and trains them on how to use the rating tool so they can focus on observing and evaluating behaviors. Rater error training presents the various types of rater errors so that certain implicit and explicit biases can be avoided. For example, contrast effects occur when raters spuriously increase their performance ratings of an individual after observing very poor performance prior to rating that individual (Summer & Knight, 1996). Hence, their performance rating is increased because they are contrasting it with someone else's performance rather than the referent targeted skill. Performance dimension training focuses on training the rater to accurately observe the target skill by providing specific behavioral examples of the targeted skill. Finally, the objective of frame of reference training is to train raters to discriminate between variations in skill levels of the targeted skill through an iterative process whereby raters practice rating behaviors, assess reliability, and discuss discrepancies between raters.

Rater training programs can be both resource and time intensive and are implemented in various ways. Traditional rater training programs may occur within a single day in the form of a workshop lasting up to 8 hours (e.g., Graham et al., 2009). Other models may be continuous where raters train over the course of several days or weeks in smaller training periods (e.g., Evans et al., 2009). Technological solutions to rater training may include deploying practice rating videos on digital media, internet, or learning management systems and having raters discuss discrepancies virtually. Currently, evidence on the effects of rater training supports its utility for enhancing reliability and validity, but more work is needed to delineate the unique effects of the various components and implementation designs. Rater training programs can be used as part of an overall CE planning, implementation, and evaluation strategy to promote evidence on higher level behavioral outcomes and enhance reliability and validity of behavioral observational measurement tools.

STUDIES OF CE AS INTERVENTIONS

Table 2 presents a list of CE interventions, definitions, and assigned values for effectiveness in changing the behavior of health care providers. The definitions are drawn from the Cochrane Database of Systematic Reviews. Assigned values - - little or no effect; mixed effectiveness; and more consistently effective - - are judgments of the authors, derived largely from reviews of studies including Davis, 1995; Thomas, 1999; Mann, 2002; Mazmanian and Davis, 2002; Marinopoulos, 2007; IOM, 2010; Forsetlund, 2009; and Miller, 2010. Reflecting the bulk of research in continuing professional education, most of the systematic reviews center on continuing medical education and physician behavior (Neimeyer et al., 2009). Generalization and transfer of findings to psychology may be limited but they are worthy of consideration as psychology continues to explore the roots of competent performance, the role of lifelong learning, and the value continuing education.

Table 2. Continuing Education Interventions, Definitions, and Effectiveness in Changing Behavior

Intervention	Definition	Effectiveness in Behavior Change
Educational materials	Distribution of published or printed recommendations for clinical care, including clinical practice guidelines, audiovisual materials, and electronic publications	Little or no effect
Conferences	Participation in conferences, lectures, workshops, or traineeships outside the practice setting	Mixed effectiveness
Outreach visits	Use of a trained person who meets with providers in their practice settings to provide information for improving the providers' performance	Mixed effectiveness
Local opinion leaders	Use of providers explicitly nominated by their colleagues as educationally influential	Mixed effectiveness
Patient-mediated interventions	Interventions for which information was sought from or given directly to patients by others (e.g., direct mailings to patients, patient counseling delivered by others, or clinical information collected directly from patients and given to the physician)	Mixed effectiveness
Audit and feedback	Any summary of clinical performance of health care over a specified period, with or without recommendations for clinical action; the information may have been obtained from medical records, computerized databases, patients, or by observation	Mixed effectiveness
Reminders	Any intervention (manual or computerized) that prompts the physician to perform a clinical action (e.g., concurrent or intervisit reminders to professionals about desired actions such as screening or other preventive services, enhanced laboratory reports, or administrative support [e.g., follow-up appointment systems or stickers on charts])	More consistently effective
Multifaceted interventions	Select combinations of the above 7 interventions (e.g., outreach visits followed by clinical information collected directly from patients and a computer reminder to counsel certain patients regarding a specific disorder)	More consistently effective
Interprofessional Education	Any type of education, training, teaching, or learning session in which two or more health and social care professionals are learning interactively	Mixed effectiveness
Interprofessional Collaboration	Practice-based interventions put into place in health care settings to improve work interventions and processes between two or more types of health care professionals	Mixed effectiveness

In 2007, Marinopoulos et al. summarized the evidence from 136 studies and nine systematic reviews of the effectiveness of continuing medical education (CME) in imparting knowledge and skills, changing attitudes and practice behavior, and improving clinical outcomes. The investigators could not determine the effectiveness of all CME methods studied, but CME was found, in general, to be effective for acquiring and sustaining knowledge, attitudes, and skills for changing behaviors, and for improving clinical outcomes. There is additional evidence to support the overall effectiveness of CE in select instances (Baker, 2010; Davis, 1995; Robertson, 2003), but too little evidence exists to make a compelling case for the effectiveness of CE in every circumstance (IOM, 2009). For example print media have been found to be generally ineffective, with exceptions, such as brief messaging techniques (Farmer, 2009). Educational meetings alone or combined with other interventions can improve professional practice and health care outcomes for patients (Forsetlund, 2009), although education meetings did not appear to be effective for complex behaviors. Mixed interactive and didactic education meetings were found more effective than either didactic meetings or interactive meetings alone (Forsetlund, 2009). Outreach visits to clinicians where they practice can improve the care delivered to patients (O'Brien, 2008) when information is delivered by persons trained to help with changes in practice (Wentz, 2003). On-screen, point-of-care reminders generally achieve small to moderate improvements in provider behavior and in patient health (Shojania, 2009). Opinion leaders alone or in combination with other interventions may successfully promote evidence-based practice, but effectiveness varies within and between studies (Flodgren, 2010). Audit and feedback that includes clinical performance data can be effective, especially when delivered more frequently and over longer periods of time (Ganz, 2007; Jamtvedt, 2006). Methods that include sequenced activities or multiple exposures to activities display mixed results, though tending to produce more positive results than one-time methods (Davis, 1995; Davis, 1992; Davis, 2009; Mansouri, 2007; Marinopoulos, 2007; Mazmanian, 2009; Mazmanian et al., 2011)

A recent report of the Josiah Macy Jr. Foundation, the ABIM Foundation, and the Robert Wood Johnson Foundation (2011) suggests teams of providers bring their collective knowledge and experience and provide a broader foundation for decision making that may be more robust than any single clinician can offer alone. Accountability should be shared appropriately with other professions, patients, and communities for improved outcomes relating to prevention and health care. The status quo for educating health professionals in silos, without preparing them for the realities of every day practice is no longer tenable, the report concludes (Macy, ABIM and Johnson, 2011).

Interprofessional education (IPE) may be defined as any type of education, training, teaching, or learning session in which two or more health and social care professions are learning interactively. In a recent review by Reeves et al., four of six studies found IPE projects improved some ways that professionals worked together and the care they provided, including decreased errors in an emergency department and improved management of care delivered to domestic violence victims (Reeves et al., 2009). Additional studies are required to determine the relative value of component interventions on individual health professions and teams (Mazmanian et al., 2011).

Zwarenstein et al. (2009) recently reviewed studies of interprofessional collaboration, defined as practice-based interventions put into place in health care settings, to improve work interventions and processes between two or more types of health care professionals. The studies evaluated interprofessional rounds, interprofessional meetings, and externally facilitated interprofessional audit. Three studies found improvements in patient care, such as use of pharmaceuticals, length of hospital stay, and total hospital charges. Locally developed provider protocols show promise for teams to improve care using system organizers, standardization of procedures, communication, and cross training to complete roles (Huber et al., 2007). However, further studies are required to understand the effects of the various interventions, how they affect interprofessional collaboration and lead to changes in health care, including under what circumstances the interventions may be most useful (Mazmanian et al., 2011).

Although further research is necessary to determine whether interprofessional education and interprofessional collaboration improve outcomes at levels 5, 6, and 7, it is sensible that the content of a continuing education activity designed to improve access and quality of depression care for ethnic and racial minorities would involve multiple professions, including physicians, nurses, pharmacists, and psychologists as well as community health workers (Mayfield-Johnson, 2011). The psychologist and others might serve alternately as leader of the team depending upon the required action, but accountability for patient/client outcomes appropriately is shared in this more egalitarian philosophy of care (Schmitt, 2011).

ACCOUNTING AND NEGOTIATING FOR WHAT WORKS IN EDUCATION

The most widely recognized approaches to CE planning include five major steps: 1) assess learners' needs, 2) define objectives based on these needs, 3) identify learning experiences to enable learners' achievement of the objectives, 4) organize the learning experiences, and 5) evaluate the program in terms of the objectives (Houle, 1972; Knowles, 1970). Most theories intended to improve CE planning account for planners as problem solvers who rigorously apply principles in their practice; organizational and social contexts are seen as noise that impedes application of the principles (Cervero &Wilson, 1994). But planning continuing professional education is not a neutral activity; it involves the negotiation of diverse and sometimes divergent interests. As psychologists choose to participate in some CE activities but not others, workplace setting plays a central role (Neimeyer, Taylor & Wear, 2010b). To the CE planner, for example, the perspective of the employed psychologist may differ from the perspective of the psychologist's employer regarding what topic or topics might be needed, in what priority order, and through what delivery methods, such as online internet offerings available after work, or face-to-face workshops convened during standard work hours. The CE planner brings his or her values to the planning process and so too will the participating patient or client who receives services, or the invited third party who pays for service delivery. All these perspectives and interests must be negotiated, as professional schools (American Association of Colleges of Nursing, 2010; Interprofessional Education Collaborative Expert Panel, 2011), private foundations (Macy, ABIM & RWJ, 2011), and public institutions (IOM, 2003; IOM 2010) recommend the integration of interprofessional education.

One strategy for interprofessional education proposed by the American Association of Colleges of Nursing (AACN, 2010) recommends: 1) design and implementation of continuing interprofessional education specific to work settings, 2) the development and assessment of interprofessional competencies by oversight bodies in conjunction with health professions organizations, 3) creation of outcomes-oriented continuing interprofessional education (CIPE) learning strategies by CE providers, faculty members, and certification and CE accreditation bodies, and 4) incorporation of CIPE experiences, including performance feedback, into standards and policies of healthcare institutions' accrediting and regulatory bodies.

A recent IOM report (2010) reviewed more than 18,000 articles from fields including CE, knowledge translation, and faculty development across a broad range of health professions.

The IOM found that effective CE activities: 1) incorporate needs assessments to ensure that the activity is controlled by, and meets the needs of, the health professionals, 2) include interaction (e.g., group reflection, opportunities to practice behaviors), 3) employ ongoing feedback to engage health professionals in the learning process, 4) use multiple methods of learning and provide adequate time to digest and incorporate knowledge, and 5) simulate the clinical setting. Although these attributes indicate ways in which CE providers can best affect the learning of health professionals, the report also found regulatory and financing mechanisms for CE disconnected from and poorly aligned with the goals of improving health professionals' performance (IOM, 2010).

The effectiveness of accreditation and credit systems in the health professions continues to draw fire from a public concerned about clinical competence and about the continuing education systems intended to assure competence. It is important that continuing education in psychology is not seen as an opportunity to nominally fulfill state licensing requirements. It is equally important that the public and all other stakeholders see no conflicts of interest or marketing initiatives in the continuing education to which psychologists subscribe; yet, there appears to be no overarching curriculum of lifelong learning to guide approximately 35 years of professional practice and few costs and benefits studies of CE or of the accreditation and credit systems in place to drive quality in the CE enterprise. Health professionals themselves are primarily responsible for being self-directed, lifelong learners: they must take personal responsibility for developing their own short and long-term learning goals for using the best available evidence to address clinical questions (IOM, 2010) and for selecting the best CE values.

RECOMMENDED: AN INSTITUTE FOR CONTINUING PROFESSIONAL DEVELOPMENT IN THE HEALTH PROFESSIONS

The history of psychology in the United States involves scholarship, service delivery, and social contract. From the turn of the 20th Century through the return of WWII veterans in the 1940s and the subsequent flourishing of American families, studies of psychoanalysis and outpatient treatment tend to show that useful psychological services were provided to the public during periods of widespread immigration and large scale industrialization. The transition from psychotherapy to empirically tested psychoeducational and behavioral interventions features contemporary treatment protocols that are integrated into the lives of millions, but also challenged by payment and health care delivery systems in the US (Cautin, 2011; DeLeon, 2011). Psychologists and their professional schools must continually advocate for themselves to assure the American public they will produce the types of psychologists society needs; in return, society provides professional psychologists and their schools with the resources required to conduct education and research and to offer psychological services (DeLeon et al., 2006; Fox, 2008).

In 2010, the IOM recommended that the Secretary of the Department of Health and Human Services should, as soon as practical, commission a planning committee to develop a public-private institute for continuing health professional development. Leaders in psychology should consider whether the profession should support that recommendation and participate in its planning. The resulting institute would coordinate and guide efforts to align approaches in the areas of: 1) content and knowledge of continuing professional development (CPD) among health professions, 2) regulation across states and national CPD providers, 3) financing of CPD for the purpose of improving professional performance and patient outcomes, and 4) development and strengthening of a scientific basis for the practice of CPD.

Continuing professional development (CPD), an alternative to continuing education, includes components of continuing education but involves a broader focus, such as teaching how to identify problems and apply solutions. It allows health professionals to tailor the learning process, setting, and curriculum to their needs. CPD recognizes the importance of multifaceted, lifelong learning in the lives of professionals and it takes a holistic view of their learning, with opportunities stretching from the classroom to the point-of-care. With CPD, control of learning rests squarely with the individual health practitioner, enabling them to be the architects of their own learning and performance. If coordinated nationally across health professions, a CPD system offers psychologists and others the promise of: 1) advancing evidence-based interprofessional learning, 2) engendering coordination and collaboration among professions, and 3) providing higher quality for a given amount of resources and leading to improvements in the health of the public.

A public-private institute for CPD in the health professions should maintain the tenet of collaboration among stakeholders including patients, the public, and other health care providers while focusing on community and health care quality improvement. Collaborating agencies might include the Agency for Healthcare Research and Quality, the Center for Medicine and Medicaid Services, the Joint Commission, the National Committee for Quality Assurance, the National Quality Forum, and other data measurement, collection, and reporting agencies to evaluate change in advocacy in performance and health care outcomes. With a national action plan for workforce development already in place (Hoge et al., 2009) but with limited resources to advocate for psychology services (Fox, 2008), the effect would be to coordinate advocacy efforts around national health care priorities, to build on psychology's success, and to further assure a place at the bargaining table for professional psychology, as issues of health care financing and CPD funding are decided.

With no work in psychology providing direct evidence of service-related outcomes associated with CE participation (Neimeyer et al., 2010a), the scientific basis for CE in psychology lags behind medicine (Neimeyer et al., 2009). Participation in a CPD institute promises to strengthen scholarship of CPD in psychology through shared resources intended to: 1) increase the scientific foundation of CPD to enhance health professionals' ability to provide better care; 2) develop, collect, analyze and disseminate metrics on process and outcome measures unique to CPD; 3) encourage health information technology and emerging data bases for feedback on professionals' and health system performance; 4) encourage development and sharing of improvement tools such as learning portfolios and assessment resources; 5) foster interprofessional collaboration to create and evaluate CPD; and 6) improve the value and cost-effectiveness of CPD delivery especially related to the outputs of CPD as quality and patient safety (IOM, 2009). At present, the majority of CE participation, estimated to cost $15-20 per credit hour (USBLS, 2008-2009), involves lecture, one of the least effective techniques for changing health care provider behavior for improved patient outcomes (Neimeyer et al., 2010a).

The IOM concluded that a new public-private initiative was required because the current system of CE is fragmented and its flaws cannot be remedied by anything short of a coordinated national effort. A new program within an existing government agency was not recommended because tying it to a federal program could not as readily incorporate collaborative decision making, including public and private sector actors and could also be subject to procedural or financial requirements that could diminish its effectiveness. An ad hoc coalition of current stakeholders and organizations was not recommended because expanding from the current set of stakeholders and organizations to the requisite breadth would require a strong central convener; reducing professional and state variability falls beyond the ability of such an ad hoc group for the foreseeable future. A private structure operated by professional societies and organizations could include all health professions and develop collaborations with other stakeholders (e.g., employers, researchers, state boards, and funders) to build the remaining infrastructure needed to support a CPD system, but the incentive to convene an oversight body for accountability would be missing. A new public-private structure could catalyze participation of a broad set of stakeholders in improving health care quality and patient safety, but it would also be accountable to the federal government. Of the five alternatives, creating a new organization with so many interested parties would be complicated but may represent the best of the options.

Moving to support the IOM recommendation could enable psychology to work with other health professions in an atmosphere more collaborative than heretofore available in the fragmented system of continuing education in the health professions. It would enable a stronger scientific base for development of effective continuing education interventions and for determining the effects of the educational activities planned not only for psychologists working independently but also for psychologists working in systems of care as members of teams. Where psychology has lagged in advocacy or support of itself as a profession, an institute offers opportunity for a seat at the bargaining table. And as payers may turn to the institute for monitoring quality of care, psychologists may improve their evidence base and bargaining positions as health service providers. As the structure of health care delivery changes, with managed care, higher co-pays, and provider restrictions and accountability moving to the forefront for control of costs, psychology may find opportunities to participate in reorganized systems of care and reformulated funding models to support education and research in lifelong learning, education, and practice improvement.

BIOSKETCHES

DR. PAUL MAZMANIAN serves as Associate Dean for Assessment and Evaluation Studies in the Virginia Commonwealth University (VCU) School of Medicine. He also serves as Director of Evaluation of the VCU Center for Clinical and Translational Research, a program supported by a Clinical and Translational Science Award (UL1RR031990) from the National Institutes of Health. In 2009, Dr. Mazmanian was a member of the Institute of Medicine Committee on Planning a Continuing Health Care Professional Education Institute and in December 2010, he completed his tenth and final year as editor of the *Journal of Continuing Education in the Health Professions*.

TAYLOR BERENS served as Research Assistant in the Office of Assessment and Evaluation Studies in the Virginia Commonwealth University School of Medicine through July, 2011. She also served as Editorial Assistant for the *Journal of Continuing Education and the Health Professions*. She is currently a doctoral student in Clinical Psychology and

Research Assistant in the HABITS lab at the University of Maryland Baltimore County. Her research interests include health behavior change and substance abuse treatment methods.

DR. ANGIE WETZEL currently serves as Director of Assessment for Virginia Commonwealth University School of Education. In 2011, Dr. Wetzel completed both her doctoral training in educational research and evaluation at Virginia Commonwealth University School of Education and a graduate assistantship with the Office of Assessment and Evaluation Studies at Virginia Commonwealth University School of Medicine. She has more than six years of experience in medical education including curriculum administration, student assessment, evaluation and research. Most recently her research interests focus on evaluating patient safety curricula in undergraduate medical education, modeling to explain medical student patient safety behaviors, measurement of medical student lifelong learning, and validity evidence and factor analysis in medical education instrument development.

DR. MOSHE FELDMAN is an Assistant Professor in the Office of Assessment and Evaluation Studies at Virginia Commonwealth University School of Medicine and Assistant Director of Research and Assessment at the Center for Human Simulation and Patient Safety. Dr. Feldman received his doctorate in Industrial and Organizational Psychology from the University of Central Florida where he conducted most of his work in the areas of human factors, team training, simulation, and organizational behavior. He designed and implemented immersive simulations to train basic workplace skills, problem solving, communication, and assertiveness in both healthcare and military settings. His work now focuses on the strategic integration of simulation based training and assessment methods across the continuum of medical education in the areas of surgical skills, clinical decision making, and teamwork to enhance patient safety outcomes.

DR. ALAN DOW is Assistant Dean of Medical Education and Associate Professor of Internal Medicine at Virginia Commonwealth University where he oversees the clinical education of third- and fourth-year medical students. He teaches and studies the use of techniques of theatre and standardized patients to improve doctor-patient rapport, health care team performance, and patient outcomes. Dr. Dow is a practicing hospitalist who chairs the VCU Health System's Medication Safety Committee. He recently was selected to the inaugural class of Macy Faculty Scholars, a highly competitive national program focused on developing the next generation of educational leaders in health care.

REFERENCES

Ajzen, I., & Fishbein, M. (1980). *Understanding attitudes and predicting social behavior.* Upper Saddle River, NJ: Prentice Hall.

Alegria, M., Chatterji, P., Wells, K., Cao, Z., Chen, C., Tekuchi, D.,...Meng, X. (2008). Disparity in depression treatment among racial and ethnic minority populations in the United States. *Psychiatric Services, 59,* 1264-1272.

American Association of Colleges of Nursing and the Association of American Medical Colleges. (2010). *Lifelong learning in medicine and Nursing,* A final conference report. Washington, DC.

American Educational Research Association, American Psychological Association, and National Council on Measurement in Education. (1999). *Standards for educational and psychological testing*. Washington, DC: American Educational Research Association.

American Psychological Association. (2000). *Minutes of the APA Council of Representatives*. Washington, DC: Author.

American Psychological Association. (2006). *APA task force on the assessment of competence in professional psychology*. Retrieved from http://www.apa.org/ed/resources/competency-revised.pdf.

American Psychological Association. (2006). *Approval of sponsors of continuing education for psychologists: Policies and procedures manual*. Retrieved from http://www.apa.org/ed/sponsor/about/policies/policy-manual.pdf.

American Psychological Association. (2009). *Standards and criteria for approval of sponsors of continuing education for psychologists*. Retrieved from http://www.apa.org/ed/sponsor/about/standards/manual.pdf.

American Psychological Association. (2010). *Ethical principles of psychologists and code of conduct*. Retrieved from http://www.apa.org/ethics/code/index.aspx.

Ameringer, C.F. (2008). *The health care revolution: From medical monopoly to market competition*. Berkeley and Los Angeles, CA: University of California Press.

Baker, R., Camosso-Stefinovic, J., Gillies, C., Shaw, E.J., Cheater, F., Flottorp, S., & Robertson, N. (2010). Tailored interventions to overcome identified barriers to change: Effects on professional practice and health care outcomes. *Cochrane Database System Review, 3*, CD005470.

Beckman, T.J., Ghosh, A.K., Cook, D.A., Erwin, P.J., & Mandrekar, J.N. (2004). How reliable are assessments of clinical teaching? *Journal of General Internal Medicine, 19*, 971-977.

Cautin, R.L. (2011). A century of psychotherapy: 1860-1960. In J.C. Norcross, G.R. VandenBos, & D.K. Freedheim (Eds.), *History of psychotherapy: Continuity and change* (2nd ed.) (pp. 3-38). Washington, DC: American Psychological Association.

Cervero, R.M. (1988). *Effective Continuing Education for Professionals*. San Francisco: Jossey-Bass.

Cervero, R.M., & Wilson, A.L. (1994). *Planning responsibly for adult education: A guide to negotiating power and interests*. San-Francisco: Jossey-Bass.

Commission on Accreditation, American Psychological Association. (2009). Guidelines and principles for accreditation of programs in professional psychology. Retrieved from http://www.apa.org/ed/accreditation/about/policies/guiding-principles.pdf.

Davis, D.A., & Galbraith, R. (2009). Continuing medical education effect on practice performance.: Effectiveness of continuing medical education: American College of Chest Physicians Evidence-Based Educational Guidelines. *CHEST, 135*, S425-S485.

Davis, D.A., Thomson, M.A., Oxman, A.D., & Haynes, R.B. (1992). Evidence for the effectiveness of CME: A review of 50 randomized controlled trials. *The Journal of the American Medical Association, 268*, 1111-1117.

Davis, D.A., Thomson, M.A., Oxman, A.D., & Haynes, R.B. (1995). Changing physician performance. *The Journal of the American Medical Association, 274*, 700-705.

DeLeon, P.H., Kenkel, M.B., Garcia-Shelton, L., & VanderBos, G.R. (2011). Psychotherapy: 1960 to the present. In J.C. Norcross, G.R. VandenBos, & D.K. Freedheim (Eds.),

History of psychotherapy: Continuity and change (2nd ed.) (pp. 39-62), Washington, DC: American Psychological Association.

DeLeon, P.H., Loftis, C.W., Ball, V., & Sullivan, M.J. (2006). Navigating politics, policy, and procedure: A firsthand perspective of advocacy on behalf of the profession. *Professional Psychology: Research and Practice, 37,* 146-153.

Derbyshire, R.C. (1965). What should the profession do about the incompetent physician? *The Journal of the American Medical Association, 194,* 1287-1290.

DeVellis, R.F. (2003). *Scale development: Theory and applications* (2nd ed.). Thousand Oaks, CA: Sage Publications.

Evans, L.V., Morse, J.L., Hamann, C.J., Osborne, M., Lin, Z., & D'Onofrio, G. (2009). The development of an independent rater system to assess residents' competence in invasive procedures. *Academic Medicine, 84,* 1135-1143.

Fabrigar, L.R., Wegener, D.T., MacCallum, R.C., & Strahan, E.J. (1999). Evaluating the use of exploratory factor analysis in psychological research. *Psychological Methods, 4,* 272-299.

Farmer, A.P., Légaré, F., Turcot, L., Grimshaw, J., Harvey, E., McGowan, J., &Wolf, F.M. (2009). Printed educational materials: Effects on professional practice and health care outcomes. *Cochrane Database of Systematic Reviews,* 3: CD004398.

Flexner, A. (1915, May). *Is social work a profession?* In National Conference of Charities and Corrections, *Proceedings of the National Conference of Charities and Corrections at the Forty-second annual session held in Baltimore, Maryland, May 12-16, 1915.* Chicago: Hildmann.

Flodgren, G., Parmelli, E., Doumit, G., Gattellari, M., O'Brien, M.A., Grimshaw, J., &Eccles, M.P. (2010). Local opinion leaders: Effects on professional practice and health care outcomes. *Cochrane Database of Systematic Reviews,* 1: CD000125.

Forsetlund, L., Bjørndal, A., Rashidian, A., Jamtvedt, G., O'Brien, M.A., Wolf, F.,…Oxman, A.D. (2009). Continuing education meeting and workshops: Effects on professional practice and health care outcomes. *Cochrane Database of Systematic Reviews,* 2: CD003030.

Fouad, N.A., Grus, C.L., Hatcher, R.L., Kaslow, N.J., Hutchings, P.S., Madson, M.,…Crossman, R.E. (2009). Competency benchmarks: A developmental model for understanding and measuring competence in professional psychology. *Training and Education in Professional Psychology, 3,* S5-S26.

Fox, R.E. (2008). Advocacy: The key to survival and growth or professional psychology. *Professional Psychology: Research and Practice, 39,* 633-637.

Ganz, P.A., Litwin, M.S., Hays, R.D., & Kaplan, R.M. (2007). Measuring outcomes in health-related quality of life. In R.M. Anderson, T.H. Rice, & G.F. Komnski (Eds.),*Changing the US Healthcare System* (pp. 213-244). San Francisco, CA: Jossey-Bass.

Gold M.R., Siegel J.E., Russell L.B., & Weinstein, M.C., (Eds.). (1996). *Cost-effectiveness in health and medicine.* New York, NY: Oxford University Press.

Graham, J., Giles, E., & Hocking, G. (2009). Using ANTS for workplace assessment. In R. Flin and L. Mitchell, *Safer surgery: Analysing behaviour in the operating theatre* (pp. 189-201). UK: Ashgate Publishing Limited.

Henson, R.K., & Roberts, J.K. (2006). Use of exploratory factor analysis in published research: common errors and some comment on improved practice. *Educational and Psychological Measurement, 66,* 393-416.

Henson, R.K., Capraro, R.M., & Capraro, M.M. (2004). Reporting practices and use of exploratory factor analyses in educational research journals: Errors and explanation. *Research in the Schools, 11,* 61-72.

Herman, P.M., Avery, D.J., Schemp, C.S., & Walsh, M.E. (2009). Are cost-inclusive evaluations worth the effort? *Evaluation of Program Planning, 32,* 55-61.

Hoge, M.A., Morris, J.A., Stuart, G.W., Huey, L.Y., Bergeson, S., Flaherty, M.T.,…Madenwald, K. (2009). A national action plan for workforce development in behavioral health. *Psychiatric Services, 60,* 883-887.

Houle, C.O. (1973). *The design of education.* San Francisco: Jossey-Bass.

Houle, C.O. (1980). *Continuing Learning in the Professions.* San Francisco: Jossey Bass. https://www.aamc.org/download/186752/data/team-based_competencies.pdf. Last accessed July 14, 2011.

Huber, T.P., Godfrey, M.M., Nelson, E.C., Johnson, J.K., Campbell, C., & Batalden, P.B. (2007). Developing professionals and improving worklife. In E.C. Nelson, P.B. Batalden, & M.M. Godfrey (Eds.), *A clinical microsystems approach* (pp. 106-123). San Francisco: Jossey-Bass.

Hutchinson, L., Aitken, P., & Hayes, T. (2002). Are medical postgraduate certification processes valid? A systematic review of the published evidence. *Medical Education, 36,* 73-91.

Institute of Medicine. (2003). *Health Professions Education: A Bridge to Quality.* Washington, DC: The National Academies Press.

Institute of Medicine. (2010). *Redesigning Continuing Education in the Health Professions.* Washington, DC: The National Academies Press.

Interprofessional Education Collaborative Expert Panel. (2011). *Core competencies for interprofessional collaborative practice: Report of an expert panel.* Washington, D.C.: Interprofessional Education Collaborative.

Jamtvedt, G., Young, J.M., Kristoffersen, D.T., O'Brien, M.A., & Oxman, A.D. (2006). Does telling people what they have been doing change what they do: A systematic review of the effects of audit and feedback. *Quality and Safety in Health Care, 15,* 433-436.

Jha, V., Bekker, H.L., Duffy, S.R.G., & Roberts, T.E. (2007). A systematic review of studies assessing and facilitating attitudes towards professionalism in medicine. *Medical Education, 41,* 822-829.

Josiah Macy Jr. Foundation, the ABIM Foundation and the Robert Wood Johnson Foundation. (2011, February). *Team-based competencies: Building a shared foundation for education and clinical practice.* Conference Proceedings, Washington DC.

Kaslow, N.J., Grus, C.L., Campbell, L.F., Fouad, N.A., Hatcher, R.L., & Rodolfa, E.R. (2009). Competency assessment toolkit for professional psychology. *Training and Education in Professional Psychology, 3,* S27-S45.

Knowles, M.S. (1970). *The modern practice of adult education: Androgogy versus pedagogy.*

Lubarsky, S., Charlin, B., Cook, D.A., Chalk, C., & van der Vleuten, C.P.M. (2011). Script concordance testing: A review of published validity evidence. *Medical Education, 45,* 329-338.

Maisonneuve, H., Matillon, Y., Negri, A., Pallarés, L., Vigneri, R., and Young, H.L. (2009). Continuing medical education and professional revalidation in Europe: Five case examples. *Journal of Continuing Education in the Health Professions, 29,* 58-62.

Mann K.V. (2002). Continuing medical education. In G. Norman, C. van der Vleuten, and D. Newble (Eds.), *International Handbook of Research in Medical Education* (pp. 415457). The Netherlands: Kluwer Academic Publishers.

Mansouri, M., & Lockyer, J. (2007). A meta-analysis of continuing medical education effectiveness. *Journal of Continuing Education in the Health Professions, 27,* 6-15.

Marinopoulos, S.S., Dorman, T., Ratanawongsa, N., Wilson, L.M., Ashar, B.H., Magaeziner,J.L,...Bass, E. **B.** (2007). Effectiveness of continuing medical education. Evidence Report/Technology Assessment No. 149 (Prepared by the Johns Hopkins Evidence-based Practice Center, under Contract No. 290-02-0018.) AHRQ Publication No. 07-E006. Rockville, MD: *Agency for Healthcare Research and Quality.*

Mayfield-Johnson, S. (2011). Adult learning, community education, and public health: Making the connection through community health advisors. In L.H. Hill (Ed.), *Adult education for health and wellness: New directions for adult and continuing education* (pp. 65-77), San Francisco: Jossey-Bass.

Mazmanian, P.E. (2009). Continuing education costs and benefits: Lessons for competing in a changing health care economy. *Journal of Continuing Education in the Health Professions, 29,* 133-34.

Mazmanian, P.E., & Davis, D.A. (2002). Continuing medical education and the physician as a learner. *Journal of the American Medical Association, 288,* 1057-1060.

Mazmanian, P.E., Davis, D.A., & Galbraith, R. (2009). Continuing medical education effect on clinical outcomes: Effectiveness of continuing medical education: American College of Chest Physicians Evidence-Based Educational Guidelines. *CHEST, 135,* S49-S55.

Mazmanian, P.E., Feldman, M., Berens, T.E., Wetzel, A.P., & Davis, D.A. (in press). Evaluating outcomes in continuing education and training: Theory and practice. In W.C. McGaghie (Ed.), *International Best Practices for Evaluation in the Health Professions.* Oxon, UK: Radcliffe Publishing Ltd.

Mazmanian, P.M., Richards, R.K., Tupper, R.L., & Wentz, D.K. (2011). The key role of the state medical societies in continuing medical education. In D. K. Wentz (Ed.), *Continuing medical education: Looking back, planning ahead* (pp. 300-316). Hanover, NH: University Press of New England.

Miller, A., & Archer, J. (2010). Impact of workplace based assessment on doctors' education and performance: A systematic review. *British Medical Journal, 341,* 1-6.

Moore, D.E., Green, J.S., & Gallis, H.A. (2009). Achieving the desired results and improved outcomes: Integrating planning and assessment throughout learning activities. *Journal of Continuing Education in the Health Professions, 29,* 1-15.

Neimeyer, G.J., Taylor, J.M., & Philip, D. (2010a). Continuing education in psychology: Patterns of participation and perceived outcomes among mandates and nonmandated psychologists. *Professional Psychology: Research and Practice, 41,* 435-441.

Neimeyer, G.J., Taylor, J.M., & Wear D. (2010b), Continuing education in psychology: Patterns of participation and aspects of selection. *Professional Psychology: Research and Practice, 41,* 281-287.

Neimeyer, G.J., Taylor, J.M., & Wear, D.M. (2009). Continuing education in psychology: Outcomes, evaluations, and mandates. *Professional Psychology: Research and Practice, 40,* 617-624.

Norris, M., & Lecavalier, L. (2010). Evaluating the use of exploratory factor analysis in developmental disability psychological research. *Journal of Autism and Developmental Disorders, 40,* 8-20.

O'Brien, M.A., Rogers, S., Jamtvedt, G., Oxman, A.D., Odgaard-Jensen, J., Kristofferson, D.T.,...Harvey, E.L. (2008). Educational outreach visits: Effects on professional practice and health care outcomes. *Cochrane Database of Systematic Reviews, 4,* CD000409.

Ottoson, J.M., & Patterson, I. (2000). Contextual influences on learning application in practice: An extended role for process evaluation. *Evaluation and the Health Professions, 23,* 194-211.

Park, H.S., Dailey, R., & Lemus, D. (2002). The use of exploratory factor analysis and principal components analysis in communication research. *Human Communication Research, 28,* 562-577.

Parmelli, E., Flodgren, G., Schaafsman, M.E., Baillie, N., Beyer, F., & Eccles, M.P. (2011). The effectiveness of strategies to change organisational culture to improve healthcare performance. *Cochrane Database of Systematic Reviews, 1,* CD008315.

Pohlmann, J.T. (2004). Use and interpretation of factor analysis in The Journal of Educational Research. *The Journal of Educational Research, 98,* 14-22.

Ratanawongsa, N., Thomas, P.A., Marinopoulos, S.S., Dorman, T., Wilson, L.M., Ashar, B.H.,...Bass, E.B. (2008). The reported validity and reliability of methods for evaluating continuing medical education: A systematic review. *Academic Medicine, 83,* 274-283.

Reeves, S., Zwarenstein, M., Goldman, J., Barr, H., Freeth, D., Hammick, M., & Koppel, I. (2009). Interprofessional education: Effects on professional practice and health care outcomes. *Cochrane Database of Systematic Reviews, 1,* CD002213.

Robertson, M.K., Umble, K.E., & Cervero, R.M. (2003). Impact studies in continuing education for health professions: update. *Journal of Continuing Education in the Health Professions, 23,* 146-156.

Rotter, T., Kinsman, L., James, E.L., Machotta, A., Gothe, H., Willis, J.,...Kugler, J. (2011). Clinical pathways: Effects on professional practice, patient outcomes, length of stay and hospital costs. *Cochrane Database of Systematic Reviews, 3,* CD006632.

Schmitt, M.H., DeWitt, C.B., & Reeves, S. (2011). Continuing interprofessional education: Collaborative learning for collaborative practice. In D. K. Wentz (Ed.), *Continuing medical education: Looking back, planning ahead* (pp. 300-316). Hanover, NH: University Press of New England.

Shaneyfelt, T., Baum, K.D., Bell, D., Feldstein, D., Houston, T.K., Kaatz, S.,...Green, M. (2006). Instruments for evaluating education in evidence-based practice. *Journal of the American Medical Association, 296,* 1116-1127.

Shojania, K.G., Jennings, A., Mayhew, A., Ramsay, C.R., Eccles, M.P., & Grimshaw, J. (2009). The effects of on-screen, point of care computer reminders on processes and outcomes of care. *Cochrane Database of Systematic Reviews, 3,* CD001096.

Starr, P. (1982). *The social transformation of American medicine.* New York, NY: Basic Books.

Streiner, D.L., & Norman, G.R. (2008). *Health measurement scales: A practical guide to their development and use.* New York: Oxford University Press.

Sullivan, W.M. (2005). *Work and integrity: The crisis and promise of professionalism in America.* San Francisco: Jossey-Bass.

Sumer, H., & Knight, P.A. (1996). Assimilation and contrast effects in performance ratings: Effects of rating the previous performance on rating subsequent performance. *Journal of Applied Psychology, 81*, 436-442.

Thomas, L.H., Cullum, N.A., McColl, E., Rousseau, N., Soutter, J., & Steen, N. (1999). Guidelines in professions allied to medicine. *Cochrane Database of Systematic Reviews, 1*, CD000349.

Tian, J., Atkinson, N.L., Portnoy, B., & Gold, R.S. (2007). A systematic review of evaluation in formal continuing medical education. *Journal of Continuing Education in the Health Professions, 27,* 16-27.

Tyler, R.W. (1949). *Principles of curriculum and instruction.* Chicago: University of Chicago Press.

United States Bureau of Labor Statistics. (2010). *Occupational outlook handbook: Psychologists.* Retrieved from http://www.bls.gov/oco/ocos056.htm

Van der Velden, T., Van, H.N., Quoc, H.N., Van, H.N., & Baron, R.B. (2010). Continuing medical education in Vietnam: New legislation and new roles for medical schools. *Journal of Continuing Education in the Health Professions, 30,* 144-148.

Veloski, J.J., Fields, S.K., Boex, J.R., & Blank, L.L. (2005). Measuring professionalism: A review of studies with instruments reported in the literature between 1982 and 2002. *Academic Medicine, 80,* 366-370.

Wang, P., Berglund, P., & Kessler, R. (2000). Recent care of common mental disorders in the United States: Prevalence and conformance with evidence-based recommendations. *Journal of General Internal Medicine, 15,* 284-292.

Wentz, D.K., Jackson, M.J., Raichle, L., & Davis, D. (2003). Forces for change in the landscape of CME, CPD, and health-systems linked education. In D.A. Davis, B.E. Barnes, & R. Fox (Eds.), *The continuing professional development of physicians* (pp. 25-47). Chicago, IL: AMA Press.

Wetzel, A.P. (2011). Factor analysis methods and validity evidence: A systematic review of instrument development across the continuum of medical education. *Proquest, 72,* UMI No. AAT 3453673. Retrieved from Proquest July 5, 2011.

Wiggins, G. (1998). *Educative assessment: Designing assessments to inform and improve student performance.* San Francisco: Jossey-Bass.

Wise, E.H., Sturm, C.A., Nutt, R.L., Rodolfa, E., Schaffer, J.B., & Webb, C. (2010). Lifelong learning for psychologists: Current status and a vision for the future. *Professional Psychology: Research and Practice, 41,* 288-297.

Woehr, D.J., & Huffcutt, A. I. (1994). Rater training for performance appraisal: A quantitative review. *Journal of Occupational and Organizational Psychology, 57,* 189-205.

Worthington, R.L., & Whittaker, T.A. (2006). Scale development research: A content analysis and recommendations for best practice. *The Counseling Psychologist, 34,* 806-838.

Yates, B.T. (2009). Cost-inclusive evaluation: A banquet of approaches for including costs, benefits, and cost-effectiveness and cost-benefit analyses in your next evaluation. *Evaluation of Program Planning, 32,* 52-54.

Younies, H., Berham, B., & Smith, P.C. (2010). Perceptions of continuing medical education, professional development, and organizational support in the United Arab Emirates. *Journal of Continuing Education in the Health Professions*, *30,* 251-256.

Zwarenstein, M., Goldman, J., & Reeves, S. (2009). Interprofessional collaboration: Effects of practice-based interventions on professional practice and healthcare outcomes. *Cochrane Database of Systematic Reviews, 3:* CD000072.

SECTION 6.

FUTURE DIRECTIONS

In: Continuing Professional Development ...
Editors: G. J. Neimeyer and J. M. Taylor

ISBN: 978-1-62100-767-8
© 2012 Nova Science Publishers, Inc.

Chapter 18

SPECIALIZATION AND LIFE LONG LEARNING[1]

Ronald H. Rozensky[1,*] *and Nadine J. Kaslow*[2]
[1] University of Florida, US
[2] Emory University, US

As a single footstep will not make a path on earth, so a single thought will not make a pathway in the mind. To make a deep physical path, we walk again and again. To make a deep mental path, we must think over and over the kind of thoughts we wish to dominate our lives.

--- Henry David Thoreau

ABSTRACT

This chapter defines what a *specialty* is in professional psychology and how the practicing psychologist can become a *specialist* after completing their core broad and general education and training. It will look at the implications of healthcare reform and the Patient Protection and Affordable Care Act and how changes in the structure of the healthcare system will impact the healthcare workforce of the future, including the training and continuing development of that workforce. This will include psychology's role in healthcare and why *specialization* will become increasingly important during the next epoch of healthcare services delivery. Finally, specialization will be discussed as part of the quest for personal development and as a structure upon which to build one dimension of each individual's professional lifelong learning portfolio.

Keywords: Specialization, specialist, board certification, lifelong learning, professional psychology

---

[1] This chapter is dedicated to the memory of Lynn P. Rehm, PhD, ABPP; he encouraged the authors to "think over and over ..."
[*] Correspondence concerning this chapter should be addressed to Ronald H. Rozensky, Ph.D., Professor, Department of Clinical and Health Psychology, College of Public Health and Health Professions, University of Florida, PO Box 100165, Gainesville, FL 32610. Email: rozensky@phhp.ufl.edu.

"A well-educated workforce is critical to the discovery and application of health care practices to prevent disease, promote well-being, and increase the quality life-years of the public" (Institute of Medicine, 2009 , p 11). Later in its report, *Redesigning continuing education in the health professions*, the Institute of Medicine (IOM) notes that the board certification of individuals as specialists by their professional societies and boards "acknowledge[s] competence in a particular specialty, often requiring more in-depth knowledge than licensure" (p. 16). Specialization, a distinctive mark or quality, is an inevitable and necessary product of developmental processes in a discipline and a profession (Roberts, 2006). Wise and colleagues recognize that the rapid growth of scientific and clinical information and the half life of professional knowledge can lead to a challenge for the individual psychologist to meet the ethical requirements of remaining current and competent in their area(s) of practice (Wise et al., 2010). Adding to, enhancing, and maintaining this apperceptive mass – that is, the sum of one's knowledge and experiences as organized by ethical expectations (Boring, 1950) – becomes *specialized* when the range of information acquired is focused. Rozensky and Kaslow each noted that by 'specializing,' the individual psychologist *de facto* focuses and delimits the range of information that they must acquire, renew, and maintain in order to remain current in their competence (Kaslow, 2011; Rozensky, 2010). With that specialized focus they can be more assured that they will provide the most recent, evidenced-based services to their patients. These services, of course, are based upon the foundations of a broad and general education in professional psychology that allows one to build their specialized knowledge, skills, and attitudes.

This chapter will define what a *specialty* is in professional psychology and how one can become a *specialist* once those broad and general competencies are developed. It will look at the implications of healthcare reform and the Patient Protection and Affordable Care Act and how changes in the structure of the healthcare system will impact the healthcare workforce of the future, including the training and continuing development of that workforce. This will include psychology's role in healthcare and why *specialization* will become increasingly important during the next epoch of healthcare services delivery. Finally, specialization will be discussed as part of the quest for personal development and as a structure upon which to build one dimension of each individual's lifelong learning portfolio.

SPECIALIZATION

What Is a Specialty in Psychology?

The following definition of "specialty" is currently agreed upon by the Council of Specialties in Professional Psychology (CoS): A specialty is a defined area of professional practice characterized by a distinctive configuration of competent services for specified problems and populations. Practice in a specialty requires advanced knowledge and skills acquired through an organized sequence of education and training in addition to the broad and general education and core scientific and professional foundations acquired through an APA or CPA accredited doctoral program. Specialty training may be acquired either at the doctoral or postdoctoral level as defined by the specialty.

Specialization then is based on the required core, foundational and functional competencies (Fouad et al., 2009; Kaslow, 2004; Kaslow et al., 2004; Rodolfa et al., 2005) of the broad and general education and training acquired through the scientific and clinical training in professional psychology plus "advanced knowledge and skills" that are the hallmark of each recognized specialty. Specialties are recognized by the APA based on a review provided by the Commission for the Recognition of Specialties and Proficiencies in Professional Psychology (CRSPPP). CRSPPP has policies and procedures used to review proposed specialties and then makes a recommendation to the APA's Council of Representatives for those specialties that meet the requirements for recognition as detailed in those policies. CRSPPP, working with CoS, proposed the specialty definition described above, as APA policy.

Currently there are twelve APA-recognized specialties: behavioral and cognitive psychology, clinical psychology, clinical child and adolescent psychology, clinical health psychology, clinical neuropsychology, counseling psychology, family psychology, forensic psychology, industrial-organizational psychology, psychoanalytic psychology, school psychology, and professional geropsychology. For each of those specialties a public description is listed at http://www.apa.org/ed/graduate/specialize/recognized.aspx. Criteria utilized to review a specialty include the following: how is that specialty distinct from other specialties; what is the public need for that specialty; what type of organizational or inter-organizational structure(s) exist to oversee the definition and development of the specialty; documentation of the advanced scientific and theoretical knowledge germane to the specialty; documentation of educational and training guidelines for the specialty; parameters defining practice in the specialty, populations served, problems addressed, and clinical procedures utilized by the specialty; and how are individual specialists evaluated and recognized to practice within that specialty.

The American Board of Professional Psychology (ABPP) has 14 defined specialties, most of which overlap with those of the APA recognized specialties. Both groups have accepted the following as specialties: behavioral and cognitive psychology, clinical psychology, clinical child and adolescent psychology, clinical health psychology, clinical neuropsychology, counseling psychology, couple and family psychology (referred to as family psychology by APA), counseling psychology, forensic psychology, organization and business psychology (referred to as organizational psychology by APA), psychoanalysis (referred to as psychoanalytic psychology by APA), and school psychology. ABPP, but not APA, also considers group psychology, rehabilitation psychology, and police and public safety to be specialties. Whereas professional geropsychology is a recognized specialty within APA, that is not yet the case within the ABPP organization. ABPP also delineates specialty criterion. However, ABPP recognizes that while there must be unique practice activities associated with each specialty, the practice activities in any specialty seldom are exclusive to the specialty and most practice activities are shared with the general practice of professional psychology.

Specialties and Specialists

Specialties routinely develop their expectations for education and training programs offering major areas of study or various levels of experiences in those specialties. Specialties also develop practice guidelines for their board certified specialists to use in developing their specialized, patient care services. For example, authors have offered descriptions of a specialty, training for specialists within that specialty, and services provided by those specialists within multiple specialties including, but not limited to, behavioral and cognitive psychology (Dowd, Clen, & Arnold, 2010), clinical child and adolescent psychology (Jackson, Alberts, & Roberts, 2010), clinical health psychology (Belar, 2008), clinical neuropsychology (Boake, 2008), clinical psychology (Finch, Simon, & Nezu, 2006), couple and family psychology (Kaslow, Celano, & Stanton, 2005; Nutt & Stanton, 2008), forensic psychology (Packer, 2008; Packer & Grisso, 2011), organizational and business consulting/industrial organizational psychology (Thomas, 2010), professional geropsychology (Molinari, 2011), rehabilitation psychology (Cox, Hess, Hibbard, Layman, & Stewart, 2010), and school psychology (Flanagan & Miller, 2010; Tharinger, Pryzwansky, & Miller, 2008). Those education and training expectations and practice guidelines provide direction for those interested in focusing their professional activities and lifelong learning within a defined specialty.

The Specialist

A specialist is a person who specializes in a particular field of study or who is devoted to a particular occupation or branch of study or research. For the individual professional psychologist, formal recognition as a board certified *specialist* occurs when they have been deemed to be competent to deliver high quality services within their specialty based upon the results of a peer evaluation as adjudicated by a recognized board certifying organization.

The most commonly recognized board certification organization in professional psychology that deems individuals competent as specialists is ABPP (Bent, Packard, & Goldberg, 1999; Nezu, Finch, & Simon, 2009). ABPP is a non-profit, unitary governing board that coordinates 14 affiliated psychology examining boards; one for each of its recognized specialties. ABPP recognizes new specialties and subspecialties and requires self-study and comprehensive periodic site review of its member boards. Further, ABPP conducts competency-based examinations and certifies specialists in accordance with its established professional standards, policies, and procedures. ABPP verifies board certified psychologists and lists them in its public directory, thus serving the public by certifying psychologists competent to deliver high-quality services in specialty areas of psychology (Cox, 2010; Kaslow & Ingram, 2009). The current philosophy of ABPP is that most licensed professional psychologists practicing within a specialty are competent and qualify for board certification in that specialty.

Becoming a Board Certified Specialist

The process of applying for specialty board certification through ABPP is in and of itself a lifelong learning experience. Indeed, licensure boards in many jurisdictions recognize this by offering continuing education credits for individuals who attain specialty board certification. After determining the appropriate board in which to become certified as a specialist, based upon one's interests and practice patterns (Boll, 2009), the interested psychologist can submit the generic application to ABPP, which documents their education, training, and experience. The next step in the application process for most of the specialty boards requires the candidate to complete a comprehensive written practice sample (Davidson, 2009). It typically is helpful for the candidate to secure a mentor in their specialty to help them prepare this clinical sample document, as well as to ask for assistance in preparing oneself for the subsequent oral board certification examination (Kaslow, 2009; Talley, 2008). The preparation of the practice sample requires a process of self-examination and an evaluation of one's clinical work, an articulation of one's competence in the core foundational and functional competency domains, and the sharing of representative work samples. This, in and of itself, is part of a lifelong learning process.

In two of the specialties, clinical neuropsychology and forensics psychology, a written examination must be passed prior to the completion of the practice sample (Lee & Otto, 2009). These exams are quite rigorous and require extensive knowledge in the specialty area. Thus, preparing for and taking these exams is a very intensive continuing education process as well. The final stage in the board certification process is the oral examination, which again requires preparation and review of one's clinical practice sample, knowledge of current trends in the field, and specialty-specific ethical issues (Kaslow, 2009). The oral examination experience itself is an in-depth, collegial process in which one's competence in the essential components of the specialty-specific foundational and functional competency domains are evaluated. Participation in the specialty board certification process through ABPP reflects the psychologist's commitment to the lifelong learning process, particularly in one's specialty area. The board certification process is a form of active learning and engagement and shows a willingness to subject oneself to a comprehensive and intensive peer-review and competency-based evaluation process that serves as a review and outcome measure of that ongoing learning process.

Changes to the Healthcare System and Importance of Specializationt

There are a number of changes in the healthcare system within the United States (U.S.) that underscore the importance and value of psychologists becoming board certified in one or more specialties within professional psychology. The U.S. Bureau of Labor Statistics (BLS) suggests that the professional psychology workforce will increase by 7 to 13% between 2008 and 2018. BLS goes on to say that 34% of those employed as psychologists are self employed (private practice) and 21% work in some type of healthcare setting. APA's own Center for Workforce Studies (CWS) (American Psychological Association, 2009) found that 45.5% of professional psychologists are in independent practice with the remaining (majority) practicing in some type of institutional settings. The bulk of those settings are some type of healthcare organization (e.g., hospital, academic health sciences center, Veterans Affairs Medical Centers).

The advent of accountable care organizations for the delivery of healthcare services will impact the oversight and credentialing of all healthcare providers in these settings (Rozensky, in press). The *Patient Protection and Affordable Care Act* (PPACA) (Public Law No: 111-148, March 23, 2010) supports accountable care organizations (CMS Office of Legislation, 2010; Fisher, Staiger, Bynum, & Gottlieb, 2007; Fisher, 2010) as a locus of healthcare service that can connect hospital-based care with office-based clinical practice. This may well focus more services, and reimbursement for health services, in these new organizational entities and this will, in turn, require enhanced scrutiny of all healthcare providers' credentials (Rozensky, in press). Rozensky notes that as it is currently the expectation for physician practice within a hospital setting, these new accountable care organizations will expect *all* independent practitioners to be board certified specialists as part of the organizations' quality assurance and accountability review activities. This will include psychologists. Thus we will see the call for those entering the field to seek board certification and for those already in the practice to identify their area(s) of specialization and seek board certification as a specialist. This in turn will call upon the continuing education systems in professional psychology to assist in this endeavor in order for psychology to be seen as relevant in the evolving, accountable care system.

There are a number of additional reasons for psychologists to be board certified in the current and evolving health care climate (Kaslow, 2011). Just as consumers expect their physicians to be board certified, they increasingly expect the same of their other doctoral level health care providers, such as psychologists. Healthcare systems increasingly expect the board certification credential of their providers. Policy, such as PPACA noted above, calls for it. The PPACA mentions various medical and behavioral health care specialties throughout the document, underscoring the recognition that different patient populations can benefit from professionals with different areas of expertise. Given the data on the association between board certification and positive clinical outcomes, quality improvement programs are increasingly demanding board certification of its providers (Brennan et al., 2004; Sharp, Bashook, Lipsky, Horowitz, & Miller, 2002). As reimbursement is linked in part to quality, and board certification is a mark of quality, then pay scales will partially take into account specialty board certification status. The evolving healthcare system needs specialists as members of the interprofessional workforce (Interprofessional Education Collaborative Expert Panel, 2011). Psychology's interprofessional healthcare colleagues have more respect for individuals who are board certified and thus those board certified psychologists are more likely to be invited to serve on integrated health care teams and broader panels of providers in accountable care organizations. Healthcare/medical homes have a place for specialists and these patient- and family-centered environments are the current context in which healthcare is being delivered (Rosenthal, 2008; Sia, Tonniges, Osterhus, & Taba, 2004). This is true in primary care settings where behavioral healthcare is being recognized increasingly as key to a comprehensive approach to healthcare (The Carter Center, 2011). With the growing attention to parity between medical and behavioral health services (Ostrow & Maderscheid, 2010) there is parity in terms of specialty care, as well as general care. And finally, all patients have the right to access quality specialty care.

Specialization and Lifelong Learning

In a recent review of the evolution of continuing education in professional psychology it was noted that focusing on the bridge between evidence-based lifelong learning and the larger competency movement will assure that one's professional development is committed to enhanced professional skills, practices, and outcomes (Neimeyer & Taylor, 2010). This is a natural interface between lifelong learning and preparing for specialization and the peer evaluation that is the hallmark of board certification, a clear outcome measure that reflects enhanced competence and practices. Indeed, becoming a specialist is an indicator of a desire for personal and professional growth as well as a reflection of a commitment to remaining current within one's specialty and to engaging in lifelong learning within that specialty. This process is facilitated by each specialty promulgating their educational and practice-based guidelines designed to help prepare the individual to practice as a specialist.

A self-study/self-assessment structure (Belar et al., 2001), in concert with the organized sequence of training and experience defined by each specialty, should allow structuring of a lifelong learning approach to specialization. This should occur in the context of psychologists being encouraged to be engaged in mindful practice, in which they engage in critical self-reflection that permits insight, possess a level of critical curiosity, engages in attentive observations, acknowledges their own areas for growth and errors, refines their competence, and clarifies their values so they act with a high degree of professionalism (Epstein, 1999). It may be valuable for specialty groups to organize their continuing professional education programs on mindful practice and mindful communication, as participation in such programs is associated with improvements in well-being and attitudes toward patient-centered care (Krasner et al., 2009). Such programs can build upon curricula that have been proposed to cultivate the habits of mind associated with mindful practice in action (Epstein, 2003b). In addition, since mindfulness requires practice to become habitual, maintenance of certification within a specialty should incorporate information from the psychologist about his/her self-reflections and mindful practices associated with functioning as a professional psychologist broadly, as well as within the specialty (Epstein, 2003a).

For specialists to remain current and competent there should be a culture within professional psychology that supports individuals in participating in competency-based continuing professional development both broadly, within the general practice of professional psychology, and more specifically, within their specialty (Campbell, Silver, Sherbino, Cate, & Holmboe, 2010). This participation should include the development of continuing professional development plans to determine learning priorities, integrate innovations and new evidence into practice, evaluate one's own competence and performance, and devise action plans to improve one's general and specialty-specific clinical practice. Continuing professional education activities for specialists should include engagement in those activities that fit their learning objectives, are interactive, utilize multiple instructional methods, and involve a small number of professionals. Such endeavors are found to be most effective as they are associated with the greatest improvement in knowledge, most significant change in provider behavior and patient outcomes, and greatest likelihood of participation and satisfaction (Bloom, 2005; Mansouri & Lockyer, 2007; Neimeyer, Taylor, & Philip, 2010). In addition, it is valuable for the design and implementation of such activities to utilize emerging technologies when appropriate (Daniels & Walter, 2002).

CRSPPP, in its specialty recognition review process, requires each specialty to document Continuing Professional Development and Continuing Education (Criterion VIII) that illustrates how "a specialty provides its practitioners a broad range of regularly scheduled opportunities for continuing professional development in the specialty" (CRSPPP). Further, specialties themselves should develop mechanisms for evaluating the effectiveness of the continuing professional education programs that they offer (Tian, Atkinson, Portnoy, & Gold, 2007).

There is growing support for the value of continuous monitoring to document that individuals who are board certified are keeping current with expanding knowledge and new clinical assessment and treatment skills. To ensure continuing competence within medicine, for example, the American Board of Medical Specialties (ABMS) established a Maintenance of Certification program. There are four key components to this system: professional standing, life-long learning and self-assessment, demonstrated cognitive expertise, and practice performance assessment. In a related vein, the Conjoint Committee on Continuing Medical Education encourages that medical educators stress the value of lifelong learning and assessment so that throughout their careers physicians continuously strive to upgrade their knowledge, skills, and attitudes in their specialty in order to ensure that they provide quality care to their patients (Miller, 2005).

Specialty boards within psychology, likewise, should encourage board certified specialists to participate in lifelong learning activities and engage in thoughtful and thorough self-assessment that informs them about their learning needs and supports them in utilizing methods and resources to assure satisfaction of those needs (i.e., self-directed learning) (Miller, 2005). It behooves our specialty board certifying groups within psychology to help identify new areas within the specialty with which specialists should gain familiarity and competence (directed self-learning), as well as to direct their own self-learning within the specialty. Psychologists should demonstrate that the result of their ongoing learning is documented improvement in their clinical performance and in patient outcomes (Davis & Willis, 2004). In addition, as part of the professional standing component of 'maintenance of certification' noted above, board certified psychologists should be encourage to serve as mentors and examiners of professional colleagues seeking specialty board certification. Such engagement in the mentoring process not only affords them the opportunity to give back to others in the profession, but the process of guiding others typically is associated with personal and professional development in the mentor, another component of lifelong learning and continuing education.

Conclusion

Professionalism is a core foundational competency within professional psychology (Fouad et al., 2009). A commitment to lifelong learning based on accurate self-assessment (Belar et al., 2001) is one essential component of this competency. This learning can be formal, non-formal, or informal (Knapper & Cropley, 2000). An investment in lifelong learning is likely to be associated with enhanced practice within one's specialty. When discussing the concerns about the half-life of professional knowledge in psychology (Dubin, 1972) and professional obsolescence (Willis & Dubin, 1990), Wise and colleagues (Wise et al., 2010) remind us that "it would be untenable to presume that foundational academic training, in and of itself, provides sufficient preparation for a full career of competent professional practice" (p. 289). The need for sustained learning then underlies the maintenance of clinical competencies and thus ethical practice (American Psychological Association, 2002).

Within the profession of medicine, the board certification movement emerged in response to a desire to ensure quality patient care (Brennan et al., 2004). In this new era of public accountability, with the public's growing need and desire for more effective behavioral health care, in order for psychology to maintain its privileged status in society as an independent healthcare and mental health profession, we have a responsibility to self-regulate through specialty certification (Weiss, 2010). As more and more psychologists choose to seek out specialty board certification to meet the demands of the current and evolving health care climate, it is essential that they do so in recognized specialties via accepted board certifying organizations, such as ABPP, rather than via the so-called vanity board (Datttilio, 2002).

One mark of psychologists' commitment to life-long learning is their awareness of the value of demonstrating their investment in maintaining competence in their specialty. It is likely that in the future there not only will need to be evidence of psychologists' maintenance of competence at the generic level, but also at the specialty level. As evidence accumulates showing the maintenance of competence is associated with more effective clinical care (Holmboe et al., 2008), then expectations for an investment in this process will grow. At the present time, all specialty boards within medicine require recertification. This may become the wave of the future within psychology as well. This is likely to be the case of healthcare systems requiring specialty board certification for psychologists at initial privileging (Rozensky, in press) and then recertification to maintain privileges for ongoing work in the practice environment, just as is done for physicians (Freed et al., 2006). And more importantly, as a self-regulating profession, we have a responsibility to hold ourselves accountable to the public we serve for our continuous professional growth and development in the competencies that we profess to have (Duffy & Holmboe, 2006). Lifelong learning provides the natural vehicle to reach that goal.

BIOSKETCHES

RONALD H. ROZENSKY, Ph.D., ABPP is a Professor at the University of Florida having served there as chairperson of the Department of Clinical and Health Psychology and Associate Dean for International Programs. He is board certified in clinical and clinical health psychology. He served on the American Psychological Association's (APA) Board of Directors and chaired APA's Board of Educational Affairs and Board of Professional Affairs and twice the Commission for the Recognition of Specialties and Proficiencies in Professional Psychology. Founding editor of the *Journal of Clinical Psychology in Medical Settings,* he has published five textbooks and numerous chapters and journal articles. His honors include APA's *Award for Distinguished Professional Contributions to Institutional Practice*, APA's *Heiser Presidential Award for Advocacy,* and *Distinguished Contributions to Global Psychology* from APA's International Psychology Division. The Associate of Psychologists in Academic Health Centers presented him its *Distinguished Educator Award* and the *J.D. Matarazzo Award for Distinguished Contributions to Psychology in Academic Health Centers.*

NADINE J. KASLOW, PhD, ABPP, Professor, Vice Chair, and Chief Psychologist Emory Department of Psychiatry and Behavioral Sciences, has expertise in psychology education, training, and credentialing; family violence; and suicide and mood disorders. A member of the American Psychological Association's (APA) Board of Directors, Editor of the Journal of Family Psychology, and President of the American Board of Professional Psychology, she is Past President of APA's Divisions of Clinical Psychology (12), Family Psychology (43), and Psychotherapy (29) and the American Board of Clinical Psychology.

She is Former Chair and Board Member Emeritus of the Association of Psychology Postdoctoral and Internship Centers. She has received numerous awards, including the APA Distinguished Contributions to Education and Training Award, an APA Presidential Citation, and the Dr. Rosalee Weiss Lecturer Award from the American Psychological Foundation. The recipient of multiple federally funded grants, she has over 250 publications. Dr. Kaslow is the psychologist for the Atlanta Ballet.

REFERENCES

American Psychological Association. (2002). *American Psychological Association Ethical Principles of Psychologists and Code and Conduct.* Retrieved from http://www.apa.org/ethics/code2002.html.

American Psychological Association. (2009). *2008 APA survey of psychology health service provides.* Retrieved from http://www.apa.org/workforce/publications/08-hsp/index.aspx.

Belar, C. D. (2008). Clinical health psychology: A health care specialty in professional psychology. *Profesional Psychology: Research and Practice, 39*, 229-233.

Belar, C. D., Brown, R. A., Hersch, L. E., Hornyak, L. M., Rozensky, R. H., Sheridan, E. P.,...Reed, G. W. (2001). Self-assessment in clinical health psychology: A model for ethical expansion of practice. *Professional Psychology: Research and Practice, 32*, 135-141.

Bent, R. J., Packard, R. E., & Goldberg, R. W. (1999). The American Board of Professional Psychology, 1947 to 1997: A historical perspective. *Profesional Psychology: Research and Practice, 30*, 65-73. Bloom, B. S. (2005). Effects of continuing medical education on improving physician clinical care and patient health: A review of systematic reviews. *International Journal of Technology Assessment in Health Care, 21*, 380-385.

Boake, C. (2008). Clinical neuropsychology. *Professional Psychology: Research and Practice, 39*, 234-239.

Boll, T. J. (2009). Finding the right board certification for you. In C. M. Nezu, J. A.J. Finch and N. P. Simon (Eds.), *Becoming board certfied by the American Board of Professional Psychology* (pp. 55-65). New York: Oxford University Press.

Boring, E. G. (1950). *A history of experimental psychology (2nd edition).* New York: Appleton Century-Crofts.

Brennan, T. A., Horwitz, R. I., Duffy, F. D., Cassel, C. K., Goode, L. D., & Lipner, R. S. (2004). The role of physcian specialty board certification status in the quality movement. *JAMA, 292*, 1038-1042.

Campbell, C., Silver, I., Sherbino, J., Cate, O. T., & Holmboe, E. S. (2010). Competency-based continuing professional development. *Medical Teacher, 32*, 657-662.

CMS Office of Legislation. (2010). *Medicare "Accountable care organizations" shared savings programs - New Section 1899 of Title VIII.* Retrieved from http://www.cms.gov/OpenDoorForums/05_ODF_SpecialODF.asp#TopOfPage.

Commission for the Recognition of Specialties and Proficiencies in Professional Psychology (CRSPPP). (2011). *Commission for the recognition of specialties and proficiencies in professional psychology.* Retrieved from http://www.apa.org/ed/graduate/specialize/crsppp.aspx.

Council of Specialties in Professional Psychology (CoS). (2009). *Council of Specialties in Professional Psychology*. Retrieved from http://cospp.org.

Cox, D. R. (2010). Board certification in professional psychology: Promoting competency and consumer protection. *The Clinical Neuropsychologist, 24*, 493-404.

Cox, D. R., Hess, D. W., Hibbard, M. R., Layman, D. E., & Stewart, R. K., Jr. (2010). Specialty practice in rehabilitation psychology. *Professional Psychology: Research and Practice, 41*, 82-88.

Daniels, A. S., & Walter, D. A. (2002). Current issues in continuing education for contemporary behavioral health practice. *Administration and Policy in Mental Health, 29*, 359-376.

Datttilio, F. M. (2002). Board certification in psychology: Is it really necessary? *Profesional Psychology: Research and Practice, 33*, 34-57. Davidson, C. S. (2009). Preparing the practice sample. In C. M. Nezu, J. A.J. Finch, & N. P. Simon (Eds.), *Becoming board certified by the American Board of Professional Psychology* (pp. 83-96). New York: Oxford University Press.

Davis, N. L., & Willis, C. E. (2004). A new metric for continuing medical education credit. *Journal of Continuing Education in the Health Professions, 24*, 139-144.

Dowd, E. T., Clen, S. L., & Arnold, K. D. (2010). The specialty practice of cognitive and behavioral psychology. *Professional Psychology: Research and Practice, 41*, 89-95.

Dubin, S. S. (1972). Obsolescence or lifelong learning: A choice for the professional. *American Psychologist, 27*, 486-498.

Duffy, F. D., & Holmboe, E. S. (2006). Self-assessment in life-long learning and improving performance in practice: Physician know thyself. *JAMA, 296*, 1137-1139.

Epstein, R. M. (1999). Mindful practice. *JAMA, 282*, 833-839.

Epstein, R. M. (2003a). Mindful practice in action (1): Technical competence, evidence-based medicine, and relationship-centered care. *Families, Systems, and Health, 21*, 1-9.

Epstein, R. M. (2003b). Mindful practice in action (ii): Cultivating habits of mind. *Families, Systems, and Health, 21*, 11-17.

Finch, A. J., Jr., Simon, M. P., & Nezu, C. M. (2006). The future of clinical psychology: Board certification. *Clinical Psychology: Science and Practice, 13*, 254-257.

Fisher, E. S., Staiger, D. O., Bynum, J. P. W., & Gottlieb, D. J. (2007). Creating accountable care organizations: The extended hospital medical staff. *Health Affairs, 26*, w44-w57.

Fisher, F. S. (2010). *Request for information regarding accountable care organizations (ACOs) and Medicare shared savings programs (CMS-1345-NC) letter to Donald Berwick, MD, Administrator, Centers for Medicare and Medicaid Services*. Retrieved from https://www.aamc.org/.

Flanagan, R., & Miller, J. A. (2010). *Specialty competencies in school psychology*. New York: Oxford University Press.

Fouad, N. A., Grus, C. L., Hatcher, R. L., Kaslow, N. J., Hutchings, P. S., Madson, M.,...Crossman, R. E. (2009). Competency benchmarks: A model for the understanding and measuring of competence in professional psychology across training levels. *Training and Education in Professional Psychology, 3*, S5-S26.

Freed, G. L., Uren, R. L., Hudson, E. J., Lakhani, I., Wheeler, J. R. C., & Stockman, J. A. (2006). Policies and practices related to the role of board certification and recertification of pediatricians in hospital privileging. *JAMA, 295*, 905-912.

Holmboe, E. S., Wang, Y., Meehan, T. P., Tate, J. P., Ho, S.-Y., Starkey, K. S., & Lipner, R. S. (2008). Association between maintenance of certification examination scores and quality of care for medicare beneficiaries. *Archives of Internal Medicine, 158*, 1396-1403.

Institute of Medicine. (2009). *Redesigning continuing education in the health professions*. Washington D.C.: National Academies Press.

Interprofessional Education Collaborative Expert Panel. (2011). *Core competencies for interprofessional collaborative practice: Report of an expert panel*. Washington D.C.: Interprofessional Education Collaborative.

Jackson, Y., Alberts, F. L., Jr., & Roberts, M. C. (2010). Clinical child psychology: A practice specialty serving children, adolescents, and their families. *Profesional Psychology: Research and Practice, 41*, 75-81.

Kaslow, F. W. (2009). How to prepare for the oral exam. In C. M. Nezu, J. A.J. Finch, & N.P.Simon (Eds.), *Becoming board certified by the American Board of Professional Psychology* (pp. 103-113). New York: Oxford University Press.

Kaslow, N. J. (2004). Competencies in professional psychology. *American Psychologist, 59*, 774-781.

Kaslow, N. J. (2011). *Specializing in psychology: What it means for health care reform*. Paper presented at the Association of Psychologists in Academic Health Centers Conference, March 3-5, Boston, MA.

Kaslow, N. J., Borden, K. A., Collins, F. L., Forrest, L., Illfelder-Kaye, J., Nelson, P. D.,…Willmuth, M. E. (2004). Competencies Conference: Future directions in education and credentialing in professional psychology. *Journal of Clinical Psychology, 80*, 699-712.

Kaslow, N. J., Celano, M. P., & Stanton, M. (2005). Training in family psychology: A competencies-based approach. *Family Process, 44*, 337-353.

Kaslow, N. J., & Ingram, M. V. (2009). Board certification: A competency-based perspective. In C. M. Nezu, A. J. Finch, & N. P. Simon (Eds.), *Becoming board certified by the American Board of Professional Psychology* (pp. 37-46). New York: Oxford University Press.

Knapper, C. K., & Cropley, A. J. (2000). *Lifelong learning in higher education (3rd edition)*. Sterling, VA: Stylus Publishing Inc.

Krasner, M. S., Epstein, R. M., Beckman, H., Suchman, A. L., Chapman, B., Mooney, C. J.,…Quill, T. E. (2009). Association of an educational program in mindful communication with burnout, empathy, and attitudes among primary care phyisicians. *JAMA, 302*, 1284-1293.

Lee, G. P., & Otto, R. K. (2009). How to prepare for the written examinations in clinical neuropsychology and forensic psychology. In C. M. Nezu, J. A.J. Finch, & N.P.Simon (Eds.), *Becoming board certified by the American Board of Professional Psychology* (pp. 67-81). New York: Oxford University Press.

Mansouri, M., & Lockyer, J. (2007). A meta-analysis of continuing medical education effectiveness. *Journal of Continuing Education in the Health Professions, 27*, 6-15.

Miller, S. H. (2005). American Board of Medical Specialties and repositioning for excellence in lifelong learning: Maintenance of certification. *Journal of Continuing Education in the Health Professions, 25*, 151-156.

Molinari, V. (Ed.). (2011). *Specialty competencies in geropsychology*. New York: Oxford University Press.

Neimeyer, G. J., & Taylor, J. M. (2010). Continuing education in psychology. In J.C.Norcross, G. R. Vandebos, & D. K. Freedheim (Eds.), *History of psychotherapy: Continuity and change (2nd edition)* (pp. 663-672). Washing DC: American Psychological Association.

Neimeyer, G. J., Taylor, J. M., & Philip, D. (2010). Continuing education in psychology: Patterns of participation and perceived outcomes among mandated and nonmandated psychologists. *Professional Psychology: Research and Practice, 41*, 435-441.

Nezu, C. M., Finch, A. J., Jr., & Simon, N. P. (Eds.). (2009). *Becoming board certified by the American Board of Professional Psychology*. New York: Oxford.

Nutt, R. L., & Stanton, M. (2008). Family psychology specialty practice. *Professional Psychology: Research and Practice, 39*, 519-528.Ostrow, L., & Maderscheid, R. (2010). Medicare mental health parity: A high potential change that is long overdue. *The Journal of Behavioral Health Services and Research, 37*, 285-290.

Packer, I. K. (2008). Specialized practice in forensic psychology: Opportunities and obstacles. *Profesional Psychology: Research and Practice, 39*, 245-249.

Packer, I. K., & Grisso, T. (2011). *Specialty competencies in forensic psychology*. New York: Oxford University Press.

Public Law No: 111-148, t. C. P. P. a. A. C. A. (March 23, 2010). *124 STAT.119.* Retrieved 6/4/11, from www.gpo.gov/fdsys/pkg/PLAW-111publ148/pdf/PLAW-111publ148.pdf.

Roberts, M. C. (2006). Essential tension: Specialization with broad and general training in psychology. *American Psychologist, 61*, 862-870.

Rodolfa, E. R., Bent, R. J., Eisman, E., Nelson, P. D., Rehm, L., & Ritchie, P. (2005). A cube model for competency development: Implications for psychology educators and regulators. *Professional Psychology: Research and Practice, 36*, 347-354.

Rosenthal, T. C. (2008). The medical home: Growing evidence to support a new approach to primary care. *Journal of the American Board of Family Medicine, 21*, 427-440.

Rozensky, R. H. (2010). *Specialization and specialists in professional psychology and the role of lifelong learning.* Paper presented at the APA Educational Leadership Conference, September 13, Washington DC.

Rozensky, R. H. (in press). The institutional practice of psychology: Health care reform and psychology's future workforce. *American Psychologist, 66*.

Sharp, L. K., Bashook, P. G., Lipsky, M. S., Horowitz, S. D., & Miller, S. H. (2002). Specialty board certification and clinical outcomes: The missing link. *Academic Medicine, 77*, 534-542. Sia, C., Tonniges, T. F., Osterhus, E., & Taba, S. (2004). History of the medical home concept. *Pediatrics, 113*, 1473-1478.

Talley, J. E. (2008). Working with a board-certified mento in the specialty. In C. M. Nezu, J. A.J. Finch, & N.P.Simon (Eds.), *Becoming board certified by the American Board of Professional Psychology* (pp. 97-102). New York: Oxford University Press.

Tharinger, D. J., Pryzwansky, W. B., & Miller, J. A. (2008). School psychology: A specialty of professional psychology with distinct competencies and complexities. *Professional Psychology: Research and Practice, 39*, 529-536.

The American Board of Professional Psychology (ABPP). *American Board of Professional Psychology.* Retrieved from www.abpp.org.

The Carter Center. (2011). *Proceedings from the Health Education Summit: Five prescriptions for ensuring the future of primary care*. Atlanta, GA: The Carter Center.

Thomas, J. C. (2010). *Specialty competencies in organizational and business consulting psychology*. New York: Oxford.

Tian, J., Atkinson, N. L., Portnoy, B., & Gold, R. S. (2007). A systematic review of evalution in formal continuing medical education. *Journal of Continuing Education in the Health Professions, 27*, 16-27.

The U.S. Bureau of Labor Statistics. (2009). *Occupational Outlook Handbook, 2010-11 Edition: Psychologists*. Retrieved from http://www.bls.gov/oco/ocos056.htm.

Weiss, K. B. (2010). Future of board certification in a new era of public accountability. *Journal of the American Board of Family Medicine, 23 (Supplement)*(32-39).

Willis, S. L., & Dubin, S. S. (Eds.). (1990). *Maintaining professional competence: Approaches to career enhancement, vitality and success throughout a work life*. San Francisco: Jossey-Bass Publishers.

Wise, E. H., Sturm, C. A., Nutt, R. L., Rodolfa, E., Schaffer, J. B., & Webb, C. (2010). Life-long learning for psychologists: Current status and a vision for the future. *Professional Psychology: Research and Practice, 41*, 288-297.

Chapter 19

REFLECTION, RETHINKING, AND LOOKING AHEAD

Jo Linder-Crow[*]
California Psychological Association, US

ABSTRACT

There is little opposition to the argument that professionals must continue their professional development throughout their careers in order to keep pace with new developments in their discipline. Professional codes of conduct include continuing professional education as an expectation and requirement. Licensing boards have, for many years, used the concept of mandated continuing education as the primary vehicle for ensuring that psychologists continue their professional education even after their graduate education and initial licensure. The psychology education and training communities have contributed to the conversation with commentary on the notion of competency, its meaning, and how best to achieve it throughout a career.

Over the years, however, the discussions about the mechanics of continuing education (CE) have been vigorous. These discussions have included honest debate about what we should call it, how much is needed, how we should define it, how we should measure quality, and whether or not it really improves and/or changes practice. Another interesting question has emerged concerning who gets to decide what is and isn't legitimate content for continuing education. In other words, "who gets to decide what professionals need to know?"

This chapter will offer a brief historical view of continuing professional education in order to reflect upon where we have been and where we are currently in the debate about CE. After a discussion of some of the more recent and current questions, conversations, and debates about continuing education the chapter will conclude with a preview of trends that may have an impact upon how continuing professional education might look in the future.

Keywords: Continuing education, professional development, lifelong learning, mandatory continuing education, competency

---

[*] Correspondence regarding this manuscript may be directed to Jo Linder-Crow, 1231 I Street, Suite 204, Sacramento, CA 95814. E-mail: jlindercrow@cpapsych.org.

This is a familiar scene for anyone involved in continuing professional education: You answer the telephone, or you receive an e-mail, and a frantic person says, "I need four CE credits by tomorrow at midnight! Do you know where I can get them quickly?" To be helpful, you answer them in the affirmative by directing them to online articles, magazines, or webinars from the vast array of choices that exist. A quick read or listen, a few questions, and they're done. They are grateful, and you have been helpful. Case closed.

Over the past number of years, continuing education credits have become the currency that professionals use to maintain a professional credential, most often a license to practice. It is the number of credits earned that demonstrates compliance with the requirements imposed by licensing and credentialing bodies in most jurisdictions. (Institute of Medicine, IOM, 2010; Neimeyer, Taylor & Wear, 2009; Wise et al., 2010). As long as the professional can verify participation in approved educational activities for a certain number of hours, then all is well.

There are some elements missing from this equation, however. Most importantly, we rarely know if the learner actually learned anything. We may know how satisfied the participant was with the instructor, the room, the parking availability and the food. We may know whether the participants thought the content of the program met the stated learning objectives, and we may know how well they can describe how to do what the educational activity intended to teach them. We even have some evidence that professionals see continuing education as helpful in their practice (Neimeyer et al., 2009). Still, after the many years that continuing professional education has been a part of the landscape, and with all that we know about the most effective means of delivering continuing education, we lack solid evidence that continuing professional education provides knowledge that is actually translated into improved practice in ways that change and improve patient/client health (Davis et al., 1999; IOM, 2010; Neimeyer et al., 2009; Neimeyer, Taylor & Wear, 2010b; Webster-Wright, 2009; Wise et al., 2010). Despite the decades-old call for reform in CE, little progress has been made to transform continuing professional education. In fact, a reader would be hard pressed, when reading the literature on continuing education, to distinguish between an article written ten years ago on the topic of change in continuing education and one written recently. The challenge remains; how to design programs that facilitate learning that can be translated into practice. With that challenge also come questions about what should be considered legitimate content for CE, what delivery models are best, and how we can ultimately measure the impact of our efforts.

REFLECTION

There is a long history of continuing education in the professions, and from the 1970s CE for professionals has been linked to licensing, certification, and credentialing (IOM, 2010). Houle (1980) characterized continuing education as a natural expression of a profession's evolution, and healthcare professions such as medicine and psychology have histories of continuing education that span at least 50 years (IOM, 2010; Neimeyer & Taylor, 2010).

As it turns out, this long history of emphasizing continuing education proves prescient since continuing advances in neuroscience demonstrate the importance of challenging our brains in order to keep them active. In the professions it is generally understood that continuing professional education is necessary in order to stay abreast of emerging science, changes in practice, and the changing social expectations that influence the practice environment. In the healthcare professions, continuing professional education is intended to provide a high quality of learning that ultimately improves the quality of practice and the service to clients/patients. (American Psychological Association, 2005; Bennett et al., 2000; Cantillon & Jones, 1999; Davis et al., 1999; IOM, 2010; Webster-Wright, 2009; Wise et al., 2010).

The significant changes in the environments that healthcare professionals work in today, and the rapid pace of advances in the professional practice arena, make continuing education essential almost as soon as the graduate degree is earned in order to keep pace with these changes. This need continues throughout a career in order to avoid obsolescence. The concern about obsolescence is not new. Dubin (1972) and Ross (1974) both used the term in early arguments for ongoing professional development. Bennett et al. (2000) noted the changing world of practice for physicians brought about by increasing consumerism and patient empowerment, as well as growing accountability to external bodies, as driving motivators for improved educational methodologies. Davis et al. (2003) emphasized the growing gap between what physicians know and what they practice when they addressed the challenge of shortening the time for translating evidence-based knowledge into practice. More recently, Wise et al. (2010) suggested that "it would be untenable to presume that foundational academic training, in and of itself, provides sufficient preparation for a full career of competent professional practice" (p. 289). In fact, because there so many required courses during professional training, opportunities are limited for participation in courses outside the required curriculum. CE allows for post-graduates to learn new areas and become specialized in practice techniques. This need for continued learning is compounded by the shifting professional roles brought about by societal and cultural changes that often require a retooling of competencies and practice skills (see Rozensky & Kaslow, 2012). An overlay, in recent history, is the fact that consumers have instant access, via the internet, to information that becomes part of the exchange between them and the professional with whom they interact, making it essential that professionals have at least a working knowledge of the latest developments in the field (substantiated or not), in order to adequately respond to a client or patient's questions and concerns.

Even though few would argue against the value of continued learning throughout a career, there have been honest differences of opinion about how best to ensure that this happens. Debates about the value of mandatory continuing education have been evident for years (Brown & Henry, 1970; Linder-Crow, 1998; VandeCreek, Knapp & Brace, 1990) and most likely will continue in some circles (see Adams & Sharkin, 2012). Still, mandates by licensing bodies seem here to stay in most professions. In psychology, 86% of U.S. jurisdictions endorse mandatory continuing education as a requirement for license renewal (Neimeyer et al., 2009). Continuing Medical Education is also required for physicians in most states, although requirements vary just as in other disciplines (IOM, 2010).

In addition, whether or not it is a legal obligation, continuing professional education is emphasized in professional codes of ethics as a professional responsibility. For example, the American Psychological Association's Ethics Code (APA, 2002) includes a section entitled *Maintaining Competence* stating that, "Psychologists undertake ongoing efforts to develop and maintain their competence" (p. 1064). The American Medical Association (AMA, n.d.) includes a section in the Code of Medical Ethics entitled *Continuing Medical Education* stating that "Physicians should strive to further their medical education throughout their careers, for only by participating in continuing medical education (CME) can they continue to serve patients to the best of their abilities and live up to professional standards of excellence. Fulfillment of mandatory state CME requirements does not necessarily fulfill the physician's ethical obligation to maintain his or her medical expertise."

Licensing and regulatory bodies have relied on mandated continuing education as one way of ensuring an ongoing effort by their licensees to develop and maintain competence, although in both of the Codes of Ethics noted above there are broad references to the fact that the responsibility to maintain expertise goes beyond merely fulfilling continuing education requirements. This highlights one of the potential differences between ethical guidelines and legal mandates in relation to continuing education. Ethical guidelines encourage the very highest levels of professionalism and competency, while legal mandates attempt to establish at least a minimum level of competency for practicing professionals. One of the primary arguments for legal mandates, however, is the concern that without them professionals might not engage in continuing professional education, at least not in a formal way. In psychology, for example, Neimeyer, Taylor, and Philip (2010a) found in a national survey that in jurisdictions without mandates 25% of psychologists completed less than five CE credits per year. This is not to say that psychologists in non-mandated states do not engage in continuing professional education, but this evidence points to the possibility that they do not engage in as much formal CE as in mandated jurisdictions. This leaves open the question of how they do maintain competence and also leaves those jurisdictions with no way to demonstrate any guaranteed level of participation in continued learning.

Currently, the perceived understanding by professionals that continuing education is a part of professional responsibility, along with the mandates by regulatory bodies in most professions, have created a booming CE business that shows no sign of decline. Licensing bodies rely on verification of attendance to meet mandated continuing education requirements, and professionals seek out activities that offer the credits that are accepted by their regulatory bodies because "credits" (earlier noted as the currency of the realm) are required to demonstrate compliance with the mandates. This market demand has led to the increasing number of organizations that are in the business of offering continuing professional education programs. The bottom line is that both for-profit CE providers and non-profit organizations depend on CE for non-dues revenue, and this requires a continuous stream of professional customers. The business of CE is big enough to receive a certain amount of scrutiny. For example, the funding of CE, particularly in medicine, has been widely debated for many years (IOM, 2010) because of concerns about the possible unwanted influence from pharmaceutical companies, who have poured substantial amount of money into the system.

Through the years there have been multiple and ongoing efforts to define continuing education and these efforts have come with healthy and sometimes testy debate. The debate has largely focused on trying to define what content should be considered as legitimate for continuing professional education. For example:

- Should CE be limited to scientifically documented approaches to practice, or is there room for learning about leading-edge approaches, or even popular trends in treatment, that are not yet evidence-based?

- Is information that is now standard fare in training programs "new" to individuals who earned their degrees years before, and can that information be considered post-doctoral or post-licensure, and therefore legitimate CE?
- Considering the new roles that professionals find themselves in, should both clinical and non-clinical content, such as leadership and practice management be considered as appropriate CE content since these skills are often necessary in these new roles? And who should decide this?

The answers to these questions have significant consequences, because just as the business of providing CE programs is a thriving enterprise, so is the business of approving these providers. Providers seek the "stamp of approval" from particular disciplines that will make their programs more desirable. Approval bodies are imbued with the power to determine what is valued and deemed appropriate as content for continuing education credits. By accepting some topics and excluding others, these approval bodies shape the program choices made by providers of CE and ultimately the choices that are available to professionals. Some regulatory and licensing bodies also allow certain topics while disallowing other topics not deemed to be legitimate for continuing education in that profession. All of these decisions are made according to established practices, traditions, and assumptions, but they are influenced by the individuals who happen to sit on an approval body at a given time and who therefore have the authority to render decisions about these issues. In essence, these entities have the power to determine what is considered justifiable to learn, and the substantial variation in current CE requirements across different professions and jurisdictions stands testament to the variability of their assessments (Daniels & Walter, 2002). We might question this dynamic as we think about new models of continuing professional education.

The internal debates about the legitimacy of certain CE content rarely make their way into general definitions of continuing professional education. As a result, although current definitions of continuing professional education vary slightly according to discipline, they tend to be broadly stated and share similar components in supporting the notion that CE is intended to help professionals stay abreast of changes in their discipline in order to deliver the highest quality of practice. We can use examples from psychology and medicine to demonstrate generally accepted definitions of continuing education.

The American Psychological Association (APA) defines continuing education in psychology this way:

> Continuing education (CE) in psychology is an ongoing process consisting of formal learning activities that (1) are relevant to psychological practice, education and science, (2) enable psychologists to keep pace with emerging issues and technologies, and (3) allow psychologists to maintain, develop, and increase competencies in order to improve services to the public and enhance contributions to the profession. Continuing education builds upon a completed doctoral program in psychology. It is not a substitute for the basic academic education and training needed for entry to the field of psychology, nor should it be the primary vehicle for career changes from one APA-recognized specialty area (e.g. clinical, counseling, school psychology) to another. (APA, 2005)

The Accreditation Council for Continuing Medical Education (ACCME) describes, in the definition of Continuing Medical Education (CME), what content is acceptable for activities that are certified for credit:

> Continuing medical education consists of educational activities which serve to maintain, develop, or increase the knowledge, skills, and professional performance and relationships that a physician uses to provide services for patients, the public, or the profession. The content of CME is that body of knowledge and skills generally recognized and accepted by the profession as within the basic medical sciences, the discipline of clinical medicine, and the provision of health care to the public. (ACCME, n.d.)

As already suggested, these definitions are most often generated by the bodies that approve CE providers, and the definitions then drive decisions about the programs and content that will be accepted by licensing bodies. This, in turn, affects the decisions of providers who have an interest in developing programs that will most likely draw an audience. They understand that if particular topics are disallowed by an organization that approves providers of continuing education, or by a licensing body in a particular jurisdiction, the likelihood of participation in a program focusing on that content is reduced. Likewise, if a licensing jurisdiction actually requires a particular topic such as Ethics it is certain that providers will create CE programs to meet those requirements. A continuous cycle is created, with all of these decisions influencing one another in ways that ultimately have an impact on the choices available to professionals when making decisions about continuing education.

All of these components influence our understanding of what continuing education *is* as defined by various professions. We still need to address the question of what continuing education *does* to change the professional as a result of participation. Licensing bodies have relied upon continuing education as a means of maintaining competency in practice (IOM, 2010; Wise et al., 2010), even though there is no clear evidence to determine how much continuing education is needed to actually do what is intended (IOM, 2010). These bodies have the weighty responsibility of investigating complaints against professionals and imposing disciplinary actions when that is required. They are invested, both from the perspective of the discipline and the consumer of services, in taking the necessary steps to try to reduce the necessity for such actions. Mandates for continuing professional education, at a minimum, may be useful as a means of reassuring the public by demonstrating a commitment to ensuring high standards for their licensees as a protection to consumers and a profession's willingness to monitor itself (ASPPB, 2010; IOM, 2010; Wise et al., 2010).

We need to explore further, however, the question of whether or not such mandates actually do lead to greater protection of the public, which is a function of licensing and credentialing bodies. In psychology, for example, the actual relationship between continuing professional education and the prevention of disciplinary action has not been established (Wise et al., 2010). In fact, even though some psychology boards specifically require continuing education in legal/ethical issues, the Association of State and Provincial Psychology Boards (ASPPB) reports that the top four violations for which psychology boards have taken disciplinary action are sexual misconduct, unprofessional conduct, non-sexual dual relationship, and negligence (Wise et al., 2010). Likewise, there does not seem to be a direct association between physician disciplinary actions or malpractice claims and professional competence (Reid, Freidbarg, Adams, McGlynn & Mehrotra, 2010).

If CE doesn't reduce the level of disciplinary action against professionals, can we hold out hope that it actually improves practice? Overall, the evidence about the effectiveness of CE in this regard is disturbingly inconclusive. There have been many attempts to find measures of effectiveness for both methods of delivery and outcomes, because we want to believe that continuing education makes a difference. What we do know doesn't provide much comfort because the knowledge has not produced many changes in the way that continuing education is designed. For example, we know something about the value of specific methods for teaching professionals, with several reviews of effectiveness concluding that didactic methods do little to change practice performance (Swankin, LeBuhn & Morrison, 2006). And yet, these didactic methods are still the predominate ones in the field (IOM, 2010), leading to the disquieting conclusion that the field's most common methods of instruction are also the least effective (Neimeyer et al., 2009).

Bloom (2005), for example, reviewed outcomes of continuing medical education (CME) and observed these same findings; traditional, didactic CME programs did not result in any significant impact on physicians' behaviors or patient-related outcomes. These same authors noted that interactive techniques, particularly presented in multiple sessions, were more effective, although even these effects were modest. Still, didactic methods in single sessions are widely used in CE, a practice that seems a holdover from undergraduate and graduate school frameworks (Webster-Wright, 2009). Perhaps this persists because in the business of continuing education it is easier and more cost-effective to design these less effective ways of providing CE, and practitioners are eager to engage in programs that are easily accessible, convenient, and cost-effective (Neimeyer et al, 2010b).

Within the field of psychology, relatively little is known about the impact of continuing education on professional competencies, practices, or outcomes (Neimeyer et al., 2009). This is true in other health professions as well, as demonstrated by Daniels and Walter (2002) when they observed that outside of medicine there were no controlled studies of the impact of CE in the health disciplines. In fact, there is general agreement that even though we do well in tracking participation in continuing education, we are still unable to fully demonstrate that participation alone leads to improved practice performance and outcomes for patients and clients (Davis et al., 2003; IOM 2010; Webster-Wright, 2009; Wise et al., 2010).

This leads us to consider the question of what we expect the impact of continuing professional education to be. If we cannot fully demonstrate its effectiveness in changing practice performance, and if it doesn't change behavior with regard to professional competence and ethical behavior, then what is it that we are missing? What can we take from what we do know about the process of learning, and what we have learned from professionals themselves, to build a better model for continuing professional education that will lead to meaningful learning experiences for professionals, improved competence, and positive client/patient outcomes?

One of the critical insights about how continuing professional education might contribute to changes in practice comes from Donald Schön's insistence that reflection is a key component of learning for the practitioner. In *The Reflective Practitioner*, Schön (1983) introduced the importance of reflection as a key component of how a professional learns and grows. Arguing that the world of the practitioner was complex and messy, he introduced the notion of "reflection-in-action" (thinking on your feet during an experience) and "reflection-on-action" (thinking about our actions later and exploring what we might do in a similar situation in the future), and suggested these were critical to professional practice. Webster-Wright (2009) reported other research that confirms that professionals learn through practice experience, that reflection has a valuable role in learning that requires change, and that such learning is contextually mediated.

Chris Argyris (1974), who collaborated with Schön on a theory of learning systems, was also interested in how practitioners and professionals learn. In his later work at the Harvard Business School he referenced his coined terms of "single loop learning" (the kind of reasoning used in problem solving), and "double loop learning" (learning that requires critical reflection on one's own behavior) (Argyris, 1991). He observed that highly skilled professionals are frequently good at single-loop learning but no so good at double-loop learning, reasoning that highly skilled professionals rarely experience failure, having acquired academic credentials, mastered an intellectual discipline, and set out to solve real world problems. In fact, he observed that "most people don't know how to learn" (1991, p. 4), noting that when these same professionals are expected to combine the mastery of their discipline with other skills such as working in teams, forming productive business relationships, and adapting to a changing work environment, they become defensive and their ability to learn shuts down.

We might do well to reflect ourselves on the work of Schön and Argyris as we think about the changing landscape facing professionals as they adapt to what Argyris calls "knowledge work" (1991, p. 5). It has become more evident that a system that relies merely on participation as a measure of compliance does not really encourage teaching and learning and does not allow for the "reflection-in-action" and "reflection-on-action" that Schön and Argyris describe as necessary for achieving change in practice. We can reflect on what we know about the changing professional environment and what we have learned from the research in the field as we move toward a model of continuing professional education that will meet the learning needs of professionals in a way that allows real learning to happen.

RETHINKING

Given all that we have learned from the research and writing on continuing education during the past decade, and as we reconsider what we want continuing education in the professions to be, it is good to see signs that change is in the air. We can see already that there is a growing trend to describe this continued learning of professionals in more complete and complex ways. Evidence-based models, competency-based approaches to training and practice, and renewed interest in a closer focus on learning rather than teaching offer new perspectives on what we know about continuing professional education, how professionals learn, and what we might anticipate in the future.

The terms *lifelong learning*, *continuing education* and even *continuing professional education* have, in many discussions, evolved into the term *professional development*. The Association of State and Provincial Psychology Board (ASPPB) (2010), in the draft proposal for Continuing Professional Development Guidelines, has deliberately shifted to the term Continuing Professional Development (CPD). Going further, ASPPB includes continuing education activities as one part of CPD, but emphasizes that CPD is broader than CE.

Webster-Wright (2009) reframed professional development as Authentic Professional Learning, and urged educators to go further in understanding the actual experience of learning as a means of gaining a better perspective on how learning experiences for professionals can be designed and implemented.

Table 1.

	Training	Education	Professional Development
Purpose	To impart a set of established facts and skills without the necessity of [a] trainee's understanding why [he] should act in the prescribed manner	To introduce, review, or alter knowledge and competencies	To encourage systematic maintenance, self-directed improvement, and broadening of knowledge and skills
Targets	A uniform, predictable behavior	Altered knowledge, skill, or attitudes	Outcomes-focused development of personal and professional qualities necessary through a professional career or life
Outcomes	Passive activity; conditioned reflex action	Observation, analysis, and questioning to formulate hypotheses and make conclusions; actions modified according to conclusions or solutions	Reflecting on practice, identifying problems
Description		Serves to update and reinforce knowledge (e.g., management of heart attacks, diagnosis of HIV)	Deals with personal, communication, managerial, and team-building skills in addition to content
		Frequently based on acquiring credits	May be based on acquiring credits or on processes of self-accreditation and reflection (e.g. personal portfolios)
		May be considered a subset of continuing professional development	Systems for monitoring CPD require flexibility so professionals can participate in a variety of CPD activities

The Institute of Medicine (2010) offered a bold recommendation in its report entitled *Redesigning Continuing Education in the Health Professions* by recommending the establishment of a public-private institute for continuing health professional development to be known as the Continuing Professional Development Institute (CPDI). The report stressed the need for continuing professional development that is evidence-based, inter-professional, and team-based. Key to their recommendations is the notion that a new system of continuing professional development must be flexible enough to adapt to the needs of individual practitioners, and that control of learning must be shifted to the individual professionals in order to make them the "architects of their own learning" (p. 5).

The Institute of Medicine report provided a useful distinction between *training*, *continuing education* and *professional development*, particularly in the way each is described as they relate to purpose, targets, outcomes, and description: (pp. 18-19)

The distinctions offered are important ones that help provide a context for the evolution of the language of continuing professional education. The stated purpose and targets of continuing professional development (CPD), as opposed to continuing education (CE), are very different, with CPD focusing on self-directed improvement and outcomes-focused development of professional and personal qualities. Likewise, the outcomes of CPD are focused on the higher-level of reflective reasoning described by Schön, rather than the ability to merely implement solutions. These distinctions emphasize the importance of the language we use to describe how our understanding of continuous learning has evolved.

In psychology, the ASPPB's approach to Continuing Professional Development (CPD) is based on a competency model. Their vision of CPD, like the one presented by the Institute of Medicine, presumes a broader scope of CPD that goes beyond continuing professional education. This distinction is important because it allows for a broader array of choices for professionals as they seek to continuously develop the wide range of competencies required to perform at the highest level. In fact, much like the Institute of Medicine, the draft guidelines from ASPPB acknowledge that continuing education activities provide one way to maintain skills, but that CE is not the only way. One of the key contributions we have from the field of adult education has been the acknowledgment that a professional is an adult. This recognition finally seems to be having an influence in these recent efforts to reconceptualize the thing we have called continuing education. These new models recognize that learning occurs in many settings, and this recognition helps advance us to a point where we can look more broadly than formal programs in considering how professionals can best maintain their skills and competencies. It is good to see acknowledgments that real learning occurs from formal *and* informal types of instruction that might include conscious reflection, conversation with peers, conferences, leadership roles, and the more traditional lectures and workshops (ASPPB, 2010; IOM, 2010; Webster-Wright, 2009; Wise et al., 2010). The recognition that professional learners are sophisticated and complex, and that they should be partners in identifying learning opportunities that meet their specific learning needs, begins to frame the argument for a less instructor-driven and a more learner-centered, learner-driven approach.

The business as usual approach to continuing professional education still rolls along, with the requisite rules, regulations, and financial interests that affect such efforts. It seems time now for continuing professional development to be more than a measure of how many credits an individual can accrue during a licensure period. It is time for a learning environment that will engage professionals in ways that will help them immediately connect what they are learning to their practice or work setting in meaningful ways. The changing practice environment demands this, professionals want this, and therefore bodies that approve continuing education providers, licensing entities, and those who provide continuing professional development must all be responsive to these new demands.

Looking Ahead

As described in this chapter, there is a growing body of work that should be encouraging to anyone interested in restructuring how professionals learn in ways that will result in optimal learning opportunities, improved competencies, and the very highest quality of services to clients/patients. After all, these are the outcomes desired by professionals themselves, licensing and regulatory bodies, providers of continuing professional development programs, and the approval bodies that offer credentialing to these providers. We can extract some themes from the research in the field to create a glimpse of how things might look in the future; one that offers a greater clarity about how continuing professional education can evolve in a way that brings about a true culture of lifelong learning that seemingly has eluded us.

The Language of Learning

One clear transition is an intentional shift in the use of terminology. Continuing education (CE) can be viewed as being teacher-driven, clinical in nature, and building on educational theory (IOM, 2010; Webster-Wright, 2009). It is based on the premise that the teacher has knowledge to give to the learner. This term has been used interchangeably with *continuing professional education* (CPE) in many contexts and for many years, along with the term *lifelong learning* that is also used to capture the concept that learning should be viewed on a continuum that lasts throughout one's career.

As shown earlier, the term *continuing professional development* (CPD) has recently emerged as the term of choice in literature calling for change (ASPPB, 2010; IOM, 2010; Webster-Wright, 2009), and will be used in the rest of this chapter to reflect a look ahead and a move away from current and past concepts. CPD is described as being broader than the previously-mentioned terms, although most often it is presumed to incorporate the formal activities associated with CE as one aspect (ASPPB, 2010; IOM, 2010). CPD is learner-driven and relies on a broader range of learning activities and settings than CE, allowing it to be tailored to the individual needs of the professional. The focus in these new discussions is on learning, rather than teaching, and there is a greater understanding that professionals develop and maintain competence in different ways depending on their own understanding of their practice and their individual needs.

The Institute of Medicine's 2010 report and recommendations emphasized that CPD includes both clinical content and other practice-related content such as communications and business. This is consistent with the way ASPPB is exploring the value of activities such as peer consultation, teaching, practice outcome monitoring, and professional activities as mechanisms for maintaining and enhancing competencies. It is also consistent with the expanded ACCME definition of Continuing Medical Education (ACCME, n.d.) that recognizes that all continuing education activities that assist physicians in carrying out their professional responsibilities more effectively and efficiently constitute CME. A course in management, for example, would be appropriate CME for physicians responsible for managing a health care facility; a course in educational methodology would be appropriate CME for physicians teaching in a medical school; a course in practice management would be appropriate CME for practitioners interested in providing better service to patients. And, as professionals increasingly move towards practicing in interdisciplinary and interprofessional contexts, they are likely to need broader competencies still in order to effectively address the expanding challenges and responsibilities that accompany integrated care.

This shift in terminology becomes meaningful once the distinctions between CPD and other terms are clearly delineated. CPD is distinguished as being more reflective of our knowledge about professional learning and our commitment to a shift in how we think about the role of the professional in structuring and directing their own learning environment.

The Responsibility of Learning

Another theme that emerges from recent writing on continuing professional development relates to a need for placing increased responsibility on professionals to direct their own learning. Those writing about continuing medical education have been supporting this change for at least a decade. Bennett et al. (2000) wrote that "optimal CME is highly self-directed, with content, learning methods, and learning resources selected specifically for the purpose of improving the knowledge, skills, and attitudes that physicians require in their daily professional lives that lead to improved patient outcomes" (p. 1169). This vision is based on the argument that in order to effectively construct meaning from learning, the learning must be appropriate for the practice environment (Neimeyer et al., 2010b).

The fact that codes of ethics in the professions emphasize continuing professional development as a professional responsibility implies an expectation that professionals can and should take responsibility for their own learning throughout their careers. Likewise, much of the recent literature about CPD includes a clear directive that CPD should become much more learner-centered and should be tailored to fit the individual needs of the professional.

If this is true, it is logical to ask how the professional is to know what he or she needs to know in order to best maintain and improve the competencies necessary for optimal performance in their work setting or practice. This highlights the role of self-assessment in CPD, because in order to develop a learning plan that will address practice and learning needs a professional must be able to assess where those gaps might be. There is mixed information available, however, about how successful professionals are at assessing their own level of competence in order to make well-reasoned selections (ASPPB, 2010; Bennett et al., 2000; Davis et al., 2006; Wise et al., 2010).

If we expect professionals to assume personal responsibility for developing learning plans and seeking information to close knowledge gaps, and if we truly want to make professionals the architects of their own learning, we will need to teach them to asses their own skill levels. Then, if we expect them to engage in self assessment and to take responsibility for bridging professional knowledge gaps, we must give them more choices and trust them to make those choices. Learning must be centered on their practice and work settings and include rapid information updates to respond to the rapid changes in the way work is done. New approaches must also recognize that the enormous amount of information that is available today arms clients/patients with information that they bring to the professional, and they expect to be able to have a conversation about the content. Professionals must be able to respond to this new environment.

What do we expect of professionals if these changes are to be implemented successfully? They must take responsibility for their own learning, should recognize the need for expanding their knowledge base, and be willing to put in the time to learn. All stakeholders in CPD can help by creating a structure that encourages this approach to lifelong learning.

The Context and Content of Learning

We must think of Continuing Professional Development as a way to connect learning and change. The observations that our current system of continuing professional development is fragmented, rather than systemic, contribute to the questions about whether or not CPD is intentionally and successfully used to improve the performance of professional duties (Bennett et al., 2000; Wise et al., 2010). Current models of CPD are based on the traditional model of the hierarchy of teacher and learner, with the underlying premise that knowledge can be transferred from the teacher to the learner and that this will have an impact on the behavior of the learner. This model is called into question when we view CPD as a collaborative, interactive process that involves effective learning and that is offered in a practice-related setting that takes advantage of that teachable moment that occurs when a professional doesn't know the answer.

This approach again points us in the direction of expanded learning opportunities; those that include formal learning activities but that also include contexts like case consultations that involve peer consultation on difficult cases. Such expanded views of the context and content that defines CPD bring renewed focus to the reminder from Fox and Bennett (1998) that it is the learning that takes place, rather then the teaching, that leads to change in practice.

In a related vein, Wise et al. (2010) pointed to the importance of competent educators who are not only experts in their field but who are knowledgeable about a variety of teaching methodologies and who can engage professionals in the learning experience. Continuing professional development will always have a place for what we now consider formal CE programs, or such activities as Grand Rounds in medicine, but to continue limiting the kinds of activities that can be considered as legitimate content for CPD the system will continue to limit learning opportunities.

It will be necessary for other professions to follow medicine's lead in thinking more flexibly about defining the content of CPD so that professionals can participate in a variety of CPD activities, both clinical and non-clinical in nature, tailored to their specific learning needs. The challenge of balancing evidence-based content with content that is more innovative (and unproven) will stay with us, but more flexibility in this regard will be critical to our goal of supporting the concept of learner-driven continuing professional development. Changes of this kind will put the burden on CPD providers to provide the highest quality of programs in order to earn the trust of professionals as they learn which providers they can depend upon. It will be incumbent upon approval bodies and licensing boards to work in concert with providers to make these changes possible.

Such shifts in perspective are consistent with the literature that shows that the most effective professional development occurs in an environment that supports learning, is social in context and, for professionals, is related to practice settings (Davis et al., 2003; IOM, 2010; Webster-Wright, 2009). Setting is important—what is needed in one setting may be very different from what is needed in another setting. New roles will bring about new knowledge gaps that need to be addressed. Also, the move to integrated healthcare will no doubt demand that healthcare professionals engage in inter-disciplinary continuing professional development that may include content from medicine, nursing, psychology, and other professions, and licensing bodies will need to support such learning.

Bennett et al. (2000) emphasized that if the purpose of learning is to change we must understand how individuals and organizations go about changing. This also suggests that provider approval and licensing bodies must recognize change as it is happening and stay ahead of the curve as much as possible, because understanding how the world of practice has changed informs our view of what professionals need to learn. Additionally, there is mounting evidence that professionals themselves are the best source of information about how learning best occurs (Bennett et al., 2000; Webster-Wright, 2009), so we should take advantage of this knowledge in order to expand our views of what can be considered as "approved" CPD content. We can use that information to design effective CPD opportunities, in partnership with practitioners. We can also use that information to work with approval and regulatory bodies in an effort to expand the array of CPD experiences that are recognized as meeting the requirements of participation for licensure purposes. In other words, if we are serious about bridging the gap between what we know about how professionals learn and our current practice then we must be open to a more inclusive view of the kinds of learning environments that contribute to continuing professional development.

As mentioned earlier, we must consider how decisions are made regarding legitimate content for CPD. We must recognize that there is no magic in determining which content is legitimate; what is considered by one professional as necessary for their work may not be considered so by another. Webster-Wright (2009) described the traditional model of CE as a deficiency model, "where professionals are incapable ingénues needing authoritative shepherding, akin to notions of engagement with third-world communities" (p.724). She reminded us that this approach is not congruent with a notion of professionals as "engaged, agentic individuals, capable of self-directed learning" (p. 724). Adult educators have long recognized that adult learners are different; it seems time to recognize this in continuing professional development.

The Assessment of Competence

An additional theme that emerges in discussions of continuing professional development is that of how continuing competence of professionals can or should be measured. Wise et al. (2010) outlined the calls for assessment of ongoing competency in the health professions, including reports by the Pew Health Professions Commission and the Federation of State Medical Boards (FSMB). Swankin et al. (2006) also reported that new models of viewing competency and how it is maintained are emerging from all of the health care professions. This is true in psychology as well, with increased attention to a competency-based model of training that is now being considered in new models of continuing professional development (ASPPB, 2010).

The notion of assessment after licensure will most likely be considered in coming discussions about redesigning and transforming continuing professional development. There are some barriers to moving forward with this concept, however, the most serious one being the resistance shown to the idea by professionals. Psychologists, for example, demonstrated on a national survey their reluctance not only to needing to demonstrate ongoing competence throughout their career, but even to objective learning assessments following CPD activities (Neimeyer et al., 2009).

There appear to be an increasing number of assessment tools that might be employed to assess ongoing competency (Bennett et al., 2000; IOM, 2010; Wise et al., 2010). Keeping in mind the caveats about self-assessment reliability noted earlier, we should still expect to see a move toward some kind of assessment of competency as a part of new models of continuing professional development.

The Effectiveness of Learning

A final theme that emerges is a strong call for research, both to learn more about how professionals learn and to determine the effectiveness of continuing professional development.

Naturally, a primary focus of interest is on the effectiveness of CPD as it relates to actual translation into change in practice. Demonstrated effectiveness would offer some concrete support for mandated CPD, might open opportunities for additional funding for research and program development, and would further demonstrate to the public that the professions have systems in place to protect them. Research related to actual changes in practice is more difficult in professions like psychology, where issues of confidentiality and client-professional relationships must be considered, but there are suggested models for this kind of research, including the use of some of the tools to assess competence, and these can be explored further (Bennett et al, 2000; IOM, 2010; Swankin et al., 2006; Wise et al., 2010).

In addition to needing definitive research on the effectiveness of continuing professional development, we also need more research on what it really means to be a professional learner in order to know better how to encourage meaningful learning that translates into behavioral change. Webster-Wright (2009) emphasized that research is needed that views the learner, the learning context, and learning itself as interrelated rather than merely related, noting that in her research on professional learning (PL) "it was only when the participants were asked to describe situations where they *had* actually learned that the rich, diverse descriptions of authentic PL emerged" (p. 725). We all know that real learning takes place in places other than formal workshops but we need research that supports what we already know in order to build effective new models for learning.

CONCLUSION

We want continuing professional development to make a difference in the career of a professional. We want to know that there is something more to the experience than simply collecting credits in order to fulfill a mandated requirement. The themes that emerge from current discussions about CPD are those of a broadening perspective, learning opportunities that are more closely tied to what we know about how professionals learn, and recognition that there is more to learning than a didactic transfer of knowledge from a teacher to a student. Changes like this will require that we disrupt current assumptions about what constitutes CPD. It will require acknowledgement that professionals learn from a diverse range of activities that may include formal programs, interaction with work colleagues, experiences outside work, or a combination of all of these. It will also require acknowledgement that both clinical and non-clinical content are critical in order to maintain and improve competency in our rapidly changing culture.

We know, through research and our own experiences, that most professionals are enthusiastic and responsible learners. It is up to us to listen to them tell us how they want to learn, what they want to learn, and where they want to learn. We should work to support that by giving them more choices, more opportunities to direct their own learning, and also our trust in their judgment as they sort through their choices. This would be a step forward in fulfilling the promise of Continuing Professional Development.

BIOSKETCH

JO LINDER-CROW, PhD is the Executive Director of the California Psychological Association. In this role she oversees the Mandatory Continuing Education Program Accrediting Agency (MCEPAA) that is regulated by the California Board of Psychology. Previously, as the Associate Executive Director for Education at the American Psychological Association, she was responsible for APA's Continuing Education Program, including the Sponsor Approval System. A past Chair of the Council of Executives of State, Provincial, and Territorial Psychological Associations, she was named the Outstanding Staff Member in a State Psychological Association by APA in 2008. She received a Presidential Citation from APA President Dr. James Bray in 2009 for her outstanding service to the profession of psychology.

REFERENCES

Accreditation Council for Continuing Medical Education. (n.d.) *CME content.* Retrieved from http://www.accme.org/index.cfm/fa/Policy.policy/Policy_id/16f1c694-d03b-4241-bd1a-44b2d072dc5e.cfm.

Adams, A., & Sharkin, B.S. (2012). Should continuing education be mandatory for re-licensure? Arguments for and against. In G. J. Neimeyer, & J. M. Taylor (Eds.), *Continuing professional development and lifelong learning: Issues, impacts and outcomes* (pp. 157-178). Hauppauge, NY: Nova Science Publishers.

American Medical Association. (n.d.) *AMA code of medical ethics: Opinion 9.011 (Continuing Medical Education).* Retrieved from http://www.ama-ssn.org/ama/pub/physician-resources/medical-ethics/code-medical-ethics/opinion9011.page?

American Psychological Association. (2005). *Standards and criteria for approval of sponsors of continuing education for psychologists.* Retrieved from http://apa.org/ed/sponsor/about/standards/manual.pdf.

American Psychological Association. (2002). Ethical principles of psychologists and code of conduct. *American Psychologist, 57,* 1060-1073.

Argyris, C. (1991). Teaching smart people how to learn. *Harvard Business Review, 4,* 4-15.

Argyris, C., & Schön, D. (1974). *Theory in practice: Increasing professional effectiveness.* San Francisco: Jossey-Bass.

Association of State and Provincial Psychology Boards. (2010). *Draft proposal: Continuing professional development (CPD) guidelines.* Retrieved from http://www.asppb.net/files/Final_draft_CPD_report[1].pdf.

Bennett, N. L., Davis, D. A., Easterling, W. E., Friedmann, P., Green, J. S., Koeppe, B. M., ...Waxman, H. S. (2000). Continuing medical education: A new vision of the professional development of physicians. *Academic Medicine, 73,* 1167-1172.

Bloom, B. S. (2005). Effects of continuing medical education on improving physician clinical care and patient health: A review of systematic reviews. *International Journal of Technology Assessment in Healthcare, 21,* 380-385.

Brown, C. R., & Henry, S. M. (1970). Mandatory continuing education: Sense or nonsense? *Journal of the American Medical Association, 213,* 1660-1668.

Cantillon, P., & Jones, R., (1999). Does continuing medical education in general practice make a difference? *British Medical Journal, 318,* 1276-1279.

Daniels, A. S., & Walter, D. A. (2002). Current issues in continuing education for contemporary behavioral health practice. *Administration and Policy in Mental health, 29,* 359-376.

Davis, D., Evans, M., Jadad, L. P., Rath, D., Ryan, D., Sibbald, G., ...Zwarenstein, M. (2003). The case for knowledge translation: Shortening the journey from evidence to effect. *British Medical Journal, 327,* 33-35.

Davis, D., O'Brien, M. A., Freemantle, N., Wolf, F., Mazmanian, P., & Taylor-Vaisey, A. (1999). Impact of formal continuing medical education: Do conferences, workshops, rounds, and other traditional continuing education activities change physician behavior or health care outcomes? *Journal of the American Medical Association, 282,* 867-874.

Davis, D., Maxmanian, P. E., Fordis, M., Harrison, R. V., Thorpe, M., & Perrier, L. P. (2006). Accuracy of physician self-assessment compared with observed measures of competence. *Journal of the American Medical Association, 296,* 1094-1102.

Dubin, S. S. (1972). Obsolescence or lifelong education: A choice for the professional. *American Psychologist, 27,* 486-498.

Fox, D., & Bennett, N.L. (1998). Continuing medical education: Learning and change: Implication for continuing medical education. *British Medical Journal, 316,* 466-468.

Houle, C.O. (1980). *Continuing learning in the professions.* San Francisco: Jossey-Bass.

Institute of Medicine Committee on Planning a Continuing Health Professional Education Institute. (2010). *Redesigning continuing education in the health professions.* Retrieved from http://www.nap.edu/catalog/12704.html

Linder-Crow, J. (1998, August). Continuing professional education in psychology: Lemons or lemonade? *The California Psychologist,* 18-19.

Neimeyer, G. J., & Taylor, J. M. (2010). Continuing education in psychology. In J. C. Norcross, G. R. VandenBos, & D. K. Freedheim (Eds.), *History of psychotherapy: Continuity and change* (pp. 663-671). Washington, DC: American Psychological Association.

Neimeyer, G. J., Taylor, J. M., & Philip, D. (2010a). Continuing education in psychology: Patterns of participation and perceived outcomes among mandated and nonmandated psychologists. *Professional Psychology: Research and Practice, 41,* 435-441.

Neimeyer, G. J., Taylor, J. M., & Wear, D. M. (2009). Continuing education in psychology: Outcomes, evaluations, and mandates. *Professional Psychology: Research and Practice, 40,* 617-624.

Neimeyer, G. J., Taylor, J. M., & Wear, D. (2010b). Continuing education in psychology: Patterns of participation and aspects of selection. *Professional Psychology: Research and Practice, 41,* 281-287.

Reid, R., Friedbarg, M., Adams, J., McGlynn, E., & Mehrotra, A. (2010) Associations between physician characteristics and quality of care. *Archives of Internal Medicine. 170,* 1442-1449.

Ross, A. O. (1974). Continuing professional development in psychology. *Professional Psychology, 5,* 122-128.

Rozensky, R. H., & Kaslow, N. J. (2012). Specialization and lifelong learning. In G. J. Neimeyer, & J. M. Taylor (Eds.), *Continuing professional development and lifelong learning: Issues, impacts and outcomes* (pp. 339-352).Hauppauge, NY: Nova Science Publishers.

Schön, D., (1983). *The reflective practitioner: How professionals think in action.* London: Temple Smith.

Swankin, D., LeBuhn, R. A., & Morrison, R. (2006). *Implementing continuing competency requirements for health care practitioners.* Washington, DC: Federation of State Medical Boards.

VandeCreek, L., Knapp, S., & Brace, K. (1990). Mandatory continuing education for licensed psychologists: Its rationale and current implementation. *Professional Psychology: Research and Practice, 21,* 135-140.

Webster-Wright, A. (2009). Reframing professional development through understanding authentic professional learning. *Review of Educational Research, 79,* 702-739.

Wise, E. H., Sturm, C. A., Nutt, R. L., Rodolfa, E., Schaffer, J. B., & Webb, C. (2010). Lifelong learning for psychologists: Current status and a vision for the future. *Professional Psychology: Research and Practice, 41,* 288-297.

Chapter 20

ANTICIPATING THE FUTURE OF CE IN PSYCHOLOGY: A DELPHI POLL

Greg J. Neimeyer[1,*], Jennifer M. Taylor[1], Doug Wear[2] and Jo Linder-Crow[3]

[1] University of Florida, US
[2] Washington State Psychological Association, US
[3] California Psychological Association, US

Learning must occur throughout the lifespan and must assume new and more complex forms...Continuing education will follow the same pattern of growth; what we hardly dare prophesy today will be seen by later generations as efforts to achieve a manifest necessity.

(Houle, 1980).

ABSTRACT

What will continuing education (CE) look like in the future? A panel of nine continuing education experts were polled twice in relation to their expectations for CE and knowledge acquisition and maintenance 10 years from now. In this Delphi study, experts were asked to anticipate future methods of CE delivery, the assessment of CE outcomes, the projected impacts of CE, the specialization of knowledge in psychology and the half-life of knowledge within the discipline of psychology 10 years from now. Results suggest that some changes will occur in relation to the methods of CE delivery, increases will likely occur in relation to the assessments of outcomes associated with CE, and that increased specialization of knowledge will be accompanied by a shrinking half-life of professional knowledge. Implications are discussed in relation to current movements and future trends in the broader field of professional development and ongoing professional competencies.

---

[*] Correspondence regarding this manuscript may be directed to Greg J. Neimeyer, Department of Psychology, University of Florida, P. O. Box 112250, Gainesville, FL 32611.

Keywords: Future of continuing education, Delphi Study, Life-long learning

INTRODUCTION

The development of continuing education (CE) within the field of psychology has been the subject of longstanding discussion, including both prospective and retrospective accounts. Webster (1971) provided one of the earliest prospective visions, identifying a series of anticipated developments within the field in what he termed a "national agenda for continuing education in psychology" (p. 1016). This agenda outlined a range of critical considerations that collectively would form the basic architecture of the field in the years ahead. Key elements of this architecture included providing thoughtful attention to the development of the curricula, identifying and training capable and qualified presenters, and establishing the local, regional and national organizations that might orchestrate and regulate the processes of ongoing professional development. Ongoing attention to the study of continuing education was vital to Webster's vision, as well, including attention to its best practices and its demonstrated outcomes.

Retrospective accounts of the development of continuing education in psychology have provided a historical backdrop against which Webster's early vision can be gauged. Neimeyer and Taylor (2010), for example, have traced the trajectory of the field's development and noted the ways in which it has fulfilled, as well as fallen short of, Webster's anticipated trajectory 40 years earlier. In some important respects, for example, the field has become a better organized and more formalized undertaking, as reflected in the steady growth in mandated continuing education and the development of organizational and regulatory bodies to oversee ongoing professional development (Neimeyer & Taylor, 2010). In other respects, however, the field has fallen short of Webster's early anticipations, particularly in relation to its attention to the development and implementation of best practices, on the one hand, and the identification and documentation of their outcomes, on the other. Neimeyer and Taylor liken the successive decades since Webster's watershed publication to the construction of a building. If the early years were marked by laying the building's foundation, framing it up and then building it out, the current period is marked by inspecting the nature of its construction and assessing the extent to which it is sufficiently load-bearing in relation to its reputed purposes and objectives (Neimeyer & Taylor, 2010).

In this regard, Neimeyer and Taylor (2010) are joined by a range of other researchers who raise concerns about the quality of the construction (Daniels & Walter, 2002; Institute of Medicine, 2010; Neimeyer, Taylor & Wear, 2009; Wise et al., 2010) and wonder whether the current edifice is fully worthy of a certificate of occupancy at this time. Particular concerns have been directed at whether or not the field is willing to embrace the rigorous assessment required to document its critical outcomes. In concluding their review of the literature, Neimeyer et al. (2009) noted that:

> The study of continuing education…can best be described as a pre-experimental patchwork of isolated surveys conducted largely on localized samples of convenience. These efforts have not yet risen to the level of programmatic research and for that reason they have not yet demonstrated the methodological progression or systematic knowledge gains that would ordinarily accompany a sustained program of research. The discrepancy

between the field's reliance on CE (Rubin et al., 2007) and its scholarly dedication to the understanding of CE is a striking, and now enduring, feature of its professional landscape. (p. 623)

Together with other scholars, practitioners and researchers in the field (Institute of Medicine, 2010), Neimeyer et al. (2009) call for the future development of evidence-based CE in psychology. Evidence-based CE can be defined as "professional education that has an ongoing commitment to evaluating educational practices and assessing educational outcomes in support of understanding, promoting, and documenting the effectiveness of continuing education in psychology" (Neimeyer et al., 2009, p. 623).

Whatever developments may await the field of professional psychology, the field may benefit from gaining a clearer picture of the probable developments that might come. The identification of favorable features might encourage future efforts to promote those developments and may hasten the field's maturation in relation to anticipated directions of change. If, on the other hand, unfavorable features can be identified on the horizon of the field's future, then steps could be taken to avert those developments by addressing them proactively in support of a more positive future for the field. Either way, envisioning the future of a field provides an opportunity for "refocusing the lens" (Institute of Medicine, 2010) in order to see more clearly the probable future that lies beyond the horizon of the field's current developments. With a clearer endpoint in sight, the field's current trajectory is clarified, offering an opportunity to bring greater precision, or adjustment, to its course and direction.

The purpose of the current study was to predict the future developments within the field of CE in psychology in four primary areas: the methods of CE delivery, the measurement of CE outcomes, the documentation of CE impacts, and the future expansion and specialization of knowledge, together with its attendant implications for continuing education.

Methods of Delivery

The traditional method of delivery for continuing education in professional psychology is the face-to-face presentation or lecture, accompanied by PowerPoint slides and associated handouts. While the size of the audience may vary widely, the nature and style of the presentation remains predominantly didactic (Bloom, 2005). This is true not only within professional psychology (Wise et al., 2010) but more broadly within the allied health professions where, for example, lectures and conference sessions constitute 88% of the total activities presented by providers accredited by state medical societies (The Accreditation Council for Continuing Medical Education, 2008). Shern (2010) has referred to this didactic approach as the "Spray and Pray" method; the presenter "sprays the information" out into the crowd and "prays" that some of it sticks. Concerns about the predominance of didactic instruction have long been reported within the literature owing to the demonstrated limitations of this approach, on the one hand, and the availability of more effective methods of delivery, on the other.

Regarding its limitations, a number of researchers have questioned the efficacy of a didactic approach. In a systematic meta-analysis of thirty years of research on continuing education within medicine, Bloom (2005) concluded flatly that, despite the development of new and more effective methods of instruction, the "CE tools and techniques most commonly used are the least effective ones..." (p. 383).

Alternatives to the traditional lecture presentation are widely available but less commonly utilized. The use of experiential and self-directed learning, problem-based learning, cognitive apprenticeship models, simulations, audit and feedback systems, academic detailing, and point-of service learning interventions, among others, have all been identified within the professional training literatures as more effective alternatives (Institute of Medicine, 2010; Neimeyer, Taylor, & Philip, 2010), but they are less commonly utilized.

Among the most rapidly developing methods of delivery for CE at this time is the growing array of technology-mediated and online mechanisms (Institute of Medicine, 2010). In discussing the growing presence of technology within continuing education in psychology, Daniels and Walter (2002) were particularly prescient. They noted that "videoconferencing technology and the use of Web-based resources are becoming more broadly available," (p. 373) "however, as a tool for accredited continuing education activities, Web-based distance learning remains in an early stage of development" (p. 372).

Notwithstanding its relative infancy, Internet-based training has supported a rapidly growing array of different methods of instruction. Webinars and hybrid instruction are joined by a wide variety of high- and low-fidelity online simulations, Internet-based discussions, online portfolios, care mapping, and a range of other instructional media. These alternatives extend to portable mechanisms of learning, too, where podcasting, 4G videos, smart phone-based video conferences, and a range of decision-support tools (e.g., ePocrates, Up-to-Date) contribute to a growing array of online options for supporting professional development.

One focus of the current study was to anticipate the nature of any changes or developments in relation to the methods of CE delivery in the field of professional psychology in the years ahead. If, as Daniels and Walter (2002) suggest, there remains "a significant potential for such technologies to be incorporated in the training of behavior health care providers," then we should expect to see substantial developments in the utilization of emerging technologies in continuing education in the years ahead (p. 372). By anticipating future developments the field may be better positioned to assess the extent to which it is integrating these technologies into its array of instructional methods and expanding outward from its traditional reliance on face-to-face didactic presentations.

Measuring Outcomes

The measurement of educational outcomes and their related impacts on service delivery have been part of the vision of continuing education from the outset (Webster, 1971). And yet these images have not materialized into the realities of practice. Learning outcomes are rarely assessed and are even more rarely evaluated in relation to their consequent impact on service-related outcomes. The call for the measurement of learning outcomes has been a recurrent one with in the field, issued in the field's earliest outcries (e.g., Webster, 1971; Ross, 1974) and reissued in progressively more plaintive and strident voices in the successive decades since that time. By the time the field of professional psychology turned the corner into the 1990s, for example, frustrated scholars and practitioners were baldly declaring that, "all CE activities should include a method of objectively demonstrating that learning has occurred" (VandeCreek, Knapp, & Brace, 1990, p. 139), and yet to this day, few do (Wise et al., 2010).

As VandeCreek et al. (1990) and others have noted, the outcomes of continuing education can be measured along a continuum of progressively more rigorous assessments. The simple documentation of attendance or ratings of participant satisfaction may anchor the low end, followed by the documentation of knowledge gains, skills development, and the translation of those skills into actual practice environments. The ultimate outcomes of these educational gains should ultimately be reflected in improved services to individuals and also in reductions in disease, dysfunction, or distress (cf. Institute of Medicine, 2010).

As Neimeyer et al. (2009) have noted, however, while the future development of such an evidence-based position is broadly endorsed within the field of professional psychology, it is nonetheless resisted by a significant minority of practitioners within the discipline. In their surveys of professional psychologists, for example, Sharkin and Plageman (2003) discovered that 60% of their respondents opposed the objective assessment of their learning, with only 20% favoring it and the remainder remaining neutral. In their recent survey of more than 6,000 licensed psychologists, Neimeyer et al. (2009) likewise found that, while over 95% of the respondents agreed with the idea that they should rate their satisfaction with their CE trainings, only two-thirds of them agreed that they should be tested on their learning and only about one-third supported the idea of any sort of skills assessment associated with their learning.

The result is that the most common forms of outcomes currently being assessed are also the weakest forms of outcomes (i.e. documentation of attendance and satisfaction ratings; Neimeyer et al., 2010). And, as VandeCreek et al. (1990) have been quick to point out, "It would be surprising if participant satisfaction were anything but favorable," and therefore, "studies of this type add little to our evaluation of the effectiveness of CE" (p. 136).

The question that continues to face the field, then, concerns the future likelihood that it will embrace the methods of assessment that would document its effectiveness in terms that would satisfy the need for accountability. For this reason, a second focus of our study concerned the field's future likelihood of integrating various forms of assessment into its ongoing professional training in a way that would support the potential documentation of its reputed outcomes.

CE Impacts

In the absence of the routine assessment of its outcomes, the field of CE in psychology has produced an understandable dearth of research to support clearly demonstrated impacts. Growing evidence supports the notion that psychologists at least *perceive* their CE experiences as translating into their practices (Neimeyer et al., 2009; 2010; Sharkin & Plageman, 2003) but objective evidence to this effect is conspicuously absent in the current literature within professional psychology. In their extensive review of the CE literature, for example, Daniels and Walter (2002) conceded that, outside the field of medicine, "a search revealed no controlled studies of the impact of continuing education in the other behavioral health disciplines" (p. 368).

One recent study within psychology, however, at least provides tentative evidence in support of the knowledge gains associated with CE. Webber, Taylor, and Neimeyer (2011) conducted a randomized controlled study of the differential impact of three forms of CE delivery on objectively measured knowledge gains. The topic of their two-hour CE program was "Internet Addiction", selected on the assumption that relatively few psychologists would have had prior professional training in relation to the growing field of problematic Internet use. Webber et al. measured perceived levels of knowledge regarding this topic both before and after participants completed the training, and objective knowledge gains using a multiple-choice examination on a post-test basis. Importantly, psychologists were randomly assigned to one of three CE conditions, all of which were delivered online. In one condition, participants watched a PowerPoint presentation with synchronized voiceover (i.e. the Audio-visual condition). In the second condition, participants heard only the audio track in the absence of the slides (i.e., the Audio-only condition). And in the third condition, they received only a verbatim written transcript of the program in the absence of any audio or visual material (i.e., the Text-only condition). The content of all three programs was identical and it focused on the prevalence and types of problematic Internet use (e.g., cybersex, online gaming, gambling, auction houses, social networking, etc.), as well as the conceptualization of problematic Internet use, its co-occurring disorders, and its treatment.

Webber et al.'s (2011) findings shed light on the potential impact of CE, the potentially differential impact as a function of the method of its delivery and, critically, the importance of objective assessment. They found, for example, that participants in all three conditions perceived themselves as having learned equal amounts from the training, based on their self-reported pre- and post-test knowledge ratings. When it came to the *objective* measure of learning, however, substantial differences were found; participants in the audio-only condition showed significantly lower levels of learning when compared to those in the audio-visual and text-only conditions. While participants in the latter two conditions, on average, scored over 80% correct, those in the audio-only condition scored only around 60% correct. Webber et al.'s results generally support VandeCreek et al.'s (1990) earlier observation that CE can be effective, but underscored that all forms of delivery may not be equal. These findings provide empirical support for what the Institute of Medicine (2010) identifies as selected practices that may be predisposed to generate greater learning and more favorable outcomes, including the use of multiple methods or channels of delivery. They also call attention to the importance assessing the effectiveness of various forms of CE delivery, rather than simply presuming the equivalent effectiveness CE. This may be especially important in relation to the utilization of emerging technologies where, as Daniels and Walter (2002) have noted, "new mediums of education will require systematic evaluation of their effectiveness" (p. 373).

Apart from Webber et al.'s (2011) work, the field of professional psychology is largely left with extrapolating from the findings within medicine in order find support for the effectiveness of CE in relation to its stipulated outcomes. As an example, Davis et al. (1999) conducted a comprehensive meta-analysis of continuing medical education and the factors associated with its favorable outcomes. Their findings were sobering insofar as traditional, didactic programs failed to register any significant impact either on physician's behavior or patient-related outcomes. Interactive programs, however, particularly those that included supervised application and rehearsal of skills, did register subsequent effects on physicians 'behavior and, to a lesser extent, on the associated healthcare outcomes, as well. These findings support those of Bloom (2005), who conducted a systematic review of the CME literature across a 20-year period. From his review of the best-controlled research in the field, Bloom concluded that interactive techniques were the most effective in relation to generating changes in physicians' behavior and in patient outcomes, but he cautioned that didactic presentations had "little or no beneficial effect on changing physician practice" (p. 380).

Within the field of psychology, which remains a generation behind medicine in relation to the assessment and demonstration of CE outcomes (Neimeyer et al., 2009; Wise et al., 2010), the question becomes whether that gap is likely to close in the foreseeable future. As Wise et al. note, "Most psychologists are satisfied with their continuing education efforts, but there is no independent evidence that these efforts actually result in maintaining competence, or have any impact of their professional practice" (p. 296). The question is whether or not the field is likely to turn its attention to demonstrating the outcomes that follow from its professional development in order to redress the current dearth of data and document instead the objective impact of CE on service delivery and outcomes.

Expansion and Specialization of Knowledge

The original impetus for continuing education arose largely from the social activism of the 1970s and the public demand for greater professional accountability (Neimeyer & Taylor, 2010). This demand was made more acute by the need for continuing competencies created by the ongoing profusion of knowledge, on the one hand, and forces of specialization, on the other. Continuing Education was originally conceptualized as a mechanism to counter the otherwise naturally occurring obsolescence of knowledge, and to document a commitment to ongoing learning that would presumably reinforce professional competence and reassure public confidence (Ross, 1974).

Given that most doctoral training programs in psychology require five to six years to complete, the time spent in professional practice after the degree is roughly five or six times that long. This underscores the importance of continuing education, which necessarily must bear the substantial and sustained responsibility of continually updating knowledge and maintaining professional competencies. The concept of the "half-life" of professional knowledge is a critical factor in this regard.

Introduced into the literature in 1972, the "half-life" of professional knowledge is defined as the length of time it takes a practicing professional, without any new learning, to become roughly half as knowledgeable or competent to practice, once they complete their degree, owing to new knowledge and developments within the field of practice (Dubin, 1972). Based on measures of knowledge generation and advances in various fields, Dubin (1972) provided estimates for the "half-life" of knowledge in various professions. The half-life of knowledge within psychology was estimated to be roughly 10-12 years meaning that, without engaging in compensatory processes of new learning, a professional psychologist's knowledge would become substantially, perhaps alarmingly, out-of-date in the decade following his or her graduation. But, given Dubin's conclusion that the half-life of knowledge decreases as the rate of change and new knowledge production increases, it would, as Wise et al. (2010) note, "suggest that the current half-life of the professional psychology doctoral degree is likely to be significantly shorter" today (p. 289).

It seems likely that rapid developments in both professional specialization, on the one hand, and knowledge generation and dissemination on the other, will further reduce the half-life of knowledge within the profession within the foreseeable future. The specialization of knowledge has occurred in tandem with its profusion, making it increasingly difficult to maintain the depth of knowledge regarding new developments across a broad range of areas. In a sense, specialization can be viewed as a response to this knowledge explosion, where rapid advances require more specialization in order to retain currency and be in command of the latest advances in a given area.

Add to this the impact of emerging technologies that dramatically enhance the dissemination of new knowledge, both in relation to the breadth and the rapidity of that dissemination. Internet-based knowledge dissemination, for example, functionally "democratizes" knowledge by making it accessible almost instantly almost anywhere in the world. And, as in medicine (Institute of Medicine, 2010), we might expect to see emerging technologies hasten the profusion and dissemination of knowledge within psychology in this regard (Daniels & Walter, 2002; Issenberg et al., 1999). The question becomes, then, what will the half-life of professional knowledge within psychology be within the foreseeable future? How much is it likely to shrink in response to rapid developments in relation to the specialization, profusion, and dissemination of new knowledge?

A Delphi Study

In order to forecast probable developments within continuing education in psychology, we utilized the best-recognized forecasting tool available, the Delphi Method. The Delphi Method solicits the opinions of a group of experts within a field to obtain a consensus about future developments that are likely to occur within that field within a specified period of time. The basis of the method is the repeated administration of a questionnaire to members of an identified expert panel. After each round of polling, aggregated, anonymous feedback is provided to panel members for them to evaluate in relation to subsequent polling, until consensus begins to emerge from within the group. The Delphi Method is designed to preserve the advantages of group decision making without incurring the disadvantages often associated with face-to-face meetings. In short, the Delphi Method is predicated on the notion that several expert minds are better than one in relation to predicting future developments in a field and that experts within a controlled communication environment, free from personal pressures or persuasion, will make judgments based on rational thought and shared information, ultimately reaching sound conclusions.

Research on the effectiveness of the Delphi Method in relation to predicting future developments within a field are encouraging. Dalkey and Helmer (1963) have demonstrated that the method is superior to face-to-face methods in relation to the ability to obtain consensus, and the method has been repeatedly utilized in predicting future developments across a wide range of fields and issues, including future developments within the fields of counseling and psychotherapy (Heath, Neimeyer & Pedersen, 1988; Neimeyer & Norcross, 1997).

METHOD

The Expert Panel

The selection of expert panelists is critical to conducting an effective Delphi Poll. As Martino (1972) has noted, it is "the most important decision the panel director will make" (p. 54.). Cicarelli (1984) has echoed this sentiment, stating flatly that "A Delphi *is* its panel" and that "genuine insights into the future of a discipline are more apt to come from active scholars and practitioners…[who] will help shape the future of the discipline, if not determine it" (p.140).

Following this rationale, we decided to impose stringent criteria for membership on the expert panel in our Delphi Poll, choosing only former members of the American Psychological Association's Continuing Education Committee (CEC) for prospective panel membership. The CEC is charged with the implementation of the APA's policies regarding continuing education. The committee's responsibilities include both regulatory responsibilities and policy-related discussions and consultations. From a regulatory position, the CEC acts as the approval body for approximately 800 APA-approved CE sponsors (Tongue, personal communication, June 8, 2011), reviewing the nature and quality of their programming as well as the organizational structures designed to implement and evaluate their programs. In addition to its regulatory function, the CEC is responsible for a wide range of policy discussions and consultations regarding continuing education within the field. Policy discussions include topics such as supporting the best practices in CE delivery, identifying effective mechanisms for monitoring CE attendance, identifying mechanisms for assessing CE outcomes, and evaluating the appropriateness of various CE activities supporting professional development. In this capacity, for example, the Committee reviews over 300 convention sessions and more than 150 workshop proposals to serve as CE activities at the annual APA convention each year. Through the CEC's liaison and outreach activities, it also provides a variety of consultation and furnishes feedback regarding CE practices to current and prospective CE sponsors, as well as regulatory and advisory boards, such as the Association of State and Provincial Psychology Boards (cf., American Psychological Association, 2011).

The CEC is composed of members of the American Psychological Association who are elected by the committee itself from nominations it solicits and receives each year from within its membership. Service on the committee is for a three-year term with approximately one-third of the committee being replaced each year. In order to maximize the expertise of our panelists, we elected to solicit the participation only of members of the CEC within the last three years who had successfully completed their full three-year terms. In all, nine former members participated in the polling and constituted the expert panel. Delphi polling is based on the identification of documented expertise, rather than on statistical sampling, so traditional issues, such as random sampling in support of the generalizability of findings do not apply. Instead, inclusion is based on identified expertise, and the composition of the panel is ordinarily acknowledged, with the consent of the panelists, in publications or presentations based on the polling. We have followed that tradition by identifying the members of our expert panel (see Table 1).

Questionnaire

Item content for the Delphi Poll was derived from a review of the current literature in continuing education and lifelong psychology within professional psychology and related health professions. The survey consisted of questions within the four primary domains of interest. These included anticipated developments in relation to 1) the methods of CE delivery, 2) the assessment of CE outcomes, 3) the anticipated impacts of CE, and 4) the expansion and specialization of knowledge within the field.

Table 1. Expert Panel Members

David Glenwick, Ph.D.
Rodney Goodyear, Ph.D.
William MacGillivray
Mort McPhail, Ph.D.
Ramona Moss, Ph.D.
Joann Peeler, Ph.D.
Jeffrey Rankin, Ph.D.
Michael Roberts, Ph.D.
Tony Wu, Ph.D.

In all cases panelists were instructed to anticipate what they felt the field will be like in 10 years. Instructions emphasized that they should indicate "what you think *will* happen, regardless of whether or not you would *like* to see it happen." The purpose of the poll was explicitly to recruit their *predictions* rather than their *preferences*, and the time frame was clearly indicated as being one decade from now. Specifically, panelists were asked, "When you think about the field of continuing education in psychology over the next 10 years, to what extent do you expect each of the following…to increase or decrease?"

The methods of delivery domain addressed anticipated changes in the format(s) in which CE is offered. This included predictions regarding the future increase or decrease in on-site presentations, synchronous and asynchronous online training, and point-of-service learning, using a 5-point scale ranging from predictions that a delivery format will "decrease considerably" (1) to "increase considerably" (5).

The assessment of outcomes domain addressed predicted increases or decreases in the attention to the measurement of various outcomes. This included the overall attention to the assessment of outcomes in general, as well as a range of specific outcomes such as the assessment of new learning, skills, and actual applications, all using a 5-point scale ranging from predictions that assessments that will "decrease considerably" (1) to "increase considerably" (5).

Likewise, the third domain, which addressed the anticipated impacts of CE, asked panelists to predict the extent to which CE would generate a range of specific, documented outcomes. These included specific outcomes, such as increased learning, changes in practice, enhanced clinical outcomes, or the protection of the public, again using a 5-point scale.

The final domain assessed the perceived "half-life" of professional knowledge in psychology, using Dubin's (1972) definition (i.e. the time it takes, without any new learning, to become roughly half as knowledgeable or competent as an individual was at the completion of his or her degree). Panelists were instructed to provide two estimates of the half-life of professional knowledge: the current half-life of professional knowledge and the half-life of knowledge in professional psychology 10 years from now.

Procedure

The Delphi method involved two rounds of polling. In the first round, the expert panelists were solicited through an email to take part in the study and provided a link to complete the survey online. They were instructed to submit the completed survey within two weeks and, following their completion, panelists were sent a second survey to complete. This second survey was identical to the first except that it included for each question the means and standard deviations of the aggregated responses of all panelists from the prior round of polling. No individual's responses were disclosed, only the overall mean and standard deviation from the group in relation to each of the survey questions. Panelists were instructed "to complete the survey a second time, mindful of the aggregated responses of the full group of panelists in the prior round of polling".

The effectiveness of the Delphi method is ordinarily reflected in the movement of the group towards greater consensus. Consensus is reflected in reduced standard deviations in the responses to the survey questions, indicating a developing convergence of opinion. Table 2 depicts the means and standard deviations for each of the questions in the Delphi Poll in both rounds of polling.

Table 2. Delphi Poll Means and Standard Deviations for Round 1 and Round 2

	Round 1	Round 2
When you think about the field of continuing education in psychology over the next 10 years, to what extent do you think that each of the following delivery formats is likely to decrease or increase…		
On-site presentations and workshops	2.87 (.64)	3.00 (.58)
Workplace or point-of-service CE	3.38 (.92)	3.14 (.38)
Asynchronous internet-based training (e.g., slide shows or text-based programs)	3.63 (1.41)	3.71 (1.25)
Synchronous live internet-based training (e.g., Webinars)	3.63 (1.41)	4.00 (.58)
When you think about the field of continuing education in psychology over the next ten years, to what extent do you believe that each of the following is likely…		
Measurement of overall CE learning	3.62 (.52)	4.14 (.69)
Measurement of applications of material in CE trainings	3.50 (.54)	4.14 (.69)
Measurement of skills in CE trainings	3.50 (.54)	3.86 (.69)
Attention to clinical outcomes	3.88 (.64)	4.29 (.76)
When you envision the field of CE in psychology 10 years from now, to what extent do you believe that it will…		
Increase professional knowledge	3.88 (.84)	3.86 (.69)
Keep psychologists up-to-date	3.86 (.90)	4.14 (.90)
Translate into practice	3.63 (1.06)	3.43 (.98)
Maintain or enhance professional competency	3.88 (.84)	3.71 (.76)
Protect the public	3.63 (.92)	3.17 (.75)
Enhance clinical outcomes	3.50 (1.07)	2.86 (.90)
When considering professional development, to what extent do you believe that each of the following developments is likely to decrease or increase…		

Table 2. (Continued)

Round 1 Round 2		
Focus on specialization(s)	3.88 (.84)	3.86 (.38)
The "half-life" of professional knowledge has been described as the length of time it takes, without any new learning, to become roughly half as knowledgeable or competent as you were at the completion of your degree. On a scale of 1-30 years, what do you feel the "half-life" of professional knowledge in psychology is at this time?	13.00 (6.16)	12.43 (4.43)
What do you feel the "half-life" of professional knowledge in psychology will be in 10 years? (1-30 years)	8.86 (4.00)	9.00 (3.46)

Note. Means (and standard deviations) are represented for rounds 1 and 2 of the Delphi Poll, using a 5-point rating scale ranging from 1 (*will decrease considerably*) to 5 (*will increase considerably*) for the first two sections. The third section utilizes a 5-point rating scale, ranging from 1 (*very little*) to 5 (*a great deal*), and the forth section ranges from 1 (*definitely will decrease*) to 5 (*definitely will increase*).

RESULTS AND DISCUSSION

The results of the Delphi Poll provided a glimpse into the anticipated future of continuing education in psychology within four broad domains: the mechanisms of its delivery, the utilization of assessments, the impacts and outcomes associated with it, and the expansion and specialization of knowledge within the field 10 years from now.

Methods of Delivery

Concerning the nature of delivery, panelists predicted no change in relation to the frequency with which on-site CE trainings will occur (M=3.00) but progressively greater utilization of point-of-service learning (M=3.14), asynchronous Internet based training (M=3.71) and synchronous live Internet-based training (e.g. Webinars, M=4.00). These predictions are consistent with the earlier anticipations of Issenberg and colleagues (1999) who noted the increased utilization of innovative technologies for the delivery of continuing education. Likewise, these findings provide empirical support for the observations of Daniels and Walter (2002) that there is "a growing consensus… in post-licensing continuing education" that "technology will play an increasingly pivotal role" (p. 371). Interactive videoconferencing, Web-based dissemination of information, interactive learning, and online simulation techniques may join with an array of online point-of-service decision-support tools and other emerging technologies to expand and enrich the array of available methods of CE delivery in support of future professional development. As Wise et al. (2010) have noted, "E-learning methods have great potential to reach large numbers of psychologist, can be created in various interactive formats, and are also lower cost forms of CE" (p. 293). These may count among the factors that support the likelihood of the field's increasing utilization of emerging technologies to support its future professional development needs.

Assessment of Outcomes

Concerning the assessment of CE-related outcomes, panelists predicted increases in the frequency with which overall learning will be assessed (M=4.14), as well as the measurement of the applications of the CE material (M=4.14) and, to a lesser extent, the actual skills that the CE training provides (M=3.86). This increased commitment to the assessment of outcomes renews the field's commitment to one of the original driving factors behind CE: accountability. The routine assessment of a range of relevant outcomes would allow the field to demonstrate its commitment to accountability, on the one hand, and to provide evidence in support of the effectiveness of its professional development practices, on the other. And this, in turn, would support the field's alignment with the broader movements towards evidence-based practices that are central to the allied fields of psychotherapy and professional competencies (Kaslow et al., 2009). Evidenced-based continuing education can be regarded as "professional education that has on ongoing commitment to evaluating educational practices and assessing educational outcomes in support of understanding, promoting, and demonstrating the effectiveness of continuing education in psychology" (Neimeyer et al., 2009, p. 623). One expression of that effectiveness might be reflected in assessments of continuing professional competence. But, as noted by Wise et al. (2010) a precondition to demonstrating ongoing professional competencies is a renewed commitment to assessing them, and the results of the current Delphi Poll are encouraging in relation to the field's probable developments along these lines.

CE Impacts

Concerning the anticipated impact and outcomes associated with CE in psychology, panelists made a number of noteworthy predictions. Overall, for example, they predicted that the field would dedicate substantially greater attention to the outcomes of CE in the future (M=4.29). The consequences of this attention was predicted to be reflected in documented increases in professional knowledge (M=3.86) that would help keep psychologists up-to-date (M=4.14) and would translate into their practice (M=3.43). While CE was expected to enhance professional competency in the future (M=3.71), panelists were less sanguine about it more fully serving to protect the public (M=3.17) or actually enhancing clinical outcomes (M=2.86).

The overall picture that this paints regarding the anticipated impact of CE in the future is a generally, though not robustly, favorable one. From the perspective of the expert panelists, the field can expect to increasingly fulfill its commitment to accountability by renewed attention to CE outcomes, but the nature of the outcomes it generates was expected to vary. In general, CE was expected to better be able to keep psychologists up-to-date and generate knowledge gains, but perhaps less likely to have these knowledge gains translate into practice, to enhance clinical outcomes, or to fulfill its mission in relation to protecting the public. As noted elsewhere, there are a number of sources of professional development outside of formal CE, per se (Neimeyer et al., 2009), and these other sources may have to play important roles in relation to the objectives that are not fulfilled by formal CE alone (Institute of Medicine, 2010).

Goodyear and Lichtenberg (2008), for example, argue that in addition to formal CE there is a range of informal forms of professional development (e.g., reading journals, attending conferences, consulting with colleagues), as well as incidental forms of learning where learning is secondary to the primary objectives of the task. In this regard Skovholt and Starkey (2010) note that therapists commonly nominate their clinical experience itself as the greatest source of their knowledge and professional development. Relatedly, the attitudes and skills associated with lifelong learning have themselves been demonstrated to predict a wide range of ongoing professional activities and accomplishments (Hojat, Veloski, Nasca, Erdmann, & Gonnella, 2006; Taylor, Neimeyer, Zemansky, & Rothke, 2012). So the cultivation of those attitudes and skills, quite apart from the completion of formal CE, may play a critical role in supporting ongoing competencies and effective clinical outcomes. This is generally consistent with the work of Epstein (1999) and others in relation to cultivating "mindfulness" in clinical practice, creating both cognitive and emotional attunement to elements of practice in a way that provides a continuous infusion of novelty and feedback related to the processes and outcomes of professional practices. Also, as Skovholt and Starkey have noted, professional development can be viewed as a three-legged stool that is supported not only by formal and informal sources of learning, but by the broader developmental context of continuing personal maturation. So, while the results of this Delphi Poll suggest that the future of CE may include its increased capacity to document selected outcomes, they may also reflect the importance of relying on other mechanisms beyond formal CE to achieve the broader outcomes associated with sustained professional competencies and enhanced clinical outcomes.

Knowledge Expansion and Specialization

In relation to a future focus on specialization, panelists predicted an increased movement towards specialization within professional psychology in the years ahead (M=3.86). This is consistent with a range of current trends within the field (Kaslow et al., 2009) and, perhaps, with the increasing rate of knowledge generation and dissemination, as well.

Support for this notion comes from the panelist's assessments concerning the "half-life" of knowledge in the field of professional psychology, where they were asked to estimate the current and future half-life of that knowledge 10 years from now. Panelists estimated that the current half-life of psychological knowledge was nearly 12-and-a-half years (M=12.43), whereas in 10 years the half-life will be only 9 years (M=9.00). This represents roughly a 28% decrease in the expected half-life of knowledge within the field over the course of the next a decade which, in turn, underscores both the importance of professional development and assessing, enhancing, and documenting its effectiveness. From the outset, CE was designed to counter the otherwise naturally occurring obsolescence of knowledge over time. As that obsolescence occurs more and more rapidly, processes must be brought to bear to contend against those effects. Increased specialization may be one of the responses to the profusion of knowledge, and renewed attention to the outcomes and best practices of continuing education may well be another.

CONCLUSION

The field of continuing education is undergoing significant change, not only within psychology, but across the broader landscape of the allied health professions (Institute of Medicine, 2010). The rapid expansion, specialization and dissemination of new knowledge are further fuelling the engines of change, and the field must somehow accommodate these developments within a context of renewed accountability in an increasingly evidence-based world. The results of the current Delphi study provide a glimpse into selected features of the field's probable future, at least in relation to professional psychology. The picture that emerges is marked by an increasing integration of emerging technologies into traditional formats of CE delivery, together with a renewed dedication to the assessment of a range of outcomes associated with those efforts. The outcomes themselves are expected to vary, bringing increased evidence regarding the impact of CE on new learning and on the application of that learning, with perhaps fewer gains in relation to documenting the role of CE in enhancing clinical outcomes or protecting the public. Within the context of increasing knowledge generation and specialization, the pace of knowledge obsolescence is expected to increase, as well. This, in turn, underscores the importance of the field's embracing an evidence-based approach so that its gains can be documented and new directions can be charted. By embracing an evidence-based approach to lifelong professional learning, the field of continuing education would position itself as a participant in the allied competency-based movements. Central to these movements, across the broad spectrum of health professions, is a shared dedication to ensuring and documenting enhanced professional skills, practice and outcomes over the course of ongoing professional development. CE is only one of many mechanisms that jointly contribute to sustained and enhanced professional competencies. Yet, as the Institute on Medicine (2010) has noted recently, "it is a critical piece- one that has been overlooked for too long" (pp. ix-x). We hope that by focusing attention on the probable future of CE in psychology, the current work brings both greater visibility to its current directions and support for ongoing efforts to fashion its future developments.

BIOSKETCHES

GREG J. NEIMEYER received his Ph.D. in counseling psychology from the University of Notre Dame. He is professor of psychology in the Department of Psychology at the University of Florida and director of the Office of Continuing Education and Psychology at the APA. A fellow of the APA, he is also a member of the Department of Community Health and Family Medicine. His areas of research include professional development, epistemology and psychotherapy, and relationship development and disorder.

JENNIFER M. TAYLOR received her M.S. in counseling psychology from the University of Florida. She is currently a Ph.D. candidate in the University of Florida counseling psychology program. Her research focuses on professional development and competencies, lifelong learning, continuing education, and mentoring.

DOUGLAS M. WEAR received his Ph.D. in clinical psychology from the University of Wyoming. He is the president of Wear and Associates, Inc., executive director of the Washington State Psychological Association, director of Antioch University Seattle

Psychology and Community Counseling Clinic, chair of the APA Continuing Education Committee, and past chair of APA Council of Executive Director of State and Provincial Psychological Associations. His research and professional interests include professional development, supervision, management, consulting, and coaching.

Jo Linder-Crow, Ph.D. is the Executive Director of the California Psychological Association. In this role she oversees the Mandatory Continuing Education Program Accrediting Agency (MCEPAA) that is regulated by the California Board of Psychology. Previously, as the Associate Executive Director for Education at the American Psychological Association, she was responsible for APA's Continuing Education Program, including the Sponsor Approval System. A past Chair of the Council of Executives of State, Provincial, and Territorial Psychological Associations, she was named the Outstanding Staff Member in a State Psychological Association by APA in 2008. She received a Presidential Citation from APA President Dr. James Bray in 2009 for her outstanding service to the profession of psychology

REFERENCES

American Psychological Association. (2011). Model act for state licensure of psychologists. *American Psychologist, 66*, 214-226.

Bloom, B. S. (2005). Effects of continuing medical education on improving physician clinical care and patient health: A review of systematic reviews. *International Journal of Technology Assessment in Health Care, 231*, 380–385.

Cicarelli, J. (1984). The future of economics: A Delphi study. *Technological Forecasting and Social Change, 25*, 139-157.

Dalkey, N., & Helmer, O. (1963). *An experimental application of the Delphi Method to the use of experts. Management Science, 9*, 458-467.

Daniels, A. S., & Walter, D. A. (2002). Current issues in continuing education for contemporary behavioral health practice. *Administration and Policy in Mental Health, 29*, 359–376.

Davis, D., O'Brien, M. A. T., Feemantle, N., Wolf, F. M., Mazmanian, P., & Taylor-Vaisey, A. (1999). Impact of formal continuing medical education: Do conferences, workshops, rounds, and other traditional continuing education activities change physician behavior or health care outcomes? *Journal of the American Medical Association, 282*, 867–874.

Dubin, S. S. (1972). Obsolescence or lifelong education: A choice for the professional. *American Psychologist*, 486–498.

Epstein, R. (1999). Mindful Practice. *Journal of the American Medical Association, 282*, 383-389.

Goodyear, R. K., & Lichtenberg, J. W. (2008, August). Preparing psychologists for lifelong learning. In C. Belar (Chair), *Examining the mechanisms for lifelong learning in professional psychology*. Symposium conducted at the meeting of the 2008 American Psychological Association Conference, Boston, MA.

Heath, A. E., Neimeyer, G. J., & Pedersen, P. B. (1988). The future of cross-cultural counseling: A Delphi poll. *Journal of Counseling and Development, 67*, 27-30.

Hojat, M., Veloski, J., Nasca, T. J., Erdmann, J. B., & Gonnella, J. S. (2006). Assessing physicians' orientation toward lifelong learning. *Journal of General Internal Medicine, 21*, 931-936.

Houle, C. (1980). *Continuing Learning in Professions*, San Francisco: Jossey-Bass.

Institute of Medicine. (2010). *Redesigning continuing education in the health professions.* Washington, DC: The National Academies Press.

Issenberg, S. B., McGaghie, W. C., Hart, I. R., Mayer, J. W., Felner, J. M., Petrusa, E. R., & Ewy, G. A. (1999). Simulation technology for health care professional skills training and assessment. *Journal of the American Medical Association, 282*, 861–866.

Kaslow, N. J., Grus, C. L., Campbell, L. F., Fouad, N. A., Hatcher, R. L., & Rodolfa, E. R. (2009). Competency Assessments Toolkit for professional psychology. *Training and Education in Professional Psychology, 3*, S27-S45.

Martino, J. P. (1972). *Technological Forecasting for Decision Making*. New York: American Elsevier.

Neimeyer, G. J., & Norcross, J. C. (1997). The future of psychotherapy and counseling psychology in the USA: Delphi data and beyond. In S. Palmer, & V. Varma (Eds.), *The Future of Counselling and Psychotherapy* (pp. 65-81). Oaks, CA: Sage Publications.

Neimeyer, G. J., & Taylor, J. M. (2010). Continuing education in psychology. In J. C. Norcross, G. R. VandenBos, & D. K. Freedheim (Eds.), *History of psychotherapy*. Washington, DC: American Psychological Association.

Neimeyer, G. J., Taylor, J. M., & Philip, D. (2010). Continuing education in psychology: Patterns of participation and perceived outcomes among mandated and nonmandated psychologists. *Professional Psychology: Research and Practice, 41*, 435-441.

Neimeyer, G. J., Taylor, J. M., & Wear, D. M. (2009). Continuing education in psychology: Outcomes, evaluations, and mandates. *Professional Psychology: Research and Practice, 40*, 617–624.Ross, A. O. (1974). Continuing professional development in psychology. *Professional Psychology, 5*, 122–128.

Rubin, N. J., Bebeau, M., Leigh, I. W., Lichtenberg, J. W., Nelson, P. D., Portnoy, S., & Kasow, N. J. (2007). Competency movement within psychology: An historical perspective. *Professional Psychology: Research and Practice, 38*, 452–462.

Sharkin, B. S., & Plageman, P. M. (2003). What do psychologists think about mandatory continuing education? A survey of Pennsylvania psychologists. *Professional Psychology: Research and Practice, 34*, 318–323.

Shern, D. (2010, February). *Health care reform, chronic disease and the emerging role for psychologists*. Presentation to the Council of Chairs of Training Councils Joint Conference of Training Councils in Psychology: Assuring competence in the next generation of psychologists. Orlando, FL.

Skovolt, T. M., & Starkey, M. T. (2010). The three legs of the practitioner's learning stool: Practice, research/theory, and personal life. *Journal of Contemporary Psychotherapy, 40*, 125-130.

Taylor, J. M., Neimeyer, G. J., Zemansky, M., & Rothke, S. (2012). Exploring the relationship between lifelong learning, continuing education, and professional competencies. In G. J. Neimeyer, & J. M. Taylor (Eds.), *Continuing professional development and lifelong learning: Issues, impacts and outcome* (pp. 83-99). Hauppauge, NY: Nova Science Publishers.

The Accreditation Council for Continuing Medical Education. (2008). *ACCME annual report data 2008*.Retrieved from http://www.accme.org/dir_docs/doc_upload/1f8dc476-246a-4e8e-91d3-d24ff2f5bfec_uploaddocument.pdf.

VandeCreek, L., Knapp, S., & Brace, K. (1990). Mandatory continuing education for licensed psychologists: Its rationale and current implementation. *Professional Psychology: Research and Practice, 21*, 135–140.

Webber, E., Taylor, J. M., & Neimeyer, G. J. (2011). *Continuing education in psychology: A comparison of measured levels of learning resulting from home study methods of continuing education.* Unpublished manuscript.

Webster, T. G. (1971). National priorities for the continuing education of psychologists. *American Psychologist, 26*, 1016–1019.

Wise, E. H., Sturm, C. A., Nutt, R. L., Rodolfa, E., Schaffer, J. B., & Webb, C. (2010). Life-long learning for psychologists: Current status and a vision for the future. *Professional Psychology: Research and Practice, 41*, 288-297.

INDEX

A

Abraham, 65, 318
abuse, 251, 260
academic performance, 30, 33, 39
academic settings, 77
access, 7, 22, 23, 24, 25, 93, 95, 107, 108, 109, 172, 212, 222, 324, 325, 330, 350, 361
accessibility, 5, 173, 222
accountability, 17, 18, 162, 177, 191, 299, 330, 333, 350, 352, 358, 361, 381, 383, 389, 391
accounting, 43, 44, 270
accreditation, 20, 21, 24, 26, 27, 78, 145, 146, 214, 217, 220, 270, 272, 321, 330, 331, 335, 367
Accreditation Council for Pharmacy Education (ACPE), 11, 15
acid, 286
acquisition of knowledge, 149
activism, 191, 383
actuality, 295
adaptation, 225
adjustment, xii, 224, 249, 250, 251, 252, 253, 254, 255, 256, 257, 299, 310, 379
administrative support, 269, 328
administrators, 297, 304
adolescent development, 96, 188, 197
adolescent female, 213
adolescents, 246, 356
adult education, 273, 335, 337, 368
adulthood, 310
adults, 290, 293, 296, 314
advancement, 93, 102
adverse event, 23
advocacy, 138, 171, 318, 332, 333, 336
affective reactions, 143
affirming, 112
African-American, 195
age, 36, 38, 39, 85, 109, 179, 191, 195, 233, 235, 253

agencies, 16, 23, 138, 145, 321, 332
Alaska, 163, 164, 166
alcohol consumption, 210
alienation, 300
altruistic acts, 230
American Educational Research Association, 65, 77, 78, 335
American Nurses Association (ANA), 15
ancestors, 238
anger, 230
antidepressant, 325
anxiety, 15, 206, 214, 230, 234, 251
apathy, 300
appetite, 233, 240
appointments, 212, 217
appraisals, 252
architects, 281, 332, 367, 370
articulation, 349
assertiveness, 334
assessment models, 78, 181
assessment procedures, 148
assessment tools, 176, 372
atmosphere, 333
attachment, 251
attitudes, xi, 7, 15, 17, 19, 20, 24, 34, 58, 71, 74, 75, 76, 85, 86, 136, 139, 142, 150, 169, 171, 178, 250, 251, 253, 269, 323, 324, 325, 326, 328, 334, 337, 346, 351, 352, 356, 367, 370, 390
audit(s), 8, 140, 150, 168, 326, 329, 337, 380
Austria, 68
authenticity, 245
authority, 105, 145, 150, 363
autonomy, 175, 187
avoidance, 210
awareness, 5, 73, 76, 94, 112, 135, 162, 177, 188, 191, 195, 196, 231, 241, 256, 257, 298, 303, 312, 353

B

bad day, 207
bargaining, 332, 333
barriers, 5, 210, 221, 241, 280, 281, 291, 293, 308, 309, 325, 335, 372
barriers to entry, 280
base, 15, 18, 25, 59, 75, 140, 186, 187, 229, 235, 265, 266, 291, 293, 333, 370
basic education, 273
behavioral change, 252, 373
behavioral manifestations, 58
behavioral sciences, 66
behaviors, 19, 20, 24, 58, 69, 213, 217, 251, 326, 328, 331, 334, 365
belief systems, 210, 315
benchmarks, 82, 96, 147, 152, 180, 225, 326, 336, 355
beneficial effect, 222, 256, 383
beneficiaries, 224, 292, 356
benefits, xi, 89, 137, 186, 192, 218, 222, 231, 237, 244, 282, 288, 302, 303, 331, 338, 340
bias, 6, 19, 45, 57, 58, 66
biological sciences, 291
biosphere, 302
birth rate, 305
blame, 15, 303
blueprint, 300
borderline personality disorder, 226
bounds, 83, 212
brain, 96, 197
breathing, 234
Britain, 292
Bureau of Labor Statistics, 22, 27, 319, 320, 340
bureaucracy, 299, 300
burn, 210
burnout, 218, 219, 222, 223, 225, 251, 253, 259, 260, 356
businesses, 144
Butcher, 313

C

cancer, 241
candidates, 7, 321
career development, 74
caregivers, 226
case examples, 338
case studies, 237
category b, 74
causal inference, 255
causal interpretation, 257
causal relationship, 88, 194, 196, 257
causation, 19, 304
CEC, 145, 385
central nervous system, 300, 306
centralisation, 314
certificate, 34, 91, 378
certification, 17, 21, 23, 72, 138, 140, 144, 148, 151, 270, 272, 275, 320, 321, 330, 337, 345, 346, 348, 349, 350, 351, 352, 353, 354, 355, 356, 357, 358, 360
challenges, xiii, 3, 7, 8, 11, 82, 136, 145, 149, 153, 173, 179, 191, 203, 207, 218, 231, 308, 369
checks and balances, 15
Chicago, 69, 96, 197, 273, 274, 311, 312, 336, 340
child abuse, 108
child development, 291
childhood, 251
children, 133, 214, 246, 278, 288, 289, 290, 312, 313, 315, 356
citizens, 283
City, 59, 313
clarity, xi, xiii, 34, 369
class size, 290
classes, 138, 223
classroom, 5, 136, 234, 235, 236, 271, 289, 293, 298, 311, 314, 332
clients, 72, 94, 102, 108, 109, 110, 112, 144, 172, 209, 210, 212, 213, 217, 219, 223, 224, 230, 231, 232, 233, 235, 236, 237, 238, 239, 240, 241, 242, 243, 244, 247, 250, 251, 277, 282, 323, 324, 325, 361, 365, 368, 370
climate(s), 283, 287, 288, 302, 350, 353
clinical assessment, 352
clinical interventions, 162
clinical judgment, 267
clinical problems, 268
clinical psychology, 184, 204, 219, 220, 221, 224, 225, 258, 347, 348, 355, 391
clinical trials, 4, 43, 51, 60, 61, 269
coaches, 10
codes, 359
codes of conduct, 359
coffee, 4, 211
cognition, 83
cognitive development, 290
cognitive dissonance, 58
cognitive psychology, 347, 348
coherence, 267, 315
collaboration, 16, 56, 141, 150, 195, 222, 280, 329, 330, 332, 341
college students, 179
colleges, 144, 291, 321
commercial, 17, 144, 145

communication, 7, 8, 82, 176, 189, 212, 329, 334, 339, 351, 356, 367, 384
community(s), 6, 7, 9, 37, 51, 68, 82, 146, 147, 148, 158, 179, 213, 216, 222, 225, 287, 292, 299, 320, 323, 324, 329, 330, 332, 338, 359, 372
community psychology, 225
compassion, 237, 251, 260, 281
competing interests, 273
competition, 175, 208, 335
compilation, 280
complement, xii
complex behaviors, 329
complexity, 31, 75, 82, 83, 139, 232
compliance, 58, 105, 106, 111, 145, 168, 173, 177, 183, 322, 325, 360, 362, 366
complications, 19, 221
composition, 57, 158, 385
comprehension, 317
computer, 40, 41, 43, 44, 60, 61, 63, 64, 92, 186, 296, 328, 339
computer skills, 44
conceptual model, 253
conceptualization, xii, 31, 56, 85, 208, 250, 382
concordance, 57, 337
conference, 16, 17, 143, 179, 206, 274, 310, 334, 379
confidentiality, 34, 57, 107, 112, 176, 211, 221, 222, 373
configuration, 346
conflict, 144, 145, 251
conflict of interest, 144, 145
conformity, 186, 312
confrontation, 241, 244
Congress, 178
congruence, 106
conscious awareness, 204
consensus, 168, 176, 185, 268, 269, 270, 274, 312, 384, 387, 388
consent, 107, 109, 112, 385
construct validity, 30, 31, 32, 42, 297, 325
construction, 298, 378
consulting, 6, 192, 244, 255, 258, 348, 358, 390, 392
consumer protection, 136, 137, 355
consumers, ix, 16, 18, 140, 142, 143, 146, 150, 162, 171, 177, 178, 350, 361, 364
consumption, 305
content analysis, 42, 340
continuing education (CE), 3, 5, 8, 19, 84, 161, 191, 204, 322, 359, 368, 377, 378
continuing professional development (CPD), 3, 332, 368, 369
contradiction, 312
controlled research, 382
controlled studies, 252, 365, 381
controlled trials, 274, 335
controversial, 283
controversies, xi, xii, 184
convention, 385
convergence, 387
conversations, xi, 9, 211, 281, 359
conviction, 217
cooperation, 8, 34, 62
coordination, 270, 332
coping strategies, 216
copper, 286
Copyright, 46, 49, 51
correlation coefficient, 47
correlational analysis, 47
correlation(s), 30, 33, 37, 38, 44, 45, 46, 47, 49, 50, 51, 57, 58, 86, 89, 157, 194, 198, 253, 254, 259, 286
cost, 5, 6, 18, 21, 22, 141, 170, 173, 185, 188, 192, 221, 283, 332, 337, 340, 365, 388
counsel, 328
counseling, 77, 95, 146, 163, 179, 197, 216, 221, 222, 223, 225, 226, 230, 231, 232, 233, 234, 235, 236, 238, 241, 242, 243, 244, 246, 257, 259, 260, 320, 328, 347, 363, 384, 391, 392, 393
counseling psychology, 77, 95, 179, 197, 222, 225, 245, 257, 347, 391, 393
course content, 271
creativity, 31, 72, 105, 113, 285, 289, 298, 315
credentials, 279, 350, 366
critical thinking, 250, 279, 292
criticism, 298
cues, 289
cultivation, 390
culture, 76, 82, 89, 96, 97, 194, 214, 255, 272, 288, 292, 339, 351, 369, 373
cure, 219, 238
currency, 112, 192, 360, 362, 384
curricula, 3, 4, 5, 7, 8, 11, 220, 270, 271, 272, 334, 351, 378
curriculum, 3, 7, 9, 10, 11, 19, 53, 57, 73, 152, 223, 224, 233, 265, 270, 271, 272, 303, 309, 310, 318, 321, 331, 332, 334, 340, 361
customers, 362
cycles, 10, 112, 168

D

danger, 240
data collection, 18, 34
database, 12, 34, 35, 43, 44, 58, 61, 64, 235, 240
death rate, 305
declarative knowledge, 326
deficiency(s), 103, 106, 110, 175, 309, 372

deficit, 277
Delta, 246
demand characteristic, 88
dementia, 96, 197
democracy, 299, 303, 313
demonstrations, 139, 176, 182
Denmark, 153
Department of Education, 310, 311
Department of Health and Human Services, 331
Department of Labor, 22, 27
dependent variable, 52, 196
depression, 96, 198, 214, 250, 251, 324, 325, 330, 334
depth, 18, 173, 216, 346, 349, 384
designers, 281
despair, 230, 235, 238, 244
destiny, 289
destruction, 307
detachment, 242
developmental process, 296, 346
deviation, 387
diet, 251
diminishing returns, 215
direct mail, 328
directors, 49, 50, 216
disability, 22, 96, 109, 187, 198, 321, 339
disappointment, 207
disaster, 305
disclosure, 107, 109, 138, 145
discomfort, 211
diseases, 324
disorder, 95, 149, 197, 258, 259, 328, 391
dissatisfaction, 259
dissonance, 66
distance learning, 31, 186, 380
distortions, 242
distress, 179, 206, 210, 212, 217, 218, 219, 223, 224, 236, 258, 259, 302, 381
distribution, 38, 57, 69, 85, 156, 195, 281
District of Columbia, 163, 164, 166, 184, 192, 320
diversification, 212
diversity, 9, 108, 164, 165, 173, 175, 176, 178, 208, 224, 225, 280, 293, 298
doctors, 153, 162, 273, 282, 338
domestic violence, 164, 174, 329
dominance, 301
draft, 152, 177, 188, 366, 368, 374
drawing, xii, 233, 250, 281, 287
dream, 275
drugs, 251, 295
due process, 18

E

early warning, 210
ecology, 310
economic status, 312
economic well-being, 305
economics, 392
editors, 284
educational institutions, 16
educational materials, 336
educational objective, 17, 103, 310
educational practices, 379, 389
educational process, 281, 288, 297, 302
educational programs, 30, 41, 51, 52, 59, 60, 271, 298
educational research, 334, 337
educational system, xii, 294, 300, 301, 302, 303, 304, 305, 306, 307, 308, 309
educators, 24, 67, 74, 97, 153, 225, 247, 290, 318, 326, 352, 357, 367, 371, 372
elaboration, 268, 271
e-mail, 41, 91, 103, 105, 304, 360
emergency, 25, 52, 329
emotion, 208, 220, 230, 241
emotion regulation, 208
emotional bias, 88
emotional distress, 172, 218
emotional exhaustion, 214, 251, 252
emotional reactions, 211
emotional well-being, 251
empathy, 233, 242, 251, 356
empirical studies, 249
employees, 256, 280, 320
employers, 7, 23, 72, 279, 283, 297, 302, 307, 309, 333
employment, 172, 320
empowerment, 31, 361
endorsements, 321
energy, 209, 212, 304
enforcement, 168
engineering, 270
England, 310, 311, 313, 315
enhanced service, 197
enrollment, 206, 308
entrepreneurs, 312
environment, 4, 6, 8, 10, 13, 16, 22, 23, 25, 232, 286, 287, 288, 289, 292, 293, 319, 325, 353, 361, 366, 368, 370, 371, 384
environmental impact, 312
environmental standards, 287
environmental variables, 286
environments, 8, 31, 72, 282, 291, 350, 361, 381
epistemology, 95, 197, 235, 244, 258, 314, 391

equipment, 109, 144, 145
ERA, 65
essay question, 320
ethical issues, 84, 135, 169, 179, 209, 224, 349, 364
ethics, 82, 96, 97, 101, 109, 133, 139, 152, 155, 157, 158, 163, 164, 173, 174, 180, 185, 188, 189, 193, 197, 198, 199, 203, 204, 205, 206, 207, 208, 211, 212, 214, 217, 223, 224, 261, 271, 292, 313, 335, 354, 361, 370, 374
ethnic groups, 38
ethnic minority, 324, 325, 334
ethnicity, 38, 39, 195
EU, 283
Europe, 338
evidence-based practices, 140, 323, 389
evil, 229, 241, 307
evolution, 20, 299, 308, 350, 360, 368
examinations, 27, 35, 36, 38, 39, 47, 49, 66, 137, 139, 147, 148, 279, 303, 348, 356
execution, 139
exercise, 23, 73, 74, 75, 104, 206, 207, 251, 283
expenditures, 283
expertise, 25, 72, 139, 185, 213, 229, 234, 236, 243, 245, 246, 288, 308, 320, 322, 350, 352, 353, 362, 385
exposure, 8, 84, 96, 197, 236, 243, 269, 292
external constraints, 280
external validity, 57
extraction, 42
extrinsic motivation, 44, 45

F

face validity, 42, 56, 168, 171
factor analysis, 30, 32, 37, 40, 42, 67, 326, 334, 336, 337, 339
faculty development, 330
fairness, 23
faith, 226, 325
families, 331, 356
family conflict, 252, 260
family members, 106, 238
family physician, 68
family support, 252
family therapy, 163
family violence, 353
fantasy, 311, 312, 315
fat, 266
fear, 6, 15, 241, 294
federal government, 14, 22, 59, 108, 333
feelings, 223, 230, 251, 294, 319
ferret, 5
fidelity, 380

financial, 18, 21, 22, 139, 172, 173, 178, 183, 186, 219, 251, 270, 291, 333, 368
financial resources, 219
firewalls, 145
first dimension, 82
fish, 287
fitness, 96, 198
flaws, 17, 24, 332
flexibility, 112, 144, 184, 187, 192, 210, 217, 367, 371
flight, 226
flowers, 146
fluid, 280, 286
focus groups, 323
food, ix, 215, 304, 305, 360
food production, 305
force, 13, 14, 24, 25, 96, 169, 180, 184, 197, 240, 241, 244, 304, 310, 335
forecasting, 384
foreign language, 291
forensic psychology, 347, 348, 356, 357
formal education, 135
formula, 39
foundations, 16, 143, 330, 346
framing, 216, 378
free will, 187
freedom, 74, 113, 175, 184, 241, 310
Freud, 229, 238
funding, 332, 333, 362, 373
funds, 18, 175, 226
fusion, 234

G

gambling, 382
general education, 345, 346, 347
general surgery, 57
generalizability, 385
geography, 188
George Kelly, xiii
Georgia, 13, 151, 164, 265, 273
GNP, 283
goods and services, 300
governance, 26
governments, 14, 21, 22, 136, 162, 273, 283
governor, 14
GPA, 36
grades, 36, 39, 47, 67, 280
grading, 10, 67
graduate education, 71, 147, 359
graduate program, 75, 218, 220, 222, 223
graduate students, 89, 204, 214, 217, 218, 219, 220, 221, 222, 223, 225, 233, 238

grants, 50, 145, 354
grass, 297
gravitational force, 304
group processes, 288
growth, 6, 9, 12, 56, 82, 89, 175, 231, 236, 237, 241, 251, 257, 273, 285, 290, 312, 320, 336, 346, 351, 377, 378
guidance, 23, 176, 300, 304, 305, 306, 325
guidelines, 4, 8, 25, 46, 76, 103, 108, 133, 137, 142, 149, 150, 152, 163, 177, 178, 181, 184, 321, 322, 324, 328, 347, 348, 351, 362, 368, 374
guiding principles, 18, 235
guilt, 216

H

habitat, 307
half-life, xiii, 75, 168, 279, 352, 377, 383, 384, 386, 388, 390
happiness, 215
harassment, 241
harmony, 243
Hawaii, 164
hazards, 244
healing, 238, 241
health care costs, 22
health care professionals, 15, 20, 22, 137, 138, 139, 141, 149, 328, 329
health care system, ix, 13, 16, 24, 25, 66, 141, 268, 325
health education, 180
health information, 109, 140, 332
health psychology, 347, 348, 353, 354
health services, 66, 165, 350
health status, 141, 323, 324
heart attack, 367
high school, 35, 53
higher education, 291, 310, 313, 356
Hispanics, 38
history, xiii, 13, 14, 140, 161, 183, 207, 260, 291, 331, 354, 360, 361
HIV, 367
homes, 278, 286, 350
host, 8, 240, 302
House, 30, 306, 311, 314
human, 18, 21, 22, 26, 27, 31, 225, 229, 230, 231, 232, 234, 235, 236, 237, 238, 239, 240, 241, 242, 243, 244, 270, 278, 279, 286, 295, 300, 304, 307, 308, 310, 312, 319, 334
human behavior, 319
human condition, 230, 234, 237, 239, 242
human development, 278
human existence, 231, 244

human experience, 237
human resources, 278, 295
Hungary, 313
Hunter, 284, 297, 314
hybrid, 380
hypertension, 275

I

ID, 226
ideal, 319
ideals, 311, 319
identification, 19, 216, 280, 285, 313, 378, 379, 385
identity, 57, 73, 82, 85, 86, 88, 89, 179, 230, 235, 243
idiosyncratic, 279, 285, 288, 290, 293, 297
image(s), 192, 252, 290, 297, 300, 306, 309, 380
immersion, 5
immigration, 331
improvements, 16, 140, 173, 186, 324, 329, 332, 351
impulses, 237
in transition, 274
incidence, 19, 324
income, 21, 22, 109, 173, 186, 215
independent variable, 52, 196
individual character, 25, 287
individual characteristics, 25
individual differences, 284, 287
individual students, 293
induction, 267, 270, 271
industrial organization, 348
industrialization, 305, 331
industry(s), 68, 96, 144, 145, 175, 198, 283, 320
infancy, 267, 380
information retrieval, 71, 75
information seeking, 30, 31, 32, 33, 40, 42, 44, 83
information technology, 17, 24
infrastructure, 25, 333
initiation, 147
injury, 23, 96, 197
innocence, 246
inspectors, 311
institutions, 19, 22, 57, 96, 144, 148, 163, 188, 197, 277, 291, 293, 297, 307, 308, 309, 312, 314, 315, 319, 320, 330
instructional design, 324
instructional methods, 78, 322, 351, 380
integration, 93, 235, 330, 334, 391
integrity, xii, 20, 82, 89, 112, 192, 340
intelligence, 282, 286, 287, 288, 305, 313
interaction effect(s), 52
interdependence, 250
interface, xii, 205, 206, 208, 350

internal consistency, 32, 46
internship, 77, 82, 83, 147, 187, 204, 216, 220, 224, 226, 240, 320
interpersonal communication, 94, 271
interpersonal relations, 82, 94, 250, 257
interpersonal relationships, 82, 94, 257
interpersonal skills, 85, 86, 88, 233, 256
interpretability, 88
interrelatedness, 208
intervention, 144, 219, 223, 239, 257, 281, 295, 305, 327, 328
intrinsic motivation, 44, 226
investment, 18, 19, 21, 24, 86, 305, 352, 353
Iowa, 164, 250
Ireland, 310, 314
irony, 307
IRT, 313
isolation, 143, 186, 230, 251

J

job dissatisfaction, 253
job performance, 314
jumping, 218
jurisdiction, 18, 137, 184, 196, 364

K

knowledge acquisition, 19, 186, 377
Korea, 77

L

landscape, xi, 240, 242, 272, 340, 360, 366, 379, 391
laws, 107, 137, 308, 320
laws and regulations, 137
lawyers, 18, 281, 282
lead, 35, 58, 88, 111, 138, 141, 149, 171, 172, 173, 174, 175, 176, 177, 185, 186, 204, 212, 215, 251, 269, 284, 287, 288, 289, 290, 294, 298, 305, 306, 309, 329, 346, 364, 365, 370, 371
leadership, 14, 15, 16, 312, 314, 363, 368
learners, 12, 19, 30, 32, 44, 68, 71, 73, 86, 88, 214, 269, 272, 326, 330, 331, 368, 372, 374
learning activity, 149
learning attitudes, xi, 74, 194, 196
learning behavior, 58
learning environment, 312, 368, 370, 372
learning outcomes, 8, 171, 172, 175, 176, 177, 178, 380
learning process, 136, 271, 331, 332, 349
learning skills, 11, 31, 41, 60, 63, 64, 77

learning society, 300, 310, 312, 313, 314, 315
learning styles, 25, 113, 178
legal issues, 82, 163, 204, 205, 206
legislation, 15, 23, 108, 111, 112, 137, 162, 163, 183, 184, 187, 188, 195, 340
legs, 246, 250, 260, 393
leisure, 310
lending, 193, 194
lens, xii, 230, 379
liability insurance, 109
Liaison Committee on Medical Education (LCME), 30, 68
life cycle, 111
life experiences, 233, 251
life satisfaction, 226, 249, 250, 251, 253, 254, 255, 256, 260
lifetime, 31, 72, 221, 270
light, 22, 57, 141, 241, 267, 287, 382
Likert scale, 85, 86
local government, 283
locus, 271, 349
longevity, 260
longitudinal study, 59, 67, 310
Louisiana, 164, 166
love, 7, 10, 31, 231, 241, 244

M

magazines, 360
magnitude, 38, 39, 41, 43, 45, 46, 47, 51
majority, 3, 5, 57, 85, 105, 112, 137, 163, 169, 171, 173, 174, 176, 184, 185, 252, 253, 279, 291, 306, 307, 332, 349
malnutrition, 281
man, 284, 299
management, 18, 25, 206, 207, 222, 258, 270, 275, 278, 284, 291, 300, 302, 306, 307, 309, 310, 312, 322, 327, 329, 363, 367, 369, 392
mandatory continuing education, 13, 14, 17, 18, 20, 21, 22, 23, 25, 96, 161, 180, 181, 189, 197, 198, 260, 359, 361, 393
MANOVA, 196
mapping, 300, 304, 305, 309, 314, 380
marketing, 291, 331
marketing initiatives, 331
marriage, 163, 211
Maryland, 137, 162, 164, 170, 179, 180, 189, 194, 198, 204, 224, 317, 334, 336
mass, 346
material resources, 18, 21, 22
materials, 26, 107, 144, 328
matter, 72, 97, 189, 192, 193, 197, 198, 210, 211, 217, 226, 234, 260, 284

McGillicuddy, 289, 312, 315
measurement, 56, 58, 65, 67, 141, 198, 259, 284, 288, 295, 313, 327, 332, 334, 339, 379, 380, 386, 389
media, 50, 151, 269, 327, 329, 380
median, 33, 46
mediation, 89
Medicaid, 332, 355
medical care, 30, 33, 140, 273
medical expertise, 362
medical science, 40, 41, 60, 63, 64, 67, 364
Medicare, 26, 354, 355, 357
membership, 85, 137, 155, 156, 157, 184, 188, 189, 195, 218, 222, 226, 253, 258, 385
memory, 88, 345
mental ability, 312
mental disorder, 164, 340
mental health, 133, 137, 148, 163, 186, 203, 205, 209, 213, 221, 226, 246, 250, 320, 321, 323, 324, 325, 353, 357
mental health professionals, 186
mental illness, 204, 219, 224
mental processes, 319
mentor, 349, 352
mentoring, 95, 143, 197, 257, 352, 391
messages, 91, 205, 290
meta-analysis, 19, 269, 275, 281, 295, 338, 356, 379, 382
methodology, 19, 103, 111, 136, 141, 280, 284, 291, 299, 369
Mexico, 15, 163, 165, 166
Microsoft, 34
military, 187, 334
Minneapolis, 3, 229
minorities, 324, 325
misconceptions, 7
mission, 16, 90, 145, 235, 279, 292, 389
Missouri, 164
misunderstanding, 212
misuse, 286
modelling, 286, 295
models, 8, 11, 35, 47, 66, 69, 89, 142, 146, 176, 217, 222, 259, 271, 274, 278, 285, 292, 293, 294, 300, 304, 318, 327, 333, 360, 363, 366, 368, 371, 372, 373, 380
modern society, 313
modifications, 34, 56, 96, 198
monopoly, 335
Montana, 165
mood disorder, 353
mortality, 19, 24, 26, 305
motivation, 11, 20, 30, 31, 32, 33, 40, 42, 43, 44, 61, 83, 85, 168, 172, 178

multidimensional, 31
multimedia, 269
multiple regression, 36, 37, 47, 286
multiple regression analyses, 47
multiple regression analysis, 36
multivariate analysis, 196

N

narratives, 204
National Council of State Boards of Nursing (NCSBN), 14
National Institutes of Health, 333
natural resources, 305
negative consequences, 266, 297
negative effects, 251, 298
neglect, 170, 216, 279, 283, 291, 298, 308
negotiating, 273, 335
negotiation, 273, 330
Netherlands, 66, 68, 338
networking, 173
neuropsychology, 96, 188, 197, 347, 348, 349, 354, 356
neuroscience, 360
neutral, 58, 330, 381
New England, 68, 338, 339
New Zealand, 152
next generation, 334, 393
Nietzsche, 238
North America, 68
Northern Ireland, 310
nurses, 13, 14, 15, 16, 17, 18, 19, 20, 21, 22, 23, 24, 25, 26, 27, 282, 330
nursing, xi, 13, 14, 15, 16, 17, 18, 19, 20, 21, 22, 23, 24, 25, 26, 27, 96, 188, 197, 270, 274, 371
nursing care, 26
nursing home, 96, 188, 197, 270
nutrients, 297

O

objective criteria, 318
objectivity, 240, 243
obstacles, 139, 218, 231, 357
Oklahoma, 165, 167
one dimension, 345, 346
openness, 75, 82, 89, 241, 243
operations, 318
opportunities, 3, 6, 7, 8, 9, 11, 17, 19, 25, 30, 32, 40, 42, 44, 71, 76, 79, 85, 111, 113, 169, 174, 186, 188, 256, 280, 284, 286, 290, 291, 308, 319, 320,

322, 331, 332, 333, 351, 361, 368, 371, 372, 373, 374
optimal performance, 370
optimism, 215
organizational behavior, 334
organizational culture, 19
organize, 268, 330, 351
orthopedic surgeon, 157
outpatient, 331
outreach, 328, 339, 385
overlap, 56, 295, 347
overlay, 361
oversight, 16, 22, 138, 330, 333, 349
overweight, 251
ownership, 310
oxygen, 286

P

Pacific, 312
pain, 206, 211, 229, 230, 231, 234, 235, 236, 240, 241, 242, 244
paints, 389
pairing, 138
paradigm shift, 306, 309
parallel, 77, 150, 204, 280, 302, 303, 309
parenthood, 232
parenting, 292
parents, 278, 279, 280, 282, 283, 287, 288, 289, 290, 291, 295, 297, 298, 299, 302, 303, 307, 309, 312, 315
parity, 350, 357
pass/fail, 10
pathology, 38, 52, 57, 240
pathophysiology, 18
pathways, 339
patient care, 4, 6, 7, 16, 18, 25, 32, 34, 37, 40, 41, 56, 58, 59, 60, 63, 67, 197, 266, 269, 271, 320, 329, 348, 352
patient safety, 13, 14, 18, 22, 25, 332, 333, 334
pedagogy, 337
peer assessment, 323
peer review, 7, 37, 57, 102, 138, 139, 141, 177, 181, 293
perceived outcome, 86, 97, 181, 189, 198, 259, 338, 357, 375, 393
percentile, 46
perception of conflict, 145
performance appraisal, 340
performance ratings, 327, 340
permission, 37, 155
permit, 108, 186, 257, 295
personal benefit, 11, 244

personal communication, 21, 186, 216, 237, 385
personal contact, 174
personal development, 293, 295, 297, 345, 346
personal hygiene, 251
personal learning, 17, 101
personal life, 12, 207, 220, 229, 235, 241, 244, 245, 246, 249, 250, 253, 260, 393
personal problems, 209, 214, 226, 259
personal qualities, 233, 256, 257, 298, 368
personal responsibility, 331, 370
personality, 32, 69, 219, 237, 250, 286, 312
personality characteristics, 32
personality traits, 250
personhood, 237
persuasion, 384
pharmaceutical(s), 144, 329, 362
Philadelphia, 29, 62, 65, 66, 68
physical abuse, 260
physical health, 169, 215
physics, 285, 291, 304, 309, 310
pilot study, 31, 34
planets, 304
plants, 287, 297
Plato, 238
playing, 300
poetry, 287
police, 347
policy, 8, 9, 64, 68, 82, 93, 94, 145, 179, 266, 269, 297, 310, 318, 335, 336, 347, 374, 385
policy issues, 179
policy makers, 318
political system, 283
politics, 273, 336
polling, 173, 384, 385, 387
pollution, 287, 305
poor performance, 317, 319, 327
population, 31, 65, 108, 141, 156, 157, 173, 213, 219, 305
portability, 177
portfolio, 9, 345, 346
positive correlation, 48
positive relationship, 255
post-traumatic stress disorder, 96, 198
poverty, 215
predictive validity, 36, 58, 67, 297
preparation, 3, 5, 6, 25, 68, 71, 72, 74, 77, 166, 169, 204, 206, 214, 349, 352, 361
preparedness, 82
president, 15, 26, 96, 151, 155, 179, 197, 258, 353, 374, 391, 392
prevention, 247, 260, 329, 364

principles, 27, 78, 96, 104, 141, 143, 148, 149, 151, 178, 180, 203, 207, 208, 215, 216, 224, 319, 322, 330, 335, 374
private practice, 96, 110, 148, 151, 170, 172, 188, 197, 210, 211, 237, 349
private sector, 333
problem solving, 214, 334, 366
problem-based learning, 59, 186, 269, 380
problem-solving, 74, 279
procedural knowledge, 143, 325
professional careers, xi, 150
professional duties, 210, 218, 371
professional educators, 8
professional growth, 111, 185, 246, 322, 351, 353
professional literature, 76
professional practice of nursing, 14, 18
professionalism, 30, 37, 49, 68, 69, 82, 112, 259, 271, 283, 285, 289, 297, 326, 337, 340, 351, 362
professionalization, 319
profit, 11, 26, 74, 144, 145, 348, 362
programming, 5, 6, 96, 174, 175, 197, 216, 385
project, 25, 181, 206, 268, 287, 290, 292, 324
proliferation, 214, 282
promote innovation, 303
prosperity, 314
protection, ix, xi, xiii, 18, 102, 192, 317, 364, 386
prototype, 67
psychiatrist, 140
psychiatry, 36, 52, 57, 140, 151, 163
psychoanalysis, 238, 321, 331, 347
psychological association, 143, 144, 155, 162, 163, 170, 172, 173, 179, 180, 188, 217, 222, 321
psychological distress, 214
psychological phenomena, 238
psychological processes, 315
psychological stress, 223
psychological tools, 145
psychometric properties, 32, 37, 176
psychosis, 224
psychotherapy, 76, 78, 79, 95, 97, 151, 197, 204, 213, 221, 222, 223, 224, 230, 231, 232, 233, 234, 235, 236, 238, 240, 241, 242, 243, 244, 245, 246, 247, 251, 258, 259, 295, 296, 331, 335, 336, 357, 375, 384, 389, 391, 393
public concern, 331
public health, 338
public interest, 299, 303
public policy, 138
public safety, 347
public sector, 314
public service, 22
publishing, 37, 86, 88, 163
Puerto Rico, 162, 165

Q

qualifications, 20, 110, 146, 147, 163, 302, 318
quality assurance, 103, 133, 145, 150, 192, 350
quality control, 8, 178, 282, 293
quality improvement, 17, 25, 26, 153, 268, 271, 332, 350
quality of life, 302, 305, 307, 336
quality of service, 102, 185, 368
quality standards, 21
quantification, 237
questioning, 186, 302, 367
questionnaire, 62, 66, 143, 178, 207, 220, 225, 384

R

racial minorities, 325, 330
radar, 223
radio, 37, 51, 304
radius, 213
rate of change, 383
rating scale, 195, 254, 388
reactions, 207, 212, 301, 303
reading, 41, 59, 62, 64, 90, 144, 170, 174, 192, 236, 238, 251, 255, 287, 290, 291, 311, 315, 360, 390
reality, 68, 210, 224, 232, 275, 279, 280, 284, 299, 311
reasoning, 82, 146, 366, 368
recall, 323
recession, 216
reciprocity, 14
recognition, 7, 8, 11, 32, 60, 75, 88, 148, 210, 279, 284, 303, 308, 315, 319, 321, 347, 348, 350, 351, 354, 368, 373
recommendations, 3, 5, 17, 78, 135, 137, 139, 140, 141, 142, 163, 176, 177, 187, 203, 221, 224, 305, 328, 340, 367, 369
reconstruction, 88
recovery, 218, 250, 251
reflective practice, 78, 82, 235
reflex action, 367
reform(s), 17, 25, 30, 66, 108, 138, 178, 271, 275, 282, 304, 314, 345, 346, 356, 357, 360, 393
regression, 38, 47, 49, 50, 51
regulations, 14, 102, 107, 112, 145, 183, 184, 196, 278, 282, 283, 368
regulatory agencies, 18, 23, 135, 137, 139, 142, 187
regulatory bodies, 7, 102, 141, 144, 146, 322, 330, 362, 369, 372, 378
rehabilitation, 216, 321, 347, 348, 355
relaxation, 251
relevance, 47, 108, 173, 205, 209, 281, 286, 293

reliability, 30, 32, 35, 36, 46, 56, 58, 325, 326, 327, 339, 372
relief, xiii, 72
religion, 306
remediation, 103, 138
repair, 240
replication, 89, 326
representativeness, 38
researchers, 8, 56, 88, 169, 173, 193, 194, 237, 238, 251, 280, 295, 298, 326, 333, 378, 379
resilience, 230, 236, 242, 260
resistance, xii, 372
resolution, 211, 278
resource management, 18
resources, 4, 5, 8, 16, 21, 22, 24, 73, 96, 139, 141, 178, 204, 214, 225, 226, 270, 271, 280, 304, 305, 314, 331, 332, 335, 352, 370, 374, 380
response, 8, 17, 20, 32, 33, 34, 35, 38, 44, 45, 56, 57, 75, 85, 88, 105, 106, 112, 195, 207, 269, 282, 291, 292, 295, 296, 298, 326, 352, 384
responsiveness, 295
restrictions, 173, 333
restructuring, 368
retention rate, 19
retirement, 29, 268, 321
revenue, 18, 21, 362
rewards, 8, 319
rhetoric, 72, 311
rights, 18, 64
risk, 25, 96, 155, 157, 164, 185, 198, 206, 207, 210, 211, 213, 214, 219, 224, 251
risk assessment, 96, 198
risk management, 164, 185, 207, 214
risks, 155, 157, 213, 292
Romania, 313
root(s), 208, 278, 327
rotations, 9
Royal Society, 292
rubrics, 10
rules, 84, 184, 187, 213, 368

S

sadness, 230
safety, 4, 13, 14, 15, 16, 18, 22, 25, 141, 218, 266, 273, 281, 283, 332, 333, 334
sanctions, 145
SAS, 144, 145
savings, 354, 355
scaling, 187
schizophrenia, 224
scholarship, 77, 205, 236, 331, 332
Scholastic Aptitude Test, 35

school performance, 53
school psychology, 320, 347, 348, 355, 363
school success, 281, 290
schooling, 281, 290, 291, 292, 313
science, 17, 35, 37, 46, 68, 72, 82, 89, 93, 136, 142, 146, 163, 233, 235, 239, 246, 249, 279, 296, 297, 305, 306, 308, 312, 313, 318, 319, 321, 361, 363
scientific knowledge, 30, 82, 93, 147
scientific method, 237, 240, 319
scope, 14, 18, 23, 138, 175, 187, 212, 216, 227, 261, 305, 368
secondary schools, 320
security, 251
self-assessment, xii, 24, 69, 82, 85, 86, 88, 138, 140, 141, 157, 175, 176, 180, 203, 206, 207, 212, 218, 285, 351, 352, 370, 372, 375
self-awareness, 71, 76, 82, 234, 256, 257
self-confidence, 251, 292
self-efficacy, xii, 86, 87, 88, 249, 253, 254, 255, 257, 259
self-employed, 320
self-esteem, 19
self-evaluations, 172
self-improvement, 102
self-interest, 193
self-knowledge, 231
self-monitoring, 187
self-organization, 318
self-reflection, 18, 75, 76, 139, 218, 351
self-report data, 174
self-reports, 169, 323, 324
self-study, 76, 166, 213, 348, 351
seminars, 223
sensitivity, 176
service provider, 333
services, ix, 25, 59, 101, 102, 109, 110, 136, 137, 138, 142, 144, 146, 148, 150, 162, 168, 171, 185, 186, 212, 217, 220, 221, 249, 252, 291, 318, 319, 320, 321, 323, 328, 330, 331, 332, 345, 346, 348, 349, 363, 364, 381
sex, 109, 300
sexual contact, 156
sexual violence, 179
shame, 230
shape, xiii, 23, 217, 296, 363, 385
shortage, 53, 286
showing, 52, 269, 305, 353
signs, 210, 366
simulation(s), 19, 269, 334, 380, 388
Sinai, 68
Singapore, 245
single-loop learning, 366
skill acquisition, 172

skill competencies, 254
skills training, 393
social activities, 298
social behavior, 334
social care, 328, 329
social change, 270
social cognition, 224
social consequences, 289
social context, 315, 330
social contract, 331
social desirability, 33, 44, 45, 57, 58, 172, 174
social development, 226
social network, 382
social order, 302
social policy, 311, 314
social relations, 222
social relationships, 222
social sciences, 273, 291
social security, 34
social skills, 157
social support, 219, 222, 223
social workers, 282
society, 37, 51, 277, 279, 283, 287, 296, 297, 299, 300, 302, 303, 304, 306, 307, 308, 309, 310, 311, 312, 313, 315, 317, 319, 321, 331, 352
Socrates, 238
software, 24
solution, 56, 93, 177, 231, 281, 293, 305, 313
South Dakota, 165
specialists, 346, 347, 348, 350, 351, 352, 357
specialization, xiii, 83, 96, 148, 188, 197, 317, 319, 345, 346, 350, 351, 377, 379, 383, 384, 386, 388, 390, 391
species, 288, 307, 308
speculation, 194
spending, 40, 172, 186
Spring, 13
stability, 35, 46, 310
staff development, 294
staffing, 139
stakeholder groups, 271
stakeholders, 15, 16, 17, 23, 146, 147, 272, 273, 274, 331, 332, 333, 370
standard deviation, 33, 38, 39, 45, 52, 53, 56, 387, 388
standardization, 18, 25, 329
statistics, 45, 58
statutes, 101, 102, 107, 108, 112, 168
stigma, 221
strategic planning, 8, 26
stratification, 312

stress, 206, 207, 210, 213, 218, 219, 220, 222, 223, 224, 225, 226, 249, 250, 251, 252, 253, 254, 255, 256, 257, 258, 259, 352
stressful life events, 218
stressors, 207, 210, 216, 217, 218, 219, 223, 225, 250, 251
stretching, 332
structure, 7, 14, 41, 68, 69, 171, 175, 177, 206, 207, 212, 267, 271, 280, 290, 306, 326, 333, 345, 346, 347, 351, 370
structuring, 351, 370
style, 19, 20, 33, 44, 45, 101, 103, 111, 204, 225, 236, 379
subjective well-being, 254
substance abuse, 212, 250, 334
suicide, 241, 353
sulphur, 286
supervision, 75, 76, 77, 78, 109, 110, 112, 133, 143, 149, 163, 164, 165, 168, 172, 174, 204, 205, 240, 258, 303, 392
supervisor(s), 3, 4, 5, 6, 7, 25, 66, 75, 76, 168, 204, 217, 218, 220, 222
survey design, 254
survival, 336
Sweden, 310
symbiosis, 286
sympathy, 240
symptoms, 6, 219, 260, 304
synthesis, 269, 311

T

tactics, 17, 22
target, xii, 169, 324, 327
Task Force, 12, 78, 96, 137, 138, 141, 142, 147, 150, 151, 176, 177, 181, 188, 197, 310, 326
teachers, 18, 68, 247, 278, 279, 280, 281, 282, 283, 287, 288, 289, 290, 291, 294, 295, 297, 298, 302, 303, 304, 307, 309, 311, 313, 314, 315
teaching strategies, 312, 315
teams, 17, 25, 143, 268, 329, 333, 350, 366
techniques, 6, 78, 88, 145, 178, 187, 212, 215, 234, 286, 296, 327, 329, 332, 334, 361, 365, 380, 382, 388
technological advances, 149
technology(s), 16, 30, 75, 136, 140, 173, 176, 212, 275, 305, 332, 351, 380, 382, 384, 388, 391, 393
telephone, 109, 213, 360
telephone numbers, 109
temperature, 306
tension(s), 58, 212, 229, 232, 235, 357
tenure, 77
territory, 230, 243

test scores, 46, 295, 298
testing, 46, 56, 57, 65, 284, 298, 325, 326, 335, 337
test-retest reliability, 46, 56
textbooks, 64, 353
theatre, 334, 336
therapeutic approaches, 6
therapeutic change, 234
therapeutic relationship, 238, 241, 242, 251
therapist, 173, 203, 219, 222, 226, 230, 231, 233, 234, 235, 239, 240, 242, 245, 246, 247, 250, 251, 254, 255, 257
therapy, 207, 211, 221, 222, 230, 231, 232, 233, 235, 239, 240, 242, 243, 244, 245, 246, 247, 251, 260
third dimension, 82
Third World, 302
thoughts, 294, 345
threats, 216
threshold level, 72
time constraints, 219
time frame, 144, 184, 386
Title V, 354
traditions, 363
trainees, 78, 146, 220, 222, 223, 225, 247
training programs, xi, 7, 71, 74, 75, 76, 77, 146, 150, 176, 220, 221, 223, 226, 320, 327, 347, 363, 383
traits, 219, 250
trajectory, 218, 307, 378, 379
transformation(s), 272, 286, 296, 304, 339
ttranslation, 84, 88, 324, 330, 373, 375, 381
transmission, 312
trauma, 210, 230, 251, 259, 260
traumatic experiences, 251
treatment, 18, 75, 107, 112, 142, 149, 150, 164, 172, 212, 213, 219, 224, 225, 230, 231, 232, 233, 234, 238, 239, 240, 247, 250, 259, 260, 261, 324, 331, 334, 352, 362, 382
treatment methods, 334
turbulence, 288
Turkey, 245
turnover, 24
twist, 293

U

U.S. Bureau of Labor Statistics, 349, 358
UK, 69, 152, 283, 310, 314, 336, 338
undergraduate education, 90
unhappiness, 215
uniform, 146, 150, 161, 178, 367
unique features, 31
United, xii, 14, 20, 22, 23, 27, 36, 57, 133, 136, 152, 161, 193, 216, 267, 271, 272, 273, 274, 275, 318, 319, 324, 331, 334, 340, 341, 349

United States, xii, 14, 20, 22, 23, 27, 36, 57, 133, 136, 152, 161, 193, 216, 267, 271, 272, 273, 274, 275, 318, 319, 324, 331, 334, 340, 349
universality, 237, 242
universe, 239
universities, 144, 145, 267, 273, 291, 293, 295, 320, 321
updating, 40, 41, 60, 63, 64, 82, 89, 112, 187, 253, 256, 265, 267, 383
USA, 29, 393

V

validation, 68, 293, 310, 313
variables, 19, 20, 21, 24, 25, 35, 36, 38, 39, 46, 47, 49, 57, 84, 85, 86, 88, 89, 196, 232, 237, 245, 253, 254, 256, 257, 281, 286, 295, 296, 305, 326
variations, 146, 168, 327
varieties, 282
varimax rotation, 37, 40, 42
vein, 233, 268, 352, 371
victims, 329
videos, 144, 327, 380
Vietnam, 340
Viking, 310
vision(s), xii, xiii, 68, 140, 153, 189, 199, 204, 268, 270, 273, 275, 340, 358, 368, 370, 375, 376, 378, 380, 394
vocational rehabilitation, 320
vote, 300
vulnerability, 230
Vygotsky, 289, 315

W

waiver, 187
Washington, 12, 26, 27, 65, 68, 78, 96, 97, 152, 153, 165, 179, 180, 181, 189, 198, 226, 245, 246, 258, 259, 273, 274, 275, 334, 335, 336, 337, 356, 357, 375, 376, 391, 393
waste, 279
water, 266, 287
watershed, 378
weakness, 19, 84, 101, 102, 103, 106, 192
wealth, 188, 215, 302, 313, 315
web, 24, 226
websites, 64, 108
welfare, ix, 18, 102
well-being, xii, 203, 215, 217, 219, 220, 222, 223, 226, 250, 251, 253, 255, 256, 257, 312, 346, 351
wellness, 225, 338
WHO, 324

Wisconsin, 165, 167
word processing, 43, 44, 61
work environment, 5, 319, 366
workers, 283, 330
workforce, 13, 15, 18, 22, 138, 139, 258, 318, 332, 337, 345, 346, 349, 350, 354, 357
workload, 209, 218
workplace, 143, 173, 180, 218, 256, 268, 284, 285, 314, 330, 334, 336, 338

World Health Organization, 324
worldwide, 295
writing time, 167

Y

yield, 43, 44, 47, 296, 302